Discovering AutoCAD® 2008

Discovering AutoCAD® 2008

Mark Dix

CAD Support Associates

Paul Riley

CAD Support Associates

PEARSON

Prentice Hall

Upper Saddle River, New Jersey
Columbus, Ohio

Library of Congress Control Number: 2007920977

Editor in Chief: Vernon Anthony
Acquisitions Editor: Jill Jones-Renger
Editorial Assistant: Yvette Schlarman
Development Editor: Karen Fortgang, bookworks publishing services
Production Editor: Louise N. Sette
Production Supervision: Karen Fortgang, bookworks publishing services
Design Coordinator: Diane Ernsberger
Text Designer: Kristina Holmes
Cover Designer: Harold Leber
Art Coordinator: Jill Horton
Director of Marketing: David Gesell
Production Manager: Deidra M. Schwartz
Marketing Manager: Jimmy Stephens
Marketing Coordinator: Alicia Dysert

This book was set by Aptara, Inc. It was printed and bound by Bind-Rite Graphics. The cover was printed by Coral Graphic Services, Inc.

Certain images and materials contained in this publication were reproduced with the permission of Autodesk, Inc. © 2007. All rights reserved. Autodesk and AutoCAD are registered trademarks of Autodesk, Inc., in the U.S.A. and certain other countries.

Disclaimer:

The publication is designed to provide tutorial information about AutoCAD® and/or other Autodesk computer programs. Every effort has been made to make this publication complete and as accurate as possible. The reader is expressly cautioned to use any and all precautions necessary, and to take appropriate steps to avoid hazards, when engaging in the activities described herein.

Neither the author nor the publisher makes any representations or warranties of any kind, with respect to the materials set forth in this publication, express or implied, including without limitation any warranties of fitness for a particular purpose or merchantability. Nor shall the author or the publisher be liable for any special, consequential, or exemplary damages resulting, in whole or in part, directly or indirectly, from the reader's use of, or reliance upon, this material or subsequent revisions of this material.

Pearson Education Ltd.
Pearson Education Singapore Pte. Ltd.
Pearson Education Canada, Ltd.
Pearson Education—Japan

Pearson Education Australia Pty. Limited
Pearson Education North Asia Ltd.
Pearson Educación de Mexico, S.A. de C.V.
Pearson Education Malaysia Pte. Ltd.

10 9 8 7 6 5 4 3 2
ISBN-10:   0-13-159226-2
ISBN-13: 978-0-13-159226-1

THE NEW AUTODESK DESIGN INSTITUTE PRESS SERIES

Pearson/Prentice Hall has formed an alliance with Autodesk® to develop textbooks and other course materials that address the skills, methodology, and learning pedagogy for the industries that are supported by the Autodesk® Design Institute (ADI) software products. The Autodesk Design Institute is a comprehensive software program that assists educators in teaching technological design.

Features of the Autodesk Design Institute Press Series

JOB SKILLS—Coverage of computer-aided drafting job skills, compiled through research of industry associations, job websites, college course descriptions, and the Occupational Information Network database has been integrated throughout the ADI Press books.

PROFESSIONAL and **INDUSTRY ASSOCIATIONS INVOLVEMENT**—These books are written in consultation with and reviewed by professional associations to ensure they meet the needs of industry employers.

AUTODESK LEARNING LICENSES AVAILABLE—Many students ask how they can get a copy of the AutoCAD® software for their home computer. Through a recent agreement with Autodesk®, Prentice Hall now offers the option of purchasing textbooks with either a 180-day or a 1-year student software license agreement for AutoCAD. This provides adequate time for a student to complete all the activities in the book. The software is functionally identical to the professional license, but is intended for student personal use only. It is not for professional use.

For more information about this book and the Autodesk Student Portfolio, contact your local Pearson Prentice Hall sales representative, or contact our National Marketing Manager, Jimmy Stephens, at 1-800-228-7854 x3725 or at Jimmy_Stephens@prenhall.com. For the name and number of your sales rep. please contact Prentice Hall Faculty Services at 1-800-526-0485.

This text presents a modern approach to using AutoCAD. That is, it addresses advances in technology and software evolution and introduces commands and procedures that reflect a modern, efficient use of AutoCAD 2008. Features include:

Chapter Objectives, a bulleted list of learning objectives for each chapter, provide users with a road map of important concepts and practices that will be introduced in the chapter.

Command Grids appear in the margin, alongside the discussion of the command. These grids provide a visual of the action options using the Standard Toolbar, Pull-Down Menu, Command Line, or Command Alias, ensuring that the student is in the right place at the right time and correctly following the authors' direction.

Discipline Icons are placed in the margin alongside each project and identify the discipline to which each project applies: General, Mechanical, Architectural, Electrical, Plumbing/HVAC, or Civil. These icons allow instructors to quickly identify homework assignments that will appeal to the varying interests of their students and allow students to work on projects that have the most interest and relevance depending on their course of study.

A **New to AutoCAD 2008** icon flags features that are new to the 2008 version of the AutoCAD software, creating a quick "study guide" for instructors who need to familiarize themselves with the newest features of the software to prepare for teaching the course. Additional details about these new features can be found in the Online Instructor's Manual.

Tip, Note, and **General Procedure** boxes highlight additional helpful information for the student.

CHAPTER TEST QUESTIONS

Questions

Before going on to the drawings, review the following questions and problems. Then you should be ready for Drawing 1-1.

1. What is the advantage of using the 2D dashboard instead of toolbars?
2. What are the three different modes of the coordinate display and how does each mode appear? How do you switch between modes?
3. What is heads-up design? Give three examples of heads-up design features from this chapter.
4. Explain and describe the diff̶e̶r̶e̶n̶c̶e̶ ̶a̶m̶o̶n̶g̶ absolute, rel̶

6. What function key tur̶n̶
7. You have just entered t̶ to enter the point two̶ How would you identi̶ tive, and polar coordin̶
8. What is the value and l̶
9. Name three different w̶
10. Name and describe thr̶ lection in AutoCAD.
11. What does the **U** com̶

End-of-Chapter material, easily located by shading on page edges, provides:

- Chapter Test Questions
- Chapter Projects

to help students check their own understanding of important chapter concepts.

Drawing 11-5: Garage Framing

This is a fairly complex drawing that takes lots of trimming and careful work. Changing the snapang (snap angle) variable so that you can draw slanted arrays is a method that can be used frequently in isometric drawing.

Drawing Suggestions

- You will find yourself using **COPY**, **ZOOM**, and **TRIM** a great deal. **OFFSET** also works well.
- You might want to create some new layers with different colors. Keeping different parts of the construction walls, rafters, and joists on different layers allows you to have more control over them and

Projects are organized by discipline to allow for application of skills to various fields, and numbered consistently among the chapters for easy back-and-forth reference. The end-of-chapter projects require students to use all the commands and skills they have learned cumulatively. Project types include:

- Mechanical B-Size Title Borders/ Annotation symbols
- Architectural D-Size Title Borders/ Annotation symbols
- Electrical schematics
- Plumbing/HVAC schematics
- Architectural plans
- Architectural details
- Mechanical—English
- Mechanical—Metric
- Civil plans
- Civil details

A CD, bound into the textbook, contains student data files.

INSTRUCTOR RESOURCES

The Online Instructor's Manual provides answers to chapter exercises and tests and solutions to end-of-chapter problems; drawing files to get users started; and lecture-supporting PowerPoint slides.

To access supplementary materials online, instructors need to request an instructor access code. Go to www.prenhall.com, click the Instructor Resource Center link, and then click Register Today for an instructor access code. Within 48 hours after registering you will receive a confirming e-mail including an instructor access code. Once you have received your code, go to the site and log on for full instructions on downloading the materials you wish to use.

OneKey—All instructor and student online course materials for this book are delivered in one Web-based course system—OneKey.

OneKey Blackboard—Prentice Hall's online content, combined with Blackboard's popular tools and interface, result in robust Web-based courses that are easy to implement, manage, and use—taking your courses to new heights in student interaction and learning.

OneKey WebCT—Course-management tools within WebCT include page tracking, progress tracking, class and student management, gradebook, communication, calendar, reporting tools, and more. Gold Level Customer Support, available exclusively to adopters of Prentice Hall courses, is provided free of charge on adoption and provides you with priority assistance, training discounts, and dedicated technical support.

STUDENT RESOURCES

Companion Website—This text is accompanied by a Companion Website at http://www. prenhall.com/dixriley for student access, which includes an interactive study guide.

Preface

Get Active with *Discovering AutoCAD® 2008*

Designed for introductory AutoCAD users, *Discovering AutoCAD® 2008* offers a hands-on, activity-based approach to the use of AutoCAD as a drafting tool—complete with techniques, tips, shortcuts, and insights designed to increase efficiency. Topics and tasks are carefully grouped to lead students logically through the AutoCAD command set, with the level of difficulty increasing steadily as skills are acquired through experience and practice. Straightforward explanations focus on what is relevant to actual drawing procedures, and illustrations show exactly what to expect on the computer screen when steps are correctly completed. This edition features Web-based exercises and projects included in each chapter. These optional exercises both assess and reinforce a student's understanding of the material.

Features

The book uses a consistent format for each chapter that includes:

- Chapter Objectives and Introduction
- Exercises that introduce new commands and techniques
- Exercise instructions clearly set off from the text discussion
- Lots of illustrations with AutoCAD drawings and screen shots
- Ten or more end-of-chapter Review Questions
- A conclusion with 4–6 realistic engineering drawing problems—fully dimensioned working drawings
- Optional Internet Projects at the end of each chapter
- Companion Website: **http://www.prenhall.com/dixriley**

High-quality working drawings include a wide range of applications that focus on mechanical drawings but also include architectural, civil, and electrical drawings.

Appendix A contains 18 drawing projects for additional review and practice, as well as 3D models of 36 objects drawn in 2D in earlier chapters.

Companion Website: http://www.prenhall.com/dixriley

This dedicated site is designed for both professor and student users of this text. It closely supports the book and serves as a useful tool that both complements and increases the value of the text. In particular, students will find multiple choice assessment questions for each chapter. These questions serve as checkups to see whether they have mastered new AutoCAD commands. Students can answer these questions as either checkup exercises or quizzes. They receive the results of these quizzes instantly and can email these directly to their professor. Chapters are also supported by an extended AutoCAD project. These extended projects complement the book and provide extra challenges for students.

Acknowledgments

We would like to acknowledge the reviewers of this text: Charles Bales, Moraine Valley Community College; Susan Freeman, Northeastern University; Joe Gaiser, LeTourneau University; George Gibson, Athens Technical College; and Yueh-Jaw Lin, The University of Akron.

STYLE CONVENTIONS IN *DISCOVERING AUTOCAD® 2008*

Text Element	Example
Key terms—Bold and italic on first mention (first letter lowercase) in the body of the text.	Views are created by placing *viewport* objects in the paper space layout.
AutoCAD commands—Bold and uppercase.	Start the **LINE** command.
Toolbar names, menu items, and dialog box names—Bold and follow capitalization convention in AutoCAD toolbar or pull-down menu (generally first letter capitalized).	The **Layer Manager** dialog box The **File** pull-down menu
Toolbar buttons and dialog box controls/ buttons/input items—Bold and follow capitalization convention of the name of the item or the name shown in the AutoCAD tooltip.	Choose the **Line** tool from the **Draw** toolbar. Choose the **Symbols and Arrows** tab in the **Modify Dimension Style** dialog box. Choose the **New Layer** button in the **Layer Properties Manager** dialog box. In the **Lines and Arrows** tab, set the **Arrow size:** to **.125.**
AutoCAD prompts—Dynamic input prompts are italic. Command window prompts use a different font (Courier New) and are boldface. This makes them look like the text in the command window. Prompts follow capitalization convention in AutoCAD prompt (generally first letter capitalized).	AutoCAD prompts you to *Specify first point:* AutoCAD prompts you to *Specify next point or ▽.* `Specify center point for circle or [3P/2P/Ttr (tan tan radius)]:`
Keyboard input—Bold with special keys in brackets.	Type **3.5 <Enter ↵>.** In the **Lines and Arrows** tab, set the **Arrow size:** to **.125.**

Contents

Discovering AutoCAD® 2008

Lines and Essential Tools

Chapter Objectives

- Beginning a New Drawing
- Exploring the Drawing Window
- Interacting with the Drawing Window
- Exploring Command Entry Methods
- Drawing, Undoing, and Erasing Lines
- Saving and Opening Your Drawings

INTRODUCTION

Drawing in AutoCAD can be a fascinating and highly productive activity. AutoCAD 2008 is full of features you can use to become a very proficient design professional. Throughout this book, our goal is to get you drawing as quickly and efficiently as possible. Discussion and explanation are limited to what is most useful and relevant at the moment, but this should also give you an understanding of the program to make you a more powerful user.

This chapter introduces some of the basic tools you will use whenever you draw in AutoCAD. You will begin to find your way around AutoCAD menus, toolbars, and workspaces as you learn to control basic elements of the Drawing Window. You will produce drawings involving straight lines. You will learn to undo your last command with the **U** command and to erase individual lines with the **ERASE** command. Your drawings will be saved, if you wish, using the **SAVE** and **SAVEAS** commands.

1-1 BEGINNING A NEW DRAWING

The General Procedure that follows is for reference only. We offer these General Procedures throughout the book as a convenience and quick overview. *They do not substitute for the more detailed and specific exercises that follow them.*

GENERAL PROCEDURE	1. Type Ctrl+N or select New from the **File** drop-down menu.
	2. Ensure that acad.dwt is entered in the File name box.
	3. Press **Enter** (↵).

AutoCAD can be customized in many ways, so that the exact look and sequence of what you see might be slightly different from what we show you here. We assume that you are working with "out of the box" settings, but take steps to ensure that your screens resemble ours and that you have no trouble following the sequences presented here. First, however, we have to load AutoCAD.

⊞ From the Windows desktop, double-click the AutoCAD 2008 icon to start AutoCAD.

⊞ Wait...

When you see the AutoCAD 2008 screen, as shown in Figure 1-1, you are ready to begin.

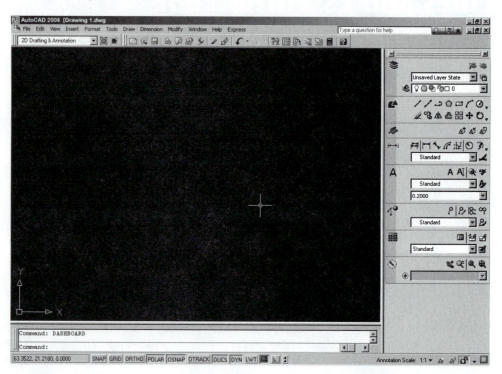

Figure 1-1

Workspaces

AutoCAD 2008 may open with a variety of different appearances, including some settings that can be customized and defined as *workspaces.* With typical settings, you open in a drawing with a generic name such as Drawing1, regardless of workspace.

In AutoCAD 2008 you have two workspaces predefined for 2D drawing and one for 3D drawing. Either the AutoCAD Classic or the 2D Drafting & Annotation workspace can be used effectively for all 2D drawings in this book. We will focus our attention on the new 2D Drafting & Annotation workspace until Chapter 12, where we switch to the 3D workspace. The most obvious difference between the 2D Drafting and the Classic workspaces is the *dashboard* on the right of the screen. The Classic workspace, shown in Figure 1-2, uses more toolbars and does not include the dashboard.

Changing workspaces is easily done using the drop-down list at the top left of the screen. If 2D Drafting & Annotation is showing in this box, you can leave it as is. Otherwise, open the list and change to this workspace as follows.

- If necessary, click the arrow on the right of the workspace drop-down list and select 2D Drafting & Annotation from the list, as shown in Figure 1-3.

- If there are elements (toolbars, windows, etc.) on your screen other than those shown in Figure 1-1, close them by clicking the **Close** button (X) in the upper right corner of each unwanted element.

Creating a New Drawing

In AutoCAD, new drawings are typically created with some form of template. A template is a drawing that contains previously defined settings. Simple drawings can be created with the acad template.

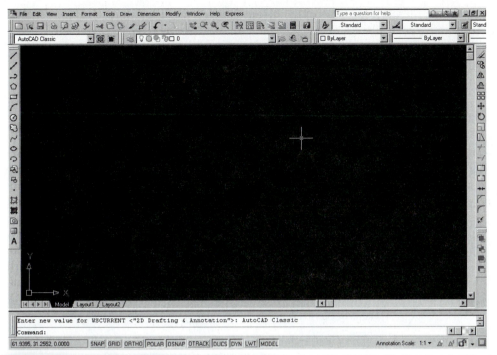

Figure 1-2

Figure 1-3

> **FOR MORE DETAILS** Template drawings are discussed in detail in Chapter 4.

⊕ Type Ctrl+N.

This opens the **Select template** dialog box shown in Figure 1-4. For now, all you need to do is look at the File name box near the bottom of the dialog box. It should read acad.dwt. Dwt is a file extension given to AutoCAD drawing

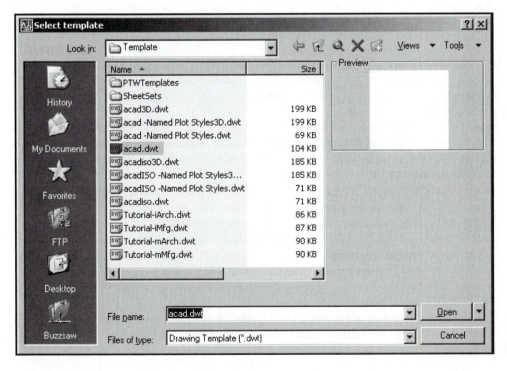

Figure 1-4

template files. If your File name box has a different template, double-click in the box and type acad.

⊕ Assuming the File name box is now showing acad or acad.dwt, press Enter to complete the dialog.

1.2 EXPLORING THE DRAWING WINDOW

You are looking at the AutoCAD Drawing Window with the 2D Drafting & Annotation workspace and the acad template. Elements of this workspace are labeled in Figure 1-5. There are many ways that you can alter the drawing window to suit a particular drawing application. We explore these throughout the book. In this section we examine some of your basic tools.

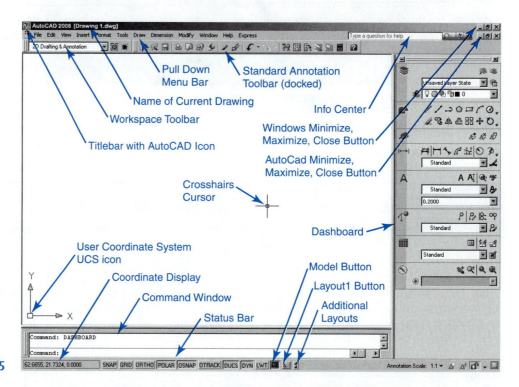

Figure 1-5

The AutoCAD Drawing Window has many features that are common to all Windows programs. At the top of the screen is the title bar, with the AutoCAD icon on the left and the standard Windows minimize, maximize, and close buttons on the right. To the right of the AutoCAD icon is the name of the current drawing.

Below the title bar is AutoCAD's pull-down menu bar, including the titles for the **File, Edit, View, Insert, Format, Tools, Draw, Dimension, Modify, Window, Help,** and **Express** pull-down menus. Pull-down menus work in AutoCAD just as in other Windows applications and are discussed later in this section.

The next line down shows the **Workspace** toolbar and the **Standard Annotation** toolbar. These are two of 37 available toolbars. These two toolbars are in a horizontal position and are docked, meaning they are locked in position along the edge of the drawing area. Toolbars can also be positioned vertically and may also float anywhere inside the drawing area. Visually, each toolbar begins with two bars on the left, in horizontal position, or on the top in vertical position. Toolbars can be created and modified. They can be moved, resized, and reshaped. They are a convenience, but they can also make your drawing area overly cluttered. For our purposes, we will find most of what we need on the dashboard.

On the right of the screen is the new 2D dashboard. It is important because the commands available on a large number of toolbars are now together in one place. Most of the commands necessary to do all the drawings in Chapters 1–11 are available on the dashboard. To the left of the dashboard is the drawing area. This is where you will do most of your work and where your drawing will appear.

Beneath the drawing area is the Command window. The most important aspect here is the command prompt area, where typed commands and options appear. Typed commands, introduced in the next section, are one of the basic ways of working in AutoCAD.

Below the Command window is the status bar, with the coordinate display on the left, currently showing three four-place decimal numbers separated by commas. To the right of the coordinate display are nine mode buttons (**Snap, Grid, Ortho, Polar, Osnap, Otrack, DUCS, Dyn, LWT** and **Model**). To the right of the mode buttons are two buttons and two arrows used to switch from drawing and modeling procedures to layout procedures when you are ready to prepare a drawing for presentation. At the right side of the status bar are several icons and selections for specifying Annotation settings. These are new in 2008 and will be explored in later chapters.

Finally, the bottom of your screen shows the Windows taskbar, with the **Start** button on the left and buttons for any open applications in the middle. You should see a button with the Auto-CAD 2008 icon here, indicating that you have an AutoCAD window open.

Note:
You might also see other windows or toolbars on your screen. If so, close each of these by clicking the X in its upper right or left corner.

TIP

You can gain more room for your drawing area by using the hide feature on the dashboard. At the top of the dashboard you will see a bar with a minimize symbol on the left (−) and a close symbol on the right. Picking the minimize button will put the dashboard in auto-hide mode. In this mode the dashboard collapses to a title bar on the right side of the screen. The rest of the dashboard appears only when you run your cursor over the title bar. To reverse the setting, pick the auto-hide button that appears at the bottom of the dashboard, just above the **Properties** button.

1.3 INTERACTING WITH THE DRAWING WINDOW

There are many ways to communicate with the Drawing Window. In this section, we explore the mouse, crosshairs, arrow, and other simple features so that we can begin to use drawing commands.

The Mouse

Most of your interaction with the Drawing Window will be communicated through your mouse. Given the graphic interfaces of AutoCAD and Windows, a two-button mouse is sufficient for most applications. In this book, we assume two buttons. If you have a digitizer or a more complex pointing device, the two button functions will be present, along with other functions that we do not address.

On a common two-button mouse the left button is called the pick button and it is used for point selection, object selection, and menu or tool selection. All mouse instructions in this book refer to the left button, unless specifically stated otherwise. The right button most often calls up shortcut menus as in other Windows applications. The menu that is called depends on the context. Learning how and when to use these menus can increase your efficiency. We show you how to use many shortcut menus as we go along. If you click the right button accidentally and open an unwanted shortcut menu, close it by left-clicking anywhere outside the shortcut menu.

Your mouse may also have a scroll wheel between the left and right buttons. This wheel has a highly useful zooming function in AutoCAD, which we will demonstrate in Chapter 3. For now, if you happen to click the mouse wheel forward or backward, just click it in the opposite direction to reverse the zooming action.

Crosshairs

The focus of action in AutoCAD is the crosshairs. This is the small cross with a box at its intersection somewhere in the display area of your screen. If you do not see it, move your pointing device until it appears. At any time, the point where the two lines of the crosshairs intersect is the point that will be specified by pressing the pick button. Try it, as follows.

⊕ Move the mouse and see how the crosshairs move in coordination with your hand movements.

⊕ Move the mouse so that the crosshairs move to the top of the screen.

When you leave the drawing area, your crosshairs are left behind and you see a standard Windows selection arrow pointing up and to the left. As in other Windows applications the arrow is used to select tools and to open menus from the menu bar.

⊕ Move the cursor back into the drawing area.

The selection arrow disappears and the crosshairs move across the drawing area again.

The Coordinate Display and Dynamic Input

The coordinate display at the left of the status bar keeps track of screen coordinates as you move the mouse. AutoCAD uses a Cartesian coordinate system to identify points in the drawing area. In this system, points are identified by an x value, indicating a horizontal position from left to right across the screen, and a y value, indicating a vertical position from bottom to top on the screen. Notice the icon at the lower left of the drawing area. This is the User Coordinate System icon, showing the alignment of the x and y axis. Typically a point near the lower left of the screen is chosen as the origin, or 0 point of the coordinate system. Its coordinates are (0,0). Points are specified by pairs of numbers, called ordered pairs, in which the horizontal x value is first, followed by the vertical y value. For example, the point (3,2) would identify a point 3 units over and 2 units up from the origin at the lower left corner of the screen. You will see many ordered pairs as you work through this book. There is also a z value in 3D Cartesian coordinates, which measures an imagined distance in front of or behind the screen, but we do not use this until Chapter 12. For now the z value will always be 0 and we can ignore it.

With this in mind, observe the coordinate display as you move the crosshairs.

⊕ Move the crosshairs around slowly and keep your eye on the three numbers at the bottom left of the screen.

The first two should be moving very rapidly through four-place decimal numbers. When you stop moving, the numbers show coordinates for the location of the crosshairs. Notice the four-place x and y values, which change rapidly, and the z value, which is always 0.0000. Coordinates shown in this form, relative to a fixed coordinate grid, are called **absolute coordinates.** As we shall see shortly, the coordinate display can also show **polar coordinates,** which are given as a length and an angle relative to a given point.

⊕ Carefully move the crosshairs horizontally and watch how the first value (x) changes and the second value (y) stays more or less the same.

⊕ Move the crosshairs vertically and watch how the second value (y) changes and the first value (x) stays more or less the same.

The coordinate display has three different modes. Switching among them is done by left-clicking directly on the coordinate display.

⊕ Move the crosshairs off the drawing area and down to the coordinate display.

The crosshairs will be replaced by the selection arrow.

⊕ With the arrow on the coordinate display numbers, press the pick button.

The numbers freeze and the coordinate display turns gray.

⊕ Move the arrow back into the drawing area and continue to move the crosshairs slowly.

Now when you move the crosshairs you see that the coordinate display does not change. You also notice that it is still grayed out.

⊕ Pick any point near the middle of your drawing area.

Notice that the coordinate display updates to the selected point even though the numbers are grayed out. This is called static mode. In this mode, the coordinate display will change only when you select a point. Previously the coordinate display was in dynamic mode, in which the numbers update constantly with the movement of the crosshairs.

You probably will see something on your screen, as shown in Figure 1-6, called the *dynamic input display.* It is a very powerful feature that in many ways duplicates the function of the coordinate display. However, this display is easier to track because it follows your cursor. Also, there are times when it can be used effectively in conjunction with the coordinate display. Dynamic input can be turned on and off using either the **Dyn** button on the status bar or the F12 key. Try this:

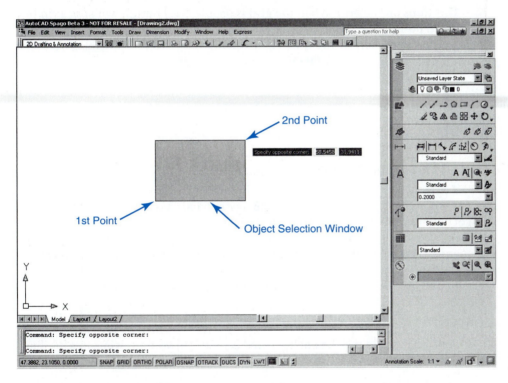

Figure 1-6

⊕ Pick the **Dyn** button or press F12.

The dynamic input numbers on your screen disappear.

⊕ Pick the **Dyn** button again or press F12.

The dynamic input display reappears.

Currently, the numbers in the dynamic display are *x* and *y* coordinates, just as in the coordinate display. The coordinate display on the status bar is static, while the dynamic display is still moving through values when you move your crosshairs. In other words, the coordinate display indicates the coordinates of the last point you picked, while the dynamic input display is showing the value of any new point you may pick.

⊕ Move the crosshairs to another point on the screen.

Something else is happening here that we must address. AutoCAD opens a box on the screen, as shown in Figure 1-6. *You are not drawing anything with this box.* This is the object selection window, used to select objects for editing. It has no effect now because there are no objects on your screen. You can give two points to define the window and then it vanishes because there is nothing there to select. Object selection is discussed in Chapter 2.

AutoCAD prompts for the other corner of the selection window. You see the following in the command area and on the dynamic input display:

Specify opposite corner:

⌖ Pick a second point.

This completes the object selection window and the window vanishes. Notice the change in the static coordinate display numbers.

The Grid

AutoCAD uses a grid with evenly spaced dots as a visual aid. The dots show a matrix of points in its Cartesian coordinate system.

⌖ Pick the Grid button on the status bar or press F7.

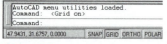

Figure 1-7

This turns on the grid. When the grid is on, the **Grid** button will appear in the depressed position on the status bar, as shown in Figure 1-7. The grid initially appears in the lower left of the drawing area, and may be barely visible. We use a simple procedure with the **ZOOM** command to enlarge and center it.

 FOR MORE DETAILS   **ZOOM** is discussed in detail in Chapter 3.

⌖ Type z ⏎ to execute the ZOOM command.

Z is a shortcut for typing zoom. Such keyboard shortcuts, called aliases, are discussed in Section 1.4. When you type a command, AutoCAD responds with a list of options at the command prompt. Options are separated by forward slashes (/) and the default option is shown at the end between arrows. If you press enter in response to the prompt you will execute the default option. Other options can be executed by typing a letter, indicated by the uppercase letter in the option. This is usually the first letter, but not always. For our purposes we want the All option, so we type "a."

⌖ Type "a" ⏎ to zoom out and show the complete grid.

Your grid should now be enlarged and centered in your drawing area, as illustrated in Figure 1-8.

The grid helps you find your way around on the screen. It does not appear on your drawing when it is plotted, and it can be turned on and off at will. You can also change the spacing between dots using the **GRID** command, as we do in Chapter 2.

The grid is currently set up to emulate the shape of an Architectural A-size (12×9 inch) sheet of drawing paper, with grid points at 0.5000 increments. There are 19 grid points from bottom to top, numbered 0, 0.5, 1.0, 1.5, and so on, up to 9.0. There are 25 points from left to right, numbered 0 to 12, including all 0.5-unit increments. The AutoCAD command that controls the outer size and shape of the grid is **LIMITS,** which is discussed in Chapter 4. Until then, continue to use the current limits setting.

Model Space

You should be aware that there is no need to scale AutoCAD drawings until you are ready to print or plot. You will always draw at full-scale, where one unit of length on the screen represents one unit of length in real space. This full-scale drawing space is called *model space.* At the time of printing, the drawing will be scaled to fit the paper. This process is handled through the creation of a drawing layout. For now, all your work will be done in model space, and you do not need to be concerned with layouts.

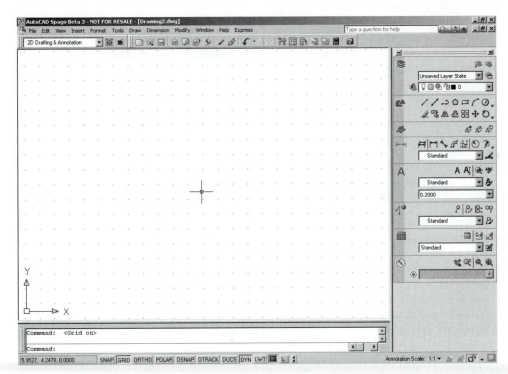

Figure 1-8

Snap

Snap is an important concept in all CAD programs. There are several AutoCAD features through which an approximate screen cursor location locks onto a precise numerical point, a point on an object, or the extension of an object. All these features enhance productivity in that the operator does not have to hunt or visually guess at precise point locations. In this chapter, we show examples of several of these related techniques, but we leave in-depth discussion and demonstration for later chapters. The simplest form of snap is called incremental snap or grid snap, because it is conceptually related to the screen grid. Try the following:

⊕ Pick the **Snap** button on the status bar or press F9.

   The **Snap** button should go into the depressed position, indicating that the snap mode is now on.

⊕ Move the crosshairs slowly around the drawing area.

   Look closely and you will see that the crosshairs jump from point to point. If your grid is on, notice that is impossible to make the crosshairs touch a point that is not on the grid. Try it.

⊕ If your coordinate display is in the static mode, left-click it to switch to dynamic mode. Move the cursor and watch the coordinate display.

   Notice that the coordinate display shows only values ending in .0000 or .5000.

⊕ Pick the **Snap** button again or press F9.

   Snap should now be off and the **Snap** button is in the released position on the status bar.

   If you move the cursor in a circle now, the crosshairs move more smoothly, without jumping. You also observe that the coordinate display moves rapidly through a full range of four-place decimal values again.

   With snap off, you can move anywhere on the screen. With snap on you can move only in predetermined increments. With the acad template default settings, snap is set to a value of .5000 so that you can move only in half-unit increments. In the next chapter, you learn how to change this setting using the **SNAP** command. For now, we leave the snap settings alone.

Using an appropriate snap increment is a tremendous time-saver. It also allows for a degree of accuracy that is not possible otherwise. If all the dimensions in a drawing fall into 1-inch increments, for example, there is no reason to deal with points that are not on a 1-inch grid. You can find the points you want much more quickly and accurately if all those in between are temporarily eliminated, and the snap setting allows you to do that.

TIP Incremental snap is more than a convenience. In most cases, it is a necessity. With snap off, it is virtually impossible to locate any point precisely. If you try to locate the point (6.5000, 6.5000, 0.0000) with snap off, for example, you might get close, but the probability is very small that you will actually be able to select that exact point. Try it.

Other Buttons on the Status Bar

All the status bar buttons are used to turn powerful features on and off. However, some of the features can interfere with your learning and ability to control the cursor when turned on at the wrong time. For this reason, we encourage you to keep some features off until you need them. *In early chapters of this book, generally Snap, Grid, Dyn, and Model should be on and other buttons should be off.* **Dyn** controls the dynamic input display. **Ortho** and **Polar** are discussed later in this chapter, and you can use them at your discretion. **Osnap,** which stands for Object Snap, is a very important feature that forces the selection of a geometrically definable point on an object, such as the endpoint or midpoint of a line. We leave Osnap alone until Chapter 6 so that you have the freedom to select points without the interference of an Object Snap selection. **Otrack** stands for Object Snap Tracking. Otrack is an outgrowth of Object Snap and we save it for Chapter 6 as well. **DUCS** stands for Dynamic User Coordinate System and is used only in 3-D modeling. **LWT** stands for Lineweight, which we introduce in Chapter 3.

The User Coordinate System Icon

At the lower left of the screen, you see the User Coordinate System (UCS) icon. These two perpendicular arrows clearly indicate the directions of the *x*- and *y*-axes, which are currently aligned with the sides of your screen. In Chapter 12, when you begin to make 3-D drawings, you will be defining your own coordinate systems. At that time, you will find that the UCS icon is an essential visual aid. However, in two-dimensional drafting it is hardly necessary. If for any reason you wish to turn it off, you can do so by following these steps:

1. Type ucsicon ↵.
2. Type off ↵.

1.4 Exploring Command Entry Methods

It is characteristic of AutoCAD that most tasks can be accomplished in a variety of ways. For example, you can enter commands by typing or by selecting an item from a toolbar, a tool palette, a pull-down menu, a shortcut menu, a dialog box, or the dashboard. Each method has its advantages and disadvantages, depending on the situation. Often a combination of two or more methods is the most efficient way to carry out a complete command sequence. The instructions in this book are not always specific about which to use. Once you get used to the range of options you will develop your own preferences.

Heads-Up Design

An important concept in the creation of AutoCAD command procedures is termed *heads-up design*. What this means is that optimal efficiency is achieved when the CAD operator can keep his or her hand on the mouse and eyes focused on the screen. The less time spent looking away from the screen, the better. A major innovation supporting heads-up technique is the dynamic input display. Because this display moves with the cursor, it allows you to stay focused on your drawing area.

We describe each of the basic command entry methods in this section. You do not have to try them all out at this time. Read them over to get a feel for the possibilities and then proceed to exploring the **LINE** command in Section 1.5.

The Keyboard and the Command Line

The keyboard is the most primitive and fundamental method of interacting with AutoCAD and it is still of great importance for all operators. Toolbars, menus, and dialog boxes all function by automating basic command sequences as they would be typed on the keyboard. Although other methods are often faster, being familiar with keyboard procedures increases your understanding of AutoCAD. The keyboard is the most basic, the most comprehensive, and changes the least from one release of AutoCAD to the next. It is literally at your fingertips, and if you know the command you want to use, you do not have to go looking for it. For this reason, some excellent CAD operators might rely too heavily on the keyboard. Do not limit yourself by typing everything. If you know the keyboard sequence, try the other methods to see how they vary and how you can use them to save time and stay screen-focused. Ultimately, you want to keep your hand on the mouse, type as little as possible, and use the command entry methods to your advantage.

As you type commands and responses to prompts, the characters you are typing appear on the command line after the colon. Also, if dynamic input is on, they may appear in the drawing area next to the crosshairs. Remember that you must press Enter to complete your commands and responses.

TIP By pressing F2 you can access a text window that gives access to all entries made in the current drawing session. Press F2 again to close the text window and return to the drawing area.

Many of the most often used commands, such as **LINE, ERASE,** and **CIRCLE,** have aliases. These one- or two-letter abbreviations are very handy. A few of the most commonly used aliases are shown in Figure 1-9. There are also a large number of two- and three-letter aliases, some of which we introduce as we go along.

COMMAND ALIAS CHART		
LETTER + ENTER		= COMMAND
A	⏎	ARC
C	⏎	CIRCLE
E	⏎	ERASE
F	⏎	FILLET
L	⏎	LINE
M	⏎	MOVE
O	⏎	OFFSET
P	⏎	PAN
R	⏎	REDRAW
S	⏎	STRETCH
Z	⏎	ZOOM

Figure 1-9

Pull-Down Menus

Pull-down menus, toolbars, and the dashboard have the great advantage that instead of typing a complete command, you can simply point and click to select an item, without looking away from the screen. The pull-down menus are always available and contain most commands that you use regularly.

Pull-down menus work in AutoCAD as they do in any Windows application. To use a menu, move the crosshairs up into the menu bar so that the selection arrow appears. Items followed by an arrow pointing to the right have cascading submenus that open automatically when an item highlighted. Items followed by an ellipsis (. . .) will call up a dialog box.

Dashboard

Toolbars and dashboards are also standard Windows features. They comprise buttons with icons that give one-click access to commands. AutoCAD 2008 emphasizes the use of dashboards in both 2D and 3D workspaces. The icons on the dashboard are the same as those used in toolbars, but there are more available in one location. In this book we will also focus on the use of the dashboard. Dashboards are made up of panels that are often the equivalent of a particular toolbar or set of toolbars. Each panel has an icon on the left that identifies the function of the tools in that panel. For example, the second panel on the 2D dashboard is the 2D Draw panel and includes tools that can also be found on the **Draw** and **Modify** toolbars.

Note:

Clicking on some of the control panel icons will open tool palettes related to the function of the panel. For now, you should close any tool palette that opens in this way.

Toolbars

Toolbars can be accessed from a shortcut menu opened by right-clicking any open toolbar. There are 37 predefined toolbars available in AutoCAD 2008. Once opened, toolbars can float anywhere on the screen or they can be docked along the edges of the drawing area.

Tool Palettes

Tool palettes are similar in many ways to toolbars. They provide access to drawing symbols, hatch patterns, commands, and previously drawn objects.

> **FOR MORE DETAILS** Tool palettes are introduced in Chapter 6 of this book.

  TIP You can temporarily remove all open toolbars, and the dashboard from the screen by picking the **Clear Screen button** at the far right of the status bar or by typing Ctrl-0. Repeating this action will return the toolbars and dashboard to the screen.

Tooltips

The icons used to represent commands are a mixed blessing. One picture may be worth a thousand words, but with so many pictures, you might find that a few words can be very helpful as well. As in other Windows applications, you can get a label for an icon by allowing the selection arrow to rest on the button for a moment without selecting it. These labels are called *tooltips*. Try the following:

⊕ Position the selection arrow on the icon on the left end of the **Standard Annotation** toolbar, as shown in Figure 1-10, but do not press the pick button.

You see a yellow label that says QNew, as shown in the figure. This label identifies this button as the **QNew** command button. QNew can be set to open with a

Figure 1-10**

default to template, but is otherwise no different from typing Ctrl-N or selecting New from the **File** menu. It calls the **Select Template** dialog box.

When a tooltip is displayed, you also see a phrase in the status bar in place of the coordinate display. This phrase describes what the tool or menu item does and is called a ***helpstring.*** The **QNew** command helpstring says, "Creates a blank drawing file: QNEW." The word following the colon identifies the command as you would type it in the command area.

Now let us get started drawing.

1.5 DRAWING, UNDOING, AND ERASING LINES

GENERAL PROCEDURE

1. Select the **Line** tool from the dashboard.
2. Pick a start point.
3. Pick an endpoint.
4. Pick another endpoint to continue in the **LINE** command, or press **Enter** or the right button on your mouse to exit the command.

Remember, the procedure just listed is a general list of how to enter and use the LINE command. It is for reference and clarity only. It does not substitute for the more detailed and specific exercise that follows.

⊕ In preparation, make sure that your status line resembles ours, as shown in Figure 1-11.

In particular, note that SNAP, GRID, DYN, and Model are in the on position (depressed), whereas ORTHO, POLAR, OSNAP, OTRACK, DUCS, and LWT are off (released). This keeps things simple and uncluttered for now. *This is very important.*

| SNAP | GRID | ORTHO | POLAR | OSNAP | OTRACK | DUCS | DYN | LWT | MODEL | **Figure 1-11**

⊕ Select the **Line** tool from the second panel of the dashboard, as shown in Figure 1-12.

As soon as you enter the command, the dynamic input prompt appears next to the crosshairs. You should see the following in the command area and the dynamic input prompt:

Specify first point:

⊕ Move your crosshairs to the point (1.0000,1.0000) and press the pick button.

Notice that you must have snap on to do this. AutoCAD registers your point selection and responds with another prompt:

Specify next point or [Undo]:

This prompts you to pick a second point. The Undo option is discussed shortly.

COMMAND GRID	
Command	Line
Alias	L
Menu	Draw
Tool	╱

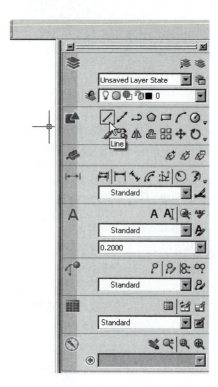

Figure 1-12

Rubber Band

⊞ Move your cursor up toward the center of your drawing area and let it rest, but do press the pick button.

There are several other new things to be aware of here. The dynamic input display has become much more complex. With typical settings, there will be three new features on the screen. There is a line called the *rubber band,* stretching from the first point to the new point. There is a dimension with a dotted line above the line. And there is an angular dimension between the line and the horizon, as illustrated in Figure 1-13. If you move the cursor, you notice that the rubber band

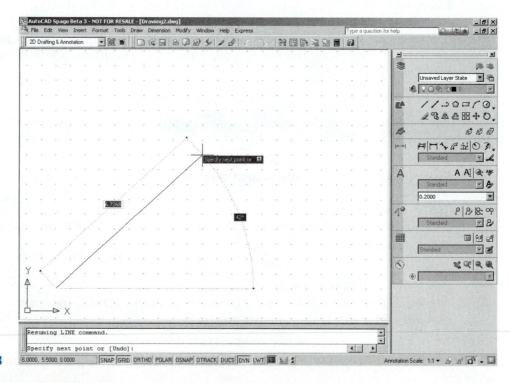

Figure 1-13

stretches, shrinks, or rotates like a tether, keeping you connected to the starting point of the line. Rubber bands have various functions in AutoCAD commands. In this case, the rubber band represents the line you are about to draw.

Polar Coordinates

The two dimensions in the dynamic input display show a visual display of polar coordinates. Polar coordinates are given as a length and an angle relative to a starting point. In this case, you see the length of the line you are drawing and the angle it forms from the horizon, straight out to the right. Typically, the coordinate display will also show polar coordinates. If not, we need to change the coordinate display mode.

⊞ If necessary, click on the coordinate display once or twice until it shows something like 6.7268 < 42,0.0000.

There are three values in the polar coordinate display. For example, 6.7268, 42, and 0.0000. The first number (6.7268) is the distance from the starting point of the line to the crosshairs as shown by the linear dimension in the dynamic display. The second (42) is an angle of rotation, measuring counterclockwise, with 0 degrees being straight out to the right. The third value (0.0000) is the z coordinate, which remains at 0 in 2-D drawings.

Working with Absolute and Polar Coordinates

The presence of the coordinate display with the dynamic display allows you to use absolute (*x, y, z*) coordinates and polar coordinates simultaneously. Try this:

⊞ Pick the coordinate display several times and watch what it displays.

As you do this you will notice that there are three coordinate display modes: static (values grayed out, with no change until you select a point), absolute *xyz* (*x*, *y*, and *z* values separated by a comma), and polar (length < angle, *z*).

⊞ Pick the coordinate display until you see absolute (*x, y, z*) coordinates in black.

With absolute coordinates showing, you can use the coordinate display to pick a point in your drawing, while the dynamic display continues to show the polar coordinates of the line you are drawing.

⊞ Move the cursor to the point with absolute coordinates (8.0000, 8.0000,0.0000).

Notice that the dynamic input display shows that this line is 9.8995 units long and makes a 45-degree angle with the horizon.

⊞ Pick the point (8.0000,8.0000,0.0000).

Your screen should now resemble Figure 1-14. AutoCAD has drawn a line between (1,1) and (8,8) and is asking for another point.

Specify next point or [Undo]:

The repetition of this prompt allows you to stay in the **LINE** command to draw a whole series of connected lines if you wish. You can draw a single line from

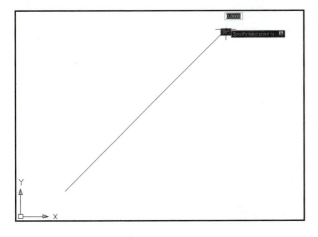

Figure 1-14

point to point, or a series of lines from point to point to point to point. In either case, you must end the command by pressing **Enter** or the spacebar.

⊞ Press Enter or the spacebar to end the LINE command.

You should be back to the *Command:* prompt again, and the dynamic input display disappears from the screen.

> **Note:**
> When you are drawing a continuous series of lines, the polar coordinates on either display are given relative to the most recent point, not the original starting point.

Spacebar and Enter Key

In most cases, AutoCAD allows you to use the spacebar as a substitute for the **Enter** key. Although this is one of the oldest Auto-CAD features, it is a major contributor to the goal of heads-up drawing. It is a great convenience, because the spacebar is easy to locate with one hand (your left hand if the mouse is on the right side) while the other hand is on the mouse and your eyes are on the screen. The major exception to the use of the spacebar as an **Enter** key is when you are entering text in your drawing (Chapter 7). Because a space can be part of a text string, the spacebar must have its usual significance within text commands and some dimension commands.

TIP   Another great convenience provided by the spacebar and **Enter** key is that pressing either at the *Command:* prompt causes the last command entered to be repeated.

Right-Click Button and Shortcut Menus

The right button on your mouse can also be used in place of the **Enter** key sometimes, but in most cases, there will be an intervening step involving a shortcut menu with choices. This, too, is a major heads-up feature, which we explore as we go along. For now, the following steps give you an introduction to shortcut menus.

⊞ Press the right button on your mouse. (This action is called right-clicking from now on.)

This opens a shortcut menu, as shown in Figure 1-15. The top line is a Repeat Line option that can be used to reenter the **LINE** command. (Remember, you can

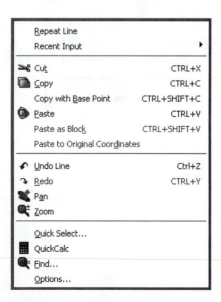

Figure 1-15

also do this by pressing the spacebar at the command prompt.) You have no use for the other options on this shortcut menu until later chapters.

Shortcut menus are context sensitive, so the menu that is called depends on the situation.

⊞ Pick any point outside the shortcut menu.

The shortcut menu disappears, but AutoCAD takes the picked point as the first point in an object selection window.

⊞ Pick any second point to the right of the first to close the object selection window.

There are many context-sensitive shortcut menus in AutoCAD. We do not attempt to present every one, but encourage you to explore them along the way. You will find many possibilities simply by right-clicking while in a command or dialog box.

Relative Coordinates and @

Besides typing or picking points on the screen, AutoCAD allows you to enter points by typing co-ordinates relative to the last point selected. To do this, use the @ symbol. For example, after picking the point (1,1) in the last exercise, you could have specified the point (8,8) by typing @7,7 as the second point is over 7 and up 7 from the first point.

Dynamic Input

You can also enter values directly to the dynamic input display. For example, you can pick the first point of a line and then show the direction of the line segment you wish to draw, but instead of picking the other endpoint you type in a value for the length of the line. Try this:

⊞ Repeat the LINE command by pressing Enter or the spacebar.

AutoCAD prompts for a first point.

TIP   If you press **Enter** or the spacebar at the *Specify first point:* prompt, AutoCAD selects the last point entered, so that you can begin drawing from where you left off.

⊞ Press Enter or the spacebar to select the point (8,8,0), the endpoint of the previously drawn line.

AutoCAD prompts for a second point.

⊞ Pull the rubber band diagonally down to the right, as shown in Figure 1-16.

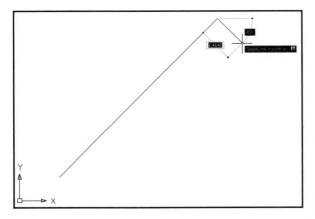

Figure 1-16

Use the dynamic input display to ensure that you are moving along the diagonal at a 45-degree angle, as shown. The length of the rubber band does not matter, only the direction. Notice that the length is highlighted.

⊕ With the rubber band stretched out as shown, type 3.

Notice that the 3 is entered directly on the dynamic input display as the length of the line.

⊕ Press Enter or hit the spacebar.

AutoCAD draws a 3.0000 line segment at the angle you have specified.

You can also use this method to input an angle. Try this:

⊕ With the length highlighted on the dynamic input display, type 2, but *do not press Enter.*

Pressing **Enter** will complete the line segment at whatever angle is showing, as you did in the last step. To move from the length value to the angle value, use the **Tab** key on your keyboard before pressing **Enter.**

⊕ Press the Tab key once.

The value 2.0000 is locked in as the length, as shown in Figure 1-17. You will see a lock icon on the length display and will notice that the rubber band no longer stretches, though it can still be rotated. Now you can manually specify an angle.

⊕ Place the rubber band above the horizontal.

⊕ Type 45 ⏎.

⊕ Press Enter or the spacebar to exit the LINE command.

> **Note:**
> Be aware that in other contexts this angle, which is 45 degrees below the horizon, would be identified as negative 45 degrees to distinguish it from the angle that is 45 degrees above the horizon. This convention is ignored in dynamic input because the visual information removes any ambiguity.

> **Note:**
> Because you are now entering numbers rather than showing an angle on the screen, there is room for ambiguity here. If you place the rubber band above the horizon AutoCAD will draw the segment along the positive 45-degree angle. If you place the rubber band below the horizon it will draw the negative angle. You can also force a negative angle by typing –45.

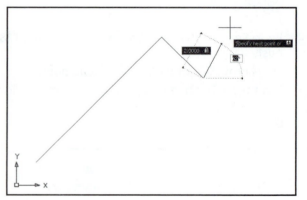

Figure 1-17

Your screen should resemble Figure 1-18.

Undoing Commands with U

⊕ To undo the line you just drew, type U ⏎, or select the Undo tool from the Standard Annotation toolbar, as shown in Figure 1-19.

U undoes the last command, so if you have done anything else since drawing the line, you need to enter it more than once. In this way, you can walk backward

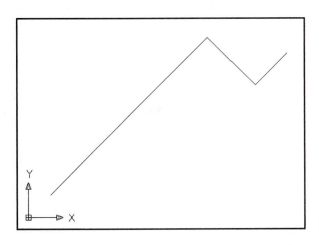

Figure 1-18

Figure 1-19

through your drawing session, undoing your commands one by one. As mentioned previously, there is also an Undo option within the **LINE** command so that you can undo the last segment drawn without leaving the command.

⊕ Click the Redo tool, which is to the right of the Undo tool on the Standard Annotation toolbar.

This redoes the line you have just undone. AutoCAD keeps track of everything undone in a single drawing session, so you can redo a number of undone actions.

> **Note:**
> Typing U actually executes the simple U command, which undoes the last command. Selecting the **Undo** tool executes a command called **UNDO.** Although the two commands often have the same effect, U is not an alias for UNDO, which has more elaborate capabilities. **REDO** can be used to reverse either U or UNDO. Also note that R is not an alias for REDO.

Erasing Lines

The **ERASE** command is explored fully in Chapter 2, but for now you might want to have access to this important command in its simplest form. Using **ERASE** brings up the techniques of object selection that are common to all editing commands. The simplest form of object selection requires that you point to an object and press the pick button. Try the following:

⊕ Select the Erase tool from the dashboard, as shown in Figure 1-20.

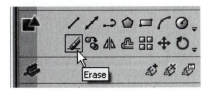

Figure 1-20

When you enter a modify command, such as **ERASE,** the crosshairs disappear, leaving only the pickbox for selecting objects.

⊕ Move the pickbox so that it is over one of the lines on your screen, as shown in Figure 1-21.

When the pickbox touches the line, the line becomes thickened and dashed, as shown in the figure. This is an AutoCAD feature called ***rollover highlighting.*** As your pickbox rolls over an object, it is highlighted before you select it, so that you can be certain that you are selecting the object you want.

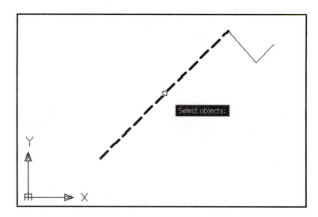

Figure 1-21

⊕ Press the pick button to select the line.

    The line becomes dotted, indicating that it has been selected.

⊕ Right-click or press **Enter** or the spacebar to complete the command.

    The line disappears.

⊕ Before going on, use U or ERASE to remove all lines from your drawing, leaving a blank drawing area.

    Be aware that undoing **ERASE** causes a line to reappear.

Ortho

Before completing this section on line drawing, we suggest that you try the Ortho and Polar tracking modes.

⊕ Select the Line tool from the dashboard or type L ↵.

⊕ Pick a starting point. Any point near the center of the screen will do.

⊕ Pick the DYN button or press F12 to turn off dynamic input.

    Turning dynamic input off will make it easier to see what is happening with Ortho and Polar tracking.

⊕ Pick the Ortho button or press F8 to turn Ortho on.

    The Ortho button should be in the on position.

⊕ Move the cursor in slow circles.

    Notice how the rubber band jumps between horizontal and vertical without sweeping through any of the angles between. Ortho forces the pointing device to pick up points only along the horizontal and vertical quadrant lines from a given starting point. With Ortho on, you can select points at 0, 90, 180, and 270 degrees of rotation from your starting point only (see Figure 1-22).

    The advantages of Ortho are similar to the advantages of snap mode, except that it limits angular rather than linear increments. It ensures that you get precise and true right angles and perpendiculars easily when that is your intent. Ortho becomes more important as drawings grow more complex. In this chapter it is hardly necessary, but it is convenient in Drawings 1 and 3.

Figure 1-22

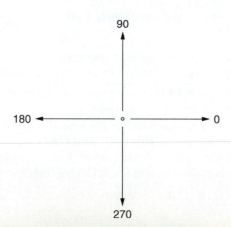

Polar Tracking

Polar tracking is an AutoCAD feature that can replace Ortho in many instances. Try it using the following steps:

⊕ Pick the **Polar** button or press F10 to turn on polar tracking.

Notice that Polar and Ortho are mutually exclusive. They cannot both be on at the same time. When you turn Polar on, Ortho shuts off automatically.

⊕ Move your cursor in a slow circle around the starting point of your line, just as you did with Ortho on.

With polar tracking on, when the rubber band crosses a vertical or horizontal axis (i.e., when the rubber band is at 0, 90, 180, or 270 degrees), a dotted line appears that extends to the edge of the drawing area. You also see a tooltip label, similar to the dynamic input display, giving a value such as Polar 4.3835 < 0°. (See Figure 1-23.) The value is a polar coordinate. By default, polar tracking is set to respond on the orthogonal axes. In Chapter 5, you will see that it can be set to track at any angle. In fact, if your polar tracking is picking up angles other than 0, 90, 180, and 270 degrees, it means that someone has changed this setting in your system.

⊕ Pick the **Polar** button or press F10 to turn polar tracking off.

Move the crosshairs in a circle and observe that polar tracking is no longer in effect.

Figure 1-23

The Esc Key

⊕ While still in the LINE command, press the Esc (escape) key.

This aborts the **LINE** command and brings back the Command: prompt. **Esc** is used to cancel a command that has been entered. Sometimes it is necessary to press **Esc** twice to exit a command and return to the command prompt.

1.6 SAVING AND OPENING YOUR DRAWINGS

Saving a drawing in AutoCAD is just like saving a file in other Windows applications. Use **SAVE** to save an already named drawing. Use **SAVEAS** to name a drawing or to save an already named drawing under a new name. In all cases, a .dwg extension is added automatically to file names to identify them as AutoCAD drawing files.

The SAVE Command

To save your drawing without leaving the Drawing Window, select **Save** from the **File** pull-down menu, or select the **Save** tool from the **Standard** toolbar, as shown in Figure 1-24.

If the current drawing has been previously saved, AutoCAD saves it without an intervening dialog box. If it has not, AutoCAD opens the **Save Drawing As** dialog box and allows you to give the file a new name and location before it is saved.

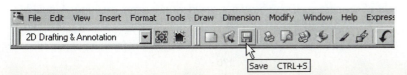

Figure 1-24

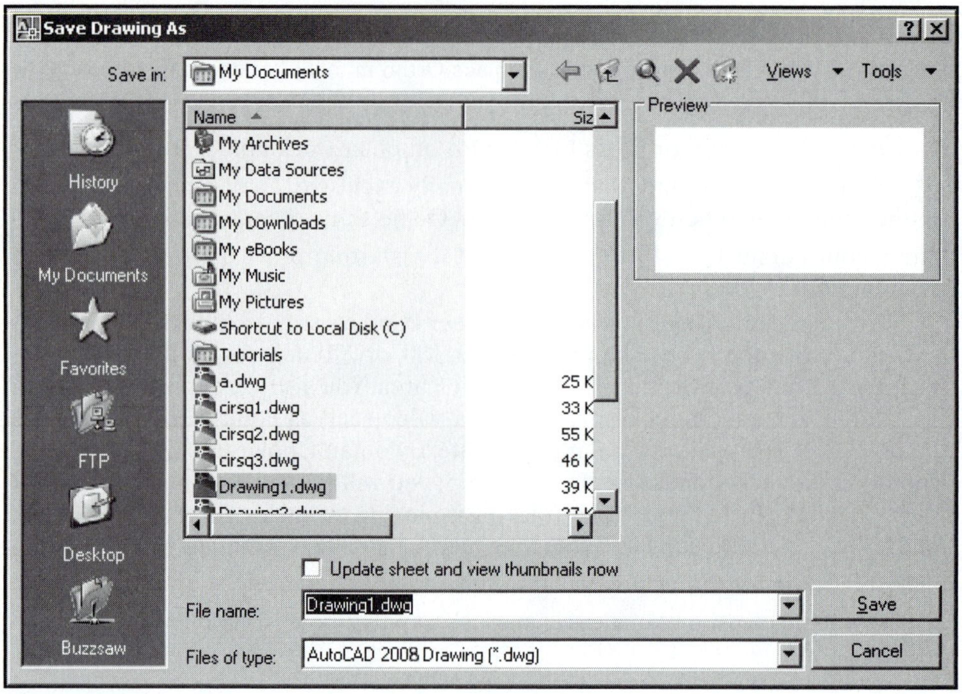

Figure 1-25

The SAVEAS Command

To rename a drawing or to save a drawing in a new location, type Saveas or select Save As from the **File** pull-down menu.

Any of these methods open the **Save Drawing As** dialog box (see Figure 1-25). The cursor blinks in the area labeled File name:, waiting for you to enter a new file name. If needed, you can browse by clicking on the arrow next to the box at the top labeled Save in:. A list of drives and folders opens and you can select a location from the list.

The **Save Drawing As** dialog box is one of several standard file selection dialog boxes. These boxes all have a very similar format. There is a File name and a file type edit box at the bottom, a list of places to look or places to save a file on the left, and a Look in or Save in list at the top. The places list on the left includes standard locations on your own computer. There is a History folder, a My Documents folder, a Favorites folder, your computer's Desktop, a folder for File Transfer Protocol (FTP) sites for downloading from the Internet, and Autodesk's Buzzsaw website. Buzzsaw provides project sites where designers can make versions of their drawings available to others on a project team so that collaboration can be facilitated through Internet access.

Opening Saved Drawings

To open a previously saved drawing, select **Open** from the **File** menu or the **Open** tool from the **Standard Annotation** toolbar, just to the left of the **Save** tool.

Any of these methods brings up the **Select File** dialog box. This is another standard file selection dialog box. It is identical to the **Save Drawing As** dialog box, except that Save in has been replaced by Look in. In this **Select File** dialog box, you can select a file folder or Internet location from the places list on the left or from a directory in the middle. When you select a file, AutoCAD shows a preview image of the selected drawing in the Preview image box at the right. This way you can be sure that you are opening the drawing you want.

Exiting the Drawing Window

To leave AutoCAD, open the **File** pull-down menu and select Exit, or click the Windows close button (X) at the upper right of the screen. If you have not saved your current drawing, AutoCAD asks you if you want to save your changes before exiting.

CHAPTER TEST QUESTIONS

Questions

Before going on to the drawings, review the following questions and problems. Then you should be ready for Drawing 1-1.

1. What is the advantage of using the 2D dashboard instead of toolbars?
2. What are the three different modes of the coordinate display and how does each mode appear? How do you switch between modes?
3. What is heads-up design? Give three examples of heads-up design features from this chapter.
4. Explain and describe the differences among absolute, relative, and polar coordinates.
5. Explain how dynamic input and the coordinate display can be used simultaneously to provide different types of information.
6. What function key turns the Dynamic Input on and off?
7. You have just entered the point (1,1,0) and you now wish to enter the point two units straight up from this point. How would you identify this point using absolute, relative, and polar coordinates?
8. What is the value and limitation of having Snap on?
9. Name three different ways to enter the **LINE** command.
10. Name and describe three different methods of point selection in AutoCAD.
11. What does the **U** command do?
12. What is the keyboard alias for the **LINE** command?
13. What key do you use to cancel a command?
14. What command would you use to save a new version of a drawing under a new file name? How would you enter it?

Drawing Problems

1. Draw a line from (3,2) to (4,8) using the keyboard only.
2. Draw a line from (6,6) to (7,5) using the mouse only.
3. Draw a line from (6,6) to (6,8) using dynamic input.
4. Undo (U) all lines on your screen.
5. Draw a square with the corners at (2,2), (7,2), (7,7), and (2,7). Then erase it using the **ERASE** command.

WWW Exercise 1 (Optional)

AutoCAD is a fully integrated Internet program. If you have Internet access you can access websites directly from within the AutoCAD program. You must first be connected to your Internet service provider. Once connected, you can move easily in and out of AutoCAD as you access all the resources available on the Web. AutoCAD drawings can be published to the Web, transferred as email attachments, uploaded, downloaded, and included as part of websites and home pages. Later in this book you learn how objects in a drawing can be designated as hyperlinks so that selecting them takes you directly from the drawing to an associated Uniform Resource Locator (URL). Also, you learn how common symbols and predrawn objects can be accessed and inserted into your drawings to reduce duplicated effort. To facilitate your learning, this book has its own companion website that you are encouraged to access. At this site you will find self-scoring tests for each chapter of the book, special Web projects related to the material in the chapter, and links to other important and interesting CAD-related websites.

In this chapter we show you how to access Autodesk.com and then take you to our companion website. Once there, take the test or go to the Web Project page for further instructions.

⊞ First, you must be sure that you are connected to an Internet service provider.

You might already be connected to the Internet, depending on your system. If you are not, you need to go through a sign-on procedure. In most cases, AutoCAD automatically initiates your sign-on procedure when you enter a Web command. If this does not happen, do not exit AutoCAD, but use the minimize button (the third button from the right at the top of the screen, with the minus sign) to temporarily leave the AutoCAD Drawing Window. We cannot give you specific instructions for connecting to the Internet from your system. For these, consult your Internet software documentation, instructor, or system manager.

⊞ If necessary, after connecting to the Internet, click the AutoCAD icon on the Windows taskbar to return to the AutoCAD Drawing Window.

⊞ At the command prompt, type "browser."

This is the **BROWSER** command, through which you can access Internet addresses, local network addresses, or locations on your own computer. AutoCAD prompts for an address:

```
Enter Web location (URL)<http:www.autodesk.com>:
```

The default location is shown within the brackets (<>) and might be different from the one shown here. It can be any valid location on your computer or on the Internet. In Chapter 2, we show you how to change the default location. As shown, the out-of-the-box default Internet location is Autodesk's own website, *http://www.autodesk.com*. Pressing **Enter** at this prompt takes you directly to this website.

⊞ Press Enter to accept the default website.

If your Internet connection is in order, you will see the Autodesk website home page, as shown in Figure 1-26, or whatever website is the default location on your system.

Note:
All descriptions and illustrations of Web pages were current as of the printing of this book. Websites can and should change, so by the time you are reading this, things might look different.

Our Companion Website

This book has its own useful companion website. On the site, you will find self-scoring tests for each chapter of the book, special Web projects related to the material in the chapters, and links to other important and interesting CAD-related websites. To reach any website that is not the current default Web location, type the address at the command line.

⊞ Close the Autodesk website.

⊞ At the command prompt, type "browser," or press Enter to repeat the BROWSER command.

AutoCAD prompts for an address:

```
Enter Web location (URL) <http:www.autodesk.com.>:
```

⊞ Type prenhall.com/dixriley ↵.

Figure 1-26

Figure 1-27

If you are properly configured and connected, this opens our companion website home page, shown in Figure 1-27.

⊕ Maximize the window, as shown, select the Discovering AutoCAD 2008 image, and enjoy your visit!

CHAPTER PROJECTS

Drawing 1-1: Grate

Before beginning, look over the drawing page. The first two drawings in this chapter are given without dimensions. Instead, we have drawn them as you will see them on the screen, against the background of a half-unit grid. All these drawings were done using the default half-unit snap, but all points are found on one-unit increments.

Note:
Units in AutoCAD can represent many different units of measurement. In some cases we use the word unit generically when there is no need to refer to specific units such as feet, inches, centimeters, or kilometers.

Drawing Suggestions

- If you are beginning a new drawing, type or select **New.**
- Ensure that acad is entered in the **File** name box of the Select template dialog box, and press **Enter** to complete the dialog.
- Remember to watch the coordinate display or dynamic input display when searching for a point.
- Be sure that Snap, Grid, Model, and the coordinate display are all turned on and that Osnap, Otrack, DUCS, and LWT are turned off. Ortho, Polar, and Dyn can be on or off as you wish.
- Draw the outer rectangle first. It is six units wide and seven units high, and its lower left-hand corner is at the point (3.0000,1.0000). The three smaller rectangles inside are 4 × 1.
- The Close option can be used in all four of the rectangles.

TIP   For drawing an enclosed figure like the one in Problem 5 on page 23, the **LINE** command provides a convenient Close option. Close connects the last in a continuous series of lines back to the starting point of the series. In drawing a square, for instance, you would simply type c in lieu of drawing the last of the four lines. For this to work, the whole square must be drawn without leaving the **LINE** command.

If You Make a Mistake—U

This is a reminder that you can stay in the **LINE** command as you undo the last line you drew, or the last two or three if you have drawn a series.

- Type U ↵. The last line you drew will be gone or replaced by the rubber band, awaiting a new endpoint. If you want to go back more than one line, type U again, as many times as you need to.
- If you have already left the **LINE** command, the **U** command undoes the last continuous series of lines.
- Remember, if you have mistakenly undone something, you can get it back by using the **Redo** tool. You cannot perform other commands between U and REDO, but you can redo several **UNDO** commands if they have been done sequentially.

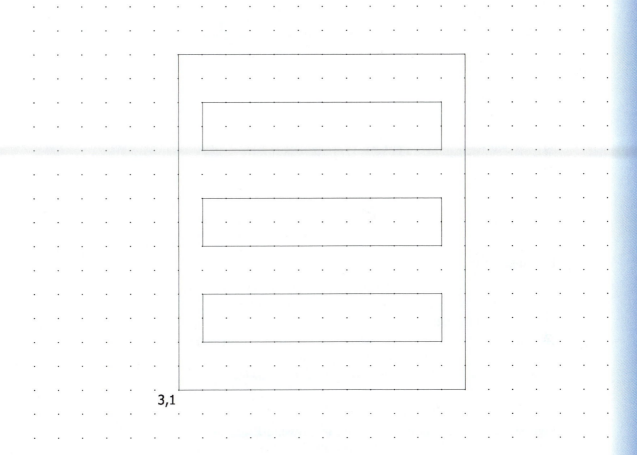

3,1

GRATE
Drawing 1-1

Drawing 1-2: Design

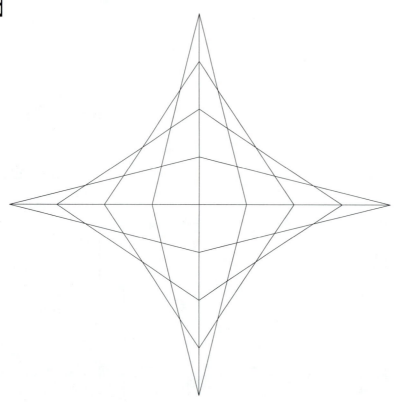

Drawing Suggestions

- If you are beginning a new drawing, type or select New, check to see that you are using the acad template, and press **Enter.**
- Draw the horizontal and vertical lines first. Each is eight units long.
- Notice how the rest of the lines work—outside point on horizontal to inside point on vertical, then working in, or vice versa.
- You will need to make sure Ortho is off to do this drawing.

Repeating a Command

Remember, you can repeat a command by pressing **Enter** or the spacebar at the *Command:* prompt. This is useful in this drawing because you have several sets of lines to draw.

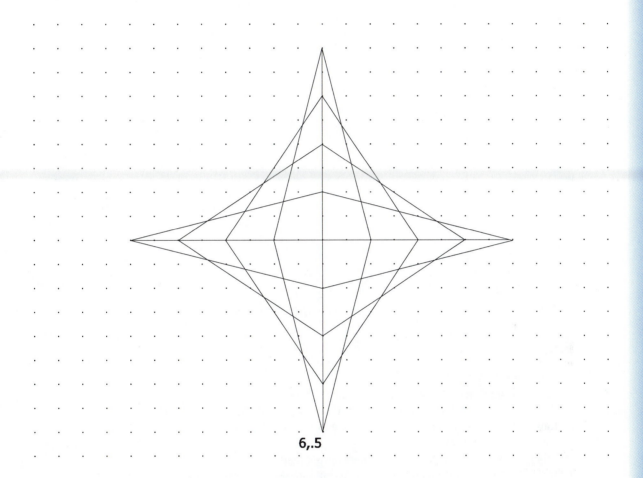

6,.5

DESIGN #1
Drawing 1-2

Drawing 1-3: Shim

This drawing gives you further practice with the **LINE** command. In addition, it gives you practice in translating dimensions into distances on the screen. Note that the dimensions are included only for your information; they are not part of the drawing at this point. Your drawing should appear like the reference drawing on this page. Dimensioning is the subject of Chapter 8.

Drawing Suggestions

- Create a new drawing with the acad template.
- It is most important that you choose a starting point that positions the drawing so that it fits on your screen. If you begin with the bottom left-hand corner of the outside figure at the point (3,1), you should have no trouble.
- Read the dimensions carefully to see how the geometry of the drawing works. It is good practice to look over the dimensions before you begin drawing. Often the dimension for a particular line might be located on another side of the figure or might have to be extrapolated from other dimensions. It is not uncommon to misread, misinterpret, or miscalculate a dimension, so take your time.

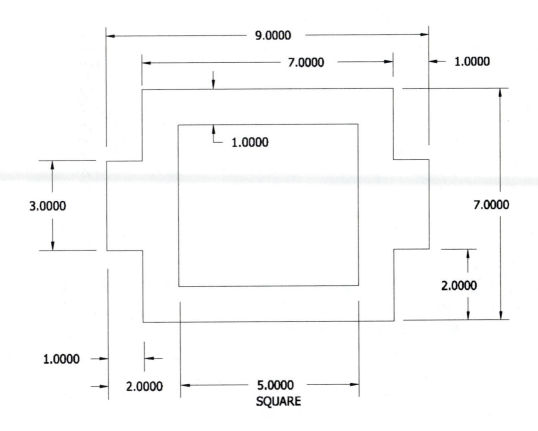

SHIM

Drawing 1-3

Drawing 1-4: Stamp

This drawing gives you practice in point selection. You can begin anywhere and use any of the point selection methods introduced in this chapter. We recommend that you try them all, including the use of dynamic input and the **Tab** key.

Drawing Suggestions

- Create a new drawing with the acad template.
- Ortho should be off to do this drawing.
- The entire drawing can be done without leaving the **LINE** command if you wish.
- If you do leave LINE, remember that you can repeat LINE by pressing **Enter** or the spacebar, and then select the last point as a new start point by pressing **Enter** or the spacebar again.
- Plan to use point selection by typing, by pointing, and by dynamic input. Make use of absolute, relative, and polar coordinates.

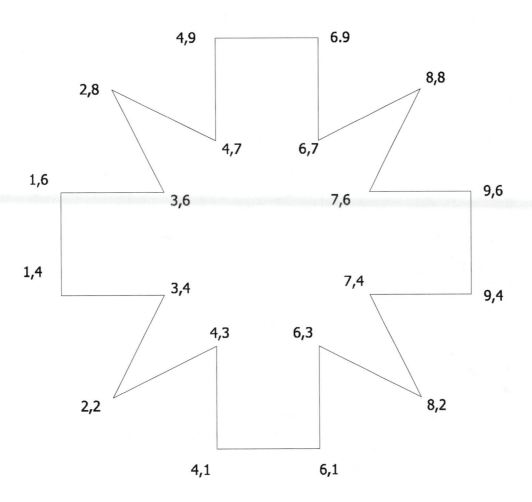

STAMP
Drawing 1-4

Drawing 1-5: Tiles

This drawing will give you lots of practice with the **LINE** command. All points are on the 0.50 grid and the dimensions on the drawing page give all the information you need to complete the drawing.

Drawing Suggestions

- Begin by drawing an 8 × 8 square.
- Be sure to make frequent use of the spacebar to repeat the **LINE** command.
- Add sixteen 2″ square tile outlines.
- Fill in the geometry in each of the 2″ squares.

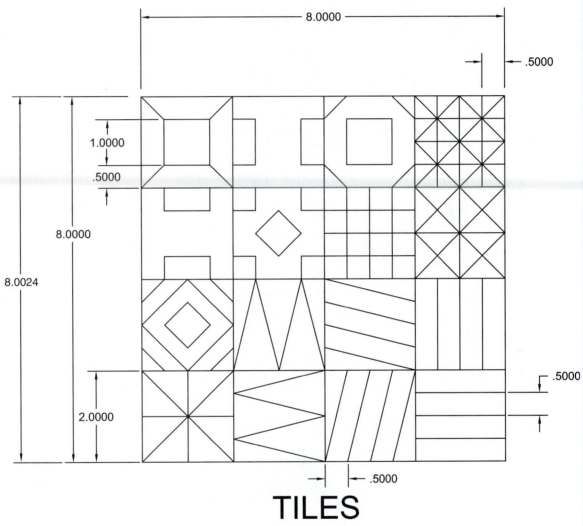

TILES
Drawing 1-5

Circles and Drawing Aids

2

Chapter Objectives

- Changing the Grid Setting
- Changing the Snap Setting
- Changing Units
- Drawing Circles Giving Center Point and Radius
- Drawing Circles Giving Center Point and Diameter
- Accessing AutoCAD Help Features
- Using the ERASE Command
- Using the RECTANGLE Command
- Using the DIST Command
- Plotting or Printing a Drawing

INTRODUCTION

This chapter is loaded with new material and techniques. Here you begin to gain control of your drawing environment by changing the spacing of the grid and snap and the units in which coordinates are displayed. You add to your repertoire of objects by drawing circles with the **CIRCLE** command and rectangles with the **RECTANGLE** command. You explore the many methods of object selection as you continue to learn editing procedures with the **ERASE** command. You gain access to convenient Help features and begin to learn AutoCAD's extensive plotting and printing procedures.

2-1 CHANGING THE GRID SETTING

GENERAL PROCEDURE	1. Type grid ↵. 2. Enter a new value.

When you begin a new drawing using the acad template, the grid and snap are set with a spacing of 0.5000 units. In Chapter 1, all drawings were completed without altering the grid and snap spacings from the default value. Usually you want to change this to a value that reflects your application. You might want a 10-mile snap for a mapping project or a 0.010-inch snap for a printed circuit diagram. The grid can match the snap setting or can be set independently.

⊞ Create a new drawing by selecting the **QNew** tool from the **Standard Annotation** toolbar.

⊞ Check to see that acad is in the File name box and press Enter.

Once again, this ensures that you begin with the settings we have used in preparing this chapter.

⊞ Turn on Grid and Snap.

⊞ Type z ↵ to execute the **ZOOM** command.

⊞ Type a ↵ to zoom all.

⊞ Type grid ↵.

The command area prompt appears like this, with options separated by slashes (/):

Specify grid spacing(X) or [ON/OFF/Snap/Major/aDaptive/
Limits/Follow/Aspect]<0.5000>:

If dynamic input is on, you also see part of this prompt next to the crosshairs. You can ignore the options for now. The number <0.5000> shows the current setting.

⊞ In answer to the prompt, type 1 ↵ and watch what happens.

The screen changes to show a 1-unit grid.

⊞ Move the cursor around to observe the effects of the new grid setting.

The snap setting has not changed, so you still have access to all half-unit points, but the grid shows only single-unit increments.

⊞ Try other grid settings. Try 2, 0.25, and 0.125.

Remember that you can repeat the last command, **GRID,** by pressing **Enter** or the spacebar.

⊞ Before going on to Section 2.2, set the grid back to 0.5000.

2.2 CHANGING THE SNAP SETTING

GENERAL PROCEDURE	1. Select Drafting Settings from the **Tools** pull-down menu, or right-click the **Grid** or **Snap** button and select Settings. 2. Enter a new snap value. 3. Click **OK** to exit the dialog box.

Grid and snap are similar enough to cause confusion. The grid is only a visual reference. It has no effect on selection of points. Snap is invisible, but it dramatically affects point selection. Grid and snap might or might not have the same setting.

Using the Drafting Settings Dialog Box

Snap can be changed using the **SNAP** command at the prompt, as we did with the **GRID** command in the last section. Both can also be changed in the **Drafting Settings** dialog box, as we do here.

⊞ Right-click on the Snap or Grid button and select Settings from the Shortcut menu, as shown in Figure 2-1.

This opens the **Drafting Settings** dialog box shown in Figure 2-2. **DSETTINGS** is the command that calls up this dialog box, and ds is the command alias. Look at the dialog box. It contains

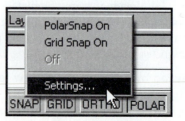

Figure 2-1

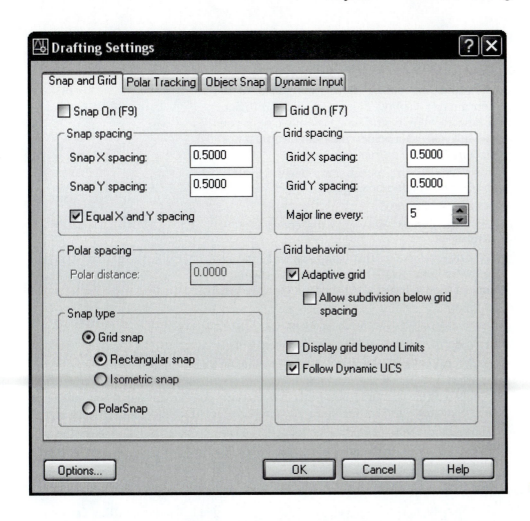

Figure 2-2

some common features, including tabs, check boxes, panels, and edit boxes. When you open from the shortcut menu, the **Snap and Grid** tab should be selected as shown. If not, select it now.

⊞   If the Snap and Grid card is not on top, click its tab to bring it up.

Below the tabs you will see check boxes labeled Snap On (F9) and Grid On (F7). You can turn snap and grid on and off by picking the appropriate check box. In your dialog box, check boxes should show that both snap and grid are on.

The snap and grid settings are shown in edit boxes, labeled Snap X spacing, Snap Y spacing, Grid X spacing, and Grid Y spacing. You can double-click in the edit box to high-light the entire text, or point and click once anywhere inside the box to do partial editing.

To change the snap setting, do the following:

> **Note:**
> The dialog box has places to set both x and y spacing. It is un-likely that you want to have a grid or snap matrix with dif-ferent horizontal and vertical increments, but the capacity is there if you do.

⊞   Double-click inside the edit box labeled Snap
     X spacing.

     The entire number 0.5000 in the Snap X
     spacing box should be highlighted.

⊞   Type 1 ↵.

Pressing **Enter** at this point is the same as clicking **OK** in the dialog box. It takes you out of the dialog box and back to the screen.

Snap is now set at 1 and grid is still at 0.5. This makes the snap setting larger than the grid setting.

⊞   Move the cursor around the screen.

     You will see that you can access only half of the grid points. This type of arrangement is not too useful. Try some other settings.

⊕ Open the dialog box again by right-clicking the **Snap** button on the status bar and then choosing Settings from the shortcut menu.

⊕ Change the Snap X spacing value to 0.25.

Move the cursor slowly and observe the coordinate display. This is a more efficient arrangement. With grid set coarser than snap, you can still pick exact points easily, but the grid is not so dense as to be distracting.

⊕ Press **Enter** or the spacebar to open the Drafting Settings dialog box again.

⊕ Set the snap to 0.05.

⊕ Move the cursor and watch the coordinate display.

Observe how the snap setting is reflected in the available coordinates. How small a snap will AutoCAD accept?

⊕ Try 0.005.

Move the cursor and observe the coordinate display.

⊕ Try 0.0005.

You could even try 0.0001, but this would be like turning snap off, because the coordinate display is registering four decimal places anyway. Unlike the grid, which is limited by the size and resolution of your screen, you can set snap to any value you like. If you try a grid setting that is too small, AutoCAD will default to a larger grid.

⊕ Finally, before you leave this section, set the snap back to 0.25 and leave the grid at 0.5.

> **Note:**
> Commands that call dialog boxes, like other commands, can be repeated by pressing the spacebar or **Enter**.

TIP If you wish to keep snap and grid the same, set the grid to 0 in the **Drafting Settings** dialog box, or enter the **GRID** command and type "s" for the Snap option. The grid then changes to match the snap and continues to change anytime you reset the snap. To free the grid, just give it its own value again.

2.3 CHANGING UNITS

GENERAL PROCEDURE	1. Type Units ↵, or select Units from the **Format** menu.
	2. Answer the prompts.

The Drawing Units Dialog Box

The **Drawing Units** dialog box makes use of drop-down lists, another common dialog box feature.

⊕ Type Units ↵, or select Units from the Format menu.

This opens the **Drawing Units** dialog box shown in Figure 2-3. This dialog box has six drop-down lists for specifying various characteristics of linear and angular drawing units. Drop-down lists show a current setting next to an arrow that is used to open the list of other possibilities. Your dialog box should show that the current Length Type in your drawing is decimal units precise to 0.0000 places, and Angle Type is decimal degrees with 0 places. Notice also the Sample Output area that gives examples of the current units.

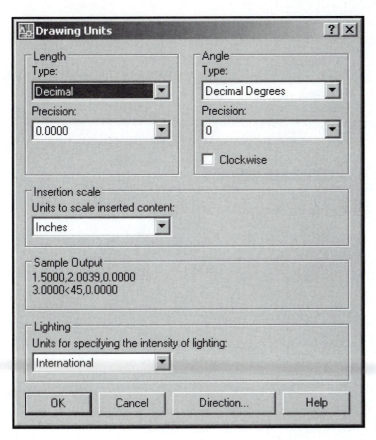

Figure 2-3

⊕ Pick the arrow to the right of the word Decimal, under Type in the Length panel of the dialog box.

A list drops down with the following options:

```
Architectural
Decimal
Engineering
Fractional
Scientific
```

Architectural units display feet and fractional inches (1′ − 3½), engineering units display feet and decimal inches (1′ − 3.50″), fractional units display units in a mixed number format (15½), and scientific units use exponential notation for the display of very large or very small numbers (1.55E + 01). With the exception of engineering and architectural formats, these formats can be used with any basic unit of measurement. For example, decimal mode works for metric units as well as English units.

Throughout most of this book, we stick to decimal units. If you are designing a house you are more likely to use architectural units. If you are building a bridge, you might want engineering-style units. You might want to use scientific units if you are mapping subatomic particles.

Whatever your application, once you know how to change units, you can do so at any time. However, as a drawing practice it is best to choose appropriate units when you first begin work on a new drawing.

⊕ Select Decimal, or click anywhere outside the list box to close the list without changing the setting.

Now we will change the precision setting to two-place decimals.

⊕ Click the down arrow next to 0.0000 in the Precision list box in the Length panel.

This opens a list with options ranging from 0 to 0.00000000, as shown in Figure 2-4.

Drawing Units

Length
Type:
Decimal

Precision:
0.00

0
0.0
0.00
0.000
0.0000
0.00000
0.000000
0.0000000
0.00000000

Angle
Type:
Decimal Degrees

Precision:
0

☐ Clockwise

Sample Output
1.5000,2.0039,0.0000
3.0000<45,0.0000

Lighting
Units for specifying the intensity of lighting:
International

OK   Cancel   Direction...   Help

Figure 2-4

We use two-place decimals because they are more common than any other choice.

⊕ Pick 0.00 from the list, as shown in Figure 2-4.

The list closes and 0.00 replaces 0.0000 as the current precision for units of length. Notice that the Sample Output has also changed to reflect the new setting.

The area to the right allows you to change the units in which angular measures, including polar coordinates, are displayed. If you open the Angle Type list, you see the following options:

        Decimal Degrees
        Deg/Min/Sec
        Grads
        Radians
        Surveyor's Unit

The default system is standard decimal degrees with 0 decimal places, measured counterclockwise, with 0 being straight out to the right (3 o'clock), 90 straight up (12 o'clock), 180 to the left (9 o'clock), and 270 straight down (6 o'clock). We will leave these settings alone.

⊕ Check to see that you have two-place decimal units for length and zero-place decimal degree units for angles.

⊕ Pick OK to close the dialog box.

TIP   All dialog boxes can be moved on the screen by picking the gray title area at the top of the dialog box, holding down the pick button, and dragging the box across the screen.

2.4 DRAWING CIRCLES GIVING CENTER POINT AND RADIUS

GENERAL PROCEDURE	1. Pick the **Circle** tool from the 2D Draw control panel on the dashboard. 2. Pick a center point. 3. Enter or show a radius value.

COMMAND GRID	
Command	Circle
Alias	C
Menu	Draw
Tool	

Circles can be drawn by giving AutoCAD a center point and a radius, a center point and a diameter, three points on the circle's circumference, two points that determine a diameter, or two tangent points on other objects and a radius. In this chapter, we use the first two options.

We begin by drawing a circle with radius 3 and center at the point (6,5). Then we draw two smaller circles centered at the same point. Later we erase them using the ERASE command.

⊕ Grid should be set to 0.50, snap to 0.25, and units to two-place decimal.

⊕ Pick the **Circle** tool from the dashboard, as illustrated in Figure 2-5.

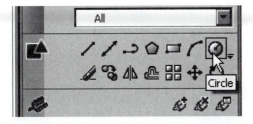

Figure 2-5

The prompt that follows looks like this:

```
Specify center point for circle or
[3P/2P/Ttr (tan tan radius)]:
```

⊕ Pick the center point of the circle you want to draw. In our case, it is the point (6,5).

AutoCAD assumes that a radius or diameter will follow and shows the following prompt:

```
Specify radius of circle or [Diameter]:
```

If we type or point to a value now, AutoCAD takes it as a radius because that is the default. Diameter is the only other option. We will get to it momentarily.

⊕ Move your cursor and observe the rubber band and dragged circle. If your dynamic input display is not on, turn it on by picking the **Dyn** button.

Dynamic input is a great feature for drawing circles. It will give you the radius or diameter of the circle you are drawing.

⊕ Watch the dynamic input display and pick a point 3.00 away from the center point.

With snap on, you will find that you can move exactly 3.00 only if you are at 0, 90, 180, or 270 degrees.

Your first circle should now be complete.

⊕ Draw two more circles using the same center point, radius method. They should be centered at (6,5) and have radii of 2.50 and 2.00. Use the spacebar to repeat the command.

The results are illustrated in Figure 2-6.

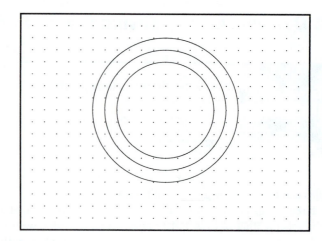

Figure 2-6

2.5 DRAWING CIRCLES GIVING CENTER POINT AND DIAMETER—

GENERAL PROCEDURE	1. Pick the **Circle** tool from the dashboard. 2. Pick a center point. 3. Type "d" ↵. 4. Enter or pick a diameter value.

We will draw three more circles centered on (6,5) having diameters of 1, 1.5, and 2. This method of drawing circles is almost the same as the radius method, except you do not use the default, and you will see that the rubber band and dynamic input display work differently.

⊕ Press Enter or the spacebar to repeat the CIRCLE command.

⊕ Pick the center point at (6,5).

⊕ Answer the prompt by typing d for diameter.

⊕ Move the crosshairs away from the center point.

Notice that the crosshairs are now outside the circle you are dragging on the screen (see Figure 2-7). This is because AutoCAD is looking for a diameter, but the last point you gave was a center point. So the diameter is being measured from the center point out, twice the radius. Also notice that the dynamic input display has responded to the diameter specification and is now

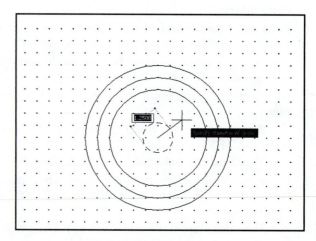

Figure 2-7

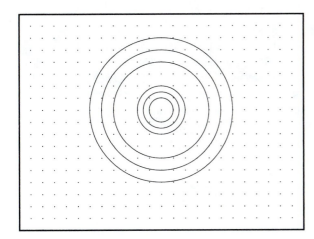

Figure 2-8

measuring the diameter of the circle. Move the cursor around, in and out from the center point, to get a feel for this.

⊕ Pick a diameter of 1.00.

   You should now have four circles.

⊕ Draw two more circles with diameters of 1.50 and 2.00.

   When you are done, your screen should look like Figure 2-8.

   Studying Figure 2-9 and using the **HELP** command, as discussed in the next section, will give you a good introduction to the remaining options in the **CIRCLE** command.

2 POINT

Pick two points.
The distance between points
defines the diameter of circle.

3 POINT

Pick three points.
The arc through all three points
is completed to from circle.
Circle is visible on screen after
second point is selected.

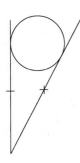

TANGENT, TANGENT, RADIUS

Select two objects on the screen.
Type or show radius length.
AutoCAD constructs the circle
that has the given radius and is
tangent to both objects.

Figure 2-9

TIP   Here are two ways to stay heads-up and avoid going to the keyboard to type "d" for the diameter option: (1) After entering the **CIRCLE** command and picking a center point, right-click to open a shortcut menu. Select Diameter. (2) If you enter the **CIRCLE** command from the **Draw** pull-down menu and select one of the options on the submenu, some of the command steps are automated. For example, if you select the Center, Diameter option, the command behaves as if Diameter is the default and you do not have to enter a "d."

2.6 ACCESSING AUTOCAD HELP FEATURES

GENERAL PROCEDURE
1. Pick the **Help** tool from the **Standard Annotation** toolbar or press F1.
2. Click the **Index** tab.
3. Type the name of a command or topic.
4. Highlight the item you want.
5. Double-click the **Display** button.

The AutoCAD **HELP** command gives you access to an extraordinary amount of information in a comprehensive library of AutoCAD references and information. The procedures for using HELP are standard Windows procedures and access the User's Guide, the Command Reference, the Driver and Peripheral Guide, the Installation and Licensing Guide, and the Customization Guide. In this section, we focus on the use of the Index feature, which pulls information from all the references, depending on the topic you select. For a demonstration, we look for further information on the **CIRCLE** command.

⊕ To begin you should be at the command prompt.

HELP is context sensitive; it goes directly to the AutoCAD Command Reference if you ask for help while in the middle of a command sequence. You should try this later.

⊕ Pick the Help tool from the Standard Annotation toolbar, as shown in Figure 2-10.

Figure 2-10

This opens the AutoCAD **Help** dialog box shown in Figure 2-11. If the **Contents** tab is showing, you see the list of available references. You can browse through the contents of each reference, but it is usually quicker to use the **Index** tab. You also see a **Search** tab. Search is similar to index, but does not show you a list of topics until after you enter words as a search criterion.

⊕ If necessary, pick the Index tab.

You should see the Index as shown in Figure 2-11. The list of topics is very long, so it is rare that you use the scroll bar on the right. Most often you type in a command or topic. The list updates as you type, so you might not need to type the complete word or command.

⊕ Type "ci" without pressing Enter.

Do this slowly, one letter at a time, and you can see how the index follows along. When you have typed ci, the list shows entries beginning with circle. Adding the rest of the letters rcle has no further effect.

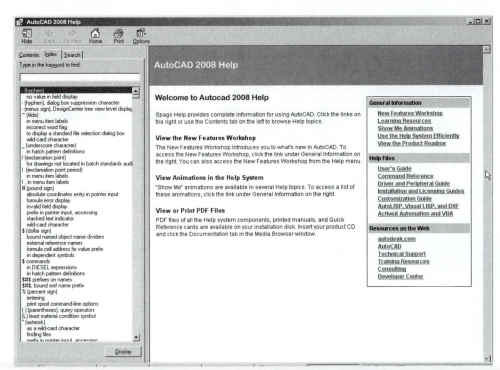

Figure 2-11

⊕ Double-click CIRCLE command.

This opens a smaller **Topics Found** dialog box.

⊕ Double-click CIRCLE again, press Enter, or click the Display button.

AutoCAD displays the **CIRCLE** command page from the AutoCAD Command Reference, as shown in Figure 2-12. Links to additional information on items on this page are available for words underlined and shown in blue.

⊕ Pick Ttr (tan tan radius).

This takes you to the information for the Tangent, Tangent, Radius option of the **CIRCLE** command, shown in Figure 2-13.

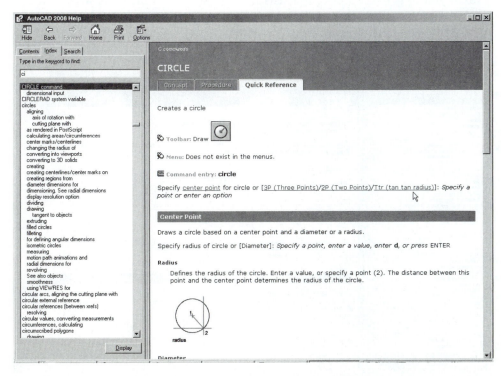

Figure 2-12

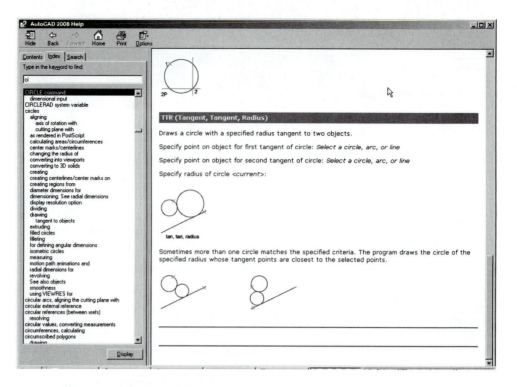

Figure 2-13

Concepts, Procedures, and Quick Reference

⊞ Scroll back up to the top of the page.

There are three tabs at the top of the Command Reference page, labeled Concepts, Procedures, and Quick Reference. These give you access to further discussion of the command or topic you have reached through the index. For example, consider the following:

⊞ Click the Concepts tab.

This calls up a page of discussion of concepts related to the topic you have chosen, in this case, drawing circles, as shown in Figure 2-14. The **Procedures** tab takes you to general procedures lists that are similar to the ones we use at the

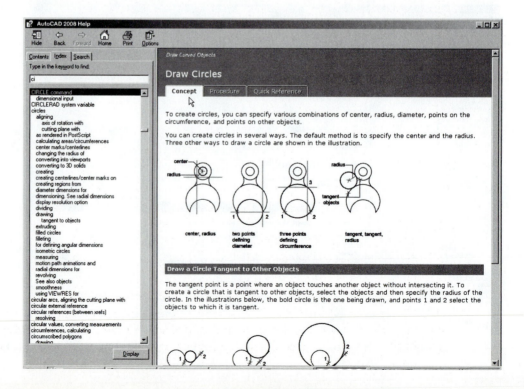

Figure 2-14

beginning of many of the sections in this book. Try it. The **Commands** tab shows you glossary-like entries for commands and system variables relating to the topic you have chosen. Try that, too.

⊕ To exit Help, pick the Close button.

This terminates the **HELP** command and brings you back to the command prompt.

2.7 USING THE **ERASE** COMMAND

GENERAL PROCEDURE	1. Pick the **Erase** tool from the dashboard. 2. Select objects. 3. Press **Enter** to carry out the command. or 1. Select objects. 2. Pick the **Erase** tool from the dashboard.

AutoCAD allows for many different methods of editing and even allows you to alter some of the basics of how edit commands work. Fundamentally, there are two different sequences for using most edit commands. These are called the noun/verb and the verb/noun methods.

In this section, we review the verb/noun sequence and then introduce the noun/verb or "pick first" method along with some of the many methods for selecting objects.

COMMAND GRID	
Command	Erase
Alias	E
Menu	Modify
Tool	

Verb/Noun Editing

⊕ To begin this section you should have the six circles on your screen, as shown previously in Figure 2-8.

We use verb/noun editing to erase the two outer circles. This is the same method introduced in Chapter 1. Here we pick two objects before erasing.

⊕ Pick the Erase tool from the dashboard.

In the command area and the dynamic input display, you see the prompt

Select objects:

This is a very common prompt. You will find it in all edit commands and many other commands as well.

⊕ Pick the outer circle.

TIP In many situations, you might find it convenient or necessary to turn snap mode off while selecting objects because this gives you more freedom of motion.

The circle will be highlighted.

⊕ Use the box to pick the second circle moving in toward the center.

It too should now be dotted.

⊕ Press the right button on your mouse to carry out the command.

This is typical of the verb/noun sequence in most edit commands. Once a command has been entered and a selection set defined, a press of the **Enter** key or right button is required to complete the command. At this point the two outer circles should be erased.

Noun/Verb Editing

Now let's try the noun/verb sequence.

⊕ Pick the Undo tool or type u to undo the ERASE command and bring back the circles.

⊕ Use the pick box to select the outer circle.

The circle is highlighted, and your screen should now resemble Figure 2-15. Those little blue boxes are called *grips*. They are part of AutoCAD's autoediting system, which we begin exploring in Chapter 3. For now, you can ignore them.

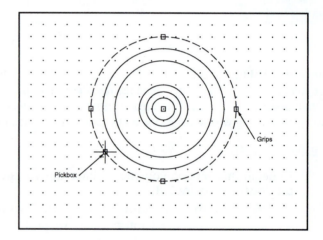

Figure 2-15

⊕ Pick the second circle in the same fashion.

The second circle also becomes dotted, and more grips appear.

⊕ Pick the Erase tool from the dashboard.

Alternatively, you can type "e" or press the Delete button. Your two outer circles disappear.

The two outer circles should now be gone. As you can see, there is not a lot of difference between the two sequences. One difference that is not immediately apparent is that there are numerous selection methods available in the verb/noun system that cannot be activated when you pick objects first. We cover other object selection methods momentarily, but first try the **OOPS** command.

Note:
If you try to use the right mouse button in place of **Enter** in this sequence it would call a shortcut menu. Avoid it unless you have use for the options on the menu.

OOPS

⊕ Type oops and watch the screen.

If you have made a mistake in your erasure, you can get your selection set back by typing oops. **OOPS** is to **ERASE** as **REDO** is to **UNDO.** You can use **OOPS** to undo an **ERASE** command, as long as you have not performed another **ERASE** in the meantime. In other words, AutoCAD saves only your most recent **ERASE** selection set.

You can also use **U** to undo an **ERASE,** but notice the difference: **U** simply undoes the last command, whatever it might be; **OOPS** works specifically with **ERASE** to recall the last set of erased objects. If you have drawn other objects in the meantime, you can still use **OOPS** to recall a previously erased set. However, if you tried to use **U,** you would have to backtrack, undoing any newly drawn objects along the way.

Other Object Selection Methods

You can select individual entities on the screen by picking them one by one, as we have done previously, but in complex drawings this is often inefficient. AutoCAD offers a variety of other methods. In this exercise, we select circles by the windowing and crossing methods, by indicating last or L, for the last entity drawn, and by indicating previous or P for the previously defined set. There are also options to add or remove objects from the selection set and other variations on windowing and crossing. We suggest that you study Figure 2-16 to learn about other methods. The number of selection options available might seem a bit overwhelming at first, but time learning them is well spent. These same options appear in many AutoCAD editing commands (**MOVE, COPY, ARRAY, ROTATE, MIRROR**) and will become part of your CAD vocabulary in time.

OBJECT SELECTION METHOD	DESCRIPTION	ITEMS SELECTED
(W) WINDOW	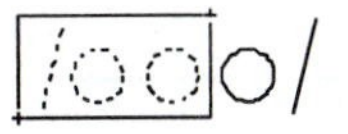	The entities within the box.
(C) CROSSING	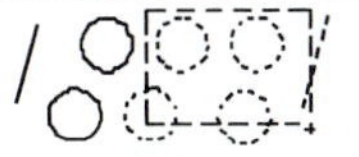	The entities crossed by or within the box.
(P) PREVIOUS		The entities that were previously picked.
(L) LAST	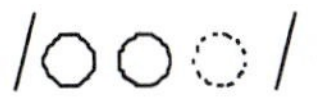	The entity that was drawn last.
(R) REMOVE	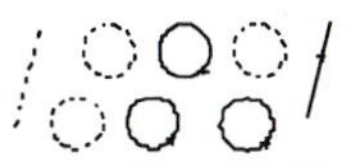	Removes entities from the items selected so they will not be part of the selected group.
(A) ADD	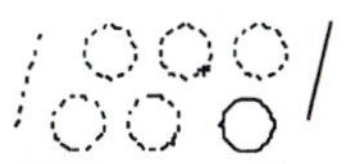	Adds entities that were removed and allows for more selections after the use of remove.
ALL	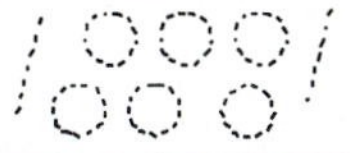	All the entities currently visible on the drawing.
(F) FENCE	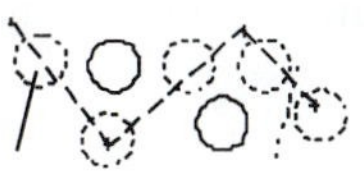	The entities crossed by the fence.
(WP) WPOLYGON	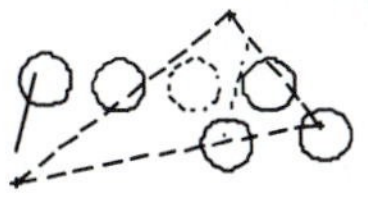	All the entities completely within the window of the polygon.
(CP) CPOLYGON	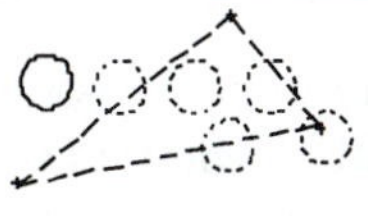	All the entities crossed by the polygon.

Figure 2-16

Selection by Window

The object selection window was demonstrated in Chapter 1 but without objects to select. Now we put it to use. Window and crossing selections, like individual object selection, can be initiated without entering a command. In other words, they are available for noun/verb selection. Whether you select objects first or enter a command first, you can force a window or crossing selection simply by picking points on the screen that are not on objects. AutoCAD assumes you want to select by windowing or crossing and asks for a second point.

Let's try it. We will show AutoCAD that we want to erase all the inner circles by throwing a temporary selection window around them. The window is defined by two points moving left to right that serve as opposite corners of a rectangular window. Only entities that lie completely within the window are selected (see Figure 2-17).

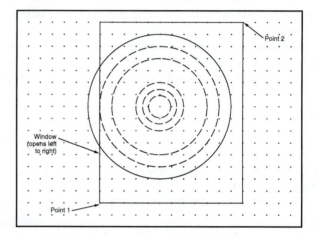

Figure 2-17

⊕ Pick point 1 at the lower left of the screen, as shown.

> Any point in the neighborhood of (3.5,1) will do.
>
> AutoCAD prompts for another corner:

> > Specify opposite corner:

⊕ Pick point 2 at the upper right of the screen, as shown.

> Any point in the neighborhood of (9.5,8.5) will do. To see the effect of the window, be sure that it crosses the outside circle, as shown in Figure 2-17.

⊕ Pick the Erase tool from the dashboard.

> The inner circles should now be erased.

⊕ Type oops ↵ to retrieve the circles once more. Because ERASE was the last command, typing u or selecting the Undo tool also works.

Selection by Crossing Window

Crossing is an alternative to windowing that is useful in many cases where a standard window selection cannot be performed. The selection procedure is similar, but a crossing box opens to the left instead of to the right and all objects that cross the box are chosen, not just those that lie completely inside the box.

We use a crossing box to select the inside circles.

⊕ Pick point 1 close to (8.0,3.0), as in Figure 2-18.

> AutoCAD prompts

> > Specify opposite corner:

⊕ Pick a point near (4.0,7.0).

> This point selection must be done carefully to demonstrate a crossing selection. Notice that the crossing box is shown with dashed lines and a green color, whereas the window box was shown with solid lines and a blue color.

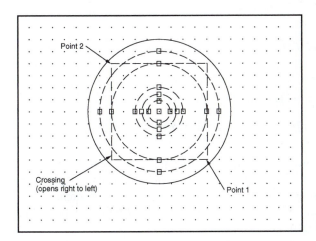

Figure 2-18

Also, notice how the circles are selected: those that cross and those that are completely contained within the crossing box, but not those that lie outside.

At this point we could enter the **ERASE** command to erase the circles, but instead we demonstrate how to use the **Esc** key to cancel a selection set.

⊕ Press the Esc key on your keyboard.

This cancels the selection set. The circles are no longer highlighted and the grips disappear.

Selecting the "Last" Entity

AutoCAD remembers the order in which new objects have been drawn during the course of a single drawing session. As long as you do not close the drawing, you can select the last drawn entity using the "last" option.

⊕ Pick the Erase tool.

Notice that there is no way to specify "last" before you enter a command. This option is available only as part of a command procedure. In other words, it works only in a verb/noun sequence.

⊕ Type L ↵.

One of the smaller circles should be highlighted.

⊕ Right-click to carry out the command.

The circle should be erased.

Selecting the "Previous" Selection Set

The P or previous option works with the same procedure, but it selects the previous selection set rather than the last drawn entity.

Remove and Add

Together, the remove and add options form a switch in the object selection process. Under ordinary circumstances, whatever you select using any of the aforementioned options is added to your selection set. By typing "r" at the *Select objects:* prompt, you can switch to a mode in which everything you pick is deselected or removed from the selection set. Then by typing "a," you can return to the usual mode of adding objects to the set.

Undoing a Selection

The **ERASE** command and other edit commands have an internal undo feature, similar to that found in the **LINE** command. By typing "u" at the *Select objects:* prompt, you can undo your last selection without leaving the edit command you are in and without undoing previous selections. You can also type "u" several times to undo your most recent selections one by one. This allows you to back up one step at a time without canceling the command and starting all over again.

Other Options

If you press any key other than the ones AutoCAD recognizes, at the *Select objects:* prompt, you see the following:

```
Expects a point or
Window/Last/Crossing/Box/All/Fence/WPolygon/CPolygon/Group/Class/
Add/Remove/
Multiple/Previous/Undo/AUto/SIngle/SUbobject/Object
Select objects:
```

Notice that some options require that you enter two letters, as shown by the uppercase letters. Along with the options already discussed, All, Fence, WPolygon, and CPolygon are shown in Figure 2-16. Box, Multiple, AUto, and SIngle are used primarily in programming customized applications. Subobject and Object are used in 3D modeling. Look up the **SELECT** command in the AutoCAD Help index for additional information on object selection.

2.8 USING THE **RECTANGLE** COMMAND

GENERAL PROCEDURE	1. Select the **Rectangle** tool from the dashboard.
	2. Pick the first corner point.
	3. Pick another corner point.

COMMAND GRID	
Command	Rectangle
Alias	Rec
Menu	Draw
Tool	

Now that you have created object selection windows, the **RECTANGLE** command comes naturally. Creating a rectangle in this way is just like creating an object selection window.

⊕ To prepare for this exercise, erase all objects from your screen.

⊕ Select the Rectangle tool from the dashboard, as shown in Figure 2-19.

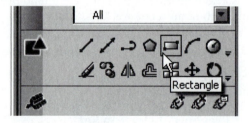

Figure 2-19

AutoCAD prompts for a corner point:

```
Specify first corner point or
[Chamfer/Elevation/Fillet/Thickness/Width]:
```

You can ignore the options for now and proceed with the defaults.

⊕ Pick (3.00,3.00) for the first corner point, as shown in Figure 2-20.

AutoCAD prompts for another point:

```
Specify other corner point or [Area/Dimensions/Rotation]:
```

TIP Notice how the coordinate display and dynamic display work differently after you have entered the **RECTANGLE** command. The coordinate display continues to show absolute coordinates relative to the screen grid. Dynamic input shows values relative to the first corner point of the rectangle so that you can see the dimensions of the rectangle you are drawing.

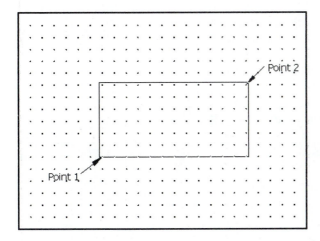

Figure 2-20

⊕ Pick a second point to create a 6 × 3 rectangle.

The dynamic input display will show 6.00 and 3.00, while the coordinate display will show that the second corner point is at (9.00,6.00), as shown in Figure 2-20.

As soon as you enter the second corner, AutoCAD draws a rectangle between the two corner points and returns you to the command prompt. This is a faster way to draw a rectangle than drawing it line by line. There are also some other advantages that we examine in Chapter 3.

Leave the rectangle on your screen for the plotting demonstration in Section 2.10.

2.9 USING THE DIST COMMAND

GENERAL PROCEDURE	1.	Open the **Tools** menu, highlight Inquiry, and select Distance.
	2.	Pick a first point.
	3.	Pick a second point.
	4.	Read the information in the command area.

The **DIST** command is one of AutoCAD's most useful inquiry commands. Inquiry commands give you information about your drawing or objects within it. **DIST** works like a simple **LINE** command procedure, but it gives you distances instead of actually drawing a line. Let us say that you need to know the distance from corner point 1 to corner point 2, the diagonal in the rectangle you just drew. Try the following:

⊕ Select Tools→Inquiry→Distance from the pull-down menu, as shown in Figure 2-21.

AutoCAD prompts you to pick a point:

                    Specify first point:

⊕ Pick (3,3) again.

Notice that AutoCAD gives you a rubber band, just as if you were drawing a line. You are also prompted for a second point:

                    Specify second point:

⊕ Pick (9,6) again.

You are returned to the command prompt and no line is drawn between the two points. However, you should see something like this in the command prompt area:

Distance = 6.71 Angle in XY Plane = 27, Angle from XY Plane = 0
Delta X = 6.00, Delta Y = 3.00, Delta Z = 0.00

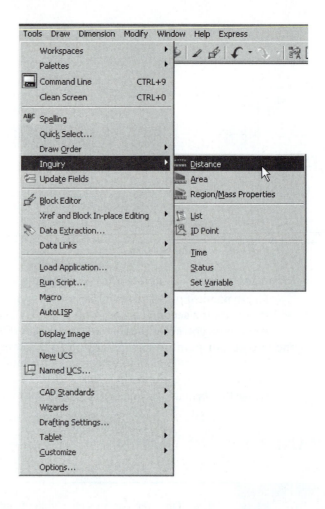

Figure 2-21

You may have to press F2 to open the text window to see all this.

Distance gives the straight-line distance between the two selected points. Angle in XY Plane gives the angle that a line between the two points would make within the coordinate system in which 0 degrees represents a horizontal line out to the right. Angle from XY Plane is a 3D feature and is always 0 in 2D drawings. Delta X is the horizontal displacement, which can be either positive or negative. Similarly, Delta Y is the vertical displacement. Delta Z is the displacement in the z direction. It is always 0 in 2D drafting.

Compare what is in your command prompt area with Figure 2-22.

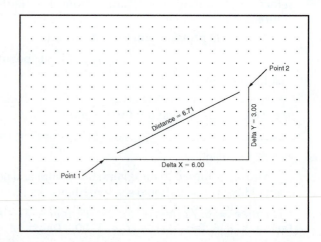

Figure 2-22

2.10 PLOTTING OR PRINTING A DRAWING

GENERAL PROCEDURE

1. Pick the **Plot** tool from the **Standard Annotation** toolbar.
2. Select Window from the What to plot list.
3. Pick two points to define a window.
4. Ensure Fit to paper is showing in the Scale list box.
5. Prepare printer or plotter.
6. Click OK.

AutoCAD's printing and plotting capabilities are extensive and complex. In this book, we introduce you to them a little at a time. We try to keep you moving and get your drawing on paper as efficiently as possible. You will find discussions of plotting and printing in Chapters 2 through 8, before the review material and drawings in each chapter.

In this chapter, we perform a very simple type of plot, going directly from your current model space objects to a sheet of drawing paper, changing only one or two plot settings. Different types of plotters and printers work somewhat differently, but the procedure we use here should achieve reasonably uniform results. It assumes that you do not have to change devices or fundamental configuration details. It should work for all plotters and printers and the drawings in this chapter. We use a window selection to define a plot area and scale this to fit on whatever size paper is in your plotter or printer.

⊞ Pick the Plot tool from the Standard Annotation toolbar, as shown in Figure 2-23.

This opens the **Plot** dialog box illustrated in Figure 2-24. You will become very familiar with it as you work through this book. It is one of the most important dialog boxes in AutoCAD. It contains many options and can be

Figure 2-23

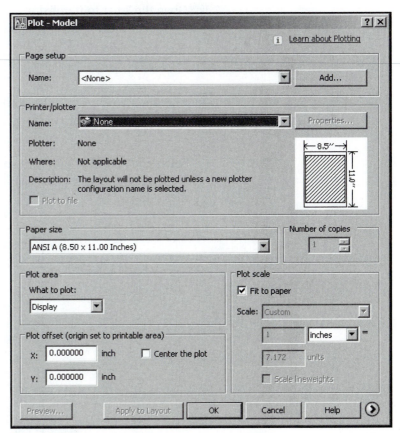

Figure 2-24

expanded to allow even more options by clicking the > button at the bottom right. (If your dialog box is already expanded, you can reduce it by clicking the < button.)

First, you need to specify a plotter or printer. The second panel from the top is the Printer/plotter selection area. Look to see if the name of a plotting device is showing in the Name list box.

⊕ If None is displayed in the list box, click the arrow on the right and select a plotter or printer.

If you are unsure what plotter to use, you can work with AutoCAD's DWF6 ePlot.pc3 utility, which should be present.

Look at the Plot scale panel in the lower right of the dialog box. Locate the Fit to paper check box. If your plot scale is configured to plot to fit your paper, as it should be by default, then AutoCAD plots your drawing at maximum size based on the paper size and the window you specify.

⊕ If for any reason Fit to paper is not checked, click in the box to check it.

On the Custom line below Plot scale, you should see edit boxes with numbers like 1 = 4.768. Right now the plot area is based on the shape of your display area and these numbers are inaccessible. When you use a window to create a plot area that is somewhat smaller, these scale numbers change automatically. When you use Scale rather than Fit to paper, these numbers will be accessible and you can set them manually or select from a list.

Now look at the panel labeled Plot area at the lower left. The drop-down list labeled "What to plot" gives you the choice of plotting based on what is on the Display, the Extents or Limits of the drawing, or a Window you define. For our purposes, defining a window gives more consistent results than relying on the Display area, which might differ more from one system to another. Windowing allows you to plot any portion of a drawing by defining a window in the usual way. AutoCAD bases the size and placement of the plot on the window you define.

⊕ Open the What to plot list and select Window.

The Plot dialog box disappears temporarily, giving you access to the drawing. AutoCAD prompts for point selection:

> Specify window for printing
> Specify first corner:

⊕ Pick the point (1.00,1.00), as shown in Figure 2-25.

AutoCAD prompts

> Specify opposite corner:

⊕ Select the point (11.00,8.00), as shown in Figure 2-25.

As soon as you have picked the second point, AutoCAD displays the Plot dialog box again.

You are now ready to plot.

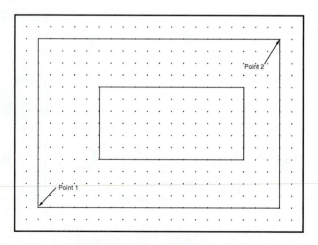

Figure 2-25

⊕ If you want to plot or print the rectangle, prepare your plotter and then click OK. Otherwise, click Cancel.

Clicking OK sends the drawing information to be printed. You can sit back and watch the plotter at work. If you need to cancel for any reason, click Cancel.

For now, that's all there is to it. If your plot does not look perfect—if it is not centered on your drawing sheet, for example—don't worry; you will learn more about plotting in later chapters.

CHAPTER TEST QUESTIONS

Questions

1. Which is likely to have the smaller setting, Grid or Snap? Why? What happens if the settings are reversed?
2. Name three ways to open the **Drafting Settings** dialog box.
3. How do you switch from decimal units to architectural units?
4. Where is 0 degrees located in AutoCAD's default units setup? Where is 270 degrees? Where is −45 degrees?
5. How do you enter the **CIRCLE** command?
6. Why does the rubber band touch the circumference of the circle when you are using the radius option, but not when you are using the diameter option?
7. What does the dynamic input display show when you are drawing a circle using a diameter dimension?
8. What does the dynamic input display show when you are selecting the second point of a rectangle in the **RECTANGLE** command?
9. How does AutoCAD know when you want a crossing selection instead of a window selection?
10. What is the difference between a Last selection and a Previous selection?
11. What is the difference between noun/verb and verb/noun editing?
12. How do you access the AutoCAD Help index?

Drawing Problems

1. Leave the grid at 0.50 and set snap to 0.25.
2. Use the 3P option to draw a circle that passes through the points (2.25,4.25), (3.25,5.25), and (4.25,4.25).
3. Using the 2P option, draw a second circle with a diameter from (3.25,4.25) to (4.25,4.25).
4. Draw a third circle centered at (5.25,4.25) with a radius of 1.00.
5. Draw a fourth circle centered at (4.75,4.25) with a diameter of 1.00.

WWW Exercise 2 (Optional)

In this second voyage to the World Wide Web, we show you how to change the default Uniform Resource Locator (URL) so that you don't have to type a long, ugly address every time you go out to the Web.

We show you how to change the default Web location to the companion website for this book. Whether or not you actually want to retain our website as the default, we encourage you to go there now, take the self-scoring review test, and try the Web project.

⊕ Type inetlocation ↵.

INETLOCATION is a system variable that stores the name of the default URL. AutoCAD prompts

    Enter new value for inetlocation <http:www.autodesk.com>:

Remember that the address within the arrows is the current default. This value is replaced by the address you enter.

⊕ Type prenhall.com/dixriley.

The new value is stored, and AutoCAD returns you to the command prompt. Now all you need to do is enter the **BROWSER** command and press **Enter** at the prompt.

⊕ Type browser ↵.

The AutoCAD prompt shows the new default URL:

        Enter web location (URL) <prenhall.com/dixriley>:

⊕ Press Enter to accept the default location.

Away you go. Good luck on the test.

CHAPTER PROJECTS

Drawing 2-1: Aperture Wheel

This drawing gives you practice creating circles using the center point, radius method. Refer to the table following the drawing for radius sizes. With snap set at 0.25, some of the circles can be drawn by pointing and dragging. Other circles have radii that are not on a snap point. These circles can be drawn by typing in the radius.

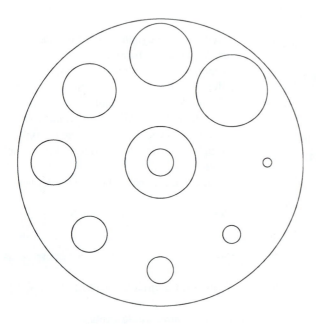

Drawing Suggestions

GRID = 0.50
SNAP = 0.25

- A good sequence for doing this drawing would be to draw the outer circle first, followed by the two inner circles (h and c) in Drawing 2-1. These are all centered on the point (6.00,4.50). Then begin at circle a and work around clockwise, being sure to center each circle correctly.

- Notice that there are two circles c and two h. The two circles having the same letter are the same size.

- Remember, you can type any value you like, and AutoCAD gives you a precise graphic image. However, you cannot always show the exact point you want by pointing. Often it is more efficient to type a few values than to turn Snap off or change its setting for a small number of objects.

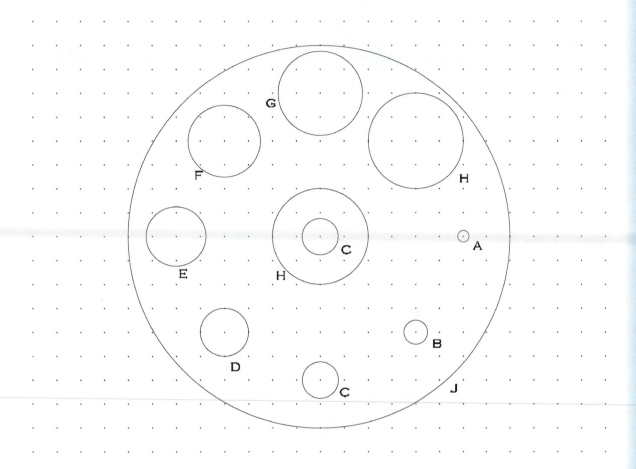

LETTER	A	B	C	D	E	F	G	H	J
RADIUS	.12	.25	.38	.50	.62	.75	.88	1.00	4.00

APERTURE WHEEL

DRAWING 2-1

Drawing 2-2: Roller

This drawing gives you a chance to combine lines and circles and to use the center point, diameter method. It also gives you some experience with smaller objects, a denser grid, and a tighter snap spacing.

TIP Even though units are set to show only two decimal places, it is important to set the snap using three places (0.125) so that the grid is on a multiple of the snap (0.25 = 2 × 0.125). AutoCAD shows you rounded coordinate values, such as 0.13, but keeps the graphics on target. Try setting snap to either 0.13 or 0.12 instead of 0.125, and you will see the problem for yourself.

Drawing Suggestions

```
GRID = 0.25
SNAP = 0.125
```

- The two views of the roller appear fairly small on your screen, making the snap setting essential. Watch the coordinate display as you work and get used to the smaller range of motion.
- Choosing an efficient sequence makes this drawing much easier to complete. Because the two views must line up properly, we suggest that you draw the front view first, with circles of diameter 0.25 and 1.00, and then use these circles to position the lines in the right side view.
- The circles in the front view should be centered in the neighborhood of (2.00,6.00). This puts the upper left-hand corner of the 1 × 1 square at around (5.50,6.50).

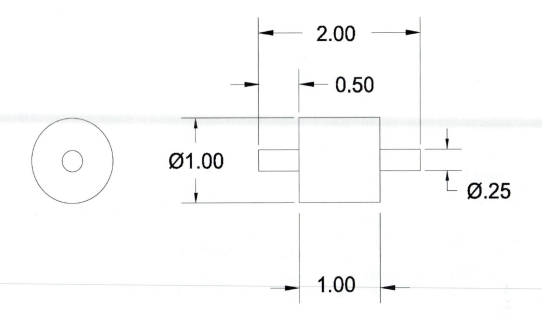

ROLLER

Drawing 2-2

Drawing 2-3: Fan Bezel

This drawing should be easy for you at this point. Set grid to 0.50 and snap to 0.125 as suggested, and everything falls into place nicely.

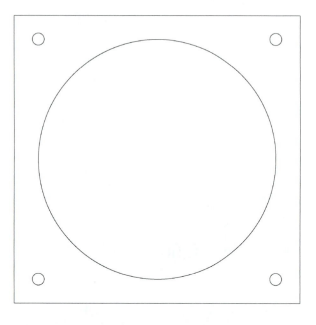

Drawing Suggestions

GRID = 0.50
SNAP = 0.125

- Notice that the outer figure in Drawing 2-3 is a 6 × 6 square and that you are given diameters for the circles.
- You should start with the lower left-hand corner of the square somewhere near the point (3.00,2.00) if you want to keep the drawing centered on your screen.
- Be careful to center the large inner circle within the square.

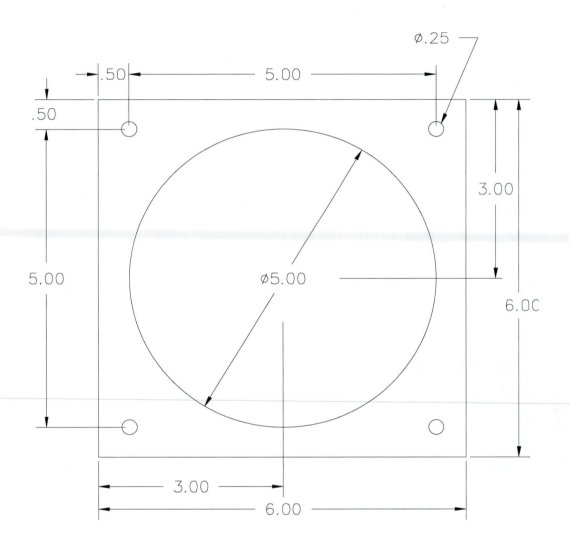

FAN BEZEL

Drawing 2-3

Drawing 2-4: Switch Plate

This drawing is similar to the last one, but the dimensions are more difficult, and a number of important points do not fall on the grid. The drawing gives you practice using grid and snap points and the coordinate display. Refer to the table that follows Drawing 2-4 for dimensions of the circles, squares, and rectangles inside the 7 × 10 outer rectangle. The placement of these smaller figures is shown by the dimensions on the drawing itself.

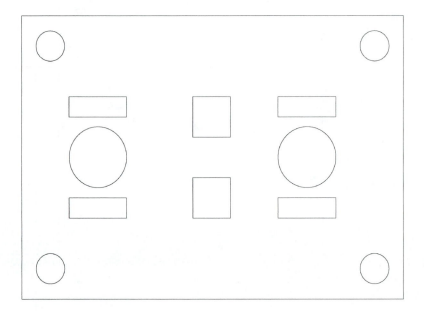

Drawing Suggestions

GRID = 0.50
SNAP = 0.25

- Turn on Ortho or Polar snap to do this drawing.
- A starting point in the neighborhood of (1,1) keeps you well positioned on the screen.

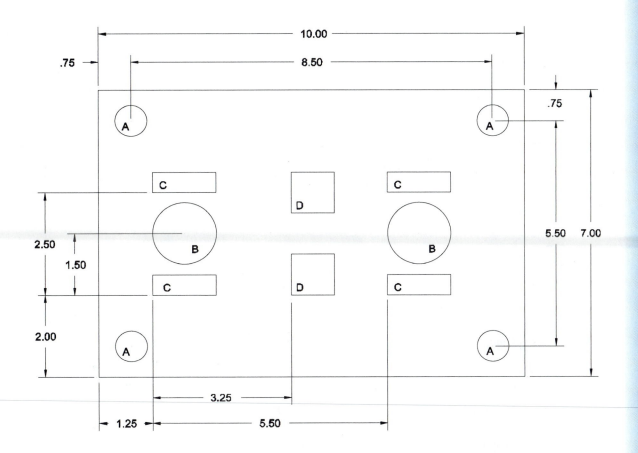

HOLE	SIZE
A	Ø.75
B	Ø1.50
C	.50 H x 1.50 W
D	1.00 SQ

SWITCH PLATE
Drawing 2-4

Drawing 2-5: Gasket

Drawing 2-5 gives you practice creating simple lines and circles while utilizing Grid and Snap. The circles in this drawing have a 0.50 diameter. With snap set at 0.25, the radii are on a snap point. These circles can be drawn easily by dragging the circle out to show the radius or by typing in the diameter.

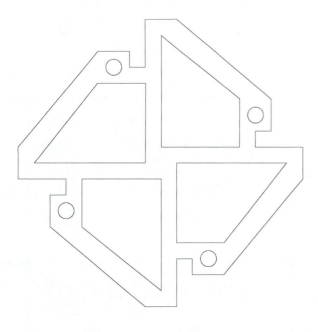

Drawing Suggestions

$$GRID = 0.50$$
$$SNAP = 0.25$$

- A good sequence for completing this drawing would be to draw the outer lines first, followed by the inner lines and then the circles.
- Notice that all endpoints of all lines fall on grid points; therefore, they are on a snap point.

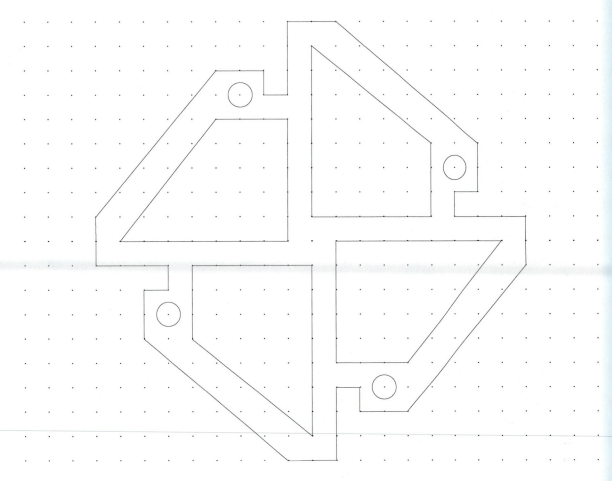

GASKET
Drawing 2-5

Layers, Colors, and Linetypes

3

Chapter Objectives

- Creating New Layers
- Assigning Colors to Layers
- Assigning Linetypes
- Assigning Lineweight
- Changing the Current Layer
- Editing Corners Using FILLET
- Editing Corners Using CHAMFER
- Using the ZOOM Command
- Zooming with the Scroll Wheel
- Using Realtime ZOOM and PAN
- Entering Single-Line Text
- Using Plot Preview

INTRODUCTION

CAD is much more than a computerized way to do drafting. CAD programs have many powerful features that have no correlation in manual drawing. Layering is a good example. Layers are used to separate different aspects of a drawing so that they can be treated independently. Layers exist in the same space and the same drawing, but can be set up and controlled individually, allowing for greater control, precision, and flexibility. In the first two chapters, all of your drawings were completed on a single layer called 0. In this chapter, you create and use three new layers, each with its own associated color and linetype.

The **ZOOM** command is another bit of CAD magic, allowing your drawings to accurately represent real-world detail at the largest and smallest scales within the same drawing. In this chapter, you also learn to **FILLET** and **CHAMFER** the corners of previously drawn objects and to move between adjacent portions of a drawing with the **PAN** command. You gain further control of the **PLOT** command by using partial and full previews. All these new techniques add considerably to the professionalism of your developing CAD technique.

3.1 CREATING NEW LAYERS

GENERAL PROCEDURE	1. Select the **Layer Properties Manager** tool from the dashboard.
	2. Click the New layer icon.
	3. Type in a layer name.
	4. Repeat for other new layers.
	5. Click **OK** to close the dialog box.

Layers allow you to treat specialized groups of entities in your drawing separately from other groups. For example, all the dimensions in this book were drawn on a special dimension layer so that we could turn them on and off at will. We turned off the dimension layer to prepare the reference drawings for Chapters 1 through 7, which are shown without dimensions. When a layer is turned off, all the objects on that layer become invisible, although they are still part of the drawing database and can be recalled at any time. In this way, layers can be viewed, edited, manipulated, and plotted independently.

It is common practice to put dimensions on a separate layer, but there are many other uses of layers as well. Fundamentally, layers are used to separate colors and linetypes, and these, in turn, take on special significance, depending on the drawing application. It is standard drafting practice, for example, to use small, evenly spaced dashes to represent objects or edges that would, in reality, be hidden from view. On a CAD system, these hidden lines can also be given their own color to make it easy for the designer to remember what layer he or she is working on.

In this book, we use a simple layering system, most of which is presented in this chapter. You should remember that there are countless possibilities. AutoCAD allows a full range of colors and as many layers as you like.

You should also be aware that linetypes and colors are not restricted to being associated with layers. It is possible to mix linetypes and colors on a single layer. Although this might be useful for certain applications, we do not recommend it at this point.

- ⊕ Create a new drawing by selecting the QNew tool from the Standard Annotation toolbar.
- ⊕ Check to see that acad is in the File name box and press Enter.
- ⊕ Turn on the grid.
- ⊕ Type "z" ⏎ to enter the ZOOM command and then "a" ⏎ to zoom all.

The Layer Properties Manager Dialog Box

The creation and specification of layers and layer properties in AutoCAD is handled through the **Layer Properties Manager** dialog box. This dialog box consists of a table of layers. Clicking the appropriate row and column changes a setting or takes you to another dialog box where a setting can be changed.

- ⊕ Select the Layer Properties Manager tool from the dashboard, as shown in Figure 3-1.

Figure 3-1

Either method opens the **Layer Properties Manager** dialog box illustrated in Figure 3-2. The large open space to the right shows the names and properties of all layers defined in the current drawing. Layering systems can become very complex, and for this reason there is a system to limit or filter the layer names shown on the layer list. This is controlled by the icons at the top left. With no filters specified, the layer list shows all used layers. Currently, 0 is the only defined layer. The icons on the line after the layer name show the current state of various properties of that layer. We get to these shortly.

Now we will create three new layers. AutoCAD makes this easy.

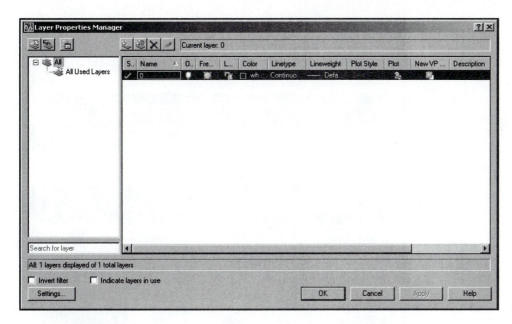

Figure 3-2

⊕ Pick the New layer icon, just above the top left of the layer list.

A newly defined layer, Layer1, is created immediately and added to the Layer name window. The new layer is given the characteristics of layer 0. We alter these in Section 3.2. First, however, we give this layer a new name and then define three more layers.

Layer names can be long or short. We have chosen single-digit numbers as layer names because they are easy to type and we can match them to AutoCAD's index color numbering sequence.

⊕ Type 1 for the layer name.

Layer 1 changes to simply 1. It is not necessary to press **Enter** after typing the name.

⊕ Click the New layer icon again.

A second new layer is added to the list. It again has the default name Layer 1. Change it to 2.

⊕ Type 2 for the second layer name.

⊕ Click the New layer icon again.

⊕ Type 3 for the third layer name and press Enter to complete the process.

At this point, your layer name list should show Layers 0, 1, 2, and 3, all with identical properties.

3.2 ASSIGNING COLORS TO LAYERS

GENERAL PROCEDURE

1. From the **Layer Properties Manager** dialog box, pick the color icon in the row for the layer you want to change.
2. In the **Color** dialog box, select a color from the index color chart or type a color name or number in the edit box.
3. Click **OK.**

We now have four layers, but they are all pretty much the same. We have more changes to make before our new layers have useful identities.

Layer 0 has some special features, which are discussed in Chapter 10. Because of these, it is common practice to leave it defined the way it is. We begin our changes on Layer 1.

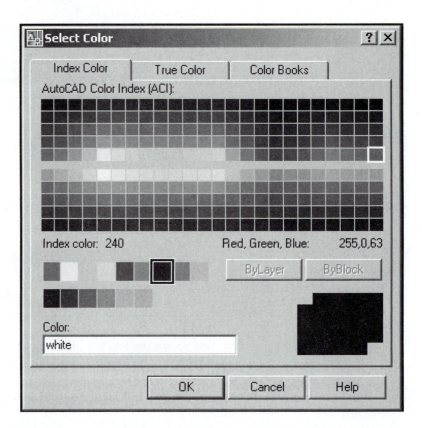

Figure 3-3

⊕ In the **Layer Properties Manager** dialog box, pick the white square under Color in the Layer 1 line.

Picking the white square in the Color column of Layer 1 selects Layer 1 and opens the **Select Color** dialog box illustrated in Figure 3-3. The three tabs in this dialog box show three ways in which colors can be defined in AutoCAD. By default, the **Index Color** tab is probably selected, as shown in Figure 3-3. The index color system is a simple numbered selection of 255 colors and shades. The True Color and Color Books systems are standard color systems commonly used by graphic designers. The **True Color** tab can be set to access either the Hue, Saturation, and Luminance (HSL) color model or the Red, Green, and Blue (RGB) model. Both of these systems work by mixing colors and color characteristics. The **Color Books** tab gives access to DIC, Pantone, and RAL color books. These standard color sets are also numbered, but they provide many more choices than the AutoCAD index color set. In this book we confine ourselves to the **Index Color** tab.

⊕ If necessary, click the Index Color tab.

The Index Color tab shows the complete selection of 255 colors. At the top is a full palette of shades 10 through 249. Below that are the nine standard colors, numbered 1 through 9, followed by gray shades, numbered 250 through 255.

⊕ Move your cursor freely inside the dialog box.

When your cursor is on a color, it is highlighted with a white box.

⊕ Let your cursor rest on any color.

Notice that the number of the color is registered under the palette next to the words Index color. This is the AutoCAD index color number for the color currently highlighted. Notice also the three numbers on the right following the words Red, Green, Blue. This is the RGB color model equivalent. RGB colors are combinations of red, green, and blue, with 255 shades of each.

⊕ Pick any color in the palette.

When a color is selected, it is outlined with a black box and a preview "patch" is displayed on the bottom right of the dialog box against a patch of the current color for comparison. The color is not actually selected in the drawing until you click OK to exit the dialog box. For our purposes, we want to select standard red, color number 1 on the strip in the middle of the dialog box.

⊕ Move the white cursor box to the red box, the first of the nine standard colors in the middle of the box.

Notice that this is index color number 1 and its RGB equivalent is 255, 0, 0, pure red with no green or blue added.

⊕ Pick the red box.

You should see the word red and the color red shown in the preview area at the bottom of the dialog box. Note that you can also select colors by typing names or numbers directly in this edit box. Typing red or the number 1 is the same as selecting the red color box from the chart.

⊕ Click OK.

Layer 1 is now defined with the color red in the Layer Name list box.

Next we assign the color yellow to Layer 2.

⊕ Pick the white square under Color in the Layer 2 line, and assign the color yellow to Layer 2 in the Select Color dialog box.

⊕ Click OK.

⊕ Select Layer 3 and set this layer to green.

Look at the layer list. You should now have Layers 0, 1, 2, and 3 defined with the colors white, red, yellow, and green.

3.3 ASSIGNING LINETYPES

GENERAL PROCEDURE	1. From the **Layer Properties Manager** dialog box, click in the Linetype column of the layer you want to set. 2. In the **Select Linetype** dialog box, select a linetype. If necessary, load linetypes first. 3. Click **OK.** 4. Click **OK** again to exit the dialog box.

AutoCAD has a standard library of linetypes that can easily be assigned to layers. There are 45 standard types in addition to continuous lines. In addition to continuous lines, we use hidden and center lines. We put hidden lines in yellow on Layer 2 and center lines in green on Layer 3. Layers 1 and 0 retain the continous linetype.

The procedure for assigning linetypes is almost identical to the procedure for assigning colors, except that you have to load linetypes into the drawing before they can be used.

⊕ In the Layer Properties Manager pick Continuous in the Linetype column of the Layer 2 line.

This selects Layer 2 and opens the **Select Line-type** dialog box illustrated in Figure 3-4. The box containing a list of loaded linetypes currently shows only the continuous linetype. We can fix this by clicking the **Load** button at the bottom of the dialog box.

Note:
Make sure that you actually click the word Continuous. If you click one of the icons in the Layer 2 line, you might turn the layer off or freeze it so that you cannot draw on it. These properties are discussed at the end of Section 3.5.

⊕ Click Load.

This opens the **Load or Reload Linetypes** dialog box illustrated in Figure 3-5. Here you can pick from the list of linetypes available from the standard acad file or from

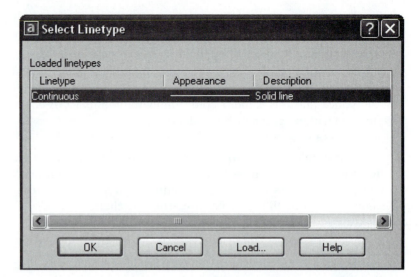

Figure 3-4

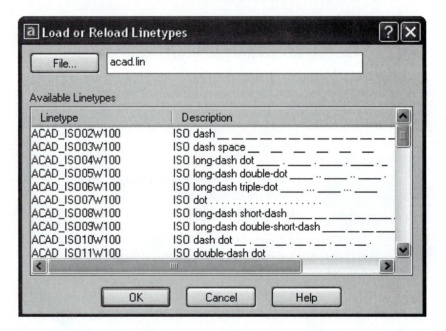

Figure 3-5

other files containing linetypes, if there are any on your system. You also have the option of loading all linetypes from any given file at once. The linetypes are then defined in your drawing, and you can assign a new linetype to a layer at any time. This makes things easier. It does, however, use up more memory.

For our purposes, we load only the hidden and center linetypes we are going to be using.

⊕ Scroll down until you see the linetype labeled CENTER.

⊕ Click CENTER in the Linetype column at the left.

⊕ Scroll down again until you see the linetype labeled HIDDEN.

⊕ Hold down the Ctrl key and click HIDDEN in the Linetype column.

The **Ctrl** key lets you highlight two separate items in a list.

⊕ Click OK to complete the loading process.

You should now see the center and hidden linetypes added to the list of loaded linetypes. Now that these are loaded, we can assign them to layers.

⊕ Click HIDDEN in the Linetype column.

⊕ Click OK to close the dialog box.

> You should see that Layer 2 now has the hidden linetype.

> Next assign the center linetype to Layer 3.

⊕ Click Continuous in the Linetype column of the Layer 3 line.

⊕ In the Select Linetype dialog box, select the Center linetype.

⊕ Click OK.

> Examine your layer list again. It should show Layer 2 with the hidden linetype and Layer 3 with the center linetype. Before exiting the **Layer Properties Manager,** we create one additional layer to demonstrate AutoCAD's lineweight feature.

3.4 ASSIGNING LINEWEIGHT

GENERAL PROCEDURE	1. From the **Layer Properties Manager,** click in the Lineweight column of the layer you want to change. 2. In the **Lineweight** dialog box, select a lineweight. 3. Click **OK.** 4. Click **OK** again to exit the dialog box.

Lineweight refers to the thickness of lines as they are displayed and plotted. All lines are initially given a default lineweight. Lineweights are assigned by layer and are displayed only if the **LWT** button on the status bar is in the on position. In this section, we create a new layer and give it a much larger lineweight for demonstration purposes.

First, we create a new layer because we do not want to change our previous layers from the default lineweight setting.

⊕ If Layer 3 is not highlighted, select it now.

⊕ Pick the New layer icon in the dialog box.

> Notice that the new layer takes the characteristics of the previously highlighted layer. Our last action was to give Layer 3 the center linetype, so your new layer should have green center lines and the other characteristics of Layer 3.

⊕ Type 4 ↵ for the new layer name.

⊕ Click Default in the Lineweight column of Layer 4.

> This opens the Lineweight dialog box, shown in Figure 3-6. We use a rather large lineweight to create a clear demonstration. Be aware that printed lineweights may not exactly match lineweights as shown on the screen.

⊕ Scroll down until you see 0.50 mm on the list.

⊕ Pick the 0.50 mm line.

> Below the list you can see that the original specification for this layer was the default and is now being changed to 0.50 mm.

⊕ Click OK to return to the Layer Properties Manager.

> It is now time to leave the dialog box and see what we can do with our new layers.

⊕ Click OK to exit the Layer Properties Manager.

> Before proceeding, you should be back in your Drawing Window with your new layers defined in your

Note:
Do not exit the dialog box by clicking the close button. Exit only by clicking OK. If you use the close button, or if you cancel the dialog box, all of your changes, new layers, and so on, will be lost.

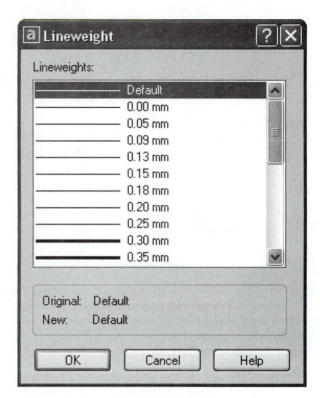

Figure 3-6

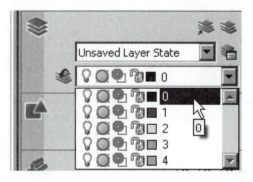

Figure 3-7

drawing. To verify that you have successfully defined new layers, open the **Layer** drop-down list on the dashboard, as shown in Figure 3-7.

⊕ To open the Layer list, click the arrow or anywhere in the list box.

Your list should resemble the one in Figure 3-7.

3.5 CHANGING THE CURRENT LAYER

GENERAL PROCEDURE	1. Open the Layer list from the dashboard. 2. Select a layer name. or 1. Select the **Make Object's Layer Current** tool from the dashboard. 2. Select an object on the layer you wish to make current.

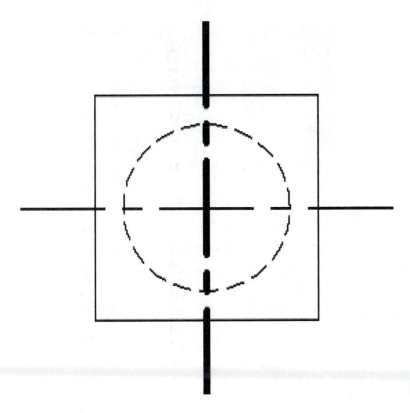

Figure 3-8

In this section, we make each of your new layers current and draw objects on them. You can immediately see how much power you have added to your drawing by the addition of new layers, colors, linetypes, and lineweight.

To draw new entities on a layer, you must make it the currently active layer. Previously drawn objects on other layers are also visible, but new objects go on the current layer.

There are two quick methods to establish the current layer. The first works the same as any drop-down list. The second makes use of previously drawn objects. We use the first method to draw the objects in Figure 3-8.

⊞ Click anywhere in the Layer list box on the dashboard.

This opens the list, as shown previously in Figure 3-7.

⊞ Select Layer 1 by clicking to the right of the layer name 1 in the drop-down list.

Layer 1 replaces Layer 0 as the current layer on the Object Properties toolbar.

⊞ Using the RECTANGLE command, draw the 6 × 6 square shown in Figure 3-8, with the first corner at (3,2) and other corner at (9,8).

Your rectangle should show the red, continuous lines of Layer 1.

⊞ Click anywhere in the Layer list box.

⊞ Click to the right of the layer name 2.

Layer 2 becomes the current layer.

⊞ With Layer 2 current, draw the hidden circle in Figure 3-8, centered at (6,5) with radius 2.

Your circle should appear in yellow hidden lines.

⊞ Make Layer 3 current and draw a horizontal center line from (2,5) to (10,5).

This line should appear as a green center line.

⊞ Pick the LWT button on the status bar to turn LWT on.

⊞ Make Layer 4 current and draw a vertical line from (6,1) to (6,9).

This line should appear as a green center line with noticeable thickness.

⊞ Pick the LWT button again to put it in the off position.

With LWT off, the lineweight of the horizontal center line is not displayed.

Figure 3-9

Making an Object's Layer Current

Finally, we use another method to make Layer 1 current before moving on.

⊕ Select the Make Object's Layer Current tool from the dashboard, as shown in Figure 3-9.

This tool allows us to make a layer current by selecting any object on that layer. AutoCAD shows the prompt

```
Select object whose layer will become current:
```

⊕ Select the red rectangle drawn on Layer 1.

Layer 1 replaces Layer 4 in the **Current Layer** box.

Other Properties of Layers

There are several other properties that can be set in the **Layer Properties Manager,** or, more conveniently, in the Layer list box. These settings probably will not be useful to you until later on, but we introduce them briefly here for your information.

On and Off

Layers can be turned on or off with the lightbulb icon. On and off status affects only the visibility of objects on a layer. Objects on layers that are off are not visible or plotted, but are still in the drawing and are considered when the drawing is regenerated. Regeneration is the process by which AutoCAD translates the precise numerical data that makes up a drawing file database into the less precise values of screen graphics. Regeneration can be a slow process in large, complex drawings. As a result, it might be useful not to regenerate all layers all the time.

Freeze and Thaw

Frozen layers are not only invisible, but are ignored in regeneration. Thaw reverses this setting. Thawed layers are always regenerated. Freeze and thaw properties are set using the sun icon, to the right of the lightbulb icon. Layers are thawed by default as indicated by the yellow sun. When a layer is frozen, the sun icon is replaced by a snowflake.

Freeze or Thaw in Current Viewport

The sun icon freezes or thaws layers in all viewports. Next to the sun icon is an icon with a sun and a square. The square represents a drawing viewport. Viewports are introduced in Chapter 6. This setting is off by default. It allows you to freeze a layer in the current viewport while leaving it thawed in other viewports.

Lock and Unlock

Next is the lock icon. The Lock and Unlock setting does not affect visibility, but does affect availability of objects for editing. Objects on locked layers are visible, but they cannot be edited. Unlocking reverses this setting.

Deleting Layers

You can delete layers using the **Delete** button in the **Layer Properties Manager** dialog box. However, you cannot delete layers that have objects drawn on them. Also, you cannot delete the current layer or Layer 0.

3.6 Editing Corners Using FILLET

GENERAL PROCEDURE	1. Select the **Fillet** tool from the dashboard, or type "F" ↵. 2. Type "r" ↵ for radius. 3. Enter a radius value. 4. Select two lines that meet at a corner.

Now that you have a variety of linetypes to use, you can begin to make more realistic mechanical drawings. Often this will require the ability to create filleted, rounded, or chamfered corners. Fillets are concave curves on corners and edges, while rounds are convex. AutoCAD uses the **FILLET** command to refer to both. Chamfers are cut on an angle rather than a curve. The **FILLET** and **CHAMFER** commands work similarly.

We modify only the square in this exercise, but instead of erasing the other objects, turn them off, as follows:

⊕ If you have not already done so, set Layer 1 as the current layer.

⊕ Open the Layer list on the dashboard, and click the lightbulb icons on Layers 2, 3, and 4 so that they turn from yellow to gray, indicating that they are off.

⊕ Click anywhere outside the list box to close it.

When you are finished, you should see only the square. The other objects are still in your drawing and can be recalled anytime simply by turning their layers on again.

We use the square to practice fillets and chamfers.

⊕ Type "f" ↵ or select the Fillet button from the dashboard, as shown in Figure 3-10.

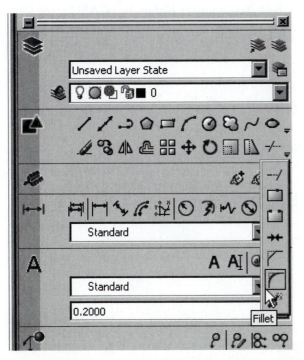

Figure 3-10

Using the dashboard requires opening the flyout, as shown. Flyouts are extensions to tool sets that drop down when you pick the small downward pointing arrow at the end of the set of visible tools. The list that drops down is like a pull-down menu, but uses tool icons instead of words.

TIP Since you have to access the **Fillet** tool on the flyout, this may be a case where you find the keyboard alias quicker. You can easily press the F key with your left index finger and use your left thumb on the spacebar to enter the command.

When the command is entered, a prompt with options appears as follows:

```
Current settings: Mode=TRIM, Radius=0.50
Select first object or [Undo/Polyline/Radius/Trim/Multiple]:
```

Polylines are discussed in Chapter 9, but we have something to show you about this option in a moment. Trim mode is discussed at the end of this exercise.

The first thing you must do is determine the degree of rounding you want. Because fillets appear as arcs, they can be defined by a radius.

⊕ Type "r" or right-click and select Radius from the shortcut menu.
   AutoCAD prompts

```
                    Specify fillet radius <0.00>:
```

The default is 0.00.

⊕ Type .75 ↲.

   You have set 0.75 as the current fillet radius for this drawing. You can change it at any time. Changing does not affect previously drawn fillets.

   The prompt is the same as before:

```
Select first object or [Undo/Polyline/Radius/Trim/Multiple]:
```

   Notice that you have the pick box on the screen now without the crosshairs.

⊕ Pick a point on the vertical line on the right near the top corner.

   Pick a point on the horizontal line at the top near the top right corner.

   Behold! A fillet! You did not even have to press **Enter.** AutoCAD knows that you are done after selecting two lines.

The Multiple Option

We use the Multiple option to fillet the remaining three corners of the square. Multiple allows you to create multiple fillets without leaving the **FILLET** command.

⊕ Press Enter or the spacebar to repeat FILLET.
⊕ Type "m" ↲ for the Multiple option.
⊕ Select two lines to fillet another corner.

   You do not have to enter a radius value again because the last value is retained. Also, because you entered the multiple option you do not have to reenter the command.

⊕ Proceed to fillet all four corners.

   When you are done, your screen should resemble Figure 3-11.

⊕ Press Enter to exit FILLET.

Trim Mode

Trim mode allows you to determine whether you want AutoCAD to remove square corners as it creates fillets and chamfers. Examples of fillets created with Trim mode on and off are shown in

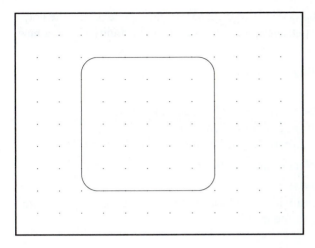

Figure 3-11

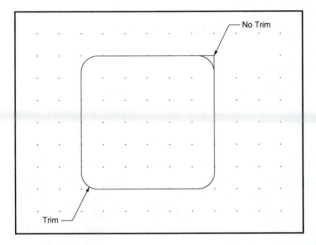

Figure 3-12

Figure 3-12. In most cases, you want to leave Trim mode on. To turn it off, enter FILLET and type "t" for Trim and then "n" for No Trim.

TIP — FILLET may also be used to connect two lines that do not intersect. By setting a fillet radius of 0 and then selecting two lines that do not meet, both lines will be extended to the point where they intersect. Lines do not need to be perpendicular, but they must not be parallel for this to work.

3.7 Editing Corners Using CHAMFER

GENERAL PROCEDURE

1. Select the Chamfer tool from the dashboard, or select Chamfer from the **Modify** menu.
2. Type "d" for the Distance option.
3. Enter a chamfer distance.
4. Enter a second chamfer distance or press **Enter** for an even chamfer.
5. Select two lines that meet at a corner.

The **CHAMFER** command sequence is almost identical to the **FILLET** command, with the exception that chamfers can be uneven. That is, you can cut back farther on one side of a corner than on the other. To do this, you must give AutoCAD two distances instead of one.

Figure 3-13

In this exercise, we draw even chamfers on the four corners of the square. Using the Polyline option, we chamfer all four corners at once. We also take the opportunity to use a new shortcut menu.

⊕ Select Chamfer from the **Modify** menu, as shown in Figure 3-13.

AutoCAD prompts:

```
(TRIM mode) Current chamfer Dist1=0.00, Dist2=0.00
              Select first line or
[Undo/Polyline/Distance/Angle/Trim/mEthod/Multiple]:
```

You can type a letter to select an option, but there is also a shortcut menu.

⊕ Right-click anywhere in the drawing area.

This opens a shortcut menu with the Undo, Polyline, Distance, Angle, Trim, mEthod, and Multiple options in the middle panel.

⊕ Select Distance.

The next prompt is

```
Specify first chamfer distance <0.00>:
```

⊕ Type "1" ↵.

AutoCAD asks for another distance:

```
Specify second chamfer distance <1.00>:
```

The first distance has become the default and will give you a chamfer cut evenly on both sides. If you want an asymmetric chamfer, enter a different value for the second distance.

⊕ Press Enter to accept the default, making the chamfer distances symmetrical.

At this point, you could proceed to chamfer each corner of the square independently. However, if you have drawn the square using the **RECTANGLE** command, you have a quicker option. The **RECTANGLE** command draws a polyline rectangle. Polylines are discussed in Chapter 9, but for now it is useful to know that a polyline is a single entity comprised of multiple lines and arcs. If you have drawn a closed polyline and specify the Polyline option in the **CHAMFER** or **FILLET** command, AutoCAD edits all corners of the object.

⊕ Type "p" ↵ or open the shortcut menu and select Polyline.

AutoCAD prompts

```
Select 2D polyline:
```

⊕ Pick any part of the square.

You should have four neat chamfers on your square, replacing the fillets from the previous section. Your screen should resemble Figure 3-14.

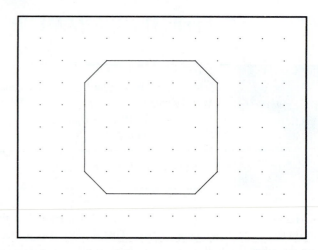

Figure 3-14

3.8 USING THE ZOOM COMMAND

GENERAL PROCEDURE	1. Enter the **ZOOM** command. 2. Enter a ZOOM method or magnification value. 3. Enter values or points, if necessary, depending on choice of method.

The capacity to zoom in and out of a drawing is one of the more impressive benefits of working on a CAD system. When drawings get complex, it often becomes necessary to work in detail on small portions of the drawing space. Especially with a small monitor, the only way to do this is by making the detailed area larger on the screen. This is done easily with the **ZOOM** command.

⊕ You should have a square with chamfered corners on your screen from the previous section.

We demonstrate zooming using the Window, All, Previous, and Realtime options.

⊕ Select the **Zoom Window** tool from the bottom panel of the dashboard, as shown in Figure 3-15.

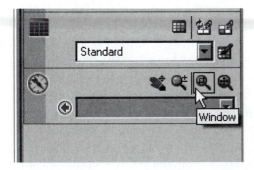

Figure 3-15

The prompt that follows looks like this:

```
[All/Center/Dynamic/Extents/Previous/Scale/
        Window/Object] <realtime>:_w
        Specify corner of window:
```

When you enter the command by way of the Zoom Window tool, the Window option (_w) is entered automatically.

⊕ Pick a point just below and to the left of the lower left-hand corner of your square (point 1 in Figure 3-16).

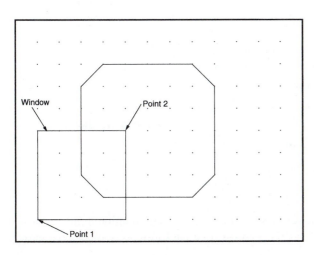

Figure 3-16

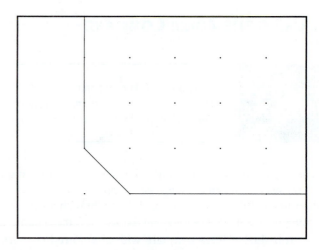

Figure 3-17

AutoCAD asks for another point:

```
Specify opposite corner:
```

You are being asked to define a window, just as in the **ERASE** command. This window is the basis for what AutoCAD displays next. Because you are not going to make a window that exactly conforms to the screen size and shape, AutoCAD interprets the window this way: Everything in the window will be shown, plus whatever additional area is needed to fill the screen. The center of the window becomes the center of the new display.

⊕ Pick a second point near the center of your square (point 2 in the figure).

AutoCAD will zoom in dynamically until the lower left corner of the square is enlarged on your screen, as shown in Figure 3-17.

⊕ Using the same method, try zooming up farther on the chamfered corner of the square. If Snap is on, you might need to turn it off.

Remember that you can repeat the **ZOOM** command by pressing **Enter** or the spacebar. When you repeat the command this way, the Window option will not be entered, but a window selection can be forced by picking two points, just as if you entered the option.

At this point, most people cannot resist seeing how much magnification they can get by zooming repeatedly on the same corner or angle of a chamfer. Go ahead. After a couple of zooms, the angle does not appear to change, though the placement shifts as the center of your window changes. An angle is the same angle no matter how close you get to it, but what happens to the spacing of the grid and snap as you move in?

When you are through experimenting with window zooming, try zooming to the previous display.

Zoom Previous

⊕ Press Enter to repeat the ZOOM command.

⊕ Type "p" ↵ or right-click and select Previous from the shortcut menu.

You should now see your previous display.

AutoCAD keeps track of up to 10 previous displays.

⊕ Zoom Previous as many times as you can until you get a message that says

```
No previous view saved.
```

3.9 ZOOMING WITH THE SCROLL WHEEL

In AutoCAD you can also zoom using the scroll wheel on your mouse. Zooming in this manner is very convenient, but less precise than using the **ZOOM** command. You occasionally get unexpected results.

Each click of the scroll wheel will cause a 10% magnification or reduction of the image in your drawing area. Turning the wheel forward (away from your hand) will cause you to zoom in. Turning it back (toward your hand) will cause zooming out. Notice that turning forward after turning back does *not* exactly reverse the zoom. The 10% factor is always applied to the current view, so that turning back after turning forward will leave you with a slightly reduced image. (For example, your first zoom in will take you to 90% of the original view. The next zoom out will take you out by 10% of 90% and you will now be at 99% of the original view. This may seem small, but it is noticeable.) Also, when you use the scroll wheel to zoom, AutoCAD uses the position of the crosshairs to determine the line of the zoom, so you can get very different zooms from different crosshair positions. This can get a little unpredictable. You will have better control if snap is on and if you don't move the cursor too much between zooms. Try it.

⊞ Check to see that the Snap button is on.
⊞ Place the cursor near the center of the chamfered square and turn the scroll wheel forward a small amount. If your scroll wheel moves in clicks, one click will do.

   Your screen image will be enlarged.
⊞ Turn the wheel forward again.

   Your screen is further enlarged.
⊞ Turn the wheel back back slightly.
⊞ Turn the wheel back again.

   Notice that your current image is slightly smaller than your original view.

Zoom All

This is the option we have been using to enlarge our grids since Chapter 1. Zoom All zooms out to display the limits of the drawing. It is useful when you have been working in a number of small areas of a drawing and are ready to view the whole scene. It also quickly undoes the effects of zooming repeatedly with the scroll wheel. You do not want to have to wade through previous displays to find your way back. Zoom All takes you there in one jump.

To see it work, you should be zoomed in on a portion of your display before executing Zoom All.

⊞ Use the scroll wheel or the ZOOM command to zoom in on a window within your drawing.
⊞ Press Enter or type z to repeat ZOOM again.
⊞ Type "a" ↵, or right-click and select All from the shortcut menu.

3.10 USING REALTIME ZOOM AND PAN

GENERAL PROCEDURE	1. Pick the **Pan Realtime** or **Zoom Realtime** tool from the dashboard. 2. Use the cursor to move your drawing within the drawing window (PAN) or increase or decrease magnification (ZOOM). 3. Press **Enter** or the spacebar to exit the command.

Realtime ZOOM and **PAN** allow you to see changes in display and magnification dynamically as you make adjustments. As soon as you start to use **ZOOM,** you are likely to need **PAN** as well. Whereas **ZOOM** allows you to magnify portions of your drawing, **PAN** allows you to move the area you are viewing in any direction.

In this section we use the **Pan Realtime** tool first and then the **Zoom Realtime** tool.

⊞ Select the Pan Realtime tool from the dashboard, as illustrated in Figure 3-18.

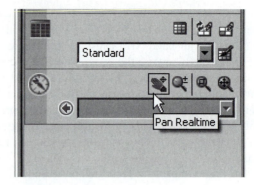

Figure 3-18

The **Realtime PAN** command cursor is in the form of a hand icon, with which you can move objects on the screen. When the mouse button is not depressed, the hand moves freely across the screen. When you move the mouse with the pick button held down, the complete drawing display moves along with the hand.

⊕ Move the hand near the middle of the screen without holding down the pick button.

⊕ Press the pick button and hold it down as you move the cursor across the screen.

⊕ Release the pick button.

The hand icon can now be moved freely again and the drawing has been moved on the screen.

Experiment with Pan Realtime, moving objects up, down, left, right, and diagonally.

Realtime Zoom

When you are in **Realtime ZOOM** or **PAN,** you can access a shortcut menu by right-clicking anywhere on the screen. Try it.

⊕ Without leaving Realtime PAN, right-click to open the shortcut menu.

⊕ Select Zoom from the shortcut menu.

Figure 3-19

The menu closes and the Realtime zoom cursor appears. As illustrated in Figure 3-19, this is represented by a magnifying glass with a plus (+) sign above and a minus (−) sign below.

⊕ Without pressing the pick button, move the Zoom cursor near the bottom of the screen.

As with the Pan cursor, you are able to move freely when the pick button is not held down.

⊕ Press and hold the pick button as you move the cursor upward.

With the pick button pressed, upward motion increases magnification, enlarging objects on the screen.

⊕ Move up and down to see the effects of the Zoom cursor movement.

⊕ Release the pick button.

When you release the button, you do not exit the command. This is important because it might take several trips up or down the screen to indicate the amount of magnification you want. Moving the cursor halfway up the screen produces a 100% magnification.

⊕ Continue to experiment with Realtime Zoom and Pan until you feel comfortable.

⊕ To exit, press Esc, the spacebar, or Enter.

Transparent Commands

You may have noticed that some entries on the command line have an apostrophe or an underline before the name of the command. If you select the Pan tool, for example, you see the following in the command area:

Command: '_pan

The apostrophe is a command modifier that makes the command transparent. This means that you can enter it in the middle of another command sequence, and when you are done you are still in that sequence. For example, you can pan while drawing a line. This is convenient if you already have selected the first point and then realize that the second point will be off the screen.

The underline character is added to commands in menu systems to ensure that AutoCAD interprets the commands in English. Foreign-language versions of AutoCAD have their own command names, but can still use menus developed in English, as long as the underline is there as a flag.

3.11 ENTERING SINGLE-LINE TEXT

<table>
<tr><td>GENERAL PROCEDURE</td><td>
1. Pick the Single Line Text tool from the dashboard.
2. Pick a start point.
3. Answer prompts regarding height and rotation.
4. Enter text on one line and press Enter.
5. Enter text on other lines or press Enter to exit the command.
</td></tr>
</table>

AutoCAD has many options for drawing text. The simplest allows you to enter single lines of text and displays them as you type. You can backspace through lines to make corrections if you do not exit the command. Text is the subject of Chapter 7. We provide this brief introduction for those who may wish to label their drawings before then. (For more details: see Chapter 7.)

For this exercise we add some simple left-justified text to your drawing. We stay on Layer 1 and add the words "chamfer square" as shown in Figure 3-20.

⊕ Pick the Pick **Single Line Text** button from the Text control panel on the dashboard, as shown in Figure 3-21.

You see a prompt with three options in the command area:

Current text style: "STANDARD" Text height:
0.20 Annotative: no
Specify start point of text or [Justify/Style]:

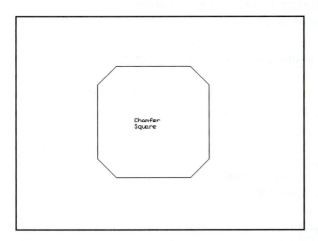

Figure 3-20

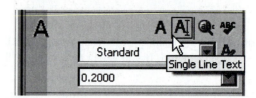

Figure 3-21

Here we use the default method by picking a start point. This gives us standard left-justified text, inserted left to right from the point we pick.

⊞ Pick a start point near the middle of the square, as shown in Figure 3-20. We chose the point (5,5).

Study the prompt that follows and be sure that you do not attempt to enter text yet:

Specify height <0.20>:

This gives you the opportunity to set the text height. The number you type specifies the height of uppercase letters in the units you have specified for the current drawing. We will specify a slightly larger text height.

⊞ Type ".3" ↵.

The prompt that follows allows you to place text in a rotated position:

Specify rotation angle of text <0>:

The default of 0 degrees orients text in the usual horizontal manner. Other angles can be specified by typing a degree number relative to the polar coordinate system or by showing a point. If you show a point, it is taken as the second point of a baseline along which the text string will be placed. For now, we stick to horizontal text.

⊞ Press **Enter** to accept the default angle (0).

Now it is time to enter the text itself. There is no prompt for text at the command line. Text is entered directly on the screen at the selected start point.

Notice that a blinking cursor has appeared at the start point on your screen. This shows where the first letter you type will be placed. Watch the screen as you type and you can see dynamic text at work.

⊞ Type "Chamfered" ↵.

Remember, you cannot use the spacebar in place of the **Enter** key when entering text. Notice that the text cursor jumps down a line when you press **Enter.**

⊞ Type "Square" ↵.

The text cursor jumps down again. This is how AutoCAD allows for easy entry of multiple lines of text directly on the screen in a drawing. To exit the command, you need to press **Enter** at the prompt.

⊞ Press **Enter** to exit the command.

This completes the process and returns you to the command prompt.

3.12 USING PLOT PREVIEW

GENERAL PROCEDURE	1. Select the **Plot** tool from the **Standard Annotation** toolbar. 2. Change parameters as needed. 3. Select Preview.

Plot preview is an essential tool in carrying out efficient plotting and printing. Plot configuration is complex, and the odds are good that you will waste time and paper by printing drawings directly without first previewing them on the screen. AutoCAD has previewing tools that help you know exactly what to expect when your drawing reaches a sheet of paper.

In this section, we are still significantly limited in our use of plot settings, but learning to use plot preview makes all your future work with plotting and printing more effective. As in Chapter 2, we suggest that you work through this section now with the objects on your screen and refer to it as necessary after you have done any of the drawings at the end of this chapter.

⊕ To begin this section you should have objects or a drawing on your screen ready to preview.

⊕ If you are using the objects drawn in this chapter, turn all layers on using the Layer list on the dashboard.

⊕ Select the Plot tool from the Standard Annotation toolbar.

This opens the **Plot** dialog box, familiar from the last chapter. The **Preview** button is at the bottom left of the dialog box. The button will call up a full preview image of your drawing on a sheet of drawing paper. Without going to a full preview, however, you already have a partial preview on the right side of the Printer/plotter panel. It shows you an outline of the effective plotting area in relation to the paper size, but does not show an image of the plotted drawing. This preview image will change as you change other plot settings, such as plot area and paper size. Let's look at a full preview.

Note: We address paper sizes in the next chapter. For now, we assume that your plot configuration is correctly matched to the paper in your printer or plotter.

⊕ Check to see that a plotter or printer has been selected in the Printer/plotter name box. If not, select one now.

The **Preview** button will not be accessible if you have not chosen a plotter.

⊕ Click the Preview button.

The dialog box disappears temporarily and you see a preview image similar to the one in Figure 3-22. This image represents your drawing on paper as it is now configured for printing. The Zoom Realtime cursor appears to allow you to zoom in or out on aspects of the preview. By clicking the right button, you can access a Zoom and Pan shortcut menu similar to the one demonstrated earlier in this chapter. The scroll wheel also works here for zooming. Panning and zooming in the preview has no effect on the plot parameters. You might want to experiment with this feature now.

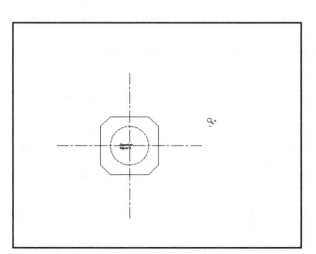

Figure 3-22

✤ When you are done experimenting with Zoom and Pan, press Esc, Enter, or the spacebar to return to the Plot dialog box.

This ends our initial preview of your drawing. In ordinary practice, if everything looked right in the preview, you would move on to plot or print your drawing now by preparing your plotter and then clicking OK. In the chapters that follow, we explore more features of the **Plot** dialog box and use full and partial plot previews extensively as we change plot parameters. For now, get in the habit of using plot preview. If things are not coming out quite the way you want, you will be able to fix them soon.

✤ To save your settings, including your plotter selection, click the Apply to Layout button.

✤ Click OK to plot or print your drawing, or click Cancel to exit without printing.

Using the Plot Preview Tool

AutoCAD also has a **Plot Preview** tool on the **Standard Annotation** toolbar, as illustrated in Figure 3-23. This icon is similar to the **Preview** tool in other Windows applications and performs the same function as the **Preview** button in the **Plot** dialog box. It gives you a quick look at your drawing positioned on a drawing sheet, but you have to go to the **Plot** dialog box if you want to make changes in plot configuration. Try it.

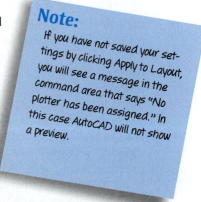

Note:
If you have not saved your settings by clicking Apply to Layout, you will see a message in the command area that says "No Plotter has been assigned." In this case AutoCAD will not show a preview.

✤ Click the Plot Preview tool, as illustrated in Figure 3-23.

You see a full preview of your printed drawing, as shown previously in Figure 3-22.

Figure 3-23

CHAPTER TEST QUESTIONS

Questions

1. What function(s) can be performed directly from the Layer list on the **Object Properties** toolbar? What functions can be performed from the **Layer Properties Manager?**

2. What linetype is always available when you start a drawing from scratch in AutoCAD? What must you do to access other linetypes?

3. How many colors are available in AutoCAD's Index Color system? What are the other color systems that are available in the **Select Color** dialog box?

4. How many different layers does AutoCAD allow you to create?

5. Name three ways to change the current layer.

6. You have been working in the **Layer Properties Manager,** and when you return to your drawing you find

that some objects are no longer visible. What happened?

7. What is a transparent command? How do you make a command transparent when entering it at the command line?

8. What happens to the grid when you zoom way out on a drawing?

9. Describe the use of the scroll wheel for zooming.

10. What is the difference between the partial preview in the Plot dialog box and a full plot preview?

11. What type of preview is created by the **Plot Preview** tool?

12. Name one setting that must be specified in the **Plot** dialog box before you can use Plot Preview.

Drawing Problems

1. Make Layer 3 current and draw a green center line cross with two perpendicular lines, each two units long and intersecting at their midpoints.
2. Make Layer 2 current and draw a hidden line circle centered at the intersection of the cross drawn in Step 1, with a diameter of two units.
3. Make Layer 1 current and draw a red square of two units on a side centered on the center of the circle. Its sides run tangent to the circle.
4. Use a window to zoom in on the objects drawn in Steps 1, 2, and 3.
5. Fillet each corner of the square with a 0.125 radius fillet.

WWW Exercise 3 (Optional)

This time we demonstrate the use of the Web toolbar. Your task is to open the toolbar, use the Browse the Web tool to go to our website, take the test, and then do the Web project. The project for this chapter takes you deeper into the world of CAD on the Internet. The Web is full of interesting and informative CAD-related websites. There are sites maintained by professional journals, CAD newsgroups, CAD industry sites, sites with drawings that can be viewed or downloaded, sites with tutorials, sites with tips on CAD technique, and sites with information on CAD-related software.

Start by opening the Web toolbar using the **Toolbars** shortcut menu. This is the quickest way to open a toolbar.

⊞ Move the cursor so that the arrow is pointing anywhere inside either of the two currently visible toolbars.

⊞ With the arrow in this position, right-click.

This opens the **Toolbars** shortcut menu, shown in Figure 3-24. This long menu includes 37 toolbar selections.

⊞ Locate Web near the bottom of the list.

⊞ Select Web.

This opens the small Web toolbar, shown in Figure 3-25. It is opened in a floating position, as shown.

⊞ Select the Browse the Web tool, as shown.

The **Browse the Web** tool executes the **BROWSER** command and automatically enters the default URL.

⊞ If you have not made our website the default, navigate to it from your default site, using the address prenhall.com/dixriley.

Away you go!

Figure 3-25

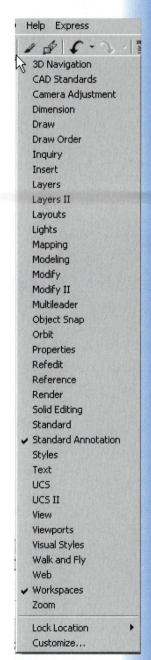

Figure 3-24

Drawing 3-1: Mounting Plate

This drawing gives you experience using center lines and chamfers. Because there are no hidden lines, you have no need for Layer 2, but we continue to use the same numbering system for consistency. Draw the continuous lines in red on Layer 1 and the center lines in green on Layer 3.

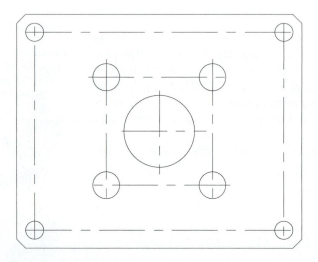

Drawing Suggestions

```
GRID = 0.5
SNAP = 0.25
LTSCALE = 0.5
```

Ltscale

The size of the individual dashes and spaces that make up center lines, hidden lines, and other linetypes is determined by a global setting called LTSCALE. By default, it is set to a factor of 1.00. In smaller drawings, this setting is too large and causes some of the shorter lines to appear continuous regardless of what layer they are on. To remedy this, change LTSCALE as follows:

1. Type lts.
2. Enter a value.

For the drawings in this chapter, use a setting of 0.50. See Figure 3-26 for some examples of the effect of changing LTSCALE.

LTSCALE = 1.00

LTSCALE = .50

Figure 3-26   LTSCALE = .25

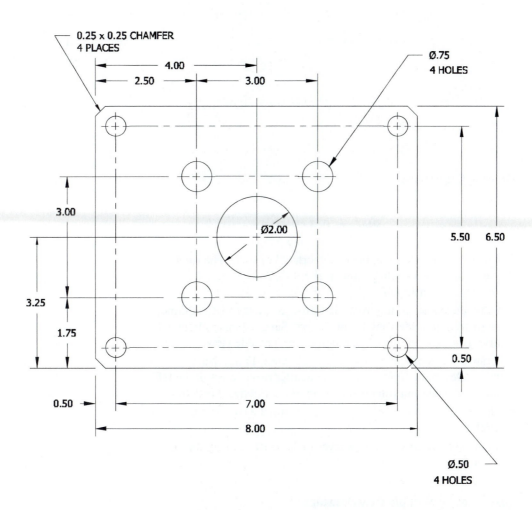

MOUNTING PLATE

Drawing 3-1

Drawing 3-2: Stepped Shaft

This two-view drawing uses continuous lines, center lines, chamfers, and fillets. You might want to zoom in to enlarge the drawing space you are actually working in, and pan right and left to work on the two views.

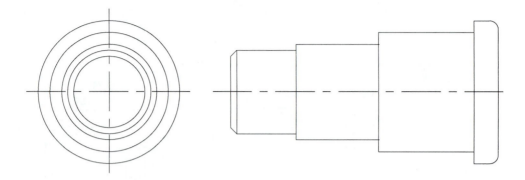

Drawing Suggestions

```
GRID = 0.25
SNAP = 0.125
LTSCALE = 0.5
```

- Center the front view in the neighborhood of (2,5). The right side view will have a starting point at about (5,4.12), before the chamfer cuts this corner off.
- Draw the circles in the front view first, using the vertical dimensions from the side view for diameters. Save the inner circle until after you have drawn and chamfered the right side view.
- Draw a series of rectangles for the side view, lining them up with the circles of the front view. Then chamfer two corners of the leftmost rectangle and fillet two corners of the rightmost rectangle.
- Use the chamfer on the side view to line up the radius of the inner circle.
- Remember to set the current layer to 3 before drawing the center lines.

3-D Models of Multiple-View Drawings

If you have any difficulty visualizing objects in the multiple-view drawings in this chapter through Chapter 11, you might wish to refer to the images in Section 14.18 at the end of Chapter 14. These are 3D solid models derived from 2D drawings done throughout the book.

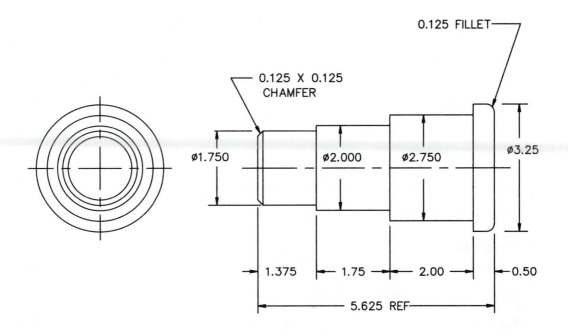

STEPPED SHAFT
Drawing 3—2

Drawing 3-3: Base Plate

This drawing uses continuous lines, hidden lines, center lines, and fillets. The side view should be quite easy once the front view is drawn. Remember to change layers when you want to change linetypes.

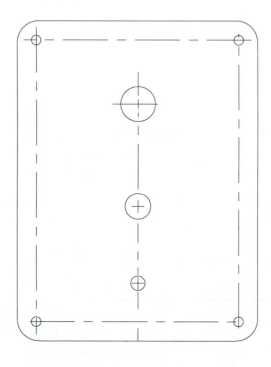

Drawing Suggestions

```
GRID = 0.25
SNAP = 0.125
LTSCALE = 0.5
```

- Study the dimensions carefully and remember that every grid increment is 0.25, and snap points not on the grid are exactly halfway between grid points. The four circles at the corners are 0.38 (actually 0.375 rounded off) over and in from the corner points. This is three snap spaces (0.375 = 3 × 0.125).

- Position the three circles along the center line of the rectangle carefully. Notice that dimensions are given from the center of the screw holes at top and bottom.

- Use the circle perimeters to line up the hidden lines on the side view, and the centers to line up the center lines.

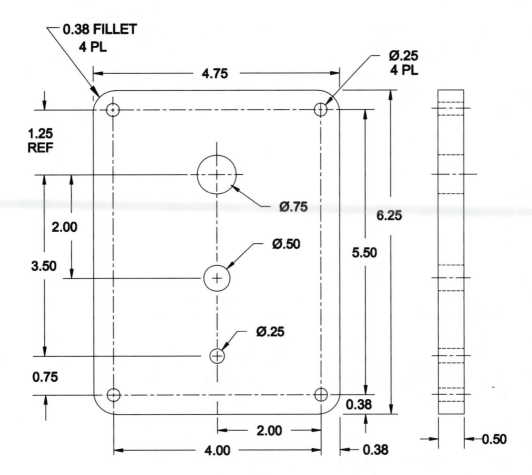

BASE PLATE

Drawing 3-3

Drawing 3-4: Bushing

This drawing gives you practice with chamfers, layers, and zooming. Notice that because of the smaller dimensions here, we have recommended a smaller LTSCALE setting.

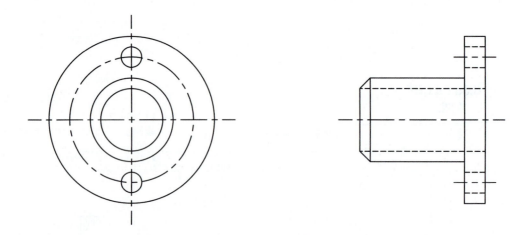

Drawing Suggestions

$$GRID = 0.25$$
$$SNAP = 0.125$$
$$LTSCALE = 0.5$$

- Because this drawing appears quite small on your screen, it would be a good idea to zoom in on the actual drawing space you are using and pan if necessary.
- Notice that the two 0.25-diameter bolt holes are 1.50 apart. This puts them squarely on grid points that you should have no trouble finding. B.C. stands for bolt circle. As indicated, the bolt circle has a 1.50 diameter.

Regen

When you change a linetype scale setting you see a message in the command area that says Regenerating model. Regeneration is the process by which AutoCAD translates drawing data into screen images. Regeneration happens automatically when certain operations are performed. You can also force a regeneration using the **REGEN** command by selecting **Regen from the View** menu.

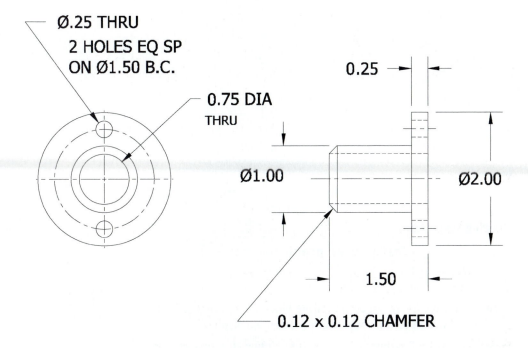

Ø.25 THRU
2 HOLES EQ SP
ON Ø1.50 B.C.

0.75 DIA
THRU

0.25

0.12 x 0.12 CHAMFER

Ø1.00

Ø2.00

1.50

BUSHING
Drawing 3-4

Drawing 3-5: Half Block

This cinder block is the first project using architectural units in this book. Set units, grid, and snap as indicated, and everything falls into place nicely.

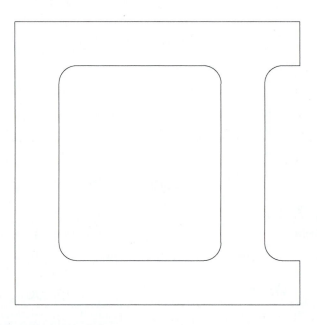

Drawing Suggestions

    UNITS = Architectural precision = 0'-0$\frac{1}{4}$"
    GRID = 1/4"
    SNAP = 1/4"

- Start with the lower left corner of the block at the point (0' −1", 0' −1") to keep the drawing well placed on the display.

- Set the FILLET radius to 1/2" or 0.5. Notice that you can use decimal versions of fractions. The advantage is that they are easier to type.

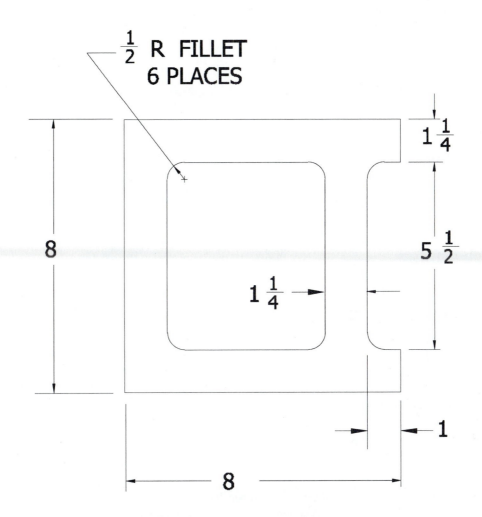

$\frac{1}{2}$ R FILLET
6 PLACES

$1\frac{1}{4}$

$5\frac{1}{2}$

$1\frac{1}{4}$

1

8

8

HALF BLOCK

Drawing 3-5

Drawing 3-6: Packing Flange

This drawing uses continuous lines, hidden lines, center lines, and fillets. The side view should be quite easy once the top view is drawn. Remember to change layers when you want to change linetypes.

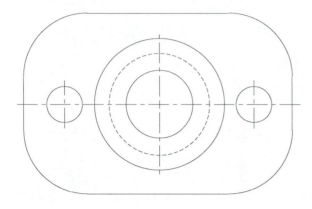

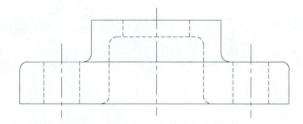

Drawing Suggestions

```
UNITS = Fractional
GRID  = 1/4"
SNAP  = 1/16"
LTSCALE = 0.5
```

- Study the dimensions carefully and remember that every grid increment is 1/4" and snap points not on the grid are exactly halfway between grid points. Notice that the units should be set to fractions.

- Begin by drawing the outline and then the three center lines in the top view. Then proceed by drawing all circles.

- The circles can be drawn using center and diameter. Position the center of the circle where the center lines cross and type in the diameter.

- Use the top view to line up all the lines on the side view.

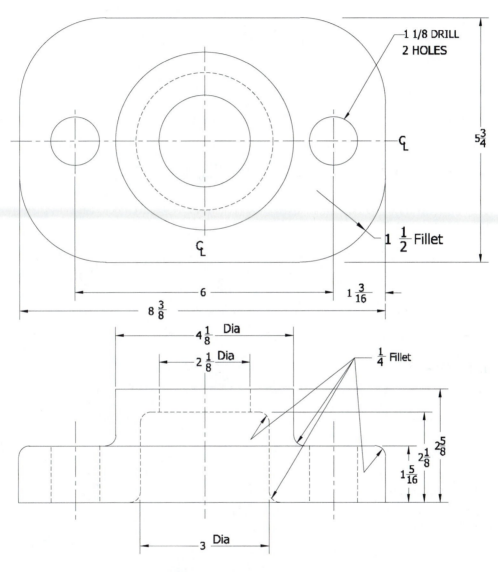

PACKING FLANGE
Drawing 3-6

Templates, Copies, and Arrays

4

Chapter Objectives

- Setting Limits
- Creating a Template
- Saving a Template Drawing
- Using the MOVE Command
- Using the COPY Command
- Using the ARRAY Command—Rectangular Arrays
- Using Single-Point Object Snap
- Changing Plot Settings

INTRODUCTION

In this chapter, you learn some real timesavers. If you have grown tired of defining the same three layers, along with units, grid, snap, and ltscale, for each new drawing, read on. You are about to learn how to create your own template drawings. With templates, you can begin each new drawing with setups you have defined and saved in previous AutoCAD sessions, or with a variety of predefined setups included in the software.

In addition, you learn to reshape the grid using the **LIMITS** command and to copy, move, and array objects on the screen so that you do not have to draw the same thing twice. We begin with the **LIMITS** command, because we want to change the limits as part of defining your first template.

4.1 SETTING LIMITS

GENERAL PROCEDURE	1. Select Drawing Limits from the Format menu. 2. Enter coordinates of a lower left corner. 3. Enter coordinates of an upper right corner. 4. Zoom All.

You have changed the density of the screen grid many times, but always within the same 12×9 space, which basically represents an Architectural A-size sheet of paper. Now you will learn how to change the shape by setting new limits to emulate other sheet sizes or any other space you want to represent. First, a word about model space and paper space.

Model Space and Paper Space

Model space is an AutoCAD concept that refers to the imaginary space in which we create and edit objects. In model space, objects are always drawn at full scale (1 screen unit = 1 unit of length in the real world). The alternative to model space is paper space, in which screen units represent units of length on a piece of paper. You encounter paper space when you begin to use AutoCAD's layout features. A layout is like an overlay on your drawing in which you specify a sheet size, a scale, and other paper-related options. Layouts also allow you to create multiple views of the same model space objects. To avoid confusion and keep your learning curve on track, however, we avoid using layouts for the time being.

In this exercise, we reshape our model space to emulate different drawing sheet sizes. This is not necessary in later practice. With AutoCAD, you can scale your drawing to fit any drawing sheet size when it comes time to plot. Ultimately model space limits should be determined by the size and shapes of objects in your drawing, not by the paper you are going to use when you plot.

Setting Limits

Figure 4-1

Limits are set using the **LIMITS** command. We begin by creating a new drawing and changing its limits from an Architectural A-size sheet (12 × 9) to an Architectural B-size sheet (18 × 12).

⊞ Pick the QNew tool from the Standard Annotation toolbar.

This brings you to the familiar **Select template** dialog box. At this point we continue to use the acad template. Once you have created your own template, it appears in this box along with all the others.

⊞ Press Enter to select the acad template.

⊞ Turn on the grid.

You are now ready to proceed with creating new limits. Leaving your grid where it is at the lower left of your screen gives you visual feedback about what is happening when you change limits.

⊞ From the Format menu, select Drawing Limits as shown in Figure 4-1.

The LIMITS command works in the command area. You see this prompt:

```
Reset Model Space limits:
Specify lower left corner or [ON/OFF] <0.0000,0.0000>:
```

The on and off options control a feature called limits checking. They determine what happens when you attempt to draw outside the drawing limits. With checking off, nothing happens. With checking on, you get a message that says Attempt to draw outside limits, and AutoCAD does not allow you to begin a new entity outside of limits. By default, limits checking is off.

The default value shows that the current lower left corner of the grid is at (0,0), where we leave it.

⊞ Press Enter to accept the default lower left corner.

AutoCAD prompts:

```
Specify upper right corner <12.0000,9.0000>:
```

Changing these settings changes the size of your grid.

⊞ Type "18,12" ↵.

Your grid is redrawn with larger limits. The usual Zoom All procedure enlarges and centers the grid on your screen.

⊞ Type "z" ↵ to enter the ZOOM command.

⊞ Type "a" ↵ to zoom all.

You should have an 18 × 12 grid on your screen.

⊞ Move the cursor to the upper right corner to check its coordinates.

This is the grid we use for your B-size template drawing.

You might want to experiment with setting limits using some of the possibilities shown in Figure 4-2, which is a table of drawing sheet sizes. It shows the two sets of standard sizes. The standard you use might be determined by your plotter. Some plotters that plot on C-size paper, for example, take a 24 × 18 sheet but do not take a 22 × 17 sheet. This information should be programmed into your plotter driver software and appears in the Plot Configuration dialog box in the Preview Image.

After you are finished exploring the **LIMITS** command, we will create the other new settings we want and save this drawing as your B-size template.

SHEET SIZE	STANDARD	"X" DIM	"Y" DIM
A	ANSI Y14.1	11"	8.5"
A	ARCHITECTURAL	12"	9"
B	ANSI Y14.1	17"	11"
B	ARCHITECTURAL	18"	12"
C	ANSI Y14.1	22"	17"
C	ARCHITECTURAL	24"	18"
D	ANSI Y14.1	34"	22"
D	ARCHITECTURAL	36"	24"
E	ANSI Y14.1	44"	34"
E	ARCHITECTURAL	48"	36"

SELECT FROM CHART UPPER RIGHT CORNER

SETTING LIMITS FOR PLOTTER CONFIGURATION

"Y" DIM

SHEET SIZE

LOWER LEFT CORNER SETTING STAYS AT 0,0

"X" DIM

Figure 4-2

4.2 CREATING A TEMPLATE

GENERAL PROCEDURE
1. Define layers and change settings (grid, snap, units, limits, ltscale, etc.) as desired.
2. Save the drawing as an AutoCAD Drawing Template file.

To make your own template so that you can begin new drawings with the settings you want, all you have to do is create a drawing that has those settings and then save it as a template. The first part should be easy for you now, because you have been doing your own setup for each new drawing in this book.

Make changes to the current drawing as follows:

GRID:	0.50 ON	COORD:	ON
SNAP:	0.25 ON	LTSCALE:	0.5
UNITS:	2-place decimal	LIMITS:	(0,0) (18,12)

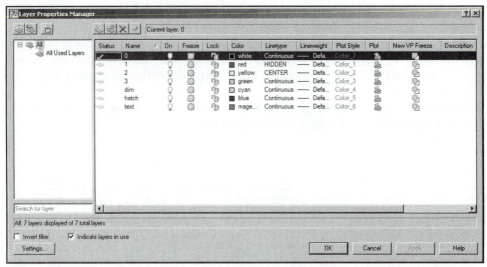

Figure 4-3

Also, ensure that the Snap, Grid, DYN, and Model buttons are on, and that Ortho, Polar, Osnap, Otrack, DUCS, and LWT are off.

⊕ Create layers and associated colors, line-types, and settings to match those in Figure 4-3.

Remember that you can make changes to your template at any time. The layers called text, hatch, and dim are not used until Chapters 7 and 8, in which we introduce text, hatch patterns, and dimensions to your drawings. Creating them now saves time and makes your template more complete later.

Note:
Do not leave anything drawn on your screen or it will come up as part of the template each time you open a new drawing. For some applications, this is quite useful, but for now, we want a blank template.

At this point, your drawing is ready to be saved as a template, which is the focus of the next task.

4.3 SAVING A TEMPLATE DRAWING

GENERAL PROCEDURE

1. Select **Save As** from the **File** menu.
2. Enter your template drawing name in the File name edit box.
3. Select AutoCAD Drawing Template (*.dwt) file in the Files of type list box.
4. Click **Save**.
5. Type a template description in the **Template Description** box.
6. Click **OK**.

A drawing becomes a template when it is saved as a template. Template files are given a .dwt extension and placed in the template file folder.

⊕ You should be in the drawing created in the last task. All the drawing changes should be made as described previously.

⊕ Open the File menu and select Save As.

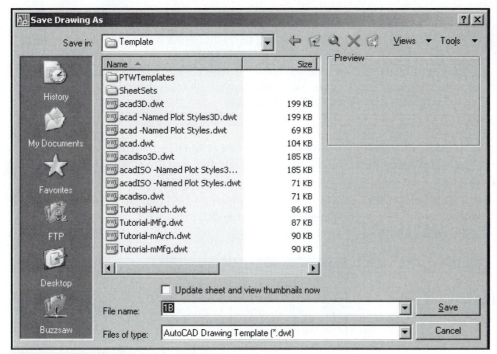

Figure 4-4

This opens the familiar **Save Drawing As** dialog box shown in Figure 4-4. The File name edit box contains the name of the current drawing. If you have not named the drawing, it is called Drawing 1.

Below the File name box is the Files of type box, which lists options for saving the drawing.

⊕ Open the Files of type list by clicking the arrow to the right of the list box.

This opens the list of file-type options. AutoCAD Drawing Template file is sixth on the list in AutoCAD 2008.

⊕ Select AutoCAD Drawing Template (*.dwt) file from the list.

This also opens the Template file folder automatically. You see the same list of templates you have seen often when creating a new drawing. There are many templates shown that are supplied by AutoCAD. These will be useful to you later. At this point, it is more important to learn how to create your own.

⊕ If necessary, double-click in the File name box.

⊕ Type 1B for the new name. Or, if others also use your computer, you may want to add your initials to identify this as your template.

Note:

In situations where several students may be using the same computer at different times during the day or week, changing AutoCAD settings may cause confusion. In this case, your instructor may not want you to save a template file, or may want it in a different location or under a different name. Ask your instructor how it is to be done in your class.

Note:

The templates included in the AutoCAD software consist of various standard sheet sizes, all with title blocks, borders, and predefined plot styles. These are convenient. At this point, however, they can cause confusion because they are created in paper space and automatically put you into a paper space layout. You have no need for titles and borders until we cover text in Chapter 7.

TIP Because template files are listed alphabetically in the file list, it can be convenient to start your template file name with a number so that it appears before the acad and ANSII standard templates that come with the AutoCAD software. Numbers precede letters in the alphanumeric sequence, so your numbered template file appears at the top of the list and saves you the trouble of scrolling down to find it.

Once you have typed your drawing name in the file name box and the Files of type box shows AutoCAD Drawing Template file, you are ready to save.

⊕ Click Save.

This opens a Template Options box, as illustrated in Figure 4-5. This is used if you select the template in the **Create New Drawing** dialog box. You can ignore it for now.

⊕ Click OK in the Template Description box.

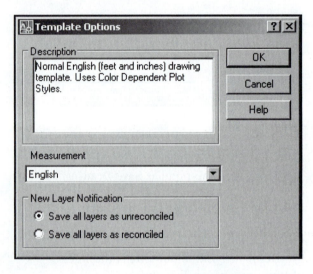

Figure 4-5

The task of creating the drawing template is now complete. All that remains is to create a new drawing using the template to see how it works.

⊕ Open the File menu and select Close to close Drawing 1B.

⊕ Pick the QNew tool from the Standard Annotation toolbar.

This opens the **Select template** dialog box as usual. However, now 1B is at the top of your list.

⊕ Highlight 1B or the file name you have used on the list of Templates.

⊕ Press Enter or click Open.

Note:
If 1B is not at the top of your list after the PTW Templates and Sheet Sets folders, it may be because your list is sorting in descending order. To reverse order, click on Name.

A new drawing opens with all the settings from 1B already in place.

4.4 USING THE MOVE COMMAND

GENERAL PROCEDURE	1. Pick the **Move** tool from the dashboard. 2. Define a selection set. (If noun/verb selection is enabled, you can reverse Steps 1 and 2.) 3. Choose the base point of a displacement. 4. Choose a second point.

The ability to copy and move objects on the screen is one of the great advantages of working on a CAD system. It can be said that CAD is to drafting as word processing is to typing. Nowhere is this analogy more appropriate than in the cut-and-paste capacities that the **COPY** and **MOVE** commands give you.

⊕ Draw a circle with a radius of 1 near the center of the screen (9,6), as shown in Figure 4-6.
⊕ Pick the Move tool from the dashboard, as shown in Figure 4-7.

Figure 4-6

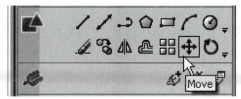

Figure 4-7

You are prompted to select objects to move.

⊕ Pick the circle.

Your circle becomes dotted.

In the command area, AutoCAD tells you how many objects have been selected and prompts you to select more. When you are through selecting objects, you need to press Enter or right-click to move on.

⊕ Right-click to end object selection.

AutoCAD prompts

`Specify base point or [Displacement] displacement:`

Most often you show the movement by picking two points that give the distance and direction in which you want the object to be moved. The base point does not have to be on or near the object you are moving. Any point will do, as long as you can use it to show the distance and direction you want your objects moved. This might seem strange at first, but it will soon become natural. Of course, you can choose a point on the object if you wish. With a circle, the center point might be convenient.

⊕ If Snap is off, turn it on.
⊕ Pick any location not too close to the right edge of the screen.

AutoCAD gives you a rubber band from the point you have indicated and asks for a second point:

`Specify second point or`
`<use first point as displacement>:`

As soon as you begin to move the cursor, AutoCAD also gives you a circle to drag so you can see the effect of the movement you are indicating. An example of how this might look is shown in Figure 4-8. Let's say you want to move the circle 3.00 to the right. Watch the dynamic input display and stretch the rubber band out until the display reads 3.00 < 0,0.

COMMAND GRID	
Command	Move
Alias	M
Menu	Modify
Tool	

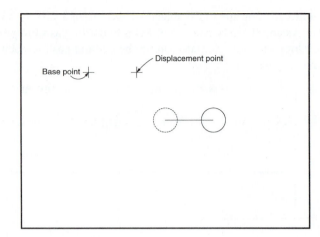

Figure 4-8

⊕ Pick a point 3.00 to the right of your base point.

    The rubber band and your original circle disappear, leaving you with a circle in the new location.

    Now try a diagonal move.

⊕ If Ortho is on, turn it off.

⊕ Select the Move tool, or press the spacebar to repeat the command.

    AutoCAD follows with the *Select objects:* prompt.

⊕ Select the circle.

⊕ Right-click to end the object selection process.

⊕ Pick a base point.

⊕ Move the circle diagonally in any direction you like.

    Figure 4-9 is an example of how this might look.

⊕ Try moving the circle back to the center of the screen.

    It might help to choose the center point of the circle as a base point this time and choose a point at or near the center of the grid for your second point.

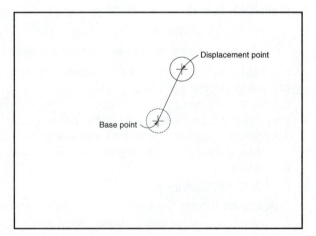

Figure 4-9

Moving with Grips

You can use grips to perform numerous editing procedures without ever entering a command. This is probably the simplest of all editing methods, called *autoediting*. It does have some limitations, however. In particular, you can only select by pointing, windowing, or crossing.

⊕ Pick the circle.

    The circle is highlighted and grips appear.

Notice that grips for a circle are placed at quadrants and at the center. In more involved editing procedures, the choice of which grip or grips to use for editing is significant. In this exercise, you will do fine with any of the grips.

⊕ Move the pick box slowly over one of the grips.

If you do this carefully, you notice that the pick box locks onto the grip as it moves over it. When the cursor locks on the grip, the grip turns green. If you are on one of the quadrant grips the number 1.00 appears, indicating the diameter of the circle.

⊕ When the crosshairs are locked onto a grip, press the pick button.

The selected grip changes colors again (from green to red).

In the command area, you see

** STRETCH **

Specify stretch point or [Base point/Copy/Undo/eXit]:

Stretching is the first of a series of five autoediting modes that you can activate by selecting grips on objects. The word *stretch* has many meanings in Auto-CAD, and they are not always what you would expect. We explore the stretch autoediting mode and the **STRETCH** command in Chapter 6. For now, we bypass stretch and use the **MOVE** mode.

AutoCAD has a convenient shortcut menu for use in grip editing.

⊕ Right-click.

This opens the shortcut menu shown in Figure 4-10. It contains all the grip edit modes plus several other options.

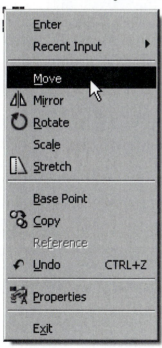

Figure 4-10

⊕ Select Move on the shortcut menu.

The shortcut menu disappears and you are in Move mode. Move the cursor and you see a rubber band from the selected grip to the same position on a dragged circle. Notice that the prompt has changed to

** MOVE **

Specify move point or [Base point/Copy/Undo/eXIt]:

⊕ Pick a point anywhere on the screen.

The circle moves where you have pointed.

⊕ Press Esc to remove grips.

Moving by Typing a Displacement

There is one more way to use the **MOVE** command. Instead of showing AutoCAD a distance and direction, you can type a horizontal and vertical displacement. For example, to move the circle three units to the right and two units up, you would use the following procedure (there is no autoediting equivalent for this procedure):

1. Pick the circle.
2. Type "m" ↵ or select the Move tool.
3. Type 3,2 in response to the prompt for base point or displacement.
4. Press **Enter** in response to the prompt for a second point.

4.5 USING THE **COPY** COMMAND

GENERAL PROCEDURE	1. Select the **Copy** tool from the dashboard. 2. Define a selection set. (Steps 1 and 2 can be reversed if noun/verb selection is enabled.) 3. Choose a base point. 4. Choose a second point. 5. Choose another second point or press **Enter** to exit the command.

The **COPY** command works much like the **MOVE** command. First, we make several copies of the circle in various positions on the screen.

⊕ Select the Copy tool from the dashboard, as shown in Figure 4-11.

COMMAND GRID

Command	Copy
Alias	Co
Menu	Modify
Tool	

Figure 4-11

Notice that c is not an alias for COPY (it is the alias for CIRCLE).

⊕ Select the circle.

⊕ Right-click to end the selection process.

AutoCAD prompts for a base point or displacement.

⊕ Pick a base point.

As in the **MOVE** command, AutoCAD prompts for a second point.

⊕ Pick a second point.

You will see a new copy of the circle. Notice also that the prompt to specify a second point of displacement has returned in the command area and that another new circle is shown at the end of the rubber band. AutoCAD is waiting for another vector, using the same base point as before.

⊕ Pick another second point.

Repeat this process as many times as you wish. If you get into this, you might begin to feel like a magician pulling rings out of thin air and scattering them across the screen. When you finish you should have several copies of the circle on your screen, as shown in Figure 4-12.

⊕ Press Enter to exit the command.

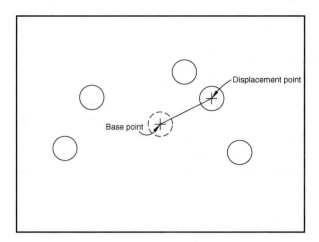

Figure 4-12

Copying with Grips

The grip editing system includes a variety of special techniques for creating multiple copies in all five modes. The function of the Copy option differs depending on the grip edit mode. For now, we use the Copy option with the Move mode, which provides a shortcut for the same kind of process you just executed with the **COPY** command.

Because you should have several circles on your screen now, we take the opportunity to demonstrate how you can copy or move more than one object at a time.

⊕ Pick any two circles.

The circles you pick should be highlighted, and grips should appear on both, as illustrated in Figure 4-13.

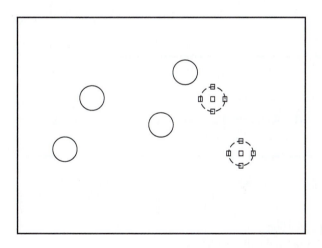

Figure 4-13

⊕ Pick any grip on either of the two highlighted circles.

The grip should change colors. This time we do not use the shortcut menu. In the command area, you see the grip edit prompt for the Stretch mode:

** STRETCH **

Specify stretch point or [/Base point/Copy/Undo/eXIt]:

Pressing **Enter** or the spacebar at this prompt will take you to the other grip edit modes. Move follows Stretch. Using the spacebar will allow you to keep your hand on the mouse.

⊕ Press the spacebar.

This brings you to the Move mode prompt:

** MOVE **

Specify move point or [/Base point/Copy/Undo/eXIt]:

⊕ Type "c" ↵ to initiate copying.

The prompt changes to

** Move (multiple) **

Specify move point or [/Base point/Copy/Undo/eXIt]:

You will find that all copying in the grip editing system is multiple copying. Once in this mode, AutoCAD continues to create copies wherever you press the pick button until you exit by typing x or pressing the spacebar.

⊕ Move the cursor and observe the two dragged circles.

⊕ Pick a point to create copies of the two highlighted circles, as illustrated in Figure 4-14.

⊕ Pick another point to create two more copies.

⊕ Press Enter or the spacebar to exit the grip editing system.

⊕ Press Esc to remove grips.

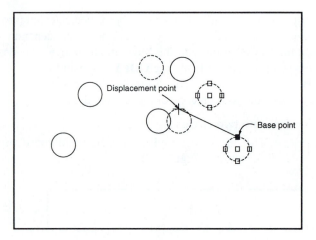

Figure 4-14

4.6 USING THE ARRAY COMMAND—RECTANGULAR ARRAYS

GENERAL PROCEDURE	1. Select the **Array** tool from the dashboard. 2. Define a selection set. (Steps 1 and 2 can be reversed if noun/verb editing is enabled.) 3. Press **Enter** to end selection. 4. Select Rectangular Array in the dialog box. 5. Enter the number of rows in the array. 6. Enter the number of columns. 7. Enter the offset distance between rows. 8. Enter the offset distance between columns.

The **ARRAY** command gives you a powerful alternative to simple copying. An array is the repetition of an image in matrix form. This command takes an object or group of objects and copies it a specific number of times in mathematically defined, evenly spaced locations.

There are two types of arrays. Rectangular arrays are linear and defined by rows and columns. Polar arrays are angular and based on the repetition of objects around the circumference of an arc or circle. The dots on the grid are an example of a rectangular array; the radial lines on any circular dial are an example of a polar array. We explore rectangular arrays in this chapter and polar arrays in the next.

In preparation for this exercise, erase all the circles from your screen. This is a good opportunity to try the Erase All option.

⊞ Select the Erase tool from the dashboard.

⊞ Type "all" ↵.

⊞ Press Enter again to complete the command.

⊞ Now draw a single circle, radius 0.5, centered at the point (2,2).

⊞ Select the Array tool from the dashboard, as shown in Figure 4-15.

This opens the **Array** dialog box shown in Figure 4-16.

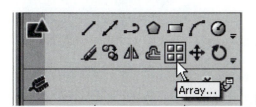

Figure 4-15

COMMAND GRID	
Command	Array
Alias	Ar
Menu	Modify
Tool	

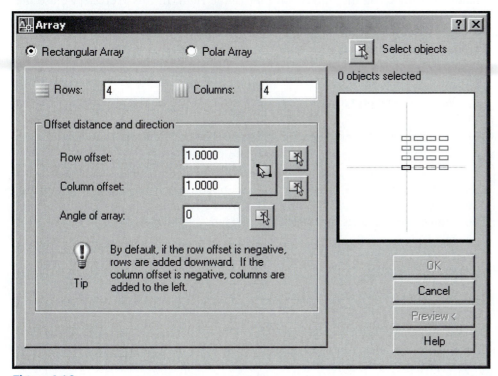

Figure 4-16

⊞ Click Select objects at the top right of the dialog box.

This step is not necessary if you use noun/verb editing and select objects before entering the ARRAY command.

⊞ Pick the circle.

⊞ Right-click to end the selection process.

AutoCAD returns you to the dialog box.

⊞ Make sure that the Rectangular Array radio button is selected at the top left of the dialog box, as it should be by default.

Next, you specify the number of rows in the array.

⊞ Type 3 in the edit box next to the word Rows.

Now you specify the number of columns in the array. Remember, rows are horizontal and columns are vertical, as shown by the blue and white icons next to the words Rows and Columns. What would an array with three rows and only one column look like?

We will construct a five-column array.

⊞ Type 5 in the edit box next to the word Columns.

Before your array definition is complete, AutoCAD needs to know how far apart to place all these circles. There will be 15 of them in this example—three rows with five circles in each row. There are three ways to specify this information. First, you can enter row and column offset values directly in the edit boxes on the left. Second, you can show two corners of a window using the large **Pick Both Offsets** button to the right. Using this option, the horizontal width of the window gives the space between columns and the vertical side gives the space between rows. Third, you can show either of the offset values independently using the buttons further to the right. In this exercise, we use the default values in the edit boxes.

⊞ Check to see that 1.00 is the value for Row offset. If not, change the value to 1.00.

⊞ Check to see that 1.00 is the value for Column offset. If not, change the value to 1.00.

We have now provided all the information we need. Use the **Preview** button to check out the results.

⊞ Check to see that the Angle of the array is 0. If not, change the value to 0.

⊞ Click Preview at the lower right of the dialog box.

You should have a 3×5 array of circles as shown in Figure 4-17. You will also see a message box with three choices: Accept completes the **ARRAY** command, Modify takes you back to the dialog box where you can change or add information, and Cancel cancels the **ARRAY** command.

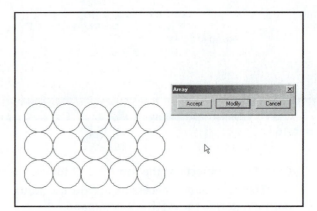

Figure 4-17

Notice that AutoCAD builds arrays up and to the right. This is consistent with the coordinate system, which puts positive values to the right on the horizontal x axis and upward on the vertical y axis. Negative values can be used to create arrays in other directions.

⊞ Click Accept to complete and exit the ARRAY command.

The message box disappears and the array remains in your drawing.

We use the array now on your screen as the selection set to create a larger array. We specify an array that has three rows and three columns, with 3.00

between rows and 5.00 between columns. This keeps our circles touching without overlapping.

⊞ Press **Enter** to repeat the **ARRAY** command.

⊞ Click Select Objects in the dialog box.

⊞ Using a window, select the whole array of 15 circles.

⊞ Right-click to end the selection process.

⊞ Enter 3 for the number of rows.

⊞ Enter 3 for the number of columns.

⊞ Enter 3 for the row offset.

⊞ Enter 5 for the column offset.

⊞ Click Preview.

You should have a screen full of circles, as shown in Figure 4-18.

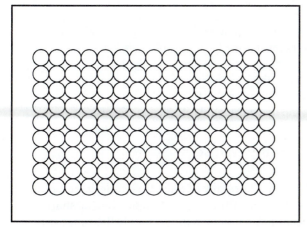

Figure 4-18

⊞ Click Accept.

When you are ready to move on, use the U command to undo the last two arrays.

⊞ Type "u" or pick the **Undo** tool to undo the second array.

⊞ Type "u" or pick the **Undo** tool to undo the first array.

Now you should be back to your original circle centered at (2,2). Notice that the **U** command works nicely to undo an incorrectly drawn array quickly. Be aware, however, that for other purposes, the objects in an array are treated as separate entities, just as if you had drawn them one by one.

Try using some negative distances and a noun/verb sequence to create an array down and to the left.

⊞ First, use the MOVE command or grips to move your circle to the middle of the screen.

⊞ If necessary, select the circle.

⊞ Pick the Array tool.

This opens the dialog box. Because you have already selected the circle, you do not have to select objects now.

⊞ Enter 3 for the number of rows.

⊞ Enter 3 for the number of columns.

⊞ Enter −2 for the row offset.

⊞ Enter −2 for the column offset.

Notice the preview image on the right of the dialog box, which shows the structure of the array and updates as you make changes.

⊞ Click Preview.

Your array should be built down and to the left. The −2 distance between rows causes the array to be built going down. The −2 distance between columns causes the array to be built across to the left.

⊞ Click Accept or Cancel to exit the command, or Modify to continue experimenting.

4.7 Single-Point Object Snap

<table>
<tr>
<td>GENERAL PROCEDURE</td>
<td>
1. Enter a drawing command, such as LINE, CIRCLE, or ARC.
2. Right-click while holding down the Shift or Ctrl key.
3. Select an object snap mode from the shortcut menu.
4. Point to a previously drawn object.
</td>
</tr>
</table>

We offer this section as a quick introduction to the powerful object snap feature, explored in detail in Chapter 6. Instead of snapping to points defined by the coordinate system, this feature snaps to geometrically specifiable points on objects that you have already drawn. It enables you to select points that you could not locate with the crosshairs or by typing coordinates. In this section we introduce single point object snaps. You can use them as the opportunity arises, but they are not strictly necessary to complete the drawings in this chapter or the next.

We use center and tangent object snaps to draw a line from one circle tangent to another.

⊞ The Osnap button should be off for this exercise.

⊞ Enter the LINE command.

We are going to draw a line from the center of one circle tangent to another, as shown in Figure 4-19. This will require the use of tangent object snaps. The center point is easily located because it is on a snap point, but the tangent point could not be located by pointing. When AutoCAD asks for a point, you select an object snap mode from the object snap shortcut menu.

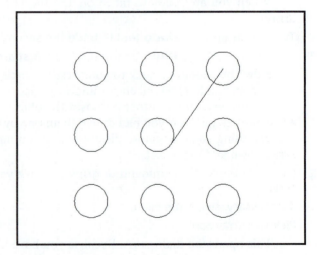

Figure 4-19

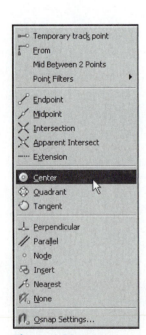

Figure 4-20

⊞ At the *Specify first point:* prompt, instead of specifying a point, hold down the Shift or Ctrl key and right-click.

This opens the shortcut menu illustrated in Figure 4-20.

⊞ Select Center from the shortcut menu.

This tells AutoCAD that you are going to select the start point of the line by using a center object snap rather than by direct pointing or by entering coordinates.

⊞ Move the crosshairs near the top right circle in the array.

When you are close to the circle, AutoCAD identifies the center point and indicates this with an orange circle surrounding the center. This object snap symbol is called a *marker*. There are different-shaped markers for each type of object snap. If you let the cursor rest here for a moment, a label appears, naming the type of object that has been recognized, as shown in Figure 4-21. This label is called a *snap-tip*.

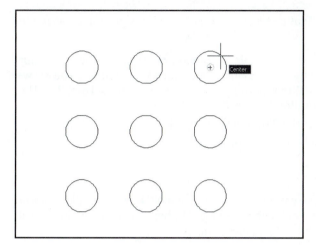

Figure 4-21

⊞ With the center object snap marker showing, press the pick button.

The orange center marker and the snap-tip disappear, and there is a rubber band stretching from the center of the circle to the crosshair position. In the command area, you see the *Specify next point:* prompt.

We use a tangent object snap to select the second point.

⊞ At the *Specify next point or [Undo]:* prompt, open the shortcut menu (Shift + right-click) and select Tangent.

⊞ Move the cursor down and to the left and position the crosshairs so that they are near the right side of the middle circle in the second row.

When you approach the tangent area, you see the orange tangent marker, as shown in Figure 4-22. Here again, if you let the cursor rest you see a snap-tip.

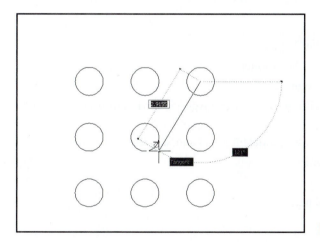

Figure 4-22

⊞ With the tangent marker showing, press the pick button.

AutoCAD locates the tangent point and draws the line. Notice the power of being able to precisely locate the tangent point in this way.

⊞ Press **Enter** to exit the **LINE** command.

Your screen should now resemble Figure 4-19, shown previously.

That's it for now.

4.8 CHANGING PLOT SETTINGS

In the previous chapter, you began using plot previews. In this chapter, we explore more options in the **Plot** dialog box. We have used no specific drawing for illustration. Now that you know how to use plot preview, you can observe the effects of changing plot parameters with any drawing you like and decide at any point whether you actually want to print the results. We remind you to look at a plot preview after making changes. Plot previewing saves you a lot of time and paper and speeds up your learning curve.

⊕ To begin this exploration, you should have a drawing or drawn objects on your screen so that you can observe the effects of various changes you make. The drawing you are in should use the 1B template so that Limits are set to 18 × 12. The circles drawn in the last task are fine for this demonstration.

⊕ Select Plot from the File menu or the Plot tool from the Standard Annotation toolbar.

This opens the **Plot** dialog box.

The Printer/Plotter Panel

One of the most basic changes you can make is your selection of a plotter. Different plotters will use different sheet sizes and will have different default settings. We begin by looking into the list of plotting devices and showing you how to add a plotter to the list.

⊕ Click the arrow at the right of the Name list in the Printer/plotter panel.

The list you see depends on your system and might include printers, plotters, and any faxing devices you have, along with AutoCAD's DWF6 ePlot, DWG to PDF, and Publish to JPG, and PNG utilities, which can be used to send drawing and plotting information to the Internet.

The Add a Plotter Wizard

For a thorough exploration of AutoCAD plotting, it is important that you have at least one plotter available. If you have only a printer, you will probably be somewhat limited in the range of drawing sheets available. You might only have an A-size option, for example. For the exercises in this book, you can use the DWF6 ePlot utility to simulate a plotter, or you can use the Add a Plotter Wizard to install one of the AutoCAD standard plotter drivers, even if you actually have no such plotter on your system. To add a plotter, follow this procedure:

1. Close the **Plot** dialog box.
2. From the **File** menu, select Plotter Manager.
3. From the Plotters window, click Add a Plotter Wizard.
4. Click Next on the Introduction page.
5. Check to see that My Computer is selected on the Add Plotter-Begin page, then click Next.
6. On the Plotter Model page, select a manufacturer and a model, then click Next.
7. Click Next on the Import Pcp or Pc2 page.
8. Click Next on the Ports page.
9. Click Next on the Plotter Name page.
10. Click Finish on the Finish page.

When the wizard is done, the new plotting device is added to your list of plotting devices in the **Plot Configuration** dialog box.

⊕ Close the Plotters dialog box.

⊕ If you have closed the Plot dialog box to install a plotter driver, reopen it. Then open the list of plotting devices again.

⊕ From the list of plotting devices, select a plotter or the DWF6 ePlot utility to simulate a plotter.

Paper Size

Now that you have a plotter selected you should have a number of paper size options.

⊞ From the Paper size list, below the plotter Name list, select a B-size drawing sheet.

The exact size depends on the plotter you have selected. An ANSI B 17 × 11 sheet is a common choice.

Drawing Orientation

Drawing orientation choices are found on the expanded **Plot** dialog box, as shown in Figure 4-23.

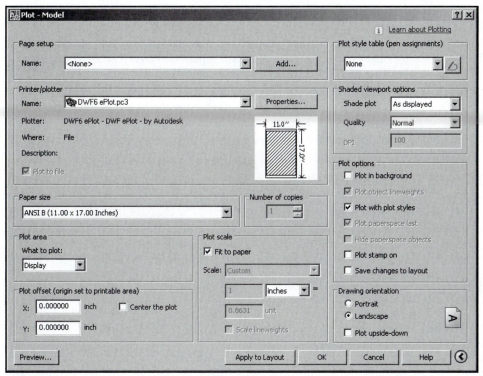

Figure 4-23

⊞ If your dialog box is not already expanded, click the right arrow button (>) at the bottom right of the dialog box.

There are basically two options for drawing orientation: portrait, in which the short edge of the paper is across the bottom, and landscape, in which the long edge is across the bottom. Portrait is typical of a letter or printed sheet of text, and landscape is typical of a drawing sheet. Your plotting device has a default orientation, but you can print either way using the radio buttons. Drawing orientation obviously has a major impact on how the plotting area of the page is used, so be sure to check out the partial preview any time you switch orientations. Try the following:

⊞ Click Preview to see how your current drawing orientation is interpreted.
⊞ Press Esc to return to the Plot dialog box.
⊞ Switch from Landscape to Portrait, or vice versa.
⊞ Click Preview again to see how drawing orientation changes the plot.

On some plotters, you have a choice of different paper orientations. You might have an 11 × 17 and a 17 × 11 option, for example. In this case, there should be a correlation between the paper you choose and the drawing orientation. If you are plotting in landscape, select the 17 × 11; in portrait, select the 11 × 17. Otherwise your paper settings will be 90 degrees off from your drawing orientation and things will get confusing.

⊕ For the following task, check to see that your drawing orientation is set to landscape.

This is the default for most plotters.

Plot Area

Look at the Plot area panel at the left of the **Plot** dialog box. This is a crucial part of the dialog box that allows you to specify the portion of your drawing to be plotted. You have some familiarity with this from Chapter 2, where you plotted using a Window selection. Other options include Display, Limits, and Extents. Changes here have a significant impact on the effective plotting area.

The list box shows the options for plotting area. Display creates a plot using whatever is actually on the screen. If you used the **ZOOM** command to enlarge a portion of the drawing before entering PLOT and then selected this option, AutoCAD would plot whatever is showing in your Drawing Window. Limits, as you know, are specified using the **LIMITS** command. If you are using our standard Architectural B-size template and Limits is selected, the plot area will be 18 × 12. Extents refers to the actual drawing area in which you have drawn objects. It can be larger or smaller than the limits of the drawing.

⊕ Try switching among Limits, Extents, Display, and Window selections and use Plot Preview to see the results.

Whenever you make a change, also observe the changes in the boxes showing inches = drawing units. Assuming that Fit to paper is checked, you will see significant changes in these scale ratios as AutoCAD adjusts scales according to the area specified.

Plot Offset

The Plot offset panel is at the bottom left of the **Plot** dialog box. Plot offset determines the way the plot area is positioned on the drawing sheet. Specifically, it determines where the plot origin is placed. The default locates the origin point (0,0) at the lower left of the plotted area and determines other locations from there. If you enter a different offset specification, (2,3), for example, the origin point of the drawing area is positioned at this point instead, and plot locations are determined from there. This has a dramatic effect on the placement of objects on paper.

The other option in Plot offset is to Center the plot. In this case, AutoCAD positions the drawing so that the center point of the plot area coincides with the center point of the drawing sheet.

⊕ Try various plot offset combinations, including Center the plot, and use Plot Preview to see the results.

CHAPTER TEST QUESTIONS

Questions

1. Name at least five settings that would typically be included in a template drawing.
2. Where are template drawings stored in a standard AutoCAD file configuration? What extension is given to template file names?
3. What is the value of using a template drawing?
4. What is the main difference between the command procedure for MOVE and that for COPY?
5. What is the main limitation of grip editing?
6. What do you have to do to remove grips from an object once they are displayed?
7. How do you access the grip edit shortcut menu?
8. Explain how arrays are a special form of copying.
9. What is a rectangular array? What is a polar array?
10. Why is it important to do a plot preview after changing plot area or plot offset?

Drawing Problems

1. Create a C-size drawing template using an ANSI standard sheet size, layers, and other settings as shown in this chapter. Start with your 1B template settings to make this process easier.
2. Open a drawing with your new C-size template and draw a circle with a two-unit radius centered at (11,8).
3. Using grips, make four copies of the circle, centered at (15,8), (11,12), (7,8), and (11,4).
4. Switch to Layer 2 and draw a 1 × 1 square with lower left corner at (1,1).
5. Create a rectangular array of the square with 14 rows and 20 columns, one unit between rows, and one unit between columns.

WWW Exercise 4 (Optional)

At Chapter 4 of our companion website, you will find a drawing project to complete in addition to the self-scoring chapter test. The drawing project challenges you to use edit commands in place of drawing commands. When you are ready, complete the following steps:

- ⊞ Make sure that you are connected to your Internet service provider.
- ⊞ Type "browser" ↵ or open the Web toolbar and select the Browse the Web tool.
- ⊞ If necessary, navigate to our companion website at prenhall.com/dixriley.
  Good luck!

CHAPTER PROJECTS

Drawing 4-1: Pattern

All the drawings in this chapter use your 1B template. Do not expect, however, that you never need to change settings. Layers stay the same throughout this book, but limits change from time to time, and grid and snap change frequently.

This drawing gives you practice using the **COPY** command. There are numerous ways in which the drawing can be done. The key is to try to take advantage of the repetition in the pattern by copying in an efficient manner. The following reference figures suggest one way to accomplish this:

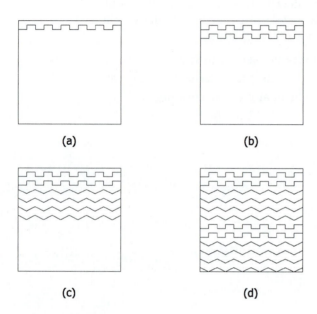

(a)   (b)

(c)   (d)

Drawing Suggestions

$$GRID = 0.5$$
$$SNAP = 0.25$$

- Begin with a 6 × 6 square. Then draw the first set of lines as in Reference 4-1a.
- Copy the first set down 0.5 to produce Reference 4-1b.
- Draw the first set of V-shaped lines. Then use a multiple copy to produce Reference 4-1c.
- Finally, make a single copy of all the lines you have so far, using a window or crossing box for selection. (Be careful not to select the outside lines.) Watch the displacement carefully and you will produce Reference 4-1d, the completed drawing.

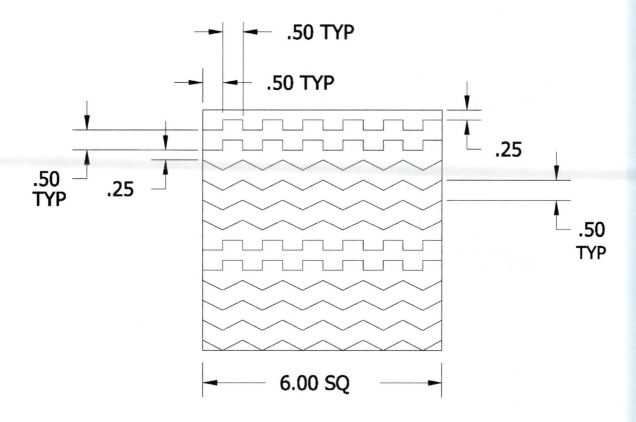

PATTERN

Drawing 4-1

Drawing 4-2: Grill

This drawing should go very quickly if you use the ARRAY command.

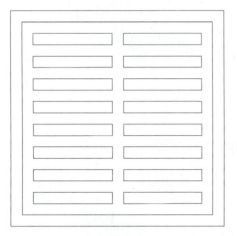

Drawing Suggestions

$$GRID = 0.5$$
$$SNAP = 0.25$$

- Begin with a 4.75 × 4.75 square.
- Move in 0.25 all around to create the inside square.
- Draw the rectangle in the lower left corner first; then use the **ARRAY** command to create the rest.
- Also remember that you can undo a misplaced array using the **U** command.

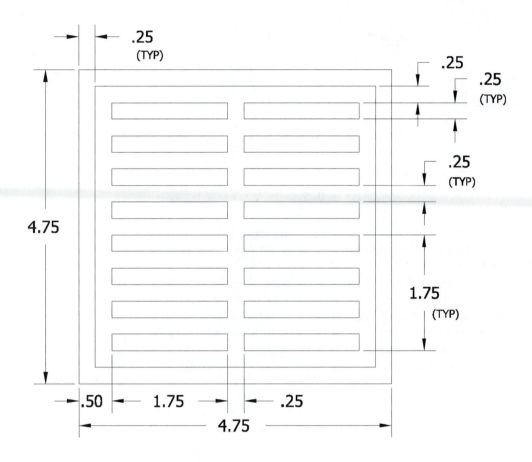

GRILL
Drawing 4-2

Drawing 4-3: Weave

As you do this drawing, watch AutoCAD work for you and think about how long it would take to do this by hand! The finished drawing looks like Reference 4-3. For clarity, the drawing shows only one cell of the array and its dimensions.

Drawing Suggestions

$$GRID = 0.5$$
$$SNAP = 0.125$$

- Draw the 6 × 6 square; then zoom in on the lower left using a window. This is the area shown in the lower left of the dimensioned drawing.

- Observe the dimensions and draw the line patterns for the lower left corner of the weave. You could use the **COPY** command in several places if you'd like, but the time gained will be minimal. Don't worry if you have to fuss with this a little to get it correct; once you have it right, the rest will be easy.

- Use **ARRAY** to repeat the lower left cell in an 8 × 8 matrix.

  If you get it wrong, use **U** and try again.

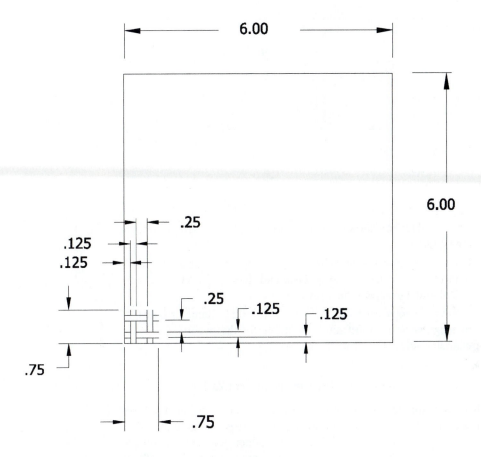

WEAVE

Drawing 4-3

Drawing 4-4: Test Bracket

This is a great drawing for practicing much of what you have learned up to this point. Notice the suggested snap, grid, ltscale, and limit settings and use the **ARRAY** command to draw the 25 circles on the front view.

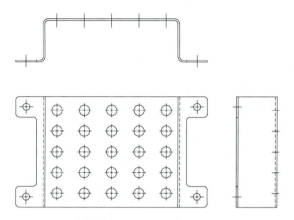

Drawing Suggestions

GRID = 0.25	SNAP = 0.125
LTSCALE = 0.50	LIMITS = (0,0)(24,18)

- Be careful to draw all lines on the correct layers, according to their linetypes.
- Draw center lines through circles before copying or arraying them; otherwise you will have to go back and draw them on each individual circle or repeat the array process.
- A multiple copy works nicely for the four 0.50-diameter holes. A rectangular array is definitely desirable for the twenty-five 0.75-diameter holes.

Creating Center Marks with the Dimcen System Variable

There is a simple way to create the center marks and center lines shown on all the circles in this drawing. It involves changing the value of a dimension variable called *dimcen* (for dimension center). Dimensioning and dimension variables are discussed in Chapter 8, but if you would like to jump ahead, the following procedure works nicely in this drawing:

1. Type "dimcen" ↵. The default setting for dimcen is 0.09, which causes AutoCAD to draw a simple cross as a center mark. Changing it to −.09 tells AutoCAD to draw a cross that reaches across the circle.
2. Type "−.09" ↵.
3. After drawing your first circle, and before arraying it, type dim. This puts you in the **DIMENSION** command.
4. Type "cen," indicating that you want to draw a center mark. This is a very simple dimension feature.
5. Point to the circle.
6. Press **Esc** to quit the **DIM** command.

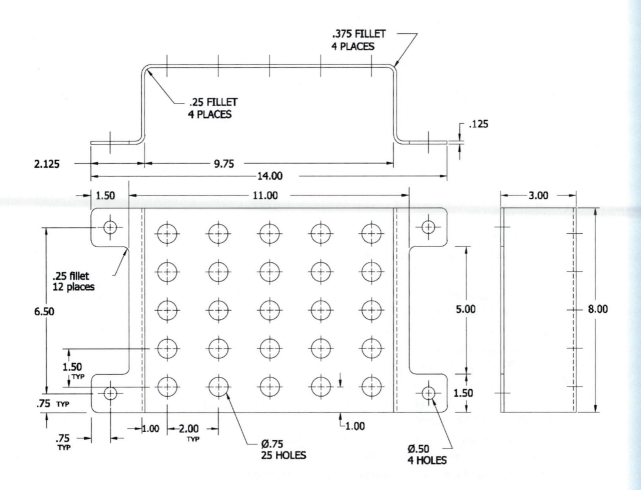

TEST BRACKET

Drawing 4-4

Drawing 4-5: Floor Framing

This architectural drawing requires changes in many features of your drawing setup. Pay close attention to the suggested settings.

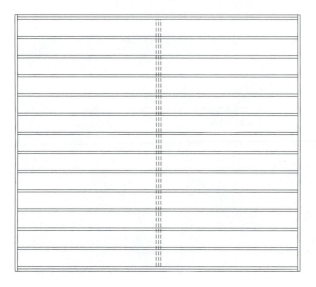

Drawing Suggestions

UNITS = Architectural, Precision = 0′ − 0″
LIMITS = 36′, 24′
GRID = 1′
SNAP = 2″
LTSCALE = 12

- Be sure to use foot (′) and inch (″) symbols when setting limits, grid, and snap (but not ltscale).
- Begin by drawing the 20′ × 17′−10″ rectangle, with the lower left corner somewhere in the neighborhood of (4′,4′).
- Complete the left and right 2 × 10 joists by copying the vertical 17′−10″ lines 2″ in from each side.
- Draw a 19′–8″ horizontal line 2′ up from the bottom and copy it 2″ higher to complete the double joists.
- Array the inner 12 × 10 in a 14-row by 1-column array, with 16″ between rows.
- Set to Layer 2, and draw the three 17′−4″ hidden lines down the center.

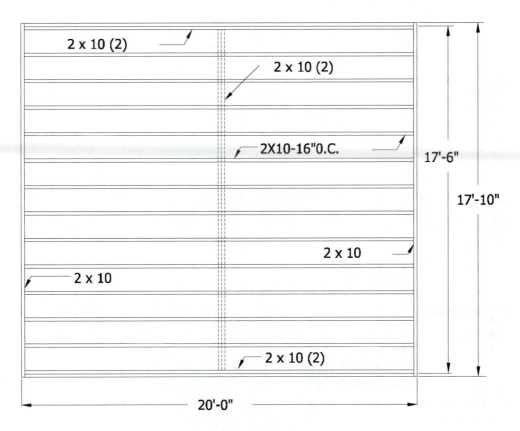

FLOOR FRAMING

Drawing 4-5

Drawing 4-6: Threaded Shaft

The finished drawing should be the top and front views without dimensions, as shown in the reference drawing. Draw the circular view first. This is the top view. Use the top view to line up the front view.

This drawing includes a typical application of rectangular **ARRAY** and **COPY** commands.

Drawing Suggestions

GRID = 1/4
SNAP = 1/8
LIMITS = (0,0)(18,12)
LTSCALE = 0.5

• Draw the circles in the top view and use these to line up the horizontal lines in the front view.

• Pay particular attention to the detail drawing when designing the ACME screw thread. Draw the outline of the zigzag shape on each side for one thread and then connect the lines, creating the full thread. Be sure the zigzag on opposite sides is offset by one thread before drawing the angular lines.

• Now that one thread is created, a simple array completes the whole shaft length.

• Complete the drawing by adding shaft lines and the square shape at the top end.

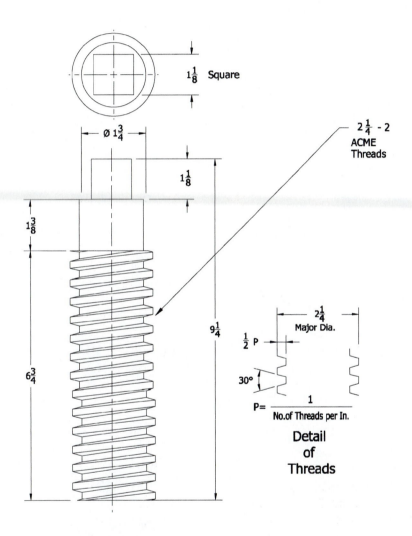

$1\frac{1}{8}$ Square

$\varnothing 1\frac{3}{4}$

$2\frac{1}{4}$ - 2
ACME
Threads

$1\frac{1}{8}$

$1\frac{3}{8}$

$9\frac{1}{4}$

$6\frac{3}{4}$

$2\frac{1}{4}$
Major Dia.

$\frac{1}{2}$ P

30°

$P= \dfrac{1}{\text{No. of Threads per In.}}$

Detail
of
Threads

THREADED SHAFT
Drawing 4-6

Arcs and Polar Arrays

Chapter Objectives

- Creating Polar Arrays
- Drawing Arcs
- Using the ROTATE Command
- Using Polar Tracking at Any Angle
- Creating Mirror Images of Objects on the Screen
- Creating Page Setups

INTRODUCTION

So far, every drawing you have done has been composed of lines and circles. In this chapter, you learn a third major entity, the ARC. In addition, you expand your ability to manipulate objects on the screen. You learn to rotate objects and create their mirror images. You learn to save Plot settings as named Page setups. First, however, we pick up where we left off in Chapter 4 by showing you how to create polar arrays.

5-1 CREATING POLAR ARRAYS

GENERAL PROCEDURE	1. Select the **Array** tool from the dashboard.
	2. Define a selection set. (Steps 1 and 2 can be reversed if noun/verb editing is enabled.)
	3. Right-click to end selection.
	4. Select Polar Array in the dialog box.
	5. Pick a center point.
	6. Enter the number of items to be in the array.
	7. Enter the angle to fill (or 0).
	8. Enter the angle between items.
	9. Indicate whether to rotate items.

The procedure for creating polar arrays is lengthy and requires some explanation. The first three steps are the same as in rectangular arrays. Step 4 is also the same, except that you select Polar instead of Rectangular. From that point on, the steps are new. First, you pick a center point, and then you have several options for defining the array.

There are three qualities that define a polar array, but two are sufficient. A polar array is defined by any combination of two of the following: a certain number of items, an angle that

COMMAND GRID	
Command	Array
Alias	Ar
Menu	Modify
Tool	⊞

these items span, and an angle between each item and the next. You also have to tell AutoCAD whether to rotate the newly created objects as they are copied.

⊕ Create a new drawing using the 1B template from Section 4.3.

⊕ In preparation for this exercise, draw a vertical 1.00 line at the bottom center of the screen, near (9.00,2.00), as shown in Figure 5-1.

We use a 360-degree polar array to create Figure 5-2.

⊕ Select the line.

⊕ Select the Array tool from the dashboard.

⊕ This opens the Array dialog box, familiar from the last chapter.

⊕ Click Polar Array.

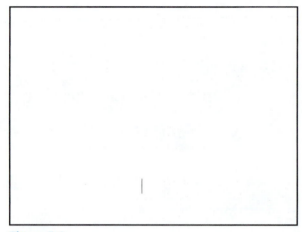

Figure 5-1

Figure 5-2

Clicking Polar Array changes the dialog box, as illustrated in Figure 5-3.

To define a polar array, you need to specify a center point. Rectangular arrays are not determined by a center. Polar arrays, however, are built by copying objects around the circumferences of circles or arcs, so we need to define one of these.

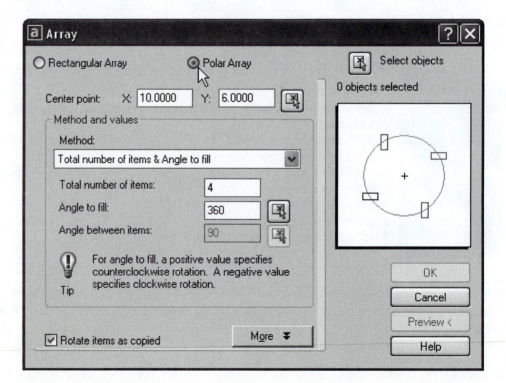

Figure 5-3

Below the **Polar Array** button is a line labeled Center point. There are two edit boxes with the *x* and *y* coordinates of a default center point, and a **Pick Center Point** button on the right that takes you out of the dialog box so that you can pick a point.

⊞ Click the Pick Center Point button.

⊞ Pick a point directly above the line and somewhat below the center of the screen.

Something in the neighborhood of (9.00,5.00) will do. As soon as you pick the point, the dialog box returns with the coordinates of the point entered in the X and Y edit boxes.

Below the Center point edit boxes is a list box labeled Method. If you open this list, you can see the three possible paired combinations of Total number of items, Angle to fill, and Angle between items. We take these in order:

⊞ If necessary, select Total number of items & Angle to fill.

With this selection, notice that the Angle between items edit box below is grayed out (unavailable).

⊞ Type "12" in the Total number of items edit box.

This time around we construct a complete 360-degree array. This is the default, but if it has been changed you might need to enter it on your computer.

⊞ If necessary, enter 360 in the Angle to fill edit box.

Notice the Tip, which tells us that if we give a positive value for angle to fill, the array is constructed counterclockwise; if we give a negative angle, it is constructed clockwise.

Notice the check box at the bottom left of the dialog box labeled Rotate items as copied. With this box checked, as it should be by default, copied objects in the array are rotated around the center point rather than retaining their vertical/horizontal orientation.

⊞ If necessary, check the Rotate items as copied check box.

⊞ Click Preview.

Your screen should resemble Figure 5-2, except that there will be a message box with the options Accept, Modify, or Cancel. Click Modify so that we can return to the dialog box and try some other arrangements.

⊞ Click Modify.

We use the same center point, but define an array that has 20 items placed 15 degrees apart and not rotated.

⊞ Open the Method list and select Total number of items & Angle between items.

Notice that the Angle to fill edit box is now grayed out and the Angle between items box has become accessible.

⊞ Type "20" for the number of items.

⊞ Type "15" for the angle between items.

All that remains is to tell AutoCAD not to rotate the lines as they are copied.

⊞ Clear the Rotate items as copied check box.

Notice how the general preview image at the right of the dialog box changes as you change your selections.

⊞ Click Preview to view a true preview.

Your screen should now resemble Figure 5-4.

⊞ Click Modify to return to the dialog box.

Try one more and then you are on your own with polar arrays. For this one, define an array that fills 270 degrees moving clockwise and has 30 degrees between each angle, as shown in Figure 5-5:

⊞ Open the Method list and select Angle to fill & Angle between items.

⊞ Type "–270" for the angle to fill.

What does the negative angle do?

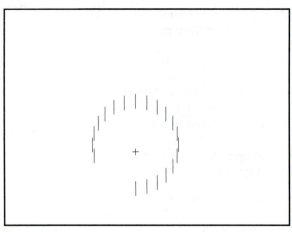

Figure 5-4   **Figure 5-5**

⊕ Type "30" for the angle between.

⊕ Select the check box to rotate items as they are copied.

⊕ Click Preview.

Your screen should resemble Figure 5-5.

⊕ Click Accept to close the dialog box and return to the command prompt.

This ends our discussion of polar arrays. With the options AutoCAD gives you, there are many possibilities that you can try. As always, we encourage experimentation. When you are satisfied, erase everything on the screen in preparation for learning the ARC command.

5-2 DRAWING ARCS

GENERAL PROCEDURE	1. Select the **Arc** tool from the dashboard. 2. Type or show where to start the arc, where to end it, and what circle it is a portion of, using any of the 11 available methods.

Learning AutoCAD's **ARC** command is an exercise in geometry. In this section, we give you a firm foundation for understanding and drawing arcs so that you are not confused by all the available options. The information we give you is more than enough to do the drawings in this chapter and most drawings you encounter elsewhere. Refer to the AutoCAD Command Reference and the chart at the end of this section (Figure 5-8) if you need additional information.

AutoCAD gives you eight distinct ways to draw arcs (11 if you count variations in order). With so many choices, some generalizations are helpful.

First, notice that every option requires you to specify three pieces of information: where to begin the arc, where to end it, and what circle it is theoretically a part of. To get a handle on the range of options, look at the list of options from the Arc submenu.

⊕ Erase any objects left on your screen from the previous section.

⊕ Open the Draw menu and highlight Arc to open the cascading submenu illustrated in Figure 5-6.

Notice that the options in the fourth panel (Center, Start, End, etc.) are simply reordered versions of those in the second panel (Start, Center, End, etc.). This is how we end up with 11 options instead of eight.

More important, Start is always included. In every option, a starting point must be specified, although it does not have to be the first point given.

The options arise from the different ways you can specify the end and the circle from which the arc is cut. The end can be shown as an actual point (all End options) or inferred from a specified angle or length of chord (all Angle and Length options).

The circle that the arc is part of can be specified directly by its center point (all Center options) or inferred from other information, such as a radius length (Radius options), an angle between two given points (Angle options), or a tangent direction (the Start, End, Direction, and Continue options).

With this framework in mind, we begin by drawing an arc using the simplest method, which is also the default, the three-points option. The geometric key to this method is that any three points not on the same line determine a circle or an arc of a circle. AutoCAD uses this in the **CIRCLE** command (the 3P option) as well as in the **ARC** command.

⊞ Select 3 Points from the Draw menu, or select the Arc tool from the dashboard, as shown in Figure 5-7.

COMMAND GRID	
Command	Arc
Alias	A
Menu	Draw
Tool	

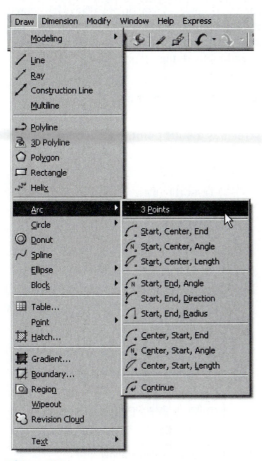

Figure 5-6

Figure 5-7

AutoCAD's response is this prompt:

      Specify start point of arc or [Center]:

Accepting the default by specifying a point leaves open all those options in which the start point is specified first.

If you instead type c, AutoCAD prompts for a center point and follows with those options that begin with a center.

⊞ Select a starting point near the center of the screen.

AutoCAD prompts

      Specify second point of arc or [Center/End]:

We continue to follow the default three-point sequence by specifying a second point. You might want to refer to the chart (Figure 5-8) as you draw this arc.

✛ Select any point one or two units away from the previous point. Exact coordinates are not important right now.

Once AutoCAD has two points, it gives you an arc to drag. By moving the cursor slowly in a circle and in and out, you can see the range of what the third point will produce.

AutoCAD also knows now that you have to provide an endpoint to complete the arc, so the prompt has only one option:

Specify end point of arc:

Any point you select will do, as long as it produces an arc that fits on the screen.

✛ Pick an endpoint.

As you can see, three-point arcs are easy to draw. It is much like drawing a line, except that you have to specify three points instead of two. In practice, however, you do not always have three points to use this way. This necessitates the broad range of options in the **ARC** command. The dimensions you are given and the objects already drawn determine what options are useful to you.

Next we create an arc using the start, center, end method, the second option illustrated in Figure 5-8.

✛ Type "u" ↵ or select the Undo tool to undo the three-point arc.

✛ Select the Arc tool from the dashboard.

✛ Select a point near the center of the screen as a start point.

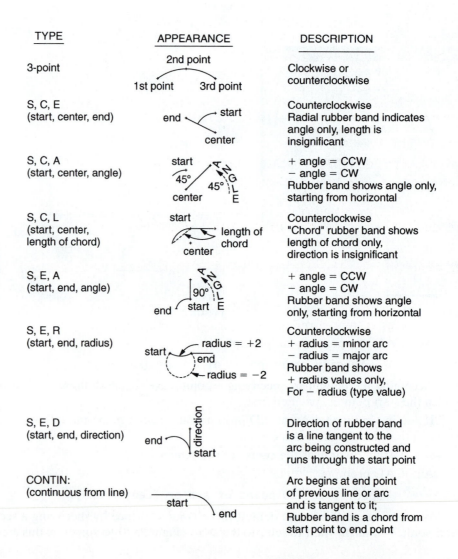

TYPE	APPEARANCE	DESCRIPTION
3-point	2nd point / 1st point / 3rd point	Clockwise or counterclockwise
S, C, E (start, center, end)	end / start / center	Counterclockwise Radial rubber band indicates angle only, length is insignificant
S, C, A (start, center, angle)	start / 45° / center / 45° / ANGLE	+ angle = CCW − angle = CW Rubber band shows angle only, starting from horizontal
S, C, L (start, center, length of chord)	start / length of chord / center	Counterclockwise "Chord" rubber band shows length of chord only, direction is insignificant
S, E, A (start, end, angle)	90° / end / start / ANGLE	+ angle = CCW − angle = CW Rubber band shows angle only, starting from horizontal
S, E, R (start, end, radius)	start / radius = +2 / end / radius = −2	Counterclockwise + radius = minor arc − radius = major arc Rubber band shows + radius values only, For − radius (type value)
S, E, D (start, end, direction)	end / direction / start	Direction of rubber band is a line tangent to the arc being constructed and runs through the start point
CONTIN: (continuous from line)	start / end	Arc begins at end point of previous line or arc and is tangent to it; Rubber band is a chord from start point to end point

Figure 5-8

The prompt that follows is the same as for the three-point option, but we do not use the default this time:

```
Specify second point of arc or [Center/End]:
```

TIP If you choose options from the **Draw** menu, some steps are automated. If you select Start, Center, End, for example, the c is entered automatically.

⊕ Type "c" ↵ or right-click and select Center from the shortcut menu.

This tells AutoCAD that we want to specify a center point next, so we see the prompt

```
Specify center point of arc:
```

⊕ Select any point roughly one to three units away from the start point.

The circle from which the arc is to be cut is now clearly determined. All that is left is to specify how much of the circle to take, which can be done in one of three ways, as the following prompt indicates:

```
Specify end point of arc or [Angle/chord Length]:
```

We pick an endpoint. First, however, move the cursor slowly in a circle and in and out to see how this method works. As before, there is an arc to drag, and now there is a radial direction rubber band as well. If you pick a point anywhere along this rubber band, AutoCAD assumes that you want the point where it crosses the circumference of the circle.

Note:
Here, as in the polar arrays in this chapter, AutoCAD is building arcs counterclockwise, consistent with its coordinate system.

⊕ Pick an endpoint to complete the arc.

We now draw one more arc, using the start, center, angle method, before going on. This method has some peculiarities in the use of the rubber band that are typical of the **ARC** command and they can be confusing. An example of how the start, center, angle method might look is shown in Figure 5-8.

⊕ Undo the last arc.
⊕ Select the Arc tool.

AutoCAD asks for a center or start point:

```
Specify start point of arc or [Center]:
```

⊕ Pick a start point near the center of the screen.

AutoCAD prompts

```
Specify second point of arc or [Center/End]:
```

⊕ Type "c" ↵ or right-click and select Center from the shortcut menu.

AutoCAD prompts for a center point:

```
Specify center point of arc:
```

⊕ Pick a center point one to three units below the start point.

AutoCAD prompts, as before,

```
Specify end point of arc or [Angle/chord Length]:
```

⊕ Type "a" ↵ or right-click and select Angle from the shortcut menu.

Notice how the shortcut menu changes to show different options available at each step.

You can type an angle specification or show an angle on the screen. Notice that the rubber band now shows an angle only; its length is insignificant. The indicated angle is being measured from the horizontal, but the actual arc begins at the start point and continues counterclockwise, as illustrated in Figure 5-8. The prompt reads

`Specify included angle:`

 Type "45" ↵ or show an angle of 45 degrees.

Now that you have tried three of the basic methods for constructing an arc, we strongly suggest that you study the chart in Figure 5-9 and then try the other options. The notes in the right-hand column serve as a guide.

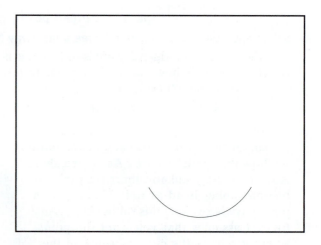

Figure 5-9

The differences in the use of the rubber band from one option to the next are important. You should understand, for instance, that in some cases the linear rubber band is only significant as a distance indicator; its angle is of no importance and is ignored by AutoCAD. In other cases, it is just the reverse: The length of the rubber band is irrelevant, whereas its angle of rotation is important.

TIP   One additional trick you should try as you experiment with arcs is as follows: If you press **Enter** or the spacebar at the *Specify start point [Center]:* prompt, AutoCAD uses the endpoint of the last line or arc you drew as the new starting point and constructs an arc tangent to it. This is the same as the Continue option on the pull-down menu.

This completes the discussion of the **ARC** command. Constructing arcs can be tricky. Another option that is available and often useful is to draw a complete circle and then use the **TRIM** or **BREAK** command to cut out the arc you want. BREAK and TRIM are introduced in the next chapter.

FOR MORE DETAILS   See Chapter 6.

5-3 USING THE **ROTATE** COMMAND

GENERAL PROCEDURE	1. Select the **Rotate** tool from the dashboard. 2. Define the selection set. (Steps 1 and 2 can be reversed if noun/verb selection is enabled.) 3. Pick a base point. 4. Indicate an angle of rotation.

ROTATE is a fairly straightforward command, and it has some uses that might not be immediately apparent. For example, it frequently is easier to draw an object in a horizontal or vertical position and then ROTATE it into position rather than drawing it in a diagonal position.

In addition to the **ROTATE** command, there is a rotate mode in the grip edit system, which we introduce later in this section.

⊞ In preparation for this exercise, clear your screen and draw a three-point arc using the points (9,6), (11.50,5), and (14,6), as in Figure 5-9.

We begin by rotating the arc to the position shown in Figure 5-10.

⊞ Select the arc.

⊞ Select the Rotate tool from the dashboard, as shown in Figure 5-11.

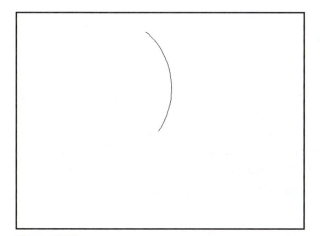

Figure 5-10

Figure 5-11

You are prompted for a base point:

    Specify base point:

This is the point around which the object is rotated. The results of the rotation, therefore, are dramatically affected by your choice of base point. Choose a point at the left tip of the arc.

⊞ Point to the left tip of the arc.

The prompt that follows looks like this:

    Specify rotation angle or [Copy/Reference]:

The default method is used to indicate a rotation angle directly. The object is rotated through the angle specified and the original object is deleted. If you specify the copy option, the original object is retained along with the rotated copy.

Move the cursor in a circle and you will see that you have an arc to drag into place visually. If Ortho is on, turn it off to see the complete range of rotation.

⊞ Type "90" ↵ or point to a rotation of 90 degrees.

The results should resemble Figure 5-10.

COMMAND GRID	
Command	Rotate
Alias	Ro
Menu	Modify
Tool	

NEW to AutoCAD 2008

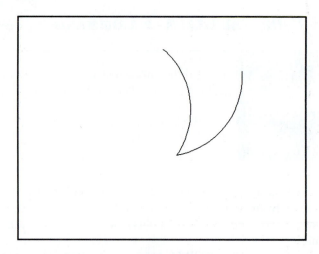

Figure 5-12

Notice that when specifying the rotation angle directly like this, the original orientation of the selected object is taken to be 0 degrees. The rotation is figured counterclockwise from there. However, there might be times when you want to refer to the coordinate system in specifying rotation. This is the purpose of the Reference option. To use it, you need to specify the present orientation of the object relative to the coordinate system, and then tell AutoCAD the orientation you want it to have after rotation. Look at Figure 5-12. To rotate the arc as shown, you can either indicate a rotation of −45 degrees or tell AutoCAD that it is currently oriented to 90 degrees and you want it rotated to 45 degrees. The following steps will rotate the arc using the Reference option and retain the original using the Copy option.

⊕ Repeat the ROTATE command.

⊕ Select the arc.

⊕ Right-click to end selection.

⊕ Choose a base point at the lower tip of the arc.

⊕ Type "c" ↵ or select Copy from the shortcut menu.

⊕ Type "r" ↵ or select Reference from the shortcut menu.

Notice that both options can be active at once.

AutoCAD prompts for a reference angle:

```
Specify the reference angle <0>:
```

⊕ Type "90" ↵.

AutoCAD prompts

```
Specify the new angle:
```

⊕ Type "45" ↵.

Your screen should now include both arcs shown in Figure 5-12.

Rotating with Grips

Rotating with grips is simple, but your choice of object selection methods is limited, as always, to pointing and windowing. Complete the following steps:

⊕ Pick the two arcs.

The arcs are highlighted and grips appear. Notice that these grips are especially designed for arcs.

⊕ Pick the grip in the middle of either arc.

⊕ Right-click to open the grip shortcut menu.

⊕ Select Rotate.

Move your cursor in a circle and you will see the arcs rotating around the grip you selected.

⊕ Right-click again and select Base Point from the menu.

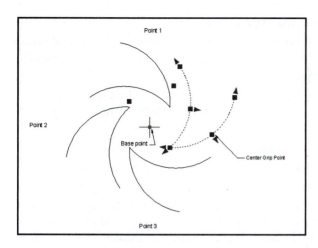

Figure 5-13

Base Point allows you to pick a base point other than the selected grip.

⊕ Pick a base point above and to the left of the grip, as shown in Figure 5-13.

Move your cursor in circles again. You can see the arc rotating around the new base point.

⊕ Type "c" ↵ or open the shortcut menu and select Copy.

Notice the command area prompt, which indicates that you are now in a rotate and multiple copy mode.

⊕ Pick a point showing a rotation angle of 90 degrees, as illustrated by the top two arcs in Figure 5-13.

⊕ Pick a second point showing a rotation angle of 180 degrees, as illustrated by the arcs at the left in the figure.

⊕ Pick point 3 at 270 degrees to complete the design shown in Figure 5-13.

⊕ Press Enter or the spacebar to exit the grip mode.

The capacity to create rotated copies is very useful, as you will find when you do the drawings at the end of this chapter.

5-4 USING POLAR TRACKING AT ANY ANGLE

You might have noticed that using Ortho or Polar Tracking to force or snap to the 90-degree, 180-degree, and 270-degree angles in the last exercise would make the process more efficient. With Polar Tracking, you can extend this concept to include angular increments other than the standard 90-degree orthogonal angles. This feature combined with the Rotate Copy technique facilitates the creation of rotated copies at regular angles. As an example, we use this process to create Figure 5-14.

Figure 5-14

⊕ To begin this task, Erase all but one arc on your screen.

This is a good opportunity to use the Remove option in the **ERASE** command. Select all the arcs and then remove one before completing the command.

⊕ Move the arc to the center of your screen.

We are going to rotate and copy this arc as before, but first we set Polar Tracking to track at 30-degree angles. This is done in the Drafting Settings dialog box.

⊕ Turn Snap off.

⊕ Click the Polar button on the status bar so that Polar Tracking is on.

⊕ Right-click the same Polar button.

⊕ Select Settings from the shortcut menu.

You see the Drafting Settings dialog box as shown in Figure 5-15. This is the same dialog box used previously to specify Snap and Grid settings, but now the **Polar Tracking** tab is selected. In the next chapter, we use the third tab, Object Snap.

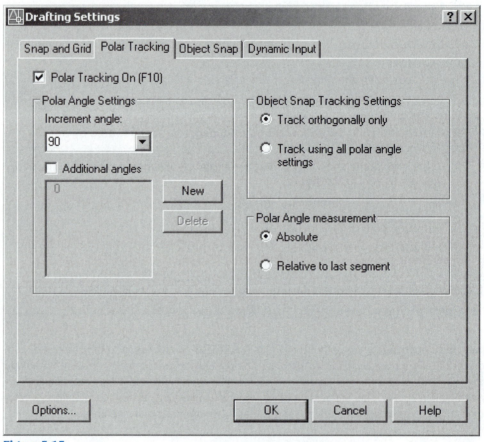

Figure 5-15

If you are using AutoCAD default settings, the increment angle is 90 degrees. Otherwise, you see whatever increment was set last in your AutoCAD system.

⊕ Open the Increment angle drop-down list.

Notice the standard selections, from 90 at the top to 5 at the bottom. Notice also that you can add custom angles by selecting the Additional angles check box, clicking New, and typing in a new value.

⊕ Select 30 from the list.

30 replaces 90 as the current increment angle. We do not use the other two panels yet.

⊕ With 30 showing as the current increment angle, click OK.

⊕ Select the arc.

⊕ Click on the grip in the middle of the arc.

⊕ Right-click to open the grip shortcut menu.

⊕ Select Rotate.

⊕ Slowly move the cursor in a wide circle around the selected grip.

Polar Tracking now tracks and snaps to every 30-degree angular increment.

⊕ Right-click to open the shortcut menu again.

⊕ Select Copy.

⊕ Carefully create a copy at every 30-degree angle until you have created a design similar to Figure 5-14.

If your design is not exactly like ours, in particular if the ends of the arcs overlap or do not meet, it is because you have used an arc that is not the same as the one we used.

5-5 Creating Mirror Images of Objects on the Screen

<table>
<tr><td>**GENERAL PROCEDURE**</td><td>1. Select the **Mirror** tool from the dashboard.
2. Define a selection set. (Steps 1 and 2 can be reversed if noun/verb selection is enabled.)
3. Point to two ends of a mirror line.
4. Indicate whether to delete the original object.</td></tr>
</table>

There are two main differences between the command procedures for MIRROR and ROTATE. First, to mirror an object you have to define a mirror line; second, you have to indicate whether you want to erase the original object or not.

There is also a mirror mode in the grip edit system, which we explore later in this section.

⊕ To begin this exercise, Erase all but one arc on your screen.

⊕ Turn Snap on.

⊕ Rotate the arc and move it so that you have a bowl-shaped arc placed to the left of the center of your screen, as in Figure 5-16.

⊕ Keep Polar Tracking on to do this exercise.

⊕ Select the arc.

⊕ Select the Mirror tool from the dashboard, as shown in Figure 5-17.

Now AutoCAD asks you for the first point of a mirror line:

        Specify first point of mirror line:

COMMAND GRID	
Command	Mirror
Alias	Mi
Menu	Modify
Tool	

Figure 5-16

Figure 5-17

A mirror line is just what you would expect; the line serves as the mirror, and all points on your original object are reflected across the line at an equal distance and opposite orientation.

We show a mirror line even with the top of the arc, so that the endpoints of the mirror images are touching.

⊕ Select a point even with the left endpoint of the arc, as in Figure 5-18.

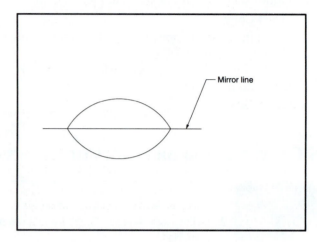

Figure 5-18

You are prompted to show the other endpoint of the mirror line:

Specify second point of mirror line:

The length of the mirror line is not important. All that matters is its orientation. Move the cursor slowly in a circle, and you see an inverted copy of the arc moving with you to show the different mirror images that are possible given the first point you have specified.

⊕ Select a point at 0 degrees from the first point, so that the mirror image is directly above the original arc and touching at the endpoints, as in Figure 5-18.

The dragged object disappears until you answer the next prompt, which asks if you want to delete the original object.

Erase source objects [Yes/No]? <N>:

This time around, do not erase the original.

⊕ Press Enter to retain the old object.

Your screen should look like Figure 5-18, without the mirror line in the middle.

Now let's repeat the process, deleting the original this time and using a different mirror line.

⊕ Repeat the MIRROR command.
⊕ Select the original (lower) arc.
⊕ Right-click to end selection.

Create a mirror image above the last one by choosing a mirror line slightly above the two arcs, as in Figure 5-19.

⊕ Select a first point of the mirror line slightly above and to the left of the figure.
⊕ Select a second point directly to the right of the first point.
⊕ Type "y" ↵ or right-click and select Yes from the shortcut menu.

Your screen should now resemble Figure 5-20.

Mirroring with Grips

The Mirror grip edit mode works exactly like the Rotate mode, except that the rubber band shows you a mirror line instead of a rotation angle. The option to retain or delete the original is obtained through the Copy option, just as in the Rotate mode. Try the following:

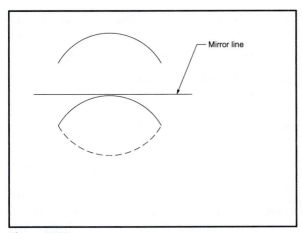

Figure 5-19

Figure 5-20

⊕ Select the two arcs on your screen by pointing or using a crossing window.

   The arcs are highlighted and grips are showing.

⊕ Pick any of the grips.

⊕ Right-click and then select Mirror from the shortcut menu.

   Move the cursor and observe the dragged mirror images of the arcs. Notice that the rubber band operates as a mirror line, just as in the **MIRROR** command.

⊕ Type "b" ↵ or right-click again and select Base point.

   This frees you from the selected grip and allows you to create a mirror line from any point on the screen. Notice the *Specify base point:* prompt in the command area.

⊕ Pick a base point slightly below the arcs.

⊕ Type "c" ↵ or right-click and select Copy from the shortcut menu.

   As in the Rotate mode, this is how you retain the original in a grip edit mirroring sequence.

⊕ Pick a second point to the right of the first.

   Your screen should resemble Figure 5-21.

⊕ Press Enter or the spacebar to exit grip edit mode.

   We suggest that you complete this exercise by using the Mirror grip edit mode with the copy option to create Figure 5-22.

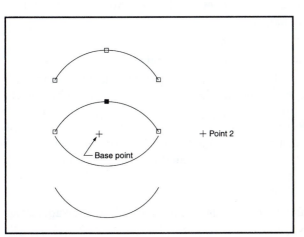

Figure 5-21

Figure 5-22

5-6 CREATING PAGE SETUPS

GENERAL PROCEDURE

1. Select the **Plot** tool from the **Standard Annotation** toolbar.
2. Make changes in Plot settings.
3. Click Add to open the **Add Page Setup** dialog box.
4. Enter a name for the page setup.
5. Click **OK.**

In this chapter and the next, you move to another level in your exploration of AutoCAD plotting. So far, we have confined ourselves to plot configurations tied directly to objects visible in your model space drawing area. In this chapter, we continue to plot from model space, but introduce the concept and technique of page setups. With page setups, you can name and save different plot configurations so that one drawing can produce several different page setups. We define two simple page setups. You do not need to learn any new options, but you do learn to save settings of the options we have covered so far so that they can be reused as part of a page setup.

⊞ To begin this section, you should be in an AutoCAD drawing using the 1B template.

Any drawing will do. We will continue using the objects drawn in Section 5.5.

The Page Setup Dialog Box

A page setup is nothing more than a group of plot settings, like the ones you have been specifying since Chapter 2. The only difference is that you give the configuration a name and save it on a list of setups. Once named, the plot settings can be restored by selecting the name and they can even be exported to other drawings.

You can define a page setup from the **Plot** dialog box or from the **Page Setup** dialog box, accessible through the **Page Setup Manager** on the **File** menu. There is little difference between the two dialog boxes. Here we continue to use the **Plot** dialog box.

⊞ Select the Plot tool from the Standard Annotation toolbar.

You should now be in the familiar **Plot** dialog box. We make a few changes in parameters and then give this page setup a name.

We create a portrait setup and a landscape setup. Besides the difference in orientation, the only difference in settings between the two is that the portrait setup is centered, whereas the landscape setup is plotted from the origin.

⊞ Make sure you have a plotter selected in the Printer/plotter list.

⊞ If necessary, open the Paper size list and select an A-size 8.50 × 11.00 sheet.

⊞ Select Limits in the plot area panel.

⊞ Select Center the plot in the Plot offset panel.

⊞ Select the Portrait button in the Drawing orientation panel.

Notice how the preview image changes. Pause a minute to make sure you understand why the preview looks this way. Assuming you are using the objects drawn in this chapter, or another drawing using the 1B template, you have model space limits set to 18 × 12. You are plotting to an 8.5 × 11 sheet of paper. The 18 × 12 limits have been positioned in portrait orientation, placed across the effective area of the drawing sheet, scaled to fit, and centered on the paper.

Now you name this page setup.

⊞ Click the Add button at the upper right of the dialog box next to the Page setup Name box.

Chapter 5   Arcs and Polar Arrays

This opens the **Add Page Setup** dialog box shown in Figure 5-23.

⊕ Type Portrait as the page setup name.

⊕ Click OK.

Figure 5-23

This brings you back to the **Plot** dialog box. Portrait is now entered in the Page setup Name box. That's all there is to it. The portrait page setup information is now part of the current drawing.

Next, we define a landscape page setup and put it on the list as well. This setup puts the drawing in landscape orientation and positions it from the origin rather than from the center.

⊕ Select the Landscape button in the Drawing orientation panel.

Notice that Portrait is no longer in the Page setup edit box now that you have changed a parameter.

⊕ Clear the check mark on Center the plot.

Notice that the preview image of the page stays in the portrait position even though the plot will be a landscape plot. This is because the sheet size is 8.5 × 11. If you wanted to rotate this image to the horizontal, you would need to select an 11 × 8.5 sheet. So now you have the 18 × 12 limits aligned with the left edge of the page, positioned at the origin of the effective area, and scaled to fit. Let's give this setup a name.

⊕ Click Add again.

⊕ Type Landscape in the User Defined Page Setup box.

⊕ Click OK.

Back in the **Plot** dialog box, you see that Landscape setup has been entered as the current page setup. You should now restore the portrait settings.

⊕ Open the Page setup Name drop-down list and select Portrait.

Your portrait settings, including the Portrait radio button and Center the plot, are restored.

⊕ Click Preview.

You should see a preview similar to Figure 5-24.

⊕ Press Esc to return to the dialog box.

⊕ Open the Page setup Name drop-down list again and select Landscape.

Your landscape settings are restored.

⊕ Click Preview.

You should see a preview similar to Figure 5-25. Notice that AutoCAD turns the paper image to landscape orientation in the full preview.

Figure 5-24

Figure 5-25

This is a simple demonstration, but remember that everything from sheet size to the plotter you are using and all the settings in the **Plot Configuration** dialog box can be included in a named page setup.

⊞ You can click OK to plot or Cancel to exit. Either way your page setups will be saved.

Importing Page Setups

A powerful feature of page setups is that they can be exchanged among drawings using the **PSETUPIN** command. This allows you to import page setups from a known drawing into the current drawing. The procedure is as follows:

1. From a drawing into which you would like to import a page setup, open the **File** menu and select Page Setup Manager.

2. In the **Page Setup Manager,** click the **Import** button.

3. In the **Select Page Setup From File** dialog box, enter the name and path of the drawing file from which you would like to import a page setup, or open the folder containing the file and select it.

4. In the Import Page Setup box, select the name of the page setup you want to import.

5. Enter the **Plot or Page Setup** dialog box and open the Page Setup Name list. The imported page setup should be there.

> **Note:**
> Once you have defined page setups, you can access them through the **Page Setup Manager,** opened from the **File** menu. This dialog box is a simple interface that allows you to select page setups from a list. It will then take you to the **Page Setup** dialog box to modify existing page setups or create new ones. In addition, you can import page setups from other drawings, as described next.

> **Note:**
> Page setups are defined in either model space or paper space as part of a layout. If you create a page setup in model space and then go into a paper space layout, you will not see it on your list. Also, if you define a page setup as part of a paper space layout, you will not see it if you begin a plot from model space.

CHAPTER TEST QUESTIONS

Questions

1. What factors define a polar array? How many are needed to define an array?
2. What factors define an arc? How many are needed for any single method?
3. How would you use Polar Tracking instead of Polar Array to create Figure 5-6?
4. What is the difference between the three-points option in the **CIRCLE** command and the three-points option in the **ARC** command?
5. Explain the significance of the rubber band in the Start, Center, Angle and the Start, End, Direction methods.
6. How would you use the Reference option to rotate a line from 60 degrees to 90 degrees? How would you accomplish the same rotation without using a reference?
7. What is the purpose of the base point option in the grip edit Rotate mode?
8. Why does MIRROR require a mirror line whereas ROTATE requires only a single point?
9. How do you create a landscape plot if your printer prints in portrait orientation?
10. What would happen if a drawing created with our 1B template were printing with a 1-to-1 scale on an A-size printer? What feature of the **Plot Configuration** dialog box would you use to find out if you weren't sure?

Drawing Problems

1. Draw an arc starting at (10,6) and passing through (12,6.5) and (14,6).
2. Create a mirrored copy of the arc across the horizontal line passing through (10,6).
3. Rotate the pair of arcs from Step 2 45 degrees around the point (9,6).
4. Create a mirrored copy of the pair of arcs mirrored across a vertical line passing through (9,6).
5. Create mirrored copies of both pairs of arcs mirrored across a horizontal line passing through (9,6).
6. Erase any three of the four pairs of arcs on your screen and re-create them using a polar array.

WWW Exercise 5 (Optional)

In addition to the self-scoring test, Chapter 5 of our companion website gives you another challenge to draw an object using a limited number of objects and edit commands. We also give you links to two new CAD-related websites. When you are ready, complete the following:

⊞ Make sure that you are connected to your Internet service provider.
⊞ Type "browser" ↵ or open the Web toolbar and select the Browse Web tool.
⊞ If necessary, navigate to our companion website at prenhall.com/dixriley.

Bon voyage!

CHAPTER PROJECTS

Drawing 5-1: Flanged Bushing

This drawing makes use of a polar array to draw eight screw holes in a circle. It also reviews the use of layers and linetypes. Please save this drawing, as noted subsequently.

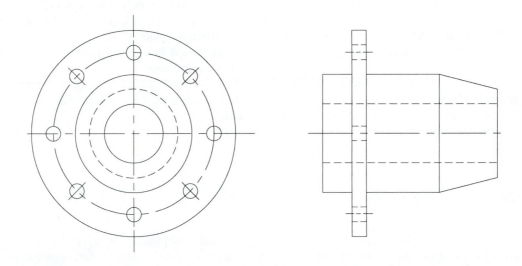

Drawing Suggestions

```
GRID = 0.25
SNAP = 0.125
LTSCALE = 0.50
LIMITS = (0,0)(12,9)
```

- Draw the concentric circles first, using dimensions from both views. Remember to change layers as needed.
- Once you have drawn the 2.75-diameter bolt circle, use it to locate one of the bolt holes. Any of the circles at a quadrant point (0 degrees, 90 degrees, 180 degrees, or 270 degrees) will do.
- Draw a center line across the bolt hole, and then ARRAY the hole and the center line 360 degrees. Be sure to rotate the objects as they are copied; otherwise, you will get strange results from your center lines.

Save This Drawing

This drawing is used in Chapter 6 to demonstrate AutoCAD drawing layouts, paper space, and the use of multiple viewports. It is important that you save the drawing so that you can use it to learn these important plotting techniques.

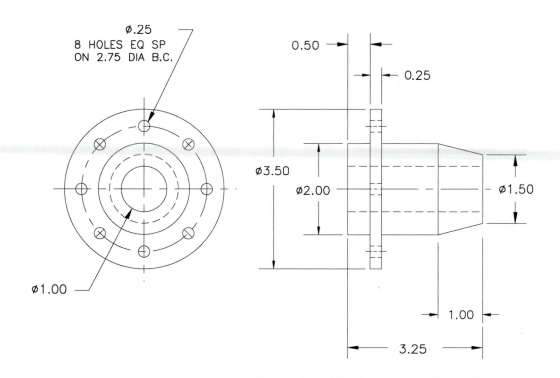

FLANGED BUSHING

Drawing 5-1

Drawing 5-2: Guide

There are six arcs in this drawing, and although some of them could be drawn as fillets, we suggest that you use the **ARC** command for practice. By drawing arcs, you also avoid a common problem with fillets. Because fillets are designed to round intersections at corners, creating a fillet in the middle of a line erases part of that line unless you turn Trim mode off. This would affect the center line on the left side of the front view of this drawing, for example.

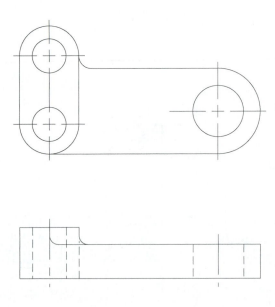

Drawing Suggestions

GRID = 0.25
SNAP = 0.125
LTSCALE = 0.50
LIMITS = (0,0)(12,9)

- The three large arcs in the top view all can be drawn easily using Start, Center, End.
- The smaller 0.375 arc in the top view could be drawn by filleting the top arc with the horizontal line to its right. However, we suggest you try an arc giving Start, Center, End or Start, Center, Angle. Note that you can easily locate the center by moving 0.375 to the right of the endpoint of the upper arc.
- The same method works to draw the 0.25 arc in the front view. Begin by dropping a line down 0.25 from the horizontal line. Start your arc at the end of this line and move 0.25 to the right to locate its center. Then the end is simply 0.25 down from the center (or you could specify an angle of 90 degrees).
- Similarly, the arc at the center line can be drawn from a start point 0.25 up from the horizontal. It has a radius of 0.25 and makes an angle of 90 degrees.

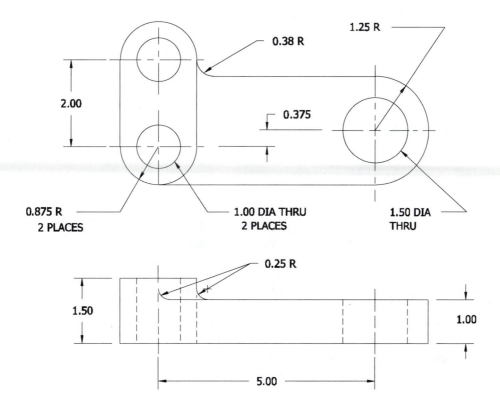

GUIDE
Drawing 5-2

Drawing 5-3: Dials

This is a relatively simple drawing that gives you some good practice with polar arrays and the **ROTATE** and **COPY** commands.

Notice that the needle drawn at the top of the next page is only for reference; the actual drawing includes only the plate and the three dials with their needles.

Drawing Suggestions

GRID = 0.25
SNAP = 0.125
LTSCALE = 0.50
LIMITS = (0,0)(18,12)

* After drawing the outer rectangle and screw holes, draw the leftmost dial, including the needle. Draw a 0.50 vertical line at the top and array it to the left (counterclockwise—a positive angle) and to the right (negative) to create the 11 larger lines on the dial. How many lines in each of these left and right arrays do you need to end up with 11?

* Draw a 0.25 line on top of the 0.50 line at the top of the dial. Then use right and left arrays with a Last selection to create the 40 small markings. How many lines are in each of these two arrays?

* Complete the first dial and then use a multiple copy to produce two more dials at the center and right of your screen. Be sure to use a window to select the entire dial.

* Finally, use the **ROTATE** command to rotate the needles as indicated on the new dials.

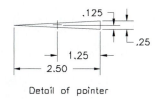

Detail of pointer

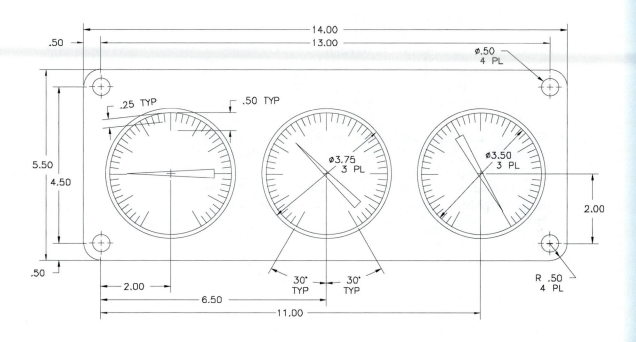

DIALS

Drawing 5-3

Drawing 5-4: Alignment Wheel

This drawing shows a typical use of the **MIRROR** command. Carefully mirroring sides of the symmetrical front view saves you from duplicating some of your drawing efforts. Notice that you need a small snap setting to draw the vertical lines at the chamfer.

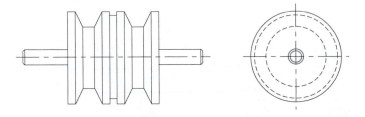

Drawing Suggestions

GRID = 0.25
SNAP = 0.0625
LTSCALE = 0.50
LIMITS = (0,0)(12,9)

- There are numerous ways to use MIRROR in drawing the front view. As the reference shows, there is top–bottom symmetry as well as left–right symmetry. The exercise for you is to choose an efficient mirroring sequence.

- Whatever sequence you use, consider the importance of creating the chamfer and the vertical line at the chamfer before this part of the object is mirrored.

- Once the front view is drawn, the right side view is easy. Remember to change layers for center and hidden lines and to line up the small inner circle with the chamfer.

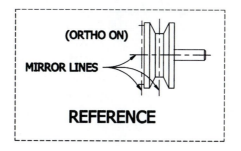

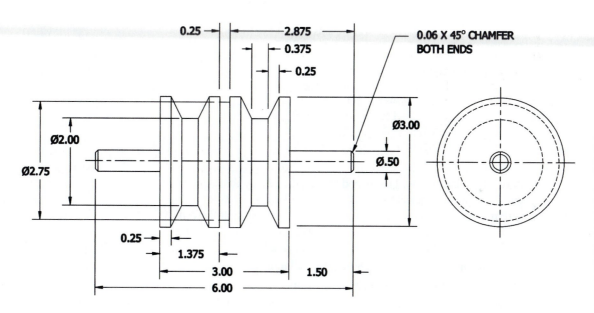

ALIGNMENT WHEEL

Drawing 5-4

Drawing 5-5: Hearth

Once you have completed this architectural drawing as it is shown, you might want to experiment with filling in a pattern of firebrick in the center of the hearth. The drawing itself is not complicated, but little errors become very noticeable when you try to make the row of 4 × 8 bricks across the bottom fit with the arc of bricks across the top, so work carefully.

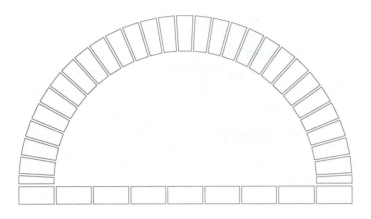

Drawing Suggestions

> UNITS = Architectural
> > Precision = 0′ − 01/8″
> LIMITS = (0,0)(12′,9′)
> GRID = 1′
> SNAP = 1/8″

- Zoom in to draw the wedge-shaped brick indicated by the arrow on the right of the dimensioned drawing. Draw half of the brick only and mirror it across the center line as shown. (Notice that the center line is for reference only.) It is very important that you use MIRROR so that you can erase half of the brick later.

- Array the brick in a 29-item, 180-degree polar array.

- Erase the bottom halves of the end bricks at each end.

- Draw a new horizontal bottom line on each of the two end bricks.

- Draw a 4 × 8 brick directly below the half brick at the left end.

- Array the 4 × 8 brick in a one-row, nine-column array, with 8.5″ between columns.

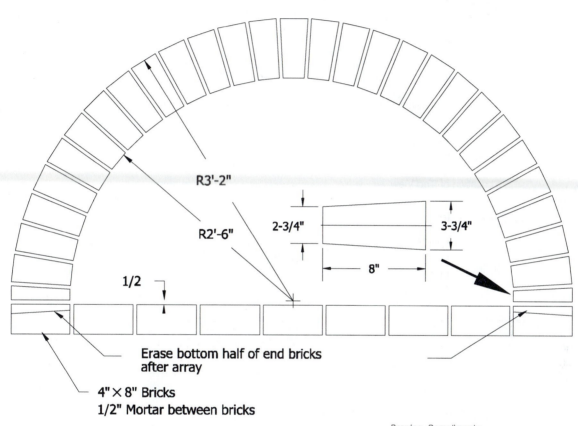

R3'-2"

R2'-6"

2-3/4"   3-3/4"

8"

1/2

**Erase bottom half of end bricks
after array**

**4" × 8" Bricks
1/2" Mortar between bricks**

Drawing Compliments
of Thomas Casey

HEARTH

Drawing 5-5

Drawing 5-6: Slotted Flange

This drawing includes a typical application of polar arrays and arcs. The finished drawing should consist of the 2-D top view and front view, not the 3-D view shown on the drawing page. The center lines and outline of the large circle in the top view are shown in the reference drawing. Use the three-dimensional view as a reference to draw the two-dimensional top and front views.

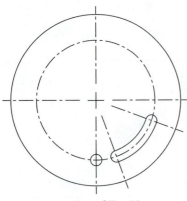

Location of Top View

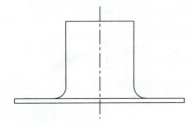

Location of Front View

Drawing Suggestions

- Begin by drawing the circles in the top view. Use the circles to line up the vertical lines in the front view.
- The small arcs in the slots can be drawn on a center line and rotated and copied into place using grips.

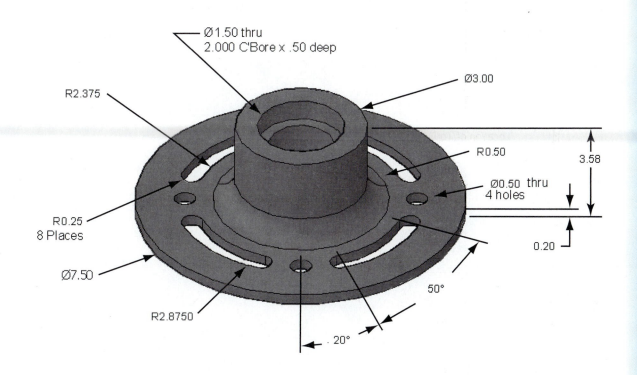

Ø1.50 thru
2.000 C'Bore x .50 deep

Ø3.00

R2.375

R0.50

3.58

Ø0.50 thru
4 holes

R0.25
8 Places

Ø7.50

R2.8750

0.20

50°

20°

SLOTTED FLANGE
Drawing 5-6

6

Object Snap

Chapter Objectives

- Selecting Points with Object Snap (Single-Point Override)
- Selecting Points with OSNAP (Running Mode)
- Object Snap Tracking
- Using the OFFSET Command (Creating Parallel Objects with OFFSET)
- BREAKing Previously Drawn Objects
- Shortening Objects with the TRIM Command
- Extending Objects with the EXTEND Command
- Using STRETCH to Alter Objects Connected to Other Objects
- Creating Plot Layouts

INTRODUCTION

This chapter completes the introduction to basic 2-D drafting and editing techniques and brings you to a very significant plateau in your developing AutoCAD technique. The techniques you have learned in Part I form the basis for everything you do in more complex two- and three-dimensional drawings.

In this chapter, you begin to use AutoCAD's very powerful Object Snap and Object Tracking features. These take you to a new level of accuracy and efficiency as a CAD operator. You also learn to BREAK entities on the screen into pieces so that they can be manipulated or erased separately, to shorten objects at intersections with other objects using the **TRIM** command, or to lengthen them with the **EXTEND** command. Finally, you move into the world of paper space as you begin to use AutoCAD's layout and multiple viewport system.

6-1 SELECTING POINTS WITH OBJECT SNAP (SINGLE-POINT OVERRIDE)

GENERAL PROCEDURE	1. Enter a drawing command, such as **LINE, CIRCLE,** or **ARC.** 2. Right-click while holding down the **Shift** or **Ctrl** key. 3. Select an object snap mode from the shortcut menu. 4. Point to a previously drawn object.

Some of the drawings in the last two chapters have pushed the limits of what you can accomplish accurately on a CAD system with incremental snap alone. Single-point object snap was introduced in Chapter 4. In this section we quickly review this procedure. In Section 6.2 we move on to the use of running object snap modes.

⊞ To prepare for this exercise, begin a new drawing using the 1B template.

⊞ Draw a 6 × 6 square with a 1.50-radius circle inside, as in Figure 6-1.

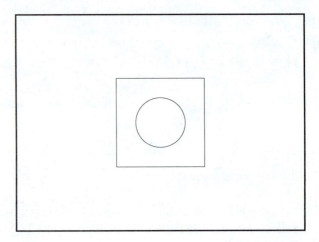

Figure 6-1

To keep the circle centered, draw the square with the **RECTANGLE** command with corners at (6,3) and (12,9). Then the circle can be centered at (9,6).

⊞ The Polar, Osnap, and Snap buttons should be off for the rest of this exercise. Dyn and DUCS may be on or off.

⊞ Enter the LINE command.

We are going to draw a line from the lower left corner of the square to a point on a line tangent to the circle, as shown in Figure 6-2. The corner is easy to locate, because you have drawn it on snap, but the tangent would not be.

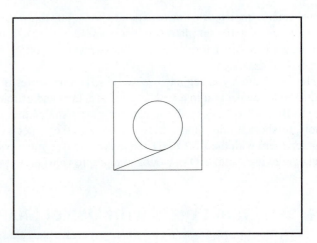

Figure 6-2

We use an endpoint object snap to locate the corner and a tangent object snap to locate the tangent point. When AutoCAD asks for a point, you can select an object snap mode from the object snap shortcut menu.

⊞ At the Specify first point: prompt, instead of specifying a point, hold down the Shift or Ctrl key and right-click.

This opens the **Object Snap** shortcut menu.

⊞ Select Endpoint.

⊞ Move the cursor near the lower left corner of the square.

The endpoint object snap marker is an orange box surrounding the endpoint.

⊞ With the endpoint object snap marker showing, press the pick button.

The orange endpoint box and the snap-tip disappear, and there is a rubber band stretching from the lower left corner of the square to the crosshair position. In the command area, you see the Specify next point: prompt.

We use a tangent object snap to select the second point.

 At the Specify next point or [Undo]: prompt, Shift + right-click and select Tangent.

 Move the cursor to the right and position the crosshairs so that they are near the lower right side of the circle.

When you approach the tangent area, you see the orange tangent marker.

 With the tangent marker showing, press the pick button.

AutoCAD locates the tangent point and draws the line.

 Press Enter to exit the LINE command.

Your screen should now resemble Figure 6-2.

That's all there is to it. Remember these steps: (1) Enter a command; (2) when AutoCAD asks for a point, Shift + right-click and specify an object snap mode; (3) position the crosshairs near an object to which the mode can be applied and let AutoCAD find the point.

6-2 Selecting Points with OSNAP (Running Mode)

GENERAL PROCEDURE
1. Select Object Snap modes from the **Drafting Settings** dialog box.
2. Click the **Osnap** button on the status bar so that it is on.
3. Enter drawing commands.
4. If there is more than one object snap choice in the area, cycle through using the **Tab** key.

So far we have been using object snap one point at a time. Because object snap is not constantly in use for most applications, this single-point method is common. Often, however, you will find that you are going to be using one or a number of object snap types repeatedly and do not need to select many points without them. In this case, you can keep object snap modes on so that they affect all point selection. This is called *running object snap*. We use this method to complete the drawing shown in Figure 6-3. Notice how each line is drawn from a midpoint or corner to a tangent point on the circle. This is easily done with running object snaps.

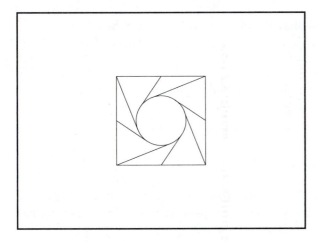

Figure 6-3

 Click the Osnap button on the status bar so that it is on.

When the Osnap button is on, you are in running object snap mode. The modes that are in effect depend on the AutoCAD default settings, or whatever settings were last selected. To change settings or see what settings are on, we open the **Drafting Settings** dialog box.

⊕ Right-click on the status bar Osnap button.

    This opens the familiar shortcut menu.

⊕ Select Settings.

⊕ This opens the Drafting Settings dialog box with the Object Snap tab on top, as shown in Figure 6-4.

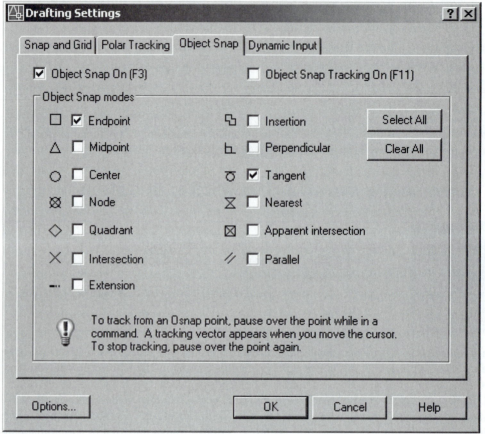

Figure 6-4

    You can find a description of all the object snap modes on the chart in Figure 6-5, but for now we use three: Midpoint, Intersection, and Tangent. Midpoint and Tangent you already know. Intersection snaps to the point where two entities meet or cross. We use an intersect instead of an endpoint to select the remaining three corners of the square, even though an endpoint could be used instead.

⊕ Select the Clear All button.

    This will clear any previous object snap selections that may have been made on your system.

⊕ Select Midpoint, Intersection, and Tangent.

    When you are finished, your dialog box should resemble Figure 6-4. Notice that Object Snap On (F3) is checked at the top of the box, and Object Snap Tracking On (F11) is not checked. We save Object Snap Tracking for Section 6.3.

⊕ Click OK.

⊕ Enter the LINE command.

⊕ Position the aperture so that the lower right corner is within the box.

    An orange X, the intersection marker, appears.

⊕ With the intersection marker showing, press the pick button.

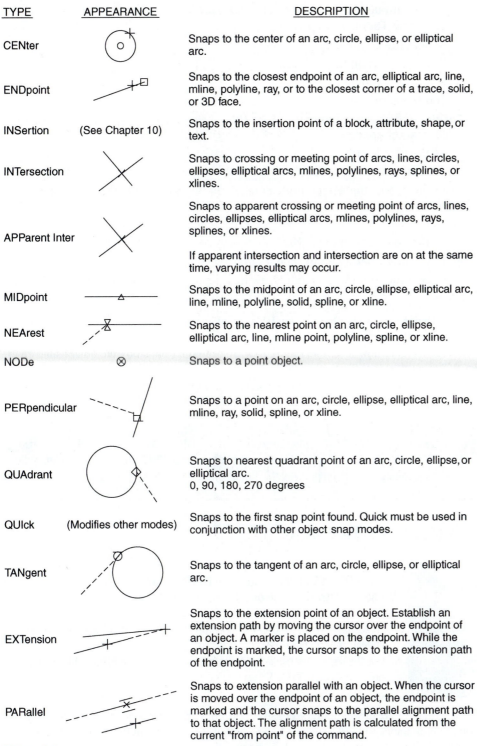

TYPE	APPEARANCE	DESCRIPTION
CENter		Snaps to the center of an arc, circle, ellipse, or elliptical arc.
ENDpoint		Snaps to the closest endpoint of an arc, elliptical arc, line, mline, polyline, ray, or to the closest corner of a trace, solid, or 3D face.
INSertion	(See Chapter 10)	Snaps to the insertion point of a block, attribute, shape, or text.
INTersection		Snaps to crossing or meeting point of arcs, lines, circles, ellipses, elliptical arcs, mlines, polylines, rays, splines, or xlines.
APParent Inter		Snaps to apparent crossing or meeting point of arcs, lines, circles, ellipses, elliptical arcs, mlines, polylines, rays, splines, or xlines. If apparent intersection and intersection are on at the same time, varying results may occur.
MIDpoint		Snaps to the midpoint of an arc, circle, ellipse, elliptical arc, line, mline, polyline, solid, spline, or xline.
NEArest		Snaps to the nearest point on an arc, circle, ellipse, elliptical arc, line, mline point, polyline, spline, or xline.
NODe		Snaps to a point object.
PERpendicular		Snaps to a point on an arc, circle, ellipse, elliptical arc, line, mline, ray, solid, spline, or xline.
QUAdrant		Snaps to nearest quadrant point of an arc, circle, ellipse, or elliptical arc. 0, 90, 180, 270 degrees
QUIck	(Modifies other modes)	Snaps to the first snap point found. Quick must be used in conjunction with other object snap modes.
TANgent		Snaps to the tangent of an arc, circle, ellipse, or elliptical arc.
EXTension		Snaps to the extension point of an object. Establish an extension path by moving the cursor over the endpoint of an object. A marker is placed on the endpoint. While the endpoint is marked, the cursor snaps to the extension path of the endpoint.
PARallel		Snaps to extension parallel with an object. When the cursor is moved over the endpoint of an object, the endpoint is marked and the cursor snaps to the parallel alignment path to that object. The alignment path is calculated from the current "from point" of the command.

Figure 6-5

AutoCAD selects the intersection of the bottom and the right sides and gives you the rubber band and the prompt for the next point.

⊕ Move the crosshairs up and along the right side of the circle until the tangent marker appears.

⊕ With the tangent marker showing, press the pick button.

AutoCAD constructs a new tangent from the lower right corner to the circle.

⊕ Press the spacebar to complete the LINE command sequence.

⊕ Press the spacebar again to repeat LINE so you can begin with a new start point.

We continue to move counterclockwise around the circle. This should begin to be easy now. There are four steps.

1. Repeat the command.

2. Select a point on the square.

3. Select the tangent point on the circle.

4. End the command.

⊕ Position the aperture along the right side of the square so that the midpoint triangle marker appears.

⊕ Press the pick button.

AutoCAD snaps to the midpoint of the side.

⊕ Move up along the upper right side of the circle so that the tangent marker appears.

⊕ Press the pick button.

⊕ Press the spacebar to exit LINE.

⊕ Press the spacebar again to repeat LINE.

Continue around the circle drawing tangents from each midpoint and intersection.

Running Osnap modes should give you both speed and accuracy, so push yourself a little to see how quickly you can complete the figure.

Your screen should now resemble Figure 6-3. Before going on, study the object snap chart, Figure 6-5. Before you can effectively analyze situations and look for opportunities to use object snap and object snap tracking, you need to have a good acquaintance with all of the object snap modes.

TIP Occasionally, you might encounter a situation in which there are several possible object snap points in a tight area. If AutoCAD does not recognize the one you want, you can cycle through all the choices by pressing the **Tab** key repeatedly.

6-3 OBJECT SNAP TRACKING

GENERAL PROCEDURE

1. Select Object Snap modes from the **Drafting Settings** dialog box.
2. Click the **Otrack** button on the status bar so that it is on.
3. Enter drawing commands.
4. To acquire a point for tracking, position the cursor so that the Osnap marker appears, but do not click.
5. Use the temporary construction lines that AutoCAD draws from this acquired point.

Object snap tracking creates temporary construction lines from designated object snap points. Once you are in a draw command, such as **LINE,** any object snap point that can be identified in an active object snap mode can be acquired. An acquired point is highlighted with a yellow cross. Once a point is acquired, object snap tracking automatically throws out temporary construction lines from this point. Construction lines are dotted lines like those used by polar tracking. They are visual and snap aids that extend to the edge of the display horizontally and vertically from the acquired point. They will also pick up specified polar tracking angles. Try the following:

⊕ To begin this task, the Osnap button should be on with the Endpoint mode in effect; all other modes from the last exercise should be turned off.

Remember the following steps:

1. Right-click the **Osnap** button.

2. Select Settings.

3. Click Clear All in the dialog box.

4. Check Endpoint.

5. Click **OK**.

⊞ Click the Dyn button to turn dynamic input off.

This is technically not necessary, but you will be able to see other things happening on your screen more easily without the dynamic input display.

⊞ Click the Otrack button on the status bar so that it is in the on position.

⊞ Enter the LINE command.

⊞ Select a first point to the left of the square and circle, as shown by Point 1 in Figure 6-6.

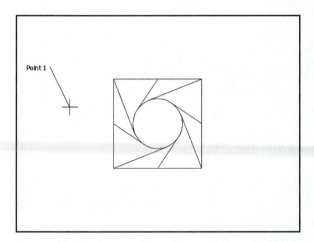

Figure 6-6

Point Acquisition

To take the next step, you need to learn a new technique called *point acquisition*. Before a point can be used for object snap tracking, it must be acquired, which is a form of selection. To acquire a point, move the cursor over it so that the object snap marker shows and pause for about a second without clicking. Try it with the following steps:

⊞ Move the cursor over the lower left corner of the square, Point 2 in Figure 6-7, so that the endpoint marker appears.

⊞ Pause.

⊞ Now move the cursor away from the corner.

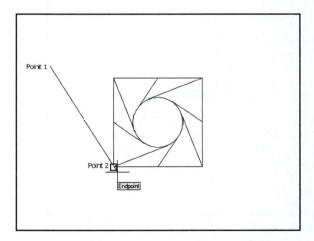

Figure 6-7

If you have done this correctly, a small orange cross appears at the corner intersection, as shown in Figure 6-8, indicating that this point has been acquired for object snap tracking. (Repeating this procedure over the same point removes the cross.)

⊕ Move the cursor to a position left of Point 2 and even with the horizontal lower side of the square, as shown in Figure 6-9.

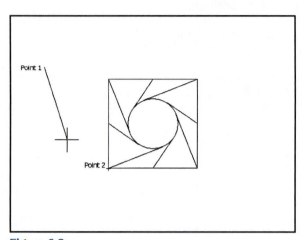

Figure 6-8

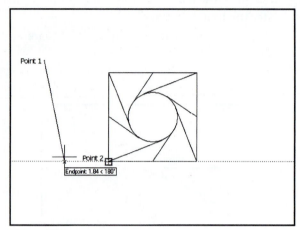

Figure 6-9

You see a construction line and a tracking tip like those shown in Figure 6-9.

⊕ Move the cursor over and down to a position even with and below the vertical left side of the square, as shown in Figure 6-10.

You see a different construction line and tracking tip, like those shown in Figure 6-10.

These construction lines are interesting, but they do not accomplish a great deal because your square is constructed on grid snap points anyway. Let's try something more difficult and a lot more interesting. Here we use two acquired points to locate a point that currently is not specifiable in either object snap or incremental snap.

⊕ Move the cursor up and acquire Point 3, as shown in Figure 6-11.

Point 3 is the endpoint of the line drawn from the midpoint of the top side of the square to a point tangent to the circle. You should now have two acquired points, with two orange crosses showing, one at Point 2 and one at Point 3.

⊕ Move the cursor slowly along the left side of the square.

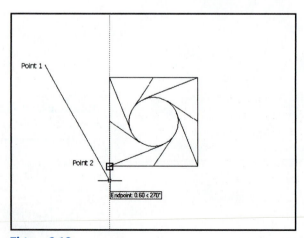

Figure 6-10

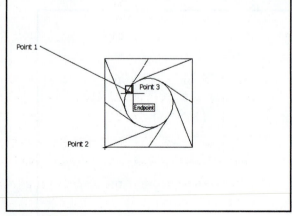

Figure 6-11

You are looking for Point 4, the point where the vertical tracking line from Point 2 intersects the horizontal tracking line from Point 3. When you near it, your screen should resemble Figure 6-12. Notice the double tracking tip Endpoint: <90, Endpoint: <180.

⊕ With the double tracking tip and the two tracking lines showing, press the pick button.

A line is drawn from Point 1 to Point 4.

⊕ Press Enter or the spacebar to exit the LINE command.

Before going on, we need to turn off the running Osnap to Endpoint mode.

⊕ Click the Osnap button or press F3 to turn off running Osnap modes.

If you have followed this exercise closely, you have already greatly increased the power of your understanding of CAD technique. You will find many opportunities to use object snap and object snap tracking from now on.

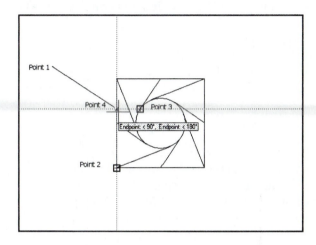

Figure 6-12

Next we move on to a very powerful editing command called **OFFSET.** Before leaving object snap, be sure that you have studied the chart in Figure 6-5, which shows examples of all the object snap modes.

6-4 USING THE OFFSET COMMAND (CREATING PARALLEL OBJECTS WITH OFFSET)

GENERAL PROCEDURE	1. Select the **Offset** tool from the dashboard. 2. Type or show an offset distance. 3. Select object to offset. 4. Show which side to offset.

OFFSET is one of the most useful editing commands in AutoCAD. With the combination of object snap and the **OFFSET** command, you can become completely free of incremental snap and grid points. Any point in the drawing space can be precisely located. Essentially, **OFFSET** creates parallel copies of lines, circles, arcs, or polylines. You can find a number of typical applications in the drawings at the end of this chapter. In this brief exercise, we perform an offset operation to draw some lines through points that would be very difficult to locate without **OFFSET.**

⊕ Select the Offset tool from the dashboard, as shown in Figure 6-13.

AutoCAD prompts

```
Specify offset distance or [Through/Erase/Layer]<Through>
```

COMMAND GRID	
Command	Offset
Alias	O
Menu	Modify
Tool	

Figure 6-13

To specify an offset distance you can type a number, show a distance with two points, or pick a point that you want the new copy to run through (the through option). As in the **ROTATE** command, the Erase option allows you to specify whether the selected object should be retained or erased when the offset object is drawn. The Layer option gives you the capacity to create the new object on the selected object's layer instead of the current layer.

✛ Type ".257"↵.

We have chosen this rather odd number to make the point that this command can help you locate positions that would be difficult to find otherwise. AutoCAD prompts for an object:

```
Select object to offset or <exit>:
```

✛ Select the diagonal line drawn in the last exercise.

AutoCAD now needs to know whether to create the offset image above or below the line:

```
Specify point on side to offset:
```

✛ Pick a point anywhere below the line.

Your screen should now resemble Figure 6-14. AutoCAD continues to prompt for objects to offset using the same offset distance. You can continue to create offset objects at the same offset distance by pointing and clicking.

✛ Pick the line just created.

✛ Pick any point below the line.

A second offset line is added, as shown in Figure 6-15. As long as you stay within the **OFFSET** command, you can select any object to offset using the same offset distance.

✛ Pick the circle in the square.

✛ Pick any point inside the circle.

An offset circle is added, as shown in Figure 6-15.

✛ Continue pointing and clicking to create additional offset circles, as shown in Figure 6-15.

✛ Press Enter to exit the OFFSET command.

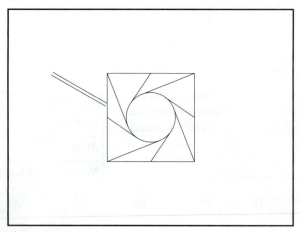

Figure 6-14

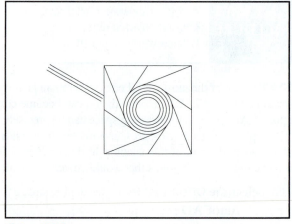

Figure 6-15

When you exit **OFFSET,** the offset distance is retained as the default, so you can return to the command and continue using the same distance.

Next we turn to five commands that allow you to shorten and lengthen objects.

6-5 BREAKing Previously Drawn Objects

<table>
<tr>
<td rowspan="2">GENERAL
PROCEDURE</td>
<td>1. Select the Break at Point tool from the Modify flyout on the dashboard.
2. Select an object to be broken.
3. Show the first point of the break.
4. Show the second point of the break.</td>
</tr>
</table>

The **BREAK** command allows you to break an object on the screen into two entities, or to cut a segment out of the middle or off the end. The command sequence is similar for all options. The action taken depends on the points you select for breaking. **BREAK** works on lines, circles, arcs, and polylines. (Polylines are discussed in Chapter 9.)

⊕ In preparation for this section, clear your screen of objects left from previous tasks and draw a 10.00 horizontal line across the middle of your screen, as in Figure 6-16.

Exact lengths and coordinates are not important. Also, be sure to turn off object snap.

Figure 6-16

AutoCAD allows for four different ways to break an object, depending on whether the point you use to select the object is also to be considered a break point. You can break an object at one point or at two points, and you have the choice of using your object selection point as a break point.

We begin by breaking the line you have just drawn into two independent lines using a single break point, which is also the point used to select the line.

⊕ Select the Break at Point tool from the dashboard, as shown in Figure 6-17.

Notice that there is a **Break** tool that is not the same as the **Break at Point** tool. All the commands we will explore in these exercises are located on the flyout, which opens downward from the end of the second line on the 2D Drafting control panel. Also, be aware that the noun/verb or pick first sequence does not work with **BREAK.**

AutoCAD prompts you to select an object to break:

SELECT OBJECT:

You can select an object in any of the usual ways, but notice that you can break only one object at a time. If you try to select more—with a window, for example—AutoCAD highlights only one.

⊕ Select the line by picking any point near its middle.

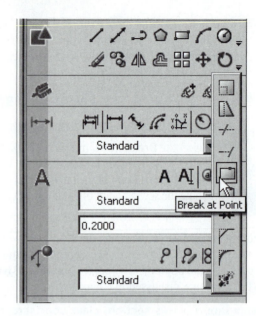

Figure 6-17

TIP   Object snap modes work well in edit commands such as **BREAK.** If you wish to break a line at its midpoint, for example, you can use the Midpoint object snap mode to select the line and the break point.

The line has now been selected for breaking, and because there can be only one object, you do not have to press **Enter** to end the selection process, as you usually do in other editing commands. AutoCAD prompts as follows:

        Specify second break point or [First point]:_f

When you are using the Break at Point tool, AutoCAD does not take the point you use for selection as the first point of the break. In the command area, notice that the "_f" for the first point option is entered automatically. This means that now you have the opportunity to select the same point or a different point as the point at which to break this line.

⊕ Point to the same point that you just used to select the line, or type @.

The @ symbol is shorthand for the last point entered. In this sequence, AutoCAD automatically enters @ for the second break point. This specifies that there is only one break point. The line will be broken, but nothing will be erased.

The break is complete. To demonstrate that the line is really two lines now, we select the right half of it for our next break.

⊕ Press Enter or the spacebar to repeat the BREAK command, or select the Break tool from the dashboard.

The **Break** tool is just below the **Break at Point** tool.

⊕ Point to the line on the right side of the last break.

The right side of the line should be highlighted, as in Figure 6-18. Clearly, the original line is now being treated as two separate entities.

We shorten the end of this dotted section of the line. Assume that the point you just used to select the object is the point where you want it to end; now all you need to do is to select a second point anywhere beyond the right end of the line.

⊕ Select a second point beyond the right end of the line.

Your line should now be shortened, as in Figure 6-19.

Next we cut a piece out of the middle of the left side.

⊕ Press Enter or the spacebar to repeat BREAK.

⊕ Select the left side of the original line with a point toward the left end.

COMMAND GRID	
Command	Break
Alias	Br
Menu	Modify
Tool	

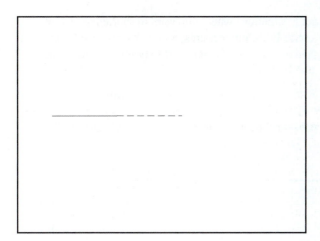

Figure 6-18

We want to cut a piece out of the middle of the left side, so the next point needs to be to the right of the first point, but still toward the middle of the left-hand line.

⊕ Select a second point on or off the line, somewhat to the right of the first point.

Your line should now have a piece cut out, as in Figure 6-20. Notice that there are now three lines on the screen, though it looks like only two. There is one to the left and two shorter connected lines to the right of the last break.

BREAK is a useful command, but there are times when it is cumbersome to shorten objects one at a time. The **TRIM** command has some limitations that **BREAK** does not have, but it is much more efficient in situations in which you want to shorten objects at intersections with other objects.

Note:
It is not necessary that the second point be on the line at all. It could be above or below it, as in Figure 6-20. AutoCAD breaks the line along a perpendicular between the point we choose and the line we are breaking. An arc or a circle would be broken along a line between the selected point and the center of the arc or circle.

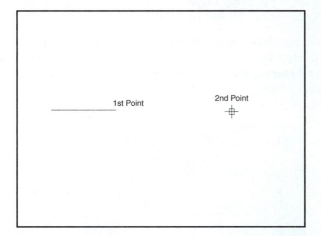

Figure 6-19

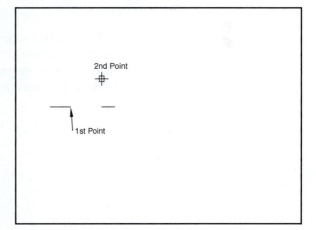

Figure 6-20

6-6 SHORTENING OBJECTS WITH THE TRIM COMMAND

GENERAL PROCEDURE	1. Select the **Trim** tool from the dashboard. 2. Select a cutting edge or edges. 3. Right-click to end the cutting-edge selection process. 4. Select an object to trim. 5. Select other objects to trim. 6. Press **Enter** to return to the command prompt.

COMMAND GRID	
Command	Trim
Alias	Tr
Menu	Modify
Tool	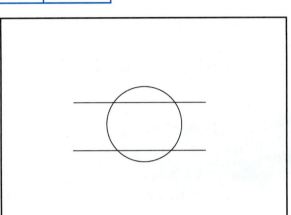

The **TRIM** command works wonders in many situations where you want to shorten objects at their intersections with other objects. It works with lines, circles, arcs, and polylines (see Chapter 9). The only limitations are that you must have at least two objects and they must cross or meet. If you are not trimming to an intersection, use **BREAK.**

⊞ In preparation for exploring TRIM, clear your screen and then draw two horizontal lines crossing a circle, as in Figure 6-21. Exact locations and sizes are not important.

First, we use the **TRIM** command to go from Figure 6-21 to Figure 6-22.

Figure 6-21

Figure 6-22

⊞ Select the Trim tool from the dashboard, as shown in Figure 6-23.

You begin by specifying at least one cutting edge. A cutting edge is an entity you want to use to trim another entity. That is, you want the trimmed entity to end at its intersection with the cutting edge.

```
Select cutting edges...
Select objects or <select all>:
```

The first line reminds you that you are selecting edges first—the objects you want to trim are selected later. The third line prompts you to select objects to use as cutting edges, or press **Enter** for the Select All option. The option of selecting all objects is demonstrated shortly.

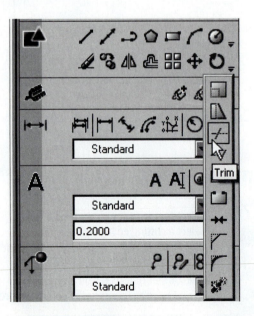

Figure 6-23

For now, select the circle as an edge and use it to trim the upper line.

⊕ Pick the circle.

The circle becomes dotted and remains so until you leave the **TRIM** command. AutoCAD prompts for more objects until you indicate that you are finished selecting edges.

⊕ Right-click to end the selection of cutting edges.

You are prompted for an object to trim:

```
Select object to trim or shift-select to extend or
        [Fence/Crossing/Project/Edge/eRase/Undo]:
```

This prompt allows you to shift over to the **EXTEND** command by holding down the **Shift** key. Otherwise, you select objects to trim using the given options. We follow a simple procedure to trim off the segment of the upper line that lies outside the circle on the left. The important thing is to point to the part of the object you want to remove, as shown in Figure 6-22.

⊕ Point to the upper line to the left of where it crosses the circle.

The line is trimmed immediately, but the circle is still dotted, and AutoCAD continues to prompt for more objects to trim.

Note that you have an undo option, so that if the trim does not turn out the way you wanted, you can back up without having to leave the command and start over. Also notice the eRase option, which allows you to erase objects without leaving the **TRIM** command.

⊕ Point to the lower line to the left of where it crosses the circle.

Now you have trimmed both lines.

⊕ Press Enter or the spacebar to end the TRIM operation.

Your screen should resemble Figure 6-22.

More complex trimming is also easy. The key is that you can select all visible objects or as many edges as you like. An entity can be selected as both an edge and an object to trim, as we demonstrate.

⊕ Repeat the TRIM command.

⊕ Press Enter to select all objects.

In this case, AutoCAD will not highlight all objects, but will proceed as if all objects had been selected. There is no need to complete object selection because everything is already selected.

⊕ Point to each of the remaining two-line segments that lie outside the circle on the right and to the top and bottom arcs of the circle to produce the bandage-shaped object in Figure 6-24.

⊕ Press Enter to exit the TRIM command.

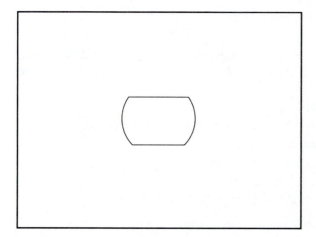

Figure 6-24

6-7 EXTENDING OBJECTS WITH THE EXTEND COMMAND

GENERAL PROCEDURE	1. Select the **Extend** tool from the dashboard. 2. Select a boundary or boundaries. 3. Press **Enter** to end the boundary selection process. 4. Select the object to extend. 5. Select other objects to extend. 6. Press **Enter** to return to the command prompt.

If you compare the procedures of the **EXTEND** command and the **TRIM** command, you notice a remarkable similarity. Just substitute the word *boundary* for *cutting edge* and the word *extend* for *trim,* and you've got it. These two commands are conceptually related and are so efficient that it is sometimes good practice to draw a temporary cutting edge or boundary on your screen and erase it after trimming or extending.

⊞ Leave Figure 6-24, the bandage, on your screen and draw a vertical line to the right of it, as in Figure 6-25.

We use this line as a boundary to which to extend the two horizontal lines, as in Figure 6-26.

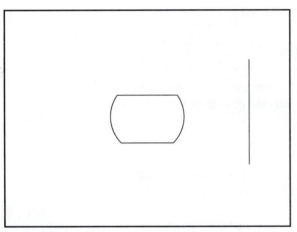

Figure 6-25

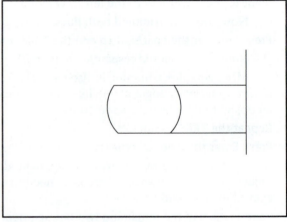

Figure 6-26

COMMAND GRID	
Command	Extend
Alias	Ex
Menu	Modify
Tool	---/

⊞ Select the Extend tool from the dashboard, as shown in Figure 6-27.

You are prompted for objects to serve as boundaries:

```
Select boundary edges . . .
Select objects or <Select All>:
```

As with the **TRIM** command, any of the usual selection methods work and there is an option for selecting all objects. For our purposes, simply point to the vertical line.

⊞ Point to the vertical line on the right.

You are prompted for more boundary objects until you exit object selection.

⊞ Right-click to end the selection of boundaries.

AutoCAD now asks for objects to extend:

```
Select object to extend or shift-select to trim
    or [Fence/Crossing/Project/Edge/eRase/Undo]:
```

⊞ Pick the right half of one of the two horizontal lines.

⊹ Pick a second point t[...]
  Having Ortho on[...]

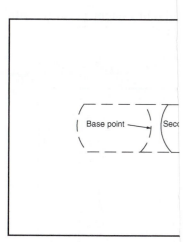

Base point ⟶ Sec[...]

The arcs are mov[...]
shown. Notice that no[...]
moved and the lines a[...]
can be used.

⊹ Try performing anothe[...]
  Here the lines are [...]
  put, so that the origina[...]

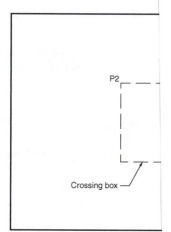

P2

Crossing box

Figure 6-31

Stretching with Grips

Stretching with grips is a simple c[...]
ones you have just performed wit[...]
they require careful selection of m[...]
it takes more time to complete the [...]
trated in the following exercise:

⊹ Pick the lower horizont[...]
  The line is highlight[...]

⊹ Pick the vertical line.

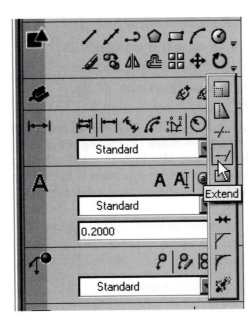

Figure 6-27

You have to point to the line on the side closer to the selected boundary. Otherwise, AutoCAD looks to the left instead of the right and gives you the following message:

        Object does not intersect an Edge

Also, you can select objects to extend only by pointing. Windowing, crossing, or last selections do not work. Arcs and polylines can be extended in the same manner as lines.

⊹ **Pick the right half of the other horizontal line. Both lines should be extended to the vertical line.**

  Your screen should resemble Figure 6-26.

⊹ **Press the spacebar to exit the EXTEND command.**

6-8 USING STRETCH TO ALTER OBJECTS CONNECTED TO OTHER OBJECTS

GENERAL PROCEDURE	1. Select the **Stretch** tool from the dashboard. 2. Select objects to stretch, using at least one crossing selection. 3. Press **Enter** to end selection. 4. Show the first point of stretch displacement. 5. Show the second point of stretch displacement.

The **STRETCH** command is a phenomenal time-saver in special circumstances in which you want to move objects without disrupting their connections to other objects. Often **STRETCH** can take the place of a whole series of moves, trims, breaks, and extends. It is commonly used in such applications as moving doors or windows within walls without having to redraw the walls.

The term *stretch* must be understood to have a special meaning in AutoCAD. When a typical stretch is performed, some objects are lengthened, others are shortened, and others are simply moved.

There is also a Stretch mode in the grip edit system, as we have seen previously. We take a look at it later in this section.

COMMAND GRID	
Command	Stretch
Alias	S
Menu	Modify
Tool	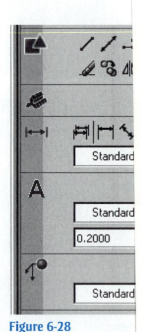

Now both lines should appear with grips, as in Figure 6-33. We use one grip on the horizontal line and one on the vertical line to create Figure 6-34.

⊞ Pick the grip at the right end of the horizontal line.

As soon as you press the pick button, the autoedit system puts you into STRETCH mode and the selected grip changes color.

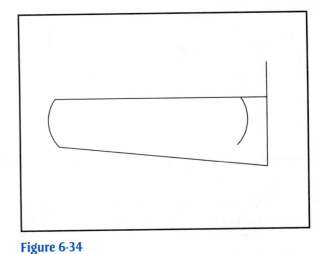

Figure 6-33   **Figure 6-34**

In the command area, you see the following:

STRETCH
Specify stretch point or [Base point/Copy/Undo/eXit]:

We stretch the line to end at the lower endpoint of the vertical line.

⊞ Move the crosshairs slowly downward and observe the screen.

If Ortho is off, you see two rubber bands. One represents the line you are stretching, and the other connects the crosshairs to the grip you are manipulating.

⊞ Pick the grip at the bottom of the vertical line.

Your screen should resemble Figure 6-34. Notice how the grip on the vertical line works like an object snap point.

⊞ Try one more grip stretch to create Figure 6-35. Stretch the endpoint of the upper line just as you did the lower.

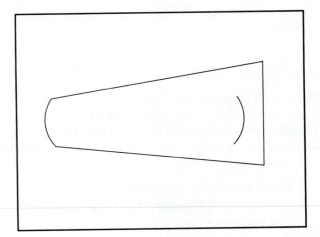

Figure 6-35

Figure 6-28

6-9 CREATING PLOT LAYOUTS

GENERAL PROCEDURE	1. Open a layout. 2. Define plot settings. 3. Create paper space viewports with associated Zoom XP factors. 4. Switch to model space to position or edit objects in the drawing. 5. Switch to paper space to plot. 6. Type or select Plot. 7. Preview plot, change parameters, and execute plotting as usual.

Up until now, we have plotted everything directly from model space. Plotting from model space has its uses, particularly in the early stages of a design process. However, when your focus shifts from modeling issues to presentation issues, paper space layouts have much more to offer. The separation of model space and paper space in AutoCAD allows you to focus entirely on modeling and real-world dimensions when you are drawing, and then shift your focus to paper output issues when you plot. On the drafting board, all drawings are committed to paper from the start. People doing manual drafting are inevitably conscious of scale, paper size, and rotation from start to finish. When draftspeople first begin using CAD systems, they still tend to think in terms of the final hard copy their plotter will produce even as they are creating lines on the screen. The AutoCAD plotting system takes full advantage of the powers of a CAD system, allowing us to ignore scale and other drawing paper issues entirely, if we wish, until it is time to plot.

In addition, the paper space world allows us to create multiple views of the same objects without copying or redrawing them, and to plot these viewports simultaneously. In this task, we create two layouts of Drawing 5-1, the flanged bushing from the last chapter. The first contains only one viewport. The second is used to demonstrate some basic principles of working with multiple viewports.

Opening Layout

⊕ To begin this exercise, open Drawing 5-1, illustrated in Figure 6-36.

If you do not have Drawing 5-1 available, you can approximate it by doing the following:

1. Erase all objects from your screen.
2. Set Limits to (0,0) and (12,9). This is critical. If you use different limits, the exercise is difficult to follow.
3. Draw a circle with diameter 3.50 centered at (3.00,4.00).
4. Draw a second circle with diameter 2.50 centered at the same point.
5. Draw a rectangle with first corner at (6.50,2.75) and second corner at (10.00,5.25).

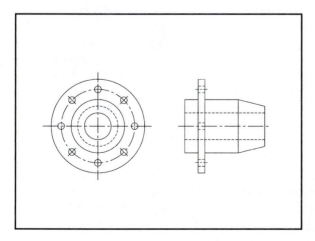

Figure 6-36

With Drawing 5-1 on your screen, or an approximation, you are ready to begin.

⊕ Before leaving model space, turn off the grid.

Layouts have their own grid, so if you leave the model space grid on you see overlapping grids that are confusing.

⊕ Pick the Layout1 button on the status line, as shown in Figure 6-37.

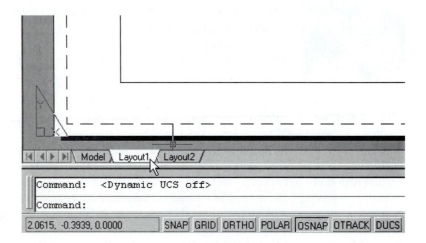

Figure 6-37

You see an image similar to the one in Figure 6-38. This is a simple one-viewport layout. AutoCAD has automatically created a single viewport determined by the extents of your drawing. Paper space viewports are sometimes called floating viewports because they can be moved and reshaped. They are like windows from paper space into model space.

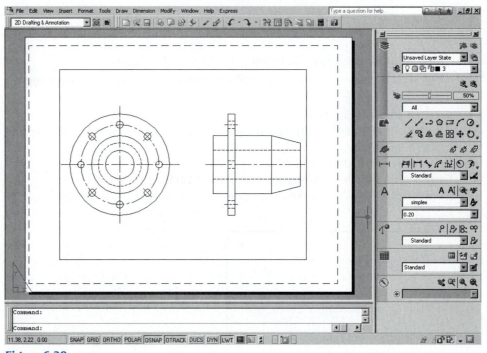

Figure 6-38

Viewports are also AutoCAD objects and are treated and stored as such. You can move them, stretch them, copy them, and erase them. Editing the viewport does not affect the model space objects within the viewport. When a viewport is selected, the border is highlighted and grips are shown at each corner.

Switching Between Paper Space and Model Space

⊞ Try selecting the viewport border, just as you would select any AutoCAD object.

If you are unable to select the viewport border, you are in still in model space. Whether you have entered Layout 1 in model space or paper space depends on recent AutoCAD activity. If you are still in model space, double-clicking anywhere outside the viewport border will you put you into paper space.

⊞ If necessary, double-click outside the viewport border to enter paper space.

⊞ Try selecting the viewport border again.

When you are in paper space you will be able to select the viewport border, but not the objects inside.

⊞ Try to select any of the objects within the viewport.

You cannot. As long as you are in paper space, model space objects are not accessible. To gain access to model space objects while in a layout view, you must double-click inside a viewport.

⊞ Double-click anywhere within the viewport.

The border of the viewport takes on a bold outline. You are now in model space. You also notice that the **MSPACE** command has been entered at the command prompt. Notice the difference between working within a viewport in a layout and switching into model space by clicking the **Model** button. If you click the **Model** button, the layout disappears and you are back in the familiar model space drawing area.

⊞ Try selecting objects in your viewport again.

Model space objects are now available for editing or positioning within the viewport. While in the model space of a viewport, you cannot select any objects drawn in paper space, including the viewport border.

⊞ Double-click anywhere outside the viewport border.

This returns you to paper space.

⊞ Pick the border of the viewport.

⊞ Type "e" ↵ or select the Erase tool from the dashboard.

This eliminates the viewport and leaves you with the image of a blank sheet of paper. Without a viewport, you have no view of model space.

Next we create a more complex layout by adding our own viewports.

Modifying a Layout

Layouts can be modified in numerous ways and can be accessed from the **Layout** buttons on the status bar. You are looking at Layout 1, which is based on the 12 × 9 drawing limits of Drawing 5-1. We modify the page setup to represent an ANSII D-size drawing sheet and then add three new viewports to the layout.

⊞ Select Page Setup Manager from the File menu.

This opens the **Page Setup Manager** illustrated in Figure 6-39. **Page Setup Manager** is familiar from Chapter 5. Layout 1 should be highlighted in the current page setup list.

⊞ Pick the Modify button on the right.

Note:
Depending on Workspace settings it is possible that you have **Model** and **Layout** buttons with icons on the status bar, instead of the tabs below the drawing area. The tabs and the buttons serve the same function and are not displayed at the same time. If you have buttons and want to display the tabs, right-click on either the **Model** button or the **Layout** button. This calls up a single-line message, which says, "Display Layout and Model Tabs." Picking this button will add the tabs to the bottom of your drawing area as shown in the figure. To hide them again, right-click any of the tabs and select "Hide Layout and Model Tabs" from the shortcut menu.

This opens the **Page Setup – Layout 1** dialog box shown in Figure 6-40. This a version of the **PLOT** dialog box.

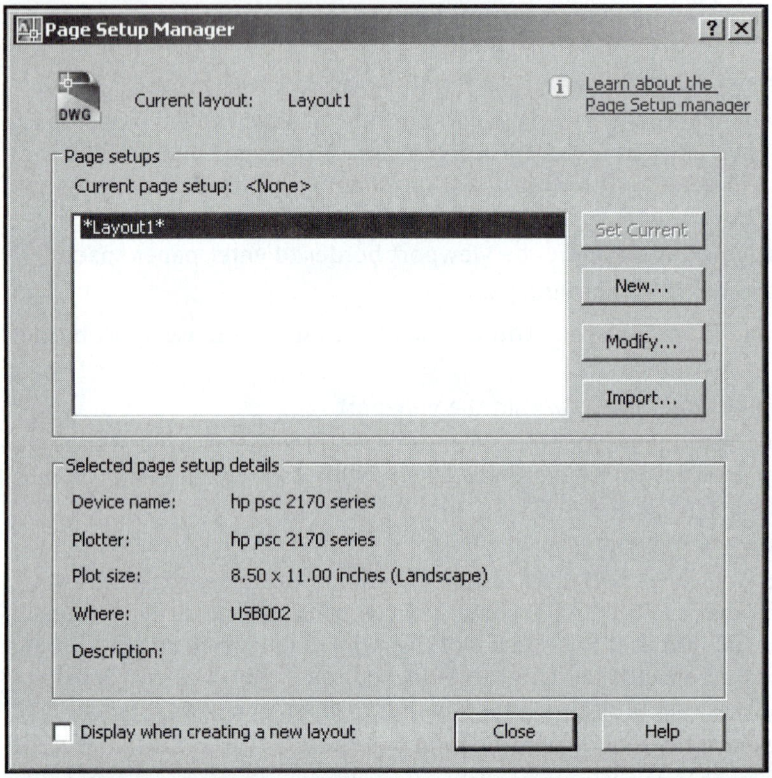

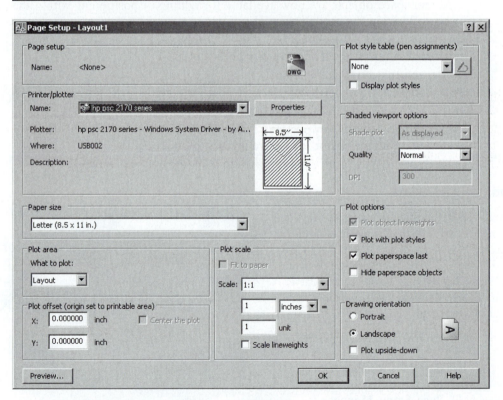

Figure 6-39

Figure 6-40

In this exercise, we use a D-size drawing sheet for our layout. If you do not have a D-size plotter, we recommend that you use AutoCAD's DWG6 ePlot driver, which is designed to create electronic plots that can be sent out over the Internet or a local network. If you prefer to use a different-size paper, you have to make adjustments as you go along. Using A-size, for example, most specifications can be divided by four. We will include A-size specifications at critical points in case you don't have access to a D-size plotter or want to use a printer.

⊞ In the Printer/plotter panel, select a plotting device that has a D-size sheet option.

⊞ In the Paper size panel, select an ANSI D (34 × 22) paper size.

Notice that Layout is now the default selection in the What to plot list. We have not encountered this selection before because it is not present when you enter the **PLOT** dialog box from model space.

⊕ If necessary, check Landscape in the Drawing orientation panel.

⊕ Click **OK.**

You return to the **Page Setup Manager.** Notice the changes in the panel labeled Selected page setup details.

⊕ Pick the Close button.

AutoCAD will adjust the layout image to represent a D-size drawing sheet in landscape.

We make a few adjustments to show the drawing sheet with a paper space grid.

⊕ Right-click the Grid button and select Settings from the shortcut menu.

⊕ In the Drafting Settings dialog box, check the Snap on box.

⊕ Check the Grid on box.

⊕ Deselect the Adaptive grid button.

⊕ Deselect the Display grid beyond limits button.

⊕ Click OK.

A grid is added to your drawing sheet giving you a better sense of the structure of your layout.

⊕ Move the cursor over the lower left corner of the paper grid and locate (0,0).

This is the origin of the plot, indicated by the corner of the dashed border that shows the effective drawing area.

⊕ Move the cursor to the upper right corner of the effective drawing area.

This is less than the limits of the grid. The exact point depends on your plotter. With the AutoCAD DWF6 ePlot driver and D-size paper, it is (33.50,21).

Your screen is now truly representative of a drawing sheet. The plot is made 1-to-1, with 1 paper space screen unit equaling 1 inch on the drawing sheet. There is little reason to do it any other way, because the whole point of paper space is to emulate the drawing sheet on the screen.

Now we add viewports.

Creating Viewports

⊕ Type mv or select View → Viewports → 1 Viewport from the pull-down menu.

These methods enter the MVIEW or VPORTS command. Either way, AutoCAD prompts:

```
Specify corner of viewport or
[ON/OFF/Fit/Shadeplot/Lock/Object/Polygonal/Restore/2/3/4]<Fit>:
```

We deal only with the Specify corner option in this exercise. With this option, you create a viewport just as you would a selection window.

⊕ Pick point (1.00,1.00) at the lower left of your screen, as shown in Figure 6-41.

If you are not using D-size paper, you can do fine by making your viewports resemble ours in size, shape, and location.

⊕ Pick an opposite corner, as shown in Figure 6-41. This is (20,13) on a D-size sheet.

Your screen is redrawn with the drawing extents at maximum scale centered within the viewport.

Now we create a second viewport to the right of the first.

⊕ Repeat MVIEW or VPORTS.

⊕ Pick point (24.00,1.00), as shown in Figure 6-41.

⊕ Pick point (32.00,13.00), as shown.

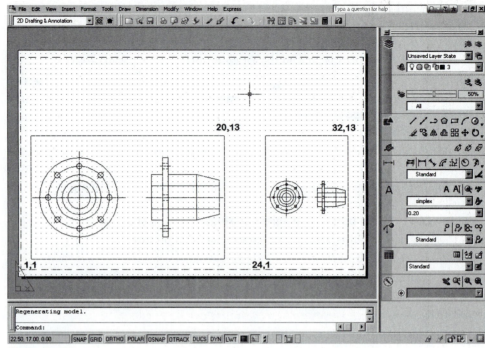

Figure 6-41

Zooming XP

You have now created a second viewport. Notice that the images in the two viewports are drawn at different scales. Each is drawn to fit within its viewport. This can create problems later when you add dimension and text. You want to maintain control over the scale of objects within viewports and have a clear knowledge of the relationships among scales in different viewports. For this, we use the ZOOM scale feature of the **ZOOM** command. We create different zoom magnifications inside the two viewports.

⊕ Double-click inside the left viewport.

This takes you into model space within the left viewport. We are going to zoom so that the two-view drawing is in a precise and known scale relation to paper space.

⊕ Enter the **ZOOM** command.

Notice the **ZOOM** command prompt:

```
Specify corner of window, enter a scale factor
(nX or nXP), or [All/Center/Dynamic/Extents/Previous/Scale/
Window] <real time>:
```

In this task, we use two new options, the paper space scale factor option (nXP) and the Center option.

⊕ Type "2xp"↵ (on A-size paper divide these factors by four, so you will use .5xp).

This creates only a slight change in the left viewport. XP means times paper. It allows you to zoom relative to paper space units. If you zoom 1xp, then a model space unit takes on the size of a current paper space unit, which in turn equals 1 inch of drawing paper. We zoomed 2xp. This means that one unit in the viewport equals two paper space units, or 2 inches on paper. We now have a precise relationship between model space and paper space in this viewport. The change in presentation size is trivial, but the change in terms of understanding and control is great.

Now we set an XP zoom factor in the right viewport so that we control not only the model space/paper space scale relations, but the scale relations among viewports as well.

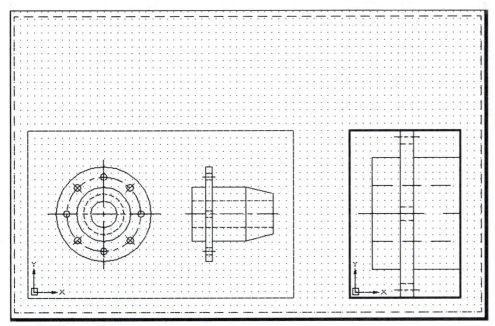

Figure 6-42

⊕ Click inside the right viewport to make it active.

   You are already in model space, so double-clicking is unnecessary.

⊕ Reenter the ZOOM command.

   In the right viewport, we are going to show a close-up image of the right side view. To accomplish this, we need a larger zoom factor and we need to be centered on the right side view.

⊕ Type "c" ↵, or right-click and select Center from the shortcut menu.

   AutoCAD asks you to specify a center point.

⊕ Pick a point on the center line near the center of the flange.

   Look at Figure 6-42. The point you select becomes the center point of the right viewport when AutoCAD zooms in.

   AutoCAD prompts:

        Enter magnification or height<3.00>:

   Accepting the default would simply center the image in the viewport. We specify an XP value here.

⊕ Type "4xp"↵.

   Your right viewport is dynamically magnified to resemble the one in Figure 6-42. In this enlarged image, one model space unit equals 4 inches in the drawing sheet (1 = 1 on A size).

Now that you have the technique, we create one more viewport, focusing this time on one of the circle of holes in the flange.

⊕ Double-click anywhere outside the two viewports to return to paper space.

⊕ Enter the MVIEW or VPORT command.

⊕ Pick point (1.00,14.00).

⊕ Pick point (9.00,20.00).

⊕ Enter model space in the new viewport and zoom in, centering on the hole at the bottom of the flange in the front view, at six times paper in the new viewport.

   This might require the use of a Center or Quadrant object snap. Remember that you can access a single-point object snap by holding down **Shift,** right-clicking, and then selecting from the **Osnap** shortcut menu.

   Your screen should resemble Figure 6-43.

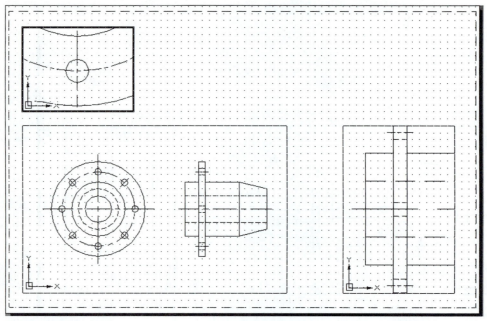

Figure 6-43

⊞ Before proceeding to plot, try a print preview to ensure that you are ready.

⊞ Select the Plot Preview tool from the Standard toolbar.

This full preview should look very much like the layout image. This is the beauty of the AutoCAD plotting system. You have a great deal of control and the ability to assess exactly what your paper output will be before you actually plot the drawing.

⊞ Press esc to exit the preview.

Maximize Viewport Button

Before going on, we introduce the maximize viewport button at the right end of the layout buttons on the status bar. This button not only will allow you to switch into model space in any viewport but also will maximize that viewport to fit the display. Once you have maximized a viewport, you can cycle through other viewports and maximize them one at a time. Try this:

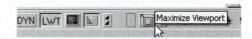

Figure 6-44

⊞ Click the Maximize Viewport button on the status bar, illustrated in Figure 6-44.

If you entered the model space of a viewport before clicking the button, AutoCAD would maximize that viewport. Otherwise, it will maximize the first viewport you defined. The maximized image will show you whatever is in the viewport, along with whatever portion of the drawing will fit the display at the magnification defined for that viewport. (If you pause with the selection arrow on the button, you will notice that it is now labeled as the **Minimize** button.)

⊞ Click the small arrow to the right or left of the button.

The arrows cycle you through other viewports in the order they were defined.

⊞ Click the arrows to continue cycling through your three viewports.

⊞ When you are done, click the Minimize button.

This will return you to the paper space layout image.

Plotting the Multiple-View Drawing

Now we are ready to plot. Plotting a multiple-viewport drawing is no different from plotting from a single view. Just make sure you are in the layout before entering the **PLOT** command.

Note: If you have done this exercise using the DWG6 ePlot driver, you will note that AutoCAD sends your plot to a file rather than to a plotter. Any drawing can be saved to a file to be plotted later. When you use the ePlot utility your plot will first be saved to a file that can be sent over the Internet.

⊕ With Layout 1 on your screen, enter the PLOT command.

At this point you should have no need to adjust settings within the **Plot** dialog box because you have already made adjustments to the page setup and the plotting device. Notice the settings that are now included in the layout.

⊕ Prepare your plotter. (Make sure you use the right size paper.)

⊕ Click OK.

Important: Be sure to save this drawing with its multiple-viewport 3view layout before leaving this chapter, because we return to it in Chapter 8 to explore scaling dimensions between model space and paper space.

CHAPTER TEST QUESTIONS

Questions

1. Why is it important to keep object snap turned off when you are not using it? What are two simple ways to turn running Osnap on and off?
2. At what point in a command procedure would you use an object snap single-point override? How would you signal the AutoCAD program that you want to use an object snap?
3. How do you access the **Object snap** shortcut menu?
4. What is an acquired point? How do you acquire a point? How do you eliminate an acquired point?
5. How do you use BREAK to shorten a line at one end? When would you use this procedure instead of the **TRIM** command?
6. You have selected a line to extend and a boundary to extend it to, but AutoCAD gives you the message "Object does not intersect an edge." What happened?
7. What selection method is always required when you use the **STRETCH** command?
8. Why is it usual practice to plot 1-to-1 in paper space?
9. Why do we use the Zoom XP option when zooming in floating model space viewports?
10. How is CAD different from manual drafting with regard to issues of scaling and paper size?

Drawing Problems

1. Draw a line from (6,2) to (11,6). Draw a second line perpendicular to the first starting at (6,6).
2. Break the first line at its intersection with the second.
3. There are now three lines on the screen. Draw a circle centered at their intersection and passing through the midpoint of the line going up and to the right of the intersection.
4. Trim all the lines to the circumference of the circle.
5. Erase what is left of the line to the right of the intersection, and trim the portion of the circle to the left, between the two remaining lines.

WWW Exercise 6 (Optional)

You conclude Part I of your exploration of online CAD with two more websites that serve as launching pads with links to many other AutoCAD and CAD-related websites. In addition, we offer a challenge to create a design using object snap and a limited number of commands.

⊕ Connect to your Internet service provider.

⊕ Type "browser"↵ or open the Web toolbar and select the Browser tool.

⊕ If necessary, navigate to our companion website at prenhall. com/dixriley.

Enjoy your visit.

CHAPTER PROJECTS

Drawing 6-1: Bike Tire

This drawing can be done very quickly with the tools you now have. It makes use of one object snap, three trims, and a polar array. Be sure to set the limits large, as suggested.

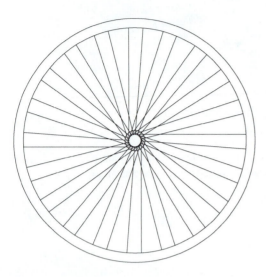

Drawing Suggestions

```
GRID = 1.00
SNAP = 0.125
LIMITS = (0,0)(48,36)
```

- Begin by drawing the 1.25, 2.50, 24.00, and 26.00 diameter circles centered on the same point near the middle of your display.

- Draw line (a) using a quadrant object snap to find the first point on the inside circle. The second point can be anywhere outside the 24 circle at 0 degrees from the first point. The exact length of the line is insignificant because you will trim it back to the circle.

- Draw line (b) from the center of the circles to a second point anywhere outside the 24 circle at an angle of 14 degrees. Use the co-ordinate display or polar tracking to construct this angle. This line also will be trimmed.

- Trim lines (a) and (b) using the 24 circle as a cutting edge.

- Trim the other end of line (b) using the 1.25 circle as a cutting edge.

- Construct a polar array, selecting lines (a) and (b). There are 20 items in the array, and they are rotated as they are copied.

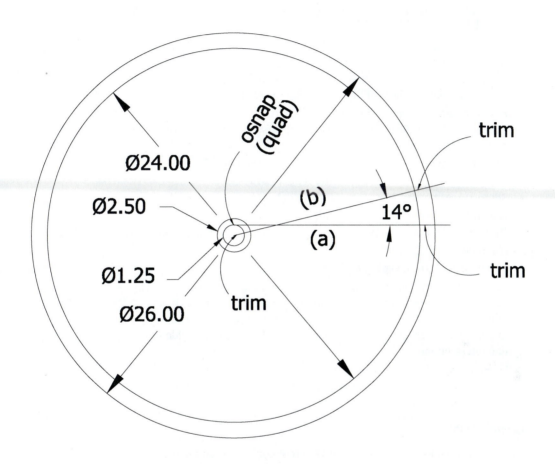

BIKE TIRE

Drawing 6-1

Drawing 6-2: Archimedes Spiral

This drawing and the next go together as an exercise you should find interesting and enjoyable. These are not technical drawings, but they give you valuable experience with important CAD commands. You create an Archimedes spiral using a radial grid of circles and lines as a guide. AutoCAD also has a **HELIX** command that creates spirals in two and three dimensions, but this spiral is different. Once the spiral is done, you use it to create the designs in Drawing 6-3.

Drawing Suggestions

```
GRID = 0.5                SNAP = 0.25
LIMITS = (0,0)(18,12)     LTSCALE = 0.5
```

- The alternating continuous and hidden lines work as a drawing aid. If you use different colors and layers, they are more helpful. Because all circles are offset 0.50, you can draw one continuous and one hidden circle, then use the OFFSET command to create all the others.

- Begin by drawing one of the continuous circles on Layer 0, centered near the middle of your display, then offset all the other continuous circles.

- Draw the continuous horizontal line across the middle of your six circles and then array it in a three-item polar array.

- Set to Layer 2, draw one of the hidden circles, then the other hidden circles.

- Draw a vertical hidden line and array it as you did the horizontal continuous line.

- Set to Layer 1 for the spiral itself.

- Turn on a running object snap to Intersection mode and construct a series of three-point arcs. Be sure to turn off any other modes that might get in your way. Start points and endpoints will be on continuous line intersections; second points always will fall on hidden line intersections.

- When the spiral is complete, turn off Layers 0 and 2. There should be nothing left on your screen, but the spiral itself. Save it or go on to Drawing 6-3.

Grouping Objects

Here is a good opportunity to use the **GROUP** command. GROUP is discussed more fully in Chapter 10, but you will find it useful here. GROUP defines a collection of objects as a single entity so that they can be selected and modified as a unit. The spiral you have just drawn is used in the next drawing, and it is easier to manipulate if you GROUP it.

FOR MORE DETAILS	See Chapter 10.

1. Type "g."
2. In the **Object Grouping** dialog box, type "Spiral" for a group name.
3. Click New.
4. Select the six arcs with a window.
5. Right-click to end selection.
6. Click **OK.**

The spiral can now be selected, moved, rotated, and copied as a single entity.

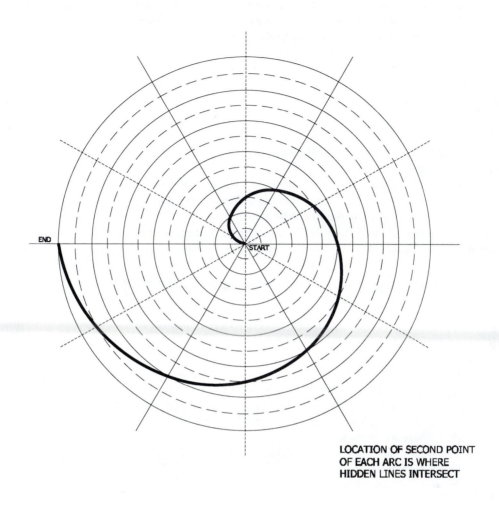

LOCATION OF SECOND POINT
OF EACH ARC IS WHERE
HIDDEN LINES INTERSECT

SOLID CIRCLE RADII	HIDDEN CIRCLE RADII
0.50	0.25
1.00	0.75
1.50	1.25
2.00	1.75
2.50	2.25
3.00	2.75

NOTE: THIS DRAWING IS USED
    ON DRAWING 6-3

SAVE THIS DRAWING!

ARCHIMEDES SPIRAL

Drawing 6-2

Drawing 6-3: Spiral Designs

These designs are different from other drawings in this book. There are no dimensions, and you use only edit commands now that the spiral is drawn. Don't be too concerned with precision. Some of your designs might come out slightly different from ours. When this happens, try to analyze the differences.

Drawing Suggestions

$$LIMITS = (0,0)(34,24)$$

These large limits are necessary if you wish to draw all these designs on the screen at once.

In some of the designs and in Drawing 6-4, you need to rotate a copy of the spiral and keep the original in place. You can accomplish this using the Copy option in the **ROTATE** command or grip edit rotate with the Copy option. Setting up Polar snap to track at various angles might also be useful. The grip edit procedure follows.

How to Rotate an Object and Retain the Original Using Grip Edit

1. Select the spiral.
2. Pick the grip around which you want to rotate, or any of the grips if you are not going to use the grip as a base point for rotation.
3. Right-click and select Rotate from the shortcut menu.
4. Right-click and type b or select Base point from the shortcut menu, if the design needs a base point not on a grip. In this exercise, the base point you choose for rotation depends on the design you are trying to create.
5. Right-click and type c or select Copy from the shortcut menu.
6. Show the rotation angle(s).
7. Press the spacebar to exit the grip edit system.

SPIRAL DESIGNS

(Make from Drawing 6-2)

Drawing 6-3

Drawing 6-4: Grooved Hub

This drawing includes another typical application of the rotation techniques just discussed. The hidden lines in the front view must be rotated 120 degrees and a copy retained in the original position. There are also good opportunities to use MIRROR, object snap, object snap tracking, and TRIM.

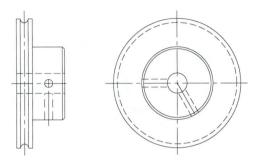

Drawing Suggestions

```
GRID = 0.5              SNAP = 0.0625
LIMITS = (0,0)(12,9)    LTSCALE = 1
```

- Draw the circles in the front view and use these to line up the horizontal lines in the left side view. This is a good opportunity to use object snap tracking. By acquiring the quadrant of a circle in the front view, you can track along the horizontal construction lines to the left side view.

- There are several different planes of symmetry in the left side view, which suggests the use of mirroring. We leave it up to you to choose an efficient sequence.

- A quick method for drawing the horizontal hidden lines in the left side view is to acquire the upper and lower quadrant points of the 0.625-diameter circle in the front view to track horizontal construction lines. Draw the lines in the left side view longer than actual length and then use TRIM to erase the excess on both sides of the left side view.

- The same method can be used to draw the two horizontal hidden lines in the front view. A slightly different method that does not use object tracking is to snap lines directly to the top and bottom quadrants of the 0.25-diameter circle in the left side view as a guide and draw them all the way through the front view. Then trim to the 2.25-diameter circle and the 0.62-diameter circle.

- Once these hidden lines are drawn, rotate them, retaining a copy in the original position.

Creating the Multiple-View Layout

Use this drawing to create the multiple-view layout shown below the dimensioned drawing. This three-view layout is very similar to the one created in Section 6.9. Exact dimensions of the viewports are not given. You should create them depending on the paper size you wish to use. What should remain consistent is the scale relationships among the three viewports. On an A sheet, for example, if the largest viewport is zoomed 0.5xp, then the left close-up is 1.0xp and the top close-up is 1.5xp. These ratios have to be adjusted for other sheet sizes.

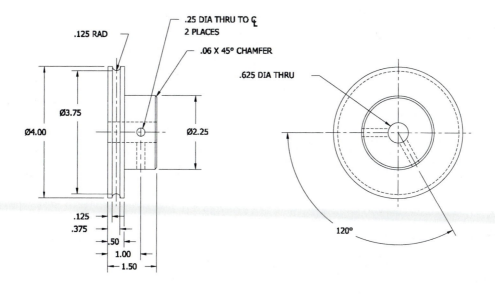

.125 RAD

.25 DIA THRU TO ℄
2 PLACES

.06 X 45° CHAMFER

.625 DIA THRU

Ø3.75

Ø4.00

Ø2.25

.125
.375
.50
1.00
1.50

120°

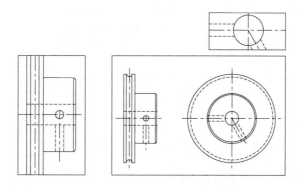

GROOVED HUB
Drawing 6-4

Drawing 6-5: Cap Iron

This drawing is of a type of blade used in a wood plane. When wood is planed, the cap iron causes it to curl up out of the plane so that it does not jam. There are several good applications for the **TRIM** command here.

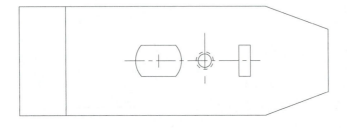

Drawing Suggestions

```
GRID = 1.00
SNAP = 0.125
LIMITS = (0,0)(18,12)
LTSCALE = 0.25
```

- The circle with a hidden line outside a continuous line represents a tapped hole. The dimension is given to the hidden line; the continuous inner line is drawn with a slightly smaller radius that is not specified.
- The figure near the center of the top view that has two arcs with 0.38 radii can be drawn exactly the same way as the bandage discussed earlier in this chapter. Draw a circle and two horizontal lines and then trim it all down.
- The small 0.54 and 0.58 arcs in the front view can be drawn using Start, End, Radius.
- The small vertical hidden lines in the front view can be drawn using techniques introduced in the last drawing. Draw lines down from snap points on the figures in the top view and then trim them, or use object snap tracking to create lines with excess length and then trim them. For the tapped hole and the arced opening in the middle, use the right and left quadrant points of the arcs and circle as acquired points or snap points.

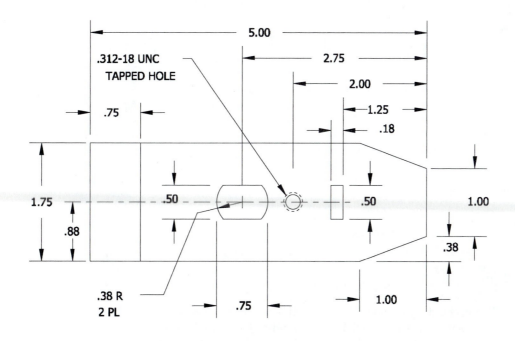

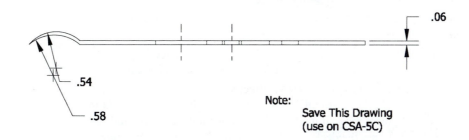

Note:
Save This Drawing
(use on CSA-5C)

CAP IRON
Drawing 6-5

Drawing 6-6: Deck Framing

This architectural drawing might take some time, although there is nothing in it you have not done before. Notice that some of the settings are quite different from our 1B template, so be sure to adjust them before beginning.

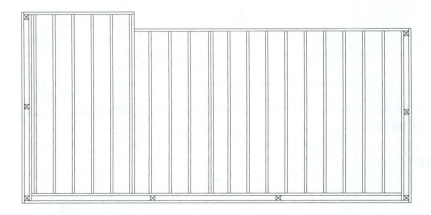

Drawing Suggestions

```
UNITS = Architectural
PRECISION = 0'-0"
LIMITS = (0', 0')(48,36')
GRID = 1'
SNAP = 2"
```

- Whatever order you choose for doing this drawing, we suggest that you make ample use of COPY, ARRAY, OFFSET, and TRIM.

- Keep Ortho on, except to draw the lines across the middle of the squares, representing upright posts.

- With snap set at 2", it is easy to copy lines 2" apart, as you have to do frequently to draw the 2 × 8 studs.

- You might need to turn Snap off when you are selecting lines to copy, but be sure to turn it on again to specify displacements.

- Notice that you can use ARRAY effectively, but there are three separate arrays. They are all 16' on center, but the double boards in several places make it inadvisable to do a single array of studs all the way across the deck. What you can do, however, is draw, copy, and array all the "vertical" studs at the maximum length first and then go back and trim them to their various actual lengths using the "horizontal" boards as cutting edges.

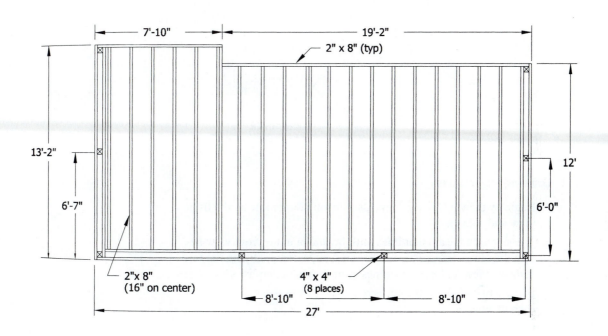

DECK FRAMING

Drawing 6-6

Drawing 6-7: Tool Block

In this drawing, you take information from a three-dimensional draw-ing and develop it into a 3view drawing. The finished drawing should be composed of the Top View, Front View, and Side View. The refer-ence drawing shows a portion of each view to be developed. You are to complete these views.

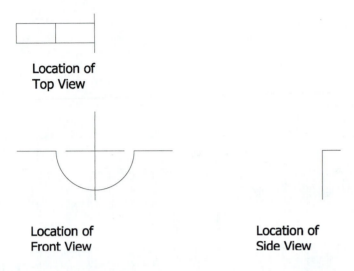

**Location of
Top View**

**Location of
Front View**

**Location of
Side View**

Drawing Suggestions

- Begin by drawing the top view. Use the top view to line up the front view and side view.

- The slot with the angular lines must be drawn in the front view be-fore the other views. These lines can then be lined up with the top and side view and used as guides to draw the hidden lines.

- Be sure to include all the necessary hidden lines and center lines in each view.

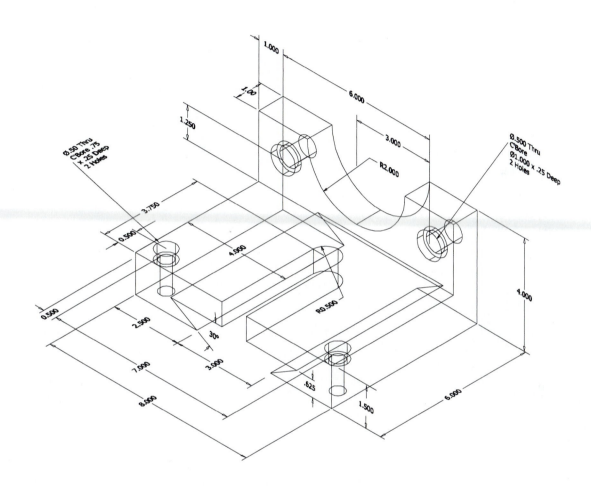

Ø.50 Thru
C'Bore .75
x .25 Deep
2 Holes

Ø.500 Thru
C'Bore
Ø1.000 x .25 Deep
2 Holes

1.000

1.00

6.000

1.250

3.000

R2.000

3.750

0.500

4.000

0.500

2.500

30°

3.000

R0.500

4.000

7.000

8.000

.625

1.500

6.000

TOOL BLOCK
Drawing 6-7

Text

7

Chapter Objectives

- Entering Single-Line Text with Justification Options
- Entering Text on an Angle and Text Using Character Codes
- Entering Multiline Text Using MTEXT
- Editing Text in Place with DDEDIT and MTEDIT
- Modifying Text with PROPERTIES
- Using the SPELL Command
- Changing Fonts and Styles
- Changing Properties with MATCHPROP
- Scaling Previously Drawn Entities
- Creating Tables and Fields
- Using AutoCAD Templates, Borders, and Title Blocks

INTRODUCTION

This chapter begins Part II of the book. Part I focused on basic 2-D entities such as lines, circles, and arcs. In the next four chapters, you learn to draw a number of AutoCAD entities that are constructed as groups of lines, circles, and arcs. Text, dimensions, polylines, and blocks are all entities made up of basic 2-D entities, but you do not have to treat them line by line, arc by arc. In addition, you learn how whole drawings can be inserted in other drawings and how this capability is used to create symbols libraries that can be shared by many users. Also in Part II, you continue to learn AutoCAD editing and plotting features and features that aid in collaborative design projects.

Now it's time to add text to your drawings. In this chapter, you learn to find your way around AutoCAD's **TEXT** and **MTEXT** commands. In addition, you learn many new editing commands that are often used with text, but are equally important for editing other objects.

7-1 ENTERING SINGLE-LINE TEXT WITH JUSTIFICATION OPTIONS

GENERAL PROCEDURE

1. Select the **Single Line Text** tool from the dashboard.
2. Choose a justification option.
3. Pick a start point.
4. Answer prompts regarding height and rotation.
5. Enter text.

AutoCAD provides two commands for entering text in a drawing. **TEXT** allows you to enter single lines of text and displays them as you type. **MTEXT** allows you to type multiple lines of text in a special text editor and then positions them in a windowed area in your drawing. Both commands provide numerous options for placing text and a variety of fonts to use and styles that can be created from them. You are already familiar with entering single lines of left-justified text from Chapter 3. Here we begin by expanding your technique to include other forms of single-line text.

⊞ To prepare for this exercise, create a new drawing using the 1B template and draw a 4.00 unit horizontal line beginning at (1,1). Then create five copies of the line 2.00 units apart, as shown in Figure 7-1.

These lines are for orientation in this exercise only; they are not essential for drawing text. Our first step is a quick review of left-justified text.

⊞ Select the Single Line Text tool from the dashboard.

⊞ Pick a start point at the left end of the upper line.

⊞ Press Enter to accept the default height (0.20).

⊞ Press Enter to accept the default angle (0).

⊞ Type "Left" ↵.

Notice that the text cursor jumps below the line when you press **Enter.**

⊞ Type "Justified" ↵.

The text cursor jumps down again and another *Enter text:* prompt appears. To exit the command, you need to press **Enter** at the prompt.

⊞ Press Enter to exit the command.

This completes the process and returns you to the command prompt.

Figure 7-2 shows the left-justified text you have just drawn.

Before proceeding with other text justification options, we demonstrate two additional features of **TEXT.**

⊞ Press Enter to repeat the TEXT command.

If you press **Enter** again at this point instead of showing a new start point or selecting a justification option, you go right back to the **Enter text:** prompt as if you had never left the command. Try it.

⊞ Press Enter.

You see the *Enter text:* prompt in the command area and the text cursor reappears on the screen just below the word *Justified.*

⊞ Type "Text" ↵.

⊞ Press Enter to exit the command.

Once you have left **TEXT,** there are other ways to edit text, which we explore in Sections 7.4 and 7.5.

Figure 7-1

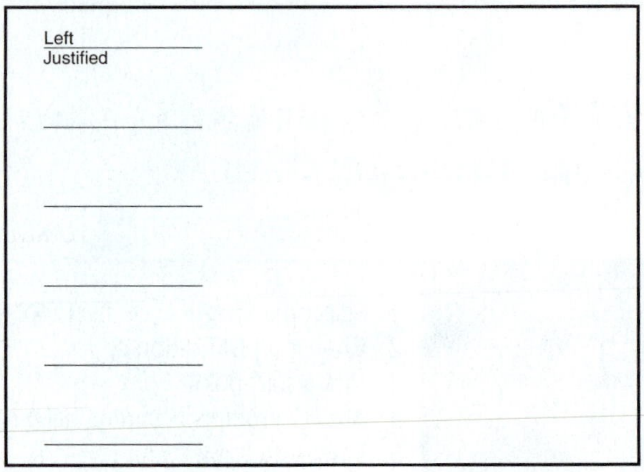

Figure 7-2

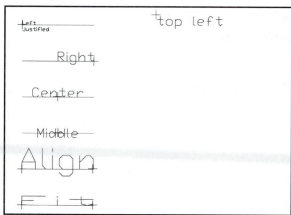

Figure 7-3

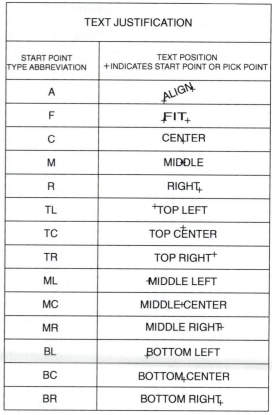

Figure 7-4

TEXT JUSTIFICATION	
START POINT TYPE ABBREVIATION	TEXT POSITION +INDICATES START POINT OR PICK POINT
A	ALIGN
F	FIT
C	CENTER
M	MIDDLE
R	RIGHT
TL	TOP LEFT
TC	TOP CENTER
TR	TOP RIGHT
ML	MIDDLE LEFT
MC	MIDDLE CENTER
MR	MIDDLE RIGHT
BL	BOTTOM LEFT
BC	BOTTOM CENTER
BR	BOTTOM RIGHT

We now proceed to some of the other text placement options, beginning with right-justified text. The options demonstrated in this exercise are all illustrated in Figure 7-3 and in the complete chart of options, Figure 7-4. For the text in this demonstration we also specify a change in height.

Right-Justified Text

Right-justified text is constructed from an endpoint backing up, right to left.

⊕ Repeat the TEXT command.

⊕ Right-click and select Justify from the shortcut menu, as shown in Figure 7-5.

This opens the dynamic input list.

⊕ Select Right from the menu.

Now AutoCAD prompts for an endpoint instead of a start point:

Specify right endpoint of text baseline:

Choose the right end of the second line.

⊕ Point to the right end of the second line.

AutoCAD prompts you to specify a text height. This time we change the height to 0.50.

⊕ Type ".5" ↵.

⊕ Press Enter to retain 0 degrees of rotation.

Notice the larger text cursor at the right end of the second line.

⊕ Type "Right" ↵.

At this point you should have the word *Right* right-justified on the second line.

⊕ Press Enter to exit the command.

Your screen should now include the second line of text in right-justified position, as shown in Figure 7-3.

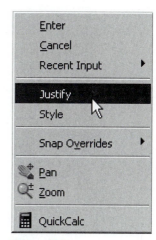

Figure 7-5

Centered Text

Centered text is justified from the bottom center of the text.

- ⊕ Repeat the TEXT command.
- ⊕ Type "c" ↵.

    AutoCAD prompts

    ```
    Specify center point of text:
    ```

- ⊕ Point to the midpoint of the third line.
- ⊕ Press Enter to retain the current height, which is now set to 0.50.
- ⊕ Press Enter to retain 0 degrees of rotation.
- ⊕ Type "Center" ↵.
- ⊕ Press Enter again to complete the command.

    The word *Center* should now be centered, as shown in Figure 7-3.

Middle Text

Middle text is justified from the middle of the text both horizontally and vertically, rather than from the bottom center.

- ⊕ Repeat TEXT.
- ⊕ Type "m" ↵.

    AutoCAD prompts

    ```
    Specify middle point of text:
    ```

- ⊕ Point to the midpoint of the fourth line.
- ⊕ Press Enter to retain the current height of 0.50.
- ⊕ Press Enter to retain 0 degrees of rotation.
- ⊕ Type "Middle" ↵.
- ⊕ Press Enter again to complete the command.

    Notice the difference between center and middle. *Center* refers to the midpoint of the baseline below the text. *Middle* refers to the middle of the text itself, so that the line now runs through the text.

Aligned Text

Aligned text is placed between two specified points. The height of the text is calculated proportional to the distance between the two points, and the text is drawn along the line between the two points.

- ⊕ Repeat TEXT.
- ⊕ Type "a" ↵.

    AutoCAD prompts

    ```
    Specify first endpoint of text baseline:
    ```

- ⊕ Point to the left end of the fifth line.

    AutoCAD prompts for another point:

    ```
    Specify second endpoint of text baseline:
    ```

- ⊕ Point to the right end of the fifth line.

    Notice that there is no prompt for height. AutoCAD calculates a height based on the space between the points you chose. There is also no prompt for an angle, because the angle between your two points (in this case 0) is used. You could position text at an angle using this option.

- ⊕ Type "Align" ↵.

    As you type, the text size will be adjusted with the addition of each letter.

- ⊕ Press Enter again to complete the command.

    Notice that the text is sized to fill the space between the two points you selected.

Text Drawn to Fit Between Two Points

The Fit option is similar to the Align option, except that the specified text height is retained.

⊕ Repeat TEXT.
⊕ Type "f" ↵.

You are prompted for two points, as in the Align option.

⊕ Point to the left end of the sixth line.
⊕ Point to the right end of the sixth line.
⊕ Press Enter to retain the current height.

As with the Align option, there is no prompt for an angle of rotation.

⊕ Type "Fit" ↵.

Once again, text size is adjusted as you type, but this time only the width changes.

⊕ Press Enter again to complete the command.

This time the text is stretched horizontally to fill the line without a change in height. This is the difference between fit and align. In the Align option, text height is determined by the width you show. With Fit, the specified height is retained and the text is stretched or compressed to fill the given space.

Other Justification Options

Before proceeding to the next task, take a moment to look at the complete list of justification options. The command line prompt looks like this:

```
[Align/Fit/Center/Middle/Right/TL/TC/TR/ML/MC/MR/BL/BC/BR]:
```

The letter options are spelled out in the chart shown in Figure 7-4. We have already explored the first five and the default Left option. For the others, study the figure. As shown on the chart, T is for top, M is for middle, and B is for bottom. L, C, and R stand for left, center, and right, respectively. Let's try one:

⊕ Repeat TEXT and then type "tl" ↵ for the Top Left option or select TL from the dynamic input list.

AutoCAD asks you to Specify top-left point of text. As shown on the chart in Figure 7-4, top left refers to the highest potential text point at the left of the word.

⊕ Pick a top left point, as shown in Figure 7-3 above the words top left.
⊕ Press Enter twice to accept the height and rotation angle settings and arrive at the *Text:* prompt.
⊕ Type "top left" ↵.

The text is entered from the top left position.

⊕ Press Enter again to complete the command.

Your screen should now resemble Figure 7-3.

7-2 ENTERING TEXT ON AN ANGLE AND TEXT USING CHARACTER CODES—

GENERAL PROCEDURE	1. Enter the **TEXT** command. 2. Specify justification option, start point, and text height. 3. Specify a rotation angle. 4. Enter text, including character codes as needed.

In this section we explore **TEXT** by entering several lines on an angle, adding special character symbols along the way. We create three lines of left-justified text, one below the other and all rotated 45 degrees, as shown in Figure 7-6.

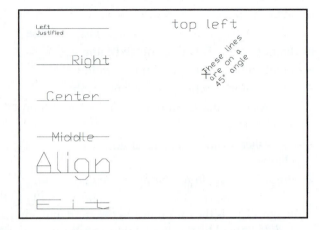

Figure 7-6

⊞ Repeat the TEXT command.

　　You see the familiar prompt:

　　　　Specify start point of text or [Justify/Style]:

⊞ Pick a starting point near (12.00,8.00), as shown by the mark next to the word *These* in Figure 7-6.

⊞ Type ".3" ↵ to specify a smaller text size.

⊞ Type "45" ↵ or show an angle of 45 degrees.

　　Notice that the text cursor is shown at the specified angle.

⊞ Type "These lines" ↵.

　　The text is drawn on the screen at a 45-degree angle, and the cursor moves down to the next line. Notice that the text box on the screen is still at the specified angle.

⊞ Type "are on a" ↵.

The Degree Symbol and Other Special Characters

The next line contains a degree symbol. Because you do not have this character on your keyboard, AutoCAD provides a special method for drawing it. Type the text with the %% signs just as shown in the following and then study Figure 7-7, which lists other special characters that can be drawn in the same way.

Control Codes and Special Characters	
Type at Text Prompt	Text on Drawing
%%O OVERSCORE %%U UNDERSCORE 180%%D 2.00 %%P.01 %%C4.00	O̅V̅E̅R̅S̅C̅O̅R̅E̅ U̲N̲D̲E̲R̲S̲C̲O̲R̲E̲ 180° 2.00 ±.01 Ø4.00

Figure 7-7

⊞ Type "45%%d."

　　TEXT initially types the percent symbols directly to the screen, just as you have typed them. When you type the d, the character code is translated and redrawn as a degree symbol.

⊞ Type "angle" ↵.

⊞ Press Enter again to complete the command sequence.

　　Your screen should now resemble Figure 7-6.

7-3 ENTERING MULTILINE TEXT USING MTEXT

GENERAL PROCEDURE	1. Select the **Multiline Text** tool from the dashboard. 2. Specify the first corner. 3. Specify the opposite corner. 4. Type text in the text editor. 5. Click **OK.**

The **MTEXT** command allows you to create multiple lines of text in a text editor and position them within a defined window in your drawing. Like **TEXT, MTEXT** has nine options for text justification and its own set of character codes.

We begin by creating a simple left-justified block of text.

⊕ Select the Multiline Text tool from the dashboard, as shown in Figure 7-8.

You see the following prompt in the command area:

```
-mtext Current text style: STANDARD Text height: 0.30
              Specify first corner:
```

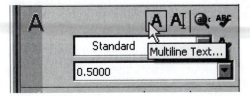

Figure 7-8

Also, notice that a multiline text symbol, "abc," has been added to the crosshair.

Fundamentally, **MTEXT** lets you define the width of a group of text lines that you create in a special text editor. As the text is entered, AutoCAD formats it to conform to the specified width and justification method and draws it on your screen. The width can be defined in several ways. The default method for specifying a width is to draw a window on the screen, but this can be misleading. **MTEXT** does not attempt to place the complete text inside the window, but only within its width. The first point of the window becomes the insertion point of the text. How AutoCAD uses this insertion point depends on the justification option. The second window point defines the width and the text flow direction (i.e., whether the text lines should be drawn above or below, to the left or right of the insertion point). Exactly how this is interpreted is also dependent on the justification option.

⊕ Pick an insertion point near the middle of your drawing area, in the neighborhood of (12.00,5.00).

AutoCAD begins a window at the selected point and gives you a new prompt:

```
Specify opposite corner or [Height/Justify/Line
          spacing/Rotation/Style/Width]:
```

We continue with the default options by picking a second corner. For purposes of demonstration, we suggest a window 3.00 wide, drawn down and to the right.

⊕ Pick a second point 3.00 to the right and about 1.00 below the first point.

As soon as you pick the opposite corner, AutoCAD opens the Multiline Text Editor and associated **Text Formatting** toolbar illustrated in Figure 7-9. The toolbar gives you the capacity to change text styles and fonts (see Section 7.7) and text height, along with some standard text features like bolding and underlining. Below the toolbar is the text editing window. When you enter text in this window, the text wraps around as it will be displayed in your drawing, according to the width you have specified. This width is represented by the small ruler at the top of the text window. Using the two small triangles at the left end of the ruler, you can also set first line indent and hanging indent tabs for paragraph formatting.

The window is placed at the actual text location and the text is shown in the window at the same size as it will appear in the drawing, unless this would make it

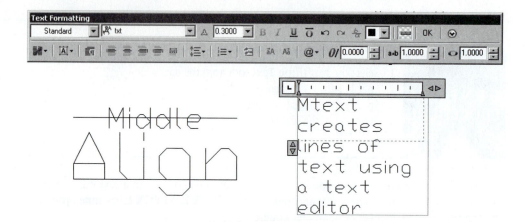

Figure 7-9

either too large or too small for convenient editing. In such cases, the text size is adjusted to a reasonable size for editing and the actual size is shown only when the command is completed.

⊕ Type "MTEXT creates lines of text using a text editor."

Text appears in the window as illustrated in Figure 7-9.

⊕ Click the OK button at the right end of the toolbar to leave the editor and complete the command.

You are returned to the drawing window and the new text is added, as shown in Figure 7-10. Notice that the text you typed has been wrapped around to fit within the 3.00 width window; the 0.30 height of the text has been retained; and the 1.00 height of the text window you defined has been ignored.

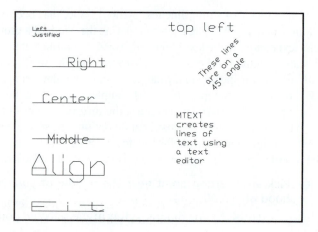

Figure 7-10

In a moment, we explore other **MTEXT** justification options by editing Mtext using **DDMODIFY**. First, however, we do some simple text editing with **DDEDIT** and **MTEDIT**.

7-4 EDITING TEXT IN PLACE WITH **DDEDIT** AND **MTEDIT**

GENERAL PROCEDURE	1. Select the text you want to edit. 2. Right-click to open the shortcut menu. 3. Select Edit or Mtext Edit from the shortcut menu. 4. Edit text. 5. If necessary click **OK**.

There are several ways to modify text that already exists in your drawing. You can change wording and spelling as well as properties such as layer, style, and justification. For simple changes in the wording of text, use the **DDEDIT** or **MTEDIT** command, accessed from the **Modify** menu; for property changes, use the **Properties Manager,** discussed in Section 7.5.

In this task, we do some simple **DDEDIT** text editing. Then we use the **MTEDIT** command to show different justification options of **Mtext** paragraphs. In both cases, it is most efficient to select the text first and then use the shortcut menu to enter commands and select options. Start by selecting the first line of the angled text.

⊞ Pick the words "These lines" by clicking on any of the letters.

The words "These lines" are highlighted and a grip appears at the start point of the line, indicating that this single line of text has been selected.

⊞ Right-click to open the shortcut menu shown in Figure 7-11.

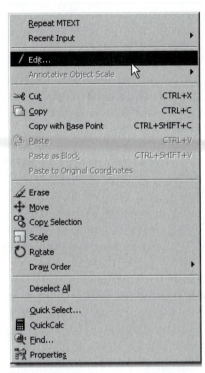

Figure 7-11

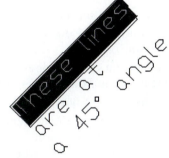

Figure 7-12

⊞ Select Edit from the shortcut menu, as shown.

When you make this selection, the shortcut menu disappears and you see the selected text line highlighted and colored as shown in Figure 7-12. This is the way **DDEDIT** functions for text created with **DTEXT**. If you had selected text created with **MTEXT,** the shortcut menu would have had an Edit Mtext option that would put you in the **Multiline Text Editor** instead.

We add the word three to the middle of the selected line, as follows.

⊞ Move the screen cursor to the center of the text, between These and lines, and press the pick button.

A flashing cursor should now be present, indicating where text will be added if you begin typing.

⊞ Type "three" and add a space so that the line reads "These three lines," as shown in Figure 7-13.

⊞ Press Enter.

The cursor disappears, but you are still in the DDEDIT command.

Now we are going to edit the text you created in **MTEXT.** The first difference you will notice is that because **MTEXT** creates multiple lines of text as a group, you cannot select a single line of text. When you click, the whole set of lines is selected.

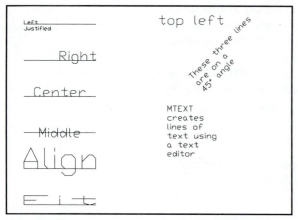

Figure 7-13

Figure 7-14

DDEDIT repeats automatically, so you should have the following prompt in the command area before proceeding:

```
Select an annotation object or [Undo]:
```

If not, repeat **DDEDIT.**

⊕ Select the text beginning with MTEXT creates.

DDEDIT recognizes that you have chosen text created with **MTEXT** and opens the Multiline Text Editor, with the text window around the chosen paragraph and the **Text Formatting** toolbar above.

⊕ Point and click just to the left of the word lines in the text editor.

You should see a white cursor blinking at the beginning of the line.

⊕ Type "multiple," so the text reads "MTEXT creates multiple lines of text using a text editor."

When you exit the command, the text is redrawn as shown in Figure 7-14. Before leaving the **Multiline Text Editor,** take a look at the available shortcut menu.

⊕ Move the cursor anywhere within the text edit window and right-click.

You see the shortcut menu illustrated in Figure 7-15. If you highlight the Symbol option, a submenu with a list of symbols appears, including the degree symbol, the plus or minus symbol, the diameter symbol and others. Selecting from this list saves you from typing the %% characters. If you select Other from the submenu, a **Character Mapping** dialog box appears with a large selection of fonts to choose from, each having its own standard set of symbols. These options are also available on the toolbars of the **Multiline Text Editor.**

⊕ Move the cursor anywhere outside the text editor and press the pick button.

The shortcut menu closes but you are still in the text editor.

⊕ Click OK to exit the command.

You return to the Drawing Window, with the new text added as shown in Figure 7-14. Next we explore **PROPERTIES** along with the Mtext justification options.

7-5 Modifying Text with **PROPERTIES**

GENERAL PROCEDURE	1. Select object. 2. Right-click and select Properties from the shortcut menu. 3. Use the **Properties** dialog box to specify property changes. 4. Click **OK.**

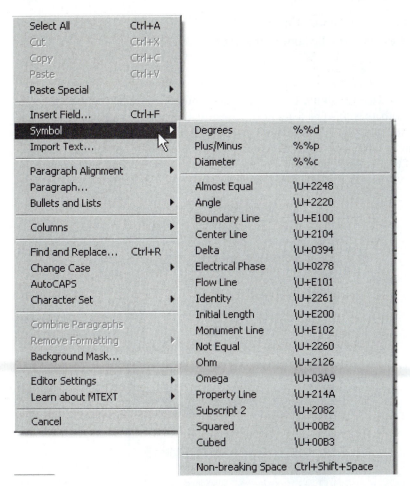

Select All	Ctrl+A		
Cut	Ctrl+X		
Copy	Ctrl+C		
Paste	Ctrl+V		
Paste Special	▶		
Insert Field...	Ctrl+F		
Symbol	▶	Degrees	%%d
Import Text...		Plus/Minus	%%p
		Diameter	%%c
Paragraph Alignment	▶	Almost Equal	\U+2248
Paragraph...		Angle	\U+2220
Bullets and Lists	▶	Boundary Line	\U+E100
		Center Line	\U+2104
Columns	▶	Delta	\U+0394
Find and Replace...	Ctrl+R	Electrical Phase	\U+0278
Change Case	▶	Flow Line	\U+E101
AutoCAPS		Identity	\U+2261
Character Set	▶	Initial Length	\U+E200
		Monument Line	\U+E102
Combine Paragraphs		Not Equal	\U+2260
Remove Formatting	▶	Ohm	\U+2126
Background Mask...		Omega	\U+03A9
		Property Line	\U+214A
Editor Settings	▶	Subscript 2	\U+2082
Learn about MTEXT	▶	Squared	\U+00B2
		Cubed	\U+00B3
Cancel			
		Non-breaking Space	Ctrl+Shift+Space

Figure 7-15

PROPERTIES is one of several commands that can be used to change properties of objects in a drawing. It is used with many kinds of objects other than text. Properties include color, layer, linetype, and lineweight, among others. In this exercise, you learn how to use **PROPERTIES** to change Mtext justification options. We begin this task with a look at the Properties tool palette.

⊕ Draw a 3.00 line just above the Mtext paragraph, as shown in Figure 7-16.

This line is only for reference to make the placement of different justification options clearer. It should begin at the same snap point that was used as the insertion point for the text. The left end of the line shows the insertion point, and the length shows the width of the paragraph. We have used the point (9.00,6.00) and the 3.00 width.

⊕ Pick the paragraph beginning with "MTEXT creates."

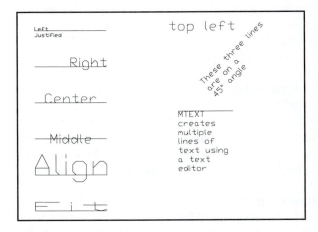

Figure 7-16

⊞ Right-click to open the shortcut menu.
⊞ Select Properties from the bottom of the shortcut menu.

Palettes

The Properties palette illustrated in Figure 7-17 is our first encounter with a palette. Palettes combine some features of toolbars with some features of regular dialog boxes, and have some unique features as well. Like toolbars, you can have more than one open at a time, they can be floating or docked, and they can be left open while other commands are executed. Tool palettes, like toolbars, are simple sets of tool buttons; however, palettes can contain a more complex interface, including multiple tabs, panels, scroll bars, drop-down lists, and edit boxes.

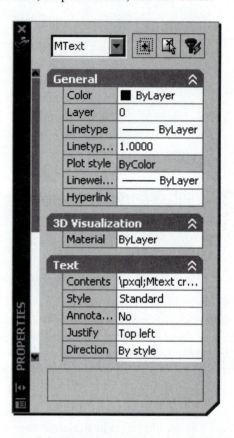

Figure 7-17

Take a look at the general format of the Properties palette. On the left is the blue title bar, with a close button (X) at the top and Properties in the middle. Below that are two symbols we explore later in this task. As usual, the dialog box can be moved on the screen by clicking and dragging on the blue title bar.

To the right of the title bar is an area with a small scroll bar, a General list, a 3D Visualization list, a Text list, and some buttons at the top. Looking closely at the palette you can see that many items are truncated, with missing text indicated by ellipses (. . .). You can expand the palette by grabbing the edge and dragging to the right.

In the top list box, you see MText. This indicates the type of object you have selected. If you had chosen multiple objects you could select from a drop-down list opening from this box.

Below the edit box are lists of all the properties that can be modified for the object you have chosen. The first list is the General list, including properties such as color and layer that apply to all objects. The second is a 3D Visualization list, which is not useful with a 2-D object. In this case the third list is the Text list, showing properties that apply only to text. There is a fourth list, called Geometry, that contains coordinates of the placement of the object within the drawing. To see the Geometry list, use the scroll bar to the left of the lists. There you find the coordinates of the start point of the MText.

We are going to make a change in text justification, but notice that there are also options here to change text content and text style (Section 7.7). To change MText content select Contents from the Text list. An ellipsis button appears in the right column. Clicking this would open the Multiline

Text Editor with the selected text. In this exercise, however, we do not change the text itself, but only the justification.

⊞ Select Justify from the Text list.

When Justify is selected, a drop-down list arrow appears in the right column, next to Top left.

⊞ Open the list.

This opens a list box with a list of nine justification options, as shown in Figure 7-18. The list should look familiar to you because it includes some of the same choices as the text justification options introduced previously for the **TEXT** command. The difference is that here you place and justify multiple lines of text as a group.

Notice that the current justification is Top left. We change it to Top center, the second option on the list.

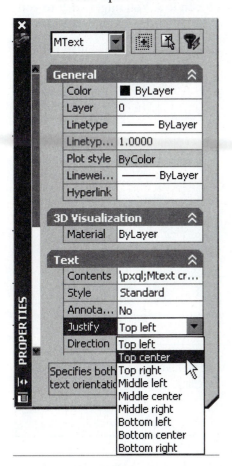

Figure 7-18

⊞ Select Top center.

The list box closes, and Top center should now be shown in the Justify edit box. You can also see that the change is immediately reflected in your drawing even while the dialog box is still open.

Auto-hide

Before leaving the Properties palette, we demonstrate one additional important feature of palettes. Just below the word Properties on the title bar, you see a symbol with a small bar on the left and two arrowheads or triangles pointing in opposite directions on the right. If you let your cursor rest on this icon you see a tooltip that says Auto-hide.

⊞ Click the Auto-hide button on the title bar.

The palette closes, but the title bar remains, as shown in Figure 7-19. Also note that the two arrowheads have been replaced by a single arrowhead. This indicates that Auto-hide is on for this palette.

Figure 7-19

⊕ Move your cursor over the title bar and let it rest a moment.

   The palette opens automatically. It is not necessary to click to open it.

⊕ Move your cursor back into the drawing area and let it rest there without clicking.

   The palette closes again, but the title bar stays open.

This is the Auto-hide feature. It allows your palette to remain accessible while taking up very little space in your drawing area. You can reverse the setting simply by clicking the Auto-hide icon again.

Finally, close the **Properties** dialog box before moving on.

⊕ Click the X button at the top of the Properties dialog box title bar.

⊕ Press Esc to clear grips.

   Your text is redrawn as shown in Figure 7-20. The paragraph is now in centered format, centered in the original insertion window. You might wish to continue with other justification options. Also, study Figure 7-21, which illustrates Mtext justification options.

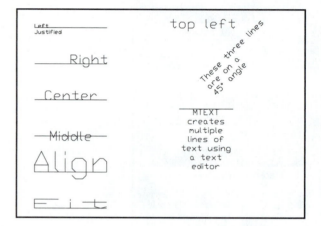

Figure 7-20

7-6 USING THE SPELL COMMAND

GENERAL PROCEDURE	1. Select the **Check Spelling** tool from the dashboard.
	2. Specify where in the drawing to check spelling.
	3. Respond to corrections.
	4. Close the dialog box.

COMMAND GRID	
Command	Spell
Alias	Sp
Menu	Tools
Tool	ABC

AutoCAD's **SPELL** command is simple to use and will appear familiar to anyone who has used spell checkers in word processing programs. We use **SPELL** to check the spelling of all the text we have drawn so far.

⊕ Pick the Spell Check tool from the dashboard, as shown in Figure 7-22.

   You see the **Check Spelling** dialog box shown in Figure 7-23.

   At the top left of the box is the Where to check list box. The options on the list are Entire drawing, Current space/layout, and Selected objects. For our purposes we use the Entire drawing option to check all the spelling in the drawing.

⊕ If necessary, select Entire drawing from the Where to check list.

⊕ Click the Start button.

   If you have followed the exercise so far and not misspelled any words along the way, you see MTEXT in the Not in dictionary box and TEXT as a suggested correction. Ignore this change, but before you leave SPELL, look at what is available: You can ignore a word the checker does not recognize or change it. You can

MULTILINE TEXT JUSTIFICATION

Mtext controls
which part of the
text aligns at the
intersection point.
This is an example
of top left text.

top left:
left-justified,
spills down

Mtext controls
which part of the
text aligns at the
intersection point.
This is an
example of top
center text.

top center:
center-justified,
spills down

Mtext controls
which part of the
text aligns at the
intersection point.
This is an
example of top
right text.

top right
right-justified,
spills down

Mtext controls
which part of the
text aligns at the
intersection point.
This is an example
of top left text.

middle left:
left-justified,
spills up and down

Mtext controls
which part of the
text aligns at the
intersection point.
This is an
example of top
center text.

middle center:
center-justified,
spills up and down

Mtext controls
which part of the
text aligns at the
intersection point.
This is an
example of top
right text.

middle right:
right-justified,
spills up and down

Mtext controls
which part of the
text aligns at the
intersection point.
This is an example
of top left text.

bottom left:
left-justified,
spills up

Mtext controls
which part of the
text aligns at the
intersection point.
This is an
example of top
center text.

bottom center:
center-justified,
spills up

Mtext controls
which part of the
text aligns at the
intersection point.
This is an
example of top
right text.

bottom right:
right-justified,
spills up

Figure 7-21

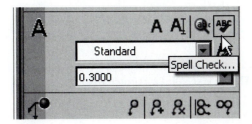

Figure 7-22

change a single instance of a word or all instances in the currently selected text. You can add a word to the main dictionary or change to another dictionary.

⊕ Click Ignore.

If your drawing does not contain other spelling irregularities, you should now see an AutoCAD message that reads

```
Spelling check complete.
```

⊕ Click OK to close the message box.

Figure 7-23

⊕ Click Close to complete the SPELL command.

If you have made any corrections in spelling, they are incorporated into your drawing at this point.

7-7 CHANGING FONTS AND STYLES

GENERAL PROCEDURE	1. Pick the Text Style from the dashboard. 2. Click New. 3. Type in a name for the new style. 4. Click **OK.** 5. Change settings in the **Text Style** dialog box. Specify height, width, and font. 6. Click **Close.**

By default, the current text style in any AutoCAD drawing is called Standard. It is a specific form of a font called txt that comes with the software. All the text you have entered so far has been drawn with the standard style of the txt font.

Also predefined in all AutoCAD 2008 drawings is a style called Annotative. The Annotative style is the same as Standard in all ways, except that it includes the Annotative property. This property is new in 2008 and allows you to create text that can be automatically scaled to match the scale of different viewports within the same layout.

FOR MORE DETAILS	See Chapter 8.

Fonts are the basic patterns of character and symbol shapes that can be used with the **TEXT** and **MTEXT** commands. *Styles* are variations in the size, orientation, and spacing of the characters in those fonts. It is possible to create your own fonts, but for most of us this is an esoteric activity. In contrast, creating your own styles is easy and practical.

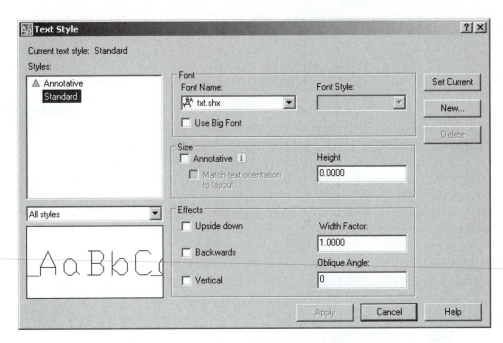

Figure 7-24

We begin by creating a variation of the Standard style you have been using:

⊞ Pick the Text Style tool from the dashboard.

You see the **Text Style** dialog box shown in Figure 7-24. You see Standard and Annotative listed in the Styles box. It is possible that other styles are listed. Standard should be selected.

We will create our own variation of the Standard style and call it Vertical. It uses the same txt character font, but is drawn down the display instead of across.

⊞ Click New.

AutoCAD opens a smaller dialog box that asks for a name for the new text style.

⊞ Type "vertical" ↵.

This returns you to the **Text Style** dialog box, with the new style listed and highlighted in the Styles box. We use the vertical text effect to make this style different.

⊞ Click the Vertical check box in the Effects area at the lower left of the dialog box.

Notice the change to vertically oriented text in the Preview panel at the lower right of the dialog box.

We also give this style a fixed height and a width factor. Notice that the current height is 0.00. This does not mean that your characters will be drawn 0.00 units high. It means that there will be no fixed height, so you can specify a height whenever you use this style. Standard currently has no fixed height, so Vertical has inherited this setting. Try giving our new Vertical style a fixed height.

⊞ Double-click in the Height edit box and then type ".5."

⊞ Double-click in the Width Factor box and type "2."

⊞ Click Apply to save Changes to the new text style.

⊞ Click Close to exit the Text Style dialog box.

The new Vertical style is now current. To see it in action you need to enter some text.

⊞ Enter the TEXT command.

⊞ Pick a start point, as shown by the placement of the letter V in Figure 7-25.

Notice that you are not prompted for a height because the current style has height fixed at 0.50. Also notice that the default rotation angle is set at 270. Your vertical text is entered moving down the screen at 270 degrees.

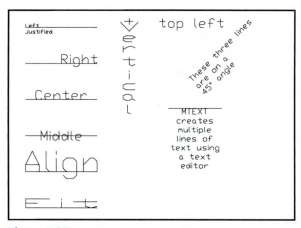

Figure 7-25

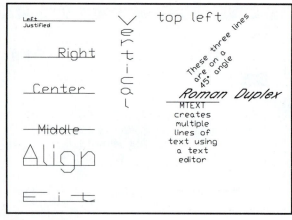

Figure 7-26

⊞ Press Enter to retain 270 degrees of rotation.

⊞ Type "Vertical" ↵.

⊞ Press Enter to end the line command.

Your screen should resemble Figure 7-25.

Next we create another style using a different font and some of the other style options. Pay attention to the Preview panel in the dialog box, which updates automatically to show your changes.

⊞ Pick the Text Style tool from the dashboard.

⊞ Click New.

⊞ In the New Text Style dialog box, give the style the name Slanted.

⊞ Click OK to close the New Text Style box.

⊞ Open the Font Name list by clicking the arrow.

A lengthy list of fonts is available.

⊞ Scroll to romand.shx and stop.

Romand stands for Roman Duplex, an AutoCAD font.

⊞ Click romand.shx to place it in the Font Name box.

⊞ If necessary, clear the Vertical check box.

⊞ Set the text Height to 0.00.

⊞ Set the Width Factor to 1.

⊞ Set Oblique Angle to 45.

This causes your text to be slanted 45 degrees to the right. For a left slant, you would type a negative number.

⊞ Click Apply to save changes to the new text style.

⊞ Click Close to exit the Text Style dialog box.

Now enter some text to see how this slanted Roman Duplex style looks.

⊞ Enter the TEXT command and answer the prompts to draw the words Roman Duplex with a 0.50 height, as shown in Figure 7-26.

Switching the Current Style

All new text is created in the current style. The style of previously drawn text can be changed, as we see later. Once you have a number of styles defined in a drawing, you can switch from one to another by using the Style option of the **TEXT** and **MTEXT** commands or by selecting a text style from the **Text Style** dialog box.

Note:
If you change the definition of a text style, all text previously drawn in that style will be regenerated with the new style specifications.

7-8 CHANGING PROPERTIES WITH MATCHPROP

GENERAL PROCEDURE	1. Select the **Match Properties** tool from the **Standard Annotation** toolbar. 2. Select a source object with properties you wish to transfer to another object. 3. If necessary, specify properties you wish to match. 4. Select destination objects. 5. Press **Enter** to end object selection.

MATCHPROP is a very efficient command that lets you match all or some of the properties of an object to those of another object. Properties that can be transferred from one object to another, or to many others, include layer, linetype, color, and linetype scale. These settings are common to all AutoCAD entities. Other properties that relate to only specific types of entities are thickness, text style, dimension style, and hatch style. In all cases, the procedure is the same.

Here we use **MATCHPROP** to change some previously drawn text to the new Slanted style.

⊕ Select the Match Properties tool from the Standard Annotation toolbar, as shown in Figure 7-27.

COMMAND GRID	
Command	Matchprop
Alias	Ma
Menu	Modify
Tool	

Match Properties

Figure 7-27

AutoCAD prompts:

Select source object:

You can have many destination objects, but only one source object.

⊕ Select the text Roman Duplex, drawn in the last task in the Slanted style.

AutoCAD switches to the Match Properties cursor, shown in Figure 7-28.

Select destination object(s) or [Settings]:

At this point, you can limit the settings you want to match, or you can select destination objects, in which case all properties are matched.

⊕ Right-click and select Settings from the shortcut menu.

This opens the **Property Settings** dialog box, shown in Figure 7-29. The Basic Properties panel shows properties that can be changed and the settings that will be used based on the source object you have selected.

At the bottom, you see nine other properties in the Special Properties panel. These refer to properties and styles that have been defined in your drawing. If any one of these is not selected, Match Properties ignores these and matches only the properties selected.

⊕ Click OK to exit the dialog box.

AutoCAD returns to the screen with the same prompt as before.

⊕ Select the words Align and Vertical.

These two words are redrawn in the Slanted style, as shown in Figure 7-30. AutoCAD returns the Select destination objects prompt so that you can continue to select objects.

⊕ Press Enter to exit the command.

Figure 7-28

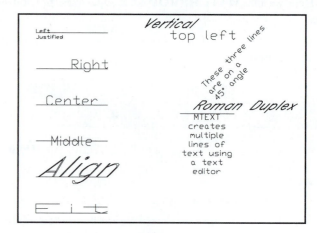

Figure 7-29

Figure 7-30

7-9 SCALING PREVIOUSLY DRAWN ENTITIES

> **GENERAL PROCEDURE**
> 1. Select the **Scale** tool from the dashboard.
> 2. Select objects.
> 3. Pick a base point.
> 4. Enter a scale factor.

Any object or group of objects can be scaled up or down using the **SCALE** command or the Grip edit scale mode. In this exercise, we practice scaling some of the text and lines that you have drawn on your screen. Remember, however, that there is no special relationship between **SCALE** and text and that other types of entities can be scaled just as easily.

⊕ Select the Scale tool from the dashboard, as shown in Figure 7-31.

   AutoCAD prompts you to select objects.

⊕ Use a crossing box (right to left) to select the set of six lines and text drawn in Section 7.1.

⊕ Right-click to end selection.

   You are prompted to pick a base point:

```
Specify base point:
```

COMMAND GRID	
Command	Scale
Alias	Sc
Menu	Modify
Tool	

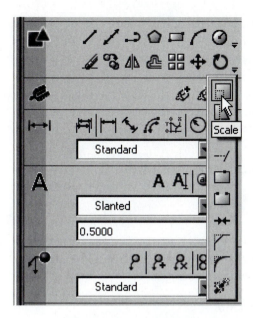

Figure 7-31

The concept of a base point in scaling is critical. Imagine for a moment that you are looking at a square and you want to shrink it using a scale-down procedure. All the sides will be shrunk the same amount, but how do you want this to happen? Should the lower left corner stay in place and the whole square shrink toward it? Or should everything shrink toward the center? Or toward some other point on or off the square? (See Figure 7-32.) This is what you specify when you pick a base point.

⊕ Pick a base point at the left end of the bottom line of the selected set (shown as Base point in Figure 7-33).

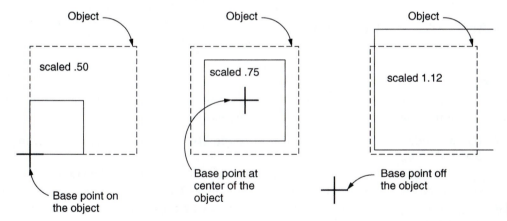

Figure 7-32

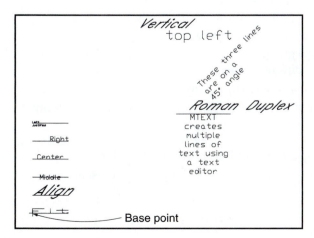

Figure 7-33

AutoCAD now needs to know how much to shrink or enlarge the objects you have selected:

`Specify scale factor or [Reference] <1.00>:`

We get to the reference method in a moment. When you enter a scale factor, all lengths, heights, and diameters in your set are multiplied by that factor and redrawn accordingly. Scale factors are based on a unit of 1. If you enter 0.5, objects are reduced to half their original size. If you enter 2, objects become twice as large.

⊕ Type ".5" ↵.

Your screen should now resemble Figure 7-33.

Scaling by Reference

This option can save you from doing the arithmetic to figure out scale factors. It is useful when you have a given length and you know how large you want that length to become after the scaling is done. For example, we know that the lines we just scaled are now 2.00. Let's say that we want to scale them again to become 2.33 long—a scale factor of 1.165 (2.33 divided by 2.00). But who wants to stop and figure that out? This could be done using the following procedure:

Note:
You can also perform reference scaling by pointing. In the foregoing procedure, you could pick the ends of the 2.00 line for the reference length and then pick the two endpoints of a 2.33 line for the new length.

1. Enter the **SCALE** command.
2. Select the lines.
3. Pick a base point.
4. Type "r" ↵ or select Reference from the short-cut menu.
5. Type "2" ↵ for the reference length.
6. Type "2.33" ↵ for the new length.

Scaling with Grips

Scaling with grips is very similar to scaling with the **SCALE** command. To illustrate this, try using grips to return the text you just scaled back to its original size.

⊕ Use a window or crossing box to select the six lines and the text drawn in Section 7.1 again.

There are several grips on the screen: three on each line and two on most of the text entities. Some of these overlap or duplicate each other.

⊕ Pick the grip at the lower left corner of the word Fit, the same point used as a base point in the last scaling procedure.

⊕ Right-click to open the shortcut menu and then select Scale.

⊕ Move the cursor slowly and observe the dragged image.

AutoCAD uses the selected grip point as the base point for scaling unless you specify that you want to pick a different base point.

Notice that you also have a reference option as in the **SCALE** command.

As in **SCALE,** the default method is to specify a scale factor by pointing or typing.

⊕ Type "2" ↵ or show a length of 2.00. (We reduced the objects by a factor of 0.5, so we need to enlarge them by a factor of 2 to return to the original size.)

Your text returns to its original size, and your screen should resemble Figure 7-30 again.

⊕ Press Esc to clear grips.

7-10 CREATING TABLES AND FIELDS

AutoCAD has many features for creating and managing tables and table data. Table styles can be created and named. Cells can be formatted with text, numerical data, formulas, and fields that update automatically. Data can be extracted from the current drawing into a table, or from an external spreadsheet. In this exercise we create a basic table showing three time and date formats and their appearances. We use a predefined Drawing Legend table style available on the **Tables** tool palette, which opens from the tables control panel on the dashboard. The table will include a title, two columns with headers, and three rows of data. We will also take the opportunity to demonstrate the use of fields, which can be inserted and easily updated when the information they hold changes.

⊞ To begin this drawing you can be in any AutoCAD drawing.

We will continue to use the text demonstration drawing created in this chapter, but will zoom into the area where we insert our table.

⊞ Zoom into an empty window of space in your drawing approximately 6.00 by 6.00.

⊞ Select the Tables button at the left side of the Tables control panel on the dashboard as shown in Figure 7-34.

Notice that this is not the same as the **Table...** tool to the right on the control panel, which opens an **Insert Table** dialog box. The **Tables** button illustrated opens the **Tables** tool palette, shown in Figure 7-35. The tool palette currently provides

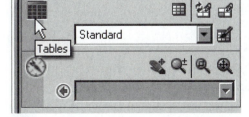

Figure 7-34   **Figure 7-35**

access to four predefined table styles. We will use the first one, labeled **Drawing Legend Table Style-Imperial.** A table is inserted from the tool palette by clicking and dragging into the drawing area.

⊕ Pick the first table on the tool palette, hold down the pick button, and drag into the drawing area.

AutoCAD shows a table that moves with your crosshairs as you drag it into place.

⊕ Select an insertion point, as shown in Figure 7-36.

Figure 7-36

⊕ Close the tool palette by picking the X in the upper right corner.

You now have an empty table in your drawing. In this table style, you see a title cell, six rows, and two columns of empty data cells. Next we fill in a title and column headers.

⊕ Click once in the title cell at the top of the table.

⊕ This opens the **Table Formatting** editor, shown in Figure 7-37. It consists of the **Table** toolbar at the top, the numbered row labels on the left, and the lettered column markers across the top of the table. The numbers and letters are for reference only. They are not permanently added to the table. The orange highlights show that the title cell is currently selected.

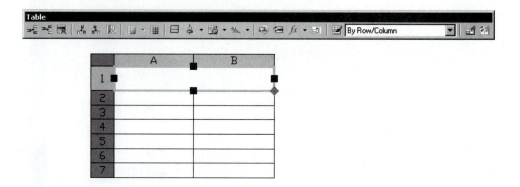

Figure 7-37

Before we enter text in this cell, it will be useful to be able to select a text format.

⊕ Double-click in the title cell.

This opens the **Text Formatting** editor, familiar from the **MTEXT** command. The text style in tables is independent of the current text style in the drawing. The Drawing Legend Table Style is defined with the Standard text style. So you should see Standard in the list box on the left of the toolbar. We will retain this style, but alter the text size. The Text Height list box is one box over to the right from the Text Style list.

⊕ Double-click in the Text Height list box and type "0.2" ⏎.

0.20 is now the text height.

⊕ For the title, type "Date and Time Formats" ⏎.

Notice that this title wraps around within the table cell. The text appears to cover up the header row, but this row will be "pushed down" when the title is completed.

⊕ When you have typed the title, press Tab.

Tabbing takes you to the next cell of the table. In this case it also moves the table cells down to make room for the two lines of the title. The text formatting toolbar remains so that you can enter and format text for the column headers.

⊕ In the first column header cell, type "Format" and then press Tab.

Tabbing takes you to the next header cell.

⊕ Type "Appearance" and press Tab.

Once again, tabbing takes you to the next table cell. You are now in the first column of the first data row. Notice that the column headings are centered in their cells, as shown in Figure 7-38. This middle center justification for the column headers is part of the definition of this table style.

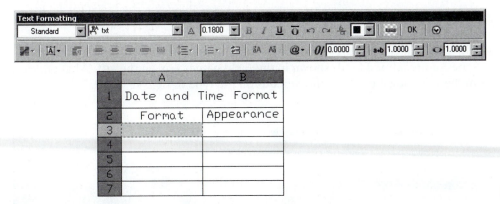

Figure 7-38

TIP   When entering data in table cells, you can move sequentially through cells using the **Tab** key. To reverse directions and move backward, hold down **Shift** while pressing **Tab.**

We will be entering time and date format symbols in the Format column and actual date and time fields in the Appearance column. The text in the Appearance column will be inserted as fields that can be updated automatically. We use dates and times because they demonstrate updating very readily.

⊕ In the first data row, first column, as shown in Figure 7-38, type "HH:mm," and press Tab.

This is the common symbol for time in an hours and minutes format. The uppercase HH indicates that this is 24-hour time (2:00 p.m. will appear as 14:00). Tabbing takes you to the second column, which we leave blank for the moment.

⊕ Press Tab again to move to the second data row.

The **Text Formatting** toolbar is still open and you are ready to enter text into the second data row, first column.

⊕ Type "h:mm:ss tt."

This symbolizes time in hours, minutes, and seconds. The tt stands for A.M. or P.M. You will see more of these symbols in a moment.

⊕ Press Tab to complete the cell and move to the second column.

⊕ Press Tab again to leave this cell blank and move to the third data row.

⊕ In the third data row, first column, type "M/d/yyyy" and press Tab once.

This represents a date in month, day, year format, with a four-place number for the year.

Inserting Fields

You are now in the third row, third column of the table and instead of typing text here, we will insert a date field, in month, day, year format. Then we return to the other rows in this column and enter time fields.

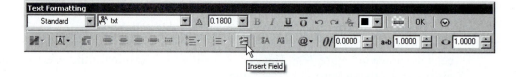

Figure 7-39

⊕ From the Text Formatting toolbar, select the Insert Field tool, shown in Figure 7-39.

This will open the **Field** dialog box, shown in Figure 7-40. There are many types of predefined fields shown in the Field names box on the left. What appears in the Format list on the right depends on the type of field selected.

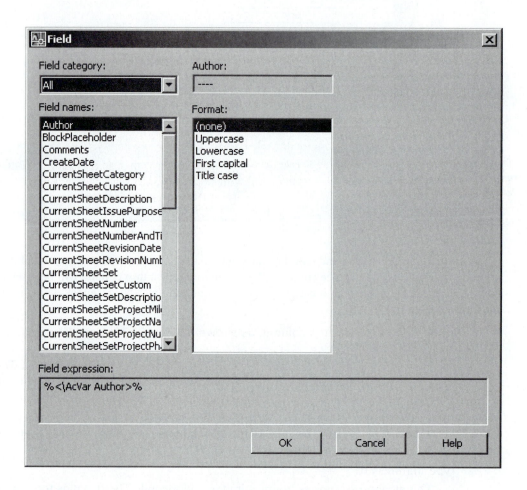

Figure 7-40

⊕ Select Date in the Field names list.

With Date selected, you see the Example formats for dates and times. There are many options and you will have to scroll to see them all. Notice that the Date format symbols for the selected format are displayed in the Date format box above the examples.

Date and Time Format	
Format	Appearance
HH:mm	
h:mm:ss tt	
M/d/yyyy	1/27/2007

Figure 7-41

⊕ Select the example at top of the list, which will be the current date in M/d/yyyy format.

⊕ With this format selected, click OK.

The date will be entered in the cell as shown in Figure 7-41. It will be displayed in gray, indicating that this is not ordinary text, but a field. If this drawing were to be plotted, the gray would not appear in the plot.

At this point we exit the table and return to the drawing.

> **Note:**
>
> Fields can be inserted anywhere in a drawing. To insert a field without a table, select Field from the Insert menu. This will call the **Field** dialog box and the rest of the process will be the same.

⊕ To return to the drawing, press Enter twice or click OK on the Text Formatting toolbar.

Your table should now resemble Figure 7-41.

We could have filled out all the table cells without leaving the table, but it is important to know how to enter data after a table has already been created. Different selection sequences will select cells in different ways. For example, if you pick a cell border, you will select the entire table. If you pick within a cell, you will select the cell, and open the Table format editor. Double-clicking within a cell will open the **Text Formatting** toolbar.

⊕ Click inside the first data row, second column, below the Appearance header.

The cell is highlighted with orange borders and the **Table Formatting** toolbar is displayed again.

⊕ Select the Insert Field tool from the middle of the toolbar.

This is the same tool and serves the same purpose as the tool on the **Text Formatting** toolbar. The **Field** dialog box opens. We select the HH:mm example to match the format we have indicated in the Format column. You will find this selection seventh up from the bottom of the examples list. It will have hours and minutes in 24-hour format, with no A.M. or P.M.

⊕ Highlight the HH:mm date format example.

When it is highlighted, HH:mm will appear in the Date Format box.

⊕ Click OK.

Finally, we use the **Table formatting** toolbar to delete the last two rows of the table before exiting. The **Delete Row(s)** button is at the left end of the toolbar, along with other basic table formatting tools. Open a window within the bottom two rows to select the four remaining cells together.

⊕ Click the Delete Row(s) tool.

⊕ Click anywhere in the drawing area to close the **Table** toolbar and return to the drawing.

Your table should now resemble Figure 7-42 with three fields in the three right-hand data cells.

Date and Time Format	
Format	Appearance
HH:mm	15:40
h:mm:ss tt	15:40:24
M/d/yyyy	1/27/2007

Figure 7-42

Updating Fields

Fields may be updated manually or automatically, individually or in groups. To update an individual field, double-click the field text to open the **Text Formatting** toolbar and right-click to open the shortcut menu. Select Update field from the shortcut menu. This also works with individual fields that are not in a table. Double-clicking on the field object will open the **Text Formatting** toolbar just as it does in a table.

For our demonstration we will update all the fields in our table at once, using the Tools menu.

⊕ Select any border of the table.

This will select the entire table. Grips will be added.

⊕ With the entire table selected, open the Tools menu and select Update Fields, at the bottom of the second section of the menu.

Notice how the two time fields are updated, while the date field remains the same.

Fields also update automatically when certain things occur, as controlled by settings in the **User Preferences** dialog box. To reach these settings, select Options from the **Tools** menu. Select the **User Preferences** tab and then the **Field Update Settings** button in the Fields panel. Fields may be automatically updated when a file is opened, saved, plotted, regenerated, or transmitted over the Internet. Any combination of these may be selected. By default, all are selected.

Note: There may be times when you wish to convert a field to regular text. This could happen if you were working on a project for some time and wished to set the date permanently on completion, for example. To convert a field to text, double-click the field to open the **Text Formatting** toolbar, right-click to open the shortcut menu, and select Convert Field to Text.

7-11 USING AUTOCAD TEMPLATES, BORDERS, AND TITLE BLOCKS

Now that you have learned how to create text in this chapter and how to use paper space layouts in the last chapter, you can take full advantage of the AutoCAD templates with predrawn borders and title blocks. In this exercise we create a new drawing using an AutoCAD D-size template, add some simple geometry, and add some text to the title block. The work you do

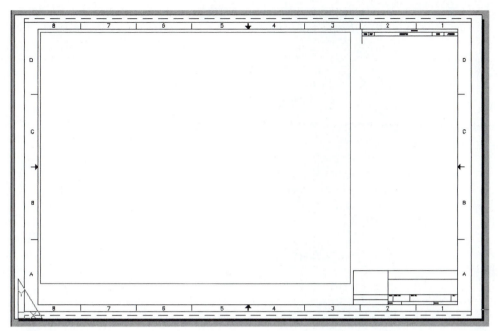

Figure 7-43

here can be saved and used as a start to completing Drawing 7-2, the gauges at the end of the chapter.

⊞ Select the QNew tool from the Standard Annotation toolbar.

⊞ In the familiar Select template dialog box, select Tutorial-iMfg.

⊞ With Tutorial-iMfg showing in the File name box, click Open.

This opens a new drawing in a paper space layout with a predrawn border and title block, as illustrated in Figure 7-43. Notice the paper space icon at the lower left of the screen and the **D-Size Layout** tab. Next we switch to model space.

⊞ Click the Model tab.

In model space you see a blank screen. Turning on the grid gives you a better sense of the drawing space.

⊞ Turn on the grid.

The grid appears at the left side of the drawing area.

⊞ Zoom All to center the grid.

By moving the cursor to the lower left and upper right corners of the grid, you notice that the model space limits for this drawing are set at (0,0) and (12,9). Note that these limits apply to model space limits only. The paper space limits are different and are set up to print to a D-size drawing sheet. As we have seen, model space and paper space limits are usually completely unrelated. The current model space limits are fine for our purposes. We are going to take the first step in creating the geometry of Drawing 7-2 by drawing a 5.00 diameter circle.

⊞ Enter the CIRCLE command.

⊞ Create a 2.50 radius circle with center point at (3.00,5.00), as shown in Figure - 7-44.

As you do this, notice also that having started this drawing with a different template, none of the layers or other settings you have previously created in your 1B template are defined in this drawing. The units are 3-place decimal and the snap is set to 0.10.

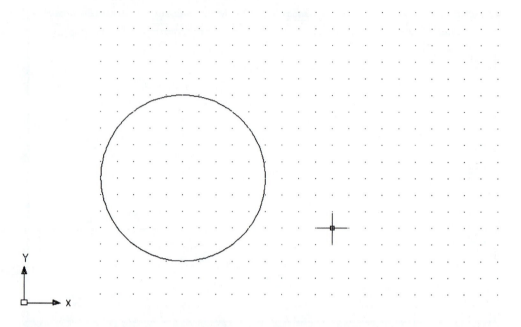

Figure 7-44

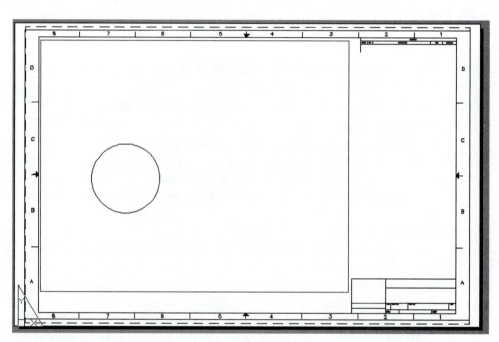

Figure 7-45

Now we return to the paper space layout.

⊞ Click the D-size Layout tab.

You return to paper space with the circle added as shown in Figure 7-45. Take a minute to explore the layout. The blue bordered area where the circle is drawn is actually a viewport.

⊞ Double-click inside the border.

The border is highlighted by bolding, indicating that the viewport is active. The paper space icon disappears and the UCS icon is displayed, indicating that you are in the viewport and do not currently have access to paper space objects.

⊞ Run your cursor over the circle.

The circle is shown with preview highlighting, indicating that you have access to the model space objects within the viewport.

⊕ Double-click outside the border.

The paper space icon returns and the viewport border is no longer bold. You are now back in paper space. Next we add two items of text to the title block. To facilitate this we make some changes to the paper space grid and snap.

⊕ Click the Grid button to turn on the paper space grid.

⊕ Click the Snap button to turn on Snap in paper space.

Notice that the paper space grid in this template is displaying dots at 2.50 intervals.

⊕ Move the crosshairs and watch the coordinate display.

You see that snap is set to 0.500.

> **Note:**
> When you pass your cursor over any part of the title block in paper space, all of the border and related numbers and symbols will be highlighted. This is because the entire object has been defined as a block.

FOR MORE DETAILS   Blocks are discussed in Chapter 10.

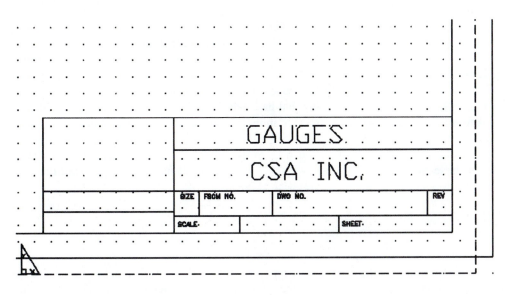

Figure 7-46

⊕ Move the crosshairs to the upper right corner of the "paper."

Notice that the layout emulates a 33.0 × 22.0 D-size drawing sheet. We are going to create text in two of the areas of the title block, as shown in Figure 7-46. However, the current snap setting makes this difficult.

⊕ Open the Drafting Settings dialog box.

The grid is set to 0.500, but the Adaptive grid setting is checked, causing AutoCAD to display the larger 2.500 grid. This effect will change when we zoom in momentarily.

⊕ Change the snap setting to .250.

⊕ Click OK to exit the dialog box.

⊕ Zoom into a window around the title block, as shown in Figure 7-46.

 You are now ready to add text.

⊕ Pick the Single Line Text tool from the dashboard and pick a start point near (28.000,2.500), as shown.

⊕ Specify a text height of .25 and a rotation angle of 0.

⊕ Type "Gauges" ↵.

⊕ Press Enter twice to exit TEXT.

⊕ Repeat TEXT and type "CSA INC." at (28.000,1.750), as shown in Figure 7-46.

⊕ Press Enter twice to exit TEXT.

⊕ Zoom All to view the complete layout.

 There you go. You are well on your way to completing Drawing 7-2, complete with title block.

CHAPTER TEST QUESTIONS

Questions

1. What is the main difference between **TEXT** and **MTEXT**?

2. You have drawn two lines of text using **TEXT** and have left the command to do some editing. You discover that a third line of text should have been entered with the first two lines. What procedure allows you to add the third line of text efficiently so that it is spaced and aligned with the first two, as if you had never left **TEXT**?

3. What is the difference between center-justified text and middle-justified text?

4. What is the purpose of %% in text entry?

5. In the **MTEXT** command, what information does Auto-CAD take from the two corners of the rectangle you specify before entering text? What else is needed to predict how AutoCAD interprets these point selections?

6. What aspect of text can be changed with **DDEDIT?** What aspects of text can be changed with **PROPERTIES?** What is the purpose of **MATCHPROP?**

7. How do you check all the spelling in your drawing at once?

8. What is the difference between a font and a style?

9. What can happen if you choose the wrong base point when using the **SCALE** command?

10. How would you use **SCALE** to change a 3.00 line to 2.75?

11. You have completed the outline of a table in your drawing, but have left the TABLE command. How would you reenter an individual cell of the table and insert a field in that cell?

12. You wish to use an AutoCAD-provided border and title block for your drawing. Where would you find the one you wish to use?

Drawing Problems

1. Draw a 6 × 6 square. Draw the word Top on top of the square, 0.4 unit high, centered on the midpoint of the top side of the square.

2. Draw the word Left 0.4 unit high, centered on the left side of the square.

3. Draw the word Right 0.4 unit high, centered on the right side of the square.

4. Draw the word Bottom 0.4 unit high, below the square so that the top of the text is centered on the midpoint of the bottom side of the square.

5. Draw the words This is the middle inside the square, 0.4 unit high, so that the complete text wraps around within a 2-unit width and is centered on the center point of the square.

WWW Exercise 7 (Optional)

In Chapter 7 of our companion website, we ask you to explore the Web and bring back information on an important innovator in the field of architecture. We define your task and give you two links to get you started. We also give you another design challenge and, as always, the self-scoring test for this chapter. So, when you are ready, complete the following:

- Make sure that you are connected to your Internet service provider.
- Type "browser" ↵ or open your system browser from the Windows taskbar.
- If necessary, navigate to our companion website at prenhall.com/dixriley.

Happy hunting!

CHAPTER PROJECTS

Drawing 7-1: Title Block

This title block gives you practice in using a variety of text styles and sizes. You might want to save it and use it as a title block for future drawings. In Chapter 10, we show you how to insert one drawing into another, so you can incorporate this title block into any drawing.

QTY REQ'D	D E S C R I P T I O N		P A R T N O.		ITEM NO.

BILL   OF   MATERIALS

UNLESS OTHERWISE SPECIFIED DIMENSIONS ARE IN INCHES	DRAWN BY: *Your Name*	DATE			

CSA INC.

REMOVE ALL BURRS & BREAK SHARP EDGES — APPROVED BY:

ISSUED: DRAWING TITLE:

TOLERANCES
FRACTIONS ± 1/64   DECIMALS
ANGLES   ± 0%%D-15'   XX ± .01
XXX ± .005

MATERIAL: FINISH:

SIZE	CODE IDENT NO.	DRAWING NO.	REV.
C	38178		

SCALE: DATE: SHEET   OF

Drawing Suggestions

GRID = 1
SNAP = 0.0625

- Make ample use of **TRIM** as you draw the line patterns of the title block. Take your time and make sure that at least the major divisions are in place before you start entering text into the boxes.
- Set to the text layer before entering text.
- Use **TEXT** with all the Standard, 0.09, left-justified text.
- Remember that once you have defined a style, you can make it current in the **TEXT** command. This saves you from restyling more than necessary.
- Use %%D for the degree symbol and %%P for the plus or minus symbol.

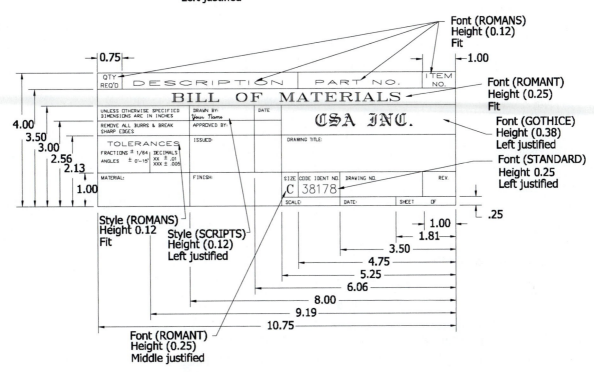

TITLE BLOCK

Drawing 7-1

Drawing 7-2: Gauges

This drawing teaches you some typical uses of the **SCALE** and **DDEDIT** commands. Some of the techniques used are not obvious, so read the suggestions carefully.

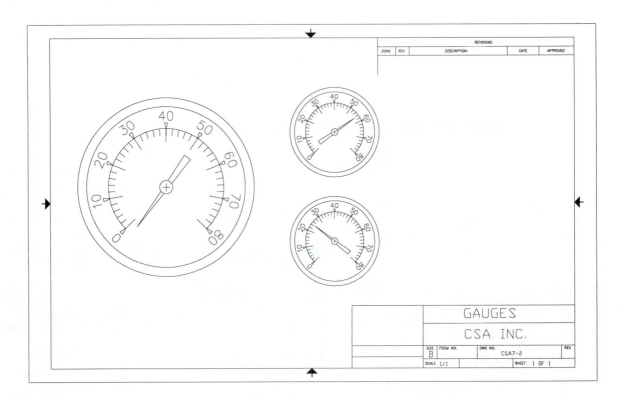

Drawing Suggestions

GRID = 0.5
SNAP = 0.125

- Draw three concentric circles at diameters of 5.0, 4.5, and 3.0. The bottom of the 3.0 circle can be trimmed later.
- Zoom in to draw the arrow-shaped tick at the top of the 3.0 circle. Then draw the 0.50 vertical line directly below it and the number 40 (middle-justified text) above it.
- These three objects can be arrayed to the left and right around the perimeter of the 3.0 circle using angles of +135 and −135 as shown.
- Use **DDEDIT** to change the arrayed numbers into 0, 10, 20, 30, and so on. You can do all of these without leaving the command.
- Draw the 0.25 vertical tick directly on top of the 0.50 mark at the top center and array it left and right. There should be 20 marks each way.
- Draw the needle horizontally across the middle of the dial.
- Make two copies of the dial; use **SCALE** to scale them down as shown. Then move them into their correct positions.
- Rotate the three needles into positions as shown.

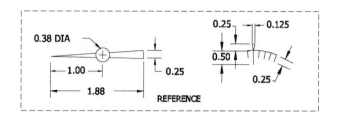

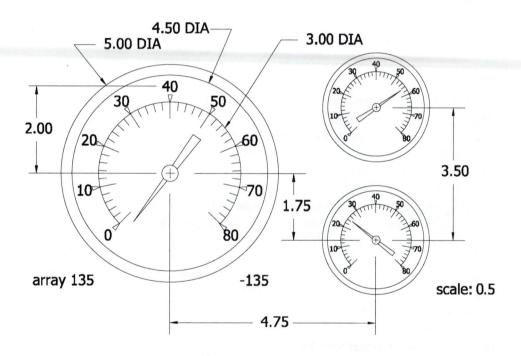

GAUGES
Drawing 7-2

Drawing 7-3: Stamping

This drawing is trickier than it appears. There are many ways that it can be done. The way we have chosen not only works well but also makes use of a number of the commands and techniques you have learned in the last two chapters. Notice that a change in limits is needed to take advantage of some of the suggestions.

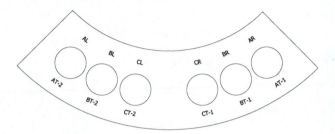

Drawing Suggestions

```
GRID = 0.50
SNAP = 0.25
LIMITS = (0,0)(24,18)
```

- Draw two circles, of radius 10.25 and 6.50, centered at about (13,15). These are trimmed later.
- Draw a vertical line down from the center point to the outer circle. We copy and rotate this line to form the ends of the stamping.
- Use the Rotate copy mode of the grip edit system to create copies of the line rotated 45 degrees and −45 degrees. (The coordinate display shows 315 degrees.)
- Trim the lines and the circles to form the outline of the stamping.
- Draw a 1.50-diameter circle in the center of the stamping, 8.50 down from (13,15). Draw middle-justified text, AR, 7.25 down, and AT-1 down 9.75 from (13,15).
- Follow the procedure given in the next subsection to create offset copies of the circle and text; then use **DDEDIT** to modify all text to agree with the drawing.

Grip Copy Modes with Offset Snap Locations

Here is a good opportunity to try another grip edit feature. If you hold down the **Shift** key while picking multiple copy points, AutoCAD is constrained to place copies only at points offset from each other the same distance as your first two points. For example, try the following steps:

1. Select the circle and the text.
2. Select any grip to initiate grip editing.
3. Select Rotate from the shortcut menu.
4. Type "b" or select Base point from the shortcut menu.
5. Pick the center of the stamping (13,15) as the base point.
6. Type "c" or select Copy from the shortcut menu.
7. Hold down the **Shift** key and move the cursor to rotate a copy 11 degrees from the original.
8. Keep holding down the **Shift** key as you move the cursor to create other copies. All copies are offset 11 degrees.

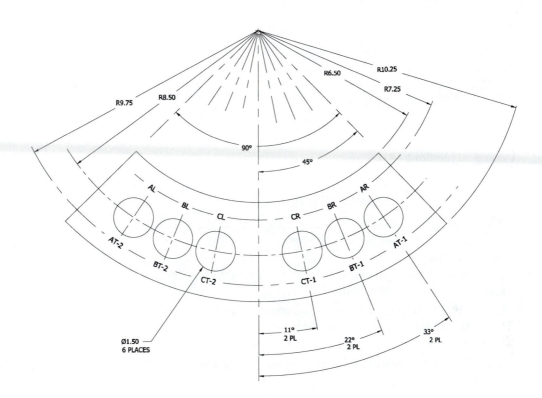

STAMPING
Drawing 7-3

Drawing 7-4: Control Panel

Done correctly, this drawing gives you a good feel for the power of the commands you now have available to you. Be sure to take advantage of combinations of **ARRAY** and **DDEDIT** as described. Also, read the suggestion on moving the origin before you begin. Moving the origin in this drawing makes it easier to read the dimensions, which are given in ordinate form measured from the (0,0) point at the lower left corner of the object.

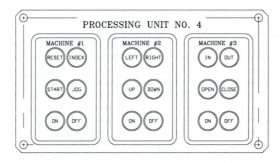

Drawing Suggestions

GRID = 0.50
SNAP = 0.0625

- After drawing the chamferred outer rectangle, draw the double outline of the left button box, and fillet the corners. Notice the different fillet radii.
- Draw the **On** button with its text at the bottom left of the box. Then array it 2 × 3 for the other buttons in the box.
- Use **DDEDIT** to change the lower right button text to Off and draw the **MACHINE** # text at the top of the box.
- **ARRAY** the box 1 × 3 to create the other boxes.
- Use **DDEDIT** to change text for other buttons and machine numbers as shown.

Moving the Origin with the UCS Command

The dimensions of this drawing are shown in ordinate form, measured from a single point of origin in the lower left-hand corner. In effect, this establishes a new coordinate origin. If we move our origin to match this point, then we can read dimension values directly from the coordinate display. This could be done by setting the lower left-hand limits to (−1, −1). However, it can be completed more efficiently using the **UCS** command to establish a user coordinate system with the origin at a point you specify. User coordinate systems are discussed in depth in Chapter 12. For now, here is a simple procedure:

1. Type "ucs."
2. Type "o" for the Origin option.
3. Point to the new origin.

That's all there is to it. Move your cursor to the new origin and watch the coordinate display. It should show 0.00,0.00,0.00, and all values are measured from there.

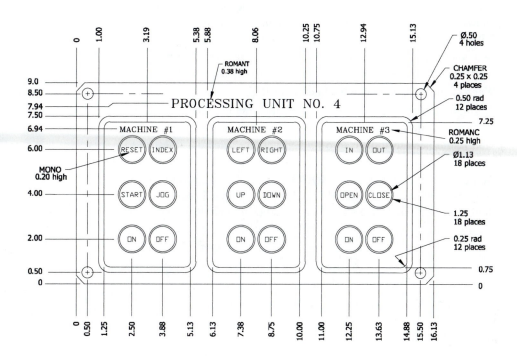

CONTROL PANEL
Drawing 7-4

Drawing 7-5: Tower

This architectural drawing takes some time, and you utilize many commands that you have learned in this and previous chapters. Notice that the settings are quite different from our standard template, so be sure to change them before beginning.

Drawing Suggestions

```
UNITS = Architectural Smallest fraction = 1
GRID = 10'
SNAP = 1'
```

- This drawing can be transferred, using the proper scale, from the book to your AutoCAD. You can use the scale provided on the drawing or use an architectural scale with the setting of 1/32″ = 1′. Either transfer method produces similar results.
- Whatever order you choose for doing this drawing, we suggest that you make ample use of **COPY, ARRAY, TRIM,** and **OFFSET.**
- Keep Ortho on, except to draw lines at an angle.
- With Snap set at 1/16, it is easy to copy and array lines and shapes, as you do frequently to reproduce the many rectangular shapes.
- You might need to turn Snap off when you are selecting lines to copy, but be sure to turn it on again to specify displacements.
- Notice that you can use polar **ARRAY** effectively to draw the text in a circle and then use **DDEDIT** to change the text. Choose a text font that is similar to that shown. (We used Dutch 801 Rm BT.)

TOWER
Drawing 7-5

Scale

This drawing courtesy of Matt Rose

Drawing 7-6: Koch Snowflake

The Koch Snowflake design can be done in numerous ways, all involving similar techniques of reference scaling, rotating, and polar arraying. We give you a few suggestions and hints, but you are largely on your own in solving this visual design puzzle.

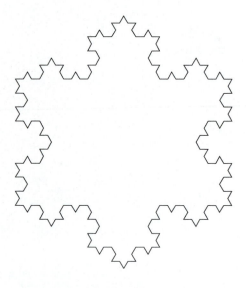

Drawing Suggestions

- Begin by creating an equilateral triangle. Because it is important to know the center point of this triangle, construct it from a circle, as shown. The radial lines are drawn by arraying a single line from the center point three times in a 360-degree polar array.

- After drawing the initial equilateral triangle you make frequent use of reference scaling.

- The number 3 is important throughout this design. Consider how you will use the number 3 in the reference scaling option.

- You will have frequent use for center, intersection, and midpoint object snaps.

- Do not move the original triangle so that you can always locate its center point. There are at least two ways to find the center point of other triangles you create. One involves constructing a 3P circle and another involves three construction lines.

- A lot of trimming and erasing is required to create the final design.

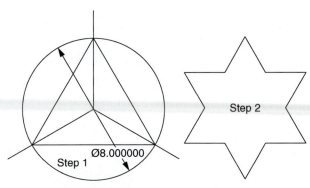

Step 1
Ø8.000000

Equilateral Triangle

Step 2

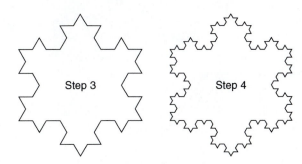

Step 3

Step 4

KOCH SNOWFLAKE
Drawing 7-6

Dimensions

8

Chapter Objectives

- Creating and Saving a Dimension Style
- Drawing Linear Dimensions
- Drawing Multiple Linear Dimensions: QDIM
- Drawing Ordinate Dimensions
- Drawing Angular Dimensions
- Dimensioning Arcs and Circles
- Dimensioning with Multileaders
- Changing Dimension Text
- Using Associative Dimensions
- Using the HATCH Command
- Scaling Dimensions Between Paper Space and Model Space

INTRODUCTION

The ability to dimension your drawings and add crosshatch patterns greatly enhances the professional appearance and utility of your work. AutoCAD's dimensioning features form a complex system of commands, subcommands, and variables that automatically measure objects and draw dimension text and extension lines. With AutoCAD's dimensioning tools and variables, you can create dimensions in a wide variety of formats, and these formats can be saved as styles. The time saved by not drawing each dimension object line by line is among the most significant advantages of CAD.

8-1 CREATING AND SAVING A DIMENSION STYLE

GENERAL PROCEDURE

1. Select the **Dimension Style** tool from the dashboard.
2. Click **New.**
3. Give your new dimension style a name.
4. Click **OK** to exit the **Create New Dimension Style** dialog box.
5. Select settings for Lines, Symbols and Arrows, Text, Fit, Primary Units, Alternate Units, and Tolerances.
6. Click **OK** to exit.

Dimensioning in AutoCAD is highly automated and very easy compared to manual dimensioning. To achieve a high degree of automation while still allowing for the broad range of flexibility required to cover all dimension styles, the AutoCAD dimensioning system is necessarily complex. In the exercises that follow, we guide you through the system, show you some of the options available, and give you a solid foundation for understanding how to get what you want from AutoCAD dimensioning. We create a basic dimension style and use it to draw standard dimensions and tolerances. We leave it to you to explore the many possible variations.

In AutoCAD, it is best to begin by naming and defining a dimension style. A *dimension style* is a set of dimension variable settings that control the text and geometry of all types of AutoCAD dimensions. We recommend that you create the new dimension style in your template drawing and save it. Then you do not have to make these changes again when you start new drawings.

⊕ To begin this exercise, open the 1B template drawing.

This is the first time that we have modified our template since Chapter 4. To modify it you must open it like any drawing. Remember to look for this file in the Template folder; it has a .dwt file extension. Use the **OPEN** command to access the **Select File** dialog box. Select Drawing Template File (*.dwt) from the File of type drop-down list. This automatically opens the Template folder. Select 1B.dwt from the list or thumbnail gallery.

We make changes in dimension style settings in the template drawing so that all dimensions showing distances are presented with two decimal places and angular dimensions have no decimals. These become the default dimension settings in any drawing created using the 1B template. 1B already uses two decimal places for drawing units, but this setting does not carry over to dimensioning.

⊕ Select the Dimension Style tool from the dashboard, as shown in Figure 8-1.

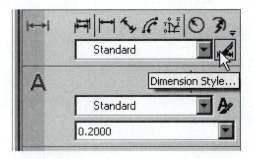

Figure 8-1

This opens the **Dimension Style Manager** shown in Figure 8-2. The current dimension style is called Standard. As with Text, the other predefined style is Annotative. Annotative is a new property in AutoCAD 2008 that allows dimensions and

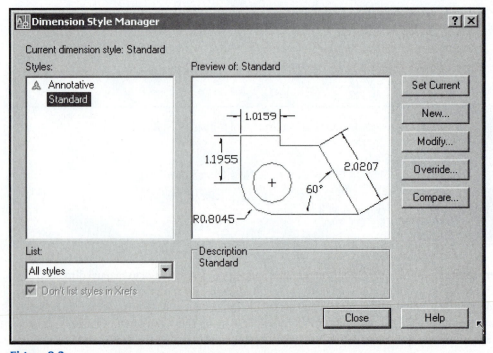

Figure 8-2

other annotative objects to be scaled to show at the correct size in paper layouts. The only difference between the Standard and Annotative styles is the addition of the Annotative property to dimensions drawn in that style. We will explore this in Section 8.11.

To the right of the Styles box is a preview that presents a sample image showing many of the settings of the style highlighted in the Styles box. The style being previewed is also named at the top of the box. The preview image is updated any time you make a change in a dimension setting.

Below the Preview image is a Description box. Right now, the description simply indicates that the style is Standard. We create our new style based on the Standard style.

⊞ Check to see that Standard is selected in the Styles box.

Now we proceed to create a new style based on the Standard style. To the right of the preview is a set of five buttons, the second of which is the **New** button.

⊞ Click the New button.

This opens the small **Create New Dimension Style** dialog box shown in Figure 8-3.

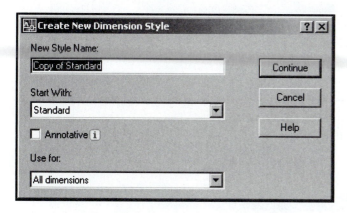

Figure 8-3

⊞ If necessary, double-click in the New Style Name edit box to highlight the words Copy of Standard.

⊞ Type "1B" ↵.

We chose this name to associate it with the template file.

This creates the new dimension style and takes us into the **New Dimension Style** dialog box, shown in Figure 8-4. Here there are seven tabs that allow us to make many changes in Dimension Lines, Symbols and Arrows, Text, Fit, Primary Units, Alternate Units, and Tolerances.

⊞ Click the Primary Units tab.

This brings up the Primary Units window, shown in Figure 8-5. There are adjustments available for linear and angular units. The lists under units and angles are similar to the lists used in the **Drawing Units** dialog box. In the Linear dimensions panel, Unit format should show Decimal. In the Angular dimensions panel, Units format should show Decimal Degrees. If for any reason these are not showing in your box, you should make these changes now. For our purposes, all we need to change is the number of decimal places showing in the Precision box. By default, it is 0.0000. We change it to 0.00.

⊞ Click the arrow to the right of the Precision box in the Linear dimensions panel.

This opens a list of precision settings ranging from 0 to 0.00000000.

⊞ Select 0.00 from the list.

This closes the list box and shows 0.00 as the selected precision. Notice the change in the preview image, which now shows two-place decimals. At this point, we are ready to complete this part of the procedure by returning to the Dimension Style Manager.

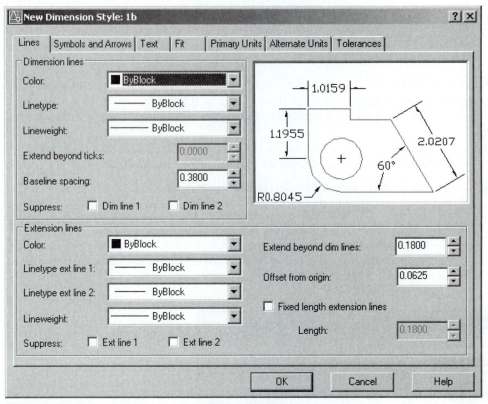

Figure 8-4

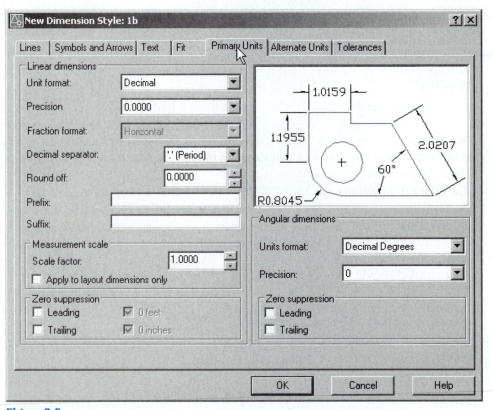

Figure 8-5

Before leaving the **New Dimension Style** dialog box, open the other tabs and look at the large variety of dimension features that can be adjusted. Each of the many options changes a dimension variable setting. Dimension variables have names and can be changed at the command line by typing in the name and entering a new value, but the dialog box makes the process much easier and the preview images give you immediate visual feedback.

In the **Lines** tab and **Symbols and Arrows** tab you find options for changing the size and positioning of dimension geometry. In Text, you are able to adjust the look and placement of dimension text. This tab includes the option of selecting different text styles previously defined in the drawing. In Fit, you can tell Auto-CAD how to manage situations in which there is a tight fit that creates some ambiguity about how dimension geometry and text should be arranged. This is also where the Annotative property is selected. Primary Units, as you know, lets you specify the units in which dimensions are displayed. Alternate Units offers the capacity to include a secondary unit specification along with the primary dimension unit. For example, you can use this feature to give dimensions in both inches and centimeters. Tolerances are added to dimension specifications to give the range of acceptable values in, for example, a machining process. The **Tolerances** tab gives several options for how tolerances are displayed.

⊕ Click OK to exit the New Dimension Style dialog box.

Back in the **Dimension Style Manager** dialog box you can see that 1B has been added to the list of styles.

At this point, you should have at least the 1B, Annotative, and Standard dimension styles defined in your drawing. 1B should be selected and will be the current style. This is indicated by the line at the top of the dialog box that says Current dimension style: 1B. You can select the other styles in the Styles box and see descriptions in the description box relating these styles to the current style. Try it.

⊕ Select Annotative in the Description box.

The description should now read "1B + Overall Scale = 0.00, Precision = 4, Tol Precision = 4." The description shows that Annotative is the same as 1B, but with a variable overall scale and different precision for dimensions and tolerances.

Conversely, if you set Annotative as the current style, the description of 1B will be relative to Annotative. Try it.

⊕ With Annotative selected in the Styles box, click the Set Current button.

Annotative now appears in the Description box.

⊕ Select 1B in the Styles box again.

The description now reads, "Annotative + Overall Scale = 1.00, Precision = 2, Tol Precision = 2." 1B is the same as Annotative, but with a fixed scale and two-place decimals.

⊕ Click Set Current to set 1B as the current dimension style again.

⊕ Click Close to exit the Dimension Style Manager dialog box.

⊕ Save and close template drawing 1B.

⊕ Create a new drawing using the 1B template.

If the new drawing is opened with the 1B template, the 1B dimension style is the current dimension style. 1B shows in the dimension style list box on the Dimension control panel of the dashboard.

8-2 DRAWING LINEAR DIMENSIONS

GENERAL PROCEDURE

1. Select the **Linear** button from the dashboard.
2. Select an object or show two extension line origins.
3. Show the dimension line location.

AutoCAD has many commands and features that aid in the drawing of dimensions, as evidenced by the fact that there is an entire pull-down menu devoted to dimensioning features. In this exercise, you create some basic linear dimensions in the now-current 1B style.

⊕ To prepare for this exercise, draw a 3.00,4.00,5.00 triangle, a 4.00 vertical line, and a 6.00 horizontal line above the middle of the display, as shown in Figure 8-6.

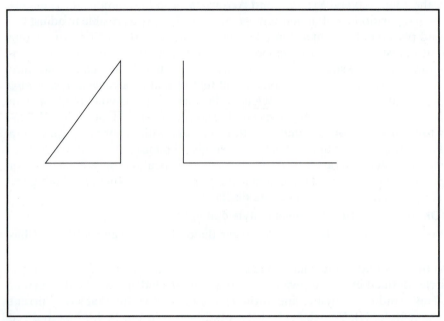

Figure 8-6

We begin by adding dimensions to the triangle.

⊕ After creating these objects, open the Layer drop-down list and make the Dim layer current.

The dimensioning commands are streamlined and efficient. Their full names, however, are long. They all begin with dim and are followed by the name of a type of dimension (e.g., **DIMLINEAR, DIMALIGNED,** and **DIMANGULAR**). Use the dashboard or the Dimension menu to avoid typing these names.

We begin by placing a linear dimension below the base of the triangle.

⊕ Select the Linear tool from the Dimension control panel of the dashboard, as shown in Figure 8-7.

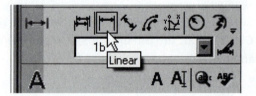

Figure 8-7

This initiates the DIMLINEAR command, with the following prompt appearing in the command area:

```
Specify first extension line origin or <select object>:
```

There are two ways to proceed at this point. One is to show where the extension lines should begin, and the other is to select the object you want to dimension and let AutoCAD position the extension lines. In most simple applications, the latter method is faster.

⊕ Press Enter to indicate that you will select an object.

AutoCAD replaces the crosshairs with a pick box and prompts for your selection:

Select object to dimension:

⊕ Select the horizontal line at the bottom of the triangle, as shown by Point 1 in Figure 8-8.

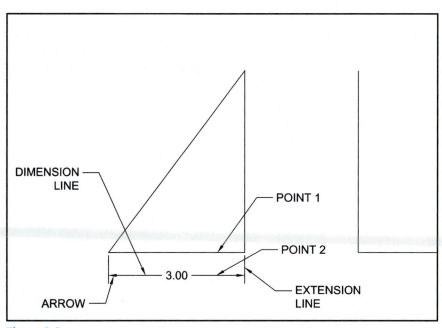

Figure 8-8

AutoCAD immediately creates a dimension, including extension lines, dimension line, and text, that you can drag away from the selected line. AutoCAD places the dimension line and text where you indicate, but keeps the text centered between the extension lines. The prompt is as follows:

Specify dimension line location or
[MText/Text/Angle/Horizontal/Vertical/Rotated]:

In the default sequence, you simply show the location of the dimension. If you wish to alter the text content, you can do so using the Mtext or Text options, or you can change it later with a command called **DIMEDIT.** Angle, Horizontal, and Vertical allow you to specify the orientation of the text. Horizontal text is the default for linear dimensions. Rotated allows you to rotate the complete dimension so that the extension lines move out at an angle from the object being dimensioned. (Text remains horizontal.)

⊕ Pick a location about 0.50 below the triangle, as shown by Point 2 in Figure 8-8.

Bravo! You have completed your first dimension. (Notice that our figure and others in this chapter are shown zoomed in on the relevant object for the sake of clarity. You can zoom or not, as you like.)

At this point, take a good look at the dimension you have just drawn to see what it consists of. As in Figure 8-8, you should see the following components: two extension lines, two arrows, a dimension line on each side of the text, and the text itself.

Notice also that AutoCAD has automatically placed the extension line origins a short distance away from the triangle base. (You might need to zoom in to see this.) This distance is controlled by a dimension variable called dimexo, which can be changed in the **Modify Dimension Style** dialog box, **Lines** tab, and **Symbols and Arrows** tab in the Extension lines panel. The setting is called Offset from origin.

Next, we place a vertical dimension on the right side of the triangle. You can see that **DIMLINEAR** handles both horizontal and vertical dimensions.

⊕ Repeat the DIMLINEAR command.

You are prompted for extension line origins as before:

    Specify first extension line origin or <select object:

This time we show the extension line origins manually.

⊕ Pick the right-angle corner at the lower right of the triangle, Point 1 in Figure 8-9.

AutoCAD prompts for a second point:

    Specify second extension line origin:

Even though you are manually specifying extension line origins, it is not necessary to show the exact point where you want the line to start. AutoCAD automatically sets the dimension lines slightly away from the line as before, according to the setting of the dimexo dimension variable.

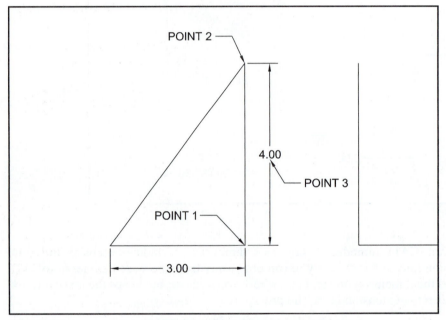

Figure 8-9

⊕ Pick the top intersection of the triangle, Point 2 in Figure 8-9.

From here on, the procedure is the same as before. You should have a dimension to drag into place, and the following prompt:

    Specify dimension line location or
    [Mtext/Text/Angle/Horizontal/Vertical/Rotated]:

⊕ Pick a point 0.50 to the right of the triangle, Point 3 in Figure 8-9.

Your screen should now include the vertical dimension, as shown in Figure 8-9.

Now let's place a dimension on the diagonal side of the triangle. For this, we need the **DIMALIGNED** command.

⊕ Select the Aligned tool from the dashboard, as shown in Figure 8-10.

⊕ Press Enter, indicating that you will select an object.

AutoCAD gives you the pick box and prompts you to select an object to dimension.

⊕ Select the hypotenuse of the triangle.

⊕ Pick a point approximately 0.50 above and to the left of the line.

Your screen should resemble Figure 8-11. Notice that AutoCAD retains horizontal text in aligned and vertical dimensions as the default.

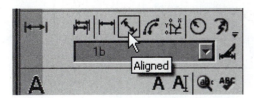

Figure 8-10

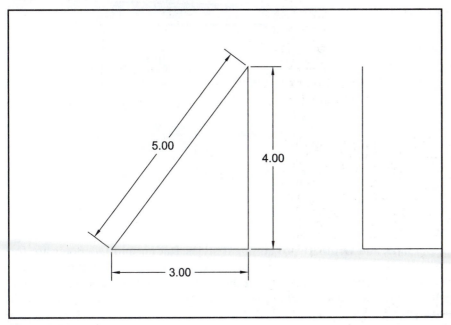

Figure 8-11

8-3 Drawing Multiple Linear Dimensions: QDIM

> **GENERAL PROCEDURE**
> 1. Select the **Quick Dimension** tool from the dashboard.
> 2. Select objects to dimension. (Steps 1 and 2 can be reversed if noun/verb editing is enabled.)
> 3. Specify a multiple dimension type.
> 4. Show dimension line location.

QDIM automates the creation of certain types of multiple dimension formats. With this command, you can create a whole series of related dimensions with a few mouse clicks. To introduce **QDIM,** we create a continuous dimension series dimensioning the bottom of the triangle, the space between the triangle and the line, and the length of the line itself. Then we edit the series to show several points along the line. Finally, we change the dimensions on the line from a continuous series to a baseline series. In later tasks, we return to QDIM to create other types of multiple dimension sets.

⊞ Erase the 3.00 dimension from the bottom of the triangle.

⊞ Select the bottom of the triangle and the 6.00 horizontal line to the right of the triangle.

　　Noun/verb editing allows you to select objects before entering **QDIM.** Your selected lines are highlighted and have grips showing.

⊞ Select the Quick Dimension tool from the dashboard, as shown in Figure 8-12.

　　AutoCAD prompts

```
Specify dimension line position, or
[Continuous/Staggered/Baseline/Ordinate/Radius/Diameter/
datumPoint/Edit/seTtings] <Continuous>:
```

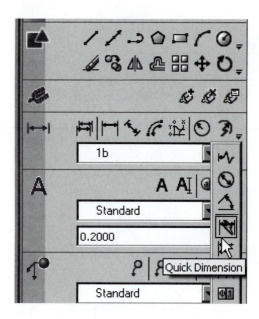

Figure 8-12

The options here are various forms of multiple dimensions. Continuous, Staggered, Baseline, and Ordinate are all linear styles. Radius and Diameter are for dimensioning circles and arcs. Datum Point is used to change the point from which a set of linear dimensions is measured, Edit has several functions we explore in a moment, and Settings allows a choice of how associated dimensions created with **QDIM** work.

Continuous dimensions are positioned end to end, as shown in Figure 8-13. AutoCAD creates three linear dimensions at once and positions them end to end.

⊕ Select a point about 0.5 units below the triangle, as shown in Figure 8-13.

Next we edit the dimension on the right, so that the line length is measured to several different lengths.

⊕ Repeat QDIM.

⊕ Select the dimension at the right, below the 6.00 line.

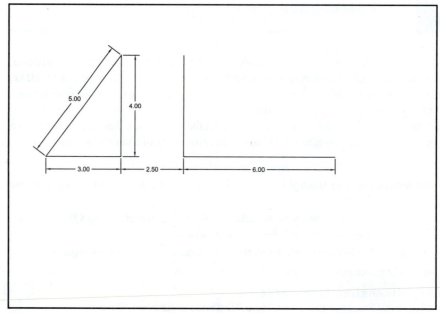

Figure 8-13

Notice that this dimension can be selected independently. The three continuous dimensions just created are separate objects, even though they were created simultaneously.

⊕ Right-click to end object selection.

AutoCAD gives you a single dimension to drag into place. If you pick a point now, the selected 6.00 dimension is re-created at the point you choose. We do something more interesting.

⊕ Right-click and select Edit from the shortcut menu.

QDIM prompts

Note:
*The objects selected for the **QDIM** command can be dimensions or objects to be dimensioned. If you select objects, **QDIM** creates new dimensions for these objects; if you select dimensions, **QDIM** edits or re-creates these dimensions depending on the options you select.*

```
Indicate dimension point to remove, or
          [Add/eXit] <eXit>:
```

We add dimension points.

⊕ Right-click and select Add from the shortcut menu.

Small white Xs are added at the endpoints of the line. These indicate the current dimension points. The prompt changes slightly as follows:

```
Indicate dimension point to add, or [Remove/eXit] <eXit>:
```

⊕ Pick Point 1, as shown in Figure 8-14.

This point is two units from the left endpoint of the line. **QDIM** continues to prompt for points.

⊕ Pick Point 2, as shown in Figure 8-14.

This point is two units from the right endpoint of the line.

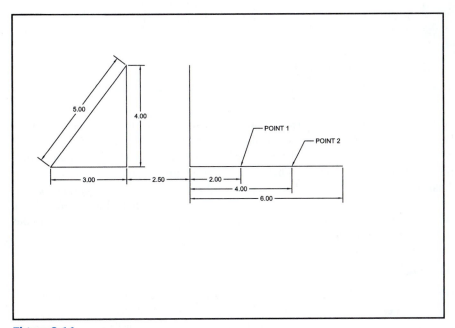

Figure 8-14

⊕ Press Enter or the spacebar to end point selection.

QDIM now divides the single 6.00 dimension into a series of three continuous 2.00 dimensions. We are not done yet. We choose to draw these three dimensions in Baseline format.

⊕ Right-click and select Baseline from the shortcut menu.

QDIM immediately switches the three dragged dimensions to a baseline form.

⊕ Pick a point so that the top, shortest dimension of the three is positioned about 0.5 below the line.

Your screen is redrawn with three baseline dimensions as shown in Figure 8-14. We have more to say about this powerful command as we go along. In the next task, we use it to create ordinate dimensions.

Note:

AutoCAD retains the last option used for drawing dimensions with **QDIM**, so if you were to enter the command now, it would default to Baseline rather than Continuous dimensions.

DIMBASELINE and DIMCONTINUE

Baseline and Continuous format dimensions can also be created one at a time using individual commands. The following general procedure is used with these commands:

1. Draw an initial linear dimension.

2. Select the **Baseline dimension** or **Continue dimension** tool from the dashboard.

3. Pick a second extension line origin.

4. Pick another second extension line origin.

5. Press **Enter** to exit the command.

8-4 DRAWING ORDINATE DIMENSIONS

GENERAL PROCEDURE

1. Define a coordinate system with the origin at the corner of the object to be dimensioned.
2. Select the **Ordinate** tool from the dashboard.
3. Select a location to be dimensioned.
4. Pick a leader endpoint.
5. Press **Enter** or change dimension text.

Ordinate dimensions are another way to specify linear dimensions. They are used to show multiple horizontal and vertical distances from a single point or the corner of an object. Because these fall readily into a coordinate system, it is efficient to show these dimensions as the x and y displacements from a single point of origin. There are two ways to create ordinate dimensions. AutoCAD ordinarily specifies points based on the point (0,0) on your screen. Using **QDIM,** you can specify a new Datum Point that serves as the origin for a set of ordinate dimensions. Using **DIMORDINATE,** it is necessary to temporarily move the origin of the coordinate system to the point from which you want dimensions to be specified. In this task, we demonstrate both.

QDIM and the Datum Point Option

We use ordinate dimensions to specify a series of horizontal and vertical distances from the intersection of the two lines to the right of the triangle. First, we use **QDIM** to add ordinate dimensions along the 4.00 vertical line. Then we use **DIMORDINATE** to add ordinate dimensions to the 6.00 horizontal line.

⊕ Enter the QDIM command.

⊕ Select the vertical line.

⊕ Right-click to end object selection.

⊕ Right-click and select Ordinate from the shortcut menu.

⊕ Select a point about 0.5 unit to the left of the line, as shown in Figure 8-15.

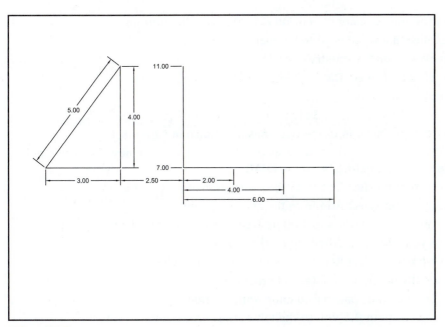

Figure 8-15

The two dimensions you see are at the ends of the line and show the y value of each endpoint. Whether in **QDIM** or in **DIMORDINATE,** AutoCAD automatically chooses the *x* or *y* value depending on the object you choose. Because the values you see are measured from the origin at the lower left corner of the grid, they are not particularly useful. A more common use would be to measure points from the intersection of the two lines. This method was used to dimension Drawing 7-4, the Control Panel, in the last chapter, for example. To complete this set of dimensions, we go back into **QDIM,** select a new datum point, and add and remove dimension points as shown in Figure 8-16.

⊕ Repeat QDIM.

⊕ Select the bottom ordinate dimension (7.00 in our illustration).

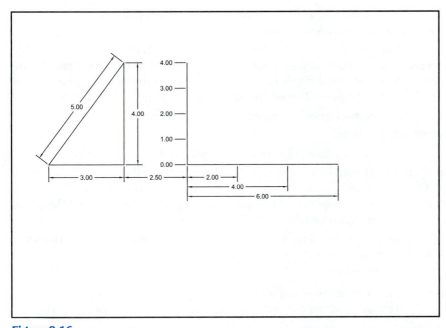

Figure 8-16

⊕ Select the top ordinate dimension (11.00 in our illustration).

Notice that these need to be selected separately.

⊕ Right-click to end geometry selection.

⊕ Right-click and select Datum Point from the shortcut menu.

QDIM prompts

```
Select new datum point:
```

⊕ Select the intersection of the two lines, as shown in Figure 8-16.

The new datum point is now established. We add three new dimension points and remove one before leaving **QDIM.**

⊕ Right-click and select Edit from the shortcut menu.

⊕ Right-click and select Add from the shortcut menu.

⊕ Add points 1.00, 2.00, and 3.00 up from the bottom of the vertical line.

As you add points, they are marked by Xs.

⊕ Right-click and select Remove from the shortcut menu.

⊕ Remove the point at the intersection of the two lines.

⊕ Press Enter or the spacebar to endpoint selection.

⊕ Pick a point about 0.5 unit to the left of the vertical line, as before.

Your screen should resemble Figure 8-16. Next we dimension the horizontal line using the **DIMORDINATE** command.

DIMORDINATE and the UCS Command

We use **DIMORDINATE** to create a series of ordinate dimensions above the horizontal 6.00 line. This method requires you to create a new origin for the coordinate system using the UCS command. User coordinate systems are crucial in 3-D drawing and are explored in depth in Chapter 12. Although **DIMORDINATE** creates only one dimension at a time, it does have some advantages over the **QDIM** system. To begin with, you do not have to go back and edit the dimension to add and remove points. Additionally, you can create a variety of leader shapes.

⊕ Select Tools → New UCS → Origin from the pull-down menu, as shown in Figure 8-17.

This selection executes the **UCS** command and automates the entry of the default Origin option. Specifying a new coordinate system by moving the point of origin is the simplest of many options in the **UCS** command. AutoCAD prompts

```
Specify new origin point <0,0,0>:
```

⊕ Pick the intersection of the two lines.

If you move your cursor to the intersection and watch the coordinate display, you can see that this point is now read as (0.00,0.00,0.00). If your user coordinate system icon is on and set to move to the origin, it moves to the new point. Also, if your grid is on, the origin will move to the new origin point.

⊕ Select the Ordinate tool from the dashboard, as shown in Figure 8-18.

AutoCAD prompts

```
Specify feature location:
```

In actuality, all you do is show AutoCAD a point and then an endpoint for a leader. Depending on where the endpoint is located relative to the first point, AutoCAD shows dimension text for either an x or a y displacement from the origin of the current coordinate system.

⊕ Pick a point along the 6.00 line, 1.00 to the right of the intersection, as shown in Figure 8-19.

AutoCAD prompts

```
Non-associative dimension created
Specify leader end point or [Xdatum/Ydatum/Mtext/Text/Angle]:
```

The first line tells you that ordinate dimensions created in this fashion are nonassociative. Associativity is discussed in Section 8.9. The second line prompts you to

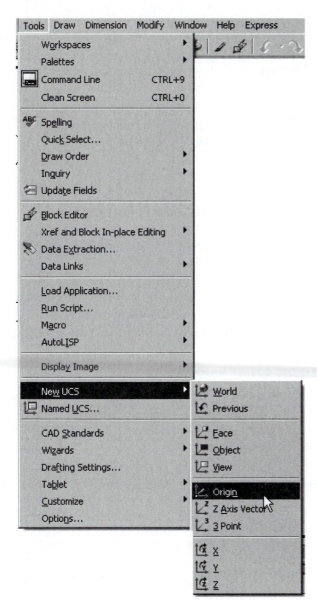

Figure 8-17

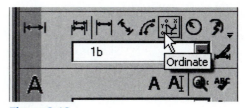

Figure 8-18

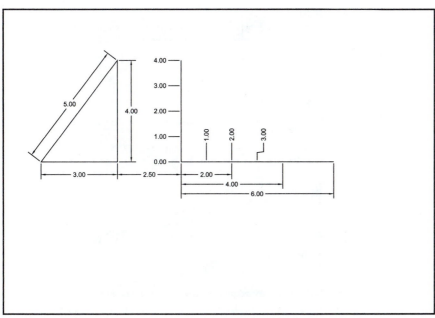

Figure 8-19

specify a leader endpoint. You can manually indicate whether you want the dimension text to show the x or y coordinate by typing x or y. However, if you choose the endpoint correctly, AutoCAD picks the right coordinate automatically. You can also provide your own text, but that would defeat the purpose of setting up a coordinate system that automatically gives you the distances from the intersection of the two lines.

⊕ Pick an endpoint 0.5 directly above the line, as shown in Figure 8-19.

Your screen should now include the 1.00 ordinate dimension shown in Figure 8-19.

⊕ Repeat DIMORDINATE and add the second ordinate dimension at a point 2.00 from the origin.

⊕ Repeat DIMORDINATE once more.

⊕ Pick a point on the line 3.00 from the origin.

⊕ Move your cursor left and right to see some of the leader shapes that DIMORDINATE creates depending on the endpoint of the leader.

⊕ Pick an endpoint slightly to the right of the dimensioned point to create a broken leader similar to the one in Figure 8-19.

When you are done, you should return to the world coordinate system. This is the default coordinate system and the one we have been using all along.

⊕ Select Tools → New UCS → World from the pull-down menu.

This returns the origin to its original position at the lower left of your screen.

8-5 DRAWING ANGULAR DIMENSIONS

GENERAL PROCEDURE	1. Select the **Angular** tool from the dashboard.
	2. Select two lines that form an angle.
	3. Pick a dimension location.

Angular dimensioning works much like linear dimensioning, except that you are prompted to select objects that form an angle. AutoCAD computes an angle based on the geometry that you select (two lines, an arc, part of a circle, or a vertex and two points) and constructs extension lines, a dimension arc, and text specifying the angle.

For this exercise, we return to the triangle and add angular dimensions to two of the angles.

⊕ Select the Angular tool from the dashboard, as shown in Figure 8-20.

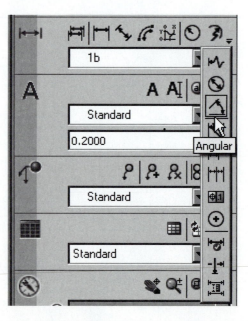

Figure 8-20

The first prompt is

        `Select arc, circle, line, or <specify vertex>:`

The prompt shows that you can use **DIMANGULAR** to dimension angles formed by arcs and portions of circles as well as angles formed by lines. If you press **Enter,** you can specify an angle manually by picking its vertex and a point on each side of the angle. We begin by picking lines.

⊕ Select the base of the triangle.

        You are prompted for another line:

                `Select second line:`

⊕ Select the hypotenuse.

        As in linear dimensioning, AutoCAD now shows you the dimension lines and lets you drag them into place. The prompt asks for a dimension arc location and also allows you the option of changing the text or the text angle:

        `Specify dimension arc line location or [Mtext/Text/Angle]:`

⊕ Move the cursor around to see how the dimension can be placed and then pick a point between the two selected lines, as shown in Figure 8-21.

        The lower left angle of your triangle should now be dimensioned, as in Figure 8-21. Notice that the degree symbol is added by default in angular dimension text.

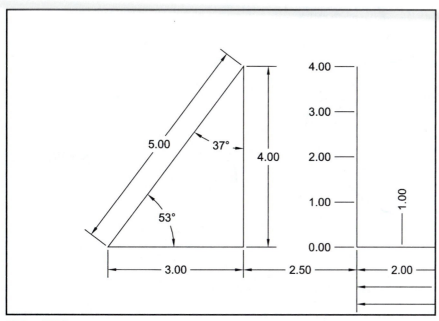

Figure 8-21

        We dimension the upper angle by specifying its vertex.

⊕ Repeat DIMANGULAR.

⊕ Press Enter.

        AutoCAD prompts for an angle vertex.

⊕ Point to the vertex of the angle at the top of the triangle.

        AutoCAD prompts

                `Specify first angle endpoint:`

⊕ Pick a point along the hypotenuse.

        To be precise, this should be a snap point. The most dependable one is the lower left corner of the triangle. AutoCAD prompts

                `Specify second angle endpoint:`

⊕ Pick any point along the vertical side of the triangle.

There should be many snap points on the vertical line, so you should have no problem.

⊕ Move the cursor slowly up and down within the triangle.

Notice how AutoCAD places the arrows outside the angle when you approach the vertex and things get crowded. Also notice that if you move outside the angle, AutoCAD switches to the outer angle.

⊕ Pick a location for the dimension arc, as shown in Figure 8-21.

Angular Dimensions on Arcs and Circles

You can also place angular dimensions on arcs and circles. In both cases, AutoCAD constructs extension lines and a dimension arc. When you dimension an arc with an angular dimension, the center of the arc becomes the vertex of the dimension angle, and the endpoints of the arc become the start points of the extension lines. In a circle, the same format is used, but the dimension line origins are determined by the point used to select the circle and a second point, which AutoCAD prompts you to select. These options are illustrated in Figure 8-22.

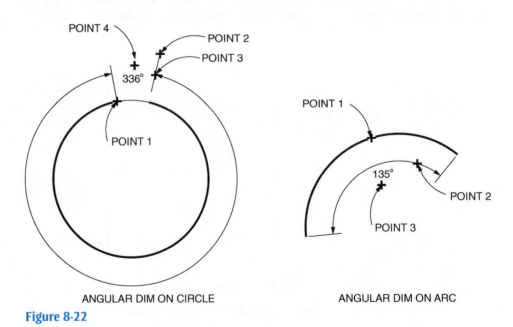

ANGULAR DIM ON CIRCLE   ANGULAR DIM ON ARC

Figure 8-22

8-6 DIMENSIONING ARCS AND CIRCLES

GENERAL PROCEDURE	1. Select the **Radius** or **Diameter** tool from the dashboard. 2. Pick an arc or circle. 3. Type "text" or press **Enter.** 4. Pick a leader line endpoint location.

The basic process for dimensioning circles and arcs is as simple as those we have already covered. It can get tricky, however, when AutoCAD does not place the dimension where you want it. Text placement can be controlled by adjusting dimension variables. In this exercise, we create a center mark and some diameter and radius dimensions. Then we return to the **QDIM** command to see how multiple circles can be dimensioned at once.

⊕ To prepare for this exercise, switch to Layer 1 and draw two circles at the bottom of your screen, as shown in Figure 8-23.

    The circles we use have radii of 2.00 and 1.50.

⊕ Return to the Dim layer.

⊕ Select the Center Mark tool from the dashboard, as shown in Figure 8-24.

    Center marks are the simplest of all dimension features to create. They are added automatically as part of some radius and diameter dimensions. AutoCAD prompts

                      Select arc or circle:

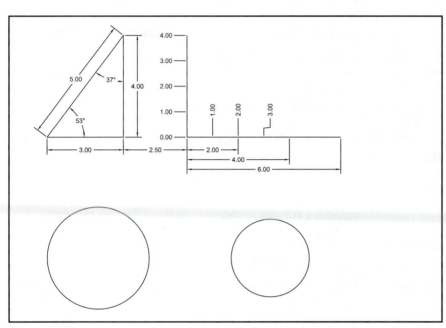

Figure 8-23

Figure 8-24

⊕ Select the smaller circle.

    A center mark is drawn in the 1.50 circle, as shown in Figure 8-25. The standard center mark is a small cross. The size of the cross can be changed in a small panel at the bottom right of the **Lines** tab and

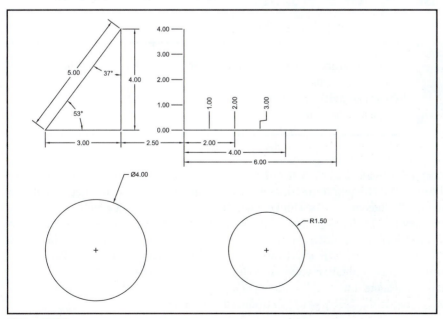

Figure 8-25

Symbols and Arrows tab of the **Modify Dimension Style** dialog box. Here you also have a choice of standard continuous lines or broken center lines to form the mark.

⊕ Now we add the diameter dimension shown on the larger circle in Figure 8-25.

⊕ Select the Diameter tool from the dashboard.

AutoCAD prompts

Select arc or circle:

⊕ Select the larger circle.

AutoCAD shows a diameter dimension and asks for a dimension line location with the following prompt:

Specify dimension line location or [Mtext/Text/Angle]:

The Text and Angle options allow you to change the dimension text or put it at an angle. If you move your cursor around, you see that you can position the dimension line anywhere around or inside the circle.

⊕ Pick a dimension position near the top of the 2.00 circle so that your screen resembles Figure 8-25.

Notice that the diameter symbol prefix and the center mark are added automatically by default.

Radius Dimensions

The procedures for radius dimensioning are exactly the same as those for diameter dimensions and the results look the same. The only differences are the radius value of the text and the use of R for radius in place of the diameter symbol.

We draw a radius dimension on the smaller circle.

⊕ Select Radius from the Dimension menu or the Radius tool from the Dimension toolbar.

⊕ Select the 1.50 (smaller) circle.

⊕ Move the cursor around the circle, inside and outside.

⊕ Pick a point to complete the dimension, as shown in Figure 8-25.

The R for radius and the center mark are added automatically.

8-7 DIMENSIONING WITH MULTILEADERS

GENERAL PROCEDURE	1. Select a Leader style from the dashboard or the **Leaders** tool palette.
	2. Select a start point.
	3. Select an endpoint.
	4. Type dimension text.

Radius and diameter dimensions, along with ordinate dimensions, make use of leaders to connect dimension text to the object being dimensioned. Leaders can also be created independently to attach annotation to all kinds of objects. Unlike other dimension formats, in which you select an object or show a length, a leader is simply a line or series of lines with an arrow at the end to visually connect an object to its annotation. Because of this, when you create a dimension with a leader, AutoCAD does not recognize and measure any selected object or distance. You need to know the dimension text or annotation you want to use before you begin.

Here we add two leaders, one with a simple tag annotation and one with text. We make use of a tool palette, similar to the Tables palette introduced in Chapter 7.

⊕ Click the Multileaders button on the left side of the Multileaders control panel of the dashboard, as shown in Figure 8-26.

This opens the **Leaders** tool palette, shown in Figure 8-27. This palette contains two sets of leader styles, Imperial styles at the top and Metric styles at the bottom. There are eight of each and they are identical except for variations is size. We will use the metric Leader - Circle style found near the bottom of the palette.

⊞ Pick the Leader - Circle style from the tool palette, as shown in Figure 8-27.

AutoCAD prompts for an arrowhead location or option:

```
Specify leader arrowhead location or
[leader Landing first/Content first/Options] <Options>:
```

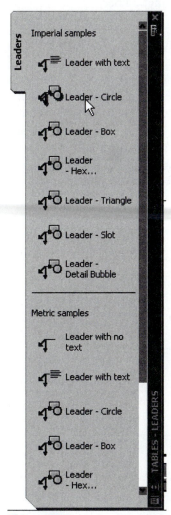

Figure 8-26   Figure 8-27

Leaders consist of an arrowhead, a leader line, and a short landing line connecting the leader to the text or annotation symbol. The options allow you to change the order in which these elements are specified.

We will use the Leader - Circle style to tag the 1.50-radius circle with a number. Nothing is being dimensioned by this leader. It is simply a tag such as might be applied to call out or number an object in a drawing.

To attach the arrow to the circle, we use a Nearest object snap.

⊞ Hold down Shift and right-click your mouse to open the object snap shortcut menu.
⊞ Select Nearest from the fourth panel of the menu.

The Nearest object snap mode specifies that you want to snap to the nearest point on whatever object you select. If you have not used this object snap mode before, take a moment to get familiar with it. As you move around the screen, you see the Nearest snaptool whenever the crosshairs approach an object. If you allow the crosshairs to rest on a point, the Nearest tooltip label appears as well.

⊕ Position the crosshairs on the upper right side of the 1.50-radius circle and press the pick button.

The leader is snapped to the circle and a rubber band appears, extending to the crosshairs. AutoCAD prompts for a second point:

Specify leader landing location:

⊕ Pick a landing location for the leader, at a 45-degree angle up and to the right of the first point, as shown in Figure 8-28.

AutoCAD draws a leader, landing line, and circle, as shown, and prompts for a tagnumber:

Enter tag number <TAGNUMBER>:

⊕ Type "5" ↵.

The number 5 has no particular significance here. It is for demonstration only. The number is added to the circle tag as shown in Figure 8-28. Many of the other leader styles would be identical to this one except for the shape of the tag (box, hex, triangle, slot, detail bubble).

Next we will add a leader with Multiline text, as shown on the larger circle. For this we use the Leader with text leader style.

⊕ Select the Leader with text style from the Leader tool palette, as shown in Figure 8-29. Either Metric or Imperial will do.

AutoCAD prompts for an arrowhead location.

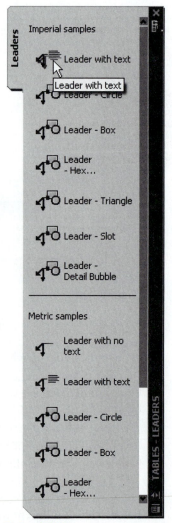

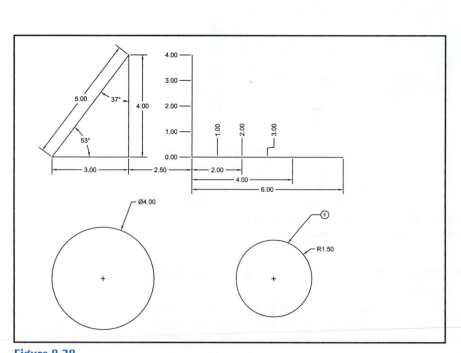

Figure 8-28

Figure 8-29

⊞ Open the Object Snap shortcut menu and select Nearest.

⊞ Pick a leader start point on the upper right side of the larger, 2.00-radius circle.

⊞ Pick a point for the leader landing about 45 degrees and 1.50 units up and to the right of the first point.

The **Multiline Text Formatting** toolbar opens. The two arrows just above where your text will be entered allow you to specify a width for the text you will enter.

⊞ Position your cursor within the small gray box with two arrows, as shown in Figure 8-30.

⊞ Hold down the pick button, drag the width box out about 2.50 units to the right, and then release the pick button.

⊞ Type "This circle is 4.00 inches in diameter" ↵.

⊞ Click OK to complete the command.

⊞ Close the Leaders tool palette.

Your screen should now resemble Figure 8-31.

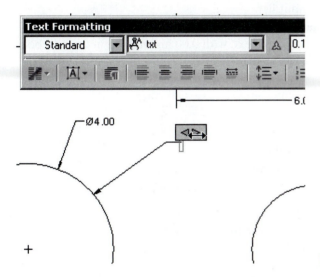

Figure 8-30

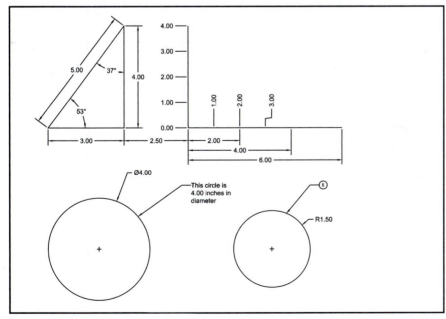

Figure 8-31

8-8 Changing Dimension Text

Dimensions can be edited in many of the same ways that other objects are edited. They can be moved, copied, stretched, rotated, trimmed, extended, and so on. There are numerous ways to change dimension text and placement. Grips can be used effectively to accomplish most changes in placement. Here we demonstrate two ways to change the text.

The DIMEDIT Command

⊕ Type "dimedit" ↵.

AutoCAD prompts with options:

```
Enter type of dimension editing [Home/New/Rotate/Oblique]
                    <Home>:
```

Home, Rotate and Oblique are placement and orientation options; New refers to new text content.

⊕ Select New from the dynamic input list.

AutoCad opens **Text Formatting** toolbar and waits for you to enter text. You see the toolbar and a small edit box for text, with 0.00 highlighted in the edit box. In this edit box you can completely change the dimension text or you can add to the existing text.

We change the 5.00 aligned dimension to read 5.00 cm.

⊕ Double-click inside the edit box.

⊕ Type "5.00 cm" ↵.

The new text appears in the edit box.

⊕ Click OK to close the editor and return to the drawing.

AutoCAD prompts for objects to receive the new text:

```
                    Select Objects:
```

⊕ Select the 5.00 aligned dimension on the hypotenuse of the triangle.

⊕ Press Enter or right-click to end object selection.

The text is redrawn, as shown in Figure 8-32.

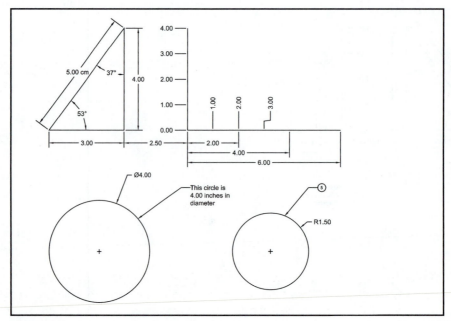

Figure 8-32

Accessing the PROPERTIES Command from the Shortcut Menu

The **PROPERTIES** command gives you direct access to many dimension variables, including text content. The **PROPERTIES** command can be opened from the **Modify** menu, or by selecting objects first and then right-clicking to open the shortcut menu. Try the following:

⊞ Pick the lower baseline dimension on the 6.00 line.

⊞ Right-click to open the shortcut menu.

⊞ From the bottom of the menu, select Properties.

This opens the Properties palette, as shown in Figure 8-33. We encountered this palette in Chapter 7. The palette is responsive to the type of object selected, however, so it appears with different lists. You need to scroll down to see all the lists. The number of lists is another indication of the complexity of dimension options. They include the General list, Miscellaneous, Lines and Arrows, Text, Fit, Primary Units, Alternate Units, and Tolerances. These tabs provide yet another way to modify dimension variables.

⊞ Scroll down the Text list to Text override, which is at the bottom of the list.

⊞ Click Text override.

⊞ Type 6.00 cm in the edit box.

⊞ Close the Properties palette.

⊞ Press Esc to clear grips.

Your screen is redrawn with the dimension text shown in Figure 8-34.

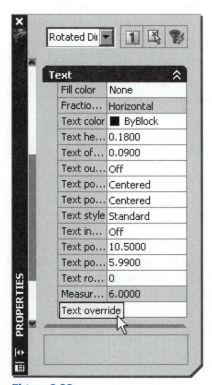

Figure 8-33

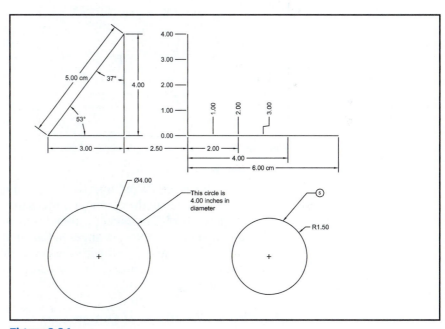

Figure 8-34

8-9 Using Associative Dimensions

By default, most dimensions in AutoCAD are associative with the geometry of the objects they dimension. This means that changes in the dimensioned objects are automatically reflected in the dimensions. If a dimensioned object is moved, the dimensions associated with it move as well. If a dimensioned object is scaled, the position and measurements associated with that object change to reflect the new size of the object. The following exercise illustrates several points about associated dimensions.

⊞ Select the 2.00 radius circle.

⊞ Click on any of the grips, move the circle about 2.00 units to the left, and click again to complete the move.

Your screen should resemble Figure 8-35. Notice that the 4.00 diameter dimension moves with the circle, and the leader from the Mtext dimension text stretches to maintain connection with the circle, but that the text does not move. We explain this in a moment, but first try the following steps:

⊞ Select any of the grips again.

⊞ Right-click to open the grip shortcut menu.

⊞ Select Scale.

⊞ Type ".5" ⏎ for a scale factor.

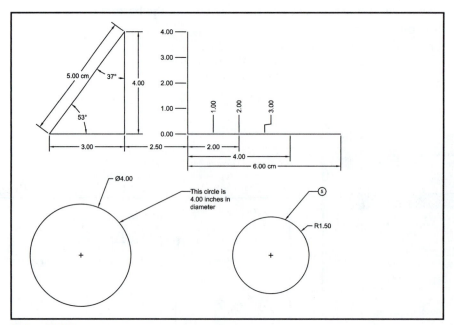

Figure 8-35

Your screen is redrawn to resemble Figure 8-36. Notice now that the scale factor is reflected in the diameter dimension (4.00 has changed to 2.00), but not in the leadered text. The diameter dimension is a true associative dimension; it moves and updates to reflect changes in the circle. The connection point of the leadered dimension is associated with the circle, but the text is not. Therefore, the leader stretches to stay connected to the circle, but the text does not move or change with the circle.

Changing Associativity of Dimensions

Nonassociative dimensions can be made associative using the **DIMREASSOCIATE** command. Associated dimensions can be disassociated with the **DIMDISASSOCIATE** command. In each case the procedure is a matter of entering the command and selecting dimensions to associate or disassociate. For example, try the following:

⊞ Type "dimdisassociate" ⏎.

Dimdisassociate is not on any toolbar or menu. AutoCAD prompts

```
Select dimensions to disassociate...
Select objects:
```

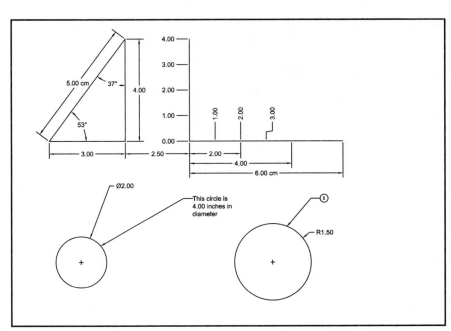

Figure 8-36

⊕ Select the 2.00 diameter dimension.

⊕ Right-click to end object selection.

Now try moving the circle again to observe the changes.

⊕ Select the circle again, select a grip, and move the circle back to the right.

This time the 2.00 diameter does not move with the circle, as shown in Figure 8-37. The leader adjusts as before to stay attached to the circle, but the diameter dimension is currently not associated to the circle. To reassociate it, use the **DIMREASSOCIATE** command, as follows:

⊕ Select Reassociate Dimensions from the bottom of the Dimension menu.

⊕ Select the 2.00 diameter dimension.

⊕ Right-click to end object selection.

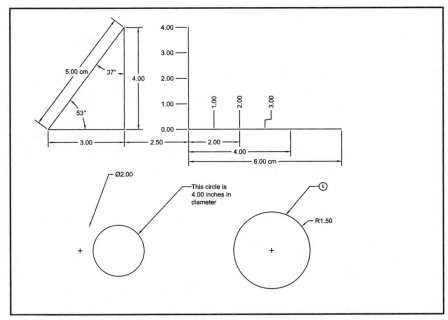

Figure 8-37

AutoCAD recognizes that this is a diameter dimension and prompts for a circle or arc to attach it to. Notice that this means you could associate the dimension to any arc or circle, not just the one to which it was previously attached.

⊕ Select the circle on the left again.

The diameter dimension moves and attaches to the 2.00 radius circle again, as shown in Figure 8-38.

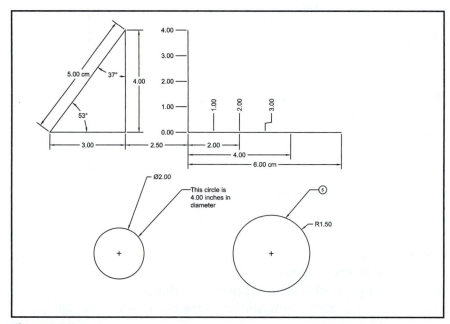

Figure 8-38

8-10 USING THE **HATCH** COMMAND

GENERAL PROCEDURE	1. Select the **Hatch** tool from the dashboard. 2. Select a pattern. 3. Define style parameters. 4. Define boundaries of object to be hatched.

Automated hatching is another immense time-saver. AutoCAD has two basic methods of hatching, both accessible through the **HATCH** command, which calls the **Hatch and Gradient** dialog box. In one method, you select a point within an area to be hatched and AutoCAD searches for the nearest boundary surrounding the point. In the other method, you specify the boundaries themselves by selecting objects. By default, AutoCAD creates associated hatch patterns. Associated hatching changes when the boundaries around change. Nonassociated hatching is completely independent of the geometry that contains it.

⊕ To prepare for this exercise, clear your screen of all previously drawn objects, return to Layer 1, and then draw three rectangles, one inside the other, with the word TEXT with a height of 1.00 at the center, as shown in Figure 8-39.

⊕ Select the Hatch tool from the dashboard, as shown in Figure 8-40.

This initiates the **HATCH** command, which calls the **Hatch and Gradient** dialog box shown in Figure 8-41. The Hatch tab gives you access to AutoCAD's library of more than 50 standard hatch patterns. Gradient creates solid fills with a wide range of gradient color schemes.

We explore the **Hatch** tab first.

COMMAND GRID	
Command	Hatch
Alias	H
Menu	Draw
Tool	

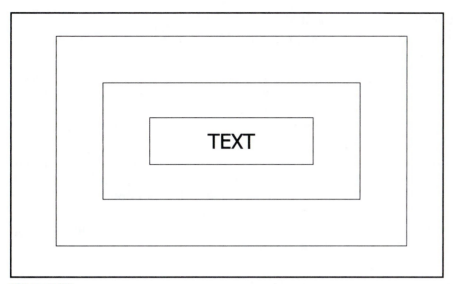

Figure 8-39

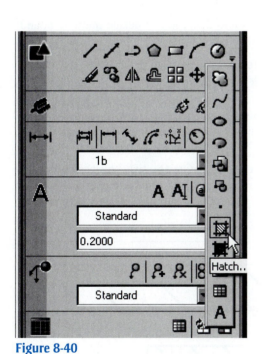

Figure 8-40

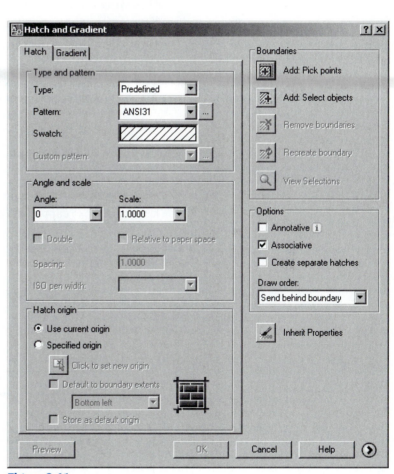

Figure 8-41

✛ If necessary, click the Hatch tab.

At the top of the **Hatch** tab window, you see the Type and pattern box. Before we can hatch anything, we need to specify a hatch pattern. Later we show Auto-CAD what we wish to hatch using the **Add: Pick points** button on the right.

The Pattern type currently shown in the Swatch image box is a predefined pattern. Before we look at predefined patterns we create a simple user-defined pattern of straight lines on a 45-degree angle.

⊞ Click on the arrow to the right of Predefined.

This opens a list including Predefined, User-defined, and Custom patterns.

⊞ Select User-defined.

When you select a user-defined pattern, the Swatch box, which shows an example of the pattern, changes to show a set of horizontal lines. To create our user-defined pattern, we specify an angle and a spacing.

⊞ Open the Angle list and select 45.

⊞ Double-click in the Spacing edit box, and then type ".5."

Next we need to show AutoCAD where to place the hatching. To the right in the dialog box is a set of buttons with icons. The first two options are *Add: Pick points* and *Add: Select* objects. Using the *Add: Pick points* option, you can have AutoCAD locate a boundary when you point to the area inside it. The *Add: Select objects* option can be used to create boundaries by selecting entities that lie along the borders of the area you wish to hatch.

⊞ Click Add: Pick points.

The dialog box disappears temporarily and you are prompted as follows:

```
Pick internal point or [Select objects/Remove boundaries]:
```

⊞ Pick a point inside the largest, outer rectangle, but outside the smaller rectangles.

AutoCAD displays the following messages, although you might have to press F2 to see them:

```
                Selecting everything...
                Selecting everything visible...
                Analyzing the selected data...
                Analyzing internal islands...
```

AutoCAD continues to prompt for internal points so that you can define multiple boundaries. Let's return to the dialog box and see what we've done so far.

⊞ Press Enter to end internal point selection.

The dialog box reappears. Several of the options that were unavailable before are now accessible. We make use of the **Preview** button at the bottom left of the dialog box. Preview allows us to see what has been specified without leaving the command, so that we can continue to adjust the hatching until we are satisfied.

⊞ Click Preview.

Your screen should resemble Figure 8-42. Notice the way the command has recognized and treated internal boundaries. Boundaries are hatched or left clear in alternating fashion, beginning with the outermost boundary and working inward.

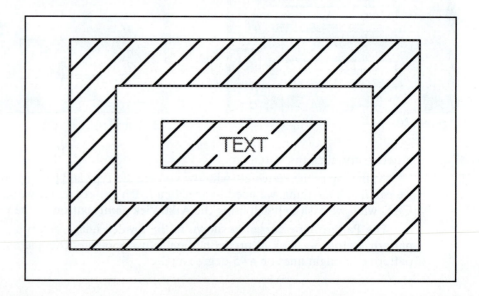

Figure 8-42

This demonstrates the "normal" style of hatching. Other styles can be achieved by clicking the **Remove boundaries** button and selecting internal boundaries to be removed. When a boundary has been removed, AutoCAD will ignore it and hatch across it to the next boundary.

⊞ Press Esc to return to the Hatch and Gradient dialog box.

Right-clicking or pressing **Enter** here would take you out of the command and apply the hatching to your drawing.

Now let's take a look at some of the more complex stored hatch patterns that AutoCAD provides.

⊞ Click the arrow to the right of User-defined and select Predefined.

⊞ Now click either the ellipsis button next to the Pattern box or the Swatch image.

Either opens the **Hatch Pattern Palette,** shown in Figure 8-43. This dialog box contains AutoCAD's library of predefined hatch patterns. They are presented in tabbed dialog box fashion with four tabs. The first three contain images of patterns. The **Custom** tab is empty unless you have created and saved your own custom patterns. To produce the hatched image in Figure 8-44, we chose the Escher pattern.

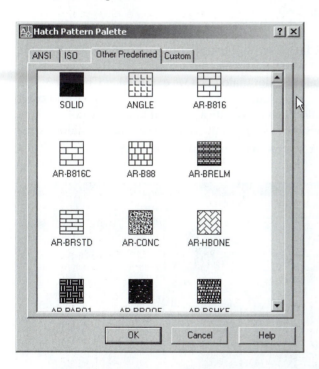

Figure 8-43

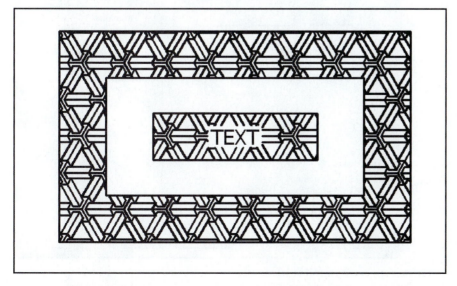

Figure 8-44

⊕ Click the Other Predefined tab.

⊕ Scroll down the images until you come to Escher.

⊕ Select Escher.

⊕ Click OK to exit the Hatch Pattern Palette.

To produce the figure, we also used a larger scale in this hatching.

⊕ Click the arrow in the Scale list box to open the list of scale factors and select 1.50.

⊕ Click the arrow in the Angle list box and select 0.

⊕ Click Preview.

Your screen should resemble Figure 8-44, but remember this is still just the preview.

⊕ Press Enter or right-click to accept the hatch.

Gradient Fill

AutoCAD has an option to create gradient fill color schemes as an additional presentation feature. We add a gradient fill to the area between the two inner rectangles that our hatch pattern has left clear.

⊕ Reenter the HATCH command.

⊕ Select the Gradient tab.

This opens the Gradient fill window, illustrated in Figure 8-45. Your screen shows gradations of blue and white that we cannot show here. By selecting the ellipsis button you open the **Select Color** dialog box we explored in Chapter 3. This gives you access to the full range of AutoCAD index colors, true colors, and color books. The **two color** button allows you to create a gradient mix of two colors. Here we apply a simple one-color gradient fill from the nine choices in the dialog box.

⊕ Select the first box in the second row, as shown in Figure 8-45.

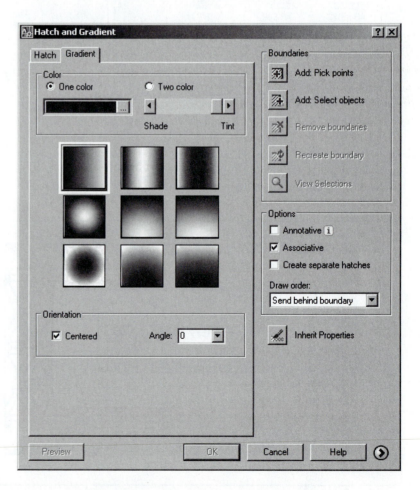

Figure 8-45

When you select the box it is highlighted with a dashed border. Next we need to define an area to fill. This is done in the same way as defining an area for hatching.

⊕ Click *Add: Pick points.*

    Pick a point in the unhatched area between the two inner rectangles.

⊕ Press Enter to return to the dialog box.

⊕ Click Preview.

    Your screen should resemble Figure 8-46.

Finally, we leave the **HATCH** command and return to the drawing.

⊕ Press Enter or right-click to exit the HATCH command and apply the hatch pattern and fill to your drawing.

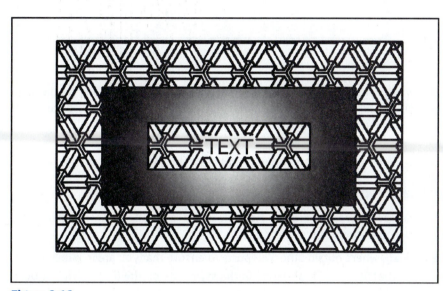

Figure 8-46

8-11 SCALING DIMENSIONS BETWEEN PAPER SPACE AND MODEL SPACE

In Chapter 6, you learned how to create multiple-viewport layouts. Now that you will be adding text and dimensions to your drawings, new questions arise about scale relationships between model space and paper space. The Zoom XP feature introduced in Chapter 6 has already allowed you to create precise scale relationships between model space viewports and paper space units. Now we will use the Annotative property to match dimension and text sizes to those zoom factors.

Important: This section begins with the three-view multiple-viewport layout of Drawing 5-1 created in Chapter 5. Hopefully, you have saved this layout and can open it now. If not, you can create an approximation of the drawing and layout as follows:

1. Set Limits to (0,0) and (12,9). This is critical. If you use different limits, the exercise is difficult to follow.

2. Draw a circle with diameter 3.50 centered at (3.00,4.00).

3. Draw a second circle with diameter 2.50 centered at the same point.

4. Draw a small 0.25-diameter circle at the lower quadrant of the 2.50 circle.

5. Draw a rectangle with first corner at (6.50,2.75) and second corner at (10.00,5.25).

6. Create a new layout with D-size limits in paper space.

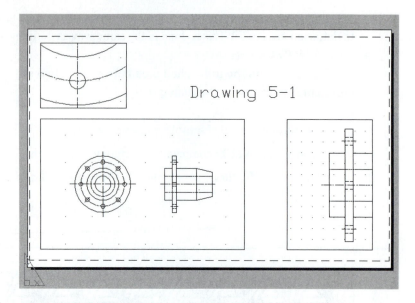

Figure 8-47

7. Create three viewports, positioned as shown in Figure 8-47. The zoom factor for the large viewport should be 2xp. The smaller viewport to the right should be at 4xp, and the smallest viewport at the top should be at 6xp. See Chapter 6, Section 6.10 for further details, if necessary.

⊞ If you have saved Drawing 5-1, open it and click the D-Size Layout tab.

Text in Paper Space and Model Space

Text drawn in paper space can be drawn at the 1:1 scale of the layout. Text drawn within viewports will be affected by the viewport scale. Try this:

⊞ Double-click anywhere outside the viewports to ensure that you are in paper space.
⊞ Check to see that Standard is showing in the style lists on the dashboard for both text and dimensions.
⊞ Pick the Single Line Text tool from the dashboard.
⊞ Pick a start point outside any of the viewports. We chose (15, 15).

    Our text begins about 2.00 units above the right side of the left viewport, as shown in Figure 8-47.

⊞ Type "1" ↵ for a text height of one unit.

This assumes that you are using the D-size paper space limits from Chapter 6. If not, you have to adjust for your own settings. On A-size paper the text height is about 0.25.

⊞ Press Enter for 0 rotation.
⊞ Type "Drawing 5-1" ↵.
⊞ Press Enter again to exit.

    Your screen should have text added, as shown in Figure 8-47.

⊞ Double-click in the lower left, largest viewport to enter model space in this viewport.
⊞ Enter the Text command again.
⊞ Pick a start point below the left view in the viewport, as shown in Figure 8-48.
⊞ Press Enter to retain a height of 1.00 units.
⊞ Press Enter for 0 rotation.
⊞ Type "Bushing" ↵.
⊞ Press Enter again to exit the command.

    AutoCAD may move objects in the viewport to make room for the text. If this happens, use pan to move things back in place.

    Your screen should resemble Figure 8-48.

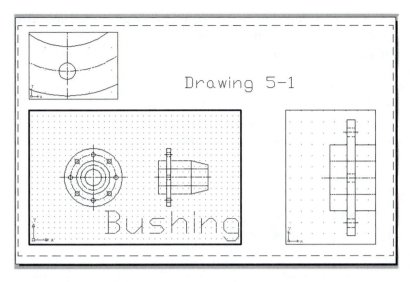

Figure 8-48

What has happened here? Why is "Bushing" drawn twice as big as "Drawing 5-1"? Do you remember the Zoom XP scale factor we used in this viewport? This viewport is enlarged by two times paper space, so any text you draw inside it is enlarged by a factor of two as well. If you want, try drawing text in either of the other two viewports. You find that text in the right viewport is magnified four times the paper space size and text in the uppermost viewport is magnified six times.

You could compensate for these enlargements by dividing text height by factors of 2, 4, and 6, but that can become very cumbersome. Furthermore, if you decide to change the zoom factor at a later date, you would have to re-create any text drawn within the altered viewport. Otherwise, your text sizes in the overall drawing would become inconsistent. The purpose of the Annotative property is to add control in situations like this.

The Annotative Property

In AutoCAD 2008, all types of objects used to annotate drawings can be defined as annotative. This annotative property allows you to attach one or more scales to the object. With the property and the correct scale, the scale of the object will match the scale of the viewport and the annotation will appear at the desired size in paper space. Objects that can have the annotative property include text, dimensions, hatch patterns, tolerances, leaders, symbols, and other types of explanatory symbols, including ones you may define yourself. The property may be applied to individual annotative objects, or may be included in a style definition.

We begin by adding the property to create text in the lower viewport at the appropriate scale.

⊕ Erase "Bushing" from the lower left viewport.

⊕ In the Text control panel on the dashboard, open the style list and switch from Standard to Annotative, as shown in Figure 8-49.

Look at the right side of the status bar. If you are in model space in the lower left viewport, you should see two scale indicators, as shown in Figure 8-50. The Viewport Scale should be 2:1, matching the scale of the current viewport, and the Annotation Scale should be the default 1:1, matching the paper space scale. By

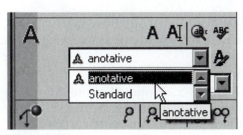

Figure 8-49

Figure 8-50

changing the Annotation scale to match the viewport scale we can cause annotative objects in this viewport to be scaled automatically.

⊕ On the status bar, pick the arrow to the right of Annotation scale and select 2:1. from the pop-up list.

At this point the viewport scale and annotation scale should match at 2:1. Now we draw text in the annotative style in the left viewport.

⊕ Pick the Single Line Text tool from the dashboard.

⊕ Pick a start point below the objects in the lower left viewport.

⊕ Type "1" ↵ for a text height.

⊕ Press Enter for 0 rotation.

⊕ Type "Bushing" ↵.

⊕ Press Enter again to exit the command.

Your screen should resemble Figure 8-51.

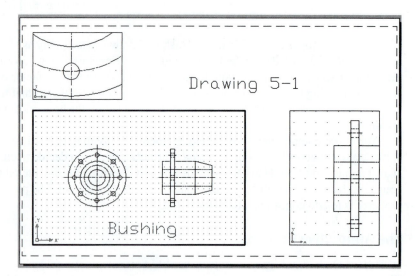

Figure 8-51

Controlling Annotation Scale Visibility

Next we add some dimensions to our viewports and learn more about how scales and viewports can be managed. First we switch to the Annotative dimension style and override the text of the style. This will be a temporary override; it does not change the default definition of the style.

⊕ Open the Dimension Style list on the dashboard and select Annotative.

⊕ Click the Dimension Style tool on the dashboard.

⊕ In the Dimension Style Manager, pick the Override button on the right.

⊕ In the Override current style dialog box, pick the Text tab.

The text style tab is shown in Figure 8-52.

⊕ As shown, change the text height to 0.50.

When properly scaled, this should make our dimension text half as large as the 1.00 unit text currently showing in paper space and in the lower left viewport.

⊕ Pick the Radius tool from the dashboard.

⊕ Pick the small bolt hole circle at the bottom quadrant of the bushing, as shown in Figure 8-53.

⊕ Pick a dimension location as shown.

Your screen should resemble Figure 8-53. Notice that the dimension just added does not appear in the top viewport, even though the bolt hole being dimensioned is clearly visible in that viewport. The annotative property has also made this possible.

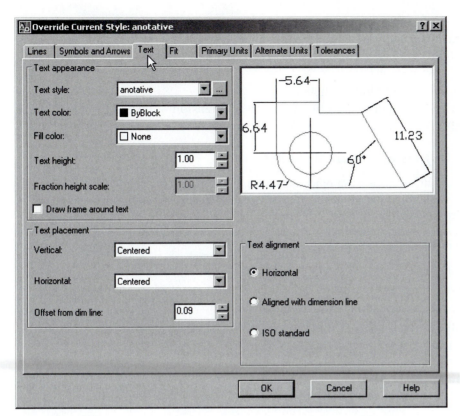

Figure 8-52

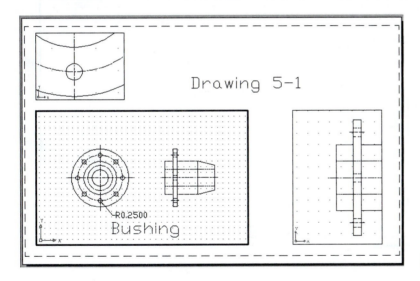

Figure 8-53

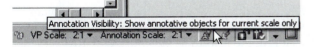

Figure 8-54

Look at the right side of the status bar again. To the right of the Annotation scale, you see the button illustrated in Figure 8-54. This is the AutoCAD annotation symbol with a tiny blue lightbulb image behind it. The tooltip for this button will say, "Annotation Visibility: Show annotation objects for the current scale only."

⊞ Click the button.

The button changes to show a yellow (on) lightbulb. The tooltip now says, "Annotation Visibility: Show annotative objects for all scales." Look closely at the upper left viewport. A large dimension leader has been added. If you were to pan to see the dimension text you would see that it is 1.50 units high, three times the 0.50 unit height of the text in the lower left viewport. This, once again, is the result of the viewport scales, with the lower viewport at 2:1 and the upper at 6:1.

⊕ Click the visibility button again.

The blue lightbulb returns and the dimension vanishes from the upper viewport.

Annotative Objects with Multiple Scales

But what if we want a dimension or other annotative object to appear in two different viewports and still retain the correct size in relation to paper space? This can be handled by assigning more than one scale to an annotative object, or group of annotative objects. To complete this exploration we will add a linear dimension to the lower left viewport and assign it two scales, so that it will appear at the same height in the right viewport.

⊕ You should be in the lower left viewport to begin this exercise.

⊕ Pick the Linear tool from the dimension control panel of the dashboard.

⊕ Right-click to select an object to dimension.

⊕ Pick the vertical side of the right view of the bushing, as shown in Figure 8-55.

⊕ Pick a dimension line location, as shown.

The dimension is drawn. Notice again that the dimension does not appear in the right viewport.

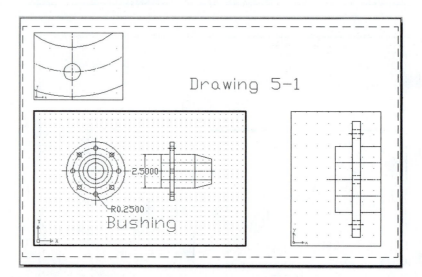

Figure 8-55

⊕ Click the Annotation Visibility button to turn all annotation objects on again.

Your screen should resemble Figure 8-56. We have the familiar problem of the dimension text appearing twice as large in the right viewport, where the Viewport Scale is 4:1 instead of 2:1, as it is in the lower left viewport. Our goal is to display this dimension in both viewports at the same size. This will require two changes. First we match the annotation scale to the viewport scale in this viewport. Second, we add a second scale to the dimension object so that it can be displayed at both scales.

⊕ Double-click in the right viewport.

Notice here that the VP Scale shows 4:1, while the Annotation Scale shows 1:1.

⊕ Open the Annotation Scale list and select 4:1.

We now have a match between the viewport scale and the annotation scale in this viewport, but the dimension is still twice as large as in the left viewport.

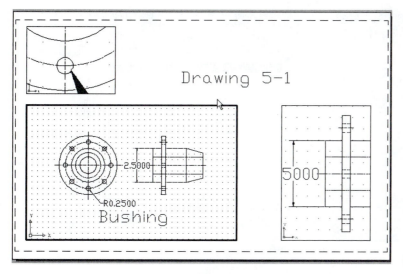

Figure 8-56

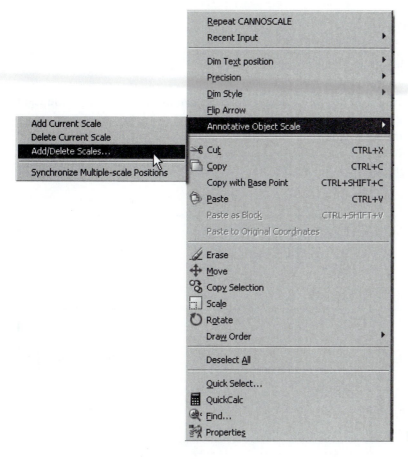

Figure 8-57

⊕ Select the dimension.

You may need to turn off snap to do this effectively. When the dimension is selected, you will see grips in both viewports.

⊕ Right-click to open the shortcut menu shown in Figure 8-57.

⊕ Highlight Annotative Object Scale and then select Add/Delete Scales as shown in the figure.

This opens the **Annotation Object Scale** dialog box shown in Figure 8-58. Notice that 2:1 is the only scale showing in the Object Scale list.

⊕ Click the Add button.

You see the **Add Scales to Object** dialog box shown in Figure 8-59.

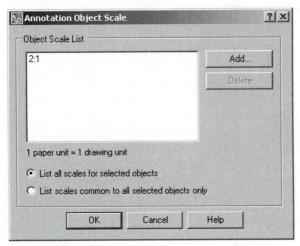

Figure 8-58

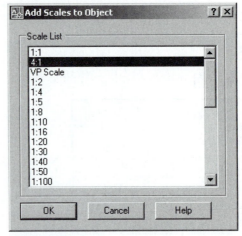

Figure 8-59

⊕ Select 4:1, as shown.

⊕ Click OK.

　　4:1 is added to the Object Scale list below 2:1.

⊕ Click OK to return to the drawing.

　　The dimension in the right viewport is redrawn at the 4:1 scale in the right viewport.

⊕ Finally, click the Annotation Visibility button again.

　　The oversized dimension in the upper viewport vanishes, but the scaled dimension in the right viewport remains. Your screen resembles Figure 8-60.

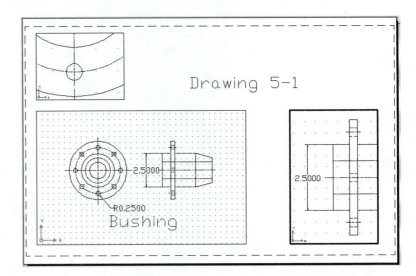

Figure 8-60

Turning Viewport Borders Off

We have used the borders of our viewports as part of our plotted drawings in this drawing layout. Frequently, you want to turn them off. In a typical three-view drawing, for example, you do not draw borders around the three views.

　　In multiple-viewport paper space drawings, the visibility of viewport borders is easily controlled by putting the viewports on a separate layer and then turning the layer off before plotting. You can make a "border" layer, for example, and make it current while you create viewports. You could also use **PROPERTIES** to move viewports to the border layer later.

CHAPTER TEST QUESTIONS

Questions

1. You are working in a drawing with units set to architectural, but when you begin dimensioning, AutoCAD provides four-place decimal units. What is the problem? What do you need to do so that your dimensioning units match your drawing units?

2. Describe at least one way to change the size of the arrowheads in the dimensions of a drawing.

3. How would you add the annotative property to a dimension style?

4. What types of changes to dimension objects can be made in the **Properties** tool palette? How do you open the tool palette?

5. What is a "nearest" object snap, and why is it important when dimensioning with leaders?

6. Why is it useful to move the origin of the coordinate system to make good use of ordinate dimensioning? What option to this is available in the QDIM command?

7. What are the elements of a multileader?

8. What is the difference between hatching by selecting internal points and by selecting objects?

9. What is associative dimensioning? What command makes a nonassociative dimension associative?

10. Name two reasons for creating dimensions with the Annotative property.

11. What is the process for adding additional scales to an annotation object?

12. Paper space is at a 1:1 plotting scale, two viewports in a layout are at 8:1 and 2:1 viewport scales. What do you have to do so that a single annotation object will appear at the same scale in both viewports?

Drawing Problems

1. Create a new dimension style called Dim-2. Dim-2 uses architectural units with 1/2″ precision for all units except angles, which use two-place decimals. Text in Dim-2 is 0.5 unit high.

2. Draw an isosceles triangle with vertexes at (4,3), (14,3), and (9,11). Draw a 2″ circle centered at the center of the triangle.

3. Dimension the base and one side of the triangle using the Dim-2 dimension style.

4. Add a diameter dimension to the circle and change a dimension variable so that the circle is dimensioned with a diameter line drawn inside the circle.

5. Add an angle dimension to one of the base angles of the triangle. Make sure that the dimension is placed outside of the triangle.

6. Hatch the area inside the triangle and outside the circle using a predefined crosshatch pattern.

WWW Exercise 8 (Optional)

In Chapter 8 of our companion website, we challenge you to find information on a great innovator in the fields of graphic arts whose name has come up in this chapter. We give you links to get you started and then send you on your way. We also offer you another design challenge and, as always, the self-scoring test for this chapter. So, when you are ready, complete the following:

⊕ Make sure that you are connected to your Internet service provider.

⊕ Type "browser" ↵ or open your system browser from the Windows taskbar.

⊕ If necessary, navigate to our companion website at prenhall.com/dixriley.

Happy hunting!

CHAPTER PROJECTS

Drawing 8-1: Tool Block

In this drawing, the dimensions should work well without editing. The hatch is a simple user-defined pattern used to indicate that the front and right views are sectioned views.

Drawing Suggestions

```
GRID = 1.0
SNAP = 0.125
HATCH line spacing = 0.125
```

- As a general rule, complete the drawing first, including all cross-hatching, and then add dimensions and text at the end.
- Place all hatching on the hatch layer. When hatching is complete, set to the dim layer and turn the hatch layer off so that hatch lines do not interfere when you select lines for dimensioning.
- The section lines in this drawing can be easily drawn as leaders. Set the dimension arrow size to 0.38 first. Check to see that Ortho is on; then begin the leader at the tip of the arrow and make a right angle as shown. After picking the other endpoint of the leader, press **Enter** to bring up the First line of annotation prompt. Type a space and press **Enter** so you have no text. Press **Enter** again to exit.
- You need to set the dimtix variable (Dimension outside align in the **Properties** dialog box) to on to place the 3.25-diameter dimension at the center of the circle in the top view and off to create the leader style diameter dimension in the front section.

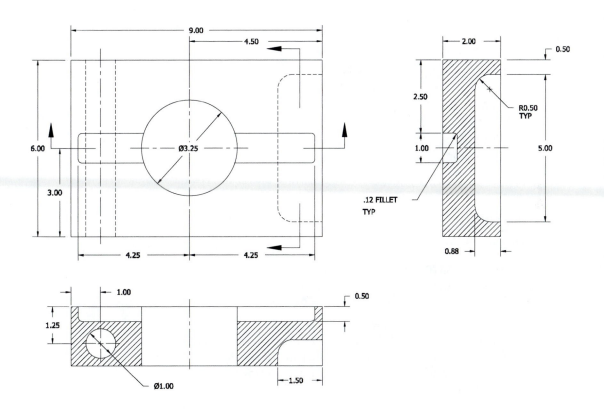

TOOL BLOCK

Drawing 8-1

Drawing 8-2: Flanged Wheel

Most of the objects in this drawing are straightforward. The keyway is easily done using the **TRIM** command. If necessary, use the **Edit** shortcut menu or grips to move the diameter dimension, as shown in the reference.

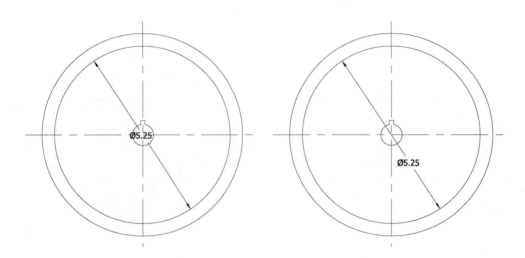

Drawing Suggestions

```
GRID = 0.25
SNAP = 0.0625
HATCH line spacing = 0.50
```

- You need a 0.0625 snap to draw the keyway. Draw a 0.125 × 0.125 square at the top of the 0.63-diameter circle. Drop the vertical lines down into the circle so they can be used to **TRIM** the circle. **TRIM** the circle and the vertical lines, using a window to select both as cutting edges.
- Remember to set to layer hatch before hatching, layer text before adding text, and layer dim before dimensioning.

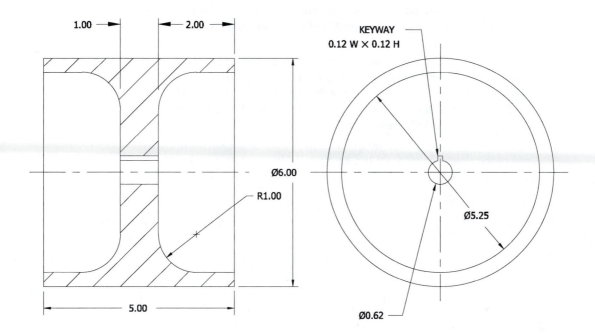

FLANGED WHEEL

Drawing 8-2

Drawing 8-3: Shower Head

This drawing makes use of the procedures for hatching and dimensioning you learned in the last two drawings. In addition, it uses an angular dimension, baseline dimensions, leaders, and %%c for the diameter symbol.

Drawing Suggestions

> GRID = 0.25
> SNAP = 0.125
> HATCH line spacing = 0.25

- You can save some time on this drawing by using **MIRROR** to create half of the right side view. Notice, however, that you cannot hatch before mirroring, because the **MIRROR** command reverses the angle of the hatch lines.
- To achieve the angular dimension at the bottom of the right side view, you need to draw the vertical line coming down on the right. Select this line and the angular line at the right end of the shower head, and the angular extension is drawn automatically. Add the text 2 PL using the **DIMEDIT** command.
- Notice that the diameter symbols in the vertical dimensions at each end of the right side view are not automatic. Use %%c to add the diameter symbol to the text.

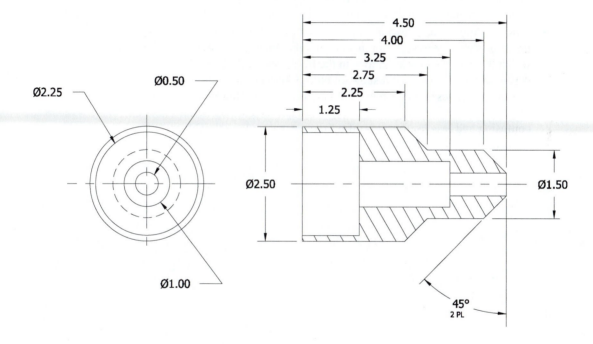

SHOWER HEAD

Drawing 8-3

Drawing 8-4: Nose Adapter

Make ample use of **ZOOM** to work on the details of this drawing. Notice that the limits are set larger than usual, and the snap is rather fine by comparison.

Drawing Suggestions

```
LIMITS = (0,0) (36,24)
GRID = 0.25
SNAP = 0.125
HATCH line spacing = 0.25
```

- You need a 0.125 snap to draw the thread representation shown in the reference. Understand that this is nothing more than a standard representation for screw threads; it does not show actual dimensions. Zoom in close to draw it, and you should have no trouble.
- This drawing includes two examples of simplified drafting practice. The thread representation is one, and the other is the way in which the counterbores are drawn in the front view. A precise rendering of these holes would show an ellipse, because the slant of the object dictates that they break through on an angle. However, to show these ellipses in the front view would make the drawing more confusing and less useful. Simplified representation is preferable in such cases.

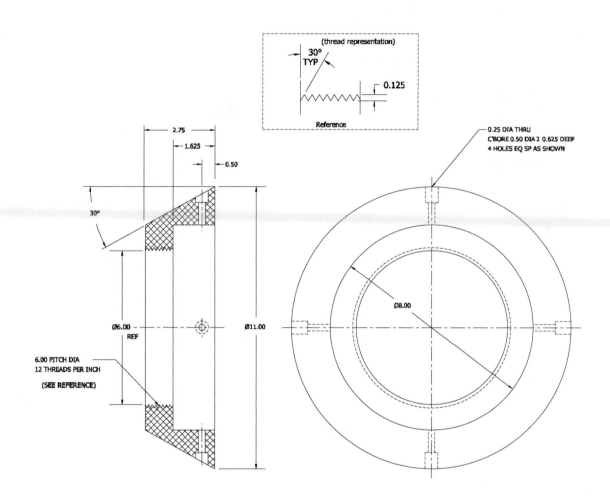

NOSE ADAPTER
Drawing 8-4

Drawing 8-5: Plot Plan

This architectural drawing makes use of three hatch patterns and several dimension variable changes. Be sure to make these settings as shown.

Drawing Suggestions

GRID = 10'
SNAP = 1'
LIMITS = 180', 120'
LTSCALE = 2'

- The "trees" shown here are symbols for oaks, willows, and evergreens.
- **HATCH** opens a space around text inside a defined boundary; however, sometimes you want more white space than **HATCH** leaves. A simple solution is to draw a rectangle around the text area as an inner boundary. Later you can erase the box, leaving an island of white space around the text.

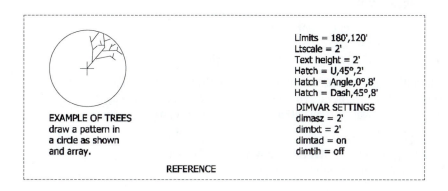

EXAMPLE OF TREES
draw a pattern in
a circle as shown
and array.

REFERENCE

Limits = 180',120'
Ltscale = 2'
Text height = 2'
Hatch = U,45°,2'
Hatch = Angle,0°,8'
Hatch = Dash,45°,8'
DIMVAR SETTINGS
dimasz = 2'
dimtxt = 2'
dimtad = on
dimtih = off

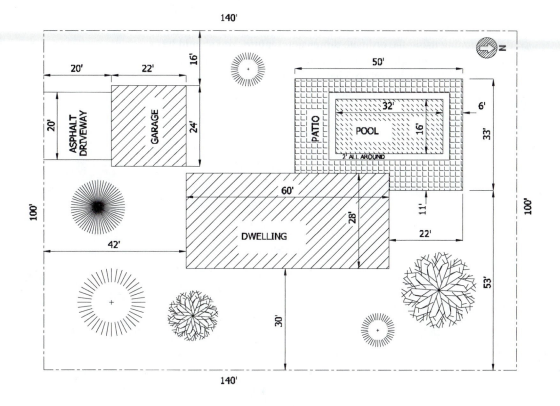

PLOT PLAN

Drawing 8-5

Drawing 8-6: Panel

This drawing is primarily an exercise in using ordinate dimensions. Both the drawing of the objects and the adding of dimensions are facilitated dramatically by this powerful feature.

Drawing Suggestions

> GRID = 0.50
> SNAP = 0.125
> UNITS = three-place decimal

- After setting grid, snap, and units, create a new user coordinate system with the origin moved in and up about one unit each way. This technique was introduced in Section 8.6. For reference, here is the procedure:

  1. Select New UCS and then Origin from the **Tools** menu.
  2. Pick a new origin point.

- From here on all the objects in the drawing can be easily placed using the x and y displacements exactly as they are shown in the drawing.

- When objects have been placed, switch to the dim layer and begin dimensioning using the ordinate dimension feature. You should be able to move along quickly, but be careful to keep dimensions on each side of the panel lined up. That is, the leader endpoints should end along the same vertical or horizontal line.

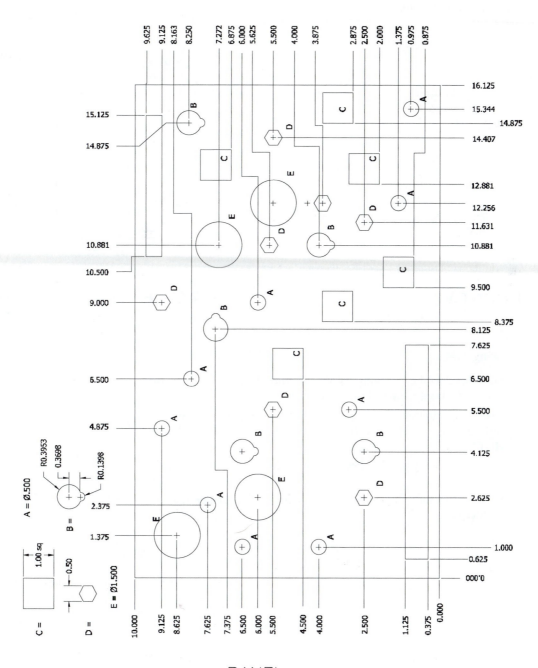

PANEL
DRAWING 8-6

Drawing 8-7: Angle Support

In this drawing, you are expected to use the 3-D view to create three orthographic views. Draw a front view, top view, and side view. The front and top views are drawn showing all necessary hidden lines, and the right side view is drawn in full section. The finished multiview drawing should be fully dimensioned.

TOP VIEW

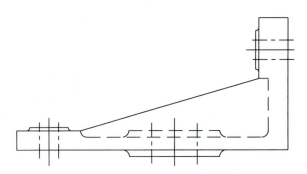

FRONT VIEW   RIGHT SIDE VIEW

Drawing Suggestions

- Start this drawing by laying out the top view. Use the top view to line up the front view and side view.
- Use the illustration of the right side view when planning out the full section. Convert the hidden lines to solid lines and use **HATCH** to create crosshatching.
- Complete the right-side view in full section, using the ANSI31 hatch pattern.
- Be sure to include all the necessary hidden lines and center lines in each view.

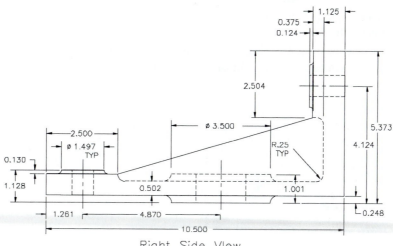

Right Side View

ANGLE SUPPORT
Drawing 8-7

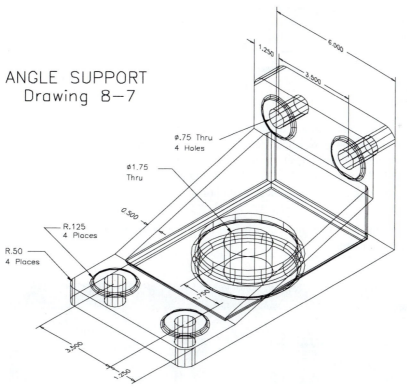

Drawing 8-8: Mirror Mounting Plate

This drawing introduces AutoCAD's geometric tolerancing capability, an additional feature of the dimension system. Geometric tolerancing symbols and values are added using a simple dialog box interface. For example, to add the tolerance values and symbols below the leadered dimension text on the .128 diameter hole at the top middle of the drawing, follow these steps. All other tolerances in the drawing are created in the same manner.

- After creating the objects in the drawing, create the leadered dimension text beginning with .128 DIA THRU . . . as shown.

- Select Tolerance from the **Dimension** menu, or the **Tolerance** tool from the **Dimension** toolbar, as illustrated in Figure 8-61.

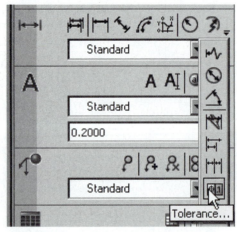

Figure 8-61

- Fill in the values and symbols as shown in Figure 8-62. To fill in the first black symbol box, click the box and select a symbol. To fill in the diameter symbol, click the second black box and the symbol is filled in automatically. To fill in any of the Material Condition boxes, click the box and select a symbol.

- Click **OK.**

- Drag the Tolerance boxes into place below the dimension text as shown in the drawing.

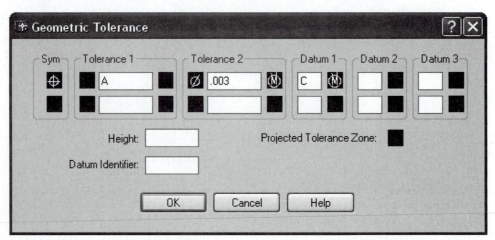

Figure 8-62

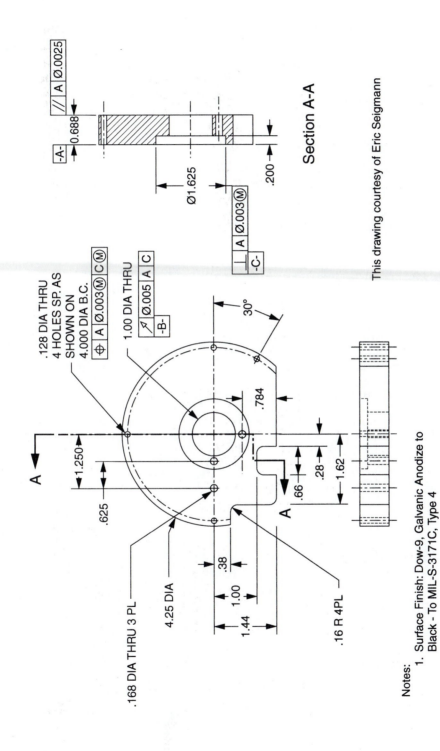

Section A-A

This drawing courtesy of Eric Seigmann

MIRROR MOUNTING PLATE
Drawing 8-8

Notes:
1. Surface Finish: Dow-9, Galvanic Anodize to
   Black - To MIL-S-3171C, Type 4

319

Polylines

Chapter Objectives

- Drawing POLYGONs
- Drawing DONUTs
- Using the FILL Command
- Drawing Straight Polyline Segments
- Drawing Polyline Arc Segments
- Editing Polylines with PEDIT
- Drawing and Editing Multilines
- Drawing SPLINEs
- Drawing Revision Clouds
- Drawing Points

INTRODUCTION

This chapter should be fun because you will be learning a large number of new commands. You will see new things happening on your screen with each command. The commands in this chapter are used to create special entities, some of which cannot be drawn any other way. All of them are complex objects made up of lines, circles, and arcs (like the text, dimensions, and hatch patterns discussed in the previous two chapters), but they are stored and treated as singular entities. Some of them, such as polygons and donuts, are familiar geometric figures, whereas others, like polylines, are peculiar to CAD.

9-1 DRAWING POLYGONS

GENERAL PROCEDURE	1. Select the **Polygon** tool from the dashboard. 2. Type the number of sides. 3. Pick a center point. 4. Indicate Inscribed or Circumscribed. 5. Show the radius of the circle.

Among the most interesting and flexible of the entities you can create in AutoCAD is the polyline. In this chapter, we begin with two regularly shaped polyline entities, polygons and donuts. These entities have their own special commands, separate from the general **PLINE** command (Sections 9.4 and 9.5), but are created as polylines and can be edited just as any other polyline would be.

Polygons with any number of sides can be drawn using the **POLYGON** command. In the default sequence, AutoCAD constructs a polygon based on the number of sides, the center point,

COMMAND GRID	
Command	Polygon
Alias	Pol
Menu	Draw
Tool	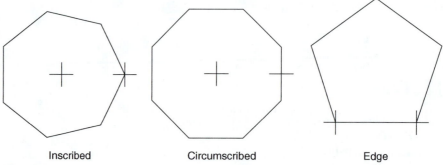

and a radius. Optionally, the edge method allows you to specify the number of sides and the length and position of one side (see Figure 9-1).

⊕ Create a new drawing using the 1B template.

⊕ Select the Polygon tool from the dashboard, as shown in Figure 9-2.

AutoCAD's first prompt is for the number of sides:

```
Enter number of sides <4>:
```

⊕ Type "8" ↵.

Inscribed   Circumscribed   Edge

Figure 9-1

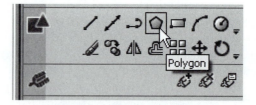

Figure 9-2

Now you are prompted to show either a center point or the first point of one edge:

```
Specify center of polygon or [Edge]:
```

⊕ Pick a center point, as shown by the center mark on the left in Figure 9-3.

From here the size of the polygon can be specified in one of two ways, as shown in Figure 9-1. The radius of a circle is given and the polygon drawn either inside or outside the imaginary circle. In the case of the inscribed polygon this means that the radius is measured from the center to a vertex of the polygon. In the circumscribed polygon the radius is measured from the center to the midpoint of a side. You indicate which option you want by typing "i" or "c"; or by selecting from the dynamic input menu. The prompt is:

```
Enter an option [Inscribed in circle/Circumscribed
about circle] <I>:
```

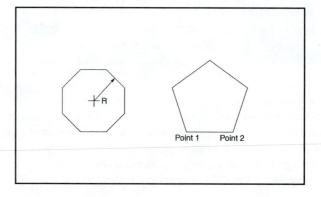

Point 1   Point 2

Figure 9-3

Inscribed is the default. We use the circumscribed method instead.

⊕ Type "c" ↵ or select Circumscribed about circle from the dynamic input menu.

Now you are prompted to show a radius of this imaginary circle (i.e., a line from the center to the midpoint of a side):

<pre>
                Specify radius of circle:
</pre>

⊕ Pick a radius similar to the one in Figure 9-3.

We leave it to you to try the inscribed option. We draw one more polygon, using the edge method.

⊕ Press Enter or the spacebar to repeat the POLYGON command.

⊕ Type "5" ↵ for the number of sides.

⊕ Type "e" ↵ or right-click and select Edge from the shortcut menu.

AutoCAD issues a different series of prompts:

<pre>
            Specify first endpoint of edge:
</pre>

⊕ Pick Point 1, as shown on the right in Figure 9-3.

AutoCAD prompts

<pre>
           Specify second endpoint of edge:
</pre>

⊕ Pick a second point as shown.

Your screen should resemble Figure 9-3.

9-2 DRAWING DONUTS

 GENERAL PROCEDURE	1. Select Donut from the **Draw** menu. 2. Type or show an inside diameter. 3. Type or show an outside diameter. 4. Pick a center point. 5. Pick another center point. 6. Press **Enter** to exit the command.

A donut in AutoCAD is a polyline object represented by two concentric circles. The donut is the space between the circles.

The **DONUT** command is logical and easy to use. You show a center point, inside and outside diameters, and then draw as many donut-shaped objects of the specified size as you like.

⊕ Clear your display of polygons before continuing.

⊕ Select Donut from the Draw menu.

You can also type the alias "do." There is no donut button on the dashboard.

AutoCAD prompts

<pre>
        Specify inside diameter of donut <0.50>:
</pre>

We change the inside diameter to 1.00.

⊕ Type "1" ↵.

AutoCAD prompts

<pre>
        Specify outside diameter of donut <1.00>:
</pre>

We change the outside diameter to 2.00.

⊕ Type "2" ↵.

AutoCAD gives you a donut to drag into place and prompts

<pre>
            Specify center of donut or [exit]:
</pre>

⊕ Pick any point.

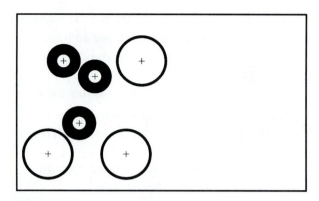

Figure 9-4

A donut is drawn around the point you chose, as shown by the "fat" donuts in Figure 9-4. (If your donut is not filled, see Section 9.3.)

AutoCAD stays in the **DONUT** command, allowing you to continue drawing donuts.

⊕ Pick a second center point.

⊕ Pick a third center point.

You should now have three "fat" donuts on your screen as shown.

⊕ Press Enter or right-click to exit the DONUT command.

Now draw the "thin" donuts in the figure.

⊕ Repeat DONUT.

⊕ Change the inside diameter to 3.00 and the outside diameter to 3.25.

⊕ Draw three or four "thin" donuts, as shown in Figure 9-4.

When you are done, leave the donuts on the screen so that you can see how they are affected by the **FILL** command.

9-3 Using the FILL Command

GENERAL PROCEDURE	1. Type "fill" ↵. 2. Select on or off. 3. Type "re" ↵ or select Regen from the **View** menu.

Donuts and wide polylines (Sections 9.4 and 9.5) are all affected by **FILL.** With **FILL** on, these entities are displayed and plotted as solid filled objects. With **FILL** off, only the outer boundaries are displayed. (Donuts are shown with radial lines between the inner and outer circles.)

⊕ For this exercise, you should have at least one donut on your screen from Section 9.2.

⊕ Type "fill" ↵.

AutoCAD prompts

Enter Mode [ON/OFF] <ON>:

These options are also shown on the dynamic input menu

⊕ Select off from the dynamic input menu.

You do not see any immediate change in your display when you do this. To see the effect, you have to regenerate your drawing.

⊕ Type "re" ↵ or select Regen from the View menu.

Your screen is regenerated with **FILL** off and should resemble Figure 9-5. Many of the special entities that we discuss in the remainder of this chapter can be filled, so we encourage you to continue to experiment with **FILL** as you go along.

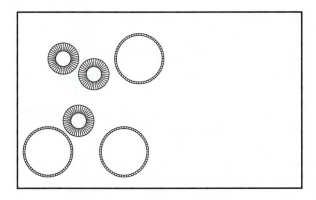

Figure 9-5

9-4 DRAWING STRAIGHT POLYLINE SEGMENTS

GENERAL PROCEDURE	1. Select the **Polyline** tool from the dashboard. 2. Pick a start point. 3. Type or select Width, Halfwidth, or other options. 4. Pick other points.

In the last two chapters, you saw how text, dimensions, and hatch patterns are all created as complex entities that can be selected and treated as single objects. In the next chapter, you see how to create groups and blocks from separate entities. In this chapter, we are focusing on the polyline. You have already drawn several polylines without going through the **PLINE** command. Donuts and polygons both are drawn as polylines and therefore can be edited using the same edit commands that work on other polylines. You can, for instance, fillet all the corners of a polygon at once, using the Pline option in the **FILLET** command. Using the **PLINE** command itself, you can draw anything from a simple line to a series of lines and arcs with varying widths. Most important, polylines can be edited using many of the ordinary edit commands as well as a set of specialized editing procedures found in the **PEDIT** command.

We begin by creating a simple polyline rectangle. The process is much like drawing a rectangular outline with the **LINE** command, but the result is a single object rather than four distinct line segments.

⊕ Clear your display of donuts before continuing.

⊕ Select the Polyline tool from the dashboard, as shown in Figure 9-6.

AutoCAD begins with a prompt for a starting point, as in the **LINE** command:

Specify start point:

⊕ Pick a start point, similar to P1 in Figure 9-7.

COMMAND GRID	
Command	Pline
Alias	Pl
Menu	Draw
Tool	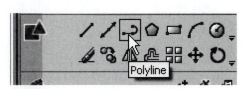

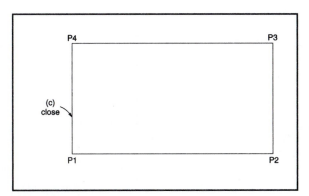

Figure 9-6

Figure 9-7

From here the **PLINE** prompt sequence becomes more complicated:

```
Current line width is 0.00
Specify next point or [Arc/Halfwidth/Length/Undo/Width]:
```

The prompt begins by giving you the current line width, left from any previous use of the **PLINE** command.

Then the prompt offers options in the usual format. Arc leads you into another set of options that deals with drawing polyline arcs. We save polyline arcs for Section 9.5. We get to the other options momentarily.

Here we draw a series of 0-width segments, just as we would in the **LINE** command.

⊕ Pick an endpoint, similar to P2 in Figure 9-7.

AutoCAD draws the segment and repeats the prompt. Notice that after you have picked two points, AutoCAD adds a Close option to the command prompt.

⊕ Pick another endpoint, P3 in Figure 9-7.

⊕ Pick another endpoint, P4 in Figure 9-7.

⊕ Type "c" ↵ or right-click and select Close from the shortcut menu to complete the rectangle, as shown in Figure 9-7.

⊕ Now select the rectangle by pointing to any of its sides.

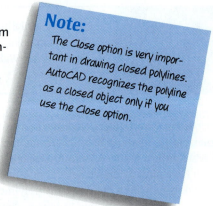

Note:
The Close option is very important in drawing closed polylines. AutoCAD recognizes the polyline as a closed object only if you use the Close option.

You can see that the entire rectangle is selected, rather than just the side you pointed to. This means, for example, that you can fillet or chamfer all four corners of the rectangle at once.

Now let's create a rectangle with wider lines.

⊕ Press Esc to remove grips.

⊕ Enter the PLINE command.

⊕ Pick a starting point, as shown by P1 in Figure 9-8.

AutoCAD prompts

```
Specify next point or [Arc/Close/Halfwidth/Length/Undo/Width]:
```

This time we need to make use of the Width option.

⊕ Type "w" ↵ or right-click and select Width from the shortcut menu.

AutoCAD responds with

```
Specify starting width <0.00>:
```

You are prompted for two widths, a starting width and an ending width. This makes it possible to draw tapered lines. For this exercise, our lines have the same starting and ending width.

⊕ Type ".25" ↵.

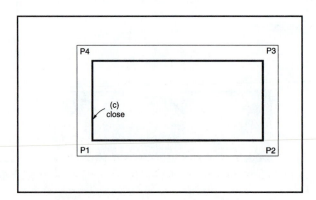

Figure 9-8

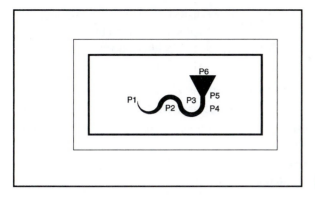

Figure 9-9

AutoCAD prompts

`Specify ending width <0.25>:`

Notice that the starting width has become the default for the ending width. To draw a polyline of uniform width, we accept this default.

✛ Press Enter or the spacebar to keep the starting width and ending width the same.

AutoCAD returns to the previous prompt and gives you a .25-wide rubber band to drag on the screen.

✛ Pick an endpoint, as shown by P2 in Figure 9-8.

✛ Continue picking Points P3 and P4 to draw a second rectangle, as shown in Figure 9-9.

✛ Use the Close option to draw the last side.

Note:
The Halfwidth option differs from Width only in that the width of the line to be drawn is measured from the center out. With either option, you can specify by showing a width rather than typing a value.

When the object is complete, AutoCAD creates joined corners. If you do not close the last side, the lower left corner overlaps rather than joins. Notice also that once a polyline has been given a width, it is affected by the **FILL** setting.

The only options we have not discussed in this exercise are Length and Undo. Length allows you to type or show a value and then draws a segment of that length starting from the endpoint of the previous segment and continuing in the same direction. (If the last segment was an arc, the length is drawn tangent to the arc.) Undo undoes the last segment, just as in LINE.

In the next task, we draw polyline arc segments.

9-5 DRAWING POLYLINE ARC SEGMENTS

GENERAL PROCEDURE

1. Enter the **PLINE** command.
2. Pick a start point.
3. Specify a width.
4. Type "a" ↵ or select arc from the shortcut menu.
5. Type or select options or pick an endpoint.

A word of caution: Because of the flexibility and power of the **PLINE** command, it is tempting to think of polylines as always having weird shapes, tapered lines, and strange sequences of lines and arcs. Remember, **PLINE** may also be used to create simple sets of lines, polygons, or arcs.

Having said that, we proceed to construct our own weird shape to show what can be done. We draw a polyline with three arc segments and one tapered line segment, as shown in Figure 9-9. We call this thing a goosenecked funnel. You might have seen something like it at your local garage.

⊞ Enter the PLINE command.

⊞ Pick a new start point, as shown by P1 in Figure 9-9.

⊞ Type "w" ↵ or right-click and select Width to set new widths.

⊞ Type "0" ↵ for the starting width.

⊞ Type ".5" ↵ for the ending width.

⊞ Type "a" ↵ or right-click and select Arc.

This opens the arc prompt, which looks like this:

```
Specify endpoint of arc or
[Angle/CEnter/Direction/Halfwidth/Line/Radius/Second
pt/Undo/Width]:
```

Let's look at this prompt for a moment. To begin with, there are four options that are familiar from the previous prompt. Halfwidth, Undo, and Width all function exactly as they would in drawing straight polyline segments. The Line option returns you to the previous prompt so that you can continue drawing straight line segments after drawing arc segments.

The other options, Angle, CEnter, Direction, Radius, Second pt, and Endpoint of arc, allow you to specify arcs in ways similar to the **ARC** command. AutoCAD assumes that the arc you are constructing will be tangent to the last polyline segment entered. You can override this assumption with the Center and Direction options, which allow you to establish different directions.

⊞ Pick an endpoint to the right, as shown by P2 in Figure 9-9, to complete the first arc segment.

TIP If you did not follow the order shown in the figures and drew your previous rectangle clockwise, or if you have drawn other polylines in the meantime, you might find that the arc does not curve below the horizontal, as shown in Figure 9-9. This is because AutoCAD starts arcs tangent to the last polyline segment drawn. Fix this by using the Direction option. Type "d" ↵ and then pick a point straight down. Now you can pick an endpoint to the right as shown.

AutoCAD prompts again:

```
Specify endpoint of arc or
[Angle/CEnter/CLose/Direction/Halfwidth/Line/Radius/Second
pt/Undo/Width]:
```

For the remaining two arc segments, retain a uniform width of 0.50.

⊞ Enter Points P3 and P4 to draw the remaining two arc segments as shown.

Now we draw two straight segments to complete the polyline.

⊞ Right-click and select Line from the shortcut menu.

This takes you back to the original prompt.

⊞ Pick P5 straight up about 1.00 units as shown.

⊞ Right-click and select Width from the shortcut menu.

⊞ Press Enter to retain 0.50 as the starting width.

⊞ Type "3" ↵ for the ending width.

⊞ Pick an endpoint up about 2.00 as shown by P6.

⊞ Press Enter or the spacebar to exit the command.

Your screen should resemble Figure 9-9.

9-6 EDITING POLYLINES WITH PEDIT

GENERAL PROCEDURE	1. Select Modify → Object → Polyline from the pull-down menu. 2. Select a polyline. 3. Type or select a PEDIT option. 4. Follow the prompts.

The **PEDIT** command provides a subsystem of special editing capabilities that work only on polylines. We do not attempt to have you use all of them. Most important is that you be aware of the possibilities so that when you find yourself in a situation calling for a **PEDIT** procedure you know what to look for. After executing the following steps, study Figure 9-12, the **PEDIT** chart.

We perform two edits on the polylines already drawn.

⊕ Type "pe" ↵ or select Modify → Object → Polyline from the pull-down menu.

This executes the **PEDIT** command. You are prompted to select a polyline:

Select polyline or [Multiple]:

⊕ Select the outer 0-width polyline rectangle drawn in Section 9.4.

Notice that PEDIT works on only one object at a time. If you want to edit more than one polyline with the same PEDIT option, use the Multiple option. You are prompted as follows:

Enter an option [Open/Join/Width/Edit
vertex/Fit/Spline/Decurve/Ltype gen/Undo]:

These same options are displayed in a drop-down menu on the dynamic input display. Open is replaced by Close if your polyline has not been closed. Undo and eXit are self-explanatory. Other options are illustrated in Figure 9-12. Edit vertex brings up the subset of options shown on the right side of the chart. When you do vertex editing, AutoCAD marks one vertex at a time with an X. You can move the X to other vertices by pressing **Enter** or typing "n."

Now we edit the selected polyline by changing its width.

⊕ Type "w" ↵ or select Width from the dynamic input display menu.

This option allows you to set a new uniform width for an entire polyline. All tapering and variation are removed when this edit is performed.

AutoCAD prompts

Specify new width for all segments:

⊕ Type ".25" ↵.

Your screen is redrawn to resemble Figure 9-10.

Figure 9-10

The prompt is returned and the polyline is still selected so that you can continue shaping it with other **PEDIT** options.

⊞ Press Enter or the spacebar to exit PEDIT.

⊞ Press Enter or the spacebar to repeat PEDIT.

This exiting and reentering is necessary to select another polyline to edit, using a different type of edit.

⊞ Select the gooseneck funnel polyline.

This time we try the Decurve option. Decurve straightens all curves within the selected polyline.

⊞ Type "d" ↵ or select Decurve from the dynamic input display menu.

⊞ Press Enter or the spacebar to exit PEDIT.

Your screen should resemble Figure 9-11.

To complete this exercise, we suggest that you try some of the other editing options. In particular, you can get interesting results from Fit and Spline. Be sure to study the **PEDIT** chart (Figure 9-12) before going on to the next task.

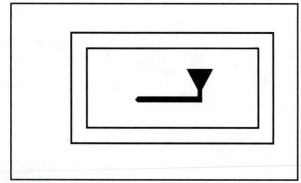

Figure 9-11

PEDIT (Editing Polylines)			
ENTIRE POLYLINE BEFORE / AFTER		**VERTEX EDITING** BEFORE / AFTER	
Close — Creates closing segment		Break — Removes sections between two specified vertices	
Open — Removes closing segment		Insert — New vertex is added after the currently marked vertex	
Join — Two objects will be joined making one polyline. Objects must be exact match. Polyline must be open		Move — Moves the currently marked vertex to a new location	
Width — Changes the entire width uniformly		Straighten — Straightens the segment following the currently marked vertex	
Fit — Computes a smooth curve		Tangent — Marks the tangent direction of the currently marked vertex for later use in fitting curves	
Spline — Computes a cubic B-spline curve		Width — Changes the starting and ending widths of the individual segments following the currently marked vertex	
Ltype gen — Set to on generates ltype in continuous pattern / Set to off generates ltype to start and end dashed at vertex			

Figure 9-12

9-7 DRAWING AND EDITING MULTILINES

GENERAL PROCEDURE	1. Type "ml" ⏎ or select Multiline from the **Draw** menu. 2. Pick a start point. 3. Pick a next point. 4. Pick another point, or press **Enter** to exit the command.

Multilines are groups of parallel lines with various forms of intersections and end caps. Each individual line is called an element, and you can have up to 16 elements in a single multiline style. Drawing multilines is about as simple as drawing lines. The complexity comes in defining multiline styles and in editing intersections. In this section, we draw standard multilines, create a new style, and edit the intersection of two multilines.

⊕ Clear the screen of objects left from previous exercises.

First, we draw some standard multilines.

⊕ Type "ml" ⏎ or select Multiline from the Draw menu.

AutoCAD issues the following prompt:

```
Current settings: Justification = Top, Scale = 1.00,
Style = STANDARD
Specify start point or [Justification/Scale/Style]:
```

If you stick with the default options, the **MLINE** sequence is exactly like drawing a line. Justification refers to the way elements are positioned in relation to the points you pick on the screen. The default justification is Top. With Top justification, the crosshairs will align with the top element of the multiline if you pick the second point to the right of the first. The crosshairs will line up with the bottom element if you move left. Try it.

⊕ Pick a start point similar to P1 in Figure 9-13.

AutoCAD gives you a standard, two-element multiline to drag and prompts for another point:

```
Specify next point:
```

Move the cursor and notice how the crosshairs continue to connect with the top element. The other two options for justification are Zero and Bottom. Zero positions the crosshairs in the middle of the elements, at the zero point or origin. Bottom lines up on the bottom element.

⊕ Pick a second point similar to P2 in Figure 9-13.

Exact lengths and angles are not important. Move the cursor around and notice how AutoCAD adjusts the corner to maintain parallel line elements.

AutoCAD has added an Undo option now that you have one multiline segment complete:

```
Specify next point or [Undo]:
```

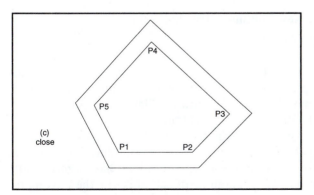

Figure 9-13

⊕ Pick P3, as in Figure 9-13.

> Once you have two complete multiline segments, AutoCAD adds a close option:
>
> Specify next point or [Close/Undo]:

⊕ Pick P4, as in Figure 9-13.

⊕ Pick P5, as in Figure 9-13.

⊕ Type "c" ↵ or right-click and select Close to close and complete the figure.

Creating Multiline Styles

The real power of multilines comes when you learn to create your own multiline style. This is done through the **Multiline Style** dialog box, called by the **MLSTYLE** command.

⊕ Select Multiline Style from the Format menu.

> This opens the dialog box shown in Figure 9-14. Standard is the name of the current multiline style, which, as we have seen, includes two continuous line elements. We begin by adding a new style to the list of multiline styles and then adding a third element to the new style.

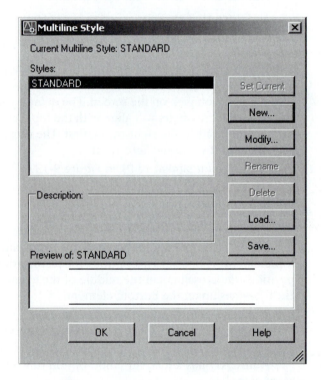

Figure 9-14

⊕ Click the New button.

> This opens a small **Create New Multiline Style** dialog box.

⊕ Type new in the New style name box.

⊕ Click Continue.

> This brings you to the **New Multiline Style** box shown in Figure 9-15. The panel on the left is labeled Caps. Here you can control the way joints and ends of multilines are treated. The variety of options is shown in Figure 9-16. For our purposes, it is not necessary to add joints or end caps at this point.
>
> Now look at the Elements panel on the right. It shows that there are now only two elements: One is offset 0.5 above the origin point of the multiline (0.0) and the other is offset −0.5, or 0.5 below the origin. Standard multilines have a zero point between the two lines, but because the default justification is top, the crosshairs

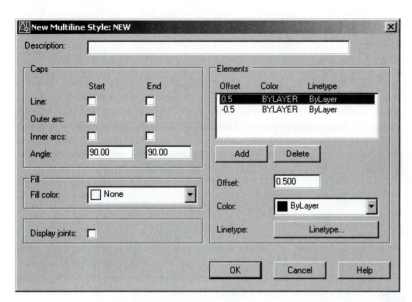

Figure 9-15

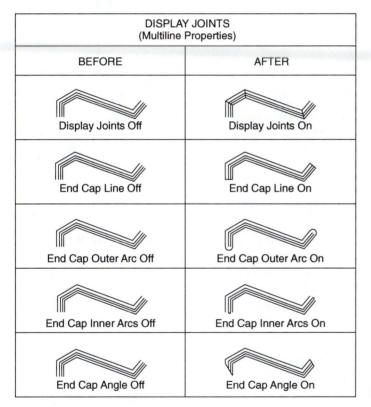

DISPLAY JOINTS (Multiline Properties)	
BEFORE	AFTER
Display Joints Off	Display Joints On
End Cap Line Off	End Cap Line On
End Cap Outer Arc Off	End Cap Outer Arc On
End Cap Inner Arcs Off	End Cap Inner Arcs On
End Cap Angle Off	End Cap Angle On

Figure 9-16

line up on the top element. With zero justification they would line up at 0.0. With bottom justification they would line up on the −0.5 element.

⊕ Click the Add button.

This is how we begin to add a new element. As soon as you click Add, a third element is added to the Elements box. Notice that it is offset 0.0. In other words, it is right on the zero line between the two offset lines. For this style, leave it there. If we needed to offset it, we would type a new offset number in the Offset box.

Next, notice that all three elements are listed as having BYLAYER color and linetype. This means that the color and linetype are determined by whatever layer the multiline is drawn on. We change the linetype of our newly added middle element. This element should be highlighted. If it is not, click on it to highlight it before proceeding.

⊕ Click the Linetype button.

This opens the **Select Linetype** dialog box shown in Figure 9-17. This box contains all the loaded linetypes in your drawing. From past exercises, you should at least have the hidden and center linetypes loaded. (If for any reason your template drawing does not have the hidden linetype, select Load in this dialog box and load it now.)

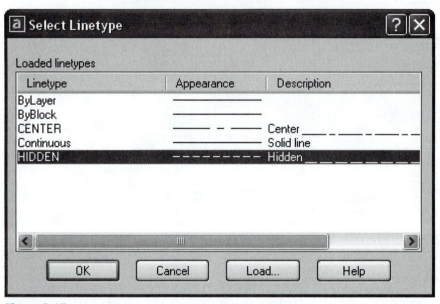

Figure 9-17

⊕ Select HIDDEN.

⊕ Click OK.

Notice that the element at 0.0 now has the hidden linetype.

⊕ Click OK again.

This returns you to the **Multiline Style** dialog box. You should see that the middle element has been added to the Preview box but is shown as a continuous line. The Preview box shows elements by position, but does not show color or linetype. Also, you see that the New style has been added to the list of styles.

⊕ Click the Set Current button to set New as the current Multiline style.

Now you are ready to leave the box and draw some new multilines.

⊕ Click OK to exit the dialog box.

⊕ Erase previously drawn multilines.

⊕ Type "ml" ↵ or select Multiline from the Draw menu.

⊕ Pick two points to draw the horizontal multiline shown in Figure 9-18.

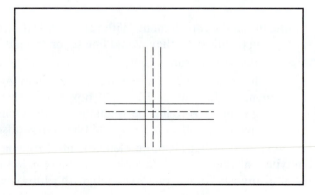

Figure 9-18

⊞ Press Enter to exit the MLINE command.

⊞ Repeat MLINE and pick two more points to draw the vertical multiline shown in Figure 9-18.

Editing Multiline Intersections

Multilines can be modified using many of the same edit commands that are used with other entities. In addition, there is a special **MLEDIT** command for editing the intersection of two multilines. The dialog box illustrates the options using a figure similar to the one you have just drawn.

⊞ Double-click either of the multiline objects in your drawing.

This opens the **Multiline Edit Tools** dialog box shown in Figure 9-19. Because the figure on your screen is similar to the one used in these image boxes, what you see is pretty much what you get when you perform any of these edits.

⊞ Click on the top left image box, labeled Closed Cross.

⊞ Pick the vertical multiline.

The order in which you pick is clearly significant with this and many of the other multiline edits. In this case, the second multiline picked does not change and appears to cross over the first.

⊞ Pick the horizontal multiline.

Your screen should resemble Figure 9-20.

⊞ Press Enter to exit the command.

With up to 16 elements, all of the AutoCAD color options, 58 standard linetypes, and the different end-cap forms and types of intersection edits, the possibilities for creating multiline styles are substantial. We encourage you to experiment before going on.

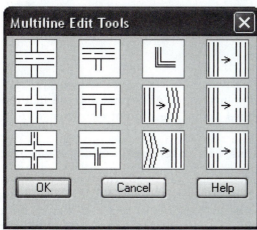

Figure 9-19

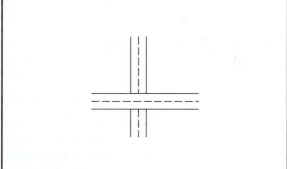

Figure 9-20

9-8 DRAWING SPLINEs

GENERAL PROCEDURE	1. Select the **Spline** tool from the dashboard. 2. Pick points. 3. Close or specify start and end tangent directions.

A spline is a smooth curve passing through a specified set of points. In AutoCAD, splines are created in a precise mathematical form called nonuniform rational B-spline (NURBS). Splines can be drawn with varying degrees of tolerance, meaning the degree to which the curve is constrained by the defined points. With zero tolerance, the curve passes through all points. With higher degrees of tolerance, the curve bends toward, but does not necessarily pass through, each point. In addition to tolerance and the set of points needed to define a spline, tangent directions are needed for the starting and ending portions of the curve. From Chapter 8, recall that dimension leaders can be drawn as splines. Polylines can be converted to spline curves. Splines can be used to create any smooth curve that can be defined by a set of control points. In this task, we use **SPLINE** to draw a curve surrounding the multilines drawn in Section 9.7.

⊕ Select the Spline tool from the dashboard, as shown in Figure 9-21.

AutoCAD prompts

```
Specify first point or [Object]:
```

⊕ Pick a point roughly 1.00 unit to the left of the top element of the horizontal multiline, P1 as shown in Figure 9-22.

AutoCAD prompts for a next point and continues to prompt for points until you press Enter.

⊕ Pick a second point about 1.00 unit above the left side of the horizontal multiline, P2 as shown in Figure 9-22.

COMMAND GRID	
Command	Spline
Alias	Spl
Menu	Draw
Tool	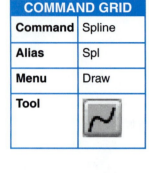

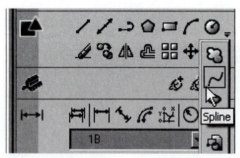

Figure 9-21

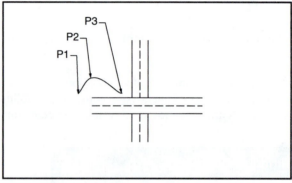

Figure 9-22

As soon as you have two points, AutoCAD shows a spline that drags with your cursor as you select a third point. The prompt also changes to add two options:

```
Specify next point or [Close/Fit tolerance] <start tangent>:
```

The Fit tolerance option determines the degree to which the curve is constrained by the selected points, as discussed previously. Close works as in other commands to create a closed object. If the object is closed, there is no need for tangent specifications. Otherwise, the start and end directions need to be specified at the end when all point selection is complete.

⊕ Pick a third point, P3 as shown in Figure 9-23.

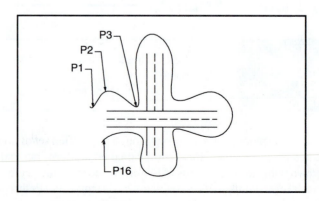

Figure 9-23

From here on, you are on your own as you continue entering points to surround the multilines. We have made no attempt to specify precise points. We used 16 points to go all the way around without crossing the multilines, as shown in Figure 9-23. The exact number of points you choose is not important for this task.

⊕ Continue selecting points to surround the multilines without touching them.

⊕ After you reach and pick a point similar to P16 in Figure 9-23, press Enter or the spacebar.

This indicates that you are finished specifying points. We left the spline open to demonstrate the tangent specifications. When you press **Enter,** the cursor is attached to the start point, P1, again, and the prompt is this:

Specify start tangent:

⊕ Pick a point above P1.

The cursor is now attached to P16 again and the prompt is this:

Specify end tangent:

⊕ Pick a point below P16.

Your screen resembles Figure 9-23.

Editing Splines

Splines can be edited in the usual ways, but they also have their own edit command, **SPLINEDIT.** Because splines are defined by sets of points, one useful option is to use grips to move grip points. The **SPLINEDIT** command gives you additional options, including the option to change the tolerance, to add fit points for greater definition, or to delete unnecessary points. An open spline can be closed, or the start and end tangent directions can be changed. To access **SPLINEDIT,** select Modify → Object → Spline from the pull-down menu.

9-9 DRAWING REVISION CLOUDS

| G E N E R A L |
| PROCEDURE |

1. Select the **Revcloud** tool from the dashboard.
2. Pick a start point and draw a rough circle around the desired area.
3. Bring the cloud outline back to the start point and let AutoCAD close the cloud automatically.

Revision clouds are a simple graphic means of highlighting areas in a drawing that have been edited. They are primarily used in large projects where a number of people are working on a drawing or a set of drawings. Revision clouds can be very quickly created to highlight an error or a place where changes have been made. They have a shape that is very unlikely to be confused with any actual geometry in your drawing. Try this:

⊕ Pick the Revcloud tool from the dashboard, as shown in Figure 9-24.

AutoCAD prompts

```
Minimum arc length: 0.50 Maximum arc length: 0.50
Specify start point or [Arc length/Object/Style] <Object>:
```

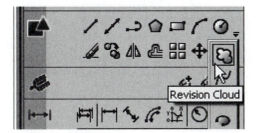

Figure 9-24

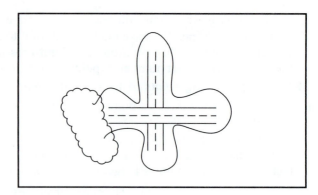

Figure 9-25

Drawing a revision cloud is a simple matter of moving the crosshairs in a circle around an area, as if you were circling it with a pencil in a paper drawing. We draw a cloud around the open end of the spline curve.

⊕ Pick any point about 1.00 away from the left end of the spline curves, as shown in Figure 9-25.

AutoCAD prompts

> Guide crosshairs along cloud path...

⊕ Move the cursor in a rough circle around the open ends of the curve to create a cloud similar to the one shown in Figure 9-25.

If snap is on, AutoCAD temporarily turns it off. When you come near the starting point, the cloud closes automatically. Revclouds can also be created from circles, rectangles, or other closed objects. These can be drawn in the usual manner and then converted to clouds using the Object option. The Arc length option allows you to change the size of the individual arcs that make up the cloud. As you might expect, a completed revision cloud is a polyline. Good practice may require that you create revision clouds on a special layer.

9-10 DRAWING POINTS

GENERAL PROCEDURE	1. Select the **Point** tool from the dashboard. 2. Pick a point.

On the surface, this is the simplest **DRAW** command in AutoCAD. However, if you look at Figure 9-26, you can see figures that were drawn with the **POINT** command that do not look like ordinary points. This capability adds a bit of complexity to the otherwise simple **POINT** command.

⊕ Erase objects from previous exercises.

⊕ Turn off the grid.

⊕ Select the Point tool from the dashboard, as shown in Figure 9-27.

⊕ Pick a point anywhere on the screen.

AutoCAD places a point at the specified location and prompts for more points. Look closely and you can see the point you have drawn. Besides those odd instances in which you might need to draw tiny dots like this, points can

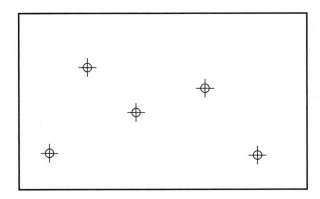

Figure 9-26

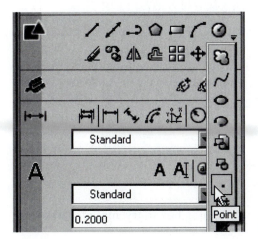

Figure 9-27

also serve as object snap nodes. See the Object Snap chart (Figure 6-5) in Chapter 6.

What about those circles and crosses in Figure 9-26? AutoCAD has 18 other simple forms that can be drawn as points. Before we change the point form, we need to see our options.

⊕ Select Point Style from the Format menu.

AutoCAD displays a **Point Style** dialog box with an icon menu, as shown in Figure 9-28. It shows you graphic images of your choices. You can pick any of the point styles shown by pointing. You can also change the size of points using the **Point Size** edit box.

⊕ Pick the style in the middle of the second row.

⊕ Click OK to exit the dialog box.

When you complete the dialog box, any points previously drawn are updated to the new point style. Notice that this means you can have only one point style in your drawing at a time. New points are also drawn with this style.

⊕ Select the Point tool from the Draw toolbar.

⊕ Pick a point anywhere on your screen.

AutoCAD draws a point in the chosen style, as shown previously in Figure 9-26.

If you have selected the **POINT** command from the toolbar, AutoCAD continues to draw points wherever you pick them until you press **Esc** to exit the command. If you have entered **POINT** from the command line or

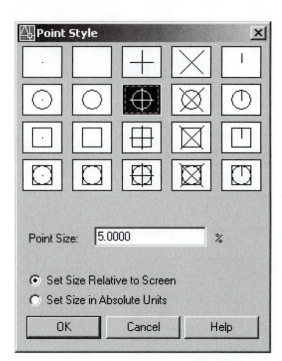

Figure 9-28

selected Single Point from the **Draw** menu, you have to repeat it to draw more points.

⊕ Pick another point.

> Draw a few more points, or return to the dialog box to try another style.

⊕ Press Esc to exit the POINT command.

> Notice that you cannot exit **POINT** by pressing **Enter** or the spacebar.

CHAPTER TEST QUESTIONS

Questions

1. If you wanted to draw a polygon around the outside of a circle so that its sides were tangent to the circle, what option of the **POLYGON** command would you use?
2. Explain this statement: Halfwidth is to width as radius is to diameter.
3. Why does **PLINE** prompt for two different widths?
4. Why is it important to use the Close option when drawing closed polygons using the **PLINE** command?
5. How does AutoCAD decide in which direction to draw a polyline arc?
6. Where is the zero point in a standard AutoCAD multi-line?
7. What properties make up a multiline style definition?
8. When is it necessary to use the **MLEDIT** command?
9. What is the difference between a spline curve constructed with a 0 tolerance and one with a 0.5 tolerance?
10. For what reason is it advisable to use the **SKETCH** command sparingly?

Drawing Problems

1. Draw a regular six-sided polygon centered at (9,6) with a circumscribed radius of 3.0 units. The top and bottom sides should be horizontal.
2. Fillet all corners of the hexagon with a single execution of the **FILLET** command, giving a radius of 0.25 unit.
3. Give the sides of the hexagon a uniform width of 0.25 unit.
4. Draw a **STANDARD** two-element multiline justified to its zero point from the midpoint of one angled side of the hexagon to the midpoint of the diagonally opposite side.
5. Draw a second multiline in the same manner, using the other two angled sides so that the two multilines cross.
6. Edit the intersection of the two multilines to create an open cross intersection.

WWW Exercise 9 (Optional)

In Chapter 9 of our companion website, we challenge you to find information on one of the twentieth century's greatest architects. We give you two links to get you started and then you are on your own. We also offer you another design challenge and the self-scoring test for this chapter. When you are ready, complete the following:

⊞ Make sure that you are connected to your Internet service provider.

⊞ Type "browser" ↵ or open your system browser from the Windows taskbar.

⊞ If necessary, navigate to our companion website at prenhall.com/dixriley.

CHAPTER PROJECTS

Drawing 9-1: Backgammon Board

This drawing should go very quickly. It is a good warm-up that gives you practice with **MLINE** and **PLINE**. Remember that the dimensions are always part of your drawing now, unless otherwise indicated.

Drawing Suggestions

GRID = 1.00
SNAP = 0.125

- First create the multiline line style for the frame with three elements 0.25, 0.00, and −0.50 and joints on as shown. Then draw the 15.50 × 17.50 multiline frame.
- Draw a 0-width 15.50 × 13.50 polyline rectangle and then **OFFSET** it 0.125 to the inside. The inner polyline is actually 0.25 wide, but it is drawn on center, so the offset must be half the width.
- Enter the **PEDIT** command and change the width of the inner polyline to 0.25. This gives you your wide filled border.
- Draw the four triangles at the left of the board and then array them across. The filled triangles are drawn with the **PLINE** command (starting width 0 and ending width 1.00); the others are just outlines drawn with **LINE** or **PLINE**. (Notice that you cannot draw some polylines filled and others not filled.)
- The dimensions in this drawing are straightforward and should give you no trouble. Remember to set to layer dim before dimensioning.

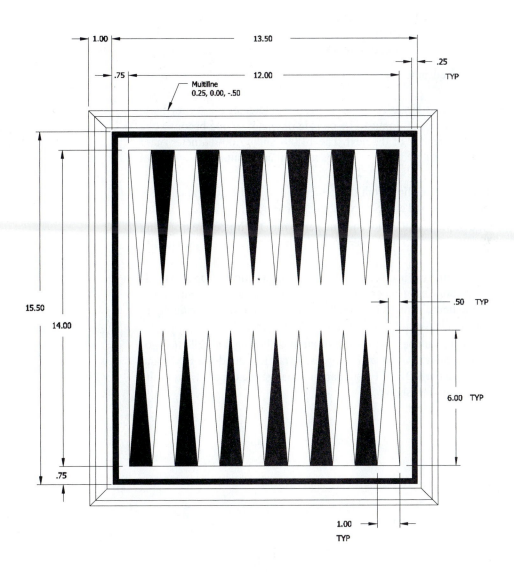

BACKGAMMON BOARD

Drawing 9-1

Drawing 9-2: Dart Board

Although this drawing might seem to resemble the previous one, it is quite a bit more complex and is drawn in an entirely different way. We suggest you use donuts and **TRIM** them along the radial lines. Using **PLINE** to create the filled areas here would be less efficient.

Drawing Suggestions

```
LIMITS = (0,0) (24,18)
GRID = 1.00
SNAP = 0.125
```

- The filled inner circle is a donut with 0 inner and 0.62 outer diameters.
- The second circle is a simple 1.50-diameter circle. From here, draw a series of donuts. The outside diameter of one becomes the inside diameter of the next. The 13.00- and 17.00-diameter outer circles must be drawn as circles rather than donuts so they are not filled.
- Draw a radius line from the center to one of the quadrants of the outer circle and array it around the circle.
- You might find it easier and quicker to turn fill off before trimming the donuts. Also, use layers to keep the donuts separated visually by color.
- To trim the donuts, select the radial lines as cutting edges. This is easily done using a very small crossing box around the center point of the board. Otherwise, you have to pick each line individually in the area between the 13.00 and 17.00 circles.
- Draw the number 5 at the top of the board using a middle text position and a rotation of 2 degrees. Array it around the circle and then use the **DDEDIT** command to change the copied fives to the other numbers shown.

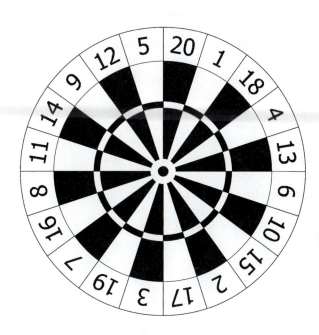

DART BOARD
Drawing 9-2

DIAMETERS
Ø.62
Ø1.50
Ø7.50
Ø8.25
Ø13.00
Ø17.00

Drawing 9-3: Printed Circuit Board

This drawing uses donuts and polylines. Also notice the ordinate dimensions.

Drawing Suggestions

```
UNITS = 4-place decimal
LIMITS = (0,0) (18,12)
GRID = 0.5000
SNAP = 0.1250
```

- Because this drawing uses ordinate dimensions, moving the 0 point of the grid using the **UCS** command makes the placement of figures very easy.

- The 26 rectangular tabs at the bottom can be drawn as polylines.

- After placing the donuts according to the dimensions, draw the connections to them using polyline arcs and line segments. These are simple polylines of uniform 0.03125 halfwidth. The triangular tabs are added later.

- Remember, AutoCAD begins all polyline arcs tangent to the last segment drawn. Often this is not what you want. One way to correct this is to begin with a line segment that establishes the direction for the arc. The line segment can be extremely short and still accomplish your purpose. Thus, many of these polylines consist of a line segment, followed by an arc, followed by another line segment.

- There are two sizes of the triangular tabs, one on top of the rectangular tabs and one at each donut. Draw one of each size in place and then use multiple **COPY, MOVE,** and **ROTATE** commands to create all the others.

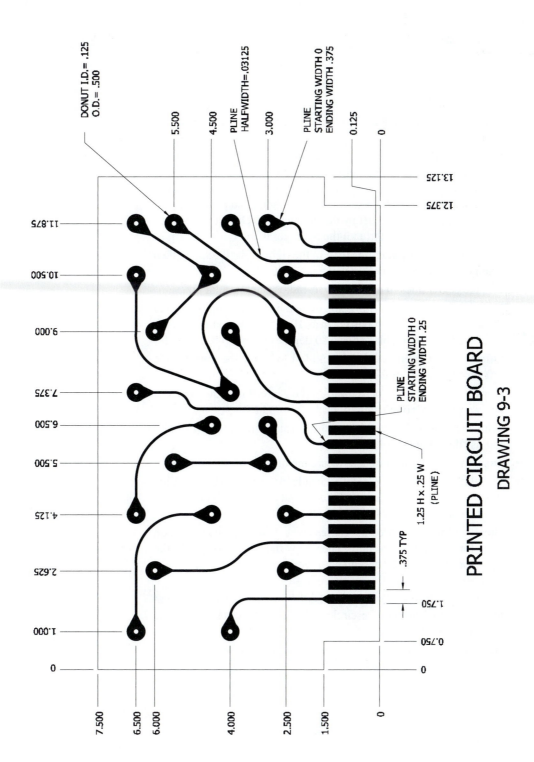

PRINTED CIRCUIT BOARD

DRAWING 9-3

Drawing 9-4: Carbide Tip Saw Blade

This is a nice drawing that requires the creation of a shape combining a donut and a polyline that can be filled to form the carbide tips. There is also an opportunity to use temporary tracking points.

Drawing Suggestions

$$GRID = 1.00$$
$$SNAP = 0.125$$

- After drawing the 7.25-diameter circle, draw a vertical line 1.50 over from the center line. This line becomes the left side of the detailed cut.

- Enter the **LINE** command and then use object snap and object snap tracking to acquire a point at the intersection of the line and the circle. Still in the **LINE** command, type "tt" or select Temporary track point from the **Osnap** shortcut menu and pick a temporary tracking point 0.58 below the intersection. Draw the horizontal center line running through the track point and out to the right.

- Offset the vertical center line 0.16 to the right of the 0.58 line, then change its layer to Layer 3 to make it a center line.

- Use the center lines to draw the 0.16-radius semicircular arc.

- From the right endpoint of the arc, draw a line extending upward at 80 degrees. The dimension is given as 10 degrees from the vertical, but the coordinate display shows 80 degrees from the horizontal.

- Offset this line 0.06 to the right and left to create the lines for the left and right sides of the carbide tip.

- Draw a horizontal line 0.12 up from the center line. You can use a temporary track point again to locate this point.

- Trim the line with the sides of the carbide tip and create 0.06-radius fillets right and left.

- Draw the 3.68-radius circle to locate the outside of the tip.

- To fill the tip, draw a donut with 0 inside diameter and 0.12 outside diameter in the lower section of the tip and a 0.12 width polyline to fill the rest of the tip. **FILL** should be on.

- Break and trim the three 80-degree lines, leaving three extension lines for use in dimensioning. Then copy the whole area up to the right for the detail. When you start working on the detail, scale it up 2.00.

- In the original view, erase the extension lines and then array the cut and carbide tip around the circle. Trim the 7.25 circle out of the new cuts and tips.

- Be sure to type in your own values as you dimension the detail because it has been scaled.

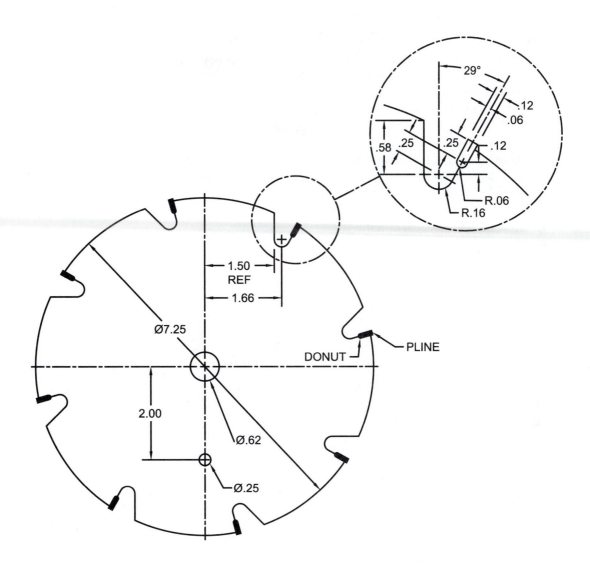

29°
.12
.06
.12
.58 .25 .25
R.06
R.16

1.50
REF
1.66

Ø7.25

PLINE
DONUT

2.00

Ø.62

Ø.25

CARBIDE TIP SAW BLADE
DRAWING 9-4

Drawing 9-5: Gazebo

This architectural drawing makes extensive use of both the **POLYGON** command and the **OFFSET** command.

Drawing Suggestions

```
UNITS = Architectural
GRID = 1'
SNAP = 2"
LIMITS =  (0',0')(48',36')
```

- All radii except the 6" polygon are given from the center point to the midpoint of a side. In other words, the 6" polygon is inscribed, whereas all the others are circumscribed.
- Notice that all polygon radii dimensions are given to the outside of the 2" × 4". Offset to the inside to create the parallel polygon for the inside of the board.
- Create radial studs by drawing a line from the midpoint of one side of a polygon to the midpoint of the side of another, or the midpoint of one to the vertex of another as shown; then offset 1" each side and erase the original. Array around the center point.
- Trim lines and polygons at vertices.
- You can make effective use of **MIRROR** in the elevation.

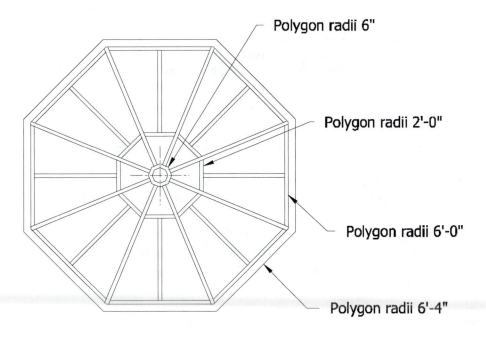

Polygon radii 6"

Polygon radii 2'-0"

Polygon radii 6'-0"

Polygon radii 6'-4"

ROOF FRAMING

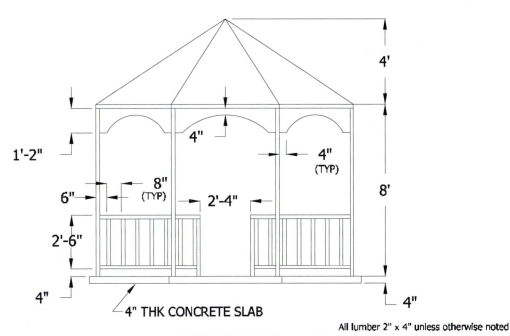

4'

1'-2"

4"

4"
(TYP)

8"
(TYP)

6"

2'-4"

8'

2'-6"

4"

4"

4" THK CONCRETE SLAB

All lumber 2" x 4" unless otherwise noted

FRONT ELEVATION

GAZEBO
Drawing 9-5

Drawing 9-6: Accident Reconstruction

This drawing can be considered a sketch. We do not offer precise dimensions or reference figures. Your task is to create a reasonable facsimile of the drawing, with all objects drawn in proportion. We used 24 × 18 limits, but the space you use is up to you. Most important, you should find opportunities to use polylines, donuts, multilines, and a revision cloud. A description of the accident would go as follows: Vehicle 1 crosses the double yellow line to avoid traffic and collides with Vehicle 2, which is merging into the left turn lane.

Drawing Suggestions

- Consider the limits of your drawing and the relative sizes of objects before you begin.
- You may want to use a scale or ruler on the drawing here in the book to give you more than a visual sense of the proportion of objects.
- All text was drawn with the Ariel Round font.
- Although not visible here, use different layers and colors to distinguish objects. Use color, for example, to represent that the three copies of Vehicle 1 in progressive positions are the same vehicle.

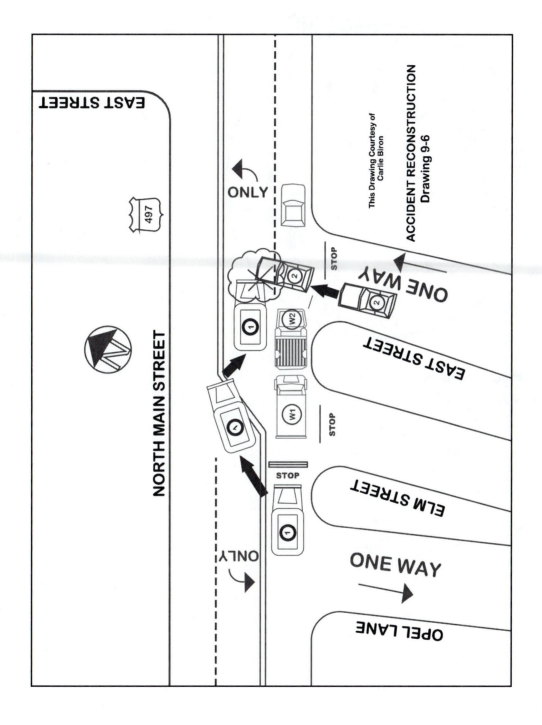

This Drawing Courtesy of
Carlie Biron

ACCIDENT RECONSTRUCTION
Drawing 9-6

353

Drawing 9-7: Clock Face

This drawing gives you practice using different filled polyline forms. All procedures for creating the clock face, ticks, hands, and numbers should be familiar from this chapter and from previous drawings in other chapters.

Drawing Suggestions

- Notice the architectural units used in the drawing. Observe the dimensions and select appropriate Limits, Grid, and Snap settings.
- All three hands can be drawn as filled polylines.
- Clock ticks are also filled polylines.
- The font is Impact.

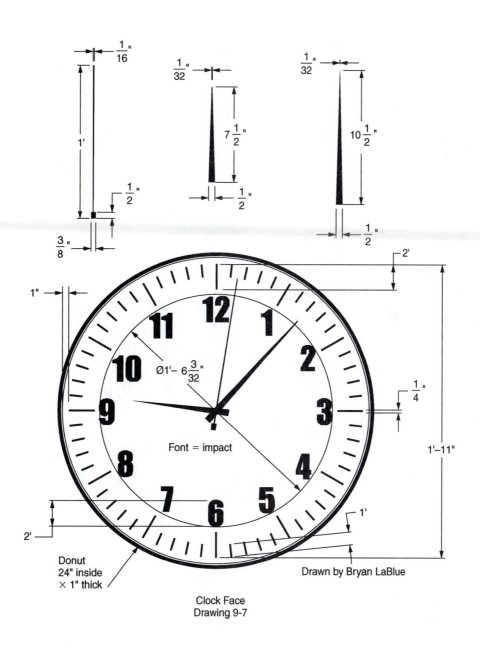

Clock Face
Drawing 9-7

Blocks, Attributes, and External References

10

Chapter Objectives

- Creating Groups
- Creating Blocks
- Inserting Blocks into the Current Drawing
- Creating Dynamic Blocks
- Using the Windows Clipboard
- Inserting Blocks and External References into Other Drawings
- Using the AutoCAD DesignCenter
- Defining Attributes
- Working with Parameters in Block References
- Working with External References
- Extracting Attribute Information from Drawings
- Creating Tool Palettes
- Exploding Blocks

INTRODUCTION

The primary goal of this book is to teach you how to be an efficient AutoCAD user. To work effectively in a professional design environment, however, requires more than proficiency in drafting techniques. Most design work is done in collaboration with other designers, engineers, managers, and customers. This chapter begins to introduce you to some of the techniques and features that allow you to communicate and share the powers of AutoCAD with others.

To begin, you learn to create groups and blocks. A *group* is a set of objects that can be selected, named, and manipulated collectively. A *block* is a set of objects defined as a single entity and saved so that it can be scaled and inserted repeatedly and potentially passed on to other drawings. Blocks become part of the content of a drawing that can be browsed, viewed, and manipulated within and between drawings using the AutoCAD DesignCenter. The DesignCenter and other functions, including the Windows clipboard and externally referenced drawings (Xrefs), allow AutoCAD objects and drawings to be shared with other drawings and applications and with CAD operators at other workstations on a local network or on the Internet. In this chapter, we also introduce you to block attributes. An *attribute* is an item of information attached to a block, such as a part number or price, that is stored along with the block definition. All the information stored in attributes can be extracted from a drawing into a spreadsheet or database program and used to produce itemized reports. Like text and dimensions, attributes and blocks can be given the annotative property and scaled automatically to match a viewport scale.

The procedures introduced in this chapter are among the most complex in this book. Particularly in the exercises where you are working with more than one drawing, it is very important to follow the text and instructions closely and to save your work if you do not complete the exercise in one session.

10-1 CREATING GROUPS

GENERAL PROCEDURE	1. Type "g" ↵.
	2. Type a name.
	3. Click New.
	4. Select objects to be included in the group definition.
	5. Press **Enter** to end object selection.
	6. Click **OK** to exit the dialog box.

The simplest way to create a collective entity from previously drawn entities is to group them into a unit with the **GROUP** command. Groups are given names and can be selected for all editing processes if they are defined as selectable.

In this exercise, we form groups from objects that also are used later to define blocks. In this way, you get a feel for the different functions of these two methods of creating collections of objects. You begin by creating simple symbols for a computer, monitor, digitizer, and keyboard. Take your time getting these right because once created, they can also be inserted when you complete Drawing 10-1 at the end of the chapter.

⊕ Create a new drawing using the 1B template and make the following changes in the drawing setup:

1. Set to Layer 0 (the reason for doing this is discussed in the note following this list).
2. Change to architectural units, with precision = $0' - 0''$.
3. Set GRID = $1'$.
4. Set SNAP = $1''$.
5. Set LIMITS = $(0',0') (12',9')$. Be sure to include the feet symbol.
6. Zoom All.

> **Note:**
> Blocks created on Layer 0 are inserted on the current layer. Blocks created on any other layer stay on the layer on which they are created. Inserting blocks is discussed in Section 10-3.

⊕ Draw the four objects shown in Figure 10-1.

Draw the geometry only; the text and dimensions in the figure are for your reference only and should not be on your screen. Notice that the computer is a simple rectangular representation of an old-style computer cpu that sits horizontally

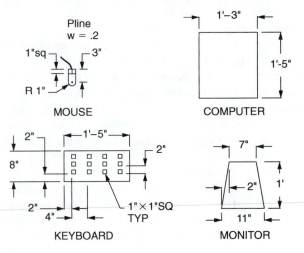

Figure 10-1

under the monitor. Later we will modify the definition of this block so that it has
the flexibility to also represent a typical tower-style computer.

⊞ Save this drawing as A.

We will be working with two drawings later in this chapter and call them A
and B for clarity. A has 12′ × 9′, A-size limits and B is based on our standard 1B
template. For now you continue working in Drawing A and do not need to create
B until later on.

We define the keyboard as a group.

⊞ Type "g" ↵.

This opens the **Object Grouping** dialog box shown in Figure 10-2. At the top
of the box is the Group Name list box. It is empty now because there are no
groups defined in this drawing. Below that is the Group Identification panel, with
edit boxes for entering a group name and a group description. The flashing cursor
bar should be in the Group Name box so that you can enter a name. Our first
group is the set of rectangles you have drawn as a symbol for a keyboard.

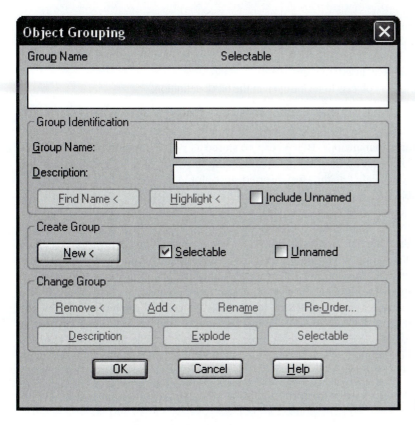

Figure 10-2

⊞ Type "keyboard" in the Group Name edit box.

Now look at the Create Group panel. The three boxes here are New, Selectable, and Unnamed. To create a group that can be selected with one pick, you
must indicate that it is a new group and defined as selectable.

⊞ Be sure that Selectable is checked.
⊞ Click the New button.

At this point the dialog box disappears to give you access to objects in your
drawing. You see a *Select Objects:* prompt at the command line.

⊞ Select the keyboard outer rectangles and small rectangles using a window.
⊞ Right-click to end object selection.

This brings back the dialog box. KEYBOARD should now be in the list box,
with a Yes to the right of it indicating that it is a selectable group.

⊕ Click OK to exit the dialog box.

The keyboard is now defined in the drawing as a selectable group. To see that this is so, try selecting it.

⊕ Position the crosshairs anywhere on the Keyboard and observe the selection preview.

You see from the highlights that the complete group is previewed. That is all you need to do with groups at this point. Groups are useful for copying and manipulating sets of objects that tend to stay together. Groups resemble blocks, which we explore in the next section. Groups are easier to define and you can edit individual objects in groups more easily than you can edit them in blocks. Blocks have other advantages, however, including the capacity to be shared with other drawings.

10-2 CREATING BLOCKS

GENERAL PROCEDURE	1. Select the **Make Block** tool from the dashboard. 2. Type a name. 3. Pick an insertion point. 4. Select objects to be included in the block definition.

Blocks have more features than groups. Blocks can be stored as part of an individual drawing or as separate drawings. They can be inserted into the drawing in which they were created, or into other drawings, and can be scaled as they are inserted. In AutoCAD, blocks can also be defined as dynamic, meaning that they are flexible and can be altered in specific ways to represent variations of the block. In general, the most useful blocks are those that can be used repeatedly in many drawings and therefore can become part of a library of predrawn objects used by you and others. In mechanical drawing, for instance, you might want a set of screws drawn to standard sizes that can be used at any time. If you are doing architectural drawing, you might find a library of doors and windows useful. You will see examples of predefined symbol libraries later in this chapter when you explore the AutoCAD DesignCenter and tool palettes.

In this chapter, we are creating a set of simple symbols for some of the tools we know you will use no matter what kind of CAD you are doing—namely, computers, monitors, keyboards, plotters, and printers. We define them as blocks, insert them, and assemble them into a workstation. Later we define the complete workstation as a block and insert workstations into an architectural drawing called CAD Room.

⊕ Select the Make Block tool from the dashboard, as shown in Figure 10-3.

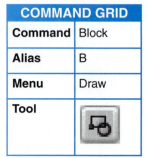

COMMAND GRID	
Command	Block
Alias	B
Menu	Draw
Tool	

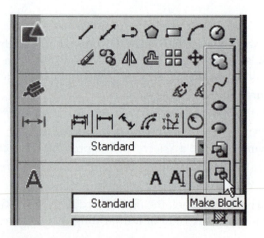

Figure 10-3

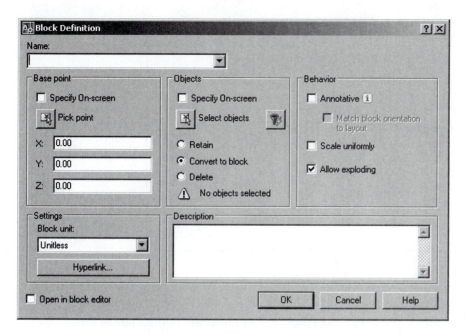

Figure 10-4

This executes the **BLOCK** command and opens the **Block Definition** dialog box shown in Figure 10-4.

TIP   Instead of running your cursor down the flyout to get to the **Make Block** tool, move to the left to avoid the other buttons and approach the button from the side. The reason for this is that the **Insert Block** button just above **Make Block** has its own flyout. Once you hit it, the flyout will open and you won't be able to access the button you want.

⊞ Type "computer" in the block Name box.

Next, choose an object to define the block.

⊞ Click the Select objects button in the middle of the dialog box.

The dialog box disappears, giving you access to objects in the drawing.

⊞ Select the computer rectangle.

AutoCAD continues to prompt for object selection.

⊞ Right-click to end object selection.

This brings you back to the dialog box.

Note:
Be sure to use the **Select objects** button, not the **Quick Select** button. **Quick Select** executes the **QSELECT** command and opens the **Quick Select** dialog box. The purpose of this dialog box is to establish filtering criteria so that defined types of objects can be selected more quickly in a complex drawing, filtering out objects that do not meet the selection criteria.

Blocks are intended to be inserted into drawings, so any block definition needs to include an insertion base point. Insertion points and insertion base points are critical in using blocks. The insertion base point is the point on the block that is at the intersection of the crosshairs when you insert the block. Therefore, when defining a block, try to anticipate the point on the block you would most likely use to position the block on the screen. If you do not define an insertion base point, AutoCAD uses the origin of the coordinate system, which might be quite inconvenient.

⊞ Click the Pick point icon on the left side of the dialog box.

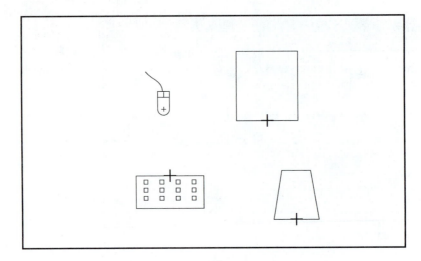

Figure 10-5

⊞ Press Shift and right-click to open the object snap shortcut menu.

⊞ Use a midpoint object snap to pick the middle of the bottom line of the computer as the insertion point, as shown in Figure 10-5.

When creating blocks, you have three choices regarding what happens to objects included in the block definition, shown by the three buttons in the Objects panel, just below the **Select objects** button. Objects can be retained in the drawing separate from the block definition, converted to an instance of the new block, or deleted from the screen. In all instances, the object data are retained in the drawing database as the block definition.

A common practice is to create a number of blocks, one after the other, and then assemble them at the end. To facilitate this method, select the **Delete** button. With this setting, newly defined blocks are erased from the screen automatically. They can be retrieved using OOPS if necessary (but not U, as this would undo the block definition). In our case, deleting blocks as we define them also helps make a clearer distinction between block references and block definitions.

⊞ Select the Delete button.

The block definition is complete.

⊞ Click OK to exit the dialog box.

You have created a "computer" block definition. The computer has vanished from your screen, but can be inserted using the **INSERT** command, which we turn to momentarily. Now repeat the **BLOCK** process to make a keyboard block.

⊞ Repeat BLOCK.

⊞ Type "keyboard" in the block Name box.

⊞ Click Select objects.

⊞ Select the keyboard.

Because you have already defined the keyboard as a selectable group, one pick selects the whole thing. In the command area, AutoCAD shows how many individual objects are in the selection set, and also that there is one group in the set. The group definition of the keyboard now becomes part of the block definition.

⊞ Press Enter to end selection.

⊞ Click the Pick point icon.

⊞ Pick the midpoint of the top line of the keyboard as the insertion base point.

⊞ Click OK.

⊞ Repeat the blocking process two more times to create monitor and mouse blocks, with insertion base points as shown in Figure 10-5.

When you are finished, your screen should be blank. At this point, your four block definitions are stored in your drawing base. In the next section, we insert them into your current drawing to create a computer workstation assembly. Before going on, take a look at these other commands that are useful in working with blocks. Many of them are used in the sections that follow.

Command	Usage
BASE	Allows you to specify a base insertion point for an entire drawing. The base point is used when the drawing is inserted in other drawings.
DBLIST	Displays information for all entities in the current drawing database. Information includes type of entity and layer. Additional information depends on the type of entity. For blocks, it includes insertion point, x scale, y scale, rotation, and attribute values.
EXPLODE	Reverses an instance of a block so that objects that have been combined in the block definition are redrawn as individual objects. Exploding a block reference has no effect on the block definition.
LIST	Lists information about a single block or entity. Information listed is the same as that in DBLIST, but for the selected entity only.
MINSERT	Multiple insert. Allows you to insert arrays of blocks. MINSERT arrays take up less memory than arrays of inserted blocks.
PURGE	Deletes unused blocks, layers, linetypes, shapes, or text styles from a drawing.
WBLOCK	Saves a block to a separate file so that it can be inserted in other drawings. Does not save unused blocks or layers and therefore can be used to reduce drawing file size.

10-3 INSERTING BLOCKS INTO THE CURRENT DRAWING

GENERAL PROCEDURE

1. Select the **Insert Block** tool from the dashboard.
2. Type or select a block name.
3. Pick an insertion point.
4. Answer prompts for horizontal and vertical scale and for rotation angle.

The **INSERT** command is used to position block references in a drawing. Here you begin to distinguish between block definitions, which are not visible and reside in the database of a drawing, and block references, which are instances of a block inserted into a drawing. The four block definitions you created in Section 10-2 are now part of the drawing database and can be inserted in this drawing or any other drawing. In this section, we focus on inserting into the current drawing. In the next section, we explore sharing blocks between drawings.

Among other things, these procedures are useful in creating assembly drawings. Assembling blocks can be done efficiently using appropriate object snap modes to place objects in precise relation to one another. Assembly drawing is the focus of the drawing problems at the end of this chapter.

In this section, we insert the computer, monitor, keyboard, and mouse back into the drawing to create the workstation assembly shown in Figure 10-6. We also discuss other options for drawing file management, including the use of complete drawings as blocks or as external references.

⊕ If you are still on Layer 0, switch to Layer 1.

⊕ Select the Insert Block tool from the dashboard, as shown in Figure 10-7.

Notice that the **Insert Block** opens a secondary flyout with four tools. The first is **Insert Block** again. Either of these tools opens the **Insert** dialog box shown in Figure 10-8. In addition to the block Name list box at the top of the dialog box, there are several scaling options that allow you to scale and rotate the block as

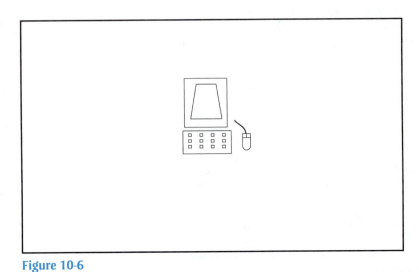

Figure 10-6

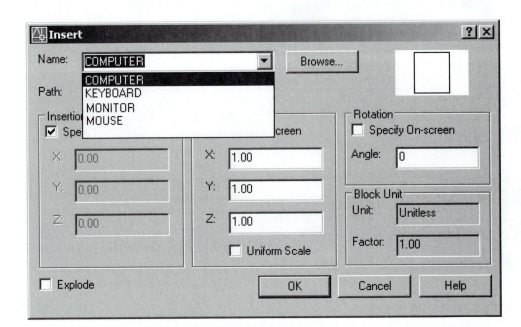

Figure 10-7

Figure 10-8

COMMAND GRID	
Command	Insert
Alias	I
Menu	Insert
Tool	

you insert it. This vastly increases the flexibility and power of the blocking system. The issue of scaling becomes particularly important when you move between drawings. What would happen if you inserted a 20-foot object into a drawing that has 12′ × 9′ limits? We shall see in Section 10-4.

Unlike the **SCALE** command, which automatically scales both horizontally and vertically, blocks can be stretched or shrunk in either direction independently as you insert them. You can type an *x* scale factor or specify both an *x* and a *y* factor. Use of *z* is reserved for 3D applications. The Uniform option scales *x*, *y*, and *z* uniformly.

Now is a good time to see that your block definitions are still in your database, even though they are no longer on the screen.

⊕ Click the arrow in the Name list box.

You should see a list like this:

```
Computer
Keyboard
Monitor
Mouse
```

⊕ Select Computer from the list.

⊕ Click OK to exit the dialog box and begin inserting the block.

From here on, you follow prompts from the command line or dynamic input display. AutoCAD now needs to know where to insert the computer, and you see this prompt:

    Specify insertion point or [Basepoint/Scale/X/Y/Z/Rotate]:

AutoCAD gives you a block to drag into place. Notice that it is positioned with the block's insertion base point at the intersection of the crosshairs.

⊕ Pick a point near the middle of the screen, as shown previously in Figure 10-6.

Notice that the block is inserted on Layer 1 even though it was created on Layer 0. Remember that this only works with blocks drawn on Layer 0. Blocks drawn on other layers stay on the layer on which they were drawn when they are inserted. This not only creates some inflexibility, but may add unwanted layers if the block was drawn on a layer that does not exist in the new drawing.

Now let's add a monitor.

⊕ Repeat the INSERT command.

Notice that the last block inserted becomes the default block name in the block Name box. This facilitates procedures in which you insert the same block in several different places in a drawing.

⊕ Select Monitor from the Name list.

⊕ Click OK.

⊕ Pick an insertion point two or three inches above the insertion point of the computer, as shown in Figure 10-6.

You should have the monitor sitting on top of the computer and be back at the command prompt. We next insert the keyboard, as shown in Figure 10-6.

⊕ Repeat INSERT.

⊕ Select KEYBOARD from the Name list.

⊕ Click OK.

⊕ Pick an insertion point one or two inches below the computer, as shown in Figure 10-6.

You should now have the keyboard in place.

⊕ Repeat INSERT once more and place a mouse block reference to the right of the other block references, as shown in Figure 10-6.

Congratulations! You have completed your first assembly. Next we modify the definition of the computer block so that it becomes dynamic and may be used to represent different styles of computer.

10-4 CREATING DYNAMIC BLOCKS

GENERAL PROCEDURE

1. Select the **Block Editor** tool from the **Standard Annotation** toolbar.
2. Select a block. (Steps 1 and 2 can be reversed.)
3. From the Block Authoring Palettes, select a Parameter.
4. Specify the parameter location.
5. From the Block Authoring Palettes, select an Action.
6. Specify the action location.

Dynamic blocks are blocks that can be altered without redefining the block. They are created using the Block Editor. The editor is a whole subsystem of screens, symbols, and commands that allows you to add dynamic parameters to newly defined or previously defined blocks. A parameter

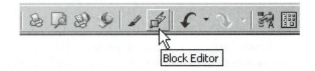

Figure 10-9

is an aspect of the geometry of a block definition that may be designated as variable. Parameters are always associated with Actions. When a dynamic block is inserted, it takes the standard form of its original definition. Unlike other blocks, however, once a dynamic block is inserted it can be selected and altered in specific ways. The ways in which a dynamic block can be altered depend on the parameters and actions that have been added to the definition.

In this exercise we will demonstrate dynamic capabilities by adding a linear parameter and a stretch action to the computer block. This will allow us to adjust the shape of the computer so that it may represent a tower style computer as well as one placed horizontally under the monitor.

⊕ To begin this task, you should be in Drawing A with the four blocks inserted in the last section, shown in Figure 10-6.

⊕ Select the computer block.

⊕ Select the Block Editor tool from the Standard Annotation toolbar, as shown in Figure 10-9.

This executes the **BEDIT** command and opens the **Edit Block Definition** dialog box shown in Figure 10-10. Because you selected the computer block before entering the dialog, the computer block should be selected in the block list and an image of the block should be displayed in the Preview box. Once inside the Block Editor, you have access to a set of commands and procedures that cannot be accessed anywhere else. All these commands begin with the letter B and work on blocks that have been selected for editing.

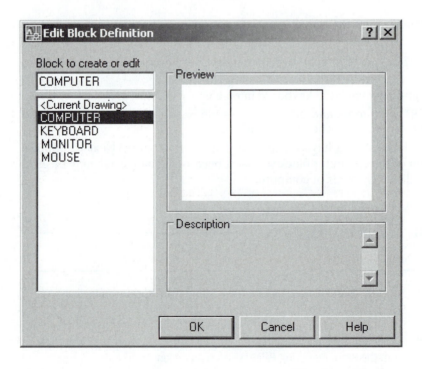

Figure 10-10

⊕ Click OK.

This brings you to the Block Authoring Palettes window shown in Figure 10-11. On the right is the block itself in a special editing window where you can work directly on the block geometry. The Block Authoring Palettes has three tabs. The first is for defining parameters, the second for actions, and the third is for sets of

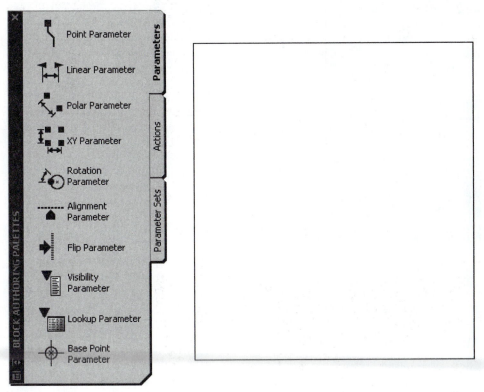

Figure 10-11

parameters and actions that are frequently paired. Here we add a linear parameter so that the width of the block can be altered, then we add a stretch action to show how the parameter can be edited after it is inserted.

⊕ From the palettes select Linear Parameter.

This executes the **BPARAMETER** command with the Linear option. Other options are shown on the palette. AutoCAD prompts:

> Specify start point or
> [Name/Label/Chain/Description/Base/Palette/Value set]:

We specify a parameter indicating that the width of the computer may be altered.

⊕ Pick a start point on one of the vertical sides of the computer block.

If the sides do not fall on snap points, you can use a Nearest object snap to locate the line precisely.

AutoCAD displays a Distance label, a line, and two arrows.

⊕ Pick a point directly across the width of the computer, as shown in Figure 10-12.

The length of the parameter is now established. AutoCAD prompts you to specify a label location.

⊕ Pick a location point for the parameter label, as shown in Figure 10-12.

The parameter is now defined, but it is incomplete because there is no action defined for altering the parameter. The yellow box with the exclamation point is an alert to remind you of this. If you let your cursor rest on the yellow alert, you will see a message that says "No actions associated with the parameter."

⊕ Click the Actions tab on the Block Authoring Palettes.

The Actions tab is shown in Figure 10-13.

⊕ Select Stretch Action from the palettes.

This executes the **BACTION** command with the Stretch option. AutoCAD prompts

> Select Parameter:

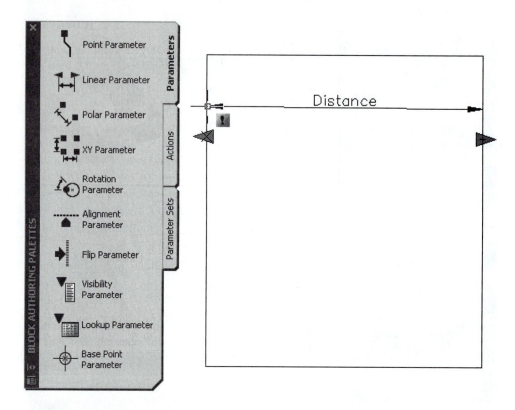

Figure 10-12

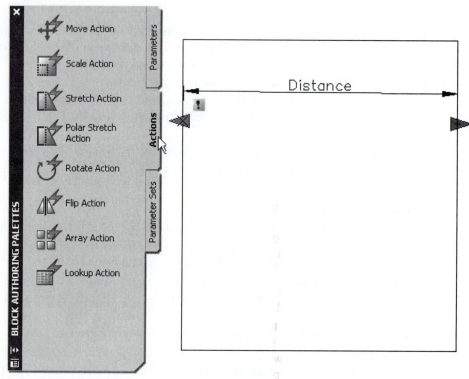

Figure 10-13

⊕ Select any part of the parameter or its label.

AutoCAD prompts

```
Specify parameter point to associate with action
    or enter [sTart point/Second point] <Start>:
```

The points you can select are the two triangles on the sides of the block. These are the start point and the endpoint of the linear parameter. The behavior of the geometry is dependent on the point you select.

⊕ Pick the right endpoint.

With this point selected we will be able to alter the width of the rectangle from the right side. AutoCAD now asks you to specify a stretch frame, just as you would do in the **STRETCH** command.

    Specify first corner of stretch frame or [CPolygon]:

This window will frame the portion of the rectangle to be stretched.

⊕ Pick two points to define a stretch frame around the right side of the rectangle, as shown in Figure 10-14.

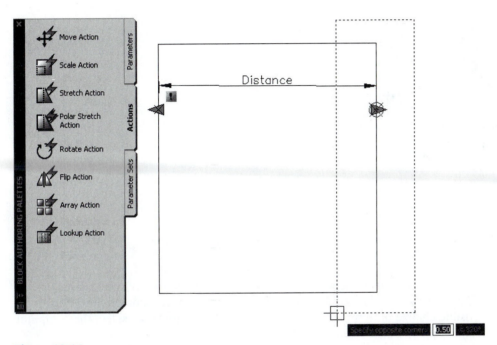

Figure 10-14

AutoCAD now asks you to select objects. For our purposes you can basically repeat the two points just selected to frame the right side again. Keep in mind, however, that in a more complex block you might not want all objects to be affected by the stretch. This prompt allows you to select objects to include in the stretch.

⊕ Pick the two points again.

⊕ Right-click or press ENTER to end object selection.

AutoCAD asks you to specify a location for the action symbol. This is merely a visual key as to the purpose of the parameter and action. The action location will not appear when the block is inserted and will not affect how the action works. Two good possibilities for this action would be along the right side of the block or on the right side of the parameter location itself, as shown in Figure 10-15.

⊕ Pick a location for the Stretch Action symbol, as shown in Figure 10-15.

⊕ Click on Close Block Editor to exit the block editing system.

This selection is located in the center of the **Block Editor** toolbar, illustrated in Figure 10-16. When you select it, AutoCAD will display a message that tells you that changes in block definitions may update existing block references.

⊕ Click Yes to save the new block definition and update block references.

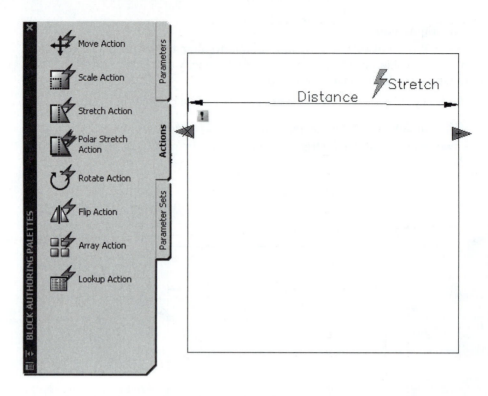

Figure 10-15

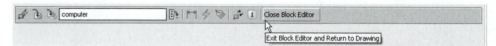

Figure 10-16

This brings us back to the drawing editor. The four block references are assembled there as before. The computer block has been updated, but there is no visible change until we select it. To complete this exercise we select the computer and implement the stretch action.

⊕ Select the computer.

The computer is highlighted, but new dynamic block grips have been added to indicate the linear parameter, as shown in Figure 10-17.

⊕ Select the dynamic block grip on the right side of the computer block. This is the point selected previously in defining the linear parameter.

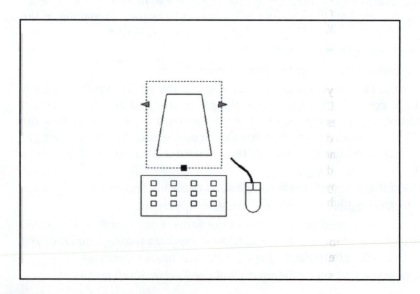

Figure 10-17

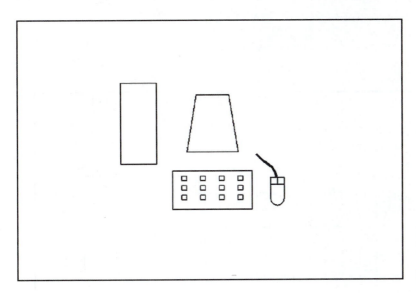

Figure 10-18

⊕ Move your cursor back and forth so that you can see how the block is stretched.

⊕ Move your cursor to the left to shrink the computer block to a 6″ width.

We now have a narrowed version of the computer block, which can represent a tower-style computer. All we need to do is to move it over to the left.

⊕ Using the square grip, move the computer 6″ to the left, as shown in Figure 10-18.

⊕ Press Esc to remove grips.

Your screen should resemble Figure 10-18.

This has been a brief introduction to the capabilities of dynamic blocks of the Block Editor. We provide another brief demonstation later to show how one aspect of a dynamic block may be moved in relation to others.

In the next two sections, we explore moving blocks between drawings and moving drawn objects between applications using the Windows clipboard.

10-5 Using the Windows Clipboard

GENERAL PROCEDURE	1. Select Copy or Cut from the **Edit menu.** 2. Select objects. (Steps 1 and 2 can be reversed.) 3. Open another drawing or a different Windows application. 4. Type "Ctrl + V," or select Paste in that drawing or application.

The Windows clipboard makes it very easy to copy objects from one AutoCAD drawing to another or into other Windows applications. **CUTCLIP** removes the selected objects from your AutoCAD drawing, whereas **COPYCLIP** leaves them in place. When you send blocks to an AutoCAD drawing via the clipboard, they are defined as blocks in the new drawing as well. Block names and definitions are maintained, but there is no option to scale as there is when you **INSERT** blocks.

In this section, we create a new drawing called B and copy the assembled workstation into it. The steps would be the same to copy the objects into another Windows application. The procedure is very simple and works with any Windows application that supports Windows Object Linking and Embedding (OLE).

⊕ To begin this task you should be in Drawing A with the assembled blocks on your screen, resembling Figure 10-18.

⊕ Open the Edit menu and select Copy, as shown in Figure 10-19.

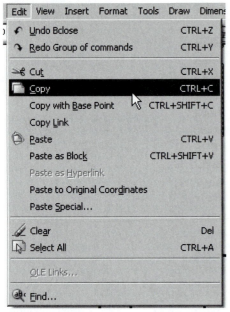

Figure 10-19

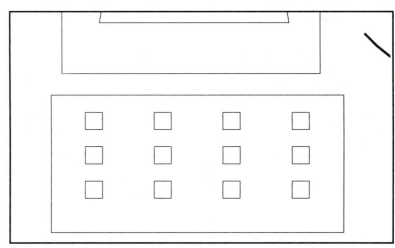

Figure 10-20

This executes the **COPYCLIP** command. AutoCAD prompts for object selection.

⊞ Using a window selection, select all the objects in the computer workstation assembled in Section 10-3.

⊞ Right-click to end object selection.

AutoCAD saves the selected objects to the clipboard. Nothing happens on your screen, but the selected objects are stored and could be pasted back into this drawing, another AutoCAD drawing, or another Windows application. Next we create a new drawing.

⊞ Create a new drawing using the 1B template.

We call this Drawing B. Notice that you can have multiple drawings open in a single AutoCAD session.

⊞ Save the new drawing, giving it the name B.

Drawing B should now be open in the drawing area with Drawing A also open in the background. You will not see A while you are in B.

⊞ In Drawing B, select Paste from the Edit menu.

AutoCAD prompts for an insertion point and gives you an image to drag into place. You see a very large image of the keyboard, as shown in Figure 10-20. Actually, the whole workstation is there, but the computer, monitor, and mouse are off the screen. They are so large because the scale of this drawing is very different from the one the objects were drawn in. The original drawing has been set up with architectural units and limits so that its block definitions can be used in Drawing 10-1, the CAD Room, at the end of the chapter. In the new drawing, based on the 1B template, the 18 × 12 units are being interpreted as inches, so the keyboard is coming in at 17″, covering most of the screen. Without the scaling capacity of the **INSERT** command, you have no control over this interpretation.

⊞ Pick an insertion point at the lower left of your screen, as shown in Figure 10-20.

That's all there is to it. It is equally simple to paste text and images from other compatible Windows applications into AutoCAD. Just reverse the process, cutting or copying from the other application and pasting into AutoCAD.

We undo this paste before moving on.

⊞ Press U until everything has been undone in Drawing B.

The issue of scaling is handled differently when you paste AutoCAD objects into other applications. In those cases, objects are automatically scaled to fit in the document that receives them. Most applications have their own editing feature, which allows you to adjust the size of the objects after they have been pasted.

10-6 INSERTING BLOCKS AND EXTERNAL REFERENCES INTO OTHER DRAWINGS

GENERAL PROCEDURE	1. Prepare a drawing or blocks to be inserted into other drawings. 2. Open a second drawing. 3. Enter the **INSERT** or **XATTACH** command. 4. Enter the name and path of the drawing to be inserted or referenced, or browse to find the file. 5. Answer prompts for scale and rotation.

Any drawing can be inserted as a block or external reference into another drawing. The process is much like inserting a block within a drawing, but you need to specify the drawing location. In this task, we attach Drawing A as an external reference in Drawing B. The process for inserting blocks into other drawings is identical to attaching an external reference.

External References

Externally referencing a drawing is a powerful alternative to inserting it as a block. The principal difference between inserted drawings and externally referenced drawings is that inserted drawings are actually merged with the current drawing database, whereas externally referenced drawings are only linked. Because attaching a reference loads only enough information to point to the externally referenced drawing, it does not increase the size of the current drawing file as significantly as **INSERT** does. If the referenced drawing is changed, the changes are reflected in the current drawing the next time it is loaded or when the Reload option of the XREF Manager is selected. This allows designers at remote locations to work on different aspects of a single master drawing, which can be updated as changes are made in the various referenced drawings. Creating this kind of dependency of one drawing on another opens up possibilities for confusion. If a file is moved or renamed, for example, the path to the external reference could be lost. The use of external references requires careful project and file management.

⊕ You should be in Drawing B to begin this task, with everything undone.

To switch back to Drawing A, use the open drawing list at the bottom of the Window menu, as follows.

⊕ Open the Window menu and select Drawing A, as shown in Figure 10-21.

This brings you back into your original drawing with the computer workstation objects displayed as shown previously in Figure 10-18. You could use this drawing as a block or external reference without further adjustment, but using the **BASE** command to add an insertion base point for the drawing is convenient. **BASE** works for either blocking or referencing.

⊕ Select Draw → Block → Base from the pull-down menu.

AutoCAD prompts

Enter base point, <0'-0", 0'-0", 0'-0">:

This indicates that the current base point is at the origin of the grid. We move it to the lower left corner of the keyboard.

⊕ Pick the lower left corner of the keyboard.

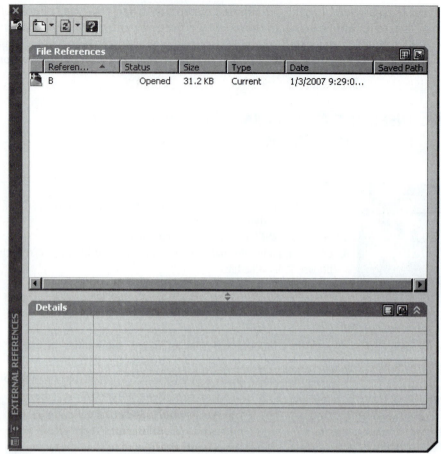

Figure 10-21

Figure 10-22

The new base point is registered, but there is no change in the drawing.

⊕ Save Drawing A.

If you don't save the drawing after changing the base point, the base point is not used when the drawing is referenced.

⊕ Open the File menu and select Close to close Drawing A.

This returns you to Drawing B. There should be no objects in this drawing.

⊕ Open the Insert menu and select External References.

This opens the External References palette, shown in Figure 10-22. Drawing B will show in the Reference name box along with other open drawings, if any.

⊕ Click the Attach file button in the upper left corner, as shown in Figure 10-22.

This will open a **Select Reference File** dialog box, as shown in Figure 10-23. This is basically the same dialog box you see when you enter any command in which you select a file.

⊕ If necessary, double-click the folder that contains Drawing A, or use the Up One Level button to locate the folder you need.

⊕ Select Drawing A from the list of files or from the thumbnail gallery, depending on your operating system and settings.

⊕ Click Open.

Note:
Be sure to pay attention to where you are saving Drawing A so that you can easily find it again.

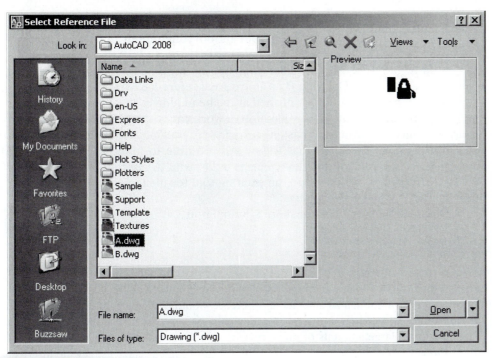

Figure 10-23

This opens the **External Reference** dialog box, shown in Figure 10-24. A should be entered in the Name box, and its path identified below the name.

⊕ Click OK to exit the dialog box.

You are now back to the Drawing B Drawing Window. As in the last task, you have a very large image of the keyboard, but this time there is a prompt for scale factors in the command area.

⊕ Type "s" ⏎ for the Scale option.

This option takes a uniform scale factor for the complete inserted drawing.

⊕ Type "1/8" ⏎.

You could also type .125, but it is worth noting that the **INSERT** and **XATTACH** commands take fractions or scale ratios at the scale factor prompt.

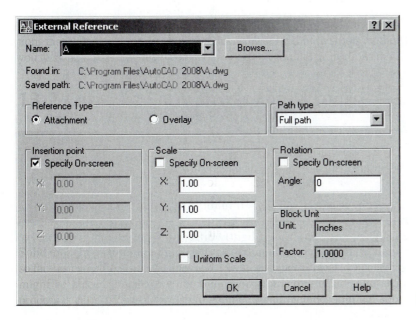

Figure 10-24

⊕ Pick an insertion point near the middle of the screen.

At this scale, the workstation appears on your screen much as it does in Drawing A.

Stop for a moment to consider your two drawings. Drawing A is closed but has been attached to Drawing B as an external reference. Drawing A has the architectural units and limits established at the beginning of the chapter. It has four separate blocks currently assembled into a workstation. Drawing B has our standard 1B units and limits and has one instance of Drawing A attached as an external reference. In the tasks that follow, we continue to make changes to these drawings. Later, you will see that changes in Drawing A are reflected in Drawing B. In the next task, we introduce an exciting tool for managing drawing data, the AutoCAD DesignCenter.

Before leaving this section, here is a final note.

Raster Images

A *raster image* is an image such as a picture or photograph that has been encoded as a matrix of dots or pixels. Any ordinary computer graphic image is an example. Such images can be brought into an AutoCAD drawing much as an external reference would be. Raster images are attached and linked to AutoCAD drawings, but they do not actually become part of the drawing database so they do not take up large amounts of memory. Once attached, raster images can be inserted repeatedly in the same drawing just like blocks. Raster images can be scaled as they are inserted. To insert a raster image, select Raster Image Reference from the **Insert** menu.

⊕ Close the External References palette before moving on.

10-7 USING THE AUTOCAD DESIGNCENTER

The AutoCAD DesignCenter enables you to manipulate drawing content similar to the way Windows Explorer handles files and folders. The interface is familiar, with a tree view on the left and a list of contents on the right. The difference is the types of data you see. With the DesignCenter you can look into the contents of open or closed drawing files and easily copy or insert content into other open drawings. Blocks, external references, layers, linetypes, dimension styles, text styles, table styles, and page layouts are all examples of content defined in a drawing that can be copied into another drawing to reduce duplicated effort.

In this task, we begin by opening the DesignCenter and examining some of the available content. Leave Drawing B open and Drawing A closed.

⊕ To begin this task you should have Drawing B open on your screen.

⊕ Click on the DesignCenter tool on the Standard Annotation toolbar, as shown in Figure 10-25.

Figure 10-25

This executes the **ADCENTER** command and opens the DesignCenter palette shown in Figure 10-26. If anyone has used DesignCenter on your computer, you are likely to see something slightly different from our illustration, because the DesignCenter stores changes and resizing adjustments. In particular, if you do not see the tree view on the left as shown, you have to use the **Tree View Toggle** button to restore the tree view to your palette before going on.

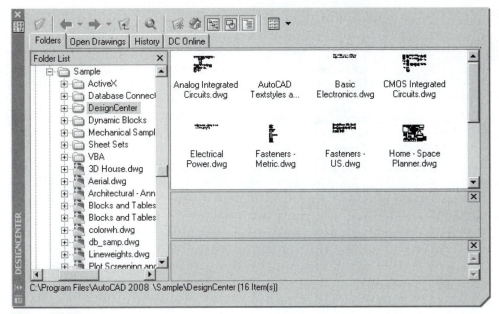

Figure 10-26

Figure 10-27

⊕ If necessary, click the Tree View Toggle button, as shown in Figure 10-27.

Your DesignCenter should now have a tree view on the left and a content area on the right. The DesignCenter has features similar to the Properties Manager, including the convenient auto-hide option, accessed by right-clicking the title bar and selecting from the shortcut menu (see Chapter 7, Section 7-6).

The DesignCenter is a complex palette that gives you access to a vast array of resources. There is a toolbar-like set of buttons at the top of the palette, including the **Tree View Toggle** button. Below these are four tabs and below these is the main work area of the palette. The tree view area shows a hierarchically arranged list of files, folders, and locations. The content area shows icons representing drawings and drawing contents of the folders or files currently selected in the tree view. What appears in the tree view depends on which tab is selected. The **Folders** tab shows the complete desktop hierarchy of your computer. The **Open Drawings** tab lists only open AutoCAD drawings. History shows a history of drawing files that have been specifically opened in the DesignCenter. If you are connected to the Internet, DC Online takes you to a comprehensive online library of standard parts and symbols for various design industries. With the **DC Online** tab selected, you also see a different set of buttons at the top of the palette.

We begin by selecting the **Open Drawings** tab and seeing what the Design-Center shows us regarding our current drawing.

⊕ Click the Open Drawings tab.

Now you have a very simple window with the open drawing and content types in the tree view and the content area, as shown in Figure 10-28.

You see icons representing standard content types: Blocks, Dimstyles, Layers, Layouts, Linetypes, Tablestyles, Textstyles, and Xrefs. All drawings show the same list, although not all drawings have content defined in each category.

In the tree view, the list of types is as far as you can go. In the palette, however, there is another level.

⊕ If necessary, highlight B.dwg in the tree view.

You don't need to do this if B is the only drawing open.

⊕ Double-click Xrefs in the tree view at the end of the list.

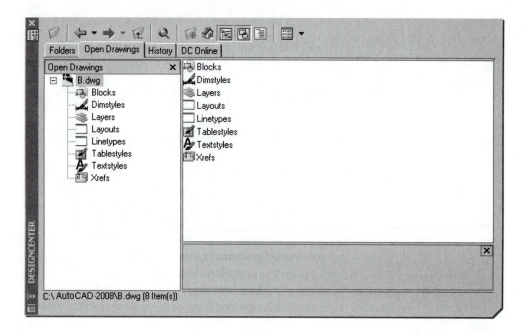

Figure 10-28

You see an icon representing the attached Drawing A in the content area, as shown in Figure 10-29. If you like, check out the other contents. In Dimstyles you find the Standard, Annotative, and 1B styles. In Layers you find all the layers defined in the 1B template. In Layouts you find Layouts 1 and 2, which are there by default. In Linetypes you find whatever linetypes have been loaded into your template. In Tablestyles you see Standard. In Textstyles you see the Standard and Annotative styles.

Now try looking into Drawing A. It is closed, but its contents are still accessible in the DesignCenter.

⊞ Click the Folders tab.

This opens the folder hierarchy for your computer's hard drive, as shown previously in Figure 10-26. You need to use the scroll bars in the tree view window to find where you have saved Drawing A.

⊞ Scroll to the folder containing Drawing A.

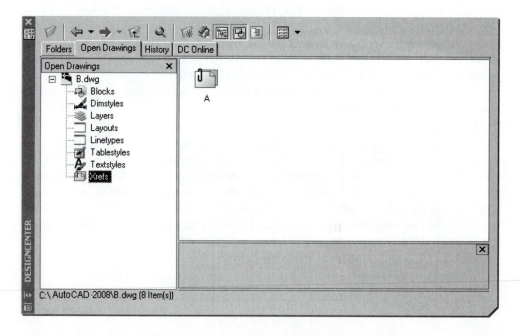

Figure 10-29

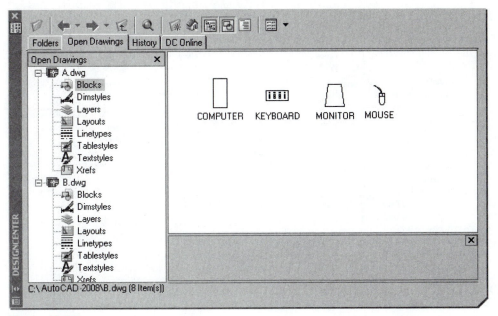

Figure 10-30

⊕ Open the folder and select Drawing A.

It is not necessary to open the list of contents under Drawing A in the tree view. As long as Drawing A is selected, you can open contents in the content area.

⊕ With Drawing A selected in the tree view, double-click the Blocks icon in the content area.

You see the familiar set of four blocks shown in Figure 10-30. At this point you could drag any of these blocks right off the palette into Drawing B. Instead, we insert a symbol from the DesignCenter's predrawn sample blocks. These are easily located using the **Favorites** button.

⊕ Click the Home button at the top of the DesignCenter palette, as shown in Figure 10-31.

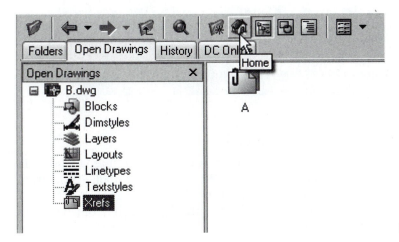

Figure 10-31

This takes you directly to the DesignCenter folder, which contains sample drawings and blocks, as illustrated in Figure 10-32. In the content area, you see a set of sample drawing thumbnails.

⊕ Scroll down and double-click Home-Space Planner.dwg.

As soon as you select this drawing, you again see the familiar set of icons for standard drawing content.

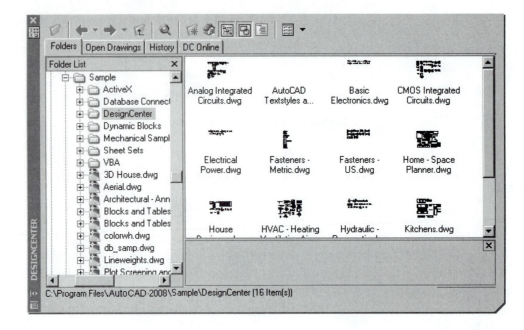

Figure 10-32

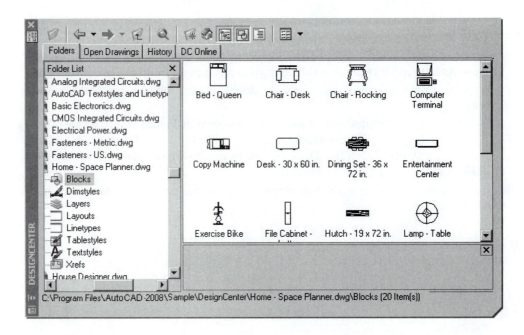

Figure 10-33

⊕ Double-click the Blocks icon in the content area.

Now you see a set of blocks representing household furniture, as shown in Figure 10-33. Look for the computer terminal. We insert this symbol, which is similar to our own workstation symbol, into Drawing B.

Blocks can be inserted from the DesignCenter by dragging, but there are some limitations, as you will see.

⊕ Select the computer terminal block in the palette.

⊕ Drag the block slowly into the Drawing B drawing area.

As soon as you are in the drawing area, you see a very large image of the computer block. This is a now familiar scaling problem.

⊕ Return your cursor to the palette without releasing the block.

We now explore a more precise and dependable method for inserting blocks from the DesignCenter. This second method allows you to scale the block as you insert it. First, however, it is convenient to put the DesignCenter palette in Auto-hide mode.

⊞ Click the Auto-hide button at the bottom of the DesignCenter title bar.

⊞ If the palette is hidden, move the cursor over the palette title bar so that the palette opens again.

⊞ Right-click on the computer block.

This opens a shortcut menu.

⊞ Select Insert Block.

You see the **Insert** dialog box with Computer Terminal in the Name edit box. From here on, the procedure is just like inserting a block within its original drawing.

⊞ Select the Uniform Scale check box.

⊞ Enter 1/8 or .125 in the X Scale box.

⊞ Click OK.

As the dialog box closes, the auto-hide feature activates and the DesignCenter collapses so that only the title bar remains. This makes it easy to pick an insertion point in the drawing area.

⊞ Select an insertion point anywhere above the workstation Xref, as shown in Figure 10-34.

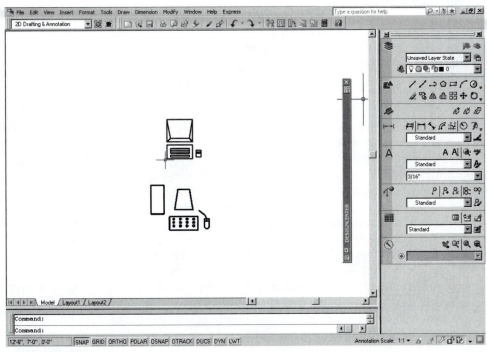

Figure 10-34

⊞ Move the cursor back into the DesignCenter title bar.

The palette opens again.

⊞ Click the Open Drawings tab.

⊞ Double-click the Blocks icon in the palette.

The ComputerTerminal block definition from the Home-Space Planner drawing is now in the database of Drawing B.

Other Features of the DesignCenter

Before leaving the DesignCenter, here are a few more features, controlled by the buttons at the top. Looking across the toolbar, the **Load** button opens a standard file selection dialog box where you can load any folder or drawing file into the DesignCenter. The **Back** and **Forward** buttons take you to previous tree view and content area displays. The **Up** button takes you up one level in whatever folder hierarchy you are exploring. The **Search** button opens a **Search** dialog box, allowing you to search for files, folders, and text in a variety of ways familiar in Windows applications. The **Favorites** button takes you to a set of defined favorite locations. By default, this includes the DesignCenter folder and the AutoCAD predefined hatch pattern sets. The **Home** button, as we have seen, takes you directly to the DesignCenter folder. The **Tree View Toggle** button opens and closes the tree view panel. With the panel closed there is more room to view contents. The **Preview** button opens and closes a panel below the content area that shows preview images of selected contents. The **Description** button opens and closes a panel below the Preview panel that displays text describing a selected block. Finally, the **Views** button allows choice over the style in which content is displayed in the content area. Before moving on, close the DesignCenter.

⊕ Click the close symbol (X) at the top of the DesignCenter title bar.

10-8 DEFINING ATTRIBUTES

GENERAL PROCEDURE	1. Select Draw → Block → Define Attributes from the pull-down menu. 2. Specify attribute modes. 3. Type an attribute tag. 4. Type an attribute prompt. 5. If desired, type a default attribute value. 6. Include the attribute in a block definition.

We have introduced many new concepts in this chapter. We have gone from simply grouping objects together to sharing drawing content between drawings. Now we add additional information to block definitions using AutoCAD's attribute feature. When you add attributes to a block definition, you create the ability to pass drawing data between drawings and nongraphic applications, typically database and spreadsheet programs. Attributes hold information about blocks in a drawing in a form that can be read out to other programs and organized into reports or bills of materials. Attributes can be confusing, and you should not spend too much time worrying about their details unless you are currently involved in an application that requires their use. On the other hand, they are a powerful tool, and if you have a basic understanding of what they can do, you could be the one in your work setting to recognize when to use them.

One of the difficulties of learning about attributes is that you have to define them before you see them in action. It is therefore a little hard to comprehend what your definitions mean the first time around. Bear with us and follow instructions closely; it is worth your effort.

In this task, we define attributes that hold information about our CAD workstations. The attributes are defined in a flexible manner so that the workstation block can represent any number of hardware configurations. One instance of the workstation block could represent a Compaq computer with a Pentium III processor and an Acer monitor, for example, whereas another instance of the same block could represent an IBM computer with a Pentium 4 processor and an NEC monitor.

When we have defined our attributes, we create a block called ws that includes the whole computer workstation assembly and its attributes. To accomplish this, we return to Drawing A and add attributes to our workstation assembly there. Because Drawing A is now attached to Drawing B as an external reference, this also gives us the opportunity to learn more about working with Xrefs and to observe the effects of editing an Xref.

Assuming you are still in Drawing B from the previous section, we begin this task by demonstrating AutoCAD's **XOPEN** command, which allows you to quickly open an Xref from within a drawing without searching through a file hierarchy to locate the referenced drawing.

⊕ Select the computer workstation in Drawing B that was inserted as an external reference to Drawing A.

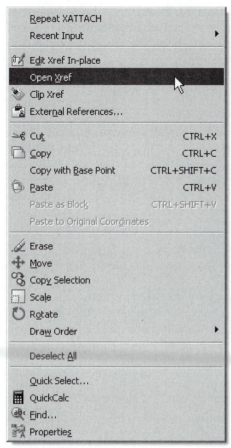

Figure 10-35

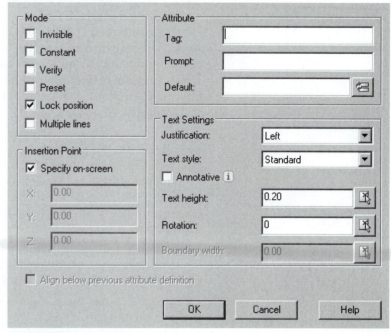

Figure 10-36

The workstation is highlighted and a grip is placed at the previously defined insertion base point.

⊕ With the external reference highlighted, right-click.

This opens the lengthy shortcut menu shown in Figure 10-35.

⊕ Select Open Xref.

Drawing A opens in the drawing area. You should see the original workstation assembly on Layer 1 in this drawing, just as you created it in Section 10-3. Drawing A is open just as if you had opened it using the **OPEN** command. You now have the two drawings open again. Drawing A is current, with Drawing B open in the background.

We are going to add attributes to these blocks in Drawing A and then define the whole assembly and its attributes as a single block called ws. First, we define an attribute that allows us to specify the type of computer in any individual reference to the ws block.

⊕ Select Draw → Block → Define Attributes from the pull-down menu.

This executes the **ATTDEF** command and opens the **Attribute Definition** dialog box shown in Figure 10-36.

Look first at the check boxes at the top left in the Mode panel. For our purposes none of these boxes should be checked. These are the default settings, which we will use in this first attribute definition. When our workstation block is inserted, the computer attribute value will be visible in the drawing (because Invisible is not selected), variable with each insertion of the block (because Constant is not selected), not verified (Verify is not selected), and not preset to a value (Preset is not selected). We will not be able to reposition the text within the block, because Lock position is selected by default, and we will use single-line text, because Multiple lines is not selected.

Next, look at the Attribute panel to the right. The cursor should be blinking in the Tag edit box. Like a field name in a database file, a tag identifies the kind of information this particular attribute is meant to hold. The tag appears in the block definition as a field name. In occurrences of the block in a drawing, the tag is replaced by a specific value. Computer, for example, could be replaced by IBM.

⊞ Type Computer in the Tag edit box.

⊞ Move the cursor to the Prompt edit box.

As with the tag, the key to understanding the attribute prompt is to be clear about the difference between block definitions and block references. Right now, we are defining an attribute. The attribute definition becomes part of the definition of the ws block and is used whenever ws is inserted. With the definition we are creating, there is a prompt whenever we insert a ws block that asks us to enter information about the computer in a given configuration.

⊞ Type "Specify computer type."

We also have the opportunity to specify a default attribute value, if we wish, by typing in the Value edit box. Here, we leave this field blank, specifying no default value in our attribute definition.

The panel labeled Text Settings allows you to specify text parameters as you would in TEXT. Visible attributes appear as text on the screen. Therefore, the appearance of the text needs to be specified. We will specify a height, and also add the annotative property so that the text could be scaled to appear at a scaled height within a layout viewport.

⊞ Click the check box next to Annotative.

⊞ Double-click in the edit box to the right of Height and then type "4"."

If you click the **Text Height** button to the right, the dialog box disappears so that you can indicate a height by picking points on the screen.

Finally, AutoCAD needs to know where to place the visible attribute information in the drawing. You can type in *x, y,* and *z* coordinate values, but you are more likely to pick a point.

⊞ Check to see that Specify On-screen is checked in the Insertion Point panel.

⊞ Click OK.

The dialog box disappears to allow access to the screen. You also see a *Start point:* prompt in the command area.

We place our attributes 3 inches below the keyboard.

⊞ Pick a start point 3 inches below the left side of the keyboard (see Figure 10-37).

The dialog box disappears and the attribute tag Computer is drawn as shown. Remember, this is an attribute definition, not an occurrence of the attribute.

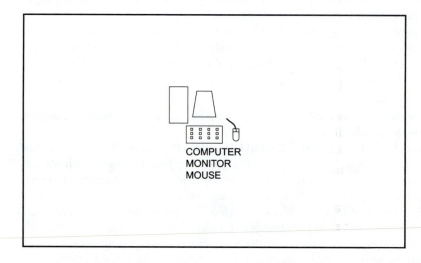

Figure 10-37

Computer is our attribute tag. After we define the workstation as a block and the block is inserted, answer the *Specify computer type:* prompt with the name of a computer type, and the name itself is shown in the drawing rather than this tag.

We proceed to define three more attributes using some different options.

⊞ Repeat ATTDEF.

We use all the default modes, but we provide a default monitor value in this attribute definition.

⊞ Type "Monitor" for the attribute tag.

⊞ Type "Specify monitor type" for the attribute prompt.

⊞ Type "20″ CRT" for the default attribute value.

> **Note:**
> The button to the right of the Attribute Value edit box allows you to insert a field as the attribute value. In this case the attribute would automatically update when the field data changed.

Now when AutoCAD shows the prompt for a monitor type, it also shows 20″ CRT as the default, as you will see.

You can align a series of attributes by selecting the Align below previous attribute definition check box at the lower left of the dialog box.

⊞ Select the Align below previous attribute definition check box.

⊞ Click OK to complete the dialog.

The attribute tag Monitor should be added to the workstation below the Computer tag, as shown in Figure 10-37.

Next, we add an invisible, preset attribute for the mouse. Invisible means that the attribute text is not visible when the block is inserted, although the information is in the database and can be extracted. Preset means that the attribute has a default value and does not issue a prompt to change it. However, unlike constant attributes, you can change preset attributes using the Attribute Manager, which we explore in Section 10-10.

⊞ Repeat ATTDEF.

⊞ Select the Invisible check box.

⊞ Select the Preset check box.

⊞ Type "Mouse" for the attribute tag.

You do not need a prompt, because the preset attribute is automatically set to the default value. There is no need to add the annotative property because the attribute is not visible when the drawing is plotted.

⊞ Type "MS Mouse" for the default attribute value.

⊞ Select the Align below previous attribute definition check box to position the attribute below Monitor in the drawing.

⊞ Click OK to complete the dialog.

The Mouse attribute tag should be added to your screen, as shown in Figure 10-37. When a workstation block is inserted, the attribute value MS Mouse is written into the database, but nothing appears on the screen because the attribute is defined as invisible.

Finally comes the most important step of all: We must define the workstation as a block that includes all our attribute definitions.

⊞ Type "b" ↵ or select the Make Block tool from the dashboard.

⊞ Type "ws" for the block name.

⊞ Click Select Objects.

⊞ Window the workstation assembly and all three attribute tags.

⊞ Right-click to end object selection.

⊞ Click Pick Point.

⊕ Pick an insertion point at the midpoint of the bottom of the keyboard.

⊕ Select the Delete button.

⊕ Click OK to close the dialog box.

The newly defined block disappears from the screen.

The ws block with its three attribute definitions is now present in the Drawing A database. Before moving on, we insert three instances of the block and provide some notes on editing attributes and attribute values.

Inserting Blocks with Attributes

Inserting blocks with attributes is no different from inserting any block, except that you will be prompted for attribute values.

⊕ To complete this task, insert three workstations, using the following procedure (note the attribute prompts):

1. Type "I" ↵ or select the **Insert Block** button from the dashboard.

2. Select ws from the Block name list.

3. Click **OK** to exit the dialog box.

4. Pick an insertion point.

5. Answer the attribute prompts for monitors and computers.

We specified two different configurations for this exercise, using processor types to designate the computers, as shown in Figure 10-38. The first two are Pentium 4 computers with the default 20″ CRT monitor. The third is a Pentium 4 Xeon computer with a 24″ LCD (flatscreen) monitor. This exercise will be easier to follow if you use the same attribute values. Notice that you are not prompted for mouse specifications because that attribute is preset.

When you are done, your screen should resemble Figure 10-38.

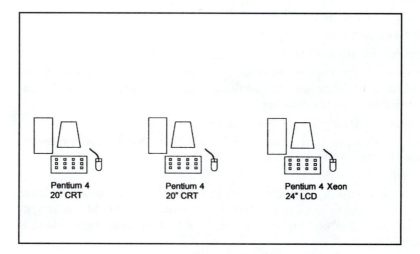

Figure 10-38

Editing Attribute Values and Definitions

Once you begin to work with defined Attributes you may have occasion to edit them. The first thing to consider whenever you edit attributes is whether you wish to edit attribute values in a block reference or whether you want to edit the actual attribute definition. There are four major commands used to edit attributes. **ATTDISP, ATTEDIT,** and **EATTEDIT** work on attribute values in inserted blocks and **BATTMAN** works directly on Attribute definitions. The following chart explains their uses.

Command	Usage
ATTDISP	Allows control of the visibility of all attribute values in inserted blocks, regardless of their defined visibility mode. There are three options. Normal means that visible attributes are visible and invisible attributes are invisible. On makes all attributes visible. Off makes all attributes invisible.
ATTEDIT	Allows single or global editing of attribute values from the command line. Global editing allows editing text strings in all attribute values that fit criteria you define.
EATTEDIT	Opens the Enhanced Attribute Edit dialog box for editing individual attribute values in inserted blocks. It allows you to change individual attribute values, text position, height, angle, style, layer, and color of attribute values.
BATTMAN	Opens the Block Attribute Manager and allows editing of attribute definitions. In this dialog box you can edit tags, prompts, default values, and modes for all blocks defined in a drawing. Changes are made directly to the block definition and reflected in blocks subsequently inserted.

10-9 Working with Parameters in Block References

Having three references to the ws block on the screen in Drawing A provides an opportunity to learn more about how parameters and actions work within dynamic blocks. WS is a nested block made up of four component blocks—the computer, the monitor, the mouse, and the keyboard. In the last section we defined attributes for three of these components. Going back to Section 10-4, recall that we added a linear parameter and a stretch action to the original computer block so that we could reshape it to represent a tower-style computer. Notice that all of our ws blocks now contain this representation. So, what has become of our original shape and the parameter and action associated with it? In this section we offer a brief exploration of the behavior of parameters and nested blocks.

⊕ To begin, you should be in Drawing A with the three ws block references shown previously in Figure 10-38.

⊕ Select any of the three block references.

The entire block will be highlighted and there will be one grip at the base point, which is the midpoint of the top of the keyboard. Notice the parameter and action that were added to the computer block back in Section 10-4 are not present. Using the grip, the entire block reference can be moved, mirrored, rotated, scaled, or stetched (the same as move in this case), but no component can be manipulated independently.

⊕ With a block reference highlighted, select the Block Editor tool from the Standard Annotation toolbar.

This opens the **Edit Block Definition** dialog box. You see all the component blocks in the Block to Create or Edit list, with ws highlighted on the list and previewed on the right.

⊕ With ws highlighted, click OK.

This brings you to the Block Editor window. The ws block is shown in the window, with the Block Authoring Palettes open on the left.

⊕ In the block editing window, select the computer rectangle.

You see the parameter grips previously defined in Section 10-4, as shown in Figure 10-39. What this means is that here in the Block Editor you can move and reshape the computer just as you have done previously. Notice the difference, though. Here you would be changing the shape of the computer within the block definition so that when you closed the Block Editor, all three block references would be updated with the new shape. The computer block is a dynamic block nested within the ws block. The ws block as a whole is not a dynamic block. In order to add dynamic capabilities to the ws block definition, we need to add them at this level. We add a simple move point and action to the monitor. This will allow

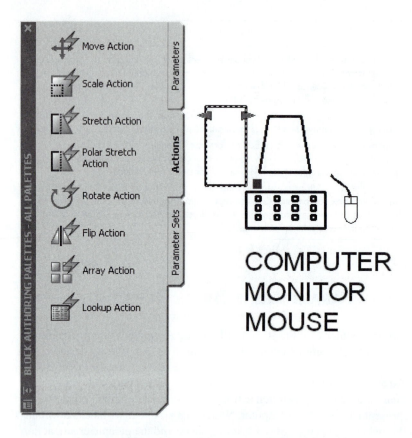

Figure 10-39

us to move the monitor independently in each block reference, and will also give you an introduction to the use of parameter sets. A parameter set is a parameter and an action paired together.

⊕ Press Esc to remove grips from the computer.

⊕ Select the monitor.

The monitor will be highlighted with a single grip at its base point.

⊕ Select the Parameter Sets tab at the bottom right on the Block Authoring Palettes.

Notice that all the selections on this tab are combinations of parameters and actions.

⊕ From the top of the list, select Point Move.

AutoCAD prompts:

```
Specify parameter location or [Name/Label/Chain/
                 Description/Palette]:
```

⊕ Shift, right-click, and select midpoint from the object snap shortcut menu.

⊕ Pick the midpoint of the top line on the monitor

AutoCAD prompts for a label location.

⊕ Pick a label location similar to that shown in Figure 10-40.

The point parameter and the move action have both been added to the block definition, but the move action must still be associated with a set of objects, as indicated by the yellow alert.

⊕ Double-click the Move action symbol.

This must be a double-click to execute the **BACTIONSET** command and allow you to select objects. You should have a Select Objects prompt on the dynamic display and the command line.

⊕ Select the monitor.

⊕ Right-click to complete object selection.

This returns you to the command prompt, but you are still in the Block Editor.

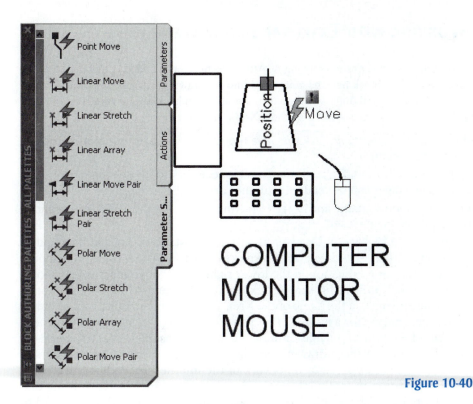

Figure 10-40

⊕ Click the Close Block Editor button on the Block Editor toolbar.

AutoCAD intervenes with a box asking if you want to save changes to the ws block.

⊕ Click Yes.

You return to the drawing with the three block references.

⊕ Select the block reference on the right.

The block reference is highlighted as before, but you now have an additional grip at the midpoint of the back of the monitor. This will allow you to move the monitor in any block reference without affecting other references.

⊕ Select the grip at the back (top) of the monitor in the selected reference.

⊕ Move the monitor back a few inches, as shown in Figure 10-41.

⊕ Press Esc to remove grips.

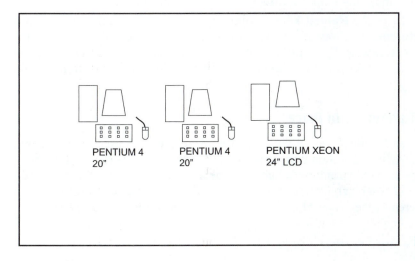

Figure 10-41

10-10 WORKING WITH EXTERNAL REFERENCES

You have made numerous changes to Drawing A. Attributes have been added, a ws block created, three references to the new block have been inserted into the drawing, and one monitor has been moved. This provides us a good opportunity to turn our attention back to Drawing B and look at the Drawing A external reference there to see how Xrefs work in action.

⊞ Before leaving Drawing A, click the Save tool on the Standard Annotation toolbar to save your changes.

This is not just to safeguard changes. It is necessary to save changes to an Xref before the changes can be read into another drawing.

⊞ Open the Window menu and select Drawing B, or use the OPEN command if Drawing B has been closed.

You should be back in Drawing B with a workstation Xref and a computer terminal block on your screen, as shown previously in Figure 10-34. You should also see a balloon notification in the lower right corner of your screen, as shown in Figure 10-42, indicating that an externally referenced drawing has been changed and giving you the name of the Xref. To clearly understand the use of this notification, imagine for a moment that you are working with a team of designers. The focus of the project is a master drawing that contains references to several external drawings and these drawings are being created or edited by designers at various locations connected by a network or the Internet. The external reference update notification instantly informs anyone looking at the master drawing that one or more of the external references have changed and should be reloaded to keep things up to date. Be aware that this notification would not appear if the changes made to Drawing A had not been saved.

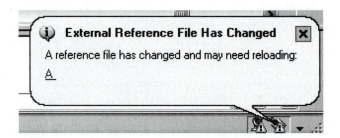

Figure 10-42

The first thing we need to do is reload the Drawing A Xref to bring our changes into Drawing B.

⊞ Click the blue underlined link to Drawing A in the notification balloon.

This executes the **Reload XREF** command and automatically updates the external reference to Drawing A, which now includes all three references to the ws block. Drawing B is updated to reflect the changes in Drawing A, as shown in Figure 10-43. Following are a few notes on working with external references.

Editing External References in Place

External references can be edited within the current drawing and even used to update the original referenced drawing. This should be done sparingly and for simple edits only; otherwise the current drawing will expand to take up more memory and the point of using an external reference instead of a block reference is lost. To edit a block or external reference in place, select the reference, then right-click and select Edit Xref in-place from the shortcut menu.

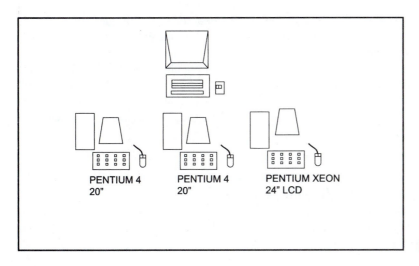

Figure 10-43

Clipping External References

External references can also be clipped so that only a portion of the referenced drawing is actually displayed in the current drawing. This would allow different users on the same network to share portions of their drawings without altering the original drawings. Clipping boundaries can be defined by a rectangular window, a polygon window, or an existing polyline. Clipping is performed with the **XCLIP** command and can be used on block references as well as external references. To clip a reference, select it, right-click, and select Clip Xref from the shortcut menu.

For example, you could clip the attributes in Drawing B so that only the workstations remained visible. The process would be:

1. In Drawing B, select the three workstation references to Drawing A.
2. Right-click to open the shortcut menu.
3. Select Clip Xref.
4. Press **Enter** to accept the default, rectangular boundary.
5. Pick two points to define a window around the workstations, but not around the attributes.

Clipping an instance of an Xref does not alter the Xref definition; it only suppresses the display of the objects outside the clipping boundary.

Parameters in External References

If you select any of the three workstations in Drawing B, all three will be highlighted. There will be only one grip at the base point defined when you inserted Drawing A as an external reference in B. The parameters defined for the computer and the monitor will not be accessible. Unlike in Drawing A, these parameters will not be accessible in the Block Editor. In fact, the ws block itself is not visible in the Block Editor, nor is the external reference to Drawing A, because it is an external reference, not a block.

In the next section, we return to our attribute information.

10-11 Extracting Data from Attributes

In AutoCAD 2008, many types of data can be extracted from a drawing and quickly formatted into tables or linked to external applications. Extracted data can be transferred to spreadsheet or database programs for use in the preparation of parts lists, bills of material, and other documentation. For example, with a well-managed system of parts and attributes you can do a drawing of a construction project and get a complete price breakdown and supply list directly from the drawing database, all processed by computer. To accomplish this, you need carefully defined attributes and a program such as Microsoft Excel that is capable of receiving the extracted information and formatting it into a useful report.

In this demonstration, you extract attribute information from blocks in Drawing A and place it in an AutoCAD table, which you insert into the drawing. The steps are the same as if you were exporting the information to a spreadsheet or database program, but can be completed successfully without leaving AutoCAD. If you are in Drawing B from the previous task, you should start by switching back to Drawing A.

⊕ Open the Window menu and select Drawing A.

The three ws blocks and their attribute values should be on your screen.

⊕ Open the Tools menu and select Data Extraction.

You see the Data Extraction Wizard, as shown in Figure 10-44. This wizard takes you through the steps of selecting data to extract and creating a table that can be exported or inserted.

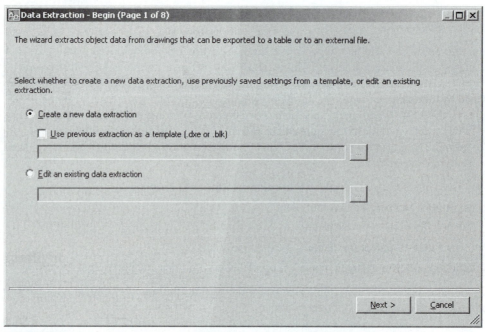

Figure 10-44

The first step in this wizard is to select a template file or to create a file from scratch. The template can be a previous extraction laid out to receive the information from your attributes.

⊕ If necessary, select the Create a new data extraction button.

⊕ Click Next.

This brings you to the **Save Data Extraction** dialog box. This is a standard file-saving dialog box. The extracted data must first be saved to a file with a dxe extension. This is true even if you are going to insert it back into your current drawing.

⊕ Type "ws data" ↵ in the File name box.

This takes you to the **Define Data Source** dialog box shown in Figure 10-45. In the Data source panel of this dialog box you can choose to extract data from the current drawing and/or drawing sheet set or from selected objects only. The panel below that gives the path of the current drawing. Drawings/Sheet set and Include current drawing should be selected in this box.

⊕ Click Next.

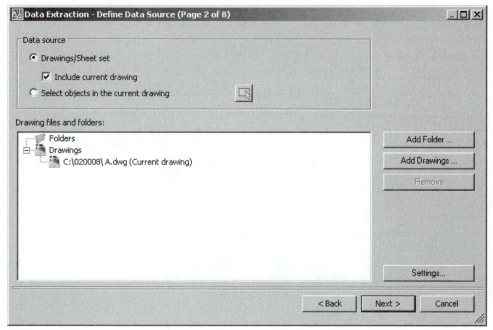

Figure 10-45

This brings you to the **Select Objects** dialog box shown in Figure 10-46. Here we begin to narrow down the type of data we want to extract. Currently all objects in the drawing are displayed. Our goal is to extract just the attribute data from the three ws blocks in the drawing.

✛ Deselect the Display all object types box.

This gives you access to the two buttons below. Display blocks only should be selected by default. On the right are two other options: Display blocks with attributes only and Display objects currently in-use only.

✛ Select Display blocks with attributes only.

At this point the only thing displayed in the Objects list should be the ws block.

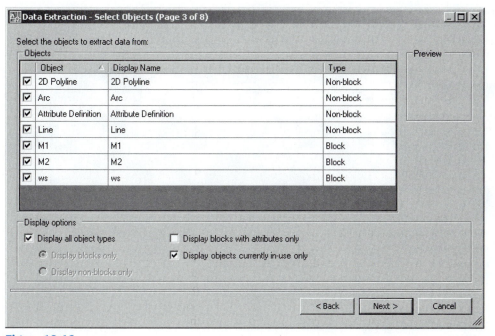

Figure 10-46

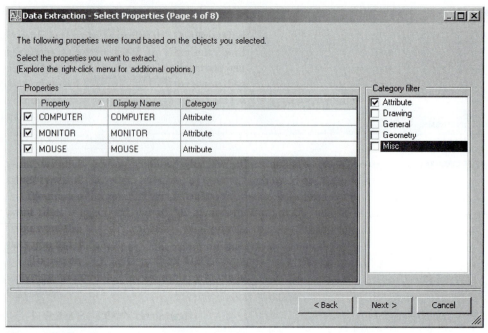

Figure 10-47

⊕ Click Next.

Now you see the **Select Properties** dialog box, shown in Figure 10-47. The category filter on the right allows us to narrow down to attributes only.

⊕ Deselect all the categories except attributes, as shown in the figure.

You should see only the computer, monitor, and mouse attributes in the properties list, as shown.

⊕ Click Next.

In the **Refine Data** dialog box, shown in Figure 10-48, the data is displayed and grouped, according to the selections made in the three boxes at the bottom:

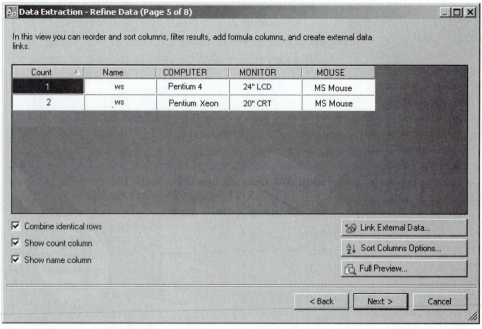

Figure 10-48

Combine identical rows, Show count column, and Show name column. They should all be selected by default.

⊞ Click Next.

The next box gives you the choice of extracting to an external file or to an AutoCAD table.

⊞ Select the first choice, Insert data extraction table into drawing.

⊞ Click Next.

You are now in a **Table Style** dialog box. We will stick with the Standard table style, but will add a title.

⊞ Double-click in the edit box below Enter a title for your table.

⊞ Type "Workstation Data."

⊞ Click Next.

⊞ Click Finish.

You have completed the attribute extraction process; all that remains is to insert the table into your drawing. You see a very small table connected to the crosshairs.

⊞ Pick a point on your screen below the middle block reference.

⊞ Zoom into a window around the inserted table.

Your screen should resemble Figure 10-49.

Workstation Data				
Count	Name	COMPUTER	MONITOR	MOUSE
1	ws	Pentium Xeon	24" LCD	MS MOUSE
2	ws	Pentium 4	20" CRT	MS MOUSE

Figure 10-49

10-12 CREATING TOOL PALETTES

Given your knowledge of blocks, Xrefs, and the DesignCenter, at this point you also have use for another AutoCAD feature. Tool palettes are simply collections of blocks placed very accessibly in a format that is much simpler than the DesignCenter palette.

The real power of tool palettes comes from the ease with which you can populate them with your own content. Try this:

⊞ Open the DesignCenter by picking the DesignCenter tool on the Standard Annotation toolbar.

⊞ If necessary, click the Open Drawings tab.

⊞ If necessary, highlight A.dwg and open the A list.

⊞ Double-click the Blocks icon.

You can see the set of blocks in Drawing A, including ws, the computer, keyboard, monitor, and mouse blocks.

⊞ Right-click anywhere in the content area.

⊞ From the shortcut menu, select Create Tool Palette at the bottom of the menu.

A tool palette is opened with a new tab, labeled A, from the name of the drawing. This palette tab has the five blocks from Drawing A, as shown in Figure 10-50. It's that simple. You now have your own tool palette to work with. The blocks on this tab can be dragged into the drawing.

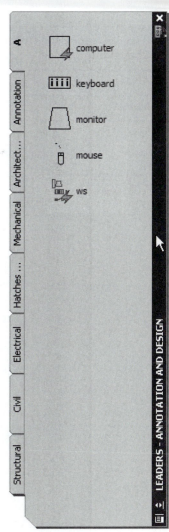

Figure 10-50

Keep in mind that the tools on a tool palette are accessible only as long as the reference is clear. If they originate from an externally referenced drawing, the reference path must be clear and accessible. If the referenced drawing is moved or deleted, the tool will no longer be available.

TIP To open all tool palettes in the tool palettes window, right-click on the double lines at the top of the bar and select All Palettes from the shortcut menu.

In the next section you learn how to reverse the block definition process.

10-13 EXPLODING BLOCKS

GENERAL PROCEDURE
1. Type "x" ↵, or select the **Explode** tool from the dashboard.
2. Select objects.
3. Press **Enter** to carry out the command.

COMMAND GRID	
Command	Explode
Alias	X
Menu	Modify
Tool	

The **EXPLODE** command undoes the work of the **BLOCK** or **GROUP** command. It takes a set of objects that have been defined as a block or group and re-creates them as independent entities. **EXPLODE** works on dimensions and hatch patterns as well as on blocks created in the **BLOCK** command or tools inserted from a tool palette. It does not work on externally referenced drawings until they have been attached permanently through the Bind option of the **XREF** command.

⊕ To begin this task, you should have Drawing A on your screen.

Let's try exploding a workstation.

⊕ Select the Explode tool from the dashboard, as shown in Figure 10-51.

You are prompted to select objects.

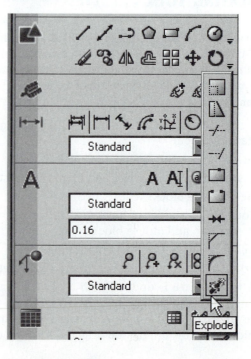

Figure 10-51

⊕ Select the center workstation.

⊕ Right-click to end object selection and carry out the command.

You should notice immediately that the attribute values are replaced by attribute tags.

⊕ Run your cursor over any part of the workstation and observe the preview highlighting.

All the component parts of the previously blocked workstation can now be selected separately, including the attribute tags. If you select the computer rectangle, you see that the parameter and action are once again accessible. If you select the monitor you see that the original grip at the front of the block has returned, but that the move parameter point, which was part of the ws block definition, is no longer present.

Note:
Exploding removes only one layer of block definition. If a block is made up of other blocks, these "nested" blocks remain as independent blocks after exploding. Attribute value information is removed by exploding, leaving the attribute tag instead.

Congratulations! This has been a tough chapter with a lot of new information and procedures to learn. You have gained a greater sense of the tools available for using AutoCAD in collaborative work environments. You should now appreciate that although the basic drafting tools available in AutoCAD are impressive themselves, there are powerful features here that go well beyond the one-person, one-workstation around to include collaboration among individuals, companies, and worksites around the globe. You can find more information on tools for collaboration in Appendix E.

CHAPTER TEST QUESTIONS

Questions

1. Why is it usually a good idea to create blocks on Layer 0?
2. What is the difference between a group and a block?
3. What is an insertion base point, as used in the **BLOCK** command? What is an insertion point, as used in the **INSERT** command?
4. Why are blocks, external references, and raster images all inserted with a scale factor?
5. How could you create a complete drawing using only the **INSERT** command?
6. What would you have to do to create blocks with geometry that could be edited after they were inserted?
7. What is the purpose of the yellow exclamation point that appears whenever you add a parameter to a block?
8. What is the difference between **COPY** and **COPYCLIP?**
9. What is an attribute tag? What is an attribute prompt? What is an attribute value?
10. What are the three settings of **ATTDISP?**
11. What is the purpose of data extraction?
12. What other complex entities can be exploded besides blocks?
13. What happens to attribute values when a block is exploded?
14. What is the main thing you can accomplish with the AutoCAD DesignCenter that cannot be done with **INSERT** or **XATTACH?**

Drawing Problems

1. Open a new drawing using the 1B prototype and create a hexagon circumscribed around a circle so that both have a 1.0-unit radius. These objects should be created so that when they are defined as a block, they are inserted on Layer 2 regardless of what layer is current at the time.

2. Define an attribute to go with the hexagon and circle. The tag should identify the two as a hex bolt; the prompt should ask for a hex bolt diameter. The attribute should be visible in the drawing, center justified 0.5 unit below the block, with text 0.3 unit high.

3. Create a block with the bolt and its attribute. Leave a clear screen when you are done.

4. Draw a rectangle on Layer 1, with lower left corner at (0,4) and upper right corner at (18,8).

5. Insert 0.5-diameter hex bolts at (2,6) and (16,6). Insert a 1.0-unit hex bolt at (9,6). The sizes of each hex bolt should appear beneath the bolt.

WWW Exercise 10 (Optional)

The new material in this chapter opens the door to several new Internet access procedures. In this task, we show you how to insert hyperlinks into drawings so that anyone using your drawing can jump from an object directly to a specified Internet address. All you have to do is insert a hyperlink and make sure that whoever wants to use that hyperlink is connected to the Internet at the time. Hyperlinks can also be used to connect to other drawing files, views, or layouts. For demonstration, we insert a hyperlink into Drawing A, attached to a workstation block. The hyperlink is defined to link to our companion website. Then we go through the procedure for connecting to the website through the hyperlink. Here we go.

⊕ To begin this task, you should be in Drawing A.

> If for any reason this drawing is not readily available, any drawing will do, but the illustrations will not match.

⊕ If you have not already done so, connect to your Internet service provider.

⊕ Open the Insert menu and select Hyperlink.

> Hyperlinks are connected to objects, so AutoCAD prompts you to select objects. The prompt is plural, indicating that you can select more than one object to connect to the same hyperlink.

⊕ Select the workstation on the left.

⊕ Select the workstation on the right.

⊕ Right-click to end object selection.

> This brings you to the Insert Hyperlink dialog box shown in Figure 10-52.

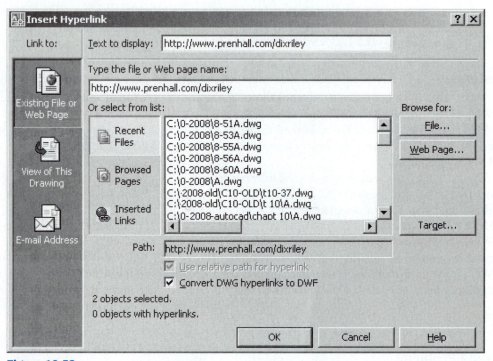

Figure 10-52

⊕ Look over the box to see the array of options you have for linking through this feature.

⊕ Type "www.prenhall.com/dixriley" in the Type the file or Web page name edit box.

⊕ Click OK to exit the dialog box.

> The dialog box disappears. The links have been inserted, but nothing happens until you select a hyperlink.

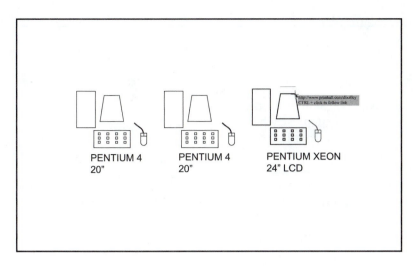

Figure 10-53

⊕ Move your cursor over either of the selected workstations. (We chose the one on the right.) When you see the hyperlink cursor as shown in Figure 10-53, let the cursor rest.

You see the hyperlink symbol and below it the hyperlink specification, as shown in Figure 10-52.

⊕ With the hyperlink symbol displayed, press the pick button.

The workstation is selected but nothing else happens.

⊕ Right-click anywhere in the drawing area.

A shortcut menu appears with Hyperlink on the bottom.

⊕ Highlight Hyperlink at the bottom of the shortcut menu.

This opens a submenu, as shown in Figure 10-54.

⊕ Select Open www.prenhall.com/dixriley.

See you at the website!

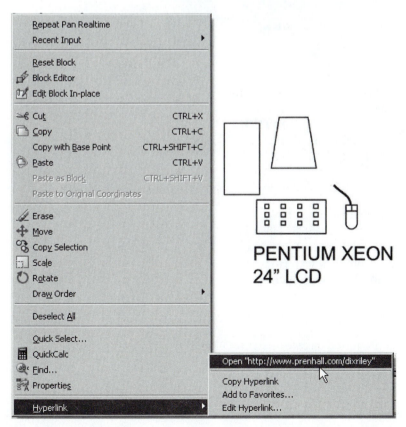

Figure 10-54

CHAPTER PROJECTS

Drawing 10-1: CAD Room

This architectural drawing is primarily an exercise in using blocks and attributes. Use your ws block and its attributes to fill in the workstations and text after you draw the walls and countertop. New blocks should be created for the plotters and printers, as described subsequently. The drawing setup is consistent with Drawing A from the chapter so that blocks can be easily inserted without scaling. When you have completed this drawing, you might want to try extracting the attribute information to a word processor or Excel file.

Drawing Suggestions

```
UNITS = Architectural, precision = 0' – 0"
GRID = 1'
SNAP = 1"
LIMITS = (0',0')(48',36')
```

- The "plotter" block is a 1 × 3 rectangle, with two visible, variable attributes (all the default attribute modes). The first attribute is for a manufacturer and the second for a model. The "printers" are 2 × 2.5 with the same type of attributes. Draw the rectangles, define their attributes eight inches below them, create the block definitions, and then insert plotters and printers as shown.

- The "8 pen plotter" was inserted with a *y* scale factor of 1.25.

Note:
Do not include the labels "plotter" and "laser printer" in the block, because text in a block is rotated with the block. This would give you inverted text on the front countertop. Insert the blocks and add the text afterward. The attribute text can be handled differently, using the mirrtext system.

The Mirrtext System Variable

The two workstations on the front counter could be inserted with a rotation angle of 180 degrees, but then the attribute text would be inverted also and would have to be turned around using **EATTEDIT**. Instead, we have reset the mirrtext system variable so that we could mirror blocks without attribute text being inverted:

1. Type mirrtext.
2. Type 0.

Now you can mirror objects on the back counter to create those on the front. With the mirrtext system variable set to 0, text included in a **MIRROR** procedure is not inverted as it would be with mirrtext set to 1. This applies to attribute text as well as ordinary text. However, it does not apply to ordinary text included in a block definition.

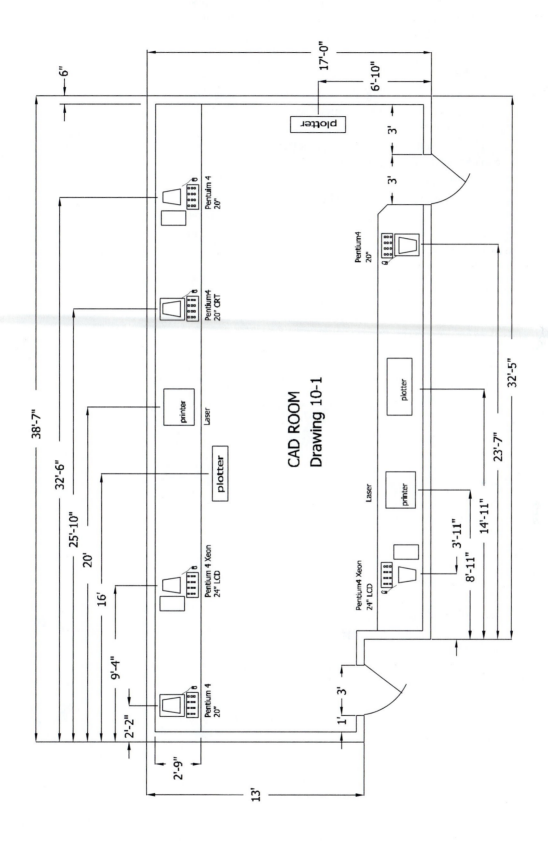

CAD ROOM
Drawing 10-1

Drawing 10-2: Office Plan

This drawing is primarily an exercise in the use of predrawn blocks and symbols. With a few exceptions, everything in the drawing can be inserted from the AutoCAD DesignCenter.

Drawing Suggestions

- Observe the overall 62′ × 33′ dimensions of the office space and choose appropriate architectural limits, snap settings, and grid settings for the drawing.
- We have not provided dimensions for the interior spaces, so you are free to choose dimensions as you wish.
- All walls can be drawn as 6″ wide filled multilines.
- All doors and furniture can be inserted from the DesignCenter.
- The large meeting room table is not predrawn. Create a simple filleted rectangle with dimensions as shown. It might be defined and saved as a block for future use.

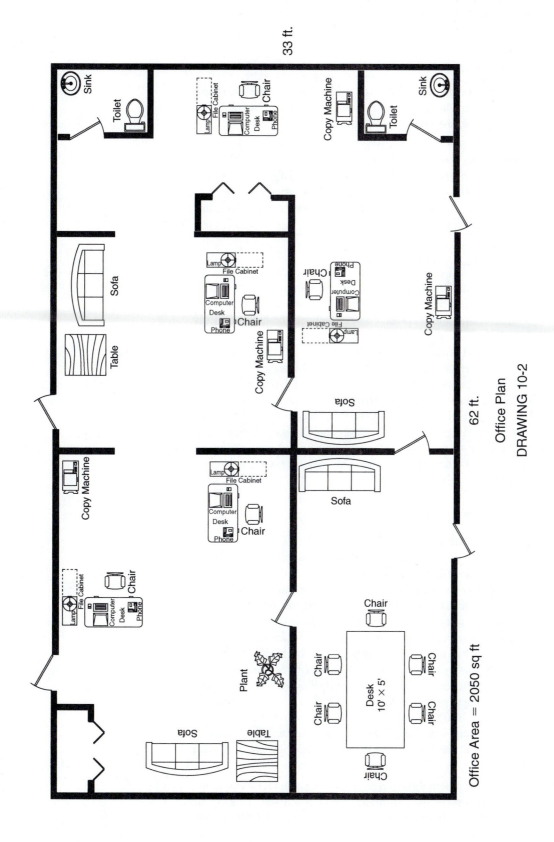

33 ft.

62 ft.

Office Plan
DRAWING 10-2

Office Area = 2050 sq ft

Drawing 10-3: Base Assembly

This is a good exercise in assembly drawing procedures. You draw each of the numbered part details and then assemble them into the base assembly.

Drawing Suggestions

We no longer provide you with units, grid, snap, and limit settings. You can determine what you need by looking over the drawing and its dimensions. Remember that you can always change a setting later if necessary.

- You can create your own title block from scratch or develop one from Title Block (Drawing 7-1), if you have saved it. Once created and saved or wblocked, a title block can be inserted and scaled to fit any drawing. AutoCAD also comes with drawing templates that have borders and title blocks.

Using Table to Create a Bill of Materials

1. To create the bill of materials in this drawing, select the **Table Styles** button from the dashboard and create a new table style with no title and no header row. (Uncheck the boxes that say Include Title row and Include Header row in the **Title** and **Column Header** tabs of the **New Table Style** dialog box.)
2. Modify the new table style row height by adjusting the text style and height in the **Modify Table Style** dialog box.
3. Select the new style and insert a table with 4 columns and 7 rows.
4. Once the table is inserted you can adjust column width by first selecting the entire table, then pressing **Ctrl** as you pick a grip at the top of a column. Moving the selected grip while you hold down **Ctrl** will move the column border without altering the rest of the table.

Managing Parts Blocks for Multiple Use

You draw each of the numbered parts (B101-1, B101-2, etc.) and then assemble them. In an industrial application, the individual part details would be sent to different manufacturers or manufacturing departments, so they must exist as separate, completely dimensioned drawings as well as blocks that can be used in creating the assembly. An efficient method is to create three separate blocks for each part detail: one for dimensions and one for each view in the assembly. The dimensioned part drawings include both views. The blocks of the two views have dimensions, hidden lines, and center lines erased.

Think carefully about the way you name blocks. You might want to adopt a naming system like the following: B101-1D for the dimensioned drawing, B101-IT for a top view without dimensions, and B101-1F for a front view without dimensions. Such a system makes it easy to call out all the top view parts for the top view assembly, for example.

- Notice that the assembly requires you to do a considerable amount of trimming away of lines from the blocks you insert. This can be easily completed, but you must remember to **EXPLODE** the inserted blocks first.

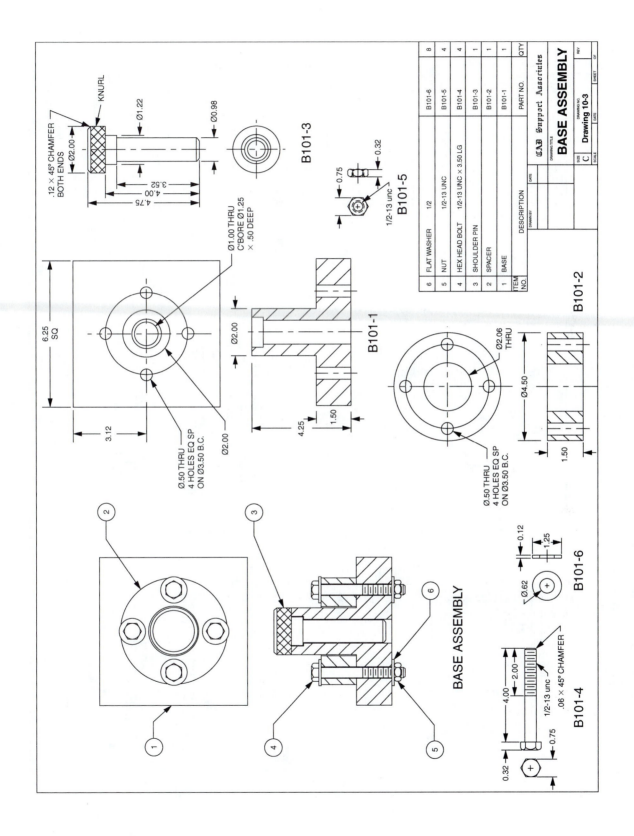

KNURL

.12 × 45° CHAMFER
BOTH ENDS

Ø2.00

Ø1.22

Ø0.98

4.75
4.00
3.52

B101-3

Ø1.00 THRU
C'BORE Ø1.25
× .50 DEEP

6.25
SQ

3.12

Ø2.00

Ø.50 THRU
4 HOLES EQ SP
ON Ø3.50 B.C.

Ø2.00

B101-1

4.25

1.50

0.75

0.32

1/2-13 unc

B101-5

ITEM NO.	DESCRIPTION		PART NO.	QTY
6	FLAT WASHER	1/2	B101-6	8
5	NUT	1/2-13 UNC	B101-5	4
4	HEX HEAD BOLT	1/2-13 UNC × 3.50 LG	B101-4	4
3	SHOULDER PIN		B101-3	1
2	SPACER		B101-2	1
1	BASE		B101-1	1

CAB Support Associates

BASE ASSEMBLY

DRAWING TITLE

DRAWING NO. Drawing 10-3

SIZE C   REV

SCALE   DATE   SHEET   OF

DRAWN BY   DATE

Ø2.06
THRU

Ø4.50

Ø.50 THRU
4 HOLES EQ SP
ON Ø3.50 B.C.

1.50

B101-2

BASE ASSEMBLY

2

1

3

4

6

5

Ø.62

0.12

1.25

B101-6

4.00

2.00

0.32

0.75

1/2-13 unc

.06 × 45° CHAMFER

B101-4

Drawings 10-4 and 10-5: Double Bearing Assembly and Scooter Assembly

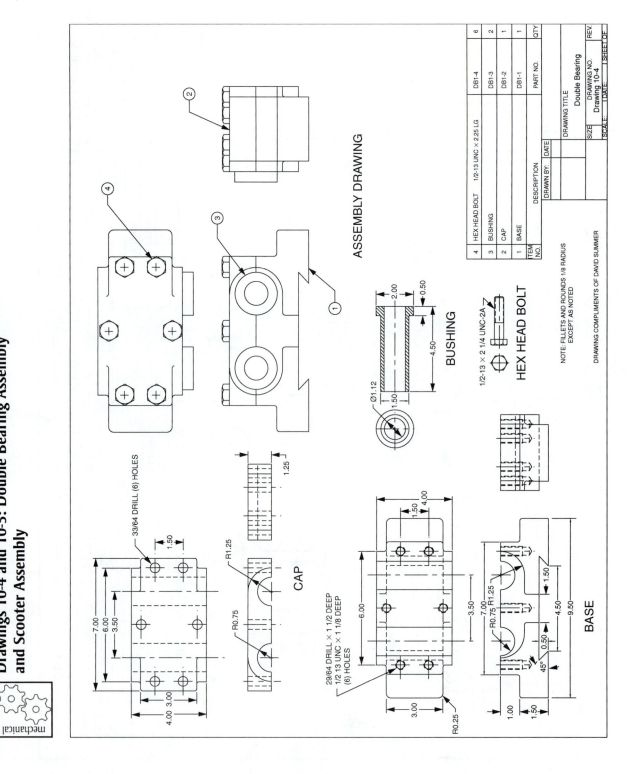

ASSEMBLY DRAWING

BUSHING

1/2-13 × 2 1/4 UNC-2A

HEX HEAD BOLT

NOTE: FILLETS AND ROUNDS 1/8 RADIUS
EXCEPT AS NOTED

DRAWING COMPLIMENTS OF DAVID SUMMER

CAP

33/64 DRILL (6) HOLES

R1.25

R0.75

29/64 DRILL × 1 1/2 DEEP
1/2 13 UNC × 1 1/8 DEEP
(6) HOLES

BASE

R0.75 R1.25

45°

ITEM NO.	PART NO.	DESCRIPTION		QTY
4	DB1-4	HEX HEAD BOLT	1/2-13 UNC × 2.25 LG	6
3	DB1-3	BUSHING		2
2	DB1-2	CAP		1
1	DB1-1	BASE		1

DRAWN BY: DATE:

DRAWING TITLE
Double Bearing

SIZE   DRAWING NO.
        Drawing 10-4   REV.

SCALE: DATE: SHEET   OF

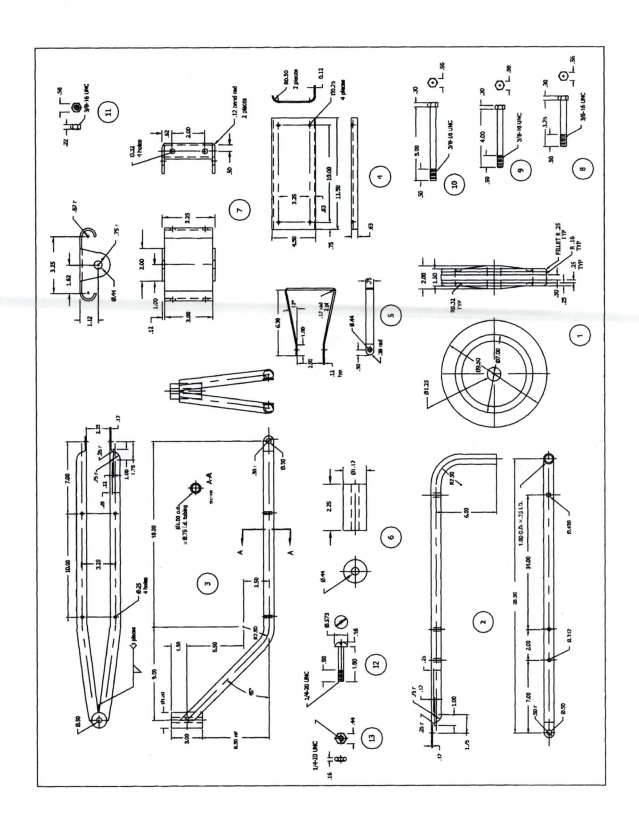

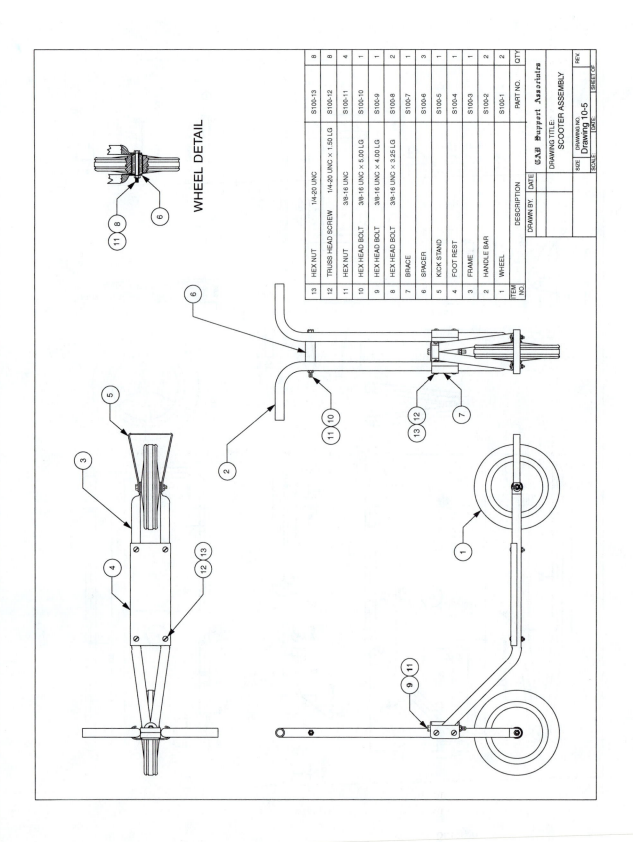

WHEEL DETAIL

ITEM NO.	DESCRIPTION		DATE	PART NO.	QTY
13	HEX NUT	1/4-20 UNC		S100-13	8
12	TRUSS HEAD SCREW	1/4-20 UNC × 1.50 LG		S100-12	8
11	HEX NUT	3/8-16 UNC		S100-11	4
10	HEX HEAD BOLT	3/8-16 UNC × 5.00 LG		S100-10	1
9	HEX HEAD BOLT	3/8-16 UNC × 4.00 LG		S100-9	1
8	HEX HEAD BOLT	3/8-16 UNC × 3.25 LG		S100-8	2
7	BRACE			S100-7	1
6	SPACER			S100-6	3
5	KICK STAND			S100-5	1
4	FOOT REST			S100-4	1
3	FRAME			S100-3	1
2	HANDLE BAR			S100-2	2
1	WHEEL			S100-1	2

DRAWN BY:	DATE

CAD Support Associates

DRAWING TITLE:
SCOOTER ASSEMBLY

DRAWING NO.
Drawing 10-5

SIZE | REV.

SCALE: | DATE: | SHEET OF:

Chapter Objectives

- Using Isometric SNAP
- Switching Isometric Planes
- Using COPY and Other Edit Commands
- Drawing Isometric Circles with ELLIPSE
- Drawing Ellipses in Orthographic Views
- Saving and Restoring Displays with VIEW

INTRODUCTION

Part III of this book takes you in a whole new direction. You begin to use the AutoCAD Drawing Window in new ways to represent isometric and 3-D spaces. Everything you know about two-dimensional drafting translates and possibilities expand as the familiar grid and snap are turned and rotated to define new coordinate systems. We begin with simple two-dimensional isometric drawing and then move on to true three-dimensional modeling.

Learning to use AutoCAD's isometric drawing features should be a pleasure at this point. There are very few new commands to learn, and anything you know about manual isometric drawing is easier on the computer. Once you know how to get into the isometric mode and change from plane to plane, you can rely on previously learned skills and techniques. Many of the commands you have learned will work readily, and you will find that using the isometric drawing planes is an excellent warm-up for 3-D wireframe drawing, which is the topic of Chapter 12.

11-1 USING ISOMETRIC SNAP

GENERAL PROCEDURE	1. Right-click on Snap or Grid on the status bar. 2. Select Settings. 3. In the **Drafting Settings** dialog box, select the **Isometric snap** radio button. 4. Click **OK**.

To begin drawing isometrically, you need to switch to the isometric snap style. You find the grid and crosshairs behaving in ways that might seem odd at first, but you quickly get used to them.

- ⊞ Begin a new drawing using the 1B template.
- ⊞ Right-click on the Snap or Grid button on the status bar.
- ⊞ Select Settings from the shortcut menu.

You see the **Drafting Settings** dialog box. Remember, you can also open this dialog by typing "ds" or selecting Drafting Settings from the **Tools** menu.

⊕ Click the Isometric snap radio button in the Snap type panel at the lower left.

⊕ Remove the check from the Adaptive check box in the Grid behavior panel at the lower right.

⊕ Click OK.

> **Note:**
> Because AutoCAD retains the isoplane setting from the most recent drawing session, it is possible that your crosshairs might be turned to the right or left isoplane instead of the top, as shown. It is not necessary to change the setting in this task.

At this point, your grid and crosshairs are reoriented so that they resemble Figure 11-1. This is the isometric grid. Grid points are placed at 30-degree, 90-degree, and 150-degree angles from the horizontal. The crosshairs are initially turned to define the top isometric plane. The three isoplanes are discussed in Section 11-2.

⊕ To get a feeling for how this snap style works, enter the LINE command and draw some boxes, as shown in Figure 11-2.

Make sure that Ortho is off and Snap is on, or you will be unable to draw the lines shown.

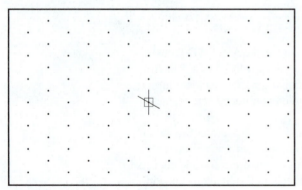

Figure 11-1

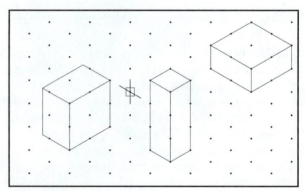

Figure 11-2

11-2 SWITCHING ISOMETRIC PLANES

GENERAL PROCEDURE	1. Press F5 once to switch to the "right" isoplane. 2. Press F5 again to switch to the "left" isoplane. 3. Press F5 again to return to the "top" isoplane.

If you tried to draw the boxes in Section 11-1 with Ortho on, you discovered that it is impossible. Without changing the orientation of the crosshairs, you can draw in only two of the three isometric planes. We need to be able to switch planes so that we can leave Ortho on for accuracy and speed. There are several ways to do this, but the simplest, quickest, and most convenient way is to use the F5 key.

Before beginning, take a look at Figure 11-3. It shows the three planes of a standard isometric drawing. These planes are often referred to as top, front, and right. However, AutoCAD's terminology is top, left, and right. We stick with AutoCAD's labels in this book.

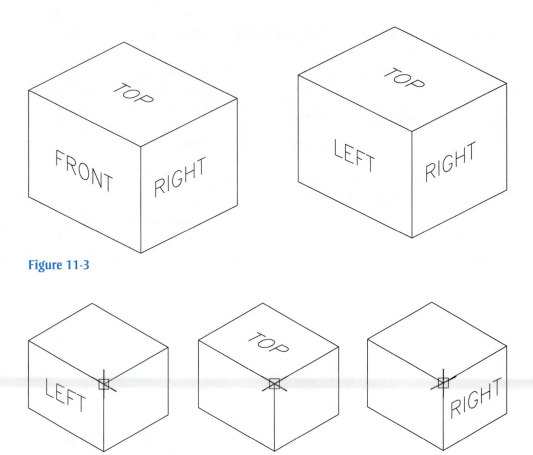

Figure 11-3

Figure 11-4

Now look at Figure 11-4 and you can see how the isometric crosshairs are oriented to draw in each of the planes.

⊞ Press F5 to switch from top to right.

⊞ Press F5 again to switch from right to left.

⊞ Press F5 once more to switch back to top.

⊞ Now turn Ortho on and draw a box outline like the one in Figure 11-5.

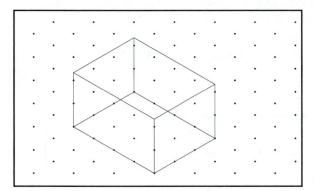

Figure 11-5

You need to switch planes several times to accomplish this. Notice that you can switch planes using F5 without interrupting the **LINE** command. If you find that you are in the wrong plane to construct a line, switch planes. Because every plane allows movement in two of the three directions, you can always move in the direction you want with one switch. However, you might not be able to hit the snap point you want. If you cannot, switch planes again.

11-3 USING COPY AND OTHER EDIT COMMANDS

Most commands work in the isometric planes just as they do in standard orthographic views. In this exercise, we construct an isometric view of a bracket using the **LINE, COPY,** and **ERASE** commands. Then we draw angled corners using **CHAMFER.** In the next task, we draw a hole in the bracket with **ELLIPSE, COPY,** and **TRIM.**

⊕ Clear your screen of boxes and check to see that Ortho is on.

⊕ Switch to the left isoplane.

⊕ Draw the L-shaped object shown in Figure 11-6.

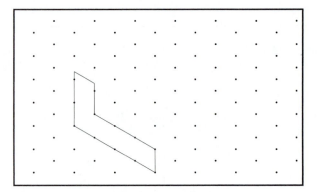

Figure 11-6

Notice that this is drawn in the left isoplane and that it is 1.00 unit wide.

Next, we copy this object 4.00 units back to the right to create the back surface of the bracket.

⊕ Select the Copy tool from the dashboard.

⊕ Use a window or crossing box to select all the lines in the L.

⊕ Right-click to end object selection.

⊕ Pick a base point at the inside corner of the L.

It is a good exercise to keep Ortho on, switch planes, and move the object around in each plane. You can move in two directions in each isoplane. To move the object back to the right, as shown in Figure 11-7, you must be in either the top or the right isoplane.

⊕ Switch to the top or right isoplane and pick a second point of displacement four units back to the right, as shown in Figure 11-7.

⊕ Press Enter to exit COPY.

⊕ Enter the LINE command and draw the connecting lines in the right plane, as shown in Figure 11-8.

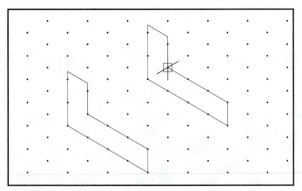

Figure 11-7

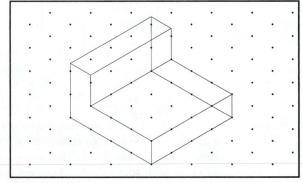

Figure 11-8

Creating Chamfers in an Isometric View

Keep in mind that angular lines in an isometric view do not show true lengths. Angular lines must be drawn between endpoints located along paths that are vertical or horizontal in one of the three drawing planes. In our exercise, we create angled lines by using the **CHAMFER** command to cut the corners of the bracket. This is no different from using **CHAMFER** in orthographic views.

⊕ Select the Chamfer tool from the dashboard.

⊕ Right-click and select Distance from the shortcut menu.

    AutoCAD prompts for a first chamfer distance.

⊕ Type "1" ↵.

⊕ Press Enter to accept 1.00 as the second chamfer distance.

⊕ Pick two edges of the bracket to create a chamfer, as shown in Figure 11-9.

⊕ Repeat CHAMFER.

⊕ Chamfer the other three corners so that your drawing resembles Figure 11-9.

⊕ Erase the two small lines left hanging at the previous corners.

⊕ To complete the bracket, enter the LINE command and draw lines between the new chamfer endpoints.

⊕ Finally, erase the two unseen lines on the back surface to produce Figure 11-10.

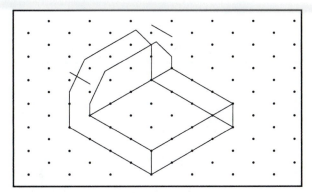

Figure 11-9

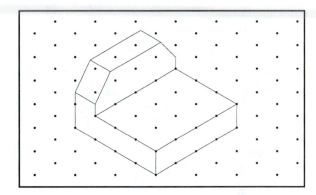

Figure 11-10

11-4 DRAWING ISOMETRIC CIRCLES WITH ELLIPSE

GENERAL PROCEDURE

1. Locate the **Center Point** for the isometric circle.
2. Select the **Ellipse** tool from the dashboard.
3. Select Isocircle from the shortcut menu.
4. Pick the center point.
5. Specify the radius or diameter.

The **ELLIPSE** command can be used to draw true ellipses in orthographic views or ellipses that appear to be circles in isometric views (called *isocircles* in AutoCAD). In this task, we use the latter capability to construct a hole in the bracket.

⊕ To begin this task you should have the bracket shown in Figure 11-10 on your screen.

    In order to draw an isocircle you need a center point. Often, it is necessary to locate this point carefully using temporary lines, object snap tracking, or point

COMMAND GRID	
Command	Ellipse
Alias	El
Menu	Draw
Tool	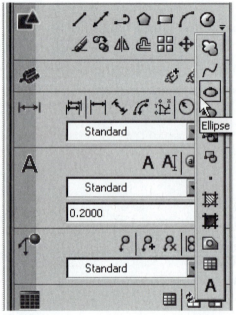

filters (see Chapter 12). You must be sure that you can locate the center point before entering the **ELLIPSE** command.

In our case, it is easy because the center point is on a snap point.

⊕ Select the Ellipse tool from the dashboard, as shown in Figure 11-11.

AutoCAD prompts

Specify axis endpoint of ellipse or [Arc/Center/Isocircle]:

The option we want is Isocircle. Ignore the others for the time being.

⊕ Type "i" ⏎, or right-click and select Isocircle from the shortcut menu.

AutoCAD prompts

Specify center of isocircle:

If you could not locate the center point, you would have to exit the command now and start over.

⊕ Use the snap and grid to pick the center of the surface, as shown in Figure 11-12.

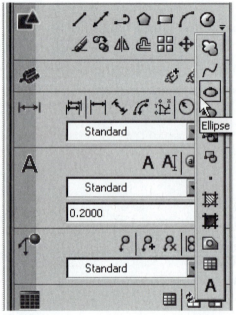

Figure 11-11

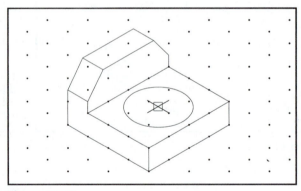

Figure 11-12

AutoCAD gives you an isocircle to drag, as in the **CIRCLE** command. The isocircle you see depends on the isoplane you are in. To understand this, try switching planes to see how the image changes.

⊕ Stretch the isocircle image out and then press F5 to switch isoplanes. Observe the isocircle. Try this two or three times.

⊕ Switch to the top isoplane before moving on.

AutoCAD is prompting for a radius or diameter:

Specify radius of isocircle or [Diameter]:

A radius specification is the default here, as it is in the **CIRCLE** command.

⊕ Pick a point so that your isocircle resembles the one in Figure 11-12.

Next, we use the **COPY** and **TRIM** commands to create the bottom of the hole.

⊕ Enter the Copy Command.

⊕ Select the isocircle.

⊕ Right-click to end object selection.

⊕ Pick a base point.

Any point could be used as the base point. A good choice would be the top front corner of the bracket. If you do this, then choosing the bottom front corner as a second point gives you the exact thickness of the bracket.

⊕ Pick a second point 1.00 unit below the base point. Make sure that you are in an isoplane that allows movement from top to bottom.

Your screen should now resemble Figure 11-13. The last thing we must do is trim the hidden portion of the bottom of the hole.

⊕ Press Enter to exit COPY.

⊕ Enter the TRIM command.

⊕ Pick the first isocircle as a cutting edge.

It may help to turn off snap to make these selections.

⊕ Right-click to end cutting edge selection.

⊕ Select the hidden section of the lower isocircle.

⊕ Press Enter to exit TRIM.

The bracket is now complete and your screen should resemble Figure 11-14.

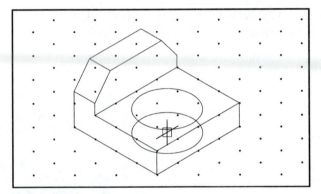

Figure 11-13

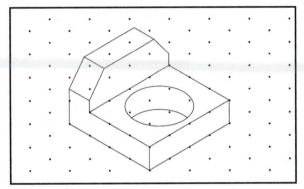

Figure 11-14

This completes the present discussion of isometric drawing. You can find more in the drawing suggestions at the end of this chapter.

Now we go on to explore the nonisometric use of the **ELLIPSE** command and then introduce the **VIEW** command for saving named views in a drawing.

11-5 DRAWING ELLIPSES IN ORTHOGRAPHIC VIEWS

GENERAL PROCEDURE	1. Select the **Ellipse** tool from the dashboard. 2. Pick one endpoint of an axis. 3. Pick the second endpoint. 4. Pick a third point showing the length of the other axis.

The **ELLIPSE** command is important not only for drawing isocircles but also for drawing true ellipses in orthographic views. There is also an option to create elliptical arcs.

An ellipse is determined by a center point and two perpendicular axes of differing lengths. In AutoCAD, these specifications can be shown in two nearly identical ways, each requiring you to show three points (see Figure 11-15). In the default method, you show two endpoints of an axis and then show half the length of the other axis, from the midpoint of the first axis out. (The midpoint

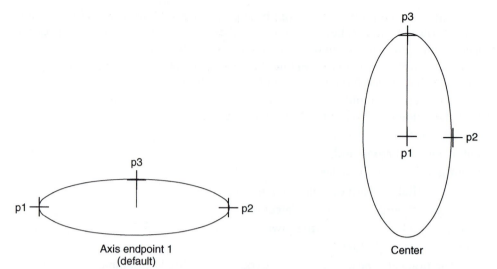

Figure 11-15

Axis endpoint 1
(default)

Center

of an axis is also the center of the ellipse.) The other method allows you to pick the center point of the ellipse first, then the endpoint of one axis, followed by half the length of the other axis.

⊕ In preparation for this exercise, return to the standard snap mode using the following procedure:

1. Right-click on Snap or Grid and open the **Drafting Settings** dialog box from the shortcut menu.
2. Click the **Rectangular snap** radio button.
3. Click **OK.**

> **Note:**
> If your grid does not return to its original shape it may be because isometric snap values have been retained in the Snap X and Grid X spacing boxes. To fix this, reenter the **Drafting Settings** dialog box and manually return Snap X spacing to 0.25 and Grid X spacing to 0.50.

Your grid is returned to the standard pattern and the crosshairs are horizontal and vertical again. Notice that this does not affect the isometric bracket you have just drawn.

We briefly explore the **ELLIPSE** command and draw some standard ellipses.

⊕ Select the Ellipse tool from the dashboard.

AutoCAD prompts

        Specify axis endpoint of ellipse or [Arc/Center]:

⊕ Pick an axis endpoint, as shown by p1 on the ellipse at the lower left in Figure 11-16.

AutoCAD prompts for the other endpoint:

                Specify other endpoint of axis:

⊕ Pick a second endpoint, as shown by p2.

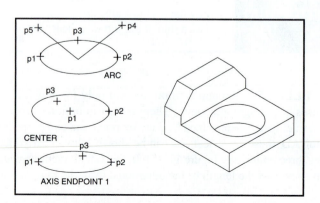

Figure 11-16

AutoCAD gives you an ellipse to drag and a rubber band so that you can show the length of the other axis. Only the length of the rubber band is significant; the angle is already determined to be perpendicular to the first axis. Because of this, the third point only falls on the ellipse if the rubber band happens to be exactly perpendicular to the first axis.

The prompt that follows allows you to show the second axis distance as before, or a rotation around the first axis:

> Specify distance to other axis or [Rotation]:

The rotation option is awkward to use, and we do not explore it here; see the AutoCAD Command Reference for more information.

⊕ Pick p3 as shown.

This point shows half the length of the other axis.

The first ellipse should now be complete. Now we draw one showing the center point first.

⊕ Repeat the ELLIPSE command.

⊕ At the first prompt, type "c" ↵ or right-click and select Center from the shortcut menu.

AutoCAD gives you a prompt for a center point:

> Specify center of ellipse:

⊕ Pick a center point, as shown by p1 at the middle left of Figure 11-16.

Now you have a rubber band stretching from the center to the end of an axis and the following prompt:

> Specify endpoint of axis:

⊕ Pick an endpoint, as shown by p2 in Figure 11-16.

The prompt that follows allows you to show the second axis distance as before, or a rotation around the first axis:

> Specify distance to other axis or [Rotation]:

⊕ Pick an axis distance, as shown by p3.

Here again the rubber band is significant for distance only. The point you pick falls on the ellipse only if the rubber band is stretched perpendicular to the first axis. Notice that it is not so in Figure 11-16.

Drawing Elliptical Arcs

Elliptical arcs can be drawn by trimming complete ellipses or by using the Arc option of the **ELLIPSE** command. Using the Arc option, you first construct an ellipse in one of the two methods shown previously and then show the arc of that ellipse that you want to keep.

⊕ Enter the ELLIPSE command.

⊕ Type "a" ↵ or right-click and select Arc from the shortcut menu.

If you select the **Ellipse Arc** tool from the **Draw** toolbar, this option is entered automatically.

⊕ Pick a first axis endpoint, as shown by p1 at the upper left in Figure 11-16.

⊕ Pick a second endpoint, p2 in the figure.

⊕ Pick p3 to show the second axis distance.

AutoCAD draws an ellipse as you have specified, but the image is only temporary. Now you need to show the arc you want drawn. The two options are Parameter and Start angle. Parameter takes you into more options that allow you to specify your arc in different ways, similar to the options of the **ARC** command. We stick with the default option.

⊕ Pick p4 to show the angle at which the elliptical arc begins.

Move the cursor slowly now and you can see all the arcs that are possible starting from this angle.

⊕ Pick p5 to indicate the end angle and complete the command.

11-6 SAVING AND RESTORING DISPLAYS WITH VIEW

GENERAL PROCEDURE

1. Select Named Views from the **View** menu.
2. Select New to create a new view.
3. Type a view name.
4. Click Define Window.
5. Select points.
6. Click **OK.**
7. Click **OK.**

The word *view* in connection with the **VIEW** command has a special significance in AutoCAD. It refers to any set of display boundaries that have been named and saved using the **VIEW** command. It also refers to a defined 3D viewpoint that has been saved with a name. Views that have been saved can be restored rapidly and by direct reference rather than by redefining the location, size, or viewpoint of the area to be displayed. **VIEW** can be useful in creating drawing layouts and any time you know that you will be returning frequently to a certain area of a large drawing. It saves you from having to zoom out to look at the complete drawing and then zoom back in again on the area you want. It can also save the time required in creating a 3D viewpoint. In this chapter, we use 2D views only. In the next chapter, we introduce 3D viewpoints.

Imagine that we have to complete some detail work on the area around the hole in the bracket and also on the top corner. We can define each of these as a view and jump back and forth at will.

⊕ To begin this exercise, you should have the bracket on your screen, as shown in Figure 11-17.

⊕ Select Named Views from the View menu, as shown in Figure 11-18.

This opens the **View Manager** dialog box shown in Figure 11-19. At the left is a list of views, including Current, Model, Layout, and Preset Views. In this

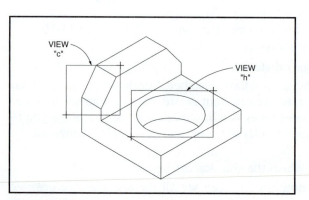

Figure 11-17

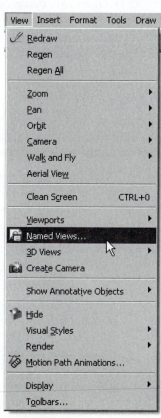

Figure 11-18

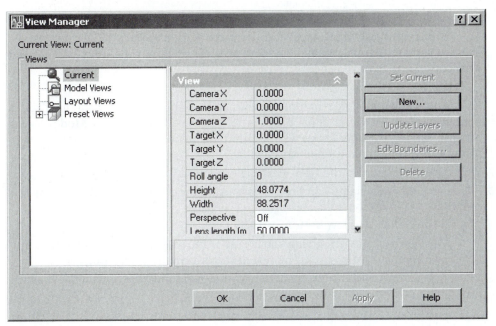

Figure 11-19

chapter we have use for only the Current view, which we will define and label
with a name.

⊞ Click the New button.

This takes you to the **New View** dialog box shown in Figure 11-20. Notice that
the **Current display** button is selected. All we have to do is give the current display
a name to save it as a named view.

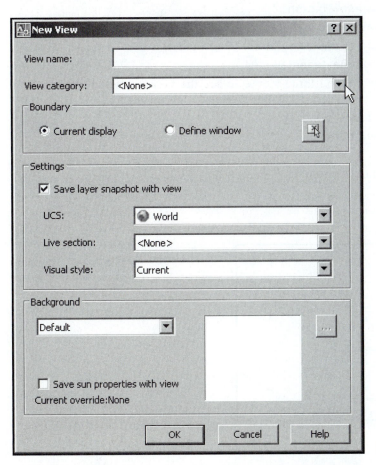

Figure 11-20

⊞ Type A in the View name edit box.

Views are designed for speed, so it makes sense to assign them short names, unless you are defining many views and need them clearly identified with longer names.

⊞ Click OK.

The **View** dialog box reappears, with A now showing under the heading of Model Views. All views defined in model space will be listed as Model Views. Views defined in paper space will be listed as Layout Views. Next we use a window to define a smaller model space view.

⊞ Click New to return to the New View dialog box.

⊞ Type H in the View name edit box. We are using the name H for hole because this view zooms in on the hole.

⊞ Select the Define window button.

The dialog box closes, giving you access to the screen. The current view is outlined within the drawing area. The rest of the drawing is grayed out.

⊞ Pick first and second corners to define a window around the hole in the bracket, as shown previously in Figure 11-17.

A window outline of the new view is shown, with the rest of the drawing grayed out.

⊞ Press Enter to return to the New View dialog box.

⊞ Click OK to complete the definition.

You are now back in the **View** dialog box with A and H on the list of Model Views. Define one more view to show the upper left corner of the bracket, as shown in Figure 11-17.

⊞ Click the New button.

⊞ Type "C" for the view name.

⊞ Select the Define window button.

⊞ Define a window, as shown in Figure 11-17.

⊞ Press Enter to return to the dialog box.

⊞ Click OK to complete the definition.

You have now defined three views. To see the views in action we must set them as current.

⊞ Highlight H in the Model Views list.

⊞ Click the Set Current button.

⊞ Click OK.

Your screen should resemble Figure 11-21.

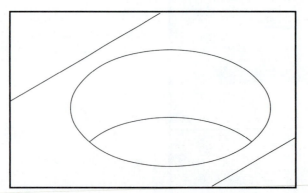

Figure 11-21

Now switch to the corner view.

⊞ Repeat the VIEW command.
⊞ Highlight C.
⊞ Click Set Current.
⊞ Click OK.

Your screen should resemble Figure 11-22.

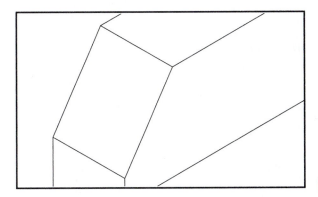

Figure 11-22

CHAPTER TEST QUESTIONS

Questions

1. What are the angles of the crosshairs and grid points in an isometric grid?
2. What function key is used to switch from one isometric plane to another?
3. What are the names for the isometric planes in AutoCAD?
4. What is an isocircle? Why are isocircles drawn in the **ELLIPSE** command?
5. How many different isocircles can you draw that have the same radius and the same center point?
6. How many points does it take to define an ellipse?
7. What do these points define in each of the two basic methods of drawing an orthographic ellipse?
8. What must you do before you can use the **VIEW** command to restore a view?
9. What are the two basic ways to define a view?
10. How do you enter the **VIEW** command? What is the name of the dialog box it calls?

Drawing Problems

1. Using the isometric grid, draw a 4-by-4 square in the right isoplane.
2. Copy the square back four units along the left isoplane.
3. Connect the corners of the two squares to form an isometric cube. Erase any lines that would be hidden in this object.
4. Use text rotation and obliquing to draw the word Top in the top plane of the cube so that the text is centered on the face and aligned with its edges. The text should be 0.5 unit high.
5. In a similar manner, draw the word Left at the center of the left side and the word Right at the center of the right side. All text should align with the face that it is on.

WWW Exercise 11 (Optional)

You are now ready for Chapter 11 of the companion website. Complete the following steps:

⊞ Make sure that you are connected to your Internet service provider.
⊞ Type "browser" or open your system browser from the Windows taskbar.
⊞ If necessary, navigate to our companion website at prenhall.com/dixriley.

Good luck on the test!

CHAPTER PROJECTS

Drawing 11-1: Mounting Bracket

This drawing is a direct extension of the exercises in the chapter. It gives you practice in basic AutoCAD isometrics and in transferring dimensions from orthographic to isometric views.

Drawing Suggestions

- When the center point of an isocircle is not on snap, as in this drawing, you need to create a specifiable point and snap onto it or use object snap and object snap tracking. For example, acquire the midpoints of the sides and then snap to the intersection of the two tracking lines.

- Often, when you try to select a group of objects to copy, there are many crossing lines that you do not want to include in the copy. This is an ideal time to use the Remove option in object selection. First, window the objects you want along with those nearby that are unavoidable, and then remove the unwanted objects one by one.

- Sometimes, you might get unexpected results when you try to **TRIM** an object in an isometric view. AutoCAD divides an ellipse into a series of arcs, for example, and only trim a portion. If you do not get the results you want, use the **BREAK** command to control how the object is broken, and then erase what you do not want.

- There is no Arc option when you use **ELLIPSE** to draw isocircles, so semicircles like those at the top and bottom of the slots must be constructed by first drawing isocircles and then trimming or erasing unwanted portions.

- Use **COPY** frequently to avoid duplicating your work. Because it might take a considerable amount of editing to create holes and fillets, do not **COPY** until edits have been completed on the original.

- The row of small arcs that show the curve in the middle of the bracket are multiple copies of the fillet at the corner.

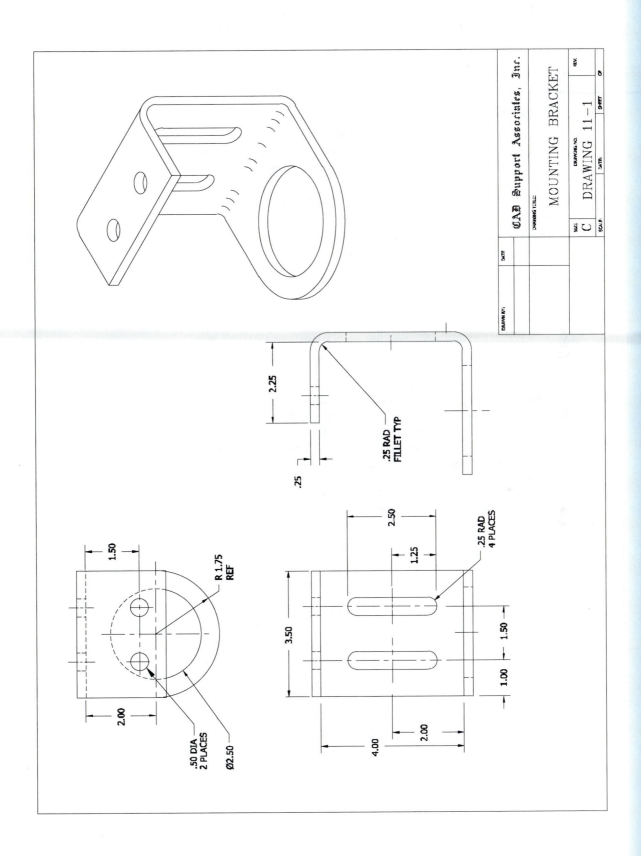

CAD Support Associates, Inc.

DRAWING TITLE: MOUNTING BRACKET

DRAWING NO. DRAWING 11-1

SIZE: C

.25 RAD
FILLET TYP

2.25

.25

R 1.75
REF

1.50

2.00

.50 DIA
2 PLACES

Ø2.50

2.50

1.25

.25 RAD
4 PLACES

3.50

1.50

1.00

4.00

2.00

Drawing 11-2: MP3 Player

This drawing introduces text and combines a complete set of 2D views with an isometric representation of the object. Placing objects on different layers so they can be turned on and off during **TRIM, BREAK,** and **ERASE** procedures makes things considerably less messy.

Drawing Suggestions

- Use the box method to create the isometric view in this drawing. That is, begin with an isometric box according to the overall outside dimensions of the MP3 player. Then trim and add the details.
- The dial is made from isocircles with copies to show thickness. You can use tangent-to-tangent object snaps to draw the front-to-back connecting lines.
- Use a gradient hatch for the video window area.
- The text is created on two different angles that line up with the left and right isoplanes.

Aligning Text to Isometric Planes

Adding text to isometric drawings has some challenges you have not encountered previously. To create the appearance that text aligns with an isometric plane, it needs to be altered in two ways. First, the whole line of text needs to be rotated to align with one side of the plane. Second, the obliquing angle of individual characters needs to be adjusted to match the tilt of the plane. Rotation angle, you recall, is handled through the command sequence of the **TEXT** command. Obliquing angle is set as a text style characteristic using the **STYLE** command (from the **Format** menu, select Text Style). In this drawing, you need the following combinations: for text in the right isoplane, specify +30 for both the rotation angle and the obliquing angle; for text in the left isoplane, specify −30 for both angles.

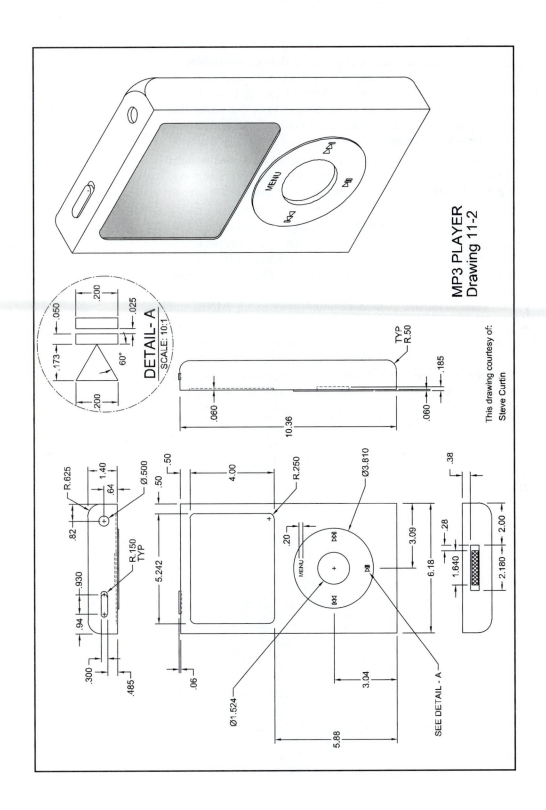

MP3 PLAYER
Drawing 11-2

This drawing courtesy of:
Steve Curtin

DETAIL - A
SCALE: 10:1

Drawing 11-3: Fixture Assembly

This is a difficult drawing. It takes time and patience, but teaches you a great deal about isometric drawing in AutoCAD.

Drawing Suggestions

- This drawing can be completed either by drawing everything in place as you see it or by drawing the parts and moving them into place along the common center line that runs through the middle of all the items. If you use the former method, draw the center line first and use it to locate the center points of isocircles and as base points for other measures.

- As you go, look for pieces of objects that can be copied to form other objects. Avoid duplicating efforts by editing before copying. In particular, where one object covers part of another, be sure to copy it before you trim or erase the covered sections.

- To create the chamfered end of Item 4, begin by drawing the 1.00 diameter cylinder 3.00 long with no chamfer. Then copy the isocircle at the end forward 0.125. The smaller isocircle is 0.875 (7/8), because 0.0625 (1/16) is cut away from the 1.00 circle all around. Draw this smaller isocircle and trim away everything that is hidden. Then draw the slanted chamfer lines using **LINE**, not **CHAMFER.** Use the same method for Item 5.

- In both the screw and the nut, you need to create hexes around isocircles. Use the dimensions from a standard bolt chart.

- Use three-point arcs to approximate the curves on the screw bolt and the nut. Your goal is a representation that looks correct. It is impractical and unnecessary to achieve exact measures on these objects in the isometric view.

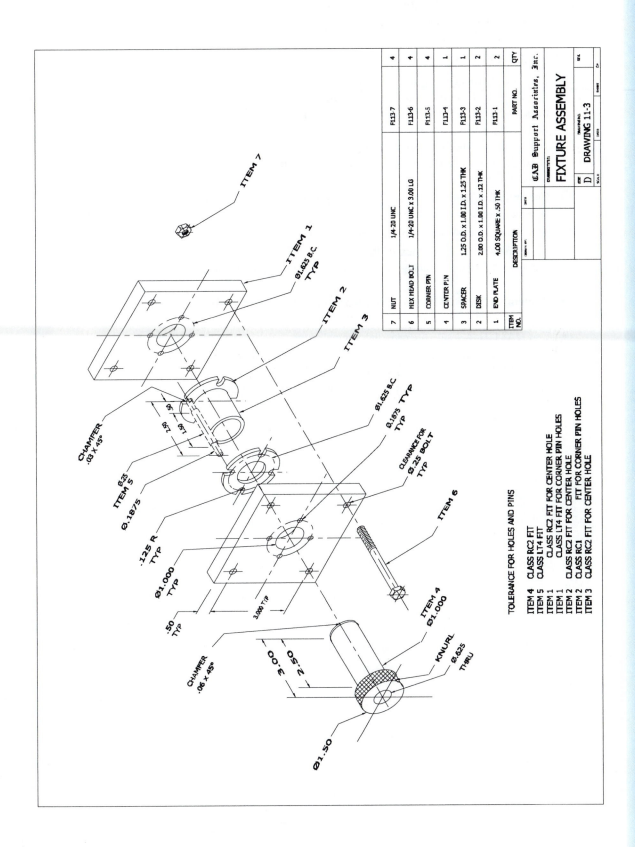

ITEM NO.	DESCRIPTION	PART NO.	QTY
7	NUT	1/4-20 UNC	F113-7	4
6	HEX HEAD BOLT	1/4-20 UNC x 3.00 LG	F113-6	4
5	CORNER PIN		F113-5	4
4	CENTER P/N		F113-4	1
3	SPACER	1.25 O.D. x 1.00 I.D. x 1.25 THK	F113-3	1
2	DISK	2.00 O.D. x 1.00 I.D. x .12 THK	F113-2	2
1	END PLATE	4.00 SQUARE x .50 THK	F113-1	2

CAD Support Associates, Inc.

FIXTURE ASSEMBLY

D DRAWING 11-3

TOLERANCE FOR HOLES AND PINS

ITEM 4   CLASS RC2 FIT
ITEM 5   CLASS LT4 FIT
ITEM 1   CLASS RC2 FIT FOR CENTER HOLE
ITEM 1   CLASS LT4 FIT FOR CORNER PIN HOLES
ITEM 2   CLASS RC2 FIT FOR CENTER HOLE
ITEM 2   CLASS RC1   FIT FOR CORNER PIN HOLES
ITEM 3   CLASS RC2 FIT FOR CENTER HOLE

Drawing 11-4: Flanged Coupling

The isometric view in this three-view drawing must be completed working off the center line.

Drawing Suggestions

- Draw the major center line first. Then draw vertical center lines at every point where an isocircle is to be drawn. Make sure to draw these lines extra long so that they can be used to trim the isocircles in half. By starting at the back of the object and working forward, you can take dimensions directly from the right side view.

- Draw the isocircles at each center line and then trim them to represent semicircles.

- Use endpoint, intersection, and tangent-to-tangent osnaps to draw horizontal lines.

- Trim away all obstructed lines and parts of isocircles.

- Draw the four slanted lines in the middle as vertical lines first. Then, with Ortho off, change their endpoints, moving them 0.125 closer.

- Remember, **MIRROR** does not work in the isometric view, although it can be used effectively in the right side view.

- Use **HATCH** to create the crosshatching.

- If you have made a mistake in measuring along the major center line, **STRETCH** can be used to correct it. Make sure that Ortho is on and that you are in an isoplane that lets you move the way you want.

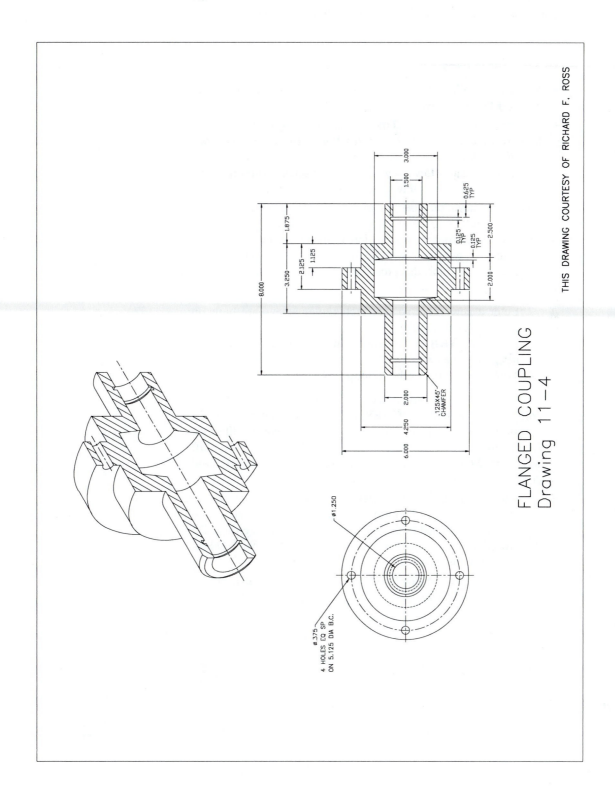

FLANGED COUPLING
Drawing 11-4

THIS DRAWING COURTESY OF RICHARD F. ROSS

429

Drawing 11-5: Garage Framing

This is a fairly complex drawing that takes lots of trimming and careful work. Changing the snapang (snap angle) variable so that you can draw slanted arrays is a method that can be used frequently in isometric drawing.

Drawing Suggestions

- You will find yourself using **COPY, ZOOM,** and **TRIM** a great deal. **OFFSET** also works well.

- You might want to create some new layers with different colors. Keeping different parts of the construction walls, rafters, and joists on different layers allows you to have more control over them and adds a lot of clarity to what you see on the screen. Turning layers on and off can considerably simplify trimming operations.

- You can cut down on repetition in this drawing by using arrays on various angles. For example, if the snapang variable is set to 150 degrees, the 22-foot wall in the left isoplane can be created as a rectangular array of studs with 1 row and 17 columns set 16 inches apart. To do so, follow this procedure:

  1. Type "snapang."
  2. Enter a new value so that rectangular arrays are built on isometric angles (30 or 150).
  3. Enter the **ARRAY** command and create the array. Use negative values where necessary.
  4. Trim the opening for the window.

- One alternative to this array method is to set your snap to 16″ temporarily and use multiple **COPY** to create the columns of studs, rafters, and joists. Another alternative is to use the grip edit offset snap method beginning with an offset snap of 16″ (i.e., press Shift when you show the first copy displacement and continue to hold down Shift as you make other copies).

- The cutaway in the roof that shows the joists and the back door is drawn using the standard nonisometric **ELLIPSE** command. Then the rafters are trimmed to the ellipse and the ellipse is erased. Do this procedure before you draw the joists and the back wall. Otherwise, you trim these as well.

- Use **CHAMFER** to create the chamfered corners on the joists.

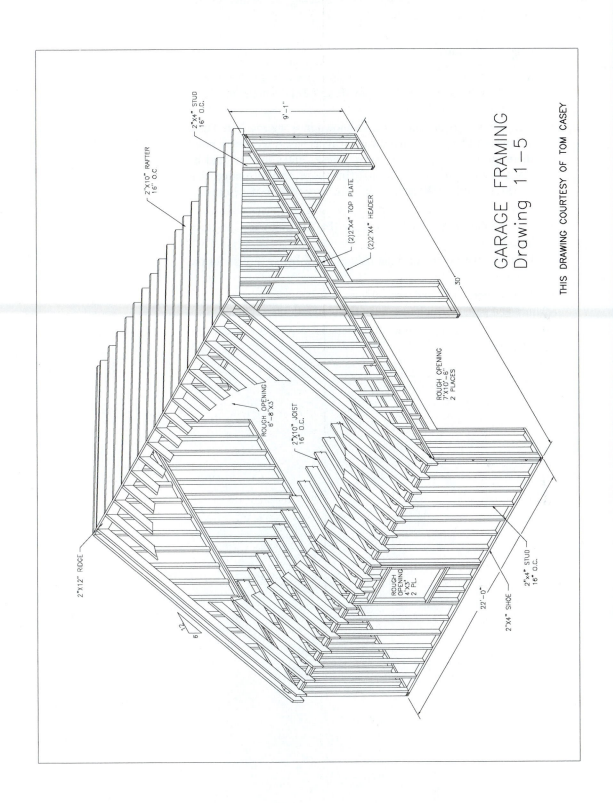

2"X4" STUD 16" O.C.

2"X10" RAFTER 16" O.C.

9'-1"

(2)2"X4" TOP PLATE

(2)2"X4" HEADER

30

GARAGE FRAMING
Drawing 11-5

THIS DRAWING COURTESY OF TOM CASEY

ROUGH OPENING
7'X10'-6"
2 PLACES

ROUGH OPENING
6'-8"X3'

2"X10" JOIST 16" O.C.

2"X12" RIDGE

ROUGH
OPENING
4'X3'
2 PL.

2"X4" STUD 16" O.C.

22'-0"

2"X4" SHOE

12

6

431

Drawing 11-6: Cast Iron Tee

The objective of this exercise is to complete the isometric view of the tee using dimensions from the three-view drawing. Begin this isometric by working off the center line.

Drawing Suggestions

- Be sure that Ortho is on and that you are in an isoplane that is correct for the lines you want to draw. Take full advantage of object snap as you lay out this drawing.
- Draw the two major center lines as shown in isometric first. Draw them to exact length. Then draw vertical center lines at every point where an isocircle is to be drawn. These center lines should be drawn longer so the isocircles trim more easily. Notice that **OFFSET** and **MIRROR** do not work very well in the isometric mode.
- After establishing the centers, draw the isocircles for the three flanges.
- When you have completed the flanges, draw the isocircles for the wall of the tee.
- Draw all horizontal and vertical lines and trim away all nonvisible lines and parts of isocircles. Fillet the required intersections.
- After completing the outline of the tee, use **HATCH** to create the crosshatching.

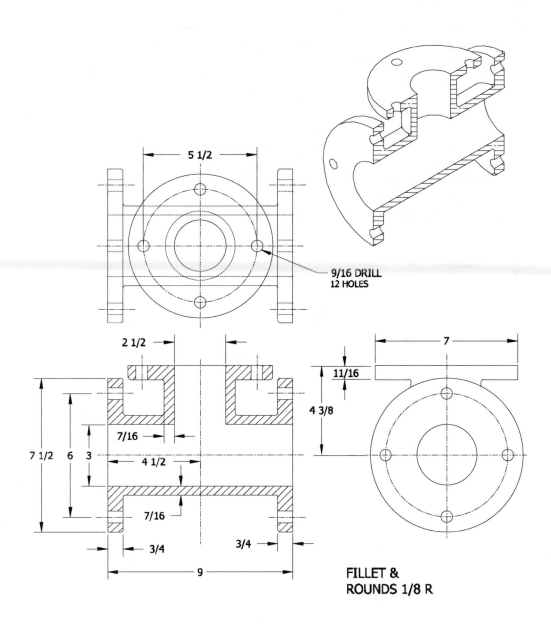

5 1/2

9/16 DRILL
12 HOLES

2 1/2

7/16

7 1/2   6   3

4 1/2

7/16

3/4   3/4

9

11/16

4 3/8

7

FILLET &
ROUNDS 1/8 R

3" CAST IRON TEE
Drawing 11-6

Drawing 11-7: Valve

For the purposes of this chapter, the isometric view is most important. The three detail views, the title block, and the border can be included or not, as assigned.

Drawing Suggestions

- Use the box method to create the isometric view in this drawing. Begin with an isometric box according to the overall outside dimensions of the valve. Then go back and cut away the excess so the drawing becomes half the valve, exposing the interior details of the object.

- As in all section drawings, no hidden lines are shown.

- In addition to flat surfaces indicated by hatching, the interior is made up of isocircles of different sizes on different planes.

- Keep all construction lines and center lines until drawing is complete (draw them on a separate layer and you can turn off that layer when you don't need them).

- The tapped holes are drawn with a series of isocircles that can be arrayed. This is only a representation of a screw thread, so it is not drawn to precise dimensions. Draw one thread and copy it to the other side.

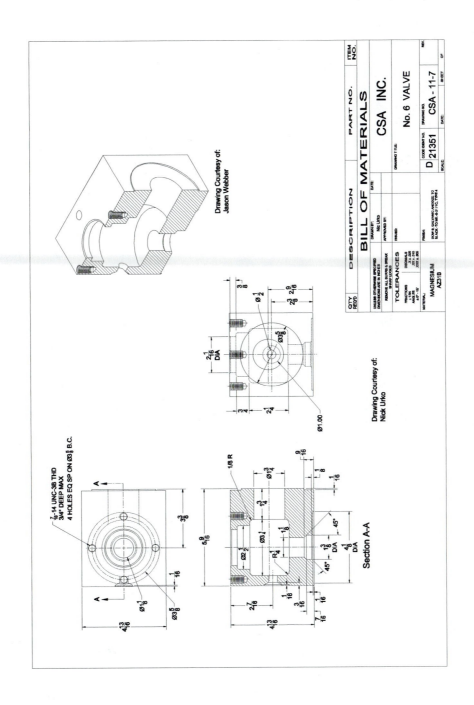

Drawing Courtesy of:
Jason Webber

Drawing Courtesy of:
Nick Urko

Section A-A

7/8-14 UNC-3B THD
3/4" DEEP MAX.
4 HOLES EQ SP ON Ø3 5/8 B.C.

1/8 R

Wireframe Models

Chapter **Objectives**

- Creating and Viewing a 3D Wireframe Box
- Defining and Saving User Coordinate Systems
- Using Draw and Edit Commands in a UCS
- Working on an Angled Surface
- Using RULESURF to Create 3D Fillets
- Adjusting Viewpoint with Constrained Orbit

INTRODUCTION

It is now time to begin thinking in three dimensions. In this chapter you will bridge the gap between 2-D and 3-D by creating wireframe models. Like isometric drawing, wireframe modeling will use all the techniques you have learned in 2-D drawing, but will extend them into a true 3-D modeling space. You will learn how AutoCAD allows you to work in three dimensions on a two-dimensional screen. Sections 12.1 through 12.5 take you through a complete 3-D wireframe modeling exercise using four different coordinate systems that we define. You learn how to define user coordinate systems to align with any specifiable plane. Your drawing will have 3-D characteristics allowing you to view it, edit it, and plot it from any point in space.

12-1 CREATING AND VIEWING A 3D WIREFRAME BOX

When you begin to create 3D models you have the option of working in the 3D modeling workspace. This workspace is designed primarily for solid modeling, and we will save it for the next chapter. We will be drawing a wireframe model line by line, similar to the way we have drawn 2D models. So, we continue to use the 2D Drafting & Annotation workspace and our 1B template as we work our way into 3D space. First, we create a simple 3D box that we can edit in later tasks to form a more complex object. If your UCS icon is not visible (see Figure 12-1), follow this procedure to turn it on:

1. Select View → Display → UCS Icon as shown in Figure 12-2.
2. Select On and Origin from the submenu, as shown.

For now, simply observe the icon as you go through the process of creating the box, and be aware that you are currently working in the same coordinate system that you have always used in AutoCAD. It is called the world coordinate system (WCS), to distinguish it from others you create yourself beginning in Section 12-2.

Currently, the origin of the WCS is at the lower left of your grid. This is the point (0,0,0) when you are thinking 3D, or simply (0,0) when you are in 2D. The *x*-coordinates increase to the right horizontally across the screen, and the *y*-coordinates increase vertically up the screen as usual. The

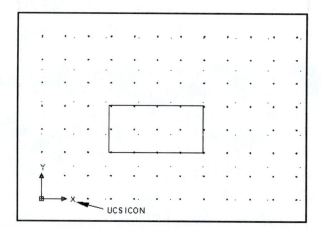

Figure 12-1

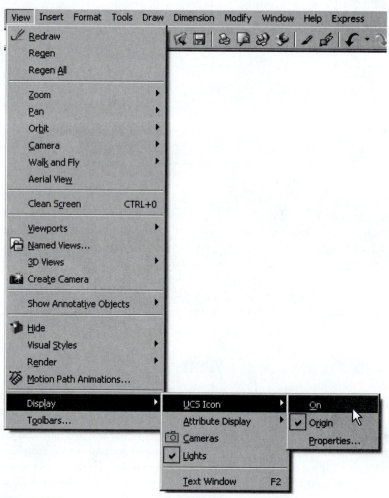

Figure 12-2

z-axis, which we have ignored until now, currently extends out of the screen toward you and perpendicular to the *x*- and *y*-axes and the plane of the screen. This orientation of the three planes is called a plan view. Soon we will switch to a front, right, top, or southeast isometric view.

Let's begin.

⊕ Create a new drawing using the 1B template.

⊕ Draw a 2.00 by 4.00 rectangle near the middle of your screen, as shown in Figure 12-1. Do not use the RECTANG command to draw this figure because we want to select individual line segments later on.

Changing Viewpoints

To move immediately into a 3D mode of drawing and thinking, our first step is to change our viewpoint on this object. There are several methods for defining 3D points of view. Of these the simplest and most efficient method is the **Named Views** dialog box introduced in the previous chapter. For now, this is the only method you need.

⊞ Open the View menu and select Named Views.

This opens the **View Manager** dialog box, which was used in Chapter 11 to create named views. In this chapter, we use the Preset Views option.

⊞ Click Preset Views in the views list.

This opens the list of simple cube images shown in Figure 12-3. These represent 10 standard preset views. Imagine your point of view to be perpendicular to the dark blue face of the cube in each case. In the six orthographic views (Top, Bottom, Left, etc.), objects are presented from points of view along each of the six axis directions. You see objects in the drawing from directly above (top, positive z) or directly below (bottom, negative z), or by looking in along the positive or negative x-axis (left and right) or the positive or negative y-axis (front and back).

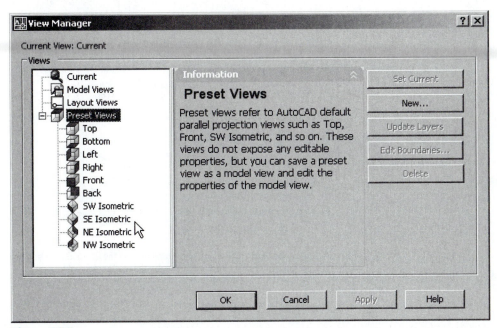

Figure 12-3

The four isometric views present objects at 45-degree angles from the XY-axis and take you up 30 degrees out of the XY plane. We use a southeast isometric view. It is simple if you imagine a compass. The lower right quadrant is the southeast. In a southeast isometric view, you are looking in from this quadrant and down at a 30-degree angle. Try it.

⊞ Select SE Isometric from the list of views.

⊞ Click Set Current.

⊞ Click OK.

The dialog box closes and the screen is redrawn to the view shown in Figure 12-4. Notice how the grid and the coordinate system icon have altered to show our current orientation. These visual aids are extremely helpful in viewing 3D objects on the flat screen and imagining them as if they were positioned in space.

At this point you might want to experiment with the other views in the **View Manager** dialog box. You will probably find the isometric views most interesting. Pay attention to the grid and the

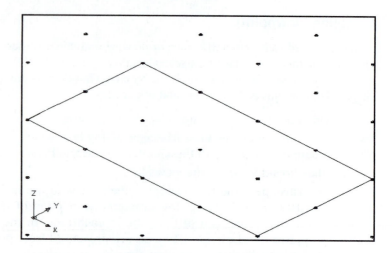

Figure 12-4

The UCS icon is displayed in various ways to help you visualize the orientation of the workplane. The following figure shows some of the possible icon displays.

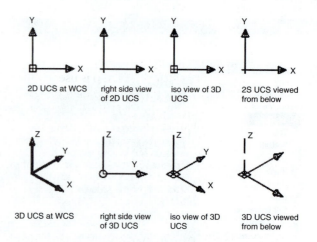

You can use the UCSICON command to switch between the 2D UCS icon and the 3D UCS icon. You can also use the command to change the size, color, arrowhead type, and icon line width of the 3D UCS icon.

Figure 12-5

icon as you switch views. Variations of the icon you might encounter here and later on are shown in Figure 12-5. With some views, you have to think carefully and watch the icon to understand which way the object is being presented.

When you have finished experimenting, be sure to return to the southeast isometric view shown in Figure 12-4. We use this view frequently throughout this chapter and the next.

Whenever you change viewpoints, AutoCAD displays the drawing extents, so that the object fills the screen and is as large as possible. Often, you need to zoom out a bit to get some space to work in. Here we do this using the Scale(X) option of the **ZOOM** command. It is different from the Zoom XP method we have used previously. The scale factor is relative to the current model space display only.

⊞ Select View → Zoom → Scale from the pull-down menu.

⊞ Type ".5x" ↵.

This tells AutoCAD to adjust the display so that objects appear half as large as before. Your screen is redrawn dynamically and the rectangle appears at half its previous magnification.

Entering 3D Coordinates

Next we create a copy of the rectangle placed 1.25 above the original. This brings up a basic 3D problem: AutoCAD interprets point selections as being in the XY plane, so how does one indicate a point or a displacement in the Z direction? In wireframe modeling there are three possibilities: typed 3D coordinates, X/Y/Z point filters, and object snaps. Object snap requires an object already drawn above or below the XY plane, so it is of no use right now. We use typed coordinates first and then discuss how point filters could be used as an alternative. Later, we use object snap extensively.

3D coordinates can be entered from the keyboard in the same manner as 2D coordinates. Often, this is an impractical way to enter individual points in a drawing. However, within **COPY** or **MOVE,** it provides a simple method for specifying a displacement in the Z direction.

⊕ Enter the COPY command.

AutoCAD prompts for object selection.

⊕ Select the complete rectangle.

⊕ Right-click to end object selection.

AutoCAD now prompts for the base point of a vector or a displacement value:

    Specify base point or displacement, or [Multiple]:

Typically, you would respond to this prompt and the next by showing the two endpoints of a displacement vector. However, we cannot show a displacement in the Z direction by pointing. This is important for understanding AutoCAD coordinate systems. Unless an object snap is used, all points picked on the screen with the pointing device are interpreted as being in the XY plane of the current UCS. Without an entity outside the XY plane to use in an object snap, there is no way to point to a displacement in the Z direction.

⊕ Type "0,0,1.25" ⏎.

AutoCAD now prompts

        Specify second point of displacement,
        or <use first point as displacement>:

You can type the coordinates of another point, or press **Enter** to tell AutoCAD to use the first entry as a displacement from (0,0,0). In this case, pressing **Enter** indicates a displacement of 1.25 in the Z direction and no change in X or Y.

⊕ Press Enter or right-click.

AutoCAD creates a copy of the rectangle 1.25 directly above the original. Your screen should resemble Figure 12-6.

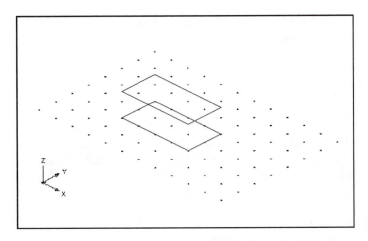

Figure 12-6

X/Y/Z Point Filters (Optional)

Point filters are very useful in 3D, although they might seem odd until you get a feel for when to use them. In a point filter, we filter out coordinates from one point and use them to create a new point. Notice that in the displacement we just entered, the only thing that changes is the Z value. Note also that we could specify the same displacement using any point in the XY plane as a base point. For example, (3,6,0) to (3,6,1.25) would show the same displacement as (0,0,0) to (0,0,1.25). In fact, we don't even need to know what X and Y are as long as we know that they don't change.

That is how an .XY point filter works. We borrow, or "filter," the X and Y values from a point, without needing to know what the values actually are, and then specify a new Z value. Other types of filters are possible, of course, such as .Z or .YZ.

You can use a point filter, like an object snap, any time AutoCAD asks for a point. After a point filter is specified, AutoCAD always prompts with "of." In our case, you are being asked, "You want the X and Y values of what point?" In response, you pick a point, and then AutoCAD asks you to fill in Z.

To use an .XY filter in the **COPY** command instead of typing coordinates, for example, you could follow this procedure:

1. Enter the **COPY** command.
2. Select the rectangle.
3. For the displacement base point, pick any point in the XY plane.
4. At the prompt for a second point, type ".xy" ↵.
5. At the *of* prompt, type "@" ↵ or pick the same point again.
6. At the *(need Z):* prompt, type "1.25" ↵. The result would be Figure 12-6, as before.

> **Note:**
> There is a Point Filters cascading submenu on the object snap shortcut menu. To access it, hold down the **Shift** key and right-click anywhere in the drawing area. From the shortcut menu, highlight Point Filters and select a point filter type from the submenu.

Using Object Snap

We now have two rectangles floating in space. Our next job is to connect the corners to form a wireframe box. This is easily managed using Endpoint object snaps, and it is a good example of how object snaps allow us to construct entities not in the XY plane of the current coordinate system.

- ⊞ Right-click the Osnap button on the status bar.
- ⊞ Select Settings from the shortcut menu.
- ⊞ Make sure that Object Snap On is checked at the top left of the dialog box.
- ⊞ Click Clear All to clear all object snap check boxes.
- ⊞ Select the Endpoint check box.
- ⊞ Click OK.

    The running Endpoint object snap is now on and affects all point selections. Object snaps can be used frequently in 3D modeling.

Now we draw some lines:

- ⊞ Enter the LINE command and connect the upper and lower corners of the two rectangles, as shown in Figure 12-7.

    We have removed the grid for clarity, but you may want to leave yours on.

Before going on, pause to take note of what you have drawn. The box on your screen is a true wireframe model. Unlike an isometric drawing, it is a 3D model that can be turned, viewed, and plotted from any point in space. It is not, however, a solid model or a surface model. It is only a set of lines in 3D space. Removing hidden lines or shading would have no effect on this model because no surfaces are represented.

In the next section, you begin to define your own coordinate systems that allow you to perform drawing and editing functions in any plane you choose.

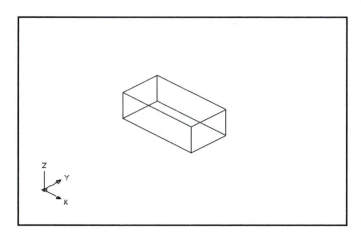

Figure 12-7

12-2 DEFINING AND SAVING USER COORDINATE SYSTEMS

GENERAL PROCEDURE	1. Select New UCS from the **Tools** menu. 2. Choose an option. 3. Specify a coordinate system. 4. Name and save the new coordinate system.

In this task, you begin to develop new vocabulary and techniques for working with objects in 3D space. The primary tool is the **UCS** command. You also learn to use the **UCSICON** command to control the placement of the coordinate system icon.

Until now, we have had only one coordinate system to work with. All coordinates and displacements have been defined relative to a single point of origin. Keep in mind that viewpoint and coordinate system are not the same, although they use similar vocabulary. In the previous section, we changed our point of view, but the UCS icon changed along with it, so that the orientations of the x-, y-, and z-axes relative to the object were retained. With the **UCS** command, you can free the coordinate system from the viewpoint and define new coordinate systems at any point and any angle in space. When you do, you can use the coordinate system icon and the grid to help you visualize the planes you are working in, and all commands and drawing aids function relative to the new system.

The coordinate system we are currently using, WCS (world coordinate system), is unique. It is the one we always begin with. The square at the base of the coordinate system icon indicates that we are working in the WCS. A UCS is nothing more than a new point of origin and a new orientation for the x-, y-, and z-axes.

We begin by defining a UCS in the plane of the top of the box, as shown in Figure 12-8.

⊕ Leave the Endpoint osnap mode on for this exercise.

⊕ Open the Tools menu and highlight New UCS.

You see options on a submenu, as illustrated in Figure 12-9. We begin by using Origin to create a UCS that is parallel to the WCS. You will remember that this is the same option we used in Chapter 8 to create ordinate dimensions.

⊕ Select Origin from the submenu.

AutoCAD prompts for a new origin:

```
Specify new origin point <0,0,0>:
```

This option does not change the orientation of the three axes. It simply shifts their intersection to a different point in space. We use this procedure to define a UCS in the plane of the top of the box.

⊕ Use the Endpoint object snap to select the top left corner of the box, as shown by the location of the icon in Figure 12-8.

The grid origin moves to the corner of the box. Notice that the square is gone from the icon, indicating that we are no longer in the WCS.

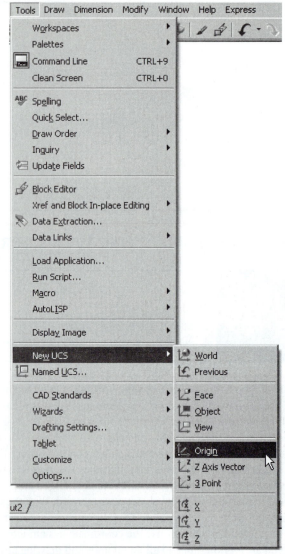

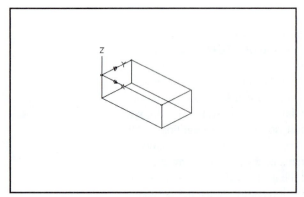

Figure 12-8

Figure 12-9

With UCSICON set to origin, the icon shifts to the new origin whenever we define a new UCS. The only exception would be if the origin were not on the screen or were too close to an edge for the icon to fit. In these cases, the icon would be displayed in the lower left corner again.

The UCS we have just created makes it easy to draw and edit entities that are in the plane of the top of the box and to perform editing in planes that are parallel to it, such as the bottom. In the next section, we begin drawing and editing using different coordinate systems, and you can see how this works. For now, we spend a little more time on the **UCS** command itself. We define two more UCSs, but first let's save this one so that we can recall it quickly when we need it later.

⊹ Open the Tools menu and highlight Named UCS.

The new UCS is on the list as Unnamed, along with World and Previous.

⊹ Double-click Unnamed.

The word *Unnamed* should be selected for editing. We name our coordinate system Top. This is the UCS we use to draw and edit in the top plane. This UCS would also make it easy for us to create an orthographic top viewpoint later on.

⊹ Type "top" ⏎.

The top UCS is now saved and can be recalled by opening this dialog box, selecting it in the name list, and picking the **Set Current** button.

Next we define a left UCS using the 3 Point option.

⊕ Click OK to close the dialog box.

⊕ Open the Tools menu, highlight New UCS, and select 3 Point from the submenu.

AutoCAD prompts

> `Specify new origin point <0,0,0>:`

In this option, you show AutoCAD a new origin point, as before, and then a new orientation for the axes as well. Notice that the default origin is the current one. If we retained this origin, we could define a UCS with the same origin and a different axis orientation.

Instead, we define a new origin at the lower left corner of the left side of the box, as shown in Figure 12-10.

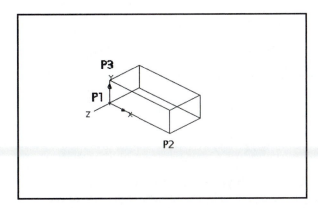

Figure 12-10

⊕ With the Endpoint osnap on, pick P1, as shown in Figure 12-10.

AutoCAD now prompts you to indicate the orientation of the *x*-axis:

> `Specify point on positive portion of the X axis`
> `<1.00,0.00,-1.25>:`

⊕ Pick the right front corner of the box, P2, as shown.

The object snap ensures that the new *x*-axis aligns with the left side of the object. AutoCAD prompts for the *y*-axis orientation:

> `Specify point on positive-Y portion of the UCS XY plane`
> `<0.00,1.00,-1.25>:`

By definition, the *y*-axis is perpendicular to the *x*-axis; therefore, AutoCAD needs only a point that shows the plane of the *y*-axis and its positive direction. Because of this, any point on the positive side of the *y* plane specifies the *y*-axis correctly. We have chosen a point that is on the *y*-axis itself.

⊕ Pick P3, as shown.

When this sequence is complete, notice that the coordinate system icon has rotated along with the grid and moved to the new origin as well. This UCS is convenient for drawing and editing in the left plane of the box, or editing in any plane parallel to the left plane, such as the back plane.

Now save the left UCS, using the command line this time.

⊕ Press Enter to repeat the UCS command.

If dynamic input is on, you will see a drop-down list of options.

⊕ Type "s" ⏎.

The Save option is not named in the prompt, but it is still available.

⊕ Type "Left" ⏎ to name the UCS.

Finally, we use the Origin and Y axis rotation options together to create a right-side UCS.

⊞ Open the Tools menu and highlight New UCS.

⊞ Select Origin from the submenu.

⊞ Pick the lower front right corner of the box for the origin, as shown in Figure 12-11.

The UCS icon moves to the selected point.

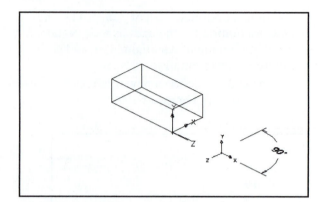

Figure 12-11

⊞ Press Enter or the spacebar to repeat the UCS command.

We rotate the UCS icon around its *y*-axis to align it with the right side of the box.

In using any of the rotation options (X, Y, and Z), the first thing you have to decide is which axis is the axis of rotation. If you look at the current position of the icon and think about how it will look when it aligns with the right side of the box, you can see that the *y*-axis retains its position and orientation while the *x*- and *z*-axes turn through 90 degrees. In other words, because *x* rotates around *y*, *y* is the axis of rotation.

⊞ Type "y" ↵.

Now AutoCAD prompts for a rotation:

      Specify rotation angle around Y axis <90>:

It takes some practice to differentiate positive and negative rotation in 3D. Use AutoCAD's right-hand rule, which can be stated as follows: If you are hitch-hiking (pointing your right thumb) in a positive direction along the axis of rota-tion, your fingers curl in the direction of positive rotation for the other axes. In this case, align your right thumb with the positive *y*-axis, and you see that your fingers curl in the direction in which we want the *x*-axis to rotate. Therefore, the rotation of *x* around *y* is positive.

⊞ Type 90 or press Enter to accept the default rotation.

You should now have the UCS icon aligned with the right side of the box, as shown in Figure 12-11. Save this UCS before going on to Section 12-3.

⊞ Press Enter to repeat the UCS command.

⊞ Type "s" ↵.

⊞ Type "Right" ↵.

12-3 Using Draw and Edit Commands in a UCS

Now the fun begins. Using our three new coordinate systems and one more we define later, we give the box a more interesting "slotted wedge" shape. In this task, we cut away a slanted sur-face on the right side of the box. Because the planes we are working in are parallel to the left side of the box, we begin by making the left UCS current. All our work in this section is done in this UCS.

- Open the Tools menu and select Named UCS.

     This opens the **Named UCS** dialog box again, with three new coordinate systems, as shown in Figure 12-12. Now that we have these coordinate systems defined, this dialog box provides a simple way to switch among them.

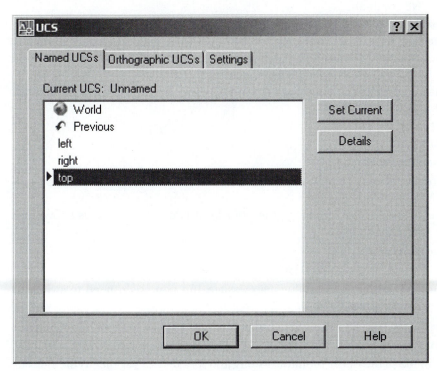

Figure 12-12

- Highlight left in the dialog box.
- Click the Set Current button.
- Click OK.

     The UCS icon returns to the left plane, but the grid may not adjust.

- Open the View menu and select Redraw.

     Look at Figure 12-13. We draw a line down the middle of the left side (Line 1) and use it to trim another line coming in at an angle (Line 2).

- Enter the LINE command.
- Hold down Shift and right-click to open the Object Snap Cursor menu.
- Select Midpoint.

     This temporarily overrides the Endpoint object snap.

- Point to the top edge of the left side of the box.

     AutoCAD snaps to the midpoint of the line.

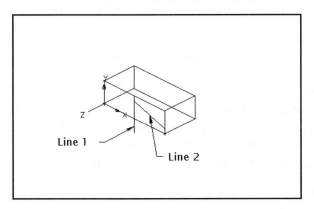

Figure 12-13

⊞ Turn Ortho on.

Notice how Ortho works as usual, but relative to the current UCS.

⊞ Pick a second point anywhere below the box.

This line is trimmed later, so the exact length does not matter.

⊞ Exit the LINE command.

Next we draw Line 2 on an angle across the left side. This line becomes one edge of a slanted surface. Your snap setting needs to be at 0.25 or smaller, and Ortho needs to be off. The grid, snap, and coordinate display all work relative to the current UCS, so it is a simple matter to draw in this plane.

⊞ Turn snap on and check your snap setting by observing the coordinate display. Change it to 0.25 if necessary.

⊞ Turn Ortho off.

⊞ Turn Osnap off.

⊞ Enter the LINE command.

⊞ Use incremental snap to pick a point 0.25 down from the top edge of the box on Line 1, as shown in Figure 12-13.

⊞ Pick a second point 0.25 up along the right front edge of the box, as shown.

⊞ Exit the LINE command.

Now trim Line 1.

⊞ Select the Trim tool from the dashboard.

AutoCAD presents the following message, but you might need to switch to the text window (press F2) to see it:

View is not plan to UCS. Command results may not be obvious.

In the language of AutoCAD 3D, a view is plan to the current UCS if the XY plane is in the plane of the monitor display and its axes are parallel to the sides of the screen. This is the usual 2D view, in which the *y*-axis aligns with the left side of the display and the *x*-axis aligns with the bottom of the display. In previous chapters, we always worked in plan view. In this chapter, we have not been in plan view since the beginning of Section 12-1.

With this message, AutoCAD is warning us that boundaries, edges, and intersections might not be obvious as we look at a 3D view of an object. For example, lines that appear to cross might be in different planes.

Having read the warning, we continue.

⊞ Select Line 2 as a cutting edge.

⊞ Right-click to end cutting edge selection.

⊞ Point to the lower end of Line 1.

⊞ Press Enter or the spacebar to exit TRIM.

Your screen should resemble Figure 12-14.

Now we copy our two lines to the back of the box. Because we will be moving out of the left plane, which is also the XY plane in the current UCS, we require the use of Endpoint object snaps to specify the displacement vector.

⊞ Select the Copy tool from the dashboard.

⊞ Pick Lines 1 and 2. (You might need to turn off incremental snap at this point to pick Line 1.)

⊞ Right-click to end object selection.

⊞ Click the Osnap button to turn object snap on.

⊞ Use the running Endpoint osnap to pick the lower front corner of the box, P1 as shown in Figure 12-15. Be careful to avoid picking the endpoint of Line 2.

⊞ At the prompt for a second point of displacement, use the Endpoint osnap to pick the lower right back corner of the box, P2 as shown.

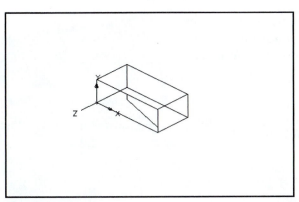

Figure 12-14

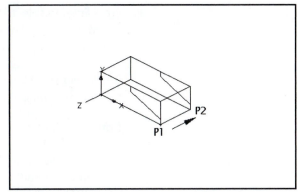

Figure 12-15

⊕ Press Enter to exit COPY.

Your screen should now resemble Figure 12-15.

What remains is to connect the edges we have just outlined and then trim away the top of the box. We continue to work in the left UCS and use Endpoint osnaps.

We use a multiple **COPY** to copy one of the previously drawn edges in three new places.

⊕ Repeat COPY.

⊕ Pick the bottom right edge for copying (the edge between P1 and P2 in Figure 12-15).

⊕ Right-click to end object selection.

⊕ Pick the front endpoint of the selected edge to serve as a base point of displacement.

⊕ Pick the top endpoint of Line 1 (P1 in Figure 12-16).

⊕ Pick the lower endpoint of Line 1 (P2) as another second point.

⊕ Pick the right endpoint of Line 2 (P3) as another second point.

⊕ Press Enter to exit the COPY command.

Finally, we need to do some trimming.

⊕ Pick the Trim button from the dashboard.

For cutting edges, we want to select Lines 1 and 2 and their copies in the back plane (Lines 3 and 4 in Figure 12-17). Because this can be difficult, a quick alternative to selecting these four separate lines is to use a crossing box to select the whole area or press **Enter** to Select All. As long as your selection includes the four lines, it will be effective.

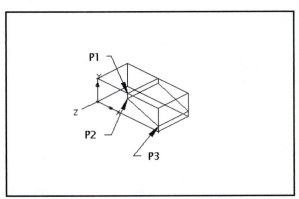

Figure 12-16

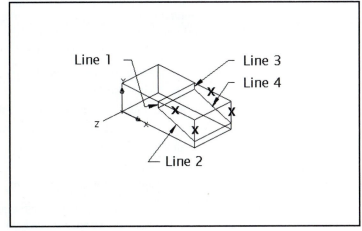

Figure 12-17

⊞ Press Enter to select all objects as cutting edges.

With this selection you do not have to press **Enter** again. Because you've already selected everything, AutoCAD does not ask for further object selection.

⊞ One by one, pick the top left and top back edges to the right of the cut, and the right front and right back edges above the cut, as shown by the Xs in Figure 12-17.

This leaves a single line hanging where the object has been trimmed. **TRIM** has a convenient eRase option designed for situations like this.

⊞ Type "r" ↵ for the eRase option.

⊞ Pick the top edge that is left hanging in space.

⊞ Press Enter to exit the TRIM command.

We use **ERASE** instead of **TRIM** here because this line does not intersect any edges. Your screen should now resemble Figure 12-18.

NEW
to AutoCAD
2008

Note:
Trimming in 3-D can be tricky. Remember where you are. Edges that do not run parallel to the current UCS might not be recognized at all.

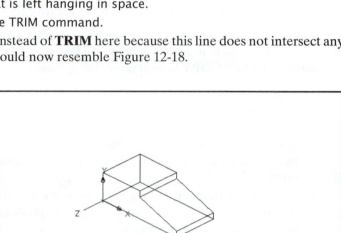

Figure 12-18

12-4 WORKING ON AN ANGLED SURFACE

In this section, we take our 3D drawing technique a step further by constructing a slot through the new slanted surface and the bottom of the object. This requires the creation of a new UCS. In completing this task, you also use the **OFFSET** command and continue to develop a feel for working with multiple coordinate systems.

Begin by defining a UCS along the angled surface.

⊞ Select Tools → New UCS → 3 Point from the pull-down menu.

⊞ Using the Endpoint osnap, pick P1, as shown in Figure 12-19.

⊞ Using an Endpoint osnap, pick P2, as shown.

⊞ Using an Endpoint osnap, pick P3, as shown.

⊞ Repeat the UCS command.

⊞ Type "s" ↵.

⊞ Type "Angle" ↵ for the name of the UCS.

Now we are ready to work in the plane of the angled surface.

From here on, we have moved our UCS icon back to the lower left of the screen for the sake of clarity in our illustrations. You can leave it at its origin on your screen, if you like, or move it by opening the **View** menu, highlighting Display, then UCS Icon, and clearing Origin.

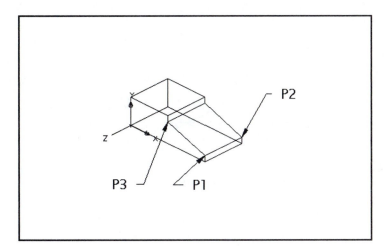

Figure 12-19

⊞ Turn Osnap off.

⊞ If Ortho is off, turn it on.

We create Line 1 across the angled surface, as shown in Figure 12-20, by off-setting the top right front edge of the wedge.

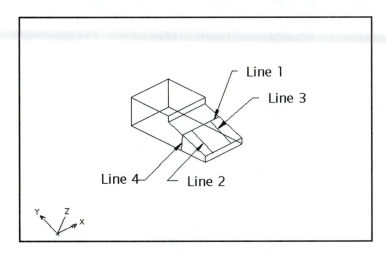

Figure 12-20

⊞ Pick the Offset tool from the dashboard.

⊞ Type "1.5" ↵.

⊞ Pick the top right front edge (the edge that lies along the *x*-axis in the current UCS).

⊞ Point anywhere above and to the left of the edge.

⊞ Exit OFFSET.

⊞ Turn Snap on and draw Lines 2 and 3 perpendicular to the first, as shown. They should be over 0.50 and 1.50 from the current *y*-axis.

Watch the coordinate display and notice how the coordinates work in this UCS as in any other.

⊞ Turn Ortho off.

⊞ Using incremental Snap for the top point and a perpendicular object snap for the lower point, drop Line 4 down to the bottom left front edge.

This is a single-point osnap. Use the Osnap shortcut menu (Shift, right-click). Notice again how object snap modes work for you, especially to locate points that are not in the XY plane of the current UCS.

⊞ Create Lines 5 and 6, as shown in Figure 12-21, by making two copies of Line 4, extending down from the ends of Lines 2 and 3, as shown.

⊞ Erase Line 4 from the left plane.

⊞ Turn Osnap on.

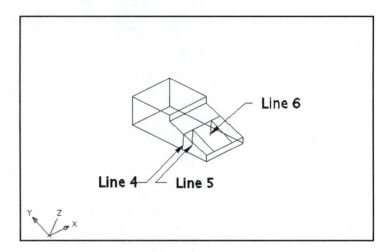

Figure 12-21

⊹ Using Endpoint object snaps, connect Lines 5 and 6 to each other in the plane of the bottom of the object.

⊹ Using Endpoint and Perpendicular object snaps, connect Lines 5 and 6 to the bottom edge of the right side.

   The running Endpoint snap is on for this; use the object snap shortcut menu for the Perpendicular snaps.

⊹ Using Endpoint object snaps, draw two short vertical lines on the right side, connecting to Lines 2 and 3.

⊹ Trim line 1 and the two lines on the right side across the opening of the slot to create Figure 12-22.

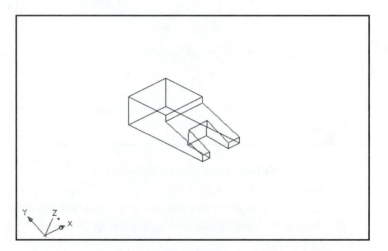

Figure 12-22

12-5 USING RULESURF TO CREATE 3D FILLETS

GENERAL PROCEDURE	1. Create fillets in two planes. 2. Select Draw → Modeling → Meshes → Ruled Mesh from the pull-down menu. 3. Pick a fillet. 4. Pick the corresponding side of the fillet in the other plane.

There are two parts to completing this task. First, we fillet the top and bottom corners of the slot drawn in the previous section. Then we use the **RULESURF** command to create filleted surfaces between the top and bottom of the slot. **RULESURF** is a surface mesh command. We use it here as the most effective way to create a 3D fillet in our wireframe model.

⊕ To begin this task you should be in the Angle UCS, as in Section 12-4, and your screen should resemble Figure 12-22.

⊕ Select the Fillet tool from the dashboard.

AutoCAD prompts as usual:

```
Current settings: Mode = TRIM, Radius = 0.50
Select first object or [Polyline/Radius/Trim]:
```

⊕ Type "r" ↵.

⊕ Type ".25" ↵ for the radius value.

⊕ Type "m" ↵ for the Multiple option.

⊕ Pick two lines that meet at one of the upper corners of the slot.

Look at Figure 12-23 to see where we are headed.

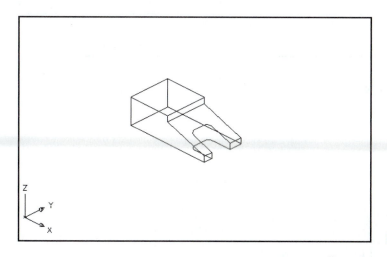

Figure 12-23

⊕ Pick two lines that meet at the other upper corner of the slot.

⊕ Pick two lines that meet at one of the lower corners of the slot.

⊕ Pick two lines that meet at the other lower corner of the slot.

⊕ Press Enter to exit FILLET.

⊕ Erase the two vertical lines left outside the fillets.

Your screen should resemble Figure 12-23.

Now we use **RULESURF** to connect the upper and lower fillets with 3D surfaces. **RULESURF** is one of several commands that create *3D polygon meshes,* which are used to represent the surfaces of 3D objects.

The **RULESURF** command creates a 3D surface between two lines or curves in 3D space. Our two curves are the upper and lower fillets at each of the two corners.

⊕ Select Draw → Modeling → Meshes → Ruled Mesh from the pull-down menu.

AutoCAD prompts

```
Select first defining curve:
```

⊕ Pick one of the top fillets, as shown by Pick fillet 1 in Figure 12-24.

AutoCAD prompts for a second curve:

```
Select second defining curve:
```

⊕ Pick the corresponding fillet in the bottom plane, with a pick point on the corresponding side, as shown by Pick fillet 2 in Figure 12-24.

AutoCAD draws a set of faces to represent the surface curving around the fillet radius, as shown in Figure 12-25.

The trick in using **RULESURF** is to be sure that you show a pick point toward one side of the curve and that you pick the next curve with a point on the

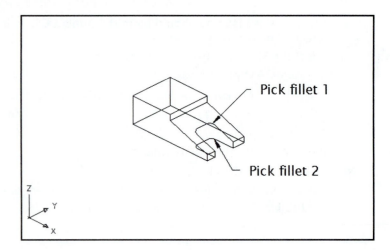

Figure 12-24

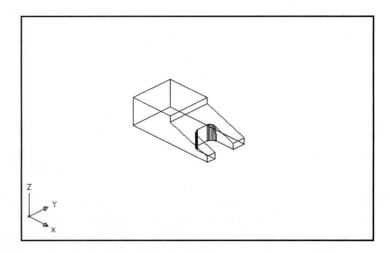

Figure 12-25

corresponding side. Otherwise, you get an hourglass effect, as shown in Figure 12-26.

⊕ To complete this task, repeat the RULESURF command and draw the fillet at the other corner of the groove.

When you are finished, your screen should resemble Figure 12-25. This completes the introduction to drawing 3D wireframe models and using UCSs.

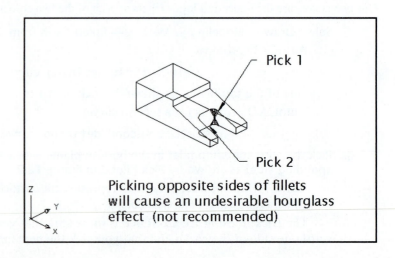

Figure 12-26

12-6 Adjusting Viewpoint with Constrained Orbit

What follows is a brief demonstration of one of several methods for dynamically adjusting point of view. Although Preset Views such as the isometric view used in this chapter are very accessible, you can also create many other viewpoints for easier editing and for presentation of your model once it is drawn. In this task we change our viewpoint on our wireframe modeling using the Constrained Orbit mode of the **3DORBIT** command.

⊞ To begin this task you should have the completed wireframe model on your screen, as shown in Figure 12-25.

⊞ Select View → Orbit → Constrained Orbit from the pull-down menu.

3D Wireframe Visual Style

This executes the **3DORBIT** command, which puts you in Constrained Orbit mode. AutoCAD will show the constrained orbit cursor and switch to a grid with lines on a gray background. This is the standard 3D wireframe visual style. Throughout this book you have been using the 2D wireframe style. We explore other visual styles in the chapters that follow.

⊞ Press the pick button and slowly move the cursor in any direction.

The wireframe model appears to move along with the cursor movement.

⊞ Move the cursor left and right, using mostly horizontal motion.

Horizontal motion creates movement parallel to the XY plane of the world coordinate system.

⊞ Move the cursor up and down, using mostly vertical motion.

Vertical motion creates movement parallel to the z axis of the world coordinate system. You can create any viewpoint on the model using these simple motions.

Camera and Target

Though the objects in your drawing appear to move, technically you are moving your point of view on the objects, rather than the objects themselves. AutoCAD uses a camera and target analogy to describe point of view. The point from which you are viewing the object is called the camera position. The point at which the camera is aimed is called the target. For the most part, you do not need to be conscious of the camera and target positions. In Constrained Orbit mode, the camera position changes and the target remains the same.

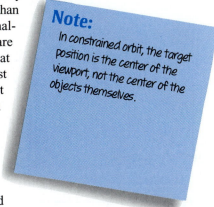

Note:
In constrained orbit, the target position is the center of the viewport, not the center of the objects themselves.

⊞ Move the cursor to create a point of view similar to the one shown in Figure 12-27.

In this view, we have moved our camera position to view the model from a northeast isometric point of view and

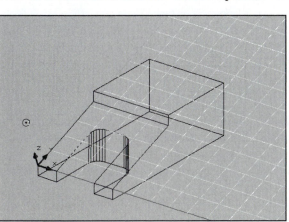

Figure 12-27

lowered the z viewing angle slightly. It could be called a northeast view, but it is not the preset northeast isometric viewpoint.

⊕ Press Enter to exit 3DORBIT.

You return to your drawing with the 2D wireframe grid and the new viewpoint. Before leaving this section, we give the new viewpoint a name so that it can be restored later. This process should be familiar to you.

⊕ Open the View menu and select Named Views.

You see the **View Manager** dialog box, as shown in Figure 12-28. The Current viewpoint is highlighted on the left and defined by the numbers on the right. You see coordinates for the camera and target positions. Your numbers will probably be different from ours.

⊕ Click the New button.

This opens the **New View** dialog box.

⊕ Type in a name for the new view.

We chose NE-2 for the name, indicating that this view is a variation of the northeast isometric view.

⊕ Click OK to leave the New View dialog box.

The NE-2 named view is now added to the list of Model Views and a set of general characteristics is added to the definition. This list includes the Angled UCS and the 2D wireframe visual style.

⊕ Click OK to complete the dialog and return to the drawing.

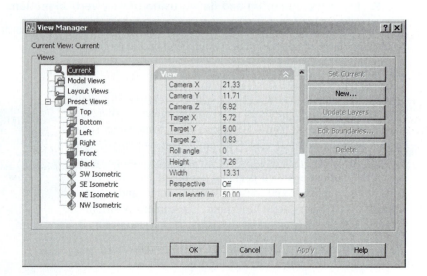

Figure 12-28

CHAPTER TEST QUESTIONS

Questions

1. It is possible to create a 3D view in which the grid is indistinguishable from an isometric snap grid. How are this grid and objects drawn on it different from the isometric grid and objects drawn on it?
2. What is a wireframe model?
3. What is the significance of the box on the UCS icon?
4. What coordinates indicate a displacement of −5 in the z direction from the point (6,6,6)?
5. Why is it usually necessary to utilize object snap to select a point on an object outside of the XY plane of the current UCS?

6. What information defines a UCS?
7. What is the right-hand rule?
8. What command did you use in this chapter to draw a surface mesh rather than a wire entity?
9. You were apparently able to draw a line from a point in the XY plane to a point above the plane without using object snap because both points appeared to be on grid snap points. What happens when you view this line from another viewpoint?
10. What angle from the XY plane defines a plan view?
11. What angle in the XY plane defines a front view?

Drawing Problems

1. Set up a southeast isometric 3D viewpoint in the WCS and draw a regular hexagon with a circumscribed radius of 4.0 units.
2. Create a half-sized scaled copy of the hexagon centered at the same center as the original hexagon; then move the smaller hexagon 5.0 units up in the *z* direction.
3. Connect corresponding corners of the two hexagons to create a tapered hexagonal prism in three dimensions.
4. Create a UCS aligned with any of the faces of the hexagonal prism.
5. Use this UCS to draw the text Lamp Shade, at 0.3 unit high, on the face that aligns with the new UCS.
6. View the object from the world plan view, the plan view of the current UCS, and a northwest isometric view.

WWW Exercise 12 (Optional)

Whenever you are ready, complete the following:

⊞ Make sure that you are connected to your Internet service provider.

⊞ Type "browser" ↵ or open your system browser from the Windows taskbar.

⊞ If necessary, navigate to our companion website at prenhall.com/dixriley.

CHAPTER PROJECTS

Drawing 12-1: Clamp

This drawing is similar to the one you did earlier in the chapter. Two major differences are that it is drawn from a different viewpoint and it includes dimensions in the 3D view. This clamp drawing gives you additional practice in defining and using UCSs. Your drawing should include dimensions, border, and title.

Drawing Suggestions

- We drew the outline of the clamp in a horizontal position and then worked from a northeast isometric point of view.
- Begin in WCS plan view, drawing the horseshoe-shaped outline of the clamp. This includes fillets on the inside and outside of the clamp. The more you can do in plan view before copying to the top plane, the less duplicate editing you need to do later.
- When the outline is drawn, switch to a northeast isometric view.
- Copy the clamp outline up 1.50.
- Define UCSs as needed, and save them whenever you are ready to switch to another UCS. You need to use these systems in your dimensioning.
- The angled face, the slots, and the filleted surfaces can be drawn just as in the chapter.

Dimensioning in 3D

The trick to dimensioning a 3D object is that you need to restore the appropriate UCS for each set of dimensions. Think about how you want the text to appear. If text is to be aligned with the top of the clamp (e.g., the 5.75 overall length), you need to draw that dimension in a top UCS; if it is to align with the front of the object (the 17-degree angle and the 1.50 height), draw it in a front UCS, and so forth.

- Define a UCS with the View option to add the border and title. Type "UCS," and then "v." This creates a UCS aligned with your current viewing angle.
- Notice that this type of dimensioning can only be done in model space. Paper space is two dimensional by definition, so you cannot align dimensions with 3D coordinate systems.

Setting Surftab 1

Notice that there are eight lines defining the **RULESURF** fillets in this drawing, compared to six in the chapter. This number of lines is controlled by the setting of the Surftab1 variable, which is discussed in Chapter 13. You can change it by typing Surftab1 and entering 8 for the new value.

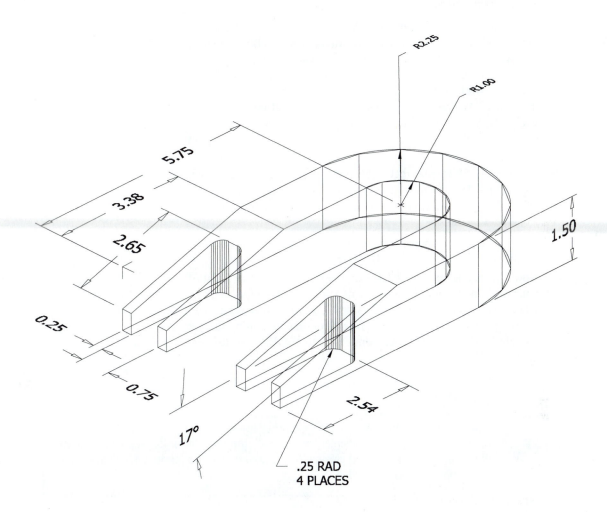

5.75

3.38

2.65

0.25

0.75

17°

R2.25

R1.00

1.50

2.54

.25 RAD
4 PLACES

CLAMP

DRAWING 12-1

Drawing 12-2: Guide Block

In this drawing, you work from dimensioned views to create a wire-frame model. This brings up some new questions: Which view should you start with? How do you translate the views into the 3D image? A good general rule is this: Draw the top or bottom in the XY plane of the WCS. Otherwise, you have trouble using the **VPOINT** command.

Drawing Suggestions

- In this drawing, it is tempting to draw the right side in WCS plan view first because that is where most of the detail is. If you do this, however, you have difficulty creating the view as shown. Instead, we suggest that you keep the bottom of the object in the WCS XY plane and work up from there, as has been the practice throughout this chapter. All preset views in the **VIEW** command are labeled relative to the WCS. Therefore, front–back, left–right, and top–bottom orientations make sense only if the top and bottom are drawn plan to the WCS.
- Draw the 12.50 × 8.00 rectangle shown in the top view and then copy it up 4.38 to form the top of the guide's base.
- Change to the same southeast isometric 3D viewpoint used in the chapter.
- Connect the four corners to create a block outline of the base of the object.
- Now you can define a new UCS on the right side and do most of your work in that coordinate system, as that is where the detail is. Once you have defined the right-side UCS, you might want to go into its plan view to draw the right-side outline, including the arc and circle of the guide. Then come back to the 3D view to copy back to the left.

> You can save some time switching viewpoints by using the **VIEW** command. When a view is saved, it includes the 3D orientation along with the zoom factor that was current at the time of the save. Also, **ZOOM** previous can be used to restore a previous 3D point of view. It does not, however, restore a UCS.

- Use **RULESURF** with Surftab 1 set to 16 to fill in surfaces between the arcs and circles.

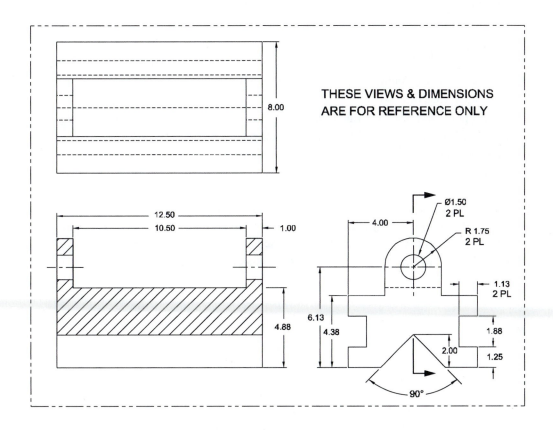

THESE VIEWS & DIMENSIONS
ARE FOR REFERENCE ONLY

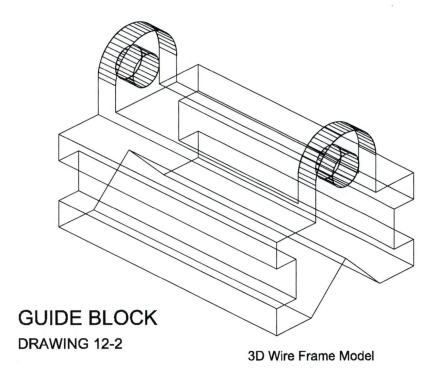

GUIDE BLOCK
DRAWING 12-2

3D Wire Frame Model

Drawing 12-3: Slide Mount

This drawing continues to use the same views, coordinate systems, and techniques as the previous drawings, but it has more detail and is a bit trickier.

Drawing Suggestions

- Draw the H-shaped outline of the top view in the WCS plan.
- Copy up in the *z* direction.
- Connect the corners to create a 3D shape.
- Define a right-side view and create the slot and holes.
- Copy back to the left side, connect the corners, and trim inside the slot.
- Return to WCS (bottom plane).
- Use **RULESURF** between circles to create mounting holes.
- Draw filleted cutout and countersunk holes. Each countersunk hole requires three circles—two small and one larger.
- Use **RULESURF** to create inner surfaces of countersunk holes.

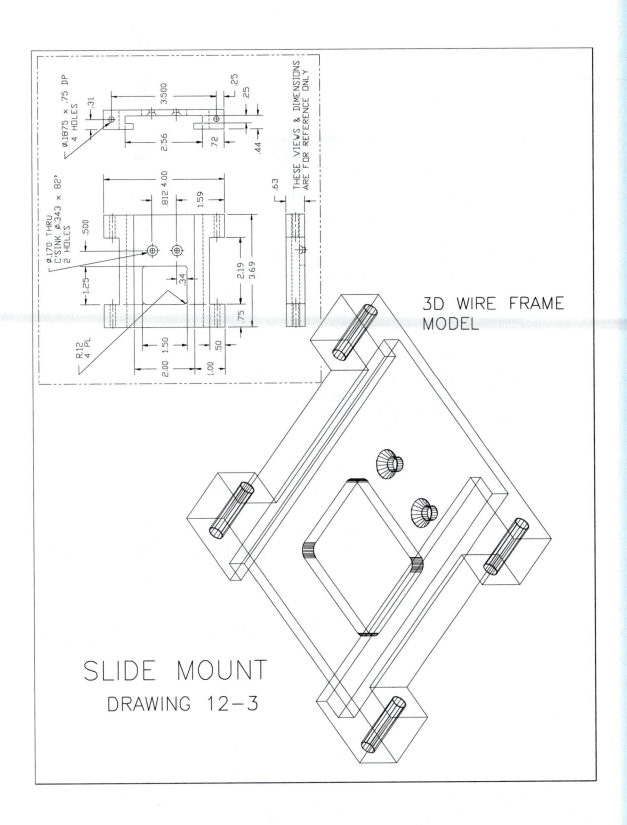

THESE VIEWS & DIMENSIONS
ARE FOR REFERENCE ONLY

3D WIRE FRAME
MODEL

SLIDE MOUNT
DRAWING 12-3

Drawing 12-4: Stair Layout

This wireframe architectural detail gives you a chance to use architectural units and limits in 3D. It requires the use of a variety of edit commands.

Drawing Suggestions

- In the WCS plan view, begin with a 2″ × 12′ rectangle that will become the bottom of a floor joist. This keeps the bottom floor in the plan view, consistent with our practice in this chapter.
- Copy the rectangle up 8″ and connect lines to form the complete joist.
- Array 16″ on center to form the first floor.
- Copy all joists up 9′6″ to form the second floor.
- Create the stairwell opening in the second floor with double headers at each end.
- Add the subfloor to the first floor.
- The outline of the stair stringers can be constructed in a number of ways. One possibility is as follows: Draw a guideline down from the front of the left double header and then another over 10′10″ to locate the end of the run. From the right end of the run, draw one riser and one tread, beginning from the top surface of the subflooring; use a multiple copy and Endpoint osnaps to create the other steps. When you get to the top, you need to trim the top tread slightly to bring it flush with the header.
- We leave it to you to construct the back line of the stringer. It needs to be parallel with the stringer line and down 1′ from the top tread, as shown.

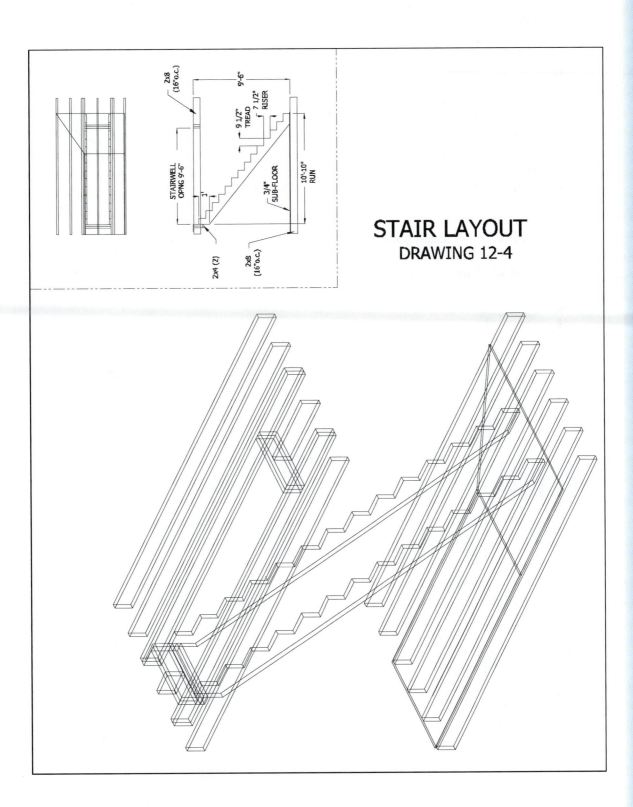

STAIR LAYOUT
DRAWING 12-4

Drawing 12-5: Housing

The objective for this drawing is to create a 3D wireframe model of the housing. The **RULESURF** command is used extensively. If you use Section B-B as your front view, you will find it easier to create the 3D wireframe.

Drawing Suggestions

- Draw the rectangular outline of the top view in the WCS plan.
- Copy up in the *z* direction to the appropriate levels.
- Change the origin of the UCS in the *z* direction to the proper height; then create the inner rectangle.
- Fillet all corners and rulesurf as necessary to create a 3D shape.
- Use **RULESURF** between circles to create cylindrical pads and semicircular cutouts. Be sure to change the UCS to the appropriate position when adding detail to a particular view.
- Each counterbore hole requires three circles—two small and one larger.
- Use **RULESURF** to create inner surfaces of counterbore holes.

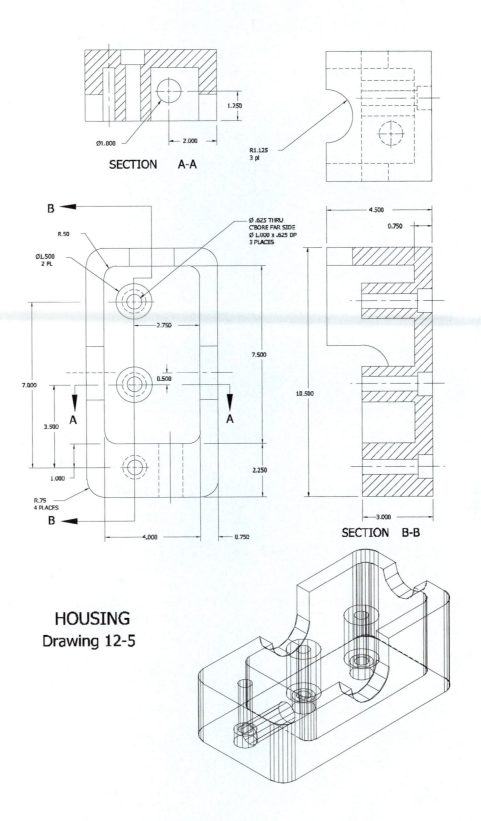

1.250

Ø1.000   2.000

SECTION   A-A

R1.125
3 pl

B

R.50

Ø1.500
2 PL

Ø .625 THRU
C'BORE FAR SIDE
Ø L.000 x .625 DP
3 PLACES

4.500

0.750

2.750

7.500

0.500

7.000

10.500

3.500

A   A

2.250

1.000

R.75
4 PLACES

B

4.000   0.750

3.000

SECTION   B-B

HOUSING
Drawing 12-5

Solid Models

13

Chapter Objectives

- Exploring the 3D Modeling Workspace
- Creating Solid Boxes and Wedges
- Creating the UNION of Two Solids
- Working with DUCS
- Creating Composite Solids with SUBTRACT
- Creating Chamfers and Fillets on Solid Objects
- RENDERing Solid Models

INTRODUCTION

In this chapter we explore a whole new way of drawing in three dimensions. Solid modeling is in many ways easier than wireframe modeling. In solid modeling, you can draw a complete solid object in a fraction of the time it would take to draw it line by line, edge by edge. Furthermore, once the object is drawn, it contains far more information than a wireframe model. In this chapter, you draw a simple solid model using several solid drawing and editing commands. The object itself is similar to the object you created in the last chapter, but you will be using many new commands and procedures, and the result will be more powerful. In this chapter we also make use of the 3D Modeling workspace for the first time.

13-1 EXPLORING THE 3D MODELING WORKSPACE

When you opened AutoCAD drawings in the early chapters of this book, you used the 2D Drafting & Annotation workspace with the acad template and default settings. Later you created your own 1B template, but continued to work in the 2D workspace. In this chapter we use the 3D Modeling workspace and the acad3D template for the first time. So, we begin by exploring this workspace and seeing how it is different.

⊕ Start AutoCAD.

⊕ Create a new drawing using the acad3D template.

> This will be just below the acad template in the **Select template** dialog box. With the acad3D template you will still be in the 2D Drafting & Annotation Workspace, but there will be a change in visual style, as shown in Figure 13-1. Notice the gray 3D grid with white gridlines instead of dots; the 3D coordinate system icon in the middle of the grid with blue arrow for the *z* axis, red arrow for the *x* axis, and green arrow for the *y* axis; and finally the 3D cursor with three narrow lines in colors similar to the UCS icon colors.

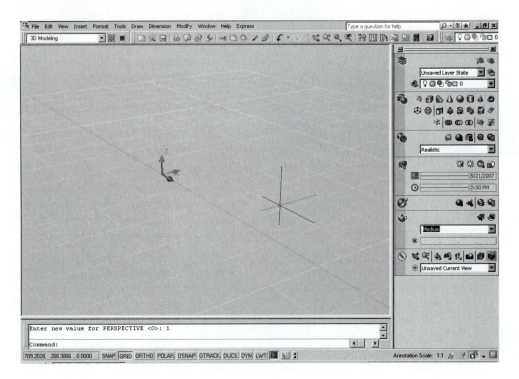

Figure 13-1

In addition to the new 3D grid, you are now in a perspective projection, with a horizon, an implied vanishing point, and a sky area beyond the grid. You can draw and edit in perspective projection just as in the familiar parallel projection.

We will discuss parallel and perspective views and visual styles momentarily, but first, we switch to the 3D Modeling workspace.

⊞ Open the Workspace list and select 3D Modeling, as shown in Figure 13-2.

⊞ Close any floating toolbars or tool palettes that may be open by default in this workspace.

Your screen should resemble Figure 13-1. This is the 3D Modeling workspace. You still have the dashboard on the right and the toolbars across the top, but there is a difference. On the dashboard, all the control panels below the layers panel have been replaced. You now have a set of control panels devoted to 3D solid modeling and rendering procedures: 3D Make, Visual Styles, Lights, Materials, Render, and 3D Navigate.

At the top of the drawing area you now have a set of three toolbars placed end to end. From the left, the first is the familiar **Workspaces** toolbar with the workspaces list, the second is the **Standard** toolbar. It is similar to the **Standard Annotation** toolbar, but has more buttons. At the right is the small **Layers** toolbar, which duplicates the function of the Layers control panel at the top of the dashboard.

Parallel and Perspective Projection

In all your 2D drawing and the wireframe 3D drawing of the last chapter, you have remained in a parallel projection. In such a view, all lines of sight are parallel and remain so at any distance from the eye of the observer. In the more realistic perspective projection, lines of sight converge toward a distant vanishing point. In 3D modeling you can draw and edit in either view. You will find perspective projections especially important for creating realistic presentation images. Before moving on, take a moment to observe how easily you can switch between the two.

⊞ To switch from perspective to parallel projection, click the Parallel Projection tool on the 3D Navigate control panel, as shown in Figure 13-3.

Your drawing area will now resemble Figure 13-4. The 3D grid, gray with white lines, is retained, but it is shown in parallel projection.

⊞ Click the Perspective Projection tool to return to perspective.

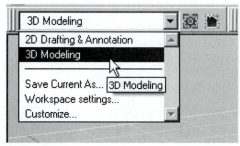

Figure 13-2

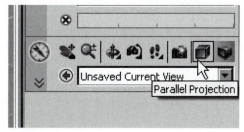

Figure 13-3

Figure 13-4

The **Perspective Projection** tool is just to the right of the **Parallel Projection** tool. In the sections that follow you create a solid model using several of the tools on the dashboard. We encourage you to switch frequently between perspective and parallel projections to get a feel for the difference.

13-2 CREATING SOLID BOXES AND WEDGES

GENERAL PROCEDURE	1. Enter BOX or WEDGE. 2. Specify corner point and distances in the XY plane of the current UCS (or define a base plane first and then specify points). 3. Specify a height.

Solid modeling requires a different type of thinking from any of the drawings you have completed so far. Instead of focusing on lines and arcs, edges and surfaces, you need to imagine how 3D objects might be pieced together by combining or subtracting basic solid shapes. This building block process is called constructive solid geometry and includes joining, subtracting, and intersecting operations. A simple washer, for example, could be made by cutting a small cylinder out of the middle of a larger cylinder. In AutoCAD solid modeling, you can begin with a flat outer cylinder, then draw an inner cylinder with a smaller radius centered at the same point, and then subtract the inner cylinder from the outer, as illustrated in Figure 13-5.

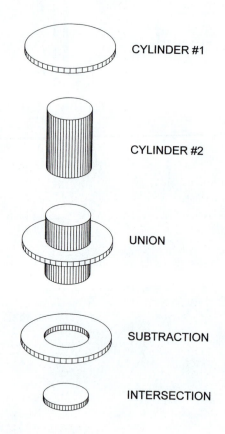

CYLINDER #1

CYLINDER #2

UNION

SUBTRACTION

INTERSECTION

Figure 13-5

This operation, which uses the **SUBTRACT** command, is the equivalent of cutting a hole and is one of three Boolean operations (after the mathematician George Boole) used to create composite solids. **UNION** joins two solids to make a new solid, and **INTERSECT** creates a composite solid in the space where two solids overlap (see Figure 13-5).

In this chapter, you create a composite solid from the union and subtraction of several solid primitives. Primitives are 3D solid building blocks—boxes, cones, cylinders, spheres, wedges, and torus. They all are regularly shaped and can be defined by specifying a few points and distances. Most are found on the 3D make control panel.

To begin drawing, we make two adjustments to your grid.

⊞ Type "Z" ↵ and then "A" ↵ to zoom to the limits of this drawing.

The acad3D template drawing has 12 by 9 limits, but the grid is initially drawn much larger to give a fuller perspective. Zooming all will take you closer to the actual limits.

⊞ Turn Snap on.

⊞ Move your cursor across the grid and observe the coordinate display.

You see that snap and grid are set to .5000, but the major lines of the grid are placed at 2.5000 intervals. We adjust this by changing grid spacing to 1.0000.

⊞ Right-click the Grid button and select settings from the shortcut menu.

⊞ Deselect the Adaptive grid check box in the Grid behavior panel.

You should now have a gridline at each 0.5000 interval and a bolder gridline at each 5.0000 interval. Snap, like Grid, is set at 0.5000. Your screen resembles Figure 13-6.

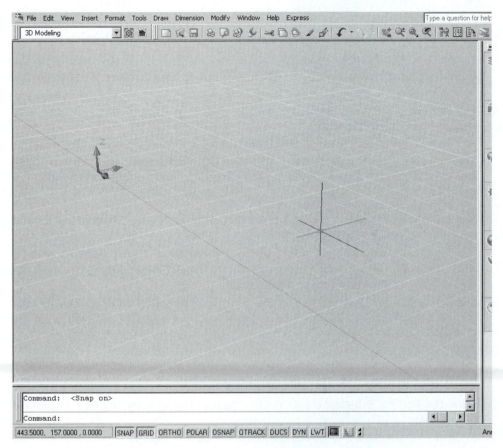

Figure 13-6

The BOX Command

- ⊕ Zoom in slightly on the area around the 3D UCS icon.
- ⊕ Select the Box tool from the dashboard, as shown in Figure 13-7.

Boxes can be drawn from the base up or they can be drawn from the center out. In either case you specify a length and width, or two corners and then a height. AutoCAD prompts

Specify first corner or [Center]:

We start with the default method, showing two corners of the base, and then typing the height.

- ⊕ Pick a first corner point at (1.0000,1.0000), P1 in Figure 13-8. (We left the adaptive grid on for our illustration so there would not be too many grid lines.)

COMMAND GRID	
Command	Box
Alias	-
Menu	Draw > Modeling
Tool	

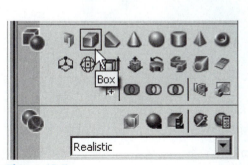

Figure 13-7

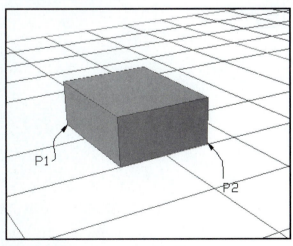

Figure 13-8

AutoCAD prompts for a second corner

Specify second corner or [Cube/Length]:

With the Cube option, length, width, and height will all be equal. With the Length option, you show length and width, rather than corners. We draw a box with a length of 4, width of 3, and height of 1.5.

⊕ Pick a point 4.00 over in the *x* direction and 3.00 back in the *y* direction, as shown by P2 in Figure 13-8.

This will be the point (5.0000,4.0000) on the coordinate display. The dynamic input display will show the *x* and *y* distances. AutoCAD will give you a box shape that can be stretched up or down in the *z* direction and prompts for a height.

Specify height or [2Point]:

⊕ Move the cursor up and down and observe the box. Also observe the height specification shown on the dynamic input display.

We are drawing a box of height 1.5000, but incremental snap does not work in the *z* direction. There is also no object above the XY plane for object snap. So, typing is the best option for specifying height.

⊕ Make sure the box is stretched in the positive *z* direction before you enter the height; otherwise AutoCAD will take the height as a negative and will draw the box below the XY plane.

⊕ Type "1.5" ↵.

Your box is complete and should resemble Figure 13-8. This is a good time to switch over to parallel perspective and back again.

⊕ Click the Parallel Projection tool on the Dashboard to view the box in parallel projection.

⊕ Click the Perspective Projection tool to return to perspective.

The WEDGE Command

Next we create a solid wedge. The process is exactly the same, but there is no Cube option. Again we use the default option of showing length and width by picking two corner points.

⊕ Select the Wedge tool from the dashboard. It is just to the right of the Box tool.

AutoCAD prompts

Specify first corner of wedge
or [Center]:

⊕ Pick the front corner point of the box, P1 in Figure 13-9.

Note:
Be careful not to rest the cursor on any of the faces of the box so that an outline is highlighted. If this happens, AutoCAD will begin drawing the wedge in the plane of that face. This is a very powerful capability we explore later in this exercise, but it will not be helpful right now.

COMMAND GRID	
Command	Wedge
Alias	We
Menu	Draw > Modeling
Tool	

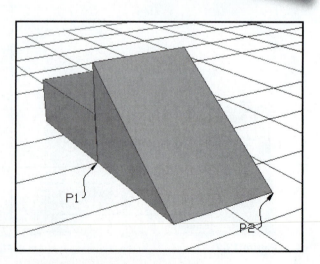

Figure 13-9

As in the **BOX** command, AutoCAD prompts for a cube, length, or the other corner:

                    Specify corner or [Cube/Length]:

⊕ Pick a point 4.00 over in the *x* direction and 3.00 back in the *y* direction, as shown by P2 in Figure 13-9.

This point should be easy to find because the back corner lines up with the back of the box already drawn.

After you pick the second corner, AutoCAD shows the wedge and prompts for a height.

⊕ Move the cursor up and down and watch the wedge stretch. Make sure that you have the wedge stretched in the positive *z* direction before you enter the height.

⊕ Type "3" ↵.

AutoCAD draws the wedge you have specified. Notice that a wedge is simply half a box, cut along a diagonal plane.

Your screen should resemble Figure 13-9. The box and wedge on your screen are true solids and are different from anything you have drawn previously. In Section 13.3, we join them to form a new composite solid.

13-3 CREATING THE UNION OF TWO SOLIDS

| **GENERAL PROCEDURE** | 1. Select the **Union** tool from the dashboard. |
| | 2. Select solid objects to join. |

Unions are simple to create and usually easy to visualize. The union of two objects is an object that includes all points that are on either of the objects. Unions can be performed just as easily on more than two objects. The union of objects can be created even if the objects have no points in common (i.e., they do not touch or overlap).

Right now we have two distinct solids on the screen; with **UNION** we can join them.

⊕ Select the Union tool from the dashboard, as shown in Figure 13-10.

AutoCAD prompts you to select objects.

⊕ Use a crossing box to select both objects.

⊕ Right-click to end object selection.

Your screen should resemble Figure 13-11.

Figure 13-10

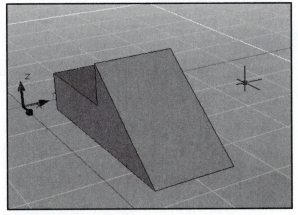

Figure 13-11

13-4 WORKING WITH DUCS

In this task, we draw another solid box while demonstrating the use of the Dynamic User Coordinate System (DUCS). This feature allows you to temporarily establish coordinate systems aligned with the faces of previously drawn solids. In this exercise we draw a thin box on top of the box from the last section and then move it to the middle of the composite object. In the next section we move it, stretch it and subtract it to form a groove.

⊕ To begin this task you should have the union of a wedge and a box on your screen, as shown in Figure 13-11.

We begin by drawing a second box positioned on top of the first box.

⊕ Pick the DUCS button on your status bar to put it in the on position.

⊕ Select the Box tool from the dashboard.

⊕ Run the cursor slowly over the faces of the composite object on your screen.

As you do this, notice that the faces are highlighted with a white dashed border as you cross them. Also notice the 3D cursor.

The 3D cursor will turn to align with each face as the face is highlighted. This includes the diagonal face, which turns the cursor on an angle.

⊕ Move the cursor over the diagonal face on the right side of the wedge and observe the orientation of the 3D cursor.

⊕ Let the cursor rest on the top of the box so that it is highlighted, as shown in Figure 13-12.

With this face highlighted and the **DUCS** button on the status bar in the on position, AutoCAD will create a temporary coordinate system aligned with the top of the box.

⊕ With the top face highlighted, carefully move the cursor to the front left corner of the top of the box and press the pick button.

This creates a coordinate system aligned with the top face and its origin at the selected point, as shown in Figure 13-13. As you move the cursor now, the base plane of the box you are drawing will be in the plane of the top of the box.

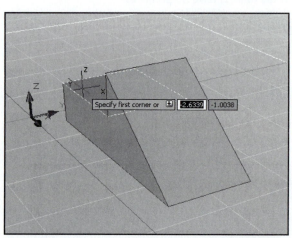

Figure 13-12

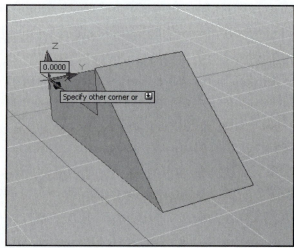

Figure 13-13

⊕ Move your cursor out along the front edge of the box 4.0000 units to the point where the box and the wedge meet. Then move over 0.50000 in the *y* direction, and press the pick button to create a 4.0000 by 0.50000 base plane.

AutoCAD prompts for a height.

⊕ Type "2" ↵.

Your screen should resemble Figure 13-14.

Next we move the new box so that the midpoint of its top front edge is at the midpoint of the top of the wedge.

Figure 13-14

13-5 CREATING COMPOSITE SOLIDS WITH SUBTRACT

GENERAL PROCEDURE	1. Create solid objects to subtract and objects to be subtracted from.
	2. Position objects relative to each other.
	3. Select the **Subtract** tool from the dashboard.
	4. Select objects to be subtracted from.
	5. Select objects to subtract.

SUBTRACT is the logical opposite of **UNION.** In a union operation, all the points contained in one solid are added to the points contained in other solids to form a new composite solid. In a subtraction, all points in the solids to be subtracted are removed from the source solid. A new composite solid is defined by what is left.

In this exercise, we use the objects already on your screen to create a slotted wedge. First, we need to move the thin upper box into place, then we stretch it to create a longer slot, and finally we subtract it from the union of the box and wedge.

⊕ To begin this task, you should have the composite box and wedge solid and the thin box on your screen, as shown in Figure 13-14.

Before subtracting, we move the box to the position shown in Figure 13-15.

⊕ Pick the 3D Move tool from the 3D Make control panel of the dashboard, as shown in Figure 13-16.

The **3DMOVE** command allows you to constrain 3D movement to a plane or an axis. It creates temporary coordinate systems similar to the DUCS system. For

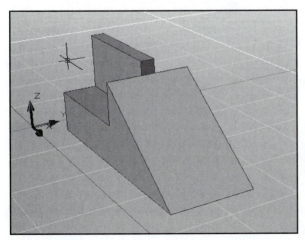

Figure 13-15

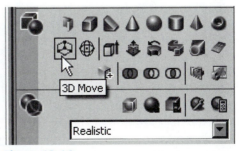

Figure 13-16

the current move we could just as easily use the regular **MOVE** command. Notice, however, that we do not have a **Move** tool on the dashboard in the 3D Modeling workspace.

This is important information, but you may not want to see it every time you select a solid object. Once you've read the information, check the Don't show me this again box. Or, click on Close if you want to continue to see this reminder.

⊕ Select the narrow box drawn in the last task.

Note:
When you make this selection you may see the message window shown in Figure 13-17. This window tells you that you can manipulate portions (subobjects) of solids by holding down the **Control** key when you make your selection.

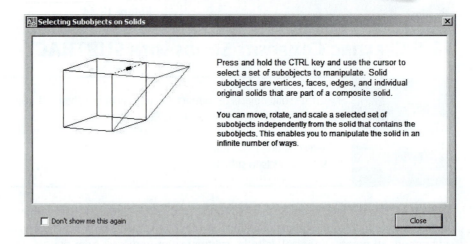

Figure 13-17

⊕ Right-click to end object selection.

With **3DMOVE,** a 3D UCS icon is added to the cursor. If you move it over the faces of the composite solid, you will see that it changes to align with the different faces. This allows moves through planes other than the current XY plane.

⊕ At the Specify base point or displacement prompt, use a midpoint object snap to pick the midpoint of the top right edge of the narrow box.

⊕ At the next Specify second point of displacement prompt, use another midpoint object snap to pick the top edge of the wedge.

This moves the narrow box over and down, as shown in Figure 13-18. If you were to perform the subtraction now, you would create a slot, but it would run only through the box, not the wedge. We can create a longer slot by stretching the narrow box over to the right using grips.

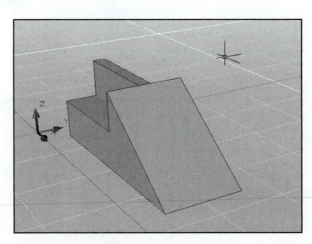

Figure 13-18

3D Solid Grips

Grips on 3D solids are more complex than our familiar 2D grips. Some grips may be used to stretch an object, whereas others might be used to move the object. It is important to select the right grip.

⊕ Select the narrow box.

Notice that some grips are triangular and some are square. The triangular grips will allow stretching in the directions they indicate. The square grips will allow stretching normal to a face of the object. We want to stretch the box out to the right, so we pick the triangle pointing in that direction.

⊕ Let your cursor rest on the arrow grip in the middle of the bottom right of the narrow box. When you lock on to this grip, you will see the value 4.0000 on the dynamic input display. This indicates that you manipulate this dimension of the box.

⊕ Pick this grip.

Now if you move the cursor in the *x* direction, you see the box stretching with you.

⊕ Move the cursor 3 or 4 units to the right and press the pick button.

If you don't go far enough, the slot will be too short.

⊕ Press Esc to clear grips.

Your screen should resemble Figure 13-19.

Subtraction

The rest is easy. Subtraction works just like Union, but the results are quite different.

⊕ Select the Subtract tool from the dashboard, as shown in Figure 13-20.

AutoCAD asks you to select objects to subtract from first:

```
Select solids and regions to subtract from...
              Select objects:
```

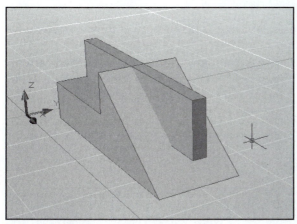

Figure 13-19

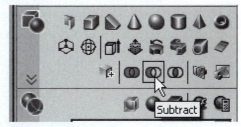

Figure 13-20

⊕ Pick the composite of the box and the wedge.

⊕ Right-click to end selection of source objects.

AutoCAD prompts for objects to be subtracted:

```
Select solids and regions to subtract...
              Select objects:
```

⊕ Pick the narrow box.

⊕ Right-click to end selection.

Your screen should resemble Figure 13-21.

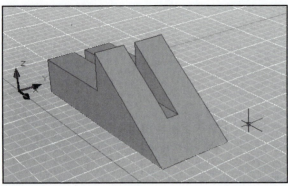

Figure 13-21

Figure 13-22

To complete this object, we draw a solid cylinder aligned with the diagonal face of the wedge and subtract it to form a hole on the right side below the slot.

⊕ Select the Cylinder tool from the dashboard, as shown in Figure 13-22.

AutoCAD prompts

```
Specify center point for base of cylinder or [3P/2P/Ttr/
                    Elliptical] <0,0,0>:
```

We use the default method of picking a center point and then specifying a base radius and a height. Be sure to move your cursor slowly and carefully so that you can observe the Dynamic User Coordinate System in action.

⊕ Move the cursor over the lower front corner of the diagonal face, as shown in Figure 13-23.

The face will be highlighted and AutoCAD will create a temporary coordinate system aligned with the face and with the lower front corner as the origin. If you moved onto the face from another corner, that would become the temporary origin. Notice in the illustration how the point where the cursor rests has become (0.5000,0.5000) in the new coordinate system. We use this coordinate system to locate the center point of the cylinder.

⊕ Move the cursor over and up to the point (1.5000,1.0000) in the new coordinate system and press the pick button.

The point is selected and the UCS icon moves to this point, aligned with the angle of the face, as shown in Figure 13-24. This point has been selected as the center point of the base of the cylinder and has also become the origin of another temporary coordinate system. AutoCAD prompts

```
Specify base radius [Diameter] <0.5000>:
```

⊕ Type ".25" ↵.

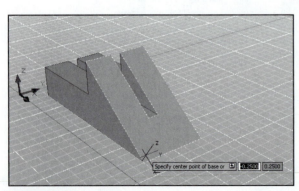

Figure 13-23

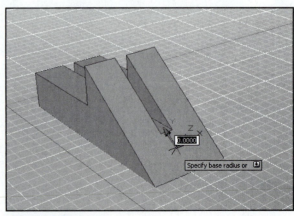

Figure 13-24

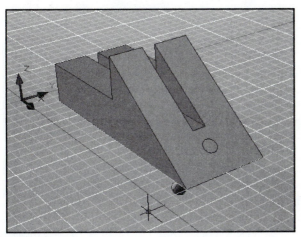

Figure 13-25

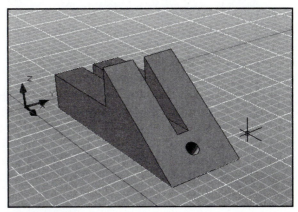

Figure 13-26

AutoCAD prompts for a height:

                Specify height [2Pt/Axis endpoint]:

⊕ Stretch the cylinder below the diagonal face and type "3" ↵.

Your screen should resemble Figure 13-25. The exact height of the cylinder is not significant because it will be subtracted from the composite object.

        Now it's time to subtract.

⊕ Select the Subtract tool from the dashboard.

⊕ Select the composite object.

⊕ Right-click to end object selection.

⊕ Select the cylinder.

⊕ Right-click to end object selection.

        Your screen should resemble Figure 13-26.

13-6 CREATING CHAMFERS AND FILLETS ON SOLID OBJECTS

GENERAL PROCEDURE

1. Select Chamfer from the **Modify** menu.
2. Pick a base surface.
3. Press **Enter** or type "n" to select the next surface.
4. Enter chamfer distances.
5. Pick edges to be chamfered.
6. Press **Enter** to end object selection.

Constructing chamfers and fillets on solids is simple, but the language of the prompts can cause confusion due to some ambiguity in the designation of edges and surfaces to be modified. We begin by putting a chamfer on the back left edge of the model.

⊕ To begin this task, you should have the solid model shown in Figure 13-26 on your screen.

⊕ Select Chamfer from the Modify menu.

        The first chamfer prompt is the same as always:

        (TRIM mode) Current chamfer Dist1 = 0.0000,
        Dist2 = 0.0000
        Select first line or [Undo/Polyline/Distance/Angel/Trim/
        mEthod/Multiple]:

Figure 13-27

⊕ Select Point 1, as shown in Figure 13-27.

The selection preview will highlight the whole solid, but when you pick Point 1, AutoCAD highlights the back left surface and prompts

```
                    Base surface selection . . .
        Enter surface selection option [Next/OK (current)] <OK>:
```

We are constructing a chamfer on the left surface of the object. However, chamfers and fillets happen along edges that are common to two surfaces. What is a base surface in relation to a chamfered edge? Actually, it refers to either of the two faces that meet at the edge where the chamfer will be. As long as you pick this edge, you are bound to select one of these two surfaces, and either will do. Which of the two surfaces is the base surface and which is the adjacent surface does not matter until you enter the chamfer distances, and then only if the distances are unequal. However, AutoCAD allows you to switch to the other surface that shares this edge, by typing "n" for the Next option or selecting Next from the dynamic input display.

⊕ Press Enter.

AutoCAD prompts

```
            Specify base surface chamfer distance
```

⊕ Type ".5" ↵ for the base surface distance.

Now AutoCAD prompts

```
        Specify other surface chamfer distance <0.5000>:
```

Now you can see the significance of base surface. The chamfer is created with the first distance on the base surface side and the second distance on the other surface side.

⊕ Type ".75" ↵ for the other base surface distance.

This constructs a chamfer that cuts 0.5 down into the left side and 0.75 forward along the top side.

Now AutoCAD prompts for the edge or edges to be chamfered:

```
            Select an edge or [Loop]:
```

Loop constructs chamfers on all edges of the chosen base surface. Selecting edges allows you to place them only on the selected edges. You have no difficulty selecting edges if you pick the edge you wish to chamfer again. The only difference is that you need to pick twice, once on each side of the slot.

⊕ Pick the top back left edge of the model, to one side of the slot (Point 1 in Figure 13-27 again).

⊕ Pick the same edge again, but on the other side of the slot (Point 2 in Figure 13-27).

⊕ Press Enter to end edge selection (right-clicking opens a shortcut menu).

Your screen should resemble Figure 13-28.

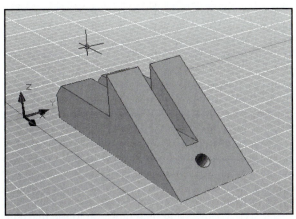

Figure 13-28

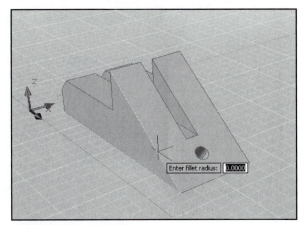

Figure 13-29

Creating Fillets

The procedure for creating solid fillets is simpler. There is one less step because there is no need to differentiate between base and other surfaces in a fillet.

⊕ Select Fillet from the Modify menu.

AutoCAD gives you current settings and prompts

```
Select first object or [Undo/Polyline/Radius/Trim/Multiple]:
```

⊕ Pick the front edge of the angled wedge face, as shown in Figure 13-29.

AutoCAD prompts

```
Enter fillet radius
```

⊕ Type ".25" ⏎.

The next prompt looks like this:

```
Select an edge or [Chain/Radius]:
```

Chain allows you to fillet around all the edges of one side of a solid object at once. For our purposes, we do not want a chain. Instead, we want to select the front and back edges of the diagonal face.

⊕ Pick the back edge of the angled wedge face.

You see this prompt again:

```
Select an edge or [Chain/Radius]:
```

The prompt repeats to allow you to select more edges to fillet.

⊕ Press Enter to end selection of edges.

Your screen should resemble Figure 13-30.

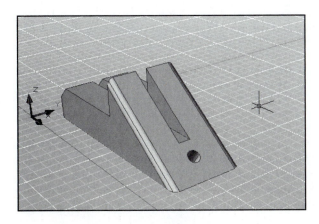

Figure 13-30

13-7 RENDERING SOLID MODELS

GENERAL PROCEDURE	1. Position lights. 2. Adjust lights. 3. Attach materials. 4. Render. 5. Name and save views.

Rendering a solid model can be a very complex process requiring a great deal of time and expertise. In this task we explore simple visual style changes and then move on to the placement and setting of lights. Knowing the various lights, how to position them, and how to understand their respective settings is a good place to begin. However, this knowledge alone will not take you very far. You need to accumulate hours of experience to know what you want and how to achieve it.

⊕ To begin this task, you should have the wedge on your screen in a southeast viewpoint, as in Figure 13-30.

Visual Styles

Visual styles are simple, default styles for presenting images of the objects in your drawing. Through most of this book you have used a 2D wireframe visual style. In this chapter you have used the Realistic style, the default in the acad3D template. Before moving on, take a minute to view your composite wedge presented in the other predefined styles. In the third panel of the dashboard you see a drop-down list box with Realistic showing as the current style.

⊕ Click the drop-down list arrow to the right of Realistic.

This opens the box of images shown in Figure 13-31. There are five preset styles and an empty box for a customized style. Styles vary in how they show edges and how they treat solid objects. To get a feel for them, select each style, one by one, and observe how they change your screen.

⊕ One by one, try each of the visual styles and observe the results.

2D Wireframe will present the edges of the object in the familiar grid of dots. 3D Hidden will show an image of the solid with hidden lines removed. 3D Wireframe will show the objects' edges just as they are in 2D Wireframe, but against the 3D grid. Conceptual will show a less detailed image of the solid, as shown in Figure 13-32.

⊕ Select Realistic again before moving on.

> **Note:**
> You may also wish to try the X-Ray mode. This mode shows wireframe edges along with a ghost image of the solid object. The **X-Ray mode** tool is the first tool on the left on the Visual Style control panel.

The Render Window and Render Presets

Our next task will be to render the object without making any lighting changes. The result will be only slightly different from the Realistic style image you already see on your screen. When you render an object, it can be shown in a special Render Window or within a viewport. The Render Window is used by default. Also, you have a choice of five different render settings that control the degree of precision in the rendering. There is a Draft setting, for example, that you might wish to use in a complex drawing where you want a quick rendering. At the other end of the spectrum is a Presentation setting, which contains more detail and is therefore drawn more slowly. The default setting is Medium.

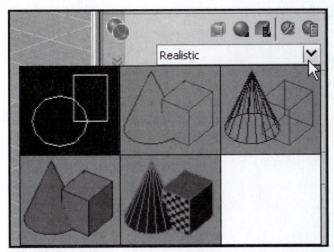

Figure 13-31

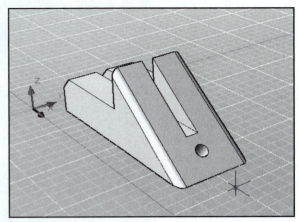

Figure 13-32

We begin by changing from Medium to Presentation.

⊕ On the bottom panel of the dashboard, click the arrow on the right of the drop-down box. The tooltip for this list says Select Render Preset.

  The opened list looks like Figure 13-33.

⊕ Select Presentation, as shown.

  We are now ready for our first rendering.

⊕ Select the Render tool, just above the drop-down list, as shown in Figure 13-34.

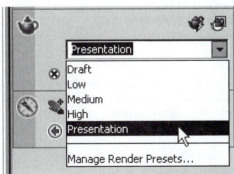

Figure 13-33

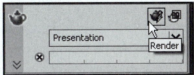

Figure 13-34

AutoCAD opens the Render Window and draws the rendered image shown in Figure 13-35. Like other windows the Render Window can be minimized and maximized. The Render Window also retains all renderings that are done in this drawing session so that you can switch back and forth and keep a record of where you have been. Rendering requires a lot of trial and error, so this history is useful. On the right are various numerical values describing your rendering.

⊕ Close the Render Window, or click the AutoCAD drawing name label on the Windows taskbar to return to the Drawing Window.

Next we add a background color to the viewport.

Changing the Background Color and Naming Views

You might find that certain rendered images are too dark against the AutoCAD background screen color. You can remedy this by changing to a different background color through the **View Manager** dialog box. When background color is changed in a viewport, it is retained in the

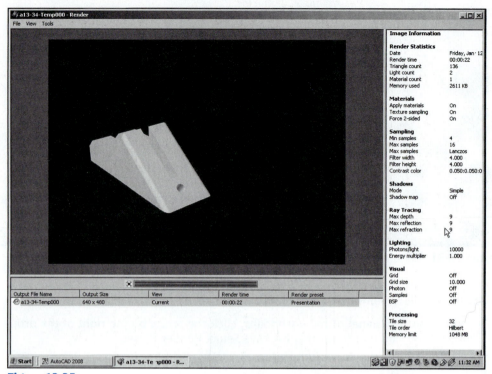

Figure 13-35

rendering of that viewport. Here we change to a gradient background for dramatic effect. We will not be able to illustrate the color effects you will see.

⊞ Open the View menu and select Named Views.

⊞ In the View Manager dialog box, click the New button.

⊞ In the New View dialog box, open the list in the Background panel at the bottom.

⊞ From the drop-down list, select Gradient.

This opens the **Background** dialog box, shown in Figure 13-36. You see a Preview panel with red, green, and blue gradient colors. At the top is a Gradient options panel that allows you to change the gradient colors and to rotate the middle border.

⊞ Click OK to accept the default gradient scheme.

This takes you back to the **New View** dialog box, where you must name the background view before you can apply it.

⊞ In the View name box, type "Gradient."

⊞ Click OK.

Back in the **View Manager** dialog box, notice the preview image at the bottom right. In order to change your viewport to this view, you must set it as current.

⊞ Click the Set Current button at the upper right.

⊞ Click OK.

You should now see your Realistic shaded model with a gradient color background.

> **Note:**
> The technique of saving named views can also be used to save more complex configurations of lights, materials, and light settings. When you have achieved a scene you wish to keep, it is a good idea to save it as a named view.

The Lights Control Panel

The Lights control panel is fourth from the top on the dashboard, just below the Visual style control panel. On the first line of this panel you see four icons, as shown in Figure 13-37. The first turns default viewport lighting on and off. Although you have done nothing to add lights to the

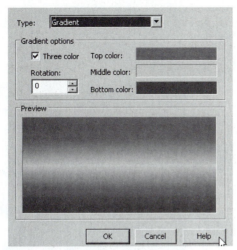

Figure 13-36

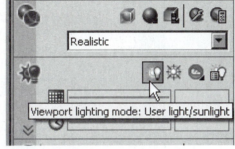

Figure 13-37

current model, there is light present. It is the default viewport lighting and is added automatically. It provides light from two sources and produces the effect you see. When you add your own lighting, default lighting will be turned off. Because you have added no lights, clicking this tool will have no effect at this point.

The second icon is the Sun status tool. Sunlight is diffuse light from overhead. It can be adjusted for location, time of year, and time of day. When you turn on sunlight, you will turn off default viewport lighting.

The third tool provides access to sky background and sky and illumination background settings that provide more precise photometric settings for natural light. The current setting has skylight off. When skylight is on, the viewport background color or gradient will be off.

The fourth button opens a palette of lights defined for this drawing. There will be nothing in this palette until we add lights.

In addition to the sun and sky, there are three additional types of lighting that can be positioned and adjusted to affect the look of a rendered or shaded model. The lights are spotlight, point light, and distant light. We begin by adding a spotlight. To define light position, it is helpful to create a three-viewport configuration so that you can see what is happening from different viewpoints simultaneously. If you do not continually examine 3D objects from different points of view, it is easy to create entities that appear correct in the current view but are clearly incorrect from other points of view. As you work, remember that these viewports are simple model space "tiled" viewports. Tiled viewports cover the complete drawing area, do not overlap, and cannot be plotted simultaneously. Plotting multiple viewports is accomplished in paper space layouts with floating viewports, as demonstrated previously in Chapter 6.

We will also move back into parallel projection at this point.

⊞ Pick the Parallel Projection tool from the dashboard.

⊞ Select View → Viewports → New Viewports from the pull-down menu.

⊞ Select Three: Right.

⊞ Select 3D from the Setup list.

⊞ Click OK.

Your screen is redrawn with a three-viewport configuration: top and front views on the left, southeast isometric view on the right, as shown in Figure 13-38. The models in your two orthographic views will probably be zoomed larger than ours. To make them more manageable, we have zoomed out a bit, using zoom scale in order to keep the two views aligned.

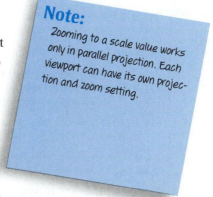

Note:
Zooming to a scale value works only in parallel projection. Each viewport can have its own projection and zoom setting.

⊞ Click in the top left viewport and zoom .5x.

⊞ Click in the bottom left viewport and zoom .5x.

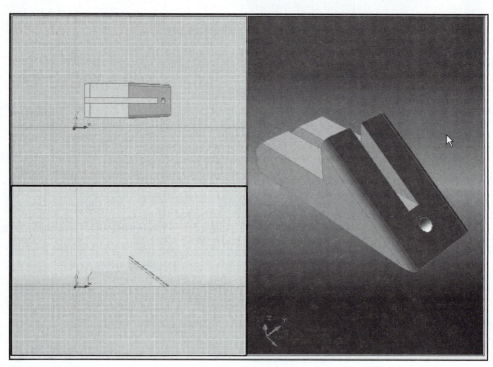

Figure 13-38

Your screen should now resemble Figure 13-38. Notice that the gradient background is applied only to the viewport on the right, which was derived from the previous single viewport.

Spotlight

We are going to add a spotlight on the right side of the object, aimed in along the slot. Light placement is probably the most important consideration in rendering. If you have used point filters previously, then you have already learned the techniques you need to position lights. Keep in mind that lights are usually positioned above the XY plane and are often alone in space. Point filters can be very helpful in this situation because there is nothing to snap the lights on to.

Note:

In AutoCAD, UCSs are defined per viewport. You can have a different UCS in each viewport if you like. The standard viewport configurations you can select from the **Viewports** dialog box use a convention of matching the UCS to the view in orthographic views. You can find a front UCS in a front view, a top UCS in a top view, and so on. The isometric view keeps the active coordinate system, in this case, the WCS, which we originally viewed in 2D plan or top view. This means that the top and south-east isometric views are now on the same grid and working with the same UCS, whereas the front view at the bottom has its own UCS. The front UCS is derived through simple rotation of the xyz-axis around the WCS origin and therefore has no specified relation to the objects in the drawing. In other words, the objects in the front view are not necessarily on the grid at all.

⊕ Pick the Lights control panel icon at the upper left of the fourth panel.

This opens the bottom half of the control panel, as shown in Figure 13-39. The first three icons create the three types of light.

In specifying light location it is extremely important that you work in either the top view or the southeast isometric view. As noted, the front view currently has a different UCS and produces very different results. You must enter the correct viewport and therefore the desired UCS before entering any of the light commands.

⊕ Click in the top viewport to make it active.

⊕ Select the Create spotlight icon, as shown.

Figure 13-39

Notice this is the second icon, not the first. We use the first in a moment to create a point light.

AutoCAD prompts

            Specify source location <0,0,0>:

Spotlights have a target and a source position. As is the case with real spotlights, AutoCAD rendering spotlights are carefully placed and aimed at a particular point in the drawing. The light falls in a cone shape and diminishes from the center of the cone. The area of the focal beam is called the hotspot. The surrounding area where the light fades is called the falloff area.

For this exercise, we place a light above and to the right of the wedge, aimed directly into the front of the slot. We use object snap and XY filters to place the target and the light source where we want them.

⊕ At the prompt for a light source, type ".xy" ↵ or open the object snap shortcut menu, highlight Point Filters, and select .XY.

AutoCAD prompts *.xy of* and waits for you to choose a point in the XY plane.

⊕ Pick a point 1.0 unit to the right of the composite wedge, the point (10,2.5,0).

AutoCAD now prompts for a *z* value:

                    (need Z):

⊕ Type "4" ↵.

This will place the source location to the right and above the wedge. Now AutoCAD prompts for the target location:

            Specify target location <0,0,-10>:

We use a midpoint object snap to place the target at the right end of the slot.

⊕ Hold down Shift, right-click, and select Midpoint from the object snap menu.

The target point is now specified and AutoCAD offers further options to adjust the spotlight. AutoCAD prompts

                  Enter option to change
[Name/Intensity factor/Photometry/Status/Hotspot/Falloff/shadoW/
        Attenuation/filter Color/eXit] <eXit>:

These same options are shown on the dynamic input display. We will not change any options at this point.

⊕ Press Enter to exit the command.

The right and top viewports will be shaded, showing the effect of the spotlight shining on the end of the slot. The shading is rather dark because the spotlight is the only light turned on. Recall that the default lighting is automatically turned off when any other light is turned on. Looking at the Light control panel on the dashboard, you see that the first icon has been turned on. This is the viewport lighting tool. Now that default lighting is off, we also turn on sunlight.

⊕ Pick in the right viewport to make it active.

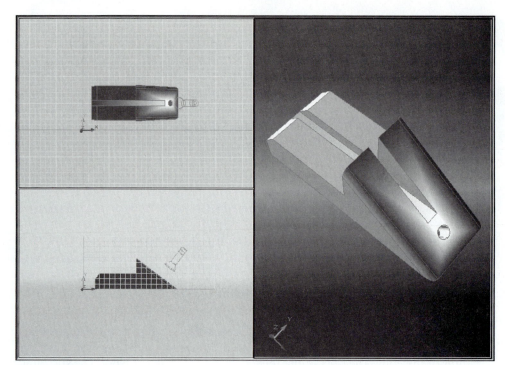

Figure 13-40

⊕ Pick the Sun status tool to turn it on. This tool is just to the right of the Viewport lighting mode tool.

    The shaded image brightens. Your right viewport should resemble Figure 13-40. Sunlight can be edited to represent different locations, times of day, and dates. The default sunlight specification is 3:00 P.M., September 21, 2007, in San Francisco. We explore these settings later.

    Before adding another light, try rendering the right viewport.

⊕ With the right viewport active, click the Render tool on the Dashboard.

    In a few moments, the image in your Render Window should resemble Figure 13-41. Notice how the spotlight is treated more precisely in the rendered model. There are numerous ways to adjust this cone of light. We adjust two settings to achieve the softer lighting effect shown in Figure 13-42.

The Light List

The **Light list** tool on the dashboard opens a palette in which you can easily make changes to light characteristics. We open it to change the hotspot and intensity settings.

⊕ Close the Render Window and return to the Drawing window.

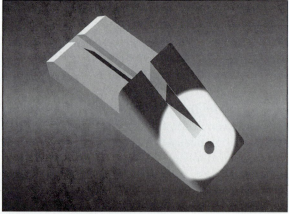

Figure 13-41

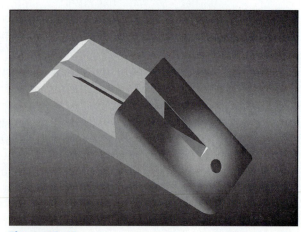

Figure 13-42

Figure 13-43

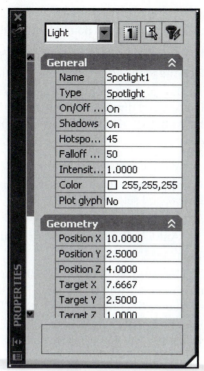

Figure 13-44

⊕ Click the Light list tool, to the right of the Sun status tool on the first line of the Light control panel.

This opens the Lights in Model palette shown in Figure 13-43. The name of your spotlight has been chosen by AutoCAD. It will be Spotlight1 or some other number.

⊕ Double-click the name of the spotlight.

This opens the Light Properties palette, shown in Figure 13-44. The first line of this palette gives you the opportunity to change the name. Here we leave it alone. The settings we change are on lines five and seven. The default spotlight cone has a large beam with a quick falloff. We shrink the hotspot and leave the falloff where it is. We also lessen the light intensity.

⊕ Click once in the Hotspot angle edit box.

⊕ Change the Hotspot specification to 20.

⊕ Click once in the Intensity edit box.

⊕ Change the Intensity setting to 0.5000.

⊕ Close the Light Properties palette.

⊕ With the right viewport active, click the Render tool.

In a few moments, your screen should resemble Figure 13-42, shown previously. Next we add a point light.

⊕ Press Esc, or click the AutoCAD drawing button on the Windows taskbar to return to the drawing.

Note:
Notice the small flashlight images that have been added to the drawing in all viewports. They indicate the placement of lights. They are called glyphs and can be turned on and off using the **Light glyphs** tool. It is second from the right on the lower part of the Light control panel.

Point Light

Point light works like a lightbulb with no shade. It radiates outward equally in all directions. The light from a point light attenuates over distance.

In this exercise, we place a point light right inside the slot of the wedge. This clearly shows the lightbulb effect of a small point of light radiating outward.

⊕ Make the upper left viewport active.

⊕ Pick the Point light tool from the Light control panel.

For a point light, you need to specify only a source location because point light has no direction other than outward from the source. AutoCAD gives you a light glyph to drag into place. The prompt is

```
Specify source location <0,0,0>:
```

We use the same point filtering system to locate this light.

⊕ At the prompt, type ".xy" ↵ or open the object snap shortcut menu, highlight Point Filters, and select .XY.

⊕ At the of prompt, pick point (4,2.5,0) in the top view.

AutoCAD prompts for a *z* value.

⊕ Type "1.25" ↵ for a *z* value.

Because the slot is at 1.00 from the XY plane, this puts the point light just above the bottom of the slot. This time around we use the dynamic input display to change the intensity. With point light there is no hotspot or falloff.

⊕ Select Intensity factor from the dynamic input display drop-down list.

⊕ Type "3" ↵ for the intensity level.

⊕ Press Enter to complete the light specification.

The effect of the point light appears immediately in the shaded image in the right viewport and top viewport.

⊕ Click in the right viewport to make it active.

⊕ Pick the Render tool.

Your rendered object should resemble Figure 13-45. In this image, you can clearly see the effect of the point light within the slot along with the spotlight falling on the right side of the object.

Distant Light

The last type of light is called distant light. We will not add a distant light to this model. Distant light is often used to achieve the effect of direct sunlight. Here we've used the **Sunlight** tool instead. In AutoCAD rendering, a distant light source emits beams of light that are parallel and travel in one direction only. Distant light does not attenuate. It is the same at any distance from the source. Distant light placement is defined by a directional vector; the command line prompt asks for a "to" point and a "from" point. You can define this vector precisely using point filters, as we have done previously. The to point will probably be on an object or in the XY plane. The from point will be above the XY plane. Most important is the angle and direction between the two points.

Sunlight Editing

Sunlight editing is easy and produces dramatic changes. The lower section of the Light control panel has an **Edit the Sun** tool on the right end of the first line. This tool opens a Sunlight Properties palette, which allows you direct access to many sunlight settings. But even more accessible are the two sliders for date and time on the second and third lines of the top section, as shown in Figure 13-46. We begin by adjusting the time of day, using the second slider.

⊕ With the right viewport active, click the slider on the Time adjustment scale, and drag it slowly left and right,

As you drag the slider, observe the changes in lighting in the viewport. As you would expect, nighttime hours will produce darkened results, whereas daylight hours will produce a wide range of sunlit effects. To achieve more control over the slider, use the arrow keys on your keyboard.

⊕ Select a point in the slider and use the arrow keys on your keyboard to take your slider to exactly 2:00 P.M.

⊕ Click the Render tool.

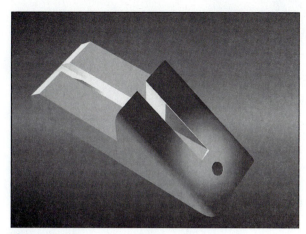

Figure 13-45

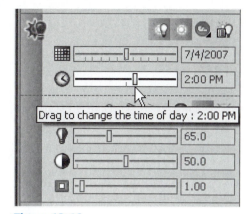

Figure 13-46

This is only a one-hour difference, but the effect is significant, as shown in Figure 13-47. You can also adjust dates and times directly by typing. Try this.

⊕ Double-click in the date edit box to the right of the first slider and type "7/4/2007."

You have adjusted your sunlight to July 4, 2007, at 2:00 P.M. The result is shown in Figure 13-48.

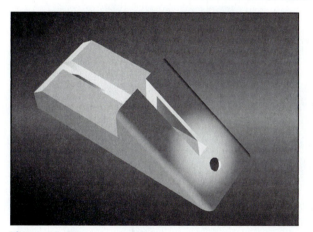

Figure 13-47

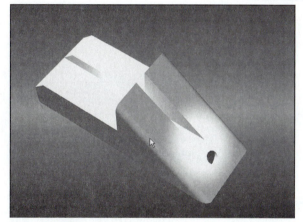

Figure 13-48

Attaching Materials

The last rendering technique we explore is the addition of materials and textures to a solid model. Materials can be created or selected from AutoCAD's materials library. Each material definition has its own characteristic color, texture, and response to light. Materials can also be created or modified. Changing an object's material dramatically affects the way it is rendered, so it usually makes sense to attach materials before adjusting light intensity and color. In this exercise, we take you through the procedure of loading materials from the AutoCAD library and attaching them to an object. When you experiment on your own, you see color effects that we cannot show in this book.

Your screen may become quite crowded as you open palettes to attach materials. It may make things a bit easier to return to a single viewport at this point.

⊕ With the right viewport active, select View → Viewports → 1 Viewport from the pull-down menu.

Below the Light control panel is the Materials control panel.

⊕ Click the Materials control panel icon on the left side of the dashboard, as shown in Figure 13-49.

This will open the tool palette window with several materials tabs visible, as shown in Figure 13-50.

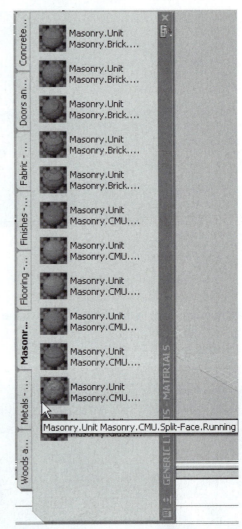

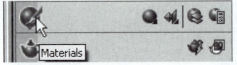

Figure 13-49   **Figure 13-50**

These palettes give access to the AutoCAD library of materials. There are eight tabs with categories of materials samples, beginning with Concrete and ending with Woods and Plastics. To see the list of tabs, pick the area of covered up tabs below the bottom tab. In order to achieve an effect that will reproduce well in gray tones, we have selected a Masonry sample.

⊕ Pick the set of "covered" tabs at the bottom of the visible tabs.

⊕ Select Masonry Materials Sample from the shortcut menu.

⊕ From the Masonry tab, select the second from the bottom sample, labeled Masonry, Unit Masonry, CMU, Split-Face, Running.

⊕ Move the cursor into the viewport drawing area.

In the drawing area, AutoCAD will show a paintbrush cursor and prompt for object selection.

⊕ Select the composite wedge.

The material and texture shown in Figure 13-51 will be added to your model.

⊕ Click the Render tool to complete the rendering.

Note:

If the attached material does not appear on your model, try clicking the Materials and Textures tool on the Materials control panel. It is the first tool on the first line. There are three settings: Materials on/Textures on, Materials on/Textures off, and Materials off/Textures off. Either of the latter two settings will not produce the results shown here.

Your screen should resemble Figure 13-51. Notice that the effect of the spot-light and point light are still visible with the materials attached.

Figure 13-51

Chapter Test Questions

Questions

1. What 3D solid objects and commands would you use to create a square nut with a bolt hole in the middle?
2. What AutoCAD feature allows you to draw outside the XY plane of the current UCS without the use of typed co-ordinates, object snap, or point filters?
3. Why is there a prompt for a base surface in **CHAMFER,** but not in **FILLET?**
4. AutoCAD allows you to drag the height of a solid primitive upward in the *z* direction. What is the major limitation of this method that caused us to type *z* values in this chapter?
5. Why do solid models have differently shaped grips? How is this useful?

6. Describe the effects of Union, Subtraction, and Intersection.
7. What are the five visual styles available in AutoCAD without customizing?
8. What is the difference between parallel and perspective projection? How do you switch between the two?
9. How would you use a point filter to place a spotlight 5.0 units above the point (3,5,0)?
10. What is a light glyph? How do you turn glyphs on and off?
11. What are the shapes and qualities of spotlights, point lights, and distant lights?
12. What is the procedure for saving a configuration of lights, light intensity, and point of view?

Drawing Problems

1. Open a new drawing with the acad3D prototype and change the snap setting to 0.25. You may wish to use two viewports, one with a 3D view and one with a plan view. Zoom in as needed.
2. Draw a solid wedge, with a 5.0 × 5.0 unit base and a height of 2.5.
3. Draw a 3.0 × 3.0 box with a height of 2.0, normal to the angled face of the wedge, with front left corner in 1.0 and over 1.0 from the two edges of the face of the wedge.

4. Draw a .75-radius cylinder with its base aligned and cen-tered at the center of the right front face of the box drawn in step 3. This cylinder should have a height of 7.0 ex-tending back through the box in the negative *z* direction of the DUCS aligned with the right front face of the box.
5. Draw a .50-radius cylinder with the same alignment and center point. This cylinder should have a height of 10.0 units extending in the same direction as the first cylinder.
6. Draw a .25-radius cylinder with height 13.0. Make it aligned and center with the previous two cylinders.

WWW Exercise 14 (Optional)

Complete the following:

⊕ Make sure that you are connected to your Internet service provider.

⊕ Type "browser" ↵ or open your system browser from the Windows taskbar.

⊕ If necessary, navigate to our companion website at prenhall.com/dixriley.

See you there.

CHAPTER PROJECTS

Drawing 13-1: Flange

We begin with three simple 3D models for this chapter. They will give you a feel for this whole new way of putting objects together on the screen. Look the objects over, and consider what primitive shapes and Boolean processes will be required to complete the models. In each case, the finished drawing is the 3D model itself. The orthographic views are presented to give the information you need to draw the solid models correctly. They may be included as part of your completed drawing, or your instructor may prefer that you just complete the model.

Drawing Suggestions

- You can complete this drawing with two commands.
- Begin with bottom of the flange in the XY plane, and draw three cylinders all with the same center point and different heights.
- Draw four .500-diameter holes on the quadrants of a 3.5 circle around the same center point.
- Subtract the middle cylinder and the four small cylinders to create the completed model.

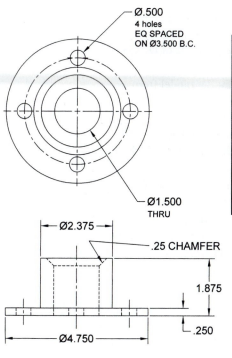

Ø.500
4 holes
EQ SPACED
ON Ø3.500 B.C.

Ø1.500
THRU

Ø2.375

.25 CHAMFER

1.875

.250

Ø4.750

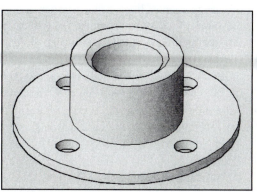

Flange
Drawing 13-1

Drawing 13-2: Link Mount

This drawing is very manageable with the techniques you learned in this chapter. When you have finished drawing this model, you may wish to experiment with adding materials, lights, and changing point of view.

Drawing Suggestions

- You will need a 0.25 snap for this drawing.

- Before you begin, notice what the model consists of and think ahead to how it will be constructed. You have a filleted 8×8 box at the base, with four cylindrical holes. A flat cylinder sits on top of this at the center. On top of the cylinder you have two upright boxes, filleted across the top and pierced through with 1.50-diameter cylindrical holes.

- Beginning the base box at (0,0,0) will make the coordinates easy to read in the WCS.

- After drawing the flat cylinder on top of the base, draw one upright box on the center line of the cylinder. Move it 0.5 left, and then make a copy 1.00 to the right. You will make frequent use of DUCS throughout the modeling process.

- Use Constrained orbit any time you need to view the model from a different angle. You may find you want to do this frequently, sometimes transparently in the middle of a command sequence.

- After drawing the base, the flat cylinder, and the upright boxes, add the four cylinders to the base and a single cylinder through the middle of the two upright boxes.

- Leave the subtracting of the cylinders until last. In particular, fillet the base and the upright boxes before you do any subtraction.

- All subtraction can be done in one step. When you do this, you will also create unions at the same time. Select the base, the flat cylinder, and the upright boxes as objects to subtract from. Select the other cylinders as objects to subtract. When you are done, the remaining object will be a single object.

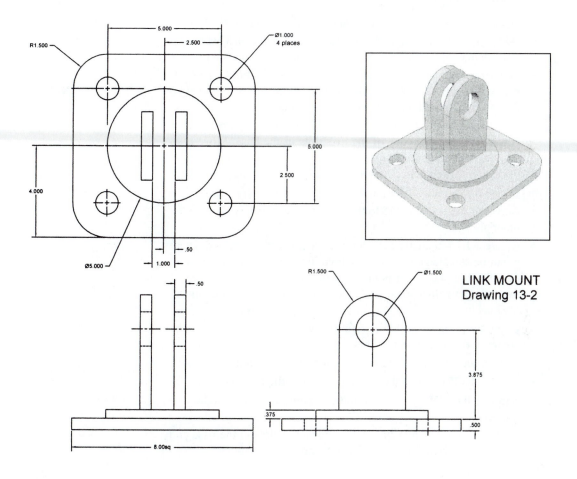

LINK MOUNT
Drawing 13-2

Drawing 13-3: Bushing Mount

This drawing gives you more practice in the techniques used in Drawing 13-2. The addition of the bushing is a primary difference. Although the geometry of the bushing can be used to create the hole in the mount, the mount and the bushing should be created and retained as separate objects.

Use an efficient sequence in the construction of all composite solids. In general, this means saving union, subtraction, and intersection operations until most of the solid objects have been drawn and positioned. This approach also allows you to continue to use the geometry of the parts for snap points as you position other parts.

Drawing Suggestions

- Use at least two views, one plan and one 3D, as you work.
- Begin with the bottom of the mount in the XY plane. This means drawing a 6.00 × 4.00 × 0.50 solid box sitting on the XY plane.
- Draw a second box, 1.50 × 4.00 × 50, in the XY plane. This becomes the upright section at the middle of the mount. Move it so that its own midpoint is at the midpoint of the base.
- Draw a third box, 1.75 × 0.75 × 0.50, in the XY plane. This is copied and becomes one of the two slots in the base. Move it so that the midpoint of its long side is at the midpoint of the short side of the base. Then, move it over 1.125 along the *x*-axis.
- Create 0.375-radius fillets at each corner of the slot.
- Copy the filleted box 3.75 to the other side of the base to form the other slot.
- Create a 1.25-diameter cylinder in the center of the mount, where it can be subtracted to create the hole in the mount upright. Using the DUCS at the center point of the upright mount, you can draw this cylinder with a height of 1.5 so that it can also be used to form the bushing.
- Copy the cylinder out to the right of the mount directly along the center line of the mount.
- Draw a second cylinder to form the top of the bushing.
- Draw a 0.375 cylinder through the center of the bushing.
- Subtract the .375 cylinder from the bushing to create the hole in the center.
- Subtract the boxes and cylinders to form the slots in the base and the bushing-sized cylinder to form the hole in the mount.

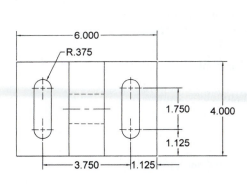

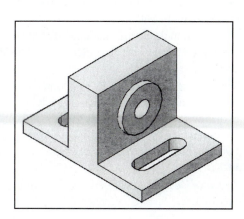

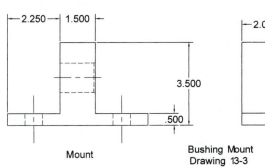

Mount

Bushing Mount
Drawing 13-3

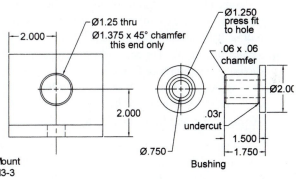

Bushing

Drawing 13-4: Picnic Table

This drawing is quite different from the previous three. It can be a challenge getting the legs correctly angled and in place. Still you will find that everything here can be done with techniques learned in this chapter.

Drawing Suggestions

- Use a three-viewport configuration, with top (plan) and front views on the left and a 3D view on the right. Be sure to keep an eye on all viewports as you go, because it is quite likely that you will create some objects that look correct in one view, but not in others.

- We recommend that you start with the XY plane at the bottom of the table legs and move everything up into the z direction. First draw nine 2″ × 6″ boards, 8′ long. You can draw one board and array the rest 1″ apart.

- The five middle boards that become the tabletop can be copied up 2′4″ in the z direction. The outer four boards that become the bench seats move up 1′4″.

- In the front view, draw a 2″ × 4″ brace even with the front edge of the table and the same width as the tabletop. Also draw the 2″ × 6″ board even with the front of the bench seats and stretching from the outer edge of one seat to the outer edge of the other. Copy these two braces to the other end of the table and then move each copy in 1′.

- Draw the center brace across the middle of the five tabletop boards.

- Draw a single 2″ × 6″ board extending down perpendicular to the tabletop. Draw it at the front edge of the table. This will later be moved to the middle of the table and become one of four legs. It will be trimmed, so draw it long: 3′ or more will do.

- Rotate the leg 30 degrees and use temporary 2″ × 6″ blocks as shown in the reference figure to trim the legs. These will be drawn overlapping the top and bottom of the leg and then subtracted to create the correctly angled leg.

- Mirror, Copy, and Move this leg to create the four table legs.

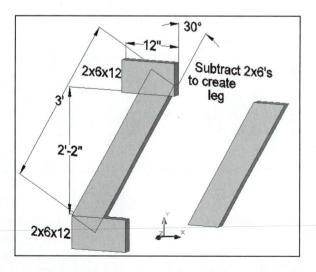

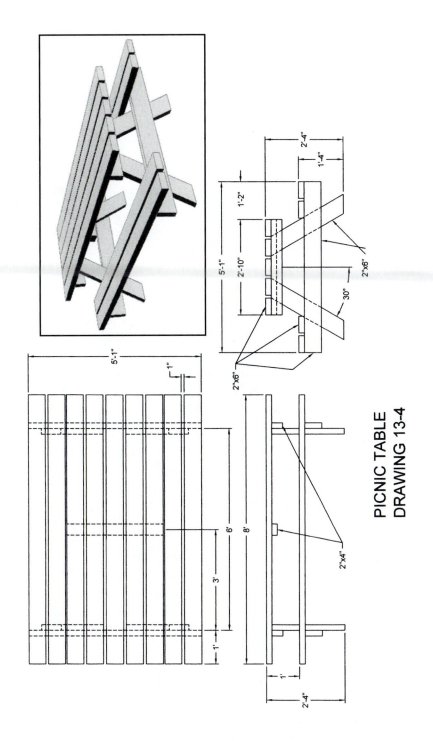

PICNIC TABLE
DRAWING 13-4

14

More Modeling Techniques and Commands

Chapter Objectives

- Drawing Polysolids
- Drawing Cones
- Drawing Pyramids
- Drawing Torus
- Slicing and Sectioning Solids
- Creating 3D Solids from 2D Outlines
- Adjusting Viewpoints with 3DORBIT
- Walking Through a 3D Landscape
- Creating an Animated Walk Through

INTRODUCTION

Chapter 13 gave you a thorough introduction to the primary methods involved in 3D solid modeling. In addition to these methods, AutoCAD has numerous other commands and techniques that facilitate the creation of particular 3D shapes. These include commands that produce regular 3D solid primitives, such as cones and spheres, and also commands that allow you to create 3D objects by revolving or extruding 2D outlines of 3D objects. These will be the focus of this final chapter. The addition of these techniques will make it possible for you to create all kinds of 3D models you could not create with the primitives introduced in Chapter 13.

14-1 DRAWING POLYSOLIDS

GENERAL PROCEDURE

1. Select the **Polysolid** tool from the dashboard.
2. Pick a start point or specify height or width.
3. Pick a second point, or type "a" to draw an arc.
4. Continue picking points or switching options.
5. Press **Enter** to end the command.

Most of this chapter is devoted to introducing commands for drawing shapes other than boxes, wedges, and cylinders. Some are created as simple solid primitives; others are derived from previously drawn lines and curves. In this first section we draw a polysolid. Polysolids are drawn just like 2D polylines, but they have a height as well as a width. Like polylines, they can have both straight line and arc segments. Ours will include both. But first, here are a few comments about drawing setup.

Drawing Setup

⊞ Create a new drawing using the acad3d template.

This should be familiar by now. You may have noticed that without the 1B template we used up until Chapter 13, we are back to redefining layers in every new drawing. In this chapter we continue to draw on Layer 0, but if you wish, you can create a new template for 3D modeling. The steps would be as follows:

1. Change Snap, Grid, Limits, and Units settings as you wish. If you change limits, Zoom all.
2. Open the DesignCenter.
3. Click the **Load** tool and navigate to the location of your template files. Typically this will be C:Documents and Settings\Owner\Local Settings\Application Data\Autodesk\Auto-CAD2007\R17.0\enu\Template.
4. When you get there, make sure that you select Drawing Template in the File type box.
5. Open 1B.
6. Select all Layers in the Content area.
7. Drag layers from the Content area into the drawing area.
8. When all layers have been brought into the new drawing, close the DesignCenter and save the drawing as a drawing template file with a new name, such as 3B.

As mentioned in Chapter 13, a major feature needed to draw effectively in 3D is the ability to view an object from several different points of view simultaneously as you work on it. Here we continue to use the 3D right viewport configuration introduced in Chapter 13.

⊞ Select View → Viewports → New Viewports from the pull-down menu.
⊞ Highlight Three: Right.
⊞ Open the Setup list and select 3D.
⊞ Click OK to exit the dialog box.
⊞ Click in the right viewport to make it active.
⊞ Turn on the grid in the right viewport.

We are now ready to begin drawing in this viewport configuration. Once you have defined viewports, any drawing or editing in the active viewport appears in all the viewports. As you draw, watch what happens in all viewports. You may need to zoom out and pan to get full views in each viewport.

⊞ Turn on Snap and Ortho.
⊞ Select the Polysolid tool from the dashboard, as shown in Figure 14-1.

AutoCAD prompts

COMMAND GRID	
Command	Polysolid
Alias	-
Menu	Draw > Modeling
Tool	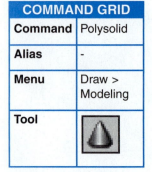

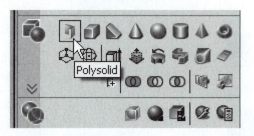

Figure 14-1

```
Specify start point or [Object/Height/Width/Justify] <Object>:
```

To ensure that your polysolid looks like ours, we will specify a height.

⊞ Right-click and select Height from the shortcut menu.
⊞ Type "4" ↵ for the height.

AutoCAD returns the original prompt.

⊞ Pick point (2.5,2.5,0) for a start point.

AutoCAD shows you a polysolid to drag. It will appear like a wall in the 3D viewport and can be stretched out, like drawing a line segment. With Ortho on it will stretch only orthogonally. AutoCAD prompts for the next point.

⊕ Pick the point (10,2.5,0) for the next point.

From here, you could continue to draw straight segments, but we switch to an arc.

⊕ Right-click and select Arc from the shortcut menu.

AutoCAD shows an arc segment and prompts for an endpoint. With Ortho on you can stretch in only two directions.

⊕ Pick the point (10,8,0) for the arc endpoint.

Now we switch back to a line segment.

⊕ Right-click and select Line from the shortcut menu.

AutoCAD shows a straight segment beginning at the endpoint of the arc and prompts for a next point.

⊕ Pick the point (2.5,8,0) for the next point.

Finally we will switch to arc again and then use the Close option to complete the polysolid.

⊕ Right-click and select Arc from the shortcut menu.

⊕ Type "c" ↵ to close.

Your screen should resemble Figure 14-2.

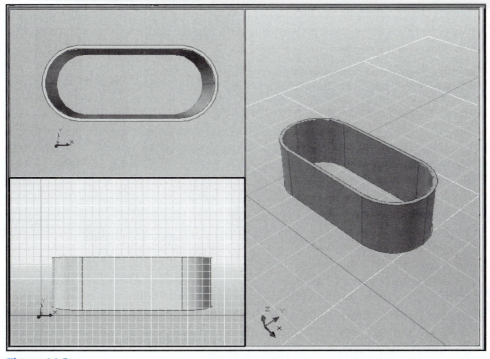

Figure 14-2

14-2 DRAWING CONES

GENERAL PROCEDURE	1. Select the **Cone** tool from the dashboard.
	2. Pick a center point for the base.
	3. Specify a base radius.
	4. Specify a height, or type "t" and specify a top radius and then specify a height.

Solid CONE Primitives

Cones are easily drawn by specifying a base and a height. The **CONE** command can also be used to draw flat-topped cones, called frustum cones, as we do in a moment.

⊞ Erase the polysolid from Section 14-1.

⊞ Select the Cone tool from the 3D Make control panel of the dashboard, as shown in Figure 14-3.

Figure 14-3

COMMAND GRID	
Command	Cone
Alias	-
Menu	Draw > Modeling
Tool	

AutoCAD prompts

    Specify center point of base or [3P/2P/Ttr/Elliptical]:

Notice the other options, including the option to create cones with elliptical bases.

You can specify the base in either the top viewport or the right viewport. Using the top viewport will give you a better view of the base and its coordinates.

⊞ Click in the top left viewport to make it active.

⊞ Pick point (5,5,0) for the center of the cone base.

AutoCAD prompts

                Specify base radius or [Diameter]:

⊞ In the top left viewport show a radius of 2.

AutoCAD draws a cone in each viewport and prompts for a height

        Specify height or [2Point/Axis endpoint/Top radius]:

⊞ Move the cursor and observe the cones in each viewport.

Notice the way the cone in the top viewport appears to tilt. This is a result of the perspective projection. If you change this viewport to parallel, you will see only the base circle, no matter what height you show.

⊞ Pick a point to indicate a height of 4.

The cone is complete and your screen will resemble Figure 14-4.

Frustum Cones

Next we create a cone with a negative z height and a different top radius.

⊞ Pick the Cone tool from the dashboard.

⊞ In the top left viewport, pick the point (10,5,0) for the base center.

⊞ As before, show a radius of 2.

Move the cursor and observe the cones in each viewport. We want to create a cone that drops down below the XY plane. Notice that we cannot do this in the active top view.

⊞ Click in the right viewport to make it active.

Drag the cone downward and notice the effects in the right and bottom left viewports. There will be no change in the top viewport.

We also want this cone to have a flat "top," so we need to specify this before specifying the height.

⊞ Type "t" ↵ for the top radius option.

AutoCAD prompts

                Specify top radius <0.0000>:

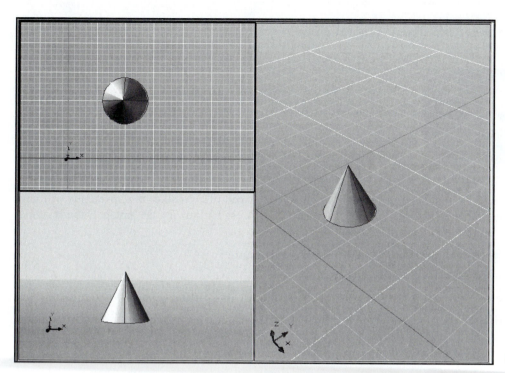

Figure 14-4

Move the cursor again to see the range of possibilities. You can create anything from a very large, wide, flat cone to a long narrow one. The top radius can be larger or smaller than the base radius. Also, the top can be below the base.

⊕ Type "5" ↵ for a top radius.

AutoCAD prompts again for a height.

⊕ Type "8" ↵ for a height.

Your screen resembles Figure 14-5.

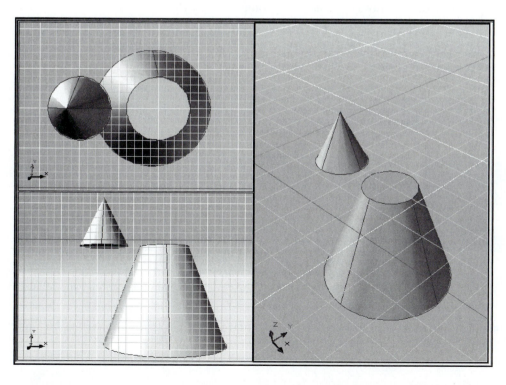

Figure 14-5

14-3 DRAWING PYRAMIDS

> **GENERAL PROCEDURE**
> 1. Select the **Pyramid** tool from the dashboard.
> 2. Specify number of sides.
> 3. Draw base.
> 4. Specify height or top radius and then height.

COMMAND GRID	
Command	Pyramid
Alias	Pyr
Menu	Draw > Modeling
Tool	

Drawing pyramids is much like drawing cones. Instead of a circular base, pyramids will have polygons at the base and possibly at the top. The process for drawing the base polygon is similar to the **POLYGON** command from Chapter 9.

⊕ Select the Pyramid tool from the dashboard.

AutoCAD prompts

```
Specify center point of base or [Edge/Sides]:
```

The default is a four-sided base. We will opt for six sides.

⊕ Right-click and select Sides from the shortcut menu.

AutoCAD prompts for the number of sides.

⊕ Type "6" ↵.

AutoCAD takes this information and repeats the initial prompt. If you pick a center point, it will then prompt for the inscribed or circumscribed polygon. Recall that for a circumscribed polygon the radius will be drawn out to a vertex; with inscribed it will be drawn to the midpoint of a side. We proceed with the Edge option instead.

⊕ Right-click and select Edge from the shortcut menu.

AutoCAD prompts for the first point of an edge.

⊕ Pick the point (13,3.5,0).

AutoCAD shows you a six-sided polygon base and prompts for the second point of the edge.

⊕ Pick the point (15,3.5,0).

AutoCAD draws the base and prompts for height:

```
Specify height or [2Point/Axis endpoint/Top radius] <8.0000>:
```

⊕ Make sure your screen shows the pyramid in the positive direction and type "4" ↵.

Your screen should resemble Figure 14-6.

14-4 DRAWING TORUS

> **GENERAL PROCEDURE**
> 1. Select the **Torus** tool from the dashboard.
> 2. Pick a center point.
> 3. Type or show an outside radius.
> 4. Type or show a tube radius

COMMAND GRID	
Command	Torus
Alias	Tor
Menu	Draw > Modeling
Tool	

Torus is another solid primitive shape that is easily drawn. It is like drawing a donut and requires an outer radius as well as a tube radius. Try this:

⊕ Pick the Torus tool from the 3D Make control panel. It is the tool at the far right on the top line, as shown in Figure 14-7.

AutoCAD prompts

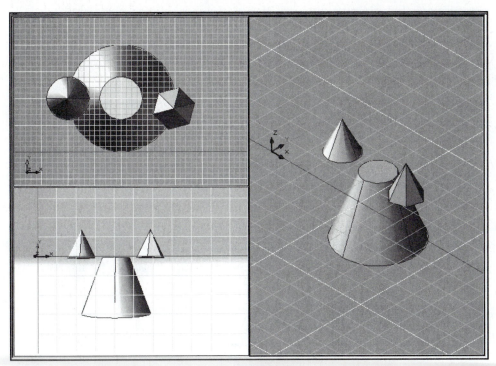

Figure 14-6

Figure 14-7

> Specify center point or [3P/2P/Ttr]:

The three point, two point, and tangent tangent radius options work just as they do in the **CIRCLE** command. We will place a torus behind and above the frustum cone.

⊕ Using an .xy point filter, specify (10,10,4) for a center point.

Notice the z coordinate of 4, which places the torus above the XY plane. AutoCAD prompts for a radius or diameter.

⊕ Show a radius of 2.

Now AutoCAD prompts for a second radius, the radius of the torus tube.

⊕ Show a radius of 0.5.

Your screen should resemble Figure 14-8.

14-5 SLICING AND SECTIONING SOLIDS

GENERAL PROCEDURE	1. Create solid objects.
	2. Select the **Slice** tool from the dashboard.
	3. Select objects to slice.
	4. Select points to define a slicing plane.

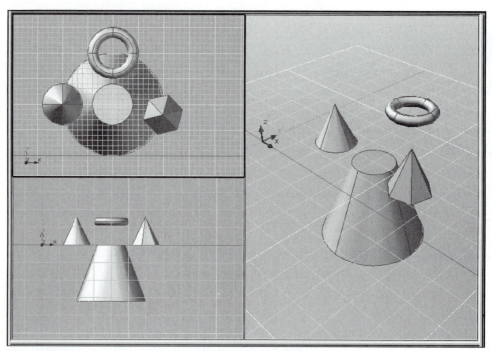

Figure 14-8

In addition to Boolean operations, there are other methods that create solid shapes by modifying previously drawn objects. In this section we will explore slicing and sectioning.

Slice

The **SLICE** command allows easy creation of objects by cutting away portions of objects on one side of a slicing plane. In this exercise we slice off the tops of a pyramid and a cone. For this purpose we will work in the front view in the lower left viewport.

⊕ Click once in the lower left viewport to make it active.

Notice the change in coloration at the base of the cone and pyramid in this viewport. This represents the XY plane in the world coordinate system, although the coordinate system in this front view has been rotated 90 degrees. Let's switch to a parallel projection in this viewport to make things clearer.

⊕ Pick the Parallel Projection tool.

Your screen should resemble Figure 14-9.

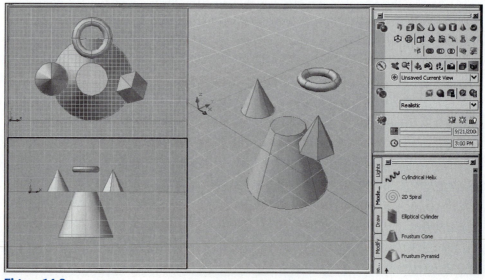

Figure 14-9

⊞ Check to see that Snap and Ortho are on.

⊞ Click the arrows at the bottom left of the 3D Make control panel at the top of the Dashboard.

    This will add a line to the control panel, as shown in Figure 14-10.

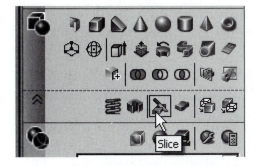

Figure 14-10

⊞ Select the Slice tool, as shown.

    AutoCAD prompts for objects.

⊞ Select the cone on the left and the pyramid on the right of the viewport.

⊞ Right-click to end object selection.

    AutoCAD prompts:

```
Specify start point of slicing plane or [planar
   Object/Surface/Zaxis/View/XY/YZ/ZX/3points]<3points>:
```

COMMAND GRID	
Command	Slice
Alias	S1
Menu	Modify > 3D Opera- tions
Tool	

This prompt allows you to define a plane by pointing, by selecting a planar object or surface of an object, or by using one of the planes of current coordinate system. We can specify a plane with two points in the front view.

⊞ Pick point (2.5,2.0) to the left of the cone.

⊞ Pick point (17.5,2.0) to the right of the pyramid.

    AutoCAD now has the plane defined but needs to know which side of the plane to cut.

    `Specify a point on desired side or [keep Both sides] <Both>:`

⊞ Pick a point below the specified plane.

    The tops of the cone and pyramid will be sliced off, as shown in Figure 14-11.

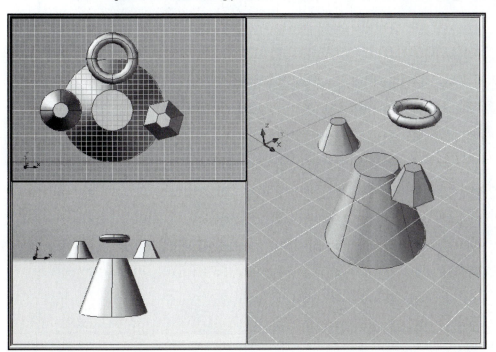

Figure 14-11

Section

Sectioning is accomplished by creating a section plane and then picking options from a shortcut menu. Here we create a section plane through three of the objects on your screen and then create 3D section images.

⊕ Click once in the top left viewport to make it active.

⊕ Select the Section Plane tool from the dashboard, as shown in Figure 14-12.

Figure 14-12

AutoCAD prompts

```
Select face or any point to locate section line or [Draw
                    section/Orthographic]:
```

We begin by using point selection.

⊕ Pick point (2.5,2.5).

AutoCAD shows a plane and prompts for a through point.

⊕ Pick point (12.5,12.5)

The section plane is drawn. Your screen should resemble Figure 14-13. At this point there is no image of the sectioning that this plane would create. To create section images, we select from a shortcut menu.

⊕ Select the section plane in any of the viewports.

A set of 3D grips will be added and the line used to create the plane will be highlighted.

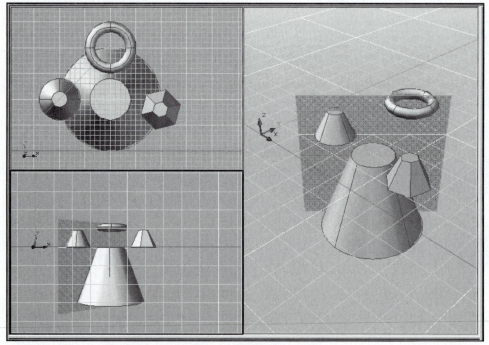

Figure 14-13

⊞ With the plane selected, right-click to open the shortcut menu shown in Figure 14-14.

Note the many options, including Rotate, Copy, Live sectioning (you can view section images as you move the section plane), and the option to create a jogged section. We use the option to generate a 3D section.

⊞ Select the Generate 2D/3D section option, as shown.

This opens the small dialog box shown in Figure 14-15.

⊞ Select the 3D Section button.

⊞ Click the Create button.

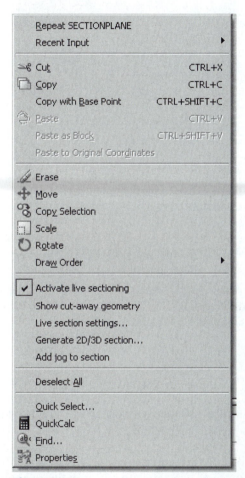

Figure 14-14

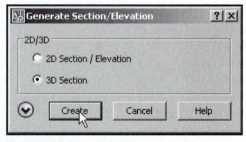

Figure 14-15

Three section images are created and can be dragged around in your viewports. Sections are like blocks and require a base point, scale factors, and rotation.

⊞ Click once in the right viewport to make it active.

⊞ Pick an insertion point behind the original objects, as shown by the placement of objects in Figure 14-16.

AutoCAD prompts for an *x* scale factor.

⊞ Press enter to specify the default scale factor of 1.

AutoCAD prompts for a *y* scale factor.

⊞ Press enter again to specify a *y* scale factor of 1.

AutoCAD prompts for a rotation.

⊞ Press Enter to retain the default 0 rotation.

Your right viewport will resemble Figure 14-16. The section images will not be visible in the other two viewports. Notice that the three section objects are treated

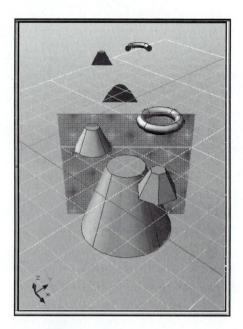

Figure 14-16

as a single object even though they are disconnected. The **EXPLODE** command can be used to separate them. Once exploded each part can be moved and edited like any other solid object on your screen.

14-6 CREATING 3D SOLIDS FROM 2D OUTLINES

An added level of flexibility in the creation of 3D objects is obtained through the use of commands that create 3D objects from 2D and 3D outlines. In this section we explore extruding, revolving, and sweeping 2D shapes to create complex 3D objects.

Extrude

⊕ To begin, erase all objects from your screen, or begin a new drawing using your 3B template.

⊕ For this section, also return to a single viewport by making the right viewport active, and then selecting View → Viewports → 1 Viewport from the pull-down menu.

You may want to work on the red Layer 1 for this section. This is not strictly necessary, but some 2D outlines will show up better in the red color of Layer 1.

⊕ If you wish, make Layer 1 current.

We begin by drawing a square and extruding it.

⊕ Open the Draw menu and select Rectangle.

⊕ Pick the point (5.0,5.0,0) for the first corner.

⊕ Pick the point (10.0,10.0,0) for the second corner.

⊕ Pick the Extrude tool from the dashboard, as shown in Figure 14-17.

AutoCAD prompts for objects to extrude.

⊕ Select the square.

⊕ Right-click to end object selection.

The **EXTRUDE** command will automatically convert the 2D square to a solid and give you an image to stretch in the positive or negative z direction. The prompts also allow you to extrude in a direction other than along the z axis by drawing a directional line or using a preexisting line as a path.

```
Specify height of extrusion or [Direction/Path/Taper angle]:
```

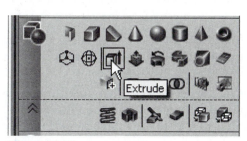

Figure 14-17

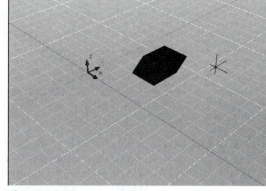

Figure 14-18

We will use the Direction option to create a slanted solid.

⊞ Right-click and select Direction from the shortcut menu.

AutoCAD prompts for the first point of a direction vector. The vector can be drawn anywhere.

⊞ Pick the point (12.5,12,5,0) for the start point.

To place the endpoint above the XY plane, we use a point filter.

⊞ At the prompt for an endpoint, type ".xy" ↵ for an XY point filter.

⊞ At the of prompt, pick the point (12.5,15.0,0).

⊞ At the need z prompt, type "2" ↵.

Your screen will resemble Figure 14-18. Before moving on to revolving, we demonstrate the technique of pressing and pulling solid objects.

Presspull

Presspull allows you to extend a solid object in a direction perpendicular to any of its faces.

⊞ Pick the Presspull tool from the dashboard, as shown in Figure 14-19.

AutoCAD prompts you to select a face. The prompt is

        Click inside bounded areas to press or pull.

⊞ Pick the front left face.

AutoCAD gives you an image to drag.

⊞ Pull in the positive and negative directions, perpendicular to the selected face.

⊞ With the object pulled in the positive direction, type "3" ↵.

Your screen should resemble Figure 14-20.

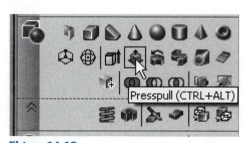

Figure 14-19

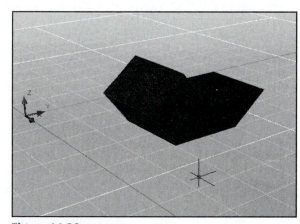

Figure 14-20

Revolve

The **REVOLVE** command creates a 3D solid by continuous extension of a 2D shape along the path of a circle or arc around a specified axis. Here we draw a rectangle and revolve it 180 degrees to create an arc-shaped model. Along the way we also demonstrate how a 2D object can be converted to a 3D planar surface.

⊞ Open the Draw menu and select Rectangle.

⊞ Pick the point (15,5,0) for the first corner point.

⊞ Pick the point (17.5,10,0) to create a 2.5 by 5.0 rectangle.

Next we use the **Convert to surface** tool to make this a rectangular surface rather than a wireframe outline. Note that this is for demonstration only. As in the **EXTRUDE** command, you can create a 3D solid directly from a 2D outline with the **REVOLVE** command.

⊞ Click the Convert to surface tool from the lower section of the 3D Make control panel from the dashboard, as shown in Figure 14-21.

Notice that there is also a **Convert to solid** button, which will convert a model made of 3D surfaces to a solid model. AutoCAD prompts for object selection.

⊞ Select the rectangle.

⊞ Press Enter to end object selection.

The rectangle will become a 3D surface and your screen will resemble Figure 14-22.

⊞ Pick the Revolve tool from the dashboard, as shown in Figure 14-23.

AutoCAD prompts for objects to revolve.

Figure 14-21

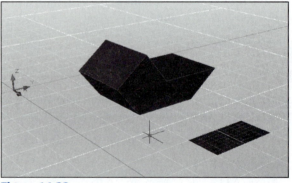

Figure 14-22

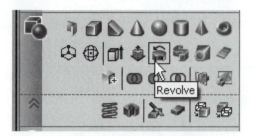

Figure 14-23

⊞ Select the rectangle.

⊞ Right-click to end object selection.

AutoCAD gives several options for defining an axis of rotation.

```
Specify axis start point or define axis by [Object/X/Y/Z] <Object>:
```

You can give start points and endpoints, select a line or polyline that has been previously drawn, or use one of the axes of the current UCS.

⊞ Pick the point (20,0,0) for a start point.

⊞ Pick the point (20,12.5,0) for an endpoint.

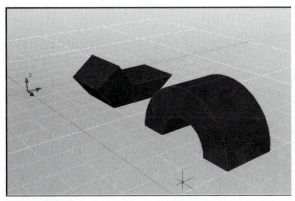

Figure 14-24

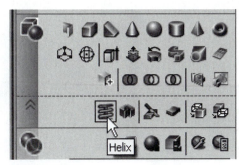

Figure 14-25

Next AutoCAD needs to know how much revolution you want. The default would be a full 360 circle.

```
Specify angle of revolution or [STart angle] <360>:
```

Here we start at the horizon, 0 degrees, and revolve through 180 degrees, placing both ends of the arc on the XY plane.

⊕ Right-click and select Start angle from the shortcut menu.

AutoCAD prompts

```
Specify Start Angle <0.0>:
```

⊕ Press Enter to accept the default start angle, or type 0 if your angle has been changed.

AutoCAD now prompts for an angle of revolution.

⊕ Type "180" ↵.

In a moment the revolved solid will be created and your screen will resemble Figure 14-24.

Helix

We have two more techniques to demonstrate before moving on. First we use the **HELIX** command to create a 3D spiral outline; then we use the **SWEEP** command to convert the helix to a solid coil.

⊕ Pick the Helix tool from the lower section of the 3D Make control panel of the dashboard, as shown in Figure 14-25.

Helix characteristics can be changed using the **Properties Manager.** Among the default specifications are two shown in the prompt area. Number of turns will be the number of times the spiral shape goes around within the height you specify. The twist will be either counterclockwise or clockwise.

```
Number of turns = 3.0000 Twist = CCW
Specify center point of base:
```

⊕ Pick the point (12.5,-5.0,0) for the center point of the helix base.

AutoCAD prompts for a base radius:

```
Specify base radius or [Diameter] <1.0000>:
```

The default will be retained from any previous usage of the command in the current drawing session.

⊕ Type "2.5" ↵ or pick two points to show a radius of 2.5000.

AutoCAD now prompts for a top radius, showing that you can taper the helix to a different top height, similar to the **CONE** and **PYRAMID** commands. We specify a smaller top radius.

⊕ Type "1" ↵ or pick two points to show a radius of 1.0000.

AutoCAD prompts for a height.

⊕ Type "4" ↵ or pick two points to show a height of 4.0.

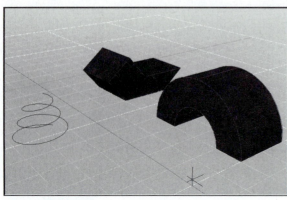

Figure 14-26

Figure 14-27

The helix is drawn, as shown in Figure 14-26. We have removed our ucsicon for clarity.

The SWEEP Command

Finally we sweep a circle through the helix path to create a solid coil.

⊕ Select Draw → Circle → Center, Radius from the pull-down menu.

⊕ Anywhere on your screen, create a circle of radius 0.5.

⊕ Pick the Sweep tool on the dashboard, as shown in Figure 14-27.

   AutoCAD prompts for objects to sweep.

⊕ Select the circle.

⊕ Right-click to end object selection.

   AutoCAD prompts

   `Select sweep path or [Alignment/Base point/Scale/Twist]:`

The default is to select a path, such as the helix. By default the object being swept will be aligned perpendicular to the sweep path. The Alignment option can be used to alter this. Base point allows you to start the sweep at a point other than the beginning of the sweep path. Scale allows you to change the scale of the objects being swept. By default the object being swept will remain perpendicular to the path at every point. To vary this and create a more complex sweep, use the Twist option. Here we use the default sweep path.

⊕ Select the helix.

   Your screen should resemble Figure 14-28.

That completes this section on modeling techniques. In the final three sections we demonstrate the Free and Continuous modes of the **3DORBIT** command, the use of **CAMERA** and **WALK** commands to move your point of view through the 3D landscape, and **ANIPATH** to create an animated walk though.

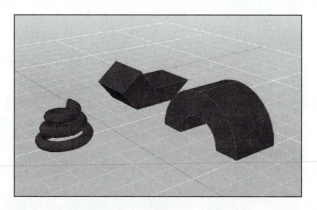

Figure 14-28

14-7 Adjusting Viewpoints with 3DORBIT

GENERAL PROCEDURE	1. Center objects within the viewport. 2. Select objects for viewing. 3. Select 3D Orbit from the **View** menu. 4. Dynamically adjust viewpoint and shading.

The **3DORBIT** command is a dramatic method for adjusting 3D viewpoints and images. **3DORBIT** has many options and works in three distinct modes. You have previously used Constrained Orbit, the simplest mode. Here we explore Free Orbit and Continuous Orbit and call your attention to some of the other features available on the **3DORBIT** shortcut menu. Using standard views such as top, front, and isometric views is generally all you need for the creation and editing of objects, and sticking with these views keeps you well grounded and clear about your position in relation to objects on the screen. However, when you move from drawing and editing into presentation, you find **3DORBIT** vastly more satisfying and freeing than the static viewpoint options.

The set of models created in the last section will work well for a demonstration of **3DORBIT.**

3DORBIT makes use of a tool called an arcball, as shown in Figure 14-29. The center of the arcball is the center of the current viewport. Therefore, to place your objects near the center of the arcball, you must place them near the center of the viewport; or, more precisely, you must place the center point of the objects at the center of the display.

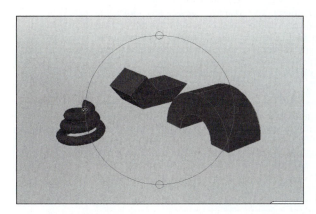

Figure 14-29

⊕ If necessary, use Zoom Center or Pan to adjust objects so that they are roughly centered on the center of the viewport.

⊕ Turn off the grid.

Before entering **3DORBIT** you can select viewing objects. **3DORBIT** performance is improved by limiting the number of objects used in viewing. Whatever adjustments are made to the viewpoint on the selected objects are applied to the viewpoint on the entire drawing when the command is exited. In our case, we have fairly simple objects to view, so we can use the whole drawing.

⊕ Select View → Orbit → Free Orbit from the pull-down menu.

Your screen is redrawn with the arcball surrounding your surface model, as shown in Figure 14-29.

The Arcball and Rotation Cursors

The arcball is a somewhat complex image, but it is very easy to use once you get the hang of it. It also gives you a more precise handle on what is happening than the Constrained Orbit mode. We already know that the center of the arcball is the center of the viewport, or the center of the drawing area in this case because we are working in a single viewport. AutoCAD uses a camera–target analogy to explain viewpoint adjustment. Your viewpoint on the drawing is called the *camera position.* The point at which the camera is aimed is called the *target.* In **3DORBIT,** the target point is fixed at the center of the arcball. As you change viewpoints, you are moving yourself around in relation to this fixed target point.

There are four modes of adjustment, which we take up one at a time. Each mode has its own cursor image, and the mode you are in depends on where you start in relation to the arcball. Try the following steps:

⊞ Carefully move the cursor into the small circle at the left quadrant of the arcball, as shown in Figure 14-29.

When the cursor is placed within either the right or the left quadrant circle, the horizontal rotation cursor appears. This cursor consists of a horizontal elliptical arrow surrounding a small sphere, with a vertical axis running through the sphere. Using this cursor creates horizontal motion around the vertical axis of the arcball. This cursor and the others are shown in Figure 14-30.

⊞ With the cursor in the left quadrant circle and the horizontal cursor displayed, press the pick button and hold it down.

⊞ Slowly drag the cursor from the left quadrant circle to the right quadrant circle, observing the model and the 3D UCS icon as you go.

As long as you keep the pick button depressed, the horizontal cursor is displayed.

3D ORBIT CURSOR	
CURSOR	DESCRIPTION
HORIZONTAL	Horizontal cursor icon displays when you move the cursor over one of the small circles on the left or right of the arcball. Clicking and dragging from either of these points rotates the view around the vertical axis that extends through the center of the arcball. The vertical axis is located on the cursor by a vertical line.
VERTICAL	Vertical cursor icon displays when you move the cursor over one of the small circles on the top or bottom of the arcball. Clicking and dragging from either of these points rotates the view around the horizontal axis that extends through the center of the arcball. The horizontal axis is located on the cursor by a horizontal line.
ROLL	Roll cursor icon displays when you move the cursor outside the arcball. Clicking outside the arcball and dragging the cursor around the arcball moves the view around an axis that extends through the center of the arcball, perpendicular to the screen. This is called a roll.
FREE ROTATION	Free rotation cursor icon displays when you move the cursor inside the arcball. Clicking inside the arcball and dragging the cursor around manipulates the view freely. It works as if your cursor were grabbing a sphere surrounding the objects and dragging the sphere around the target point. You can drag horizontally, vertically, and diagonally.
3DCORBIT	Continuous orbit cursor displays when you select it from the shortcut menu under (more). Click in the drawing area and drag the cursor in any direction to get the objects moving in the direction that you specify. The speed of the cursor movement determines the speed at which the objects spin.

Figure 14-30

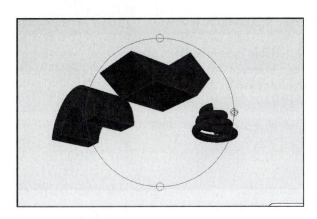

Figure 14-31

⊕ With the cursor in the right quadrant circle, release the pick button.

　　You have created a 180-degree rotation. Your screen should resemble Figure 14-31.

⊕ With the cursor in the right quadrant circle and the horizontal cursor displayed, press the pick button again and then move the cursor slowly back to the left quadrant circle.

　　You have moved the image roughly back to its original position. Now try a vertical rotation.

⊕ Move the cursor into the small circle at the top of the arcball.

　　The vertical rotation cursor appears. When this cursor is visible, rotation is around the horizontal axis, as shown in the chart in Figure 14-30.

⊕ With the vertical rotation cursor displayed, press the pick button and drag down toward the circle at the lower quadrant.

⊕ This time, do not release the pick button, but continue moving down to the bottom of the screen.

　　The viewpoint continues to adjust and the vertical cursor is displayed as long as you hold down the pick button. Notice that 3D Orbit uses the entire screen, not just the drawing area. You can drag all the way down through the command line, the status bar, and the Windows taskbar.

⊕ Spend some time experimenting with vertical and horizontal rotation.

　　Note that you always have to start in a quadrant to achieve horizontal or vertical rotation. What happens when you move horizontally with the vertical cursor displayed or vice versa? How much rotation can you achieve in one pick-and-drag sequence vertically? What about horizontally? Are they the same amount? Why is there a difference?

⊕ When you have finished experimenting, try to rotate the image back to its original position, shown previously in Figure 14-29.

　　If you are unable to get back to this position, don't worry. We show you how to do this easily in a moment. Now let's try the other two modes.

⊕ Move the cursor anywhere outside the arcball.

　　With the cursor outside the arcball you can see the roll icon, the third icon in the chart in Figure 14-30. Rolling creates rotation around an imaginary axis pointing directly toward you out of the center of the arcball.

⊕ With the roll icon displayed, press the pick button and drag the cursor in a wide circle well outside the circumference of the arcball.

　　Notice again that you can use the entire screen, outside of the arcball.

⊕ Try rolling both counterclockwise and clockwise.

⊕ Release the pick button and then start again.

　　Note that you must be in the drawing area with the roll icon displayed to initiate a roll and that you must stay outside the arcball.

Finally, try the free rotation cursor. This is the most powerful, and therefore the trickiest form of rotation. It is also the same as the Constrained Orbit mode. The free cursor appears when you start inside the arcball or when you cross into the arcball while rolling. It allows rotation horizontally, vertically, and diagonally, depending on the movement of your pointing device.

⊞ Move the cursor inside the arcball and watch for the free rotation icon.

⊞ With the free rotation icon displayed, press the pick button and drag the cursor within the arcball.

Make small movements vertically, horizontally, and diagonally. What happens if you move outside the arcball?

There is less room to work with the free icon, but it gives you a less restricted type of rotation. Making small adjustments seems to work best. Imagine that you are grabbing the objects and turning them a little at a time. Release the pick button and grab again. You might need to do this several times to reach a desired position.

⊞ Try returning the image to approximate the southeast isometric view before proceeding.

You have now explored all of the rotation modes of the **3DORBIT** command. Next we move on to some other options readily available in this powerful command. Leave everything as is on your screen. It is best to continue without leaving the **3DORBIT** command.

3DORBIT is more than an enhanced viewpoint command. While you work within the command you can adjust visual styles, projections, and even create a continuous motion effect. **3DORBIT** options are accessed through the shortcut menu shown in Figure 14-32. We explore these from the bottom up, looking at the lower two panels and one option from the second panel.

⊞ Right-click anywhere in the drawing area to open the shortcut menu.

Preset and Reset Views

In the second from the bottom panel, there is a Preset Views option that provides convenient access to the standard 10 orthographic and isometric viewpoints we have encountered in this chapter and the last, so that these views can be accessed without leaving the command. Above this is a Reset View option. This option quickly returns you to the view that was current before you entered **3DORBIT.** This is a great convenience, because you can get pretty far out of adjustment and have a difficult time finding your way back.

⊞ Select Reset View from the shortcut menu.

Regardless of where you have been within the **3DORBIT** command, your viewpoint is immediately returned to the view shown previously in Figure 14-29. If you have left **3DORBIT,** the view is reset to whatever view was current before you reentered the command. If you have attempted to return to this view manually using the cursors, you can see that there is still a slight adjustment to return your viewpoint to the precise view.

Visual Aids and Visual Styles

⊞ Right-click to open the shortcut menu again.

On the bottom panel, you can see Visual Styles and Visual Aids selections. Highlighting Visual Aids opens a submenu with three options: Compass, Grid, and UCS icon. The Grid option is useful for turning the grid on and off without leaving the command. The Compass adds an adjustable gyroscope-style image to the arcball. There are three rings of dashed ellipses showing the planes of the x-, y-, and z-axes of the current UCS. Try this if you like. We do not find it particularly helpful.

The third option on the submenu turns the 3D UCS icon on and off.

Highlighting Visual Styles opens a submenu with the four 3D visual styles: Hidden, Wireframe, Conceptual, and Realistic. We have been working in the Realistic style. Here you can change styles without leaving the command.

Figure 14-32

Continuous Orbit

Continuous orbit might or might not be the most useful feature of AutoCAD, but it is probably the most dramatic and the most fun. With continuous orbit you can set objects in motion that continues when you release the pick button.

⊞ If necessary, right-click to open the shortcut menu.

⊞ Highlight Other Navigation Modes in the second panel.

This opens a submenu shown in Figure 14-33. We explore some of the Camera and Walk and Fly options in the next section. Continuous Orbit, like Free Orbit and Constrained Orbit, can also be initiated directly from the **View** menu. The command is **3DCORBIT.**

⊞ Select Continuous Orbit from the submenu.

The arcball disappears and the continuous orbit icon is displayed, consisting of a sphere surrounded by two ellipses, as shown in Figure 14-34. The concept is simple: Dragging the cursor creates a motion vector. The direction and speed of the vector is applied to the model to set it in rotated motion around the target point. Motion continues until you press the pick button again.

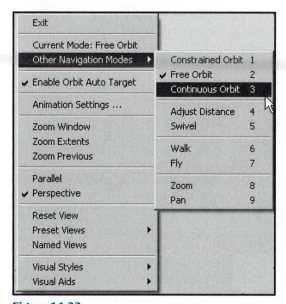

Figure 14-33   **Figure 14-34**

⊞ With the continuous orbit cursor displayed, press and hold the pick button, then drag the cursor at a moderate speed in any direction.

We cannot illustrate the effect, but if you have done this correctly, your model should now be in continuous rotation. Try it again.

⊞ Press and hold the pick button at any time to stop rotation.

⊞ Press and hold the pick button again and drag the cursor in a different direction, at a different speed.

⊞ Press and hold the pick button to stop rotation.

⊞ Press the pick button, drag, and release again.

Now try changing directions without stopping.

⊞ While the model is spinning, press and hold the pick button and drag in another direction.

Have a ball. Experiment. Play. Try to create gentle, controlled motions in different directions. Try to create fast spins in different directions. Try to create diagonal, horizontal, and vertical spins.

One more trick before we move on:

TIP The best way to achieve control over continuous orbit is to pick a point actually on the model and imagine that you are grabbing it and spinning it. It is much easier to communicate the desired speed and direction in this way. Note the similarity between the action of continuous orbit and the free rotation or constrained orbit icon. The grabbing and turning is the same, but continuous orbit keeps moving when you release the pick button, whereas free rotation stops. Also notice that however complex your dragging motion is, continuous orbit registers only one vector, the speed and direction of your last motion before releasing the pick button.

⊕ Set your model into a moderate spin in any direction.

⊕ With your model spinning, right-click to open the shortcut menu.

You might have a momentary hesitation, but the model keeps spinning. Many of the shortcut menu options can be accessed without disrupting continuous orbit.

⊕ Select Reset View from the shortcut menu.

The model makes an immediate adjustment to the original view and continues to spin without interruption.

⊕ Open the shortcut menu again.

⊕ Highlight Visual Styles and select Conceptual.

The style is changed and the model keeps spinning. Pretty impressive.

⊕ When you are done playing, press the pick button without moving for a moment to stop Continuous orbit.

⊕ Press Enter, Esc, or the spacebar to exit 3DORBIT.

You return to the command prompt, but any changes you have made in point of view and visual style are retained.

14-8 WALKING THROUGH A 3D LANDSCAPE

GENERAL PROCEDURE	1. Create 3D Solid and Surface Objects.
	2. Specify camera and target location.
	3. Select Walk or Fly from the **View** menu.
	4. Use arrow keys to navigate through 3D space.

AutoCAD has features that allow you to move your point of view through the 3D space of a drawing. This is particularly useful in architectural drawings in which you can create a simulated walk through of a model. In this section we demonstrate the use of the **WALK** command to navigate through the objects on your screen. The process involves creating a camera and a target and then using arrow keys to move the camera. Our goal will be to make it possible to navigate under the cylinder, as if we were walking under an arch.

Camera and Target

The first step will involve creating camera and target locations.

⊕ To begin, you should be in the drawing created in the previous sections, as shown in Figure 14-28.

If you are not in this exact view, it does not matter because these procedures will change your viewpoint anyway.

⊕ Turn on the grid.

⊕ Pick the Create Camera tool on the 3D Navigate control panel of the dashboard, as shown in Figure 14-35.

AutoCAD prompts for a camera location. We will start with a location on the axis of the cylinder.

Figure 14-35

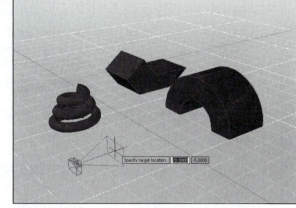

Figure 14-36

⊞ Pick the point (20,-10), as shown by the camera icon in Figure 14-36.

AutoCAD now prompts for a target location. In our case we want to point the camera along the axis of the cylinder. The distance to the target is not significant. AutoCAD shows the target with an image representing an expanding field of vision in the direction specified.

⊞ Pick the point (20,-5), as shown by the field of vision symbols in Figure 14-36.

AutoCAD shows you a set of options on the **Dynamic Input** menu in Figure 14-37. We choose the View option, which will change our display to align with the camera's point of view on the target.

⊞ Select View from the Dynamic Input menu.

With another small menu, AutoCAD asks us to verify that we wish to switch to the camera view.

⊞ Select Yes from the menu.

This completes the command and switches your view to the camera view shown in Figure 14-38. We have panned slightly to bring the complete cylindrical arc onto the screen. We are now ready to proceed with our walk.

The 3DWalk and 3DFly Commands

The **WALK** and **FLY** commands use identical procedures, but **3DWALK** keeps you in the XY plane, whereas **3DFLY** allows you to move above or below the plane. Here we enter **3DWALK,** walk through the arch, turn left toward the other objects, then turn around and walk back between the objects.

⊞ Pick the Walk tool from the 3-D Navigate control panel of the dashboard, as shown in Figure 14-39.

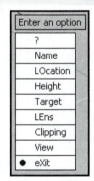

Figure 14-37

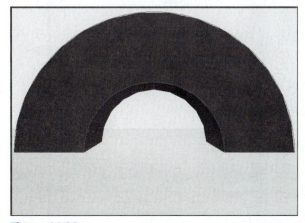

Figure 14-38

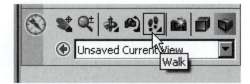

Figure 14-39

You may see the Walk and Fly Navigation mappings message box shown in Figure 14-40. This box tells you to use the arrow keys for forward, back, left, and right motion; the mouse for turning motion, and the F key to toggle between Walk and Fly. If you simply close this message, it will continue to appear each time you enter the **WALK** or **FLY** command. If you don't want to see it, you can check the box in the lower left corner.

⊕ Close the mappings message box.

AutoCAD shows the Position Locator palette in Figure 14-41. This palette shows a plan view of the objects in the drawing with a red square representing the

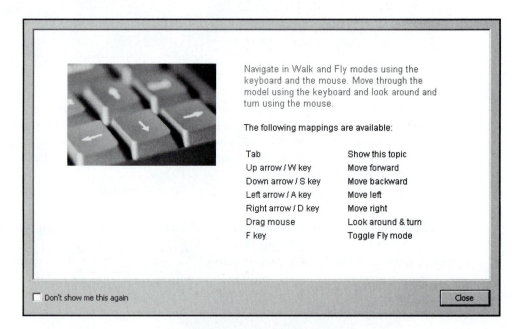

Figure 14-40

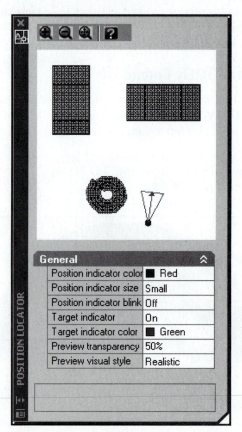

Figure 14-41

camera position and a green triangle representing the target and field of vision. We use the forward arrow to move through the arch. Notice that AutoCAD also positions a green cross on the screen, indicating the target position.

⊕ Press the up arrow key once to move forward.

You move a "step" closer to the arch. Notice also that the camera and target image move forward on the Position Locator palette.

⊕ Continue pressing the up arrow and observing the screen image as well as the Position Locator.

⊕ Walk through the arch until you reach the other side. At this point the camera location image on the Position Locator should be completely beyond the arch, as shown in Figure 14-42.

⊕ Press the left arrow and observe the Position Locator Palette.

You will see no change in the drawing area, but the camera and target image will shift to the left on the palette.

⊕ Press the left arrow again.

Notice that the camera image continues to move to the left, but the target is still straight ahead.

⊕ Continue moving to the left until the camera and target image is between the cylinder and the boxes to the left.

⊕ Move the cursor over the upper left corner of the green triangle representing the field of vision.

When the cursor is in this position it will appear with a hand icon, as used in the **PAN** command.

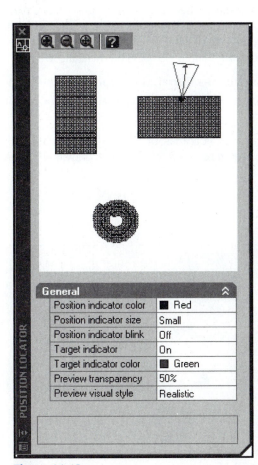

Figure 14-42

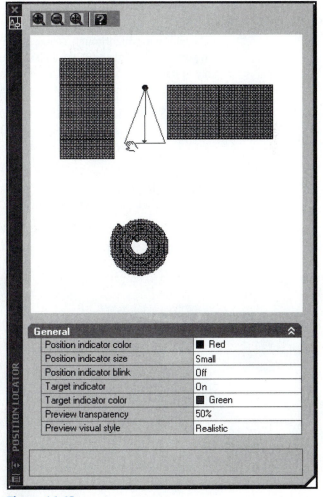

Figure 14-43

⊕ With the Pan icon showing and resting on the top left corner of the triangle, press and hold the pick button, and drag the triangle around 180 degrees.

Your camera is now pointing toward the coil. Your screen should resemble Figure 14-43.

⊕ Continue using the arrow keys and the mouse along with the Pan cursor to move through the objects on your screen.

In particular you should continue to explore the action of the Pan cursor in the Position Locator palette. You can use it to change both camera and target locations.

⊕ When you are done, press Enter to exit the command.

The objects will remain in whatever view you have created. Of course, you can return to your previous view using the **U** command.

14-9 CREATING AN ANIMATED WALK THROUGH

GENERAL PROCEDURE	1. Draw an animation path. 2. Select Motion Path Animations from the **View** menu. 3. In the Camera panel or the **Motion Path Animations** dialog box, pick the **Select Path** button. 4. Select the desired animation path in the drawing area. 5. Adjust the Duration. 6. Preview the animation. 7. Click **OK** to save the animation to a WMV file.

The ability to walk through a landscape is impressive, but for presentation purposes it may be more important to have the walk through animated so that any potential client can see the view without having to interact with AutoCAD. Here we create a simple animation of a walk through that is slightly different from the one we did manually in the last section. We begin by switching to a plan view.

⊕ Select View → 3D Views → Plan View → Current UCS from the pull-down menu.

Regardless of what was in your view previously, you should now be in the plan view shown in Figure 14-44.

Animations follow paths specified by Lines, Polylines, or 3D Polylines. For our purposes we will draw the simple polyline path shown in Figure 14-45. First we will draw it with right angles and then fillet one corner, as shown.

⊕ Select Polyline from the Draw menu.

⊕ Pick the point (20,-5) for a start point.

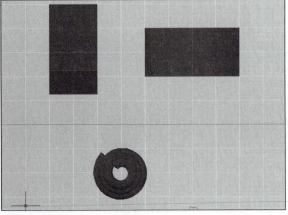

Figure 14-44

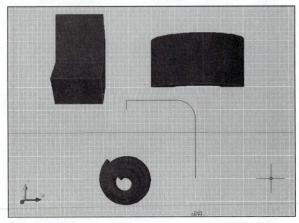

Figure 14-45

⊕ Pick the point (20,3.5) for the next point.

⊕ Pick the point (12.5,3.5) for the next point.

⊕ Pick the point (12.5,2.5) for the final point.

⊕ Press Enter to complete the polyline and exit the command.

> Now we fillet the right corner to complete the path. The fillet will have a significant impact on the animation.

⊕ Type "F" ↵ or select Fillet from the Modify menu.

⊕ Type "r" ↵ for the Radius option.

⊕ Type "2" ↵ for a radius specification.

⊕ At the prompt for a first object, select the vertical line segment on the right.

⊕ At the prompt for a second object, select the horizontal segment.

> Your screen should resemble Figure 14-45.
> We are now ready to create an animation.

⊕ Open the View menu and select Motion Path Animations.

> This opens the Motion Path Animations dialog box shown in Figure 14-46.

⊕ In the dialog box, pick the Select Path button on the right side of the Camera panel.

> The dialog box disappears, giving you access to the drawing area.

⊕ Select the polyline.

> The polyline is selected and AutoCAD asks for a Path Name, as shown in Figure 14-47.

⊕ Click OK to accept the default name (Path1).

> This brings you back to the dialog box. We make one more critical adjustment.

⊕ In the Animation settings panel on the right, change the Duration setting to 15.

> Without changing this setting the animation will move very quickly, and it will be difficult to see what is happening.

⊕ Click the Preview button on the bottom left of the dialog box.

> AutoCAD shows you an animation preview. Watch closely. What you see will be an animation based on moving a camera along the specified path. Notice the difference between the gentle turn along the fillet path and the abrupt turn

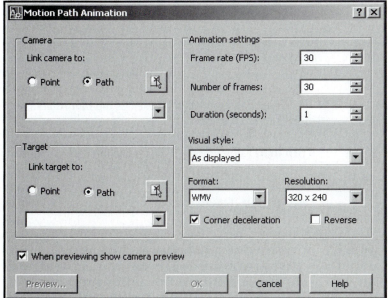

Figure 14-46

Figure 14-47

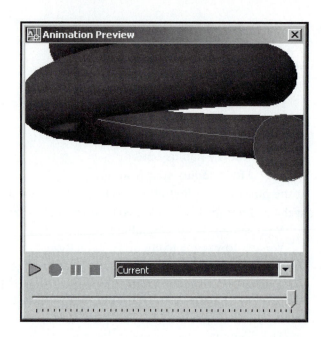

Figure 14-48

at the right angle. When the animation is done, your Animation Preview box should resemble Figure 14-48. Closing the Preview takes you back to the dialog box, where you can continue to modify and preview the animation, or save it to a WMV file.

⊞ Click the X in the upper right corner to close the Animation Preview.

At this point you can Cancel the animation and return to your drawing, or click **OK** to save it. If you click **OK,** AutoCAD will initiate a process of creating a video. It will be saved as a WMV file that can be played back by other programs such as Windows Media Player. Once created you can run the video by opening the file and following Windows Media Player procedure.

There you have it. Congratulations on your first video. You have come a long way since drawing your first line in Chapter 1.

CHAPTER TEST QUESTIONS

Questions

1. Why is it often important to keep two or more different views of an object on the screen as you are drawing and editing it?

2. Briefly describe the process for copying layers from one drawing to another.

3. What is a frustum cone? What is the procedure for drawing a 3D frustum cone?

4. You have created a section plane. What additional steps are necessary to create a sectioned image?

5. Name at least three commands that create 3D models from 2D objects.

6. Where is the center of the **3DORBIT** arcball in relation to the drawing area and the current viewport? What else is centered at the center of the arcball?

7. What action is produced by each of the four rotation cursors in **3DORBIT?**

8. Explain the camera and target metaphor used by the **3DORBIT** command. How is it used to define views?

9. What is the quickest way to return to the view you started with before entering **3DORBIT?** How do you access this feature without leaving the **3DORBIT** command?

10. How many direction vectors are specified by the motion of your mouse in the Continuous Orbit mode?

11. What elements must be present in your drawing before you can use the **3DWALK** or **3DFLY** commands?

12. What additional element must be present before you can create an animated walk through?

Drawing Problems

1. Beginning with a blank drawing using the 3B or acad3D template, draw a 0.5-radius circle anywhere on your screen.
2. Draw a helix with center point at (0,0,0), base radius 5.0, top radius 1.0, and height 5.0.
3. Sweep the circle through the helix path to create a solid coil. Erase the helix.
4. Draw a cone with base center at (0,0,0), radius 5.0, and height 6.5.
5. Subtract the coil from the cone.
6. Create a section view of the object; cut along the YZ plane.

WWW Exercise 14 (Optional)

Whenever you are ready, complete the following:

⊞ Make sure that you are connected to your Internet service provider.

⊞ Type "browser" or open your system browser from the Windows taskbar.

⊞ If necessary, navigate to our companion website at prenhall.com/dixriley.

CHAPTER PROJECTS

Drawing 14-1: REVOLVE Designs

The **REVOLVE** command is fascinating and powerful. As you get familiar with it, you might find yourself identifying objects in the world that can be conceived as surfaces of revolution. To encourage this process, we have provided this page of 12 revolved objects and designs. The next drawing is also an application of the **REVOLVE** procedure.

To complete the exercise, you need only the **PLINE** and **REVOLVE** commands. In the first six designs, we have shown the path curves and axes of rotation used to create the design. In the other six, you are on your own.

Exact shapes and dimensions are not important in this exercise, but imagination is. When you have completed our designs, we encourage you to invent your own. Also, consider adding materials and lights to any of your designs and viewing them from different viewpoints using **3DORBIT.**

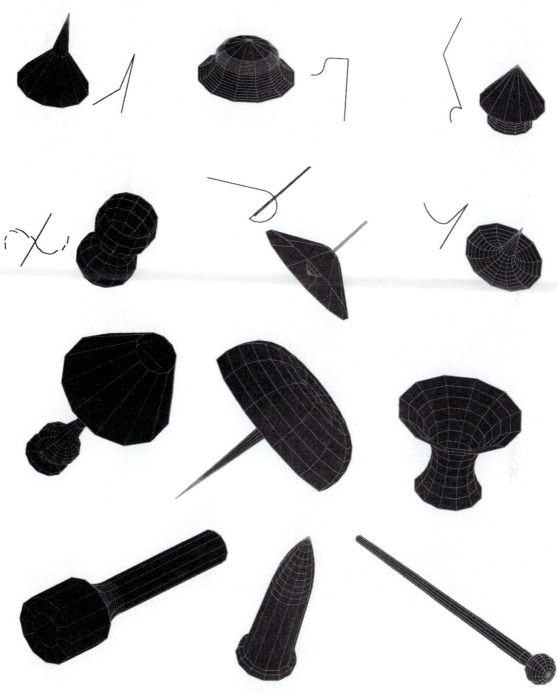

REVOLVE DESIGNS
Drawing 14-1

Drawing 14-2: Tapered Bushing

This is a more technical application of the **REVOLVE** command. By carefully following the dimensions in the side view, you can create the complete drawing using **PLINE** and **REVOLVE** only.

Drawing Suggestions

- Use at least two viewports with the dimensioned side view in one viewport and the 3D isometric view in another.
- Create the 2D outline as shown and then **REVOLVE** it 270 degrees around a center line running down the middle of the bushing.
- When the model is complete, consider how you might present it in different views on a paper space layout.

Drawing 14–2
Tapered Bushing

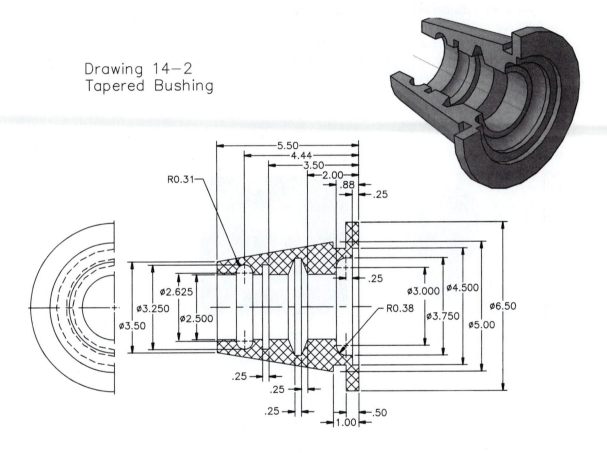

Drawing 14-3: Globe

This drawing uses a new command. The **SPHERE** command creates a 3D sphere and you should have no trouble learning to use it at this point. You will find it on the dashboard, between **CONE** and **CYLINDER.** Like a circle, it requires only a center point and a radius or diameter.

Drawing Suggestions

- Use a three-viewport configuration with top and front views on the left and an isometric 3D view on the right.
- Use 12-sided pyramids to create the base and the top part of the base.
- Draw the 12.25 cylindrical shaft in vertical position, and then rotate it around what will become the center point of the sphere, using the angle shown.
- The arc-shaped shaft holder can be drawn by sweeping or revolving a rectangle through 226 degrees. Considering how you would do it both ways is a good exercise. Then choose one method, or try both.
- As additional practice, trying adding a light and rendering the globe as shown in the reference drawing.

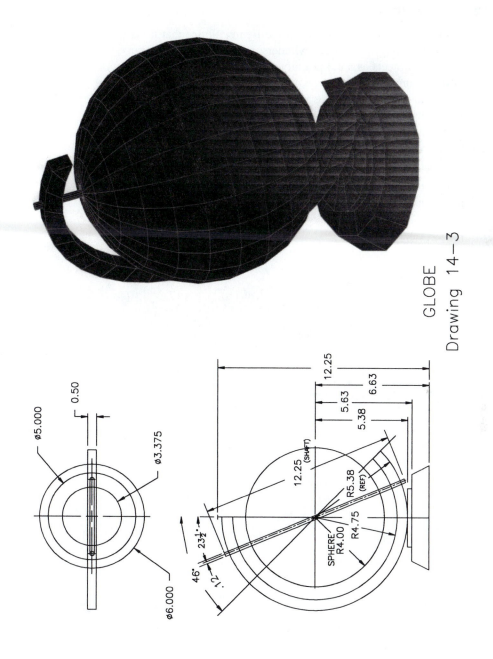

GLOBE
Drawing 14—3

Ø5.000

0.50

Ø3.375

Ø6.000

12.25

5.63

6.63

5.38

12.25
(SHAFT)

R5.38
(REF)

SPHERE
R4.00

R4.75

46°

23½°

1.2

Drawing 14-4: Pivot Mount

This drawing gives you a workout in constructive geometry, as introduced in the last chapter. We suggest you do this drawing with completely dimensioned orthographic views and the 3-D model as shown. Also, create a sliced view of the model as shown in the reference figure.

Drawing Suggestions

- Begin by analyzing the geometry of the figure. Notice that it can be created entirely with boxes, cylinders, and wedges, or you can create some objects as solid primitives and others as extruded or revolved figures. As an exercise, consider how you would create the entire model without using any solid primitive commands (no boxes, wedges, or cylinders). What commands from this chapter would be required?
- When the model is complete, create the sliced view as shown.
- Create the orthographic views and place them in paper space viewports.
- Add dimensions in paper space.

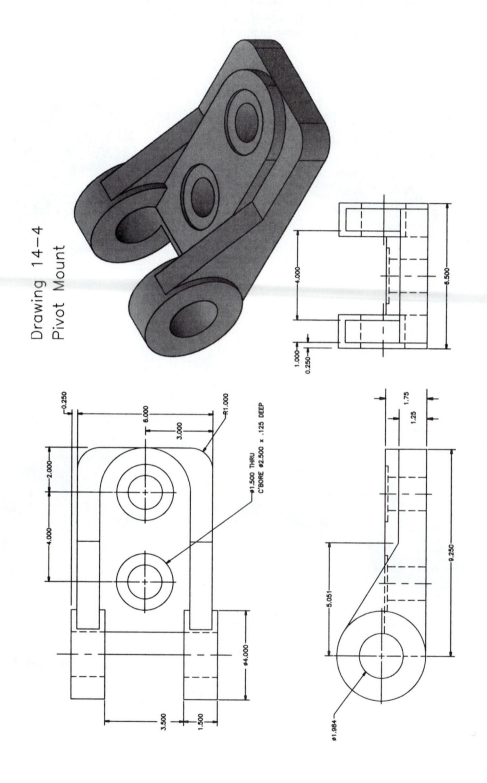

Drawing 14-4
Pivot Mount

0.250

6.000

3.000

R1.000

2.000

4.000

⌀1.500 THRU
C'BORE ⌀2.500 x .125 DEEP

⌀4.000

3.500

1.500

4.000

6.500

1.000

0.250

1.75

1.25

9.250

5.051

⌀1.984

Drawings 14-5A, B, C, and D

The drawings that follow, shown four to a page and labeled 14-5A, B, C, and D, are 3D solid models derived from drawings done earlier in the book. You can start from scratch or begin with the 2D drawing and use some of the geometry as a guide to your 3D model. The dimensions for these drawings are those shown in preceding chapters.

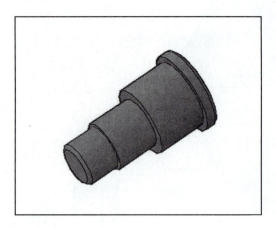

Drawing 3-2

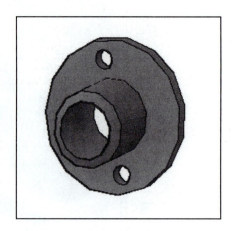

Drawing 3-4

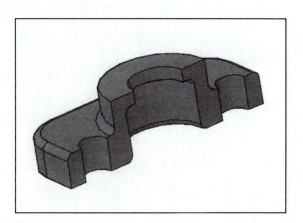

Drawing 3-6

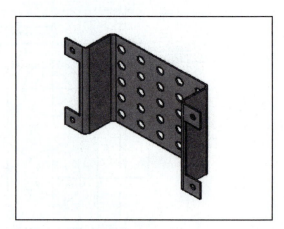

Drawing 4-4

Drawing 14-5A

Drawing 5-1

Drawing 5-4

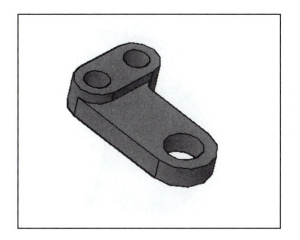

Drawing 5-2

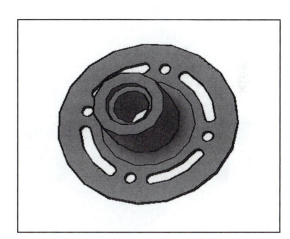

Drawing 5-6

Drawing 14-5B

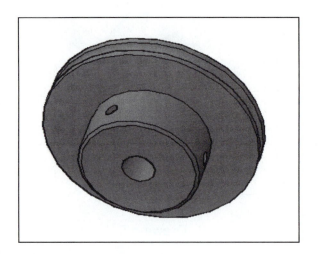

Drawing 6-4

Drawing 8-1

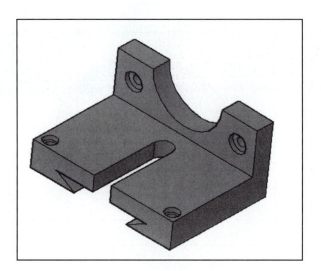

Drawing 6-7

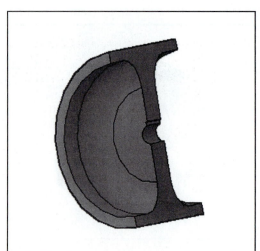

Drawing 8-2

Drawing 14-5C

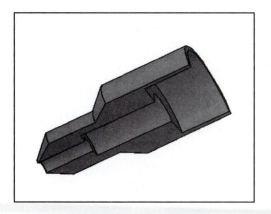

Drawing 8-3

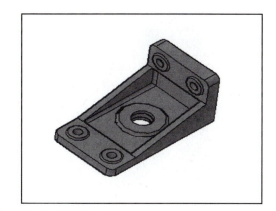

Drawing 8-7

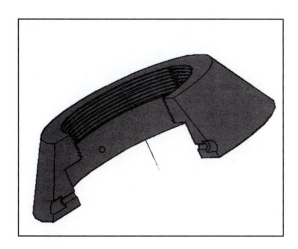

Drawing 8-4

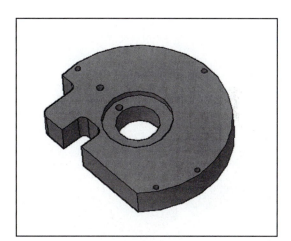

Drawing 8-8

Drawing 14-5D

Drawing Projects

The drawings on the following pages are offered as additional challenges and are presented without suggestions. They may be drawn in two or three dimensions and may be presented as multiple-view drawings, hidden line drawings, or rendered drawings. In short, you are on your own to explore and master everything you have learned in this book.

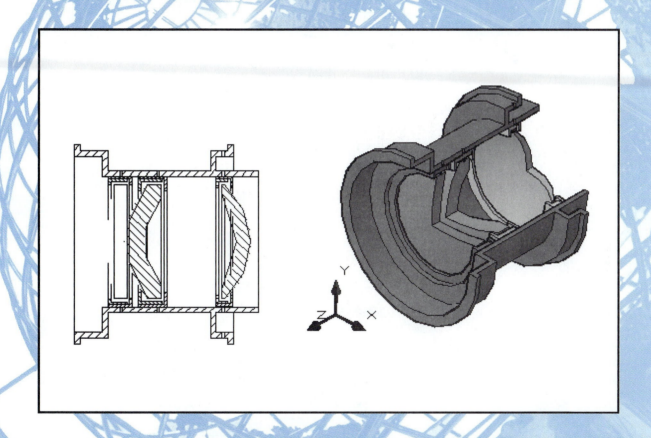

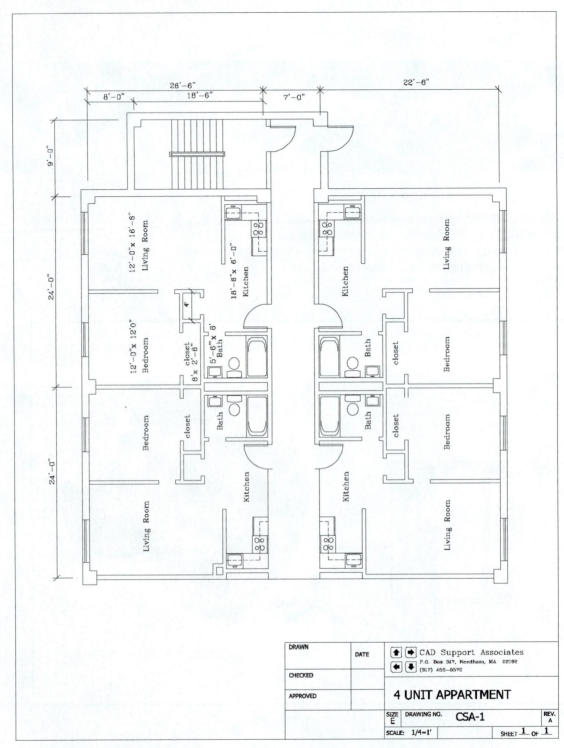

26'-6"

8'-0"

18'-6"

22'-6"

7'-0"

9'-0"

24'-0"

24'-0"

12'-0" x 16'-6"
Living Room

18'-6"x 6'-0"
Kitchen

Kitchen

Living Room

12'-0"x 12'0"
Bedroom

closet
8'x 2'-6"

4'

5'-8"'x 8'
Bath

Bath

closet

Bedroom

Bedroom

closet

Bath

Bath

closet

Bedroom

Living Room

Kitchen

Kitchen

Living Room

DRAWN		⬆️ ➡️ CAD Support Associates		
	DATE	⬅️ ⬇️ P.O. Box 317, Needham, MA 02192		
		(617) 455-8570		
CHECKED				
APPROVED		**4 UNIT APPARTMENT**		
		SIZE E	DRAWING NO. CSA-1	REV. A
		SCALE: 1/4=1'		SHEET 1 OF 1

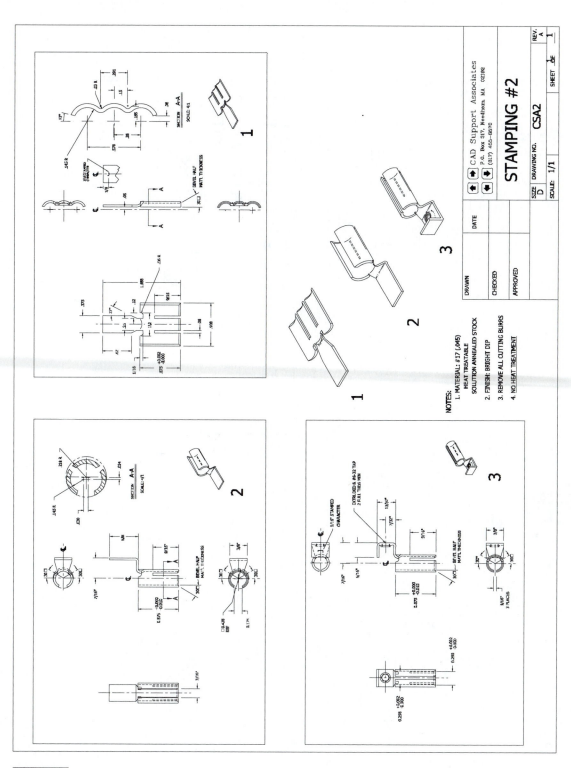

CAD Support Associates
P.O. Box 317, Needham, MA 02192
(817) 455-8670

STAMPING #2

DRAWING NO. CSA2

REV. A

SIZE D

SCALE 1/1

SHEET OF

DRAWN

CHECKED

APPROVED

DATE

NOTES:
1. MATERIAL: #17 (.045)
   HEAT TREATABLE
   SOLUTION ANNEALED STOCK
2. FINISH: BRIGHT DIP
3. REMOVE ALL CUTTING BURRS
4. NO HEAT TREATMENT

mechanical

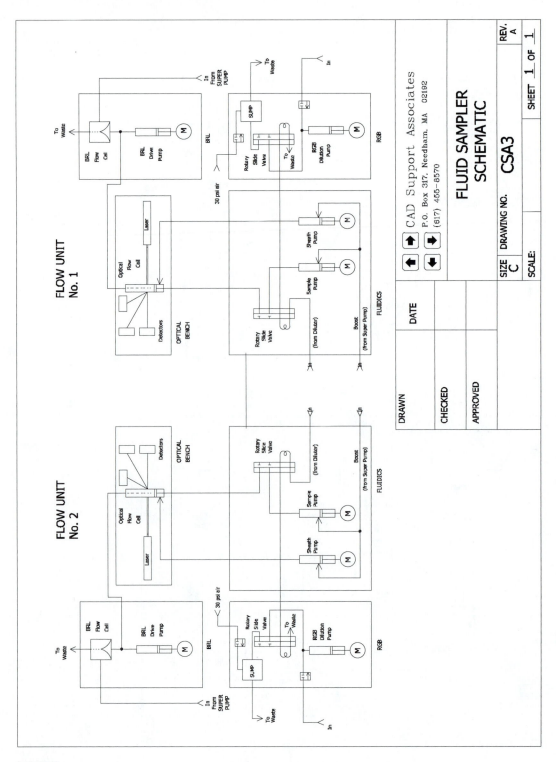

FLOW UNIT No. 1

FLOW UNIT No. 2

CAD Support Associates
P.O. Box 317, Needham, MA 02192
(617) 455-8570

FLUID SAMPLER
SCHEMATIC

DRAWING NO. CSA3

REV. A

SIZE C

SHEET 1 OF 1

SCALE:

DRAWN

CHECKED

APPROVED

DATE

electrical

550

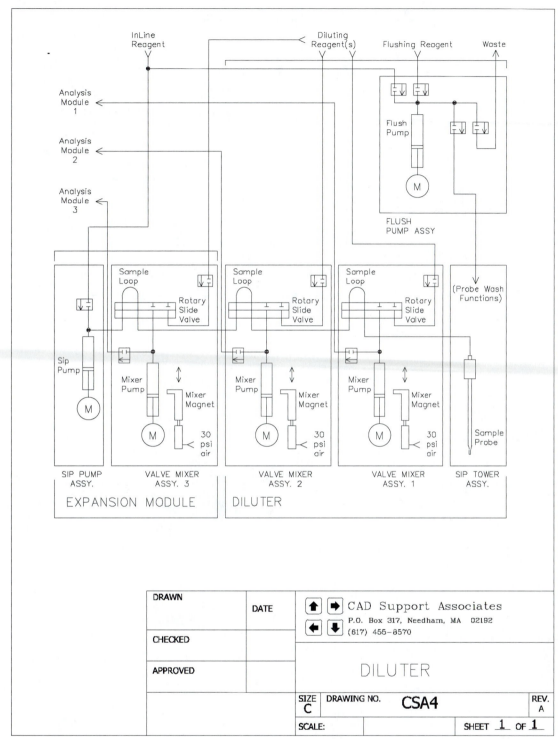

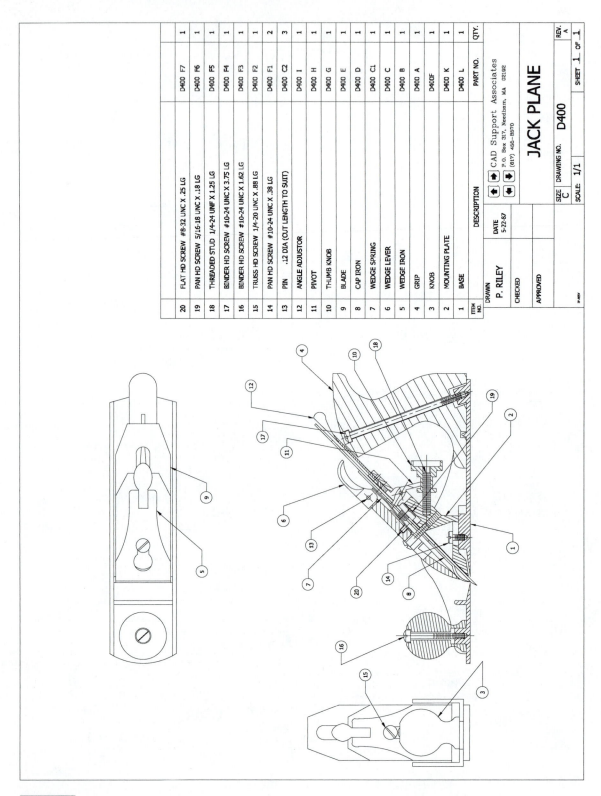

ITEM NO.	DESCRIPTION		PART NO.	QTY.
20	FLAT HD SCREW #8-32 UNC X .25 LG		D400 F7	1
19	PAN HD SCREW 5/16-18 UNC X .18 LG		D400 F6	1
18	THREADED STUD 1/4-24 UNF X 1.25 LG		D400 F5	1
17	BINDER HD SCREW #10-24 UNC X 3.75 LG		D400 F4	1
16	BINDER HD SCREW #10-24 UNC X 1.62 LG		D400 F3	1
15	TRUSS HD SCREW 1/4-20 UNC X .88 LG		D400 F2	1
14	PAN HD SCREW #10-24 UNC X .38 LG		D400 F1	2
13	PIN .12 DIA (CUT LENGTH TO SUIT)		D400 C2	3
12	ANGLE ADJUSTOR		D400 I	1
11	PIVOT		D400 H	1
10	THUMB KNOB		D400 G	1
9	BLADE		D400 E	1
8	CAP IRON		D400 D	1
7	WEDGE SPRING		D400 C1	1
6	WEDGE LEVER		D400 C	1
5	WEDGE IRON		D400 B	1
4	GRIP		D400 A	1
3	KNOB		D400F	1
2	MOUNTING PLATE		D400 K	1
1	BASE		D400 L	1

DRAWN		CAD Support Associates		
P. RILEY	DATE 5-22-87	P.O. Box 317, Needham, MA 02192		
CHECKED		(617) 466-8670		
APPROVED		JACK PLANE		REV. A
		SIZE C	DRAWING NO. D400	
		SCALE: 1/1	SHEET 1 OF 1	

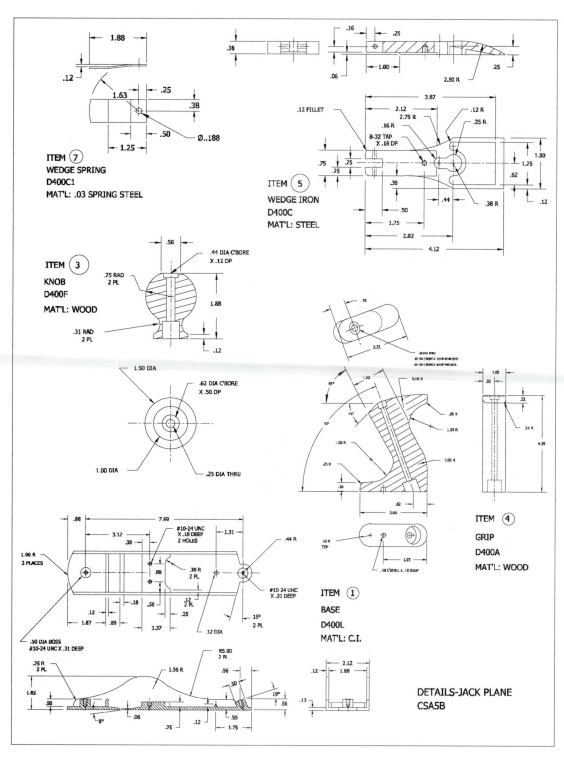

ITEM ⑦
WEDGE SPRING
D400C1
MAT'L: .03 SPRING STEEL

ITEM ⑤
WEDGE IRON
D400C
MAT'L: STEEL

ITEM ③
KNOB
D400F
MAT'L: WOOD

ITEM ④
GRIP
D400A
MAT'L: WOOD

ITEM ①
BASE
D400L
MAT'L: C.I.

DETAILS-JACK PLANE
CSA5B

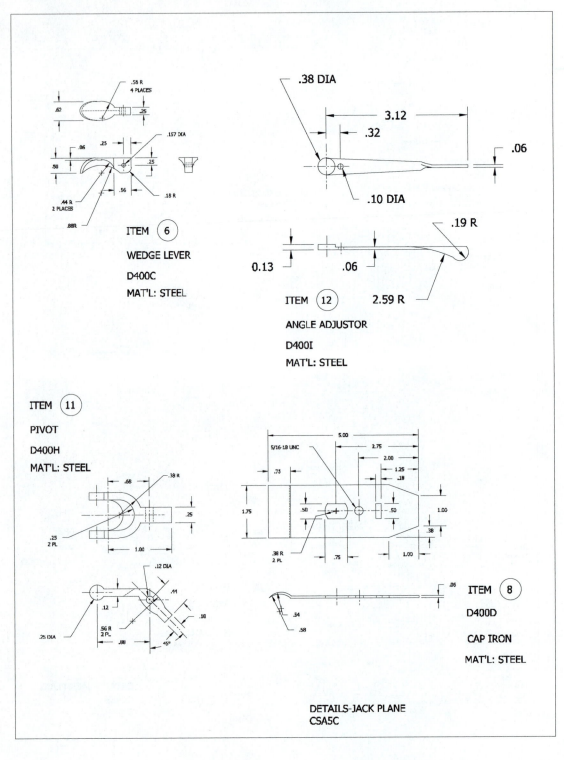

ITEM ⑥

WEDGE LEVER

D400C

MAT'L: STEEL

ITEM ⑫

ANGLE ADJUSTOR

D400I

MAT'L: STEEL

ITEM ⑪

PIVOT

D400H

MAT'L: STEEL

ITEM ⑧

D400D

CAP IRON

MAT'L: STEEL

DETAILS-JACK PLANE
CSA5C

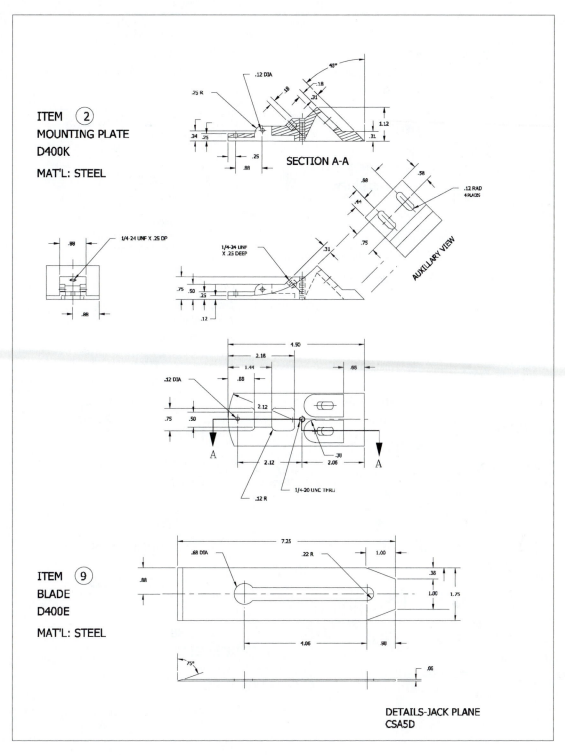

ITEM (2)
MOUNTING PLATE
D400K
MAT'L: STEEL

SECTION A-A

AUXILIARY VIEW

ITEM (9)
BLADE
D400E
MAT'L: STEEL

DETAILS-JACK PLANE
CSA5D

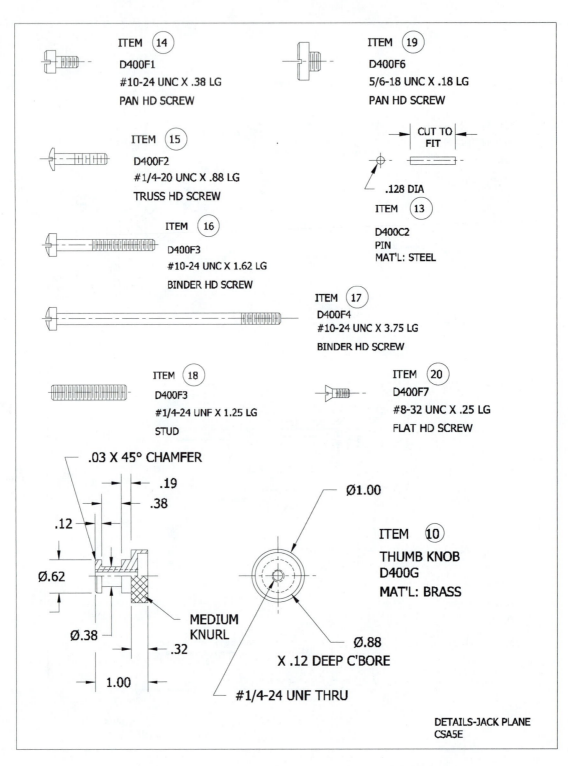

ITEM ⑭
D400F1
#10-24 UNC X .38 LG
PAN HD SCREW

ITEM ⑲
D400F6
5/6-18 UNC X .18 LG
PAN HD SCREW

ITEM ⑮
D400F2
#1/4-20 UNC X .88 LG
TRUSS HD SCREW

CUT TO FIT
.128 DIA

ITEM ⑬
D400C2
PIN
MAT'L: STEEL

ITEM ⑯
D400F3
#10-24 UNC X 1.62 LG
BINDER HD SCREW

ITEM ⑰
D400F4
#10-24 UNC X 3.75 LG
BINDER HD SCREW

ITEM ⑱
D400F3
#1/4-24 UNF X 1.25 LG
STUD

ITEM ⑳
D400F7
#8-32 UNC X .25 LG
FLAT HD SCREW

.03 X 45° CHAMFER
.19
.38
.12
Ø.62
Ø.38
.32
1.00
MEDIUM
KNURL

Ø1.00

ITEM ⑩
THUMB KNOB
D400G
MAT'L: BRASS

Ø.88
X .12 DEEP C'BORE
#1/4-24 UNF THRU

DETAILS-JACK PLANE
CSA5E

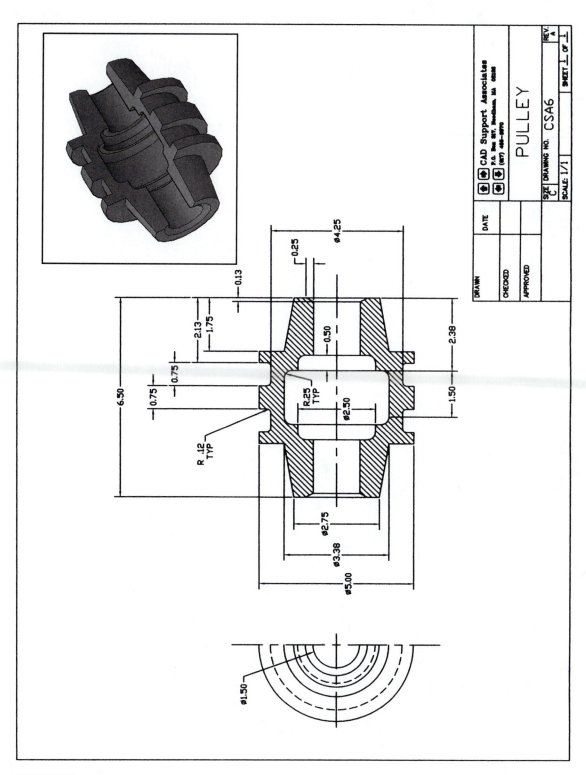

PULLEY

CAD Support Associates
P.O. Box 667, Needham, MA 02192
(617) 466-8970

DRAWN	DATE
CHECKED	
APPROVED	

SIZE C DRAWING NO. CSA6 REV. A

SCALE: 1/1 SHEET 1 OF 1

Ø4.25
0.25
0.13
2.13
1.75
0.50
6.50
0.75
0.75
R.25 TYP
Ø2.50
2.38
1.50
R .12 TYP
Ø2.75
Ø3.38
Ø5.00
Ø1.50

mechanical

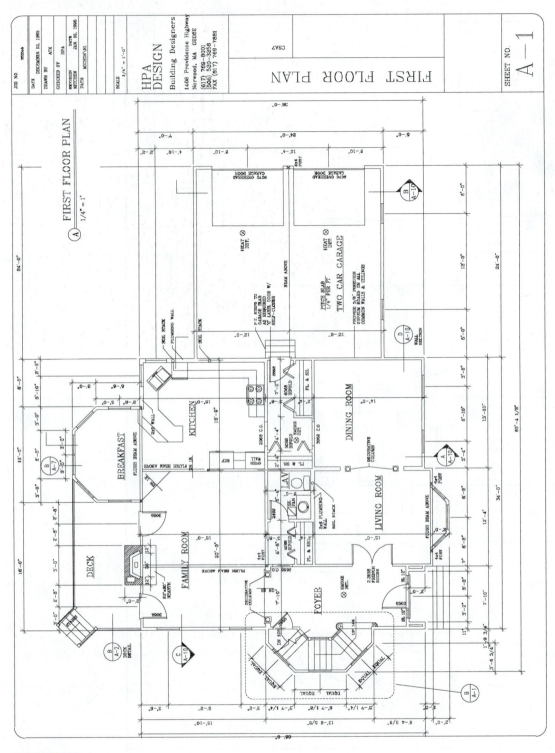

FIRST FLOOR PLAN
1/4" = 1'

TWO CAR GARAGE

PITCH SLAB
1/4" PER FT

PROVIDE 5/8" FIRECODE
GYPSUM BOARD ON ALL
COMMON WALLS & CEILINGS

90%0 OVERHEAD
GARAGE DOOR

90%0 OVERHEAD
GARAGE DOOR

HEAT
DET.

HEAT
DET.

DINING ROOM

LIVING ROOM

DECORATIVE
COLUMN

FOYER

KITCHEN

BREAKFAST

FAMILY ROOM

DECK

LAV

DECORATIVE
COLUMN

FLUSH BEAM ABOVE

FLUSH BEAM ABOVE

SMOKE
DET.

HPA
DESIGN
Building Designers
1408 Providence Highway
Norwood, MA 02062
(617) 769-8001
(508) 520-3258
FAX (617) 769-7881

FIRST FLOOR PLAN

JOB NO 95DA6
DATE DECEMBER 12, 1995
DRAWN BY ATX
CHECKED BY HPA
REVISION KITCHEN DATE JAN 16, 1996
PATH KITCHEN\B1
SCALE 1/4" = 1'-0"
CSA7

SHEET NO.
A-1

architectural

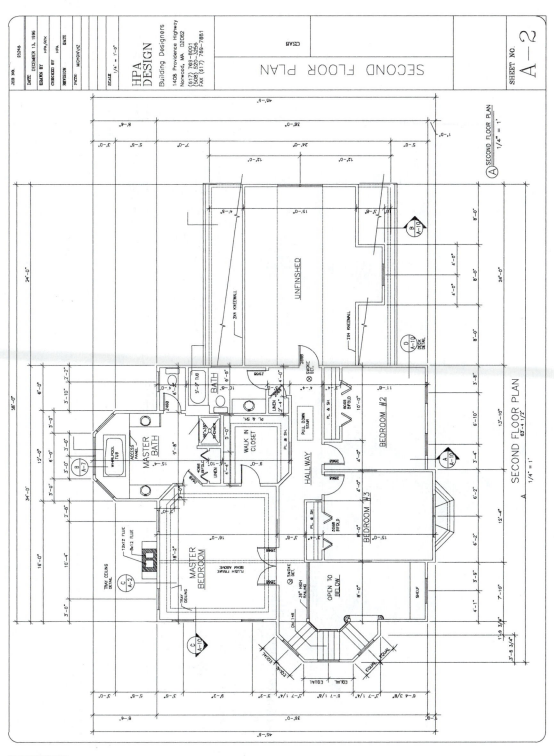

SECOND FLOOR PLAN

HPA DESIGN
Building Designers
1408 Providence Highway
Norwood, MA 02062
(617) 769-8001
(508) 520-3256
FAX (617) 769-7881

SHEET NO. A-2

MASTER BEDROOM

MASTER BATH

WALK IN CLOSET

BATH

HALLWAY

UNFINISHED

BEDROOM #2

BEDROOM #3

OPEN TO BELOW

SECOND FLOOR PLAN
1/4" = 1'

architectural

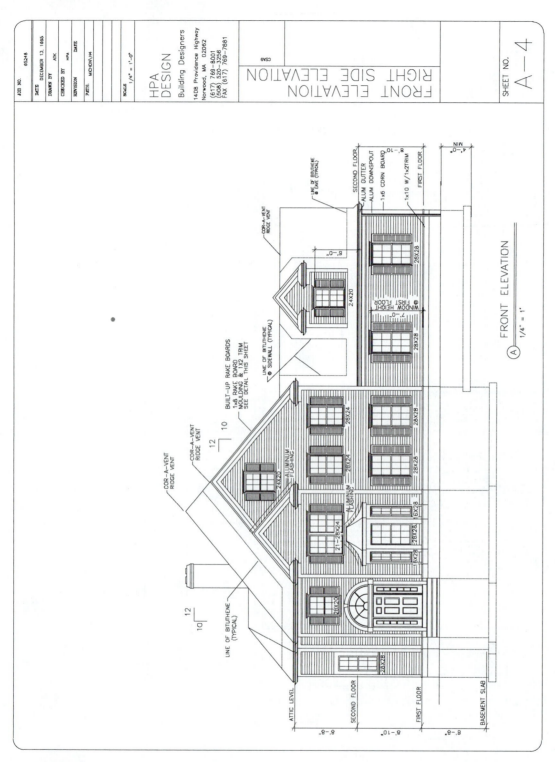

FRONT ELEVATION
RIGHT SIDE ELEVATION
FRONT ELEVATION

HPA
DESIGN

Building Designers

1408 Providence Highway
Norwood, MA 02062
(617) 769-8001
(508) 520-3256
FAX (617) 769-7881

JOB NO.   65246
DATE   DECEMBER 13, 1995
DRAWN BY   ATK
CHECKED BY   HPA
REVISION   DATE
PATH: MICHON\H4

SCALE   1/4" = 1'-0"

SHEET NO.
A-4

CSA9

architectural

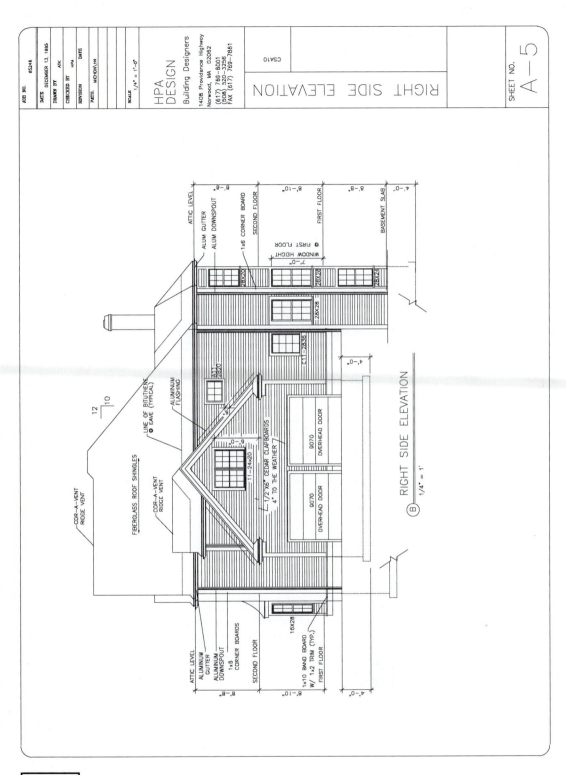

RIGHT SIDE ELEVATION

B 1/4" = 1'

HPA
DESIGN

Building Designers

1408 Providence Highway
Norwood, MA 02062
(617) 769-8001
(508) 520-3256
FAX (617) 769-7881

CSA10

JOB NO.	05248
DATE	DECEMBER 13, 1995
DRAWN BY	ATK
CHECKED BY	HPA
REVISION	DATE
PATH:	MICHON.HH
SCALE	1/4" = 1'-0"

architectural

561

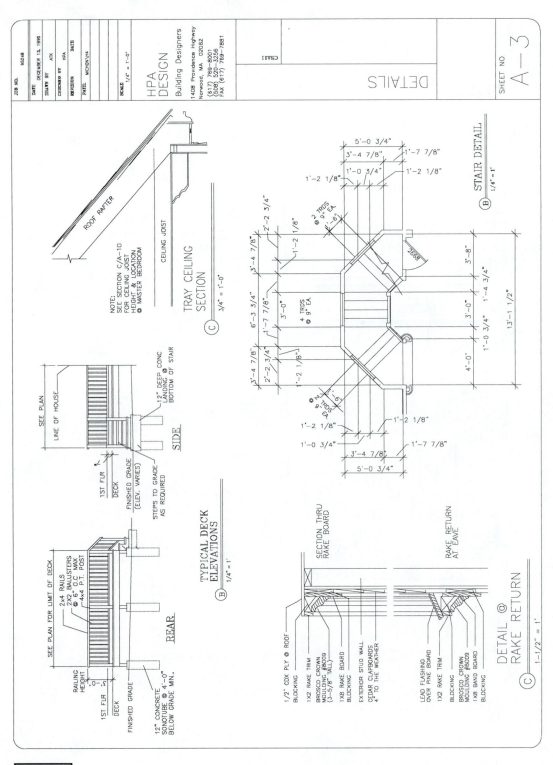

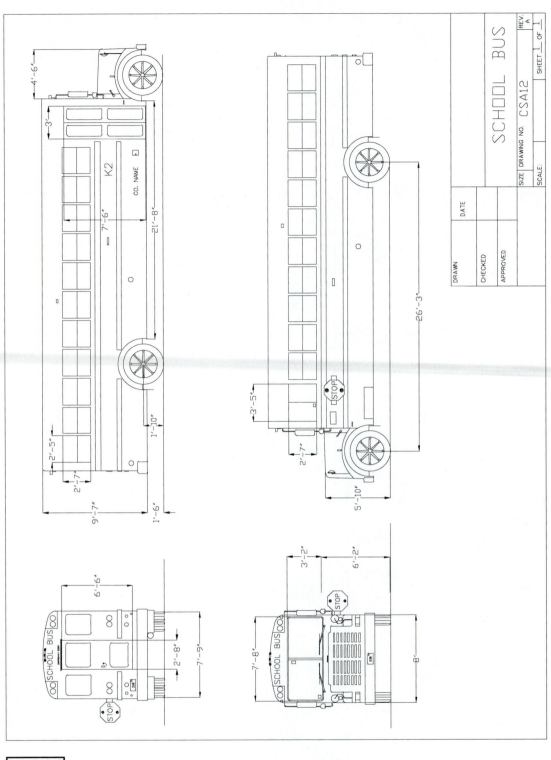

SCHOOL BUS

SIZE | DRAWING NO. CSA12 | REV. A
SCALE: | SHEET 1 OF 1

DRAWN
CHECKED
APPROVED
DATE

general

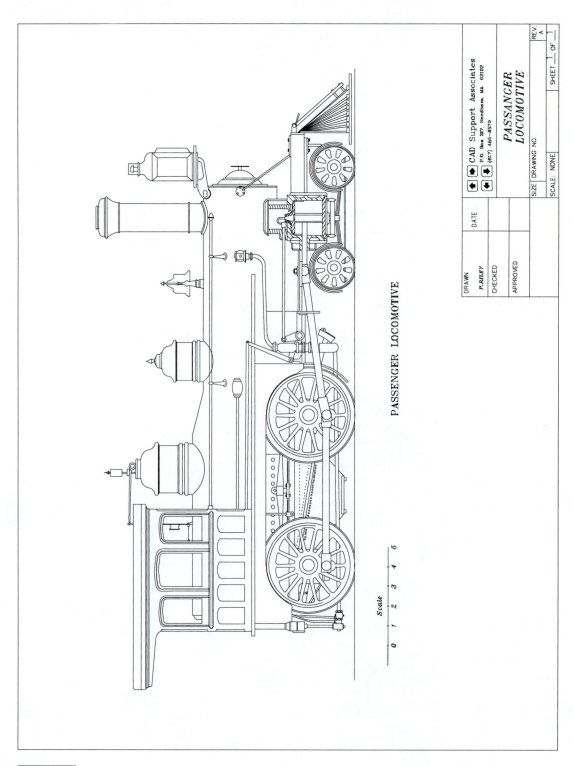

PASSENGER LOCOMOTIVE

Scale
0 1 2 3 4 5

DRAWN
P.RILEY
CHECKED
APPROVED

DATE

CAD Support Associates
P.O. Box 317, Needham, MA 02192
(617) 455-8570

PASSANGER
LOCOMOTIVE

SIZE | DRAWING NO.

SCALE: NONE

REV.
A

SHEET 1 OF 1

general

Drawing Courtesy of: Brian Tufts

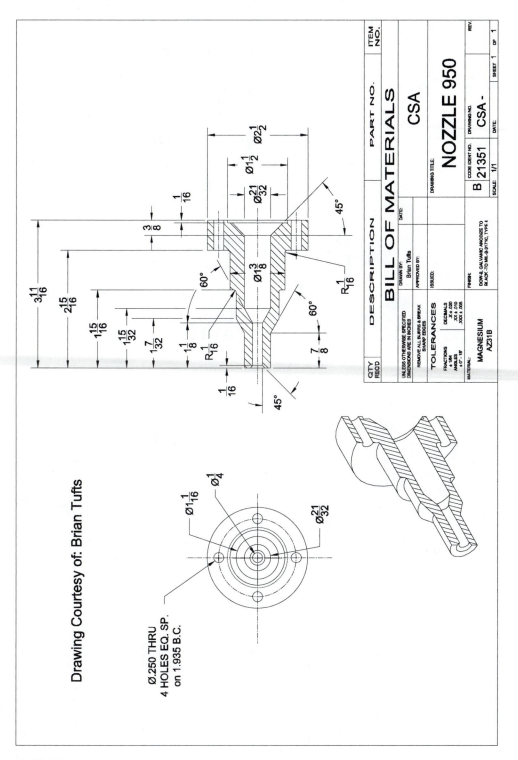

Ø.250 THRU
4 HOLES EQ. SP.
on 1.935 B.C.

Ø1 1/16
Ø1/4
Ø21/32

3 11/16
2 15/16
1 15/16
1 15/32
1 7/32
1 1/8

R1/16
60°
Ø1 3/8
60°
7/8

R1/16
45°
1/16
45°

1/16
3/8

Ø2 1/2
Ø1 1/2
Ø21/32

QTY REQD	DESCRIPTION	PART NO.	ITEM NO.
	BILL OF MATERIALS		
		CSA	

DRAWING TITLE:
NOZZLE 950

DRAWN BY: Brian Tufts DATE:

APPROVED BY:

ISSUED:

CODE IDENT NO.	DRAWING NO.	REV.
B 21351	CSA -	

SCALE: 1/1   DATE: SHEET 1 OF 1

FINISH: DOW-9, GALVANIC ANODIZE TO
BLACK -TO MIL-S-317XC, TYPE I

UNLESS OTHERWISE SPECIFIED
DIMENSIONS ARE IN INCHES
REMOVE ALL BURRS & BREAK
SHARP EDGES

TOLERANCES
FRACTIONS ± 1/64
ANGLES ± 0° - 15'
DECIMALS
.X ± .020
.XX ± .010
.XXX ± .005

MATERIAL:
MAGNESIUM
AZ31B

mechanical

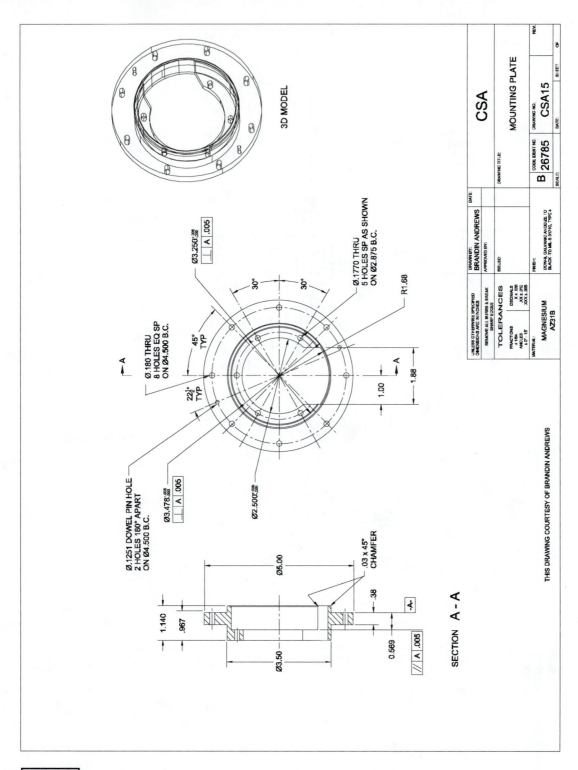

3D MODEL

Ø3.250⁺·⁰⁰⁸ | ⊥ | A | .005

30°   30°

Ø.1770 THRU
5 HOLES SP AS SHOWN
ON Ø2.875 B.C.

R1.68

45°
TYP

Ø.180 THRU
8 HOLES EQ SP
ON Ø4.500 B.C.

22½°
TYP

A

Ø.1251 DOWEL PIN HOLE
2 HOLES 180° APART
ON Ø4.500 B.C.

Ø3.478⁺·⁰⁰⁸ | ⊥ | A | .005

Ø2.500⁺·⁰⁰⁸

1.88
1.00

A

Ø5.00

.03 x 45°
CHAMFER

1.140
.967

.38

-A-

Ø3.50

0.569

// | A | .005

SECTION A - A

UNLESS OTHERWISE SPECIFIED
DIMENSIONS ARE IN INCHES
REMOVE ALL BURRS & BREAK
SHARP EDGES

TOLERANCES
FRACTIONS   DECIMALS
± 1/64   .X ± .030
ANGLES   .XX ± .010
± 0° -15'   .XXX ± .005

MATERIAL:
MAGNESIUM
AZ31B

DRAWN BY:
BRANDIN ANDREWS
APPROVED BY:

ISSUED:

FINISH:
DOW#4, GALVANIC ANODIZE, TO
BLACK, TO MIL-S-3171C, TYPE 4

DATE:

CSA

DRAWING TITLE:
MOUNTING PLATE

CODE IDENT NO.   DRAWING NO.   REV.
B 26785   CSA15
SCALE: SHEET: DATE: OF:

mechanical

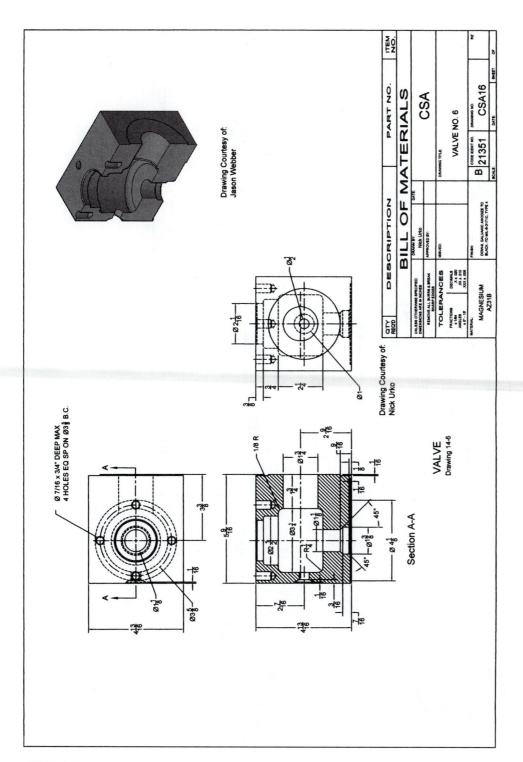

Drawing Courtesy of:
Jason Webber

Drawing Courtesy of:
Nick Urko

VALVE
Drawing 14-6

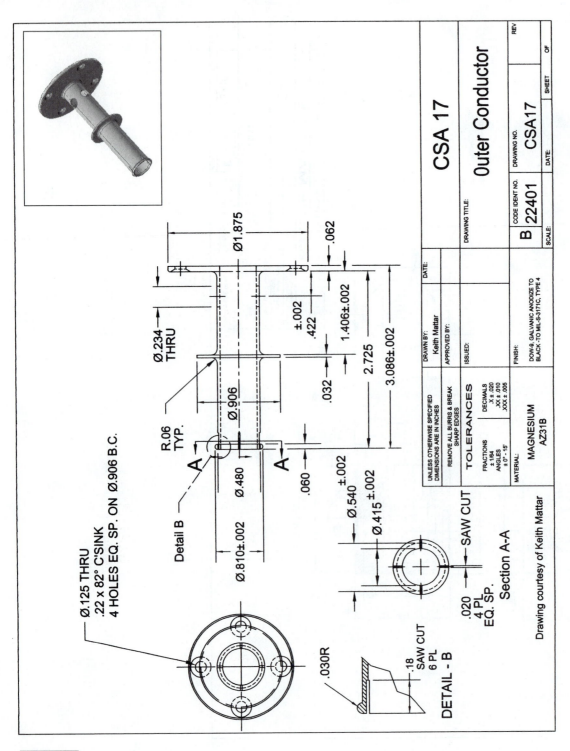

Ø1.875

.062

Ø.234
THRU

±.002

.422

1.406±.002

2.725

Ø.906

.032

3.086±.002

R.06
TYP.

A

A

Ø.480

.060

Detail B

Ø.540

±.002

Ø.415 ±.002

Ø.810±.002

Section A-A

Ø.125 THRU
.22 x 82° C'SINK
4 HOLES EQ. SP. ON Ø.906 B.C.

.020
4 PL
EQ. SP.

SAW CUT

.030R

.18

SAW CUT
6 PL

DETAIL - B

Drawing courtesy of Keith Mattar

UNLESS OTHERWISE SPECIFIED DIMENSIONS ARE IN INCHES		DRAWN BY: Keith Mattar	DATE:			
REMOVE ALL BURRS & BREAK SHARP EDGES		APPROVED BY:			CSA 17	
TOLERANCES		ISSUED:		DRAWING TITLE:		REV
FRACTIONS ± 1/64 ANGLES ±0° - 15'	DECIMALS .X ± .020 .XX ± .010 .XXX ± .005				Outer Conductor	
MATERIAL: MAGNESIUM AZ31B		FINISH: DOW-9, GALVANIC ANODIZE TO BLACK -TO MIL-S-3171C, TYPE 4		CODE IDENT NO. B 22401	DRAWING NO. CSA17	
				SCALE:	DATE:	SHEET OF

mechanical

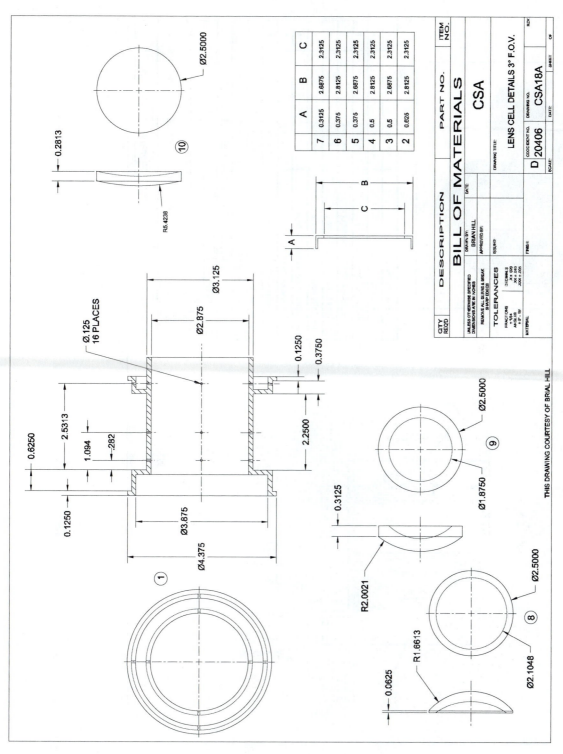

BILL OF MATERIALS

ITEM NO.			A	B	C
7			0.3125	2.6875	2.3125
6			0.375	2.8125	2.3125
5			0.375	2.6875	2.3125
4			0.5	2.8125	2.3125
3			0.5	2.6875	2.3125
2			0.625	2.8125	2.3125

QTY REQ'D	DESCRIPTION	PART NO.
		CSA

DRAWN BY: BRIAN HILL

DRAWING TITLE: LENS CELL DETAILS 3° F.O.V.

CODE IDENT NO. 20406 DRAWING NO. CSA18A

D

UNLESS OTHERWISE SPECIFIED DIMENSIONS ARE IN INCHES
REMOVE ALL BURRS & BREAK SHARP EDGES

TOLERANCES
FRACTIONS ± 1/64
ANGLES ± 0° - 15'

THIS DRAWING COURTESY OF BRIAN HILL

mechanical

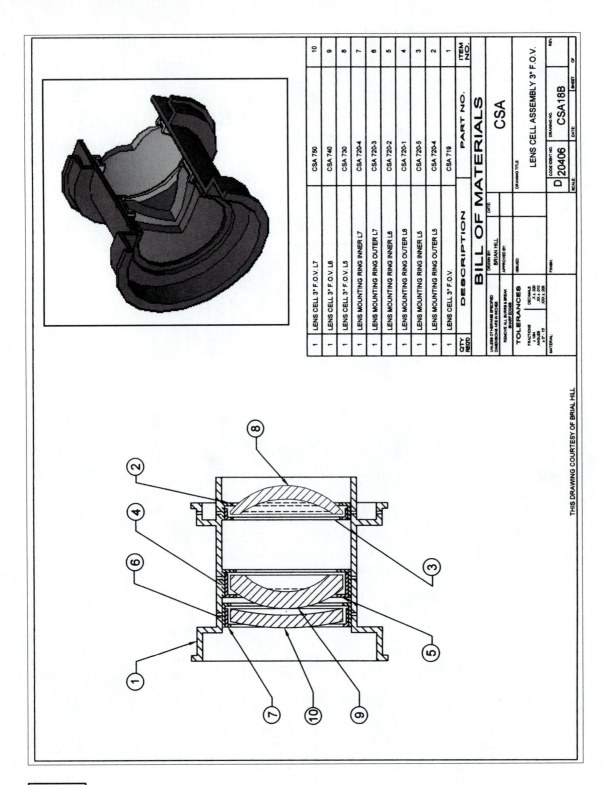

QTY REQD	DESCRIPTION	PART NO.	ITEM NO.
1	LENS CELL 3° F.O.V. L7	CSA 750	10
1	LENS CELL 3° F.O.V. L6	CSA 740	9
1	LENS CELL 3° F.O.V. L5	CSA 730	8
1	LENS MOUNTING RING INNER L7	CSA 720-4	7
1	LENS MOUNTING RING OUTER L7	CSA 720-3	6
1	LENS MOUNTING RING INNER L6	CSA 720-2	5
1	LENS MOUNTING RING OUTER L6	CSA 720-1	4
1	LENS MOUNTING RING INNER L5	CSA 720-5	3
1	LENS MOUNTING RING OUTER L5	CSA 720-4	2
1	LENS CELL 3° F.O.V.	CSA 719	1

BILL OF MATERIALS

CSA

DRAWING TITLE: LENS CELL ASSEMBLY 3° F.O.V.

DRAWN BY: BRIAN HILL
APPROVED BY:
ISSUED:
FINISH:
DATE:

UNLESS OTHERWISE SPECIFIED
DIMENSIONS ARE IN INCHES
REMOVE ALL BURRS & BREAK SHARP EDGES

TOLERANCES
FRACTIONS ± 1/64
ANGLES ± 0° – 15'
DECIMALS
.X ± .020
.XX ± .010
.XXX ± .005

MATERIAL:

CODE IDENT. NO. D | DRAWING NO. CSA18B | REV.
20406
SCALE: | DATE: | SHEET: OF

THIS DRAWING COURTESY OF BRIAN HILL

mechanical

Creating Customized Toolbars

This appendix and the next are provided to give you an introduction to some of the many ways in which AutoCAD can be customized to more efficiently fit the needs of a particular industry, company, or individual user. In Chapter 10 you learned how to create customized tool palettes. Tool palettes give you easy access to libraries of frequently used blocks, symbols, and commands. You can also create customized toolbars to store sets of frequently used commands or commands that have been modified to suit your preferences. Creating your own customized toolbars is a simple and powerful feature that also gives you some idea of the more complex customization options discussed in Appendix C.

This appendix takes you through the procedure of creating your own toolbar and modifying the behavior of some basic commands. On completing this exercise, you will have added a simple toolbar to your own system and have the knowledge necessary to create other toolbars of your own design.

There are two levels to the creation of a customized toolbar. At the first level, you simply create the toolbar, give it a name, and add whatever commands you wish to put there. This can be very handy for putting together sets of tools that would otherwise be located on different toolbars and menus. At the second level, you actually modify the function of a command, then alter its name and the look of its toolbar button so that it functions differently from the standard AutoCAD command. In this exercise, we begin by creating a toolbar with five commands and then we show how to alter three of these commands.

Note:
The ability to create and customize toolbars is a powerful feature. We strongly discourage you from making changes in the standard AutoCAD set of toolbars. Adding, removing, or otherwise changing standard commands can lead to confusion and to the need to reload the AutoCAD menu. You create less confusion if you customize only new toolbars that you create yourself.

B-1 ADDING TOOLS TO A CUSTOMIZED TOOLBAR

GENERAL PROCEDURE

1. Select Tools → Customize → Interface from the pull-down menu.
2. Right-click on Toolbars.
3. Select New Toolbar.
4. Give the new toolbar a name by overtyping in the Customizations in ALL CUI Files list.
5. Select a Category from the Command List.
6. Find tools on the Commands List and drag them up to the name of the new toolbar in the Customizations in ALL CUI Files list.
7. Click **OK** to exit the dialog box.

⊕ You can begin this exercise in any AutoCAD drawing.

⊕ Select Tools → Customize → Interface from the pull-down menu.

This opens the **Customize User Interface (CUI)** dialog box, shown in Figure B-1. This is a centralized location for customizing various elements of the AutoCAD interface. Elements that can be customized are listed in the Customizations in ALL CUI Files list on the upper left. You can learn more about CUI files in Appendix C.

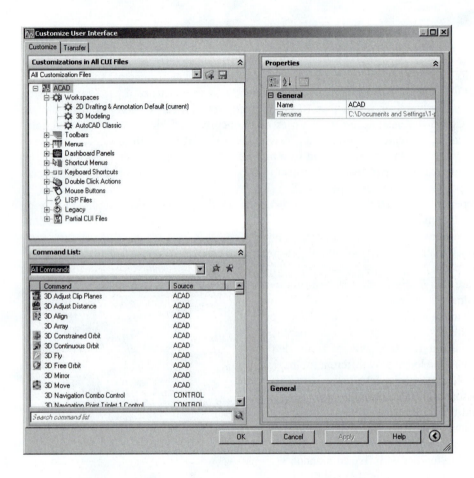

Figure B-1

⊕ Right-click the word Toolbars on the Customizations in ALL CUI Files list on the left.

⊕ Select New Toolbar.

This opens the Toolbar folder on the left and a Properties window on the right side of the **CUI** dialog box. A new toolbar is added to the bottom of the list in the list of toolbars on the left, as in Figure B-2. The default name is Toolbar1 (or Toolbar2 if someone has already created a Toolbar1 on your system). This is fine for our purposes. Feel free to type in a different name if you like. Next we add commands to the new toolbar.

The procedure for adding commands to a toolbar is simple. You select a category from the Categories list and then drag individual commands up to the name of the toolbar. For our purposes, we bring together five very common commands. These commands are available elsewhere, of course, but bringing them together in one place on a small toolbar that doesn't get in the way on the screen can be useful.

The Categories list includes all the standard pull-down menu titles, but there are commands within each of these categories that are not on the pull-down menus and there are also commands you might want that you will not find in these

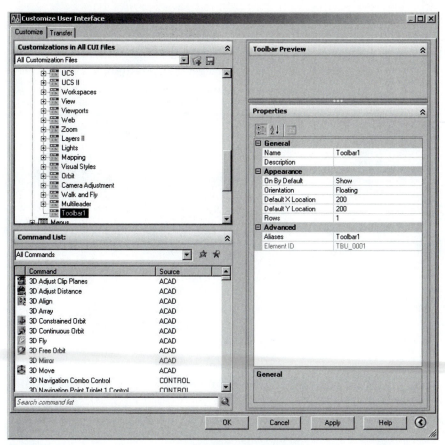

Figure B-2

default lists. We get to this issue in a moment. For now, let's begin with the **LINE** command.

⊕ Click the arrow to open the drop-down list in the Command List window at the bottom left of the dialog box.

You see a list beginning with All Commands and ending with Legacy.

⊕ In the categories list, select Draw.

This opens a list of Drawing commands in the Command List below Categories.

⊕ Scroll down the list until you see the Line command and button image.

From here, it is a simple matter of dragging the tool up to the new toolbar name.

⊕ Pick the Line button, hold down the pick button, and drag the tool up just to the right of "Toolbar1."

When you are in the correct position, there will be a small blue arrow to the right of Toolbar1.

⊕ With the blue arrow showing, drop the command by releasing the pick button.

You see a Button Image and a Properties window for this command on the right, and the **LINE** command is added to Toolbar1 in the Customizations in ALL CUI Files box, as shown in Figure B-3.

⊕ To see your new toolbar so far, right-click Toolbar1 in the Customizations in ALL CUI Files box.

This calls up a Toolbar Preview at the right, as shown in Figure B-4. Your new toolbar now has one tool and a close button. We add one more tool from the Draw category and then move on to other categories. When we are done, your new toolbar will resemble Figure B-5.

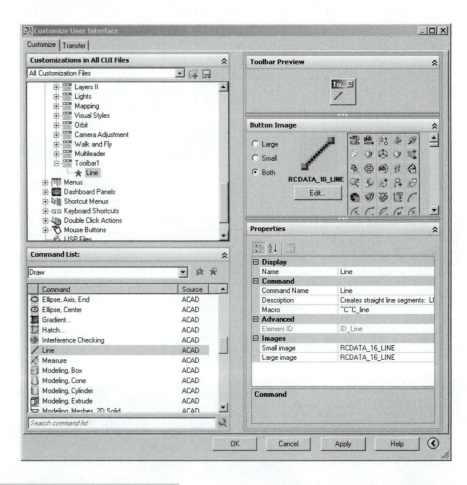

Figure B-3

Figure B-4

Figure B-5

The common **Draw** toolbar has the **CIRCLE** command with the radius option as the default. It might be useful to have the command with the diameter option as the default on our toolbar. You can find this option on the Command List in the dialog box.

⊕ Scroll up the Command List and find Center Diameter next to the Circle tool.

⊕ Drag Circle Center Diameter up to Toolbar1.

Your new toolbar now has two tools.

Let's move on to the Edit category and add the **Erase** tool to our toolbar.

⊕ Open the Categories list and select Edit.

⊕ Drag Erase up to Toolbar1.

Your customized toolbar now has three tools. The Preview updates automatically. We add two more tools to complete the first level of this exercise. First, we add the **Linear dimension** button. There is nothing new in this procedure.

⊕ Select Dimension in the Categories list.

⊕ Drag Dimension, Linear up to Toolbar1.

The last button we add is for the **Distance** command. If you are not familiar with **DIST,** see Chapter 2 (Section 2-9). DIST is an inquiry command. As you can see, Inquiry is not on the Categories list. Where will we find the **Distance** command?

⊕ Highlight All Commands in the Categories list.

⊕ Scroll down the Command List until you see the Distance button.

⊞ Drag Distance up to Toolbar1.

Your new toolbar is now complete and should resemble Figure B-5, shown previously.

B-2 CREATING CUSTOMIZED TOOLS

<table>
<tr><td>**GENERAL PROCEDURE**</td><td>1. With the **Customize User Interface** dialog box open, highlight a tool on a customized toolbar.
2. In the Properties panel, give the command a new name.
3. Edit the command macro associated with the tool button.
4. Edit the button image.
5. Assign the button image location to the tool reference.
6. Check to see that the tool works the way you want it to.</td></tr>
</table>

In this section, we offer a simple introduction to the possibilities of customization through the use of customized toolbar buttons. In Section B-1, you created a new toolbar with five tools selected from different categories. In this section, we show you how to customize three of these tools so they function differently from standard AutoCAD commands.

⊞ You should be in an AutoCAD drawing with the customized toolbar created in B.1 open on your screen. Or, you may still be in the CUI dialog box from the previous section.

⊞ If necessary, open the Customize User Interface dialog box.

⊞ With the Customize User Interface dialog box open, open Toolbar1 and then select Line.

This automatically opens the Properties panel shown in Figure B-6. This is a very powerful and interesting place in the AutoCAD system. Here you can change the command name associated with this tool, change the appearance of the toolbar button, and edit the macro that determines, to an extent, how the command functions. Note that you are not actually creating a new command, but have the ability to determine default options that are entered automatically as part of the command procedure. For example, it might be nice to have a version of the **LINE** command that draws only one line segment and then returns you to the command prompt. This is easily accomplished with a little knowledge of AutoCAD macro language. Macros are automated key sequences. By automatically entering an extra press of the **Enter** key after drawing a single line segment, we can complete the command sequence as desired.

First, though, let's give this tool button a name to differentiate it from the standard Line tool.

⊞ Click in the Name edit box under Properties and add a 1 to the name so that it reads Line1.

This is a good descriptive name and it also associates it with Toolbar1, if you have used this as your toolbar name.

Next, we modify the macro so that the command is complete after one line segment is drawn. For the purposes of this exercise, you only need to know two items of AutoCAD macro language. The semicolon (;) is the macro language equivalent to pressing **Enter**. When AutoCAD sees a semicolon in a macro, it acts as if the user has pressed **Enter** or the spacebar. The backslash character (\) is the pause for user input character. When AutoCAD reads a backslash in a macro, it waits for something to be entered through the keyboard or the pointing device.

⊞ Click in the box next to Macro and add ;\\; to the macro, so that the complete macro reads ^C^C_line;\\;

It is very important that this be entered exactly as shown, without extra spaces. Macro language, like any programming language, is very fussy.

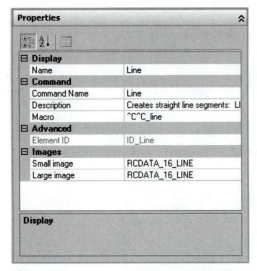

Figure B-6

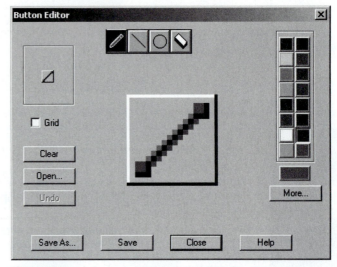

Figure B-7

Let's analyze what these characters do.

^C^C   The macro equivalent of typing Ctrl+C (or the **Esc** button) twice, which cancels any command in progress before entering the **LINE** command.

Line   Types Line at the command prompt
;   Like pressing **Enter** after typing the command
\   Waits for user to specify the first point
\   Waits for user to specify a second point
;   Like pressing **Enter** or the spacebar, ends the command sequence.

In a moment, we try this, but first let's change the button image to show that the command sequence for this customized tool is different from the standard **LINE** command.

⊞ Click Edit in the Button Image panel.

This opens the **Button Editor** dialog box illustrated in Figure B-7. This box provides simple graphics tools for creating or editing button images. The four tools include a drawing "pencil" for drawing individual grid cells, a line tool, a circle tool, and an erase tool. In addition, there is a grid and a color palette. We simply shorten the **Line** button image to differentiate it from the regular **Line** tool.

⊞ Click the Erase tool at the top right and use it to erase the lower left half of the Line button image, as shown in Figure B-8.

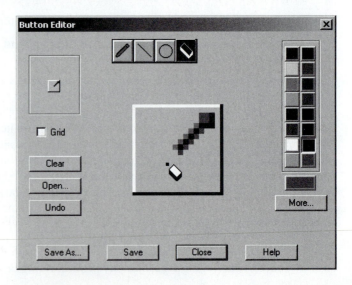

Figure B-8

⊕ Click Save.

This opens a **Create File** dialog box. It should automatically open to the correct location. Button image files are BMP files and must be saved in the same folder as the CUI file with which they are associated. Typically that file will be in C:\Documents and Settings\<owner>\Application Data\Autodesk\AutoCAD 2008\R16.2\enu\Support

⊕ Type Line1 for the name of the tool button.

Notice that there will now be two aspects of this modified **LINE** command in the CUI file: the **Line1** command, which is the **LINE** command modified by the additional macro characters, and the tool button image stored as a BMP file. We refer to both of them as Line1.

⊕ Click Save in the Create File dialog box.

⊕ Click Save in the Button Editor box.

⊕ Click Close in the Button Editor box to return to the Customize User Interface dialog box.

There is one last step to complete the creation of Line1 on your new toolbar. You must associate the button image with the modified command. This is done at the bottom of the Properties Panel to the right of the words Small image and Large image. Right now you will see "RCDATA_16_LINE" in both of these locations. This refers to the standard button image of the **LINE** command. We replace this with the modified image you just created.

⊕ Click in the edit box to the right of Large image and then click the ellipsis button at the end of the line.

This opens a **Select Image File** dialog box. Line1 should be entered as the new file name, with RCDATA_16_LINE as the current file. In the window above this you should see Line1, along with any other BMP files that may have been created and placed in this location.

⊕ If necessary select Line1 from the list.

You should see Line1 in the File name edit box.

⊕ Click Open.

This brings you back to the **Customize User Interface (CUI)** dialog box with the new location and BMP file listed next to Large image. By default, Line1 will be also entered for the Small image. If not, you can add it using the same procedure.

⊕ Click Apply to execute the changes to your customized tool button.

Now, let's close the **CUI** dialog box and try our new tool.

⊕ Click OK.

The dialog box closes, leaving you in the drawing area with Toolbar1 open.

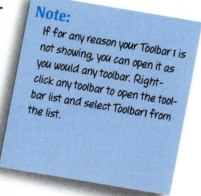

Note:
If for any reason your Toolbar1 is not showing, you can open it as you would any toolbar. Right-click any toolbar to open the toolbar list and select Toolbar1 from the list.

⊕ Select the Line1 tool from your customized toolbar.

⊕ Select a first point anywhere in your drawing area.

⊕ Select a second point.

You should be back to the command prompt. If this did not happen, check the syntax on the macro for your **Line1** tool.

Next, we return to the **CUI** dialog box and make similar changes in two more tools. We customize the **Erase** tool so that it erases a single object and then exits the command, and we customize the **Linear** tool so that it defaults to dimensioning an object.

⊕ Select Tools → Customize → Interface from the pull-down menu.

⊕ Double-click Toolbars from the list on the left.

⊕ Double-click Toolbar1 at the bottom of the list.

⊕ Double-click Erase.

⊕ Add a 1 in the Name edit box so that it reads Erase1.

⊕ In the macro associated with this button, add ;\; after erase.

The macro should read

$$\text{^C^C\_erase;\backslash;}$$

Consider how this macro works. After canceling any other command, it types erase and then the first semicolon enters the **ERASE** command. The \ tells Auto-CAD to wait for input. After the user points to one object, the second semicolon completes the command and returns to the command prompt.

⊕ Click Edit in the Button Image window to open the Button Editor.

⊕ Use the Erase tool and the Pencil tool to create the button image shown in Figure B-9.

This image shows the eraser head over a single object.

Figure B-9

⊕ Save the modified image as Erase1.

⊕ Click Close to close the Button Editor.

⊕ In the CUI dialog box, click the ellipsis buttons next to the Small or Large image edit boxes and open Erase1 to associate the button image with the tool reference.

⊕ Click Apply to apply changes to the Erase1 tool.

The Erase1 tool is now complete with a modified button image.

After one more sequence of modifications, our work will be complete.

⊕ Select Dimension Linear in the list under Toolbar1 button.

⊕ Add a 1 in the Name edit box, so that the name reads Dimension Linear1.

We use this tool to default to object selection as the method for creating a single linear dimension.

⊕ Add ;;\ to the macro associated with this button.

The macro should read

$$\text{^C^C\_dimlinear;;\backslash}$$

The first semicolon enters the command. The second enters the Select object option. The backslash creates a pause for object selection. After this there is no further instruction, so AutoCAD waits for further input. After the dimension position is selected, the command terminates. There is no need for a semicolon at the end because returning to the command prompt after dimension placement is normal procedure in this command.

⊕ Click Edit to open the Button Editor.

⊕ Using the Crayon tool, draw a short line segment below the Dimension icon, as shown in Figure B-10.

⊕ Save the modified button image as Linear1.

⊕ Close the Button Editor.

⊕ Assign the Linear1 button to the Small and Large button images for the Linear1 command.

⊕ Click Apply and then OK to close the CUI dialog box.

Figure B-10

Finally, to complete this exercise, use your customized toolbar to do the following:

1. Use the **Line1** tool to draw a single line segment.

2. Use the **Linear1** tool to dimension the line.

3. Use the **Erase1** tool to erase the line.

4. Use the **Erase1** tool again to erase the dimension.

Be aware that pressing the spacebar to repeat one of these commands repeats the regular AutoCAD command, not the macro you created for your customized toolbar.

Menus, Macros, and the CUI Dialog

When you begin to look below the surface of AutoCAD as it is configured straight out of the box, you find a whole world of customization possibilities. This open architecture, which allows you to create your own menus, commands, toolbars, tool palettes, and automated routines, is one of the reasons for AutoCAD's success. It is characteristic of all AutoCAD releases and has made room for a vast network of third-party developers to create custom software products tailoring AutoCAD to the particular needs of various industries and tasks.

The **Customize User Interface** dialog box, new in AutoCAD 2006, brought a major change to the way customization is handled. Prior to 2006 many of the customizable elements in the **CUI** dialog were accessible through different means. The largest single resource for customizing elements was the menu system. The standard acad menu (which addressed much more than pull-down menus) was contained in a file with an .mnu extension. This file could be accessed and edited in a word processing program. In AutoCAD 2006, the mnu and related files were replaced by the XML-based CUI file, and the elements formerly accessible through word processing could now be modified directly through the single interface of the **CUI** dialog box. In this appendix we will further explore the vocabulary of AutoCAD macro language and show how it is used with the elements in the **CUI** dialog. The intention of this discussion is not to make you an AutoCAD developer, but to give you a taste of what is going on in the CUI system. After reading this, you should have a sense of what elements are readily available for customization.

C-1 THE CUI DIALOG BOX

If you have worked through Appendix B, you have already gotten a taste of what is available in the **CUI** dialog box and how it works. The beauty of the system is that all elements are customized in the same way. Like toolbars, all elements are represented by starred entries in the tree view on the left and Properties panels on the right. Some elements also have Button Image panels.

Following is a list of the elements in the tree view with a brief discussion of each. In Section C-2 you will find further discussion of AutoCAD macro language characters.

⊞ To view the CUI dialog box, open the View menu and select Toolbars, or open the Tools menu, highlight Customize, and select Interface.

The tree view is in the top left panel and includes ten elements: Workspaces, Toolbars, Menus, Dashboard Panels, Shortcut Menus, Keyboard Shortcuts, Double Click Actions, Mouse Buttons, LISP Files, Legacy, and Partial CUI Files. Following is a brief description of each.

Workspaces. Workspaces are a simple form of customization. Workspaces consist of open toolbars, menus, palettes, and dockable windows. By opening or closing toolbars and selecting elements to add or remove from the drawing area, you can create unique and customized configurations. These can be saved as workspaces and then opened together as named Workspace from the **Window** pull-down menu. The AutoCAD default workspace includes all the elements you are used to seeing. A simple example of a customized workspace would be to open the **Dimension** and **Text** toolbars and then save this configuration as an "Annotation" workspace. Then whenever you want to be in this workspace you open the **Window** menu, highlight Workspace, and select Annotation.

Toolbars.   Toolbars can be created and added to the tree view list of toolbars. Everything you need to know about toolbar creation is in Appendix B. You can also modify existing toolbars using the same techniques used to create new ones. We do not recommend modifying the AutoCAD toolbars.

Menus.   These are the standard pull-down menus you see at the top of your drawing area. If you open Menus in the tree view, you see the list from File to Help. If you open File, you see the list of commands on the **File** pull-down menu, beginning with New and proceeding down to Exit. Most entries on pull-down menus refer to commands and they work exactly like the tool button entries on toolbars. For example, click New on the list and you will see the Button Image for the **New** command on the top right and the Properties panel below that. The macro for this line on the menu is ^C^C_new. If you are not familiar with the Properties panel, read Appendix B.

Dashboard Panels.   This item has been added in AutoCAD 2008. Dashboard panels are very similar in appearance and function to toolbars. They can be created and customized in the same way as toolbars, demonstrated in Appendix B. We do not recommend modifying the standard AutoCAD dashboard panels.

Shortcut Menus.   Here you will find a list of standard shortcut menus. Under Grips Cursor Menu, for example you will see familiar grip modes and options that appear when you right-click while in the grip editing system.

Keyboard Shortcuts.   This list is a good place to explore the complete keyboard shortcuts available. For example, open the tree view, then the Shortcut keys list and look under New. You will find that this is the place where Ctrl+N is established as the keyboard shortcut for entering the **New** command. There are 30 keyboard shortcuts defined here, including many you've probably never noticed. The Temporary Overrides list shows key combinations that will temporarily override a setting without changing it. Most of these use the **Shift** key in combination with another key.

Double Click Actions.   This list determines what action is taken when you double-click with the cursor resting on an object in a drawing. The action taken will depend on the type of object present and is a customizable feature. By default, many objects will call the Properties palette. Some other examples are double-clicking on a: polyline, which will execute the **PEDIT** command; multiline, which will execute **MLEDIT;** or an attribute definition, which will execute **ATTEDIT.**

Mouse Buttons.   The options with a standard two-button mouse are pretty limited, but this list gives you a place for customizing pointing devices with more than the two buttons.

LISP Files.   AutoCAD allows you to create customized routines in other languages, in addition to the macro language presented here. AutoLISP is a programming language based on LISP. LISP is a standard list processing language. You see AutoLISP statements in place of some macros in the Properties panel. LISP statements are enclosed in parentheses.

Legacy.   Legacy refers to elements of the drawing area that are no longer in common use but are still supported for those who like to use them. This includes screen menus, tablet menus, and image tile menus. You do not need to know about these unless you are working on a system that uses legacy features.

Partial CUI Files.   The way to create customized user interface files is to add partial files to the standard file. This way you do not lose the original and can go back to it at any time. If you open this entry you will see that there is currently one Partial CUI file defined under the name CUSTOM. It contains all the elements of the standard file, but there are no entries under the main element headings. To create your own partial CUI file you can start with CUSTOM and add commands and macros to any of the elements.

This completes the tour of the **CUI** dialog box. In the next section you will find additional macro characters and their meanings.

C-2 What Characters Are Used in AutoCAD Macros?

The following table lists some menu and macro characters you find in many elements of the CUI file.

Most Common AutoCAD Macro Characters	
&	Placed before a letter that can be used as an alias. The letter will be underlined on the menu.
;	Same as pressing **Enter** while typing.
^	Ctrl.
^C	Ctrl+C, same as pressing **Esc**.
^C^C	Double cancel; cancels any command, ensures a return to the *Command:* prompt before a new command is issued.
POPn	Section header, where *n* is a number between 1 and 16, identifying one of the 16 possible pull-down menu areas. POP0 refers to the cursor menu.
[]	Brackets enclose text to be written directly to the screen or pull-down menu area. Eight characters are printed on the screen menu. The size of menu items on the pull-down menu varies.
[–]	Writes a blank line on a pull-down menu.
_	English-language flag.
,	Transparent command modifier.
( )	Parentheses enclose AutoLISP and DIESEL expressions.
\	Pause for user input. Allows for keyboard entry, point selection, and object selection. Terminated by pressing **Enter** or pick button.
~	Begins a pull-down menu label that is unavailable. Can be used to indicate a function not currently in use.
*^C^C	This set of characters causes the menu item to repeat.

Data Exchange Formats

AutoCAD has the capacity to recognize and create files in a number of common file exchange formats. These allow you to translate AutoCAD drawings for use with other software and to bring drawings from other programs into AutoCAD. Following is a list of available drawing file types, listed by extension with descriptions of the purpose of each, followed by the commands used to import and export them:

File Extension	Purpose
3DS	3D Studio. 3DS files are used by Autodesk's 3D Studio software. 3D Studio is an Autodesk rendering program with advanced lighting and material capabilities. EXPORT, 3DSOUT, 3DSIN
BMP	Bitmap. Bitmap files use a pixel-by-pixel digital representation of screen images. BMPOUT, PASTECLIP
DWF	Drawing Web Format. For publishing drawings on the World Wide Web. DWF files can be viewed on the Internet by others who have a Web browser and the AutoCAD plugin WHIP! DWF files are created for viewing and publishing; they are not read by AutoCAD for editing and information exchange, as regular DWG files would be. DWFOUT, ePLOT
DXB	Drawing Exchange Binary. A binary-coded format used by AutoSHADE. DXBIN
DXF	Data Exchange Format. A text file format for exchanging drawings between different CAD programs. AutoCAD reads and writes DXF files for exchange with other systems. SAVEAS
EPS	Encapsulated Postscript. For printing and plotting on machines with postscript capability. PSOUT, PSIN
SAT	ACIS (*.sat extension) files capture regions, solids, and NURB (NonUniform Rational B-spline) surfaces in an ASCII format for exchange with other modeling software. ACISOUT, ACISIN
STL	Stereolithograph Apparatus. For translating solid object data into a format compatible with a Stereolithograph machine. Stereolithography is a technology that creates actual physical models from CAD solid model data. STLOUT
WMF	Windows Metafile. For saving objects in a raster or vector image format for use with other Windows programs. EXPORT, WMFOUT, WMFIN

In addition to these file types, also remember that images can be transferred among Windows applications using the clipboard (Chapter 10) and that raster images can be attached in a manner similar to external references (Chapter 10). The clipboard makes use of the **CUTCLIP, COPYCLIP,** and **COPYLINK** commands for exporting and **PASTECLIP, PASTELINK,** and **PASTESPEC** for importing. When importing through the clipboard, AutoCAD automatically recognizes and uses the most efficient format among its options of DWG, WMF, and BMP files. Raster images are attached using the **IMAGEATTACH** command, which supports a large

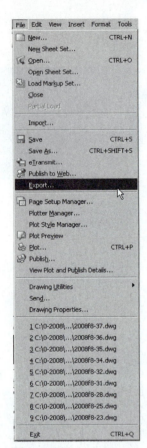

Figure D-1

number of image file types. See the *AutoCAD User's Guide* for additional information on raster images and image file types.

D-1 CREATING EXPORT FILES

Although the file formats that AutoCAD can export vary widely and are used for quite different purposes, the procedure for creating them is identical. As long as you know what type of file you want to create, all you need to do is open the **Export** dialog box from the **File** menu (Figure D-1), give the export file a name, and select the type of file you want to save it as. To create a 3DS (3D Studio file), for example, follow this procedure:

1. Open the **File** menu and select Export.
2. In the **Export Data** dialog box, type a name for the file.
3. Open the Save As Type list and select 3D Studio (*.3ds).
4. Click **Save.**

For other drawing exchange formats, follow the same procedure, selecting the file type you want from the Save As Type file list.

D-2 IMPORTING FILES IN OTHER FORMATS

Many of the drawing file types listed previously can be imported into AutoCAD as well. Importing most drawing file types is handled through the Insert menu. In most cases, you will select a file type, select a file, and open it. An example of an import procedure for a WMF follows:

1. Open the **Insert** menu and select Windows Metafile.
2. In the Import **WMF file** dialog box, select the name of a WMF file to insert.
3. Select **Open.**
4. Specify an insertion point and scale factors, just as you would when inserting a block with the **INSERT** command.

Different types of files require different insertion specifications, as shown in their respective **Import** dialog boxes. File types on the **Insert** menu are shown in Figure D-2. DXF, DWS, and DWT files are opened using the **OPEN** command, selecting the desired type from the Files of type list.

Figure D-2

Additional Tools for Collaboration

This book is designed primarily as a tutorial for a single user at a computer workstation or a student in a class with access to a workstation. In order to stay true to this goal it has been necessary to leave certain very important aspects of CAD practice alone. In addition to the programming and customizing tools introduced in Appendixes B and C, there are numerous tools that are only encountered in collaborative environments, where the work space extends beyond the individual and the individual computer. In this appendix, we briefly introduce a few of these tools, so that readers may enter a collaborative environment with some understanding of these processes. These tools are not necessary for the completion of any drawing in this book, but they belong in your repertoire of techniques.

E-1 CAD STANDARDS

The CAD Standards feature is important in work environments where drawings from one organization might be used in other organizations or departments. Using CAD Standards files allows quick checking and modifying of drawings to ensure that externally created or out-sourced drawings use standards compatible with standards in place for drawings created in-house. AutoCAD's CAD Standards feature requires the use of a drawing standards file. This can be any drawing that uses the desired standards, including layer definitions and properties, dimension styles, text styles, and linetypes. To understand the issues involved, imagine that in Your Company, Inc. all drawings have a standard layer, we'll call it Layer1, that is red. In order to support this practice, a certain Drawing A has been defined as a CAD Standards file (saved with a .dws extension). Your Company receives Drawing B from Their Company. Drawing B and Drawing A both have a layer called Layer1, but in Their Company, Layer1 is yellow. As a Your Company's CAD expert, you must ensure that Drawing B complies with Your Company's standards. You proceed as follows:

- Open Drawing B.
- Select Tools → CAD Standards → Configure from the pull-down menu.
  This opens the **Configure Standards** dialog box.
- Click the + button to add a Standards file.
- From the Select Standards file dialog box, select Drawing A as the CAD Standards file.
- In the Configure Standards dialog box click Check Standards. This opens a dialog box that shows you any discrepancies between Drawing A and Drawing B.
- Click the Fix button to alter Layer1 in Drawing B to match the standard of Drawing A.

Now that Drawing A is defined as a Standards file for Drawing B, anytime you try to change a property in Drawing B so that it does not match a standard, you will get a Standards Violation notification in the lower right corner of your screen. You can use the blue link to run a standards check and fix the problem or you can ignore and close the message.

E-2 Layer Translation

Layer translation is closely related to CAD Standards checking. It works similarly, but only addresses layers and it allows you to adjust the layers in any drawing to match layers in another drawing. You are not restricted to using drawings that have been defined as standards files, but can use any drawing to shape any other drawing. Properties that can be matched are all the properties that define layers. To translate Layer1 properties in Drawing A to Layer1 properties in Drawing B:

⊞ Open Drawing B.
⊞ Select Tools → CAD Standards → Layer Translator from the pull-down menu.

      This opens the Layer Translator. Layers in the current drawing are shown in the Translate From panel. There is nothing in the Translate To panel until we load a drawing.

⊞ Click Load.

      This opens a **Select Drawing File** dialog box. You can select a drawing, a template drawing, or a CAD Standards drawing file.

⊞ Navigate to the folder where Drawing A is located.
⊞ Select Drawing A.

      Notice that this can be any drawing. It does not have to be a .dws drawing.

⊞ Click Open.

      Layers from Drawing A are now listed in the Translate To panel.

⊞ Highlight Layer1 in both panels.
⊞ Click Map.

      The proposed translation shows in the Layer Translations Mapping panel.

⊞ Click Translate.
⊞ Click Yes to save or No to eliminate the old layer information in Drawing B.

E-3 Management of Named Objects

When managing multiple drawings from different sources, you are likely to encounter the problem of duplicate definitions. For example, what happens when a drawing that is externally referenced or block-inserted has layers, linetypes, text styles, dimension styles, blocks, or views with names that are the same as those in the current drawing? Good question. In the case of blocked drawings, name definitions in the current drawing override those in the inserted block, regardless of its origin. In the case of XREFed drawings, named objects are given special designations that eliminate the duplication. For example, if Drawing B is attached to Drawing A and both have a layer called FLOOR, a new layer is created in A called B|FLOOR.

E-4 Sheet Set Management

Most industrial design projects involve not one drawing but a set of drawings detailing different views or different aspects of a single design. When a design project is to be communicated to a client or a consultant it is likely to be represented by a whole set of related drawings. Sets of drawings like these, called Sheet Sets, may be created manually by saving particular layouts from individual drawings and then assembling all the relevant layouts and views in a single location. This process can become quite complex, especially when the individual drawings are on different computers and rely on external references, font files, plot files, and so on that may reside in different locations. To facilitate the creation of Sheet Sets, AutoCAD includes a system called the Sheet Set Manager. Through this interface, layouts from individual drawings are collected into a new drawing. Here, layouts can be easily organized into categories and subsets so that the Sheet Set presents a coherent design concept. One sheet of the set may be designated as the title sheet and this may display a table showing the organizational hierarchy of the complete Sheet Set. Sheets in the Sheet Set are given numbers and designations shown in standard symbol blocks that update automatically if the number and organization of the Sheet Set changes. Consider the following work flow:

- Create drawings in model space.
- In each drawing, create layouts presenting a design image.
- Using the Sheet Set Manager, collect layouts from all relevant drawings into a single set.
- Create a title sheet listing all layouts (sheets) and showing how they are organized.
- Create a Sheet Set package that contains the Sheet Set and all files required to view the set, all organized through the Sheet Set Manager.
- Archive the Sheet Set.
- eTransmit the Sheet Set to a client or consultant.

Index